ACCESS TO CARE, AC

Access to Care, Access to Justice:

The Legal Debate Over Private Health Insurance in Canada

Edited by

Colleen M. Flood, Kent Roach, and Lorne Sossin

UNIVERSITY OF TORONTO PRESS
Toronto Buffalo London

© University of Toronto Press Incorporated 2005
Toronto Buffalo London
Printed in Canada

ISBN-13: 978-0-8020-9420-9 (paper)
ISBN-10: 0-8020-9420-1 (paper)

Printed on acid-free paper

Library and Archives Canada Cataloguing in Publication

Access to care, access to justice : the legal debate over private health
insurance in Canada / edited by Colleen M. Flood, Kent Roach and Lorne
Sossin.

Papers from a conference held at the Faculty of Law, University of
Toronto on Sept. 16, 2005.
ISBN-13: 978-0-8020-9420-9
ISBN-10: 0-8020-9420-1

1. Insurance, Health – Law and legislation – Canada. 2. National health
insurance – Law and legislation – Canada. 3. Medical care – Law and
legislation – Canada. 4. Medical policy – Canada. I. Roach, Kent, 1961–
II. Sossin, Lorne Mitchell, 1964– III. Flood, Colleen M. (Colleen Marion),
1966–

KE3404.A66 2005   344.7102′2   C2005-905622-3
KF3605.A75A23 2005

University of Toronto Press acknowledges the financial assistance to
its publishing program of the Canada Council for the Arts and the
Ontario Arts Council.

University of Toronto Press acknowledges the financial support for
its publishing activities of the Government of Canada through the
Book Publishing Industry Development Program (BPIDP).

Contents

Preface by The Honourable Roy J. Romanow   ix

Acknowledgments   xi

List of Contributors   xv

Introduction: Kent Roach, Colleen M. Flood and Lorne Sossin   xix

What Did the Court Decide in *Chaoulli*?

Peter H. Russell, '*Chaoulli*: The Political versus the Legal Life of a Judicial Decision'   5

Bernard M. Dickens, 'The Chaoulli Decision: Less than Meets the Eye – or More?'   19

Jean-Francois Gaudreault-Desbiens and Charles-Maxime Panaccio, '*Chaoulli* and Quebec's *Charter of Human Rights and Freedoms: The Ambiguities of Distinctness*'   32

Lorraine Weinrib, 'Charter Perspectives on *Chaoulli* – The Body and the Body Politic'   56

***Chaoulli* and the Proper Role of the Courts in a Democracy**

Sujit Choudhry, 'Worse than *Lochner*?'   75

Allan Hutchinson, 'Condition Critical: The Constitution and Health Care'   101

Andrew Petter, 'Wealthcare: The Politics of the
Charter Re-visited'   116

Christopher P. Manfredi, 'Déjà vu All Over Again: *Chaoulli* and
the Limits of Judicial Policy-making'   139

Chaoulli and Prospects for Increased Access to Justice and Care

Lorne Sossin, 'Towards a Two-Tier Constitution? The Poverty
of Health Rights'   161

Kent Roach, 'The Courts and Medicare: Too Much or Too Little
Judicial Activism?'   184

Evidence in the Chaoulli Case

Hamish Stewart, 'Implications of *Chaoulli* for Fact Finding in
Constitutional Cases'   207

Morris Barer, 'Experts and Evidence: New Challenges in
Knowledge Translation'   216

Charles J. Wright, 'Different Interpretations of 'Evidence' and
Implications for the Canadian Healthcare System   220

Comparative Evidence About Private Health Insurance

Alan Maynard, 'How to defend a public health care system:
lessons from abroad'   237

André den Exter, 'Blending Private and Social Health Insurance
in the Netherlands: Challenges Posed by the EU'   257

16) Stefan Greß, 'The Role of Private Health Insurance in Social Health
Insurance Countries – Implications for Canada'   278

Colleen M. Flood, Mark Stabile and Sasha Kontic, 'Finding
Health Policy 'Arbitrary': The Evidence on Waiting, Dying,
and Two-Tier Systems'   296

The Implications of Private Insurance

Trudo Lemmens and Tom Archibald, 'The CMA's *Chaoulli* Motion
and the Myth of Promoting Fair Access to Health Care'   323

Robert G. Evans, 'Preserving Privilege, Promoting Profit: The Payoffs from Private Health Insurance'   347

Tracey Epps and David Schneiderman, 'Opening Medicare to Our Neighbours or Closing the Door on a Public System? International Trade Law Implications of *Chaoulli v. Quebec*'   369

Possible Governmental Responses to *Chaoulli*

Claude E. Forget, 'Promises, Promise – Setting Boundaries Between Public and Private'   393

Timothy Caulfield and Nola Ries, 'Politics and Paradoxes: *Chaoulli* and the Alberta Reaction'   413

Greg Marchildon, 'Private Insurance for Medicare: Policy History and Trajectory in the Four Western Provinces'   429

T. Sullivan, A. Greenberg, C. Sawka, A. Hudson, ' A Just Measure of Patience: Managing access to cancer services after *Chaoulli*'   454

Caroline Pitfield and Colleen M. Flood, 'Section 7 "Safety Valves": Appealing Wait Times Within a One-Tier System'   477

***Chaoulli* and the Future of Medicare**

Stanley Hartt, 'Arbitrariness, Randomness and the Principles of Fundamental Justice'   505

Roy Romanow, 'In Search of a Mandate?'   521

Appendix A: The Quebec Superior Court Decision   531

Appendix B: The Quebec Court of Appeal Decision   559

Appendix C: The Supreme Court of Canada Decision   565

Preface

In its best light, the Supreme Court's majority decision of June 9, 2005, in *Chaoulli v. Quebec (Attorney General)*, should provide a wake up call to the public and the governments they elect, to get on with badly needed health care reforms in an integrated and coherent manner. But the Court's decision by the majority of the seven sitting justices signals a potentially serious disruption of the Canadian balance between the individual and the community, between nation and enterprise, envisioned by the *Canadian Charter of Rights and Freedoms*.

Professor Peter Russell's contribution in this collection of essays cautions us to note the difference between what was actually written in the case at hand, and how it has been interpreted by both hasty journalists on deadline and those who wish to exploit it for the ideologically driven private alternatives in health care. Russell refers to the double life of such Supreme Court decisions, including the political life, when 'such decisions take on virtually a mythic quality and their significance depends not on what the judges actually said but on what they are alleged to have said...by their detractors and supporters.'

Therein resides the significance of this book, for both 'lives' of this decision require examination – the judicial and the political. In this case, were these 'lives' separate or intertwined? How can evidence, Canadian values, and greater understanding about the intention of the Charter, provide confused Canadians with greater clarity about the proper pathway forward?

I thank Colleen Flood, Kent Roach, Lorne Sossin and the Faculty of Law in the University of Toronto for organizing the very important conference Access to Care, Access to Justice: The Legal Debate Over Private Health Insurance in Canada that provided the basis for this remarkably important and timely book. They have done a wonderful job in assembling leading academics and practitioners who have a particular interest in the legal dimensions of health care policy. The contributing authors, under the editorship of Professors Flood, Roach and Sossin, pull back the curtain of obfuscation arising from the Court's decision. Please read it with our nation's future in mind and urge others to read it and join in on a more informed debate as a result.

HON. ROY J. ROMANOW
Former Royal Commissioner on Health Care
Professor, University of Saskatchewan and Atkinson Fellow

Acknowledgments

It would have been impossible for the three of us as editors to have organized the Access to Care, Access to Justice conference that was held on September 16, 2005 to discuss the implications of the Supreme Court's *Chaoulli* decision of June 9, 2005, let alone to produce a volume from that conference that will be published in early October, 2005. We are extremely grateful to the many colleagues and students at the University of Toronto's Faculty of Law and the University of Toronto Press who have worked so tirelessly on both the conference and the production of this volume, as well as to the all of the authors and the sponsoring institutions.

Greig Hinds, the CHSRF Medicare Basket Research Manager at the Faculty of Law, University of Toronto, was a rock for the entire project and flawlessly handled details from travel arrangements for our out of town speakers to the final production of the copy for the University of Toronto. The conference arrangements, including our last minute change to the Metro Toronto Conference Centre to handle increased registrations were done by Jennifer Tam, the events co-ordinator at the University of Toronto' Faculty of Law, with her usual skill, calm and expertise. Kathleen O'Brien handed publicity and media and ensured that the conference was well covered in the national and local media. We are extremely fortunate at the Faculty of Law to be able to call on people like Greig Hinds, Jennifer Tam and Kathleen O'Brien for assistance.

We are also extremely grateful to the experts on health policy who agreed to act as moderators of the panel discussions at the Conference. We thank Tony Clement, Ontario's former Minister of Health, Michael Decter of the Health Council of Canada, Antonia Maioni of McGill University and Peter Russell and Carolyn Tuohy of the University of Toronto for significantly contributing to the success of the conference.

We also thank Andrew Botterell, Sasha Kontic, Zimra Yetnikoff, and Lorian Hardcastle and students at the Health Law Club at the University of Toronto, Faculty of Law, who assisted both at the conference and preparing the manuscripts for publication. Bernadette Mount also provided expert assistance.

We are very grateful to the following organisations for their generous support of the conference for which these papers were prepared and this publication.

Canadian Institutes of Health Research (especially Dr. Alan Bernstein, President, and Dr. Morris Barer, Scientific Director, CIHR Institute of Health Services and Policy Research) Canadian Health Services Research Foundation (especially Dr. Jonathan Lomas, CEO)

The Law Foundation of Ontario Borden Ladner Gervais LLP (especially Guy Pratte, Freya Kristjanson, and Susan V. Zimmerman) 'The Insurance and Health Systems Implications of Genetics Project,' (Trudo Lemmens, Colleen Flood and Bernard Dickens) funded by Genome Canada, through the Ontario Genomics Institute

Of course, the views expressed in this volume are those of the individual authors and not those of our sponsor organisations.

The Faculty of Law, University of Toronto has been unwavering in its commitment to this initiative and in particular we wish to recognize the leadership of Interim Dean Brian Langille in supporting the conference and this volume. In addition to the Faculty and our sponsors, thanks must go to the University of Toronto Press for agreeing to and expertly carrying out an extremely expedited process of manuscript review and publication. Special thanks to John Yates, Bill Harnum, Marty Friedland, Don Moggridge and Virgil Duff.

In addition to this volume, the staff of the Bora Laskin Law Library have created a website for the conference which has a wealth of background information on the Chaoulli case and the issues it engages. We encourage those interested to visit our website and follow the links to the conference page at *www.law.utoronto.ca/healthlaw*. We wish to acknowledge the efforts of Susan Barker, Gian Medves and Dylan Reid in this effort.

Finally, we'd like to thank the various contributors to this book who worked long and hard; crafting their papers and presentations, reflecting on the contributions of others, and meeting our extremely tight deadlines. It was an enormous privilege to work with you all.

Colleen M. Flood, Kent Roach and Lorne Sossin

September 19, 2005.
Toronto.

Contributors

Tom Archibald, SJD Candidate, Faculty of Law, University of Toronto

Morris Barer, Scientific Director, CIHR Institute of Health Services and Policy Research, Canadian Institutes of Health Research

Timothy Caulfield, Canada Research Chair and Director, Health Law Institute, University of Alberta

Sujit Choudhry, Associate Professor, Faculty of Law, University of Toronto

André den Exter, Lecturer in European law at Radboud University Nijmegen, the Netherlands

Bernard Dickens, Dr. William M. Scholl Professor Emeritus of Health Law and Policy, Faculty of Law, University of Toronto

Tracey Epps, SJD Candidate, Faculty of Law, University of Toronto

Robert G. Evans, Professor, Department of Economics, University of British Columbia

Colleen M. Flood, Associate Professor and Canada Research Chair, Faculty of Law, University of Toronto

Claude Forget, Consultant and Chairman, Institut d'Evaluation en Santé, Quebec

Jean-Francois Gaudreault-DesBiens, Associate Professor, Faculty of Law, University of Toronto

Anna Greenberg, Manager, Cancer Quality Council, Cancer Care Ontario

Stefan Greß, Assistant Professor, Institute of Health Care Management, University of Duisburg-Essen, Germany

Stanley H. Hartt Q.C., O.C., Chairman, Citigroup Global Markets Canada Inc.

Alan Roy Hudson, O.C., Lead, Access to Services and Wait Times Strategy, Health Results Team, Ontario Ministry of Health and Long Term Care

Allan Hutchinson, Associate Dean, Osgoode Hall Law School, York University

Alexandra (Sasha) Kontic, Research Assistant, Faculty of Law, University of Toronto

Trudo Lemmens, Associate Professor, Faculty of Law, University of Toronto

Christopher Manfredi, Chair, Department of Political Science, McGill University

Gregory Marchildon, Canada Research Chair and Professor, Graduate School of Public Policy, University of Regina

Alan Maynard, Professor of Health Economics, Department of Health Sciences, University of York

Charles-Maxime Panaccio, SJD Candidate, Faculty of Law, University of Toronto

Andrew Petter, Dean, Faculty of Law, University of Victoria

Caroline Pitfield, Counsel, Department of Justice, Government of Canada

Nola Ries, Research Associate, Health Law Institute, University of Alberta; and Lecturer in Health Law, University of Victoria

Kent Roach, Professor, Faculty of Law, University of Toronto

Hon. Roy J. Romanow, Premier of Saskatchewan (1991-2001); Senior Fellow in Public Policy at the University of Saskatchewan and the University of Regina; and Visiting Fellow in the School of Policy Studies at Queen's University.

Peter H. Russell, Professor Emeritus, Department of Political Science, University of Toronto

Carol Sawka, MD, FRCPC, Provincial Vice President, Clinical Programs, Cancer Care Ontario

David Schneiderman, Associate Professor, Faculty of Law, University of Toronto

Lorne M. Sossin, Associate Dean, Faculty of Law, University of Toronto

Mark Stabile, Professor, Department of Economics and Center for Economics and Public Affairs, University of Toronto

Hamish Stewart, Professor, Faculty of Law, University of Toronto

Terry Sullivan, President and CEO, Cancer Care Ontario

Lorraine Weinrib, Professor, Faculty of Law, University of Toronto

Charles J. Wright, MB, MSc, FRCS(C,E,Ed), Consultant and Professor Emeritus, University of Toronto

Introduction

KENT ROACH, COLLEEN M. FLOOD,
AND LORNE SOSSIN

The catalyst for this book was a Supreme Court decision on whether banning private health insurance for services covered by the public system violated the Constitution. On June 9, 2005, the Supreme Court of Canada released its judgment in *Jacques Chaoulli and George Zeliotis versus the Attorney Generals of Quebec and Canada*.[1] Dr. Chaoulli, a doctor who wanted to offer private health services, and Mr. Zeliotis, a patient who had been on a waiting list in the Quebec health system, argued that that Quebec's prohibition of private health insurance for services covered by the public system violated both the Canadian and Quebec Charter of Rights and Freedoms. After hearing expert witnesses who testified to their experience as practitioners in the Quebec health system and to the comparative experience of health care systems in other countries, the trial judge concluded in 2000 that the impugned laws did not violate the Canadian or Quebec Charters.[2] This decision was upheld in 2002 by a unanimous Quebec Court of Appeal.[3]

Many believed the Supreme Court of Canada would dismiss the appellants' appeal, especially after late in 2004, the Supreme Court held that British Columbia's refusal to fund intensive therapy for autistic children did not violate the Charter.[4] To the surprise of many, the Supreme Court in *Chaoulli* reversed the Quebec courts in a 4:3 decision and held that Quebec's prohibition should be invalidated. The decision was complex because only seven of the nine judges on the Court sat on the case with three judges deciding that the prohibition was an unjustified violation of s.7 of the Canadian Charter and three judges deciding that it did not violate s.7 of the Charter. The seventh judge concluded that the Quebec law violated the Quebec Charter and found it unnecessary to decide whether the law also violated the Canadian Charter.

After considering subsequent written submissions from the parties and intervenors, the Court suspended the operation of its judgment until June 9, 2006 without giving reasons.

In *Chaoulli*, the worlds of constitutional law and health policy collided in a manner symbolized by the intertwining of the judge's gavel and the doctor's stethoscope on the front cover of this book. It remains to be seen, however, how influential the decision and subsequent decisions of the courts will be in determining health care policy. *Chaoulli* raises more questions that it answers. First, the majority decision in the case actually reflects a minority of the nine-member Court. Justices Abella and Charon had not yet been appointed to the Court when the *Chaoulli* case was argued and Justice Major will have been replaced by the time this issue next reaches the Court. Will a future majority on a changing Court follow Chief Justice McLachlin, Justice Major, and Justice Bastarache in concluding that a prohibition on private medical insurance for services provided by the public health system is arbitrary and unnecessary to preserve the public system? If so, will the growth of private insurance lead to inequities and less public engagement with the public health system? Will a future majority on the Court follow Justices Binnie, LeBel, and Fish and hold that governments do not violate the principles of fundamental justice when they restrict private health insurance? Will future courts intervene in cases where people on public waiting lists are denied needed treatment? How should Quebec respond to the *Chaoulli* decision? How should other Canadian governments respond? Will governments use the notwithstanding clause of the Constitution to override the Courts to protect public Medicare? All of these questions need to be addressed and addressed quickly, but the answers will not be easy to find because of the complex and contested nature of the law and the dynamic and contested nature of the debate and data on health care policy.

The Faculty of Law at the University of Toronto took a particular interest in the Court's decision in *Chaoulli* because many of its members are active researchers in the fields of health policy and constitutional law. At the same time, the decision raised issues that required a great range of expertise and engaged a variety of different perspectives. To this end, a conference was organized by the Faculty of Law bringing together experts in constitutional law and health policy from throughout Canada and the world to Toronto on September 16, 2005 to discuss the meaning, soundness and implications of *Chaoulli*. Papers were exchanged among the participants before this conference and then revised in light of the stimulating and intense discussions held on that day. Because of the urgency and importance of the subject matter, the University of Toronto Press graciously agreed to an expedited publication process. Many people worked long and harm with tight deadlines in the hope that this book can contribute to the current political, policy and legal debates about *Chaoulli* and the role of private medical insurance and the courts in Canadian health policy.

What Did the Court Decide in *Chaoulli*?

The first part of this collection deals with the preliminary but complex question of what the Supreme Court of Canada actually decided in *Chaoulli*. Peter H. Russell of the University of Toronto warns against taking initial media reports about the judicial creation of a two-tier health care system or a right to timely treatment too seriously. He argues that a careful reading of the lengthy reasons given by the judges in the case reveals a narrow judgment that in a legal sense only applies in Quebec and only finds that prohibition of private health insurance for public services violates the Quebec Charter. Russell argues that the position of the three judges who would have invalidated the private health insurance ban under s.7 of the Canadian Charter significantly widens the scope of judicial review and predicts that the new judges on the Court who will shape any future case will be attracted to the less activist judgment written by Justice Binnie and LeBel. Whatever the eventual legal outcome is, however, Russell also counsels attention to the parallel political life of the case. Here, the Court's decision has a meaning different from what the judges actually decided and exaggerations in the media and in the legislature about the case will have a life of their own. He predicts that the political life of *Chaoulli*, combined with political and economic pressures, may place pressures on provincial governments to loosen restrictions on private health insurance.

Bernard M. Dickens of the University of Toronto observes that the meaning of judicial decisions is often in the eye of the beholder and that *Chaoulli* is no exception. For some, the decision threatens the very essence of Canadian Medicare while for others its impact is limited to Quebec. Dickens argues that there might be less to *Chaoulli* than meets the eye. The 3:3 split on the Canadian Charter means that the judgment has no clear legal consequences outside of Quebec. Even in Quebec, the reduction of waiting times might persuade the Court that rights were no longer violated. Like Russell, however, Dickens recognizes that

Chaoulli may have a political life quite different from its legal meaning. He adds an international dimension to the political life of the case by suggesting that international health care equity may be harmed if doctors from poorer countries come to Canada because of the decision. Dickens argues that better preventive health care and public health may ultimately help reduce wait times, but notes that there may be a focus on more immediate clinical care services in the wake of *Chaoulli*.

As Peter Russell and Bernard Dickens demonstrate, the *Chaoulli* decision was actually only decided under the Quebec Charter of Human Rights and Freedoms. Justice Deschamps' judgment that the prohibition on private medical insurance violated the right to inviolability under s.1 and could not be justified under s.9.1 of the Quebec Charter is the focus of Jean-Francois Gaudreault-DesBiens and Charles-Maxime Panaccio's contribution. They outline the origins of the Quebec Charter as a distinctive Quebecois alternative to the Canadian Charter, but argue that Justice Deschamps conflated an arguably more communitarian and deferential test for justifying limits on rights under s.9.1 of the Quebec Charter with a more individualistic and rigorous justification test under s.1 of the Canadian Charter as interpreted in *R. v. Oakes*.[5] They suggest that the dissenting judgment of Justice Binnie and LeBel better articulates the meaning of s.9.1 of the Quebec Charter which requires persons exercising their fundamental rights and freedoms to 'maintain a proper regard for democratic values, public order and the general well-being of the citizens of Quebec.'[6] Gaudreault-DesBiens and Panaccio also outline some of the reactions in Quebec to the Court's decision. They suggest that Quebecers, unlike many in the rest of Canada, may not see a single payer medicare system as an integral part of their national identity and that this may influence the eventual response of the Quebec government to the Court's decision.

Although Gaudreault-DesBiens and Panaccio are relatively critical of the majority decision in *Chaoulli*, their University of Toronto colleague Lorraine Weinrib is more sympathetic. She outlines the structure of the Court's judgment in the doctrinal terms of justiciability, the affected rights, the principles of fundamental justice, the limitation clause, and the remedy. She argues that the issues posed to the Court were clearly justiciable and criticizes the dissenters for allowing misgivings about justiciability to slip into their judgment. She finds the approach taken by Chief Justice McLachlin and Justice Major to defining the principles of fundamental justice to be preferable to that taken by Justices Binnie and LeBel because the former focus on issues of arbitrariness and necessity while the latter focus more on social policy, consensus and reasonableness. Weinrib focuses on which of the two competing approaches is normatively superior in contrast to Peter Russell's more empirical predictive that the less activist Binnie and LeBel position will eventually win the day. She also, however, expresses concerns about the adequacy of the remedy requested and provided in *Chaoulli*, namely a striking down of restrictions on private health insurance. She concludes that the majority could have disposed of the issue before it by demanding more robust processes of appeal for those who suffer long wait-times and in this regard; an issue that Caroline Pitfield and Colleen Flood also consider as discussed further below.

Chaoulli and the Proper Role of the Courts in a Democracy

The next part of this collection contains four essays which all deal with whether the majority of the Supreme Court in *Chaoulli* exceeded its proper institutional role in *Chaoulli*, as well as related issues about the impact of judicial activism and the Charter on Canadian democracy. These essays tend to focus more on the majority judgments as examples of judicial reasoning and the politics of the Charter and less on the limits of what the Court actually decided, as discussed earlier by Russell and Dickens.

Sujit Choudhry of the University of Toronto raises the provocative question of whether the majority's decision in *Chaoulli* is worse than *Lochner*,[7] a 1905 decision of the United States Supreme Court that struck down a law restricting the number of hours that could be worked in a day. He recognizes that equating a case with *Lochner* is about the worst insult that a constitutional lawyer can make and observes that four of the nine intervenors who opposed the claims of Dr. Chaoulli and Mr. Zeliotis in the Supreme Court invoked the spectre of Lochner in their defence. For his part, Choudhry argues that majority's decision in *Chaoulli* is similar to *Lochner* and in some respects even worse. Faced with inconclusive and conflicting evidence about the impact of private health insurance on the public health system, he suggests that the Court should have deferred to the legislature because it had a reasonable basis for restricting private health insurance. In his view, the majority was wrong to require definitive scientific proof where none exists. Choudhry also suggests that a more deferential approach is well grounded in most of the Court's jurisprudence under s.1 of the Charter. He also argues that the majority's decision embraces the economic libertarianism of *Lochner* even though the drafters of the Charter deliberately excluded property rights and freedom of contract. He suggests that the majority of the Court intervened not to assist a discrete and insular minority, but to allow more advantaged Canadians to exit from a universal social program.

In contrast to Sujit Choudhry who sees the majority's decision in *Chaoulli* as a regrettable aberration from prior Charter decisions, the remaining essays in this section all suggest that *Chaoulli* was no surprise, but rather the culmination of the enhanced role that the Charter gives the courts. Drawing on his prior criticisms of the Charter and the court's performance under it, Allan C. Hutchinson of Osgoode Hall Law School starts and ends his essay with a 'told you so.' For him, *Chaoulli* brings home in the clearest manner the regressive politics of the Charter, one that allows vested interests in society to weaken the state and harm the disadvantaged. Even the few progressive decisions made by the Court, for example, the invalidation of restrictions on abortion in *R. v. Morgentaler*,[8] have provided ammunition for the majority's decision in *Chaoulli* to allow the advantaged to opt out of the public health system through the purchase of private medical insurance. Hutchinson concludes that the anti-state and highly individualistic politics of the Charter are based on the false idea that citizens are most free when their negative liberty is protected from state interference.

Andrew Petter of the University of Victoria's Faculty of Law (and a former Minister of Health in British Columbia) starts his essay with a discussion of how universal single payer model of medicare is a core social value and defining feature of Canada that has been validated and re-enforced through many reports, royal commissions and governmental and intergovernmental commitments. He expresses dismay that the majority of the Supreme Court in *Chaoulli* with the benefit of a one day hearing would cast aside these commitments as mere 'assertions of belief' that are 'disconnected from reality.'[9] He argues that the Court's decision should not be seen as a wake up call or a legitimate part of a dialogue with legislatures. Governments were already fully attentive and had committed themselves in 2004 to adding $41 billion over ten years to the health care system. He warns that the political force of the Charter, combined with market forces, globalization and international trade law, will restrain the ability of governments to respond to *Chaoulli* and that dialogue theorists underestimates the constraints that Charter decisions place on governments. Petter joins Hutchison in arguing that the idea that Charter decisions are only part of a dialogue with legislatures has enabled judges to write their policy preferences into law. Both also agree that *Chaoulli* was not an aberration but the culmination of the Charter's ideology of liberal legalism that protects negative liberty and imposes a formal vision of equality that harms the disadvantaged.

Christopher P. Manfredi of McGill University also argues in his essay that *Chaoulli* is an entirely predictable consequence of the growth of judicial power under the Charter. Unlike Hutchinson and Petter, however, Manfredi does not question the legitimacy of judicial review which he sees as a necessary check and balance of liberal constitutionalism. He does, however, question the expansive approach to judicial review taken by the Supreme Court by its relaxation of rules of standing that allowed Dr. Chaoulli and Mr. Zeliotis to bring the case, even though they were no longer directly affected by waiting lists. He also criticizes the Court's failure to restrict s.7 of the Charter to procedural fairness in the administration of justice. In a memorable phrase, he describes the essence of the Court's decision as 'We like Kirby, you like Romanow. We win, 4–3. Statutory provision invalidated.' He then notes that despite their influence on the Supreme Court both the Romanow and Kirby reports were released only after the trial judge had heard evidence and made her factual findings. Manfredi argues that courts are ill-suited to judging or developing policy for the future as opposed to deciding what happened in the past. He cautions that the selective and partial use of social science evidence in *Chaoulli* is similar to the Court's flawed attempt to provide an empirical foundation for speedy trial standards in *R. v. Askov.*[10] Manfredi concludes by suggesting the normative and empirical reservations about judicial review that he has outlined are good reasons for not granting the Court's Charter judgments authoritative status.

Chaoulli and the Prospects for Increased Access to Justice and Care

The next section of this collection contains two essays that are concerned with how *Chaoulli* may affect future litigation before the courts and future governmental actions with respect to Medicare. Although these two essays are critical of some aspects of *Chaoulli*, they also strike a somewhat more optimistic tone that the preceding four essays.

Lorne Sossin of the University of Toronto warns that there is a danger of a two-tier approach to Charter interpretation that will deprive the less advantaged members of society of rights to social assistance or to health care. Sossin like others in this collection examines the *Chaoulli* decision in contrast to the Court's other recent decision to deny Charter challenges to the adequacy of social assistance and to the adequacy of coverage in the public system.[11] He does not, however, view the Court's prior performance as insurmountable obstacle to judicial recognition of more equitable approach to rights. To this end, he argues that judges should reject the dichotomy between positive and negative rights and between deserving and undeserving litigants. A key to rejecting such distinctions will be increased judicial empathy for those who must rely on the state for either social assistance or health care. He predicts that *Chaoulli* may have a surprisingly progressive influence on Charter jurisprudence in cases where litigants request necessary health services from the state.

Kent Roach of the University of Toronto suggests that the majority's decision in *Chaoulli* was shaped by the fact that the litigants were not directly affected by a waiting list and only requested the negative remedy of striking down Quebec's prohibition on private insurance. He argues that it will be cruelly ironic if judges do not provide effective remedies for those who must rely on the public system. He suggests that the minority in *Chaoulli* rightly left the door open to such case by case adjudication and outlines a variety of remedies including damage awards, declarations of entitlement to health services and injunctions ordering treatment or supervising wait lists that may be available in subsequent litigation. At the same time, he concedes that administrative measures such as wait time guarantees and administrative appeals may be superior to judicial remedies. Roach also defends the idea that courts do not necessarily have the last word in their Charter dialogues with legislatures and society that is criticized by both Petter and Hutchison. Roach argues that the Supreme Court was correct to suspend its judgment to allow Quebec to decide how to respond to its judgment and to consider the use of the override. He outlines a variety of possible responses available to the Quebec government to respond to *Chaoulli*. Roach suggests that *Chaoulli* could have a surprisingly positive impact if it makes governments more concerned about the rationality of waiting lists and the treatment of individuals on waiting lists.

The Treatment of Evidence in Chaoulli

The next section provides a transition from a focus on the Court's decision in *Chaoulli* to a discussion of the available evidence on the effects of private health insurance on public health care and the range of possible governmental responses to the Court's decision.

The section begins with an examination of the Supreme Court's approach to evidence in the *Chaoulli* case by Hamish Stewart of the University of Toronto. He acknowledges that fact-finding about policies in constitutional cases is different than fact finding about discrete events in traditional non-constitutional cases. Nevertheless, he concludes that in both types of cases, appellate courts should defer to the factual findings of trial judges. Stewart concludes that there was no basis for the Supreme Court to overturn the trial judge's factual finding concerning the adverse effects of allowing private insurance on the public health care system. He warns that majority's decision in *Chaoulli* threatens to undermine the principle that the appropriate forum for resolving factual disputes is in trial courts and not on appeal.

The next essay by Morris Barer of the University of British Columbia briefly examines how health policy making in governments and hospitals is becoming more evidence-based. He then critically examines the Supreme Court's treatment of the evidence in *Chaoulli*, suggesting that it has bought into the misguided idea that private health insurance will improve health care systems. He characterizes this idea as a 'zombie' idea because it cannot be killed in popular discourse even though it is not supported in the evidence. He then poses the question of whether experts on health policy-making must adopt different strategies in order to convince judges or whether the judiciary requires training in health policy evidence. This paper is a revised version of opening remarks that Dr. Barer prepared for the conference.

Charles Wright, a surgeon and expert witness for the government in *Chaoulli* then details in his paper the various reports and studies that were referred to by him and other expert witnesses to illustrate the problems of allowing a two-tier system on the public tier. For example, a study of waiting lists for cataract surgery in Manitoba[6] found that patients attending surgeons who also work in private clinics waited far longer than patents whose surgeons worked only in the public system. The median wait for a public system patient whose surgeon also worked privately was 23 weeks compared with 10 weeks for the patients with surgeons working only in the public system. Despite the reference to these and other studies, Deschamps J. concludes in dismissing the testimony of the expert witnesses called that 'no study was produced or discussed in the Superior Court.'[12] But Wright is pragmatic about the decision. Indeed, taking a similar stance to that of Alan Maynard and providing a bridge to the next section in this book, he argues that the decision is a wake-up call to do something about waiting times. In Wright's view, rather than bemoaning the decision, we should focus on how to tackle the waiting list problem. Thus he sees to some extent the *Chaoulli* decision as opportunity rather than set-back. He notes that presently there is no systematic management of waiting lists and lists are managed in an unregulated fashion by individual physicians. They have no incentive and there is not any directive for them to co-ordinate to ensure that both needs and capacity to meet those needs are triaged and matched. Where, however, a measure of management has been applied to wait lists – for example in cardiac surgery – wait times have been wrestled back to acceptable standards. But once we finally wrestle wait lists down and eliminate demand and calls for complementary or duplicate insurance, Wright warns that there are another set of ethically complex challenges ahead. These challenges relate to the reach of the public system and the fact that many new and expensive therapies and technologies that are developed are of marginal clinical value. Tough decisions will have to be made about the boundaries of the public system, in which equity is assured, and the private system where access will be related to ability and willingness to pay.

Comparative Evidence about Private Health Insurance

This part of the collection deals with the court's treatment of evidence about the co-existence and dynamics of public and private financing in other jurisdictions. Such evidence was used by the majority to conclude that there were no dangers to the public system in allowing the purchase of private insurance for medically necessary hospital and physician services. This in turn allowed McLachlin C.J. and Major J. to conclude that the deprivation of s. 7 rights caused by long waits in the public system and the prohibition on private insurance were not in accordance with the principles of fundamental justice as these laws were arbitrary.

    Alan Maynard, from York University in the United Kingdom, argues that *Chaoulli* is a wake-up call to Canadian governments to increase the productivity of Medicare. The challenge is not how to spend more given inefficiencies in both the public and private health insurance systems, but how to spend what is available more efficiently. He refers to the enormous variations in the delivery of care that are unrelated to differences in illness or price – but rather due to differences in patterns of practice. For example, Manhattan Medicare enrollees were three times as likely as Portland enrollees to spend a week or more in an intensive care unit and had five times as many visits to a medical specialist. The result of this kind of variation is, he argues, an enormous waste of resources that could otherwise be used to solve problems of waiting times and to improve access to chronic care. Although critical of the failures in public governance, he insists that these problems are only compounded by the addition of complementary or double-cover insurance as allowed post-*Chaoulli*. If duplicate private health insurance were to emerge in Canada, to avoid exacerbating efficiency problems and to ameliorate reductions in equity, it would have to be regulated vigorously. In his view, no government has been able to regulate private health insurance to achieve efficiency or equity. He concludes that the path of duplicated public and private health, if chosen, will be very difficult to return from as the consumer and provider benefits will make electoral change costly. This is best illustrated by the Labour Party's support for private health insurance in the last Australian election in an attempt to win the votes of those who have benefited from the Conservative government's regressive policies in this regard.

The Supreme Court refers with favour to the experience of European countries like the Netherlands and Germany as evidence that allowing a two-tier system will not impact on the public system. André den Exter from the University of Erasmus in the Netherlands describes how solidarity has been the guiding principle for health insurance in the Netherlands and the mere fact of being insured privately does not buy one the right to jump waiting lists. Moreover, physicians are paid the same fee regardless of whether the funds flow from the public or the private sector and it is part of the medical code of ethics not to treat patients differently as a result of the type of insurance they hold. Den Exter is concerned that this strong sense of solidarity will be tested with the new Dutch Health Insurance Bill which aims to simultaneously eliminate the split between social and private insurers and inject competition into the system and to make social and private insurers compete for business. The theme of Andre den Exter's paper is also about the difficulty of pulling back from a path of liberalization, but not as argued by Alan Maynard because of the distribution of benefits to elites. Den Exter argues that European Union agreements on free trade may make it difficult to re-regulate liberalized regimes for private health insurance. In this regard, he makes similar claims to that of Epps and Schneiderman who in the next section of this collection discuss the ramifications of the *Chaoulli* decision in light of the effects of the North American Free Trade Agreement (NAFTA).

Stefan Greß clarifies the Supreme Court's confusion over the role of private health insurance in European countries. He distinguishes between three types or functions of insurance: The first is as an *alternative* for mandatory (statutory) social health insurance arrangements. The wealthy in the Netherlands and Germany may purchase such insurance, but it must cover them for all their needs and does not simply top-up coverage in the social insurance system. The second function is to *supplement* basic health insurance, providing coverage for services not covered by social insurance or to cover the financial risks of co-payments and coinsurance. In Canada, many have supplementary health insurance for prescription drugs. A third function of private insurance is to provide what can be termed *complementary or double-cover* coverage, in which insured purchase additional private insurance even while they have to participate in existing social schemes. Double-cover private health insurance would be allowed in Quebec after *Chaoulli* but contrary to the majority's assumption in that case, such coverage is relatively rare in European countries. Greß also describes the different kind of regulatory approaches taken to social insurance and private insurance in Europe, including regulation designed to achieve income solidarity and/or risk solidarity.

An interesting insight to arise out of Greß's contribution is his discussion of the interaction between alternative and supplementary insurance. Charles Wright, as well as Terrence Sullivan and his colleagues at Cancer Care Ontario each suggest that the hardest issues to solve will ultimately not be about competing or duplicate insurance, but rather the role of supplementary insurance or private pay for services such as some expensive cancer drugs that provide some benefits but are not covered in the public system because of concerns about their cost-effectiveness. They focus on the equity concerns about this kind of shift, but as Greß notes if services are shifted into supplementary insurance or a private pay sector that people consider important then calls will rise for increased regulation to try to better ensure access to care that is considered important. At a certain point, he contends, heavily regulated private insurance starts to take on all the characteristics of public insurance and this raises the issue of whether public insurance is preferable and more efficient than a highly regulated private insurance market.

Colleen Flood, Mark Stabile and Sasha Kontic from the University of Toronto argue that the majority decision with respect to the Quebec Charter and the decision written by McLachlin C.J. and Major J. with respect to the Canadian *Charter* each reveal a flawed understanding of the dynamics of public and private financing in health care. For example, the majority concludes that waiting lists are caused as a result of a public sector 'monopoly.' In truth, many countries that have two-tier care systems also have significant problems with waiting lists. Another problematic conclusion reached by the majority is that 'many' Quebeckers and 'ordinary' Canadians would be able to avoid suffering on long wait lists if the restriction on purchasing private health insurance was removed. In truth, evidence from other jurisdictions clearly shows that ordinary people are unlikely to be able to avail themselves of duplicate or complementary insurance. For example, in the United Kingdom, just 5% of the poorest 40% of the population have private insurance and most people must suffer waiting times in the public system that historically have been much longer than those recorded in Canada.

Flood and colleagues conclude that the majority in *Chaoulli* miss not only the equality and distributive effects of private insurance, but also the adverse impacts on the public sector of a shift of effort and time on the part of specialists from a public to a private tier. There are only a limited number of doctors and nurses available; increasing their number in short of a decade is impossible unless accreditation problems are eased and more are lured quickly into the country. Using calculations from a survey of OECD countries, they calculate that a 10% decrease in the population of specialists serving the public system would result in up to a maximum of a 9% increase in mean waiting times, and a maximum of a 16% increase in median waiting times. They acknowledge that all of these figures are debatable – but the aim of the exercise is to point out a key consideration of capacity that was simply not considered sufficiently by the majority. Although the majority in *Chaoulli* were reassured that the integrity of Medicare would not be affected by the mere existence of public or social insurance in tandem with private insurance in European countries, they did not explore to any extent waiting times in countries with two-tier systems, the various measures that countries take who value solidarity to suppress the negative effects of private financing, or the access, quality and capacity problems inherent in systems with more private financing.

The Implications of Private Health Insurance

Trudo Lemmens and Tom Archibald of the University of Toronto critically examine the positions taken by the Canadian Medical Association both in its intervention before the Supreme Court in *Chaoulli* and in its subsequent resolution that private health insurance should be available when timely access cannot be provided in the public health system. Lemmens and Archibald accept that support for private insurance may be an expression of frustration at waiting times and that private health insurance will benefit some patients, but they raise concerns about its effects on the public system as a whole and on the ethics of the physician-patient relationship. Potential ethical problems include 'diagnostic drift' that will give some patients access to the private sector and attempts by insurance companies to influence the clinical judgments of doctors. They argue that the possible expansion of private insurance requires provincial colleges of physicians to enact new ethical standards and rules.

Robert Evans of the University of British Columbia predicts that increased private insurance in Canada will follow the American model of public subsidization through tax benefits and risk rating rather than the more regulated European model that is discussed in the previous part of this book. He predicts that the wealthy will benefit from lower premiums because they generally are healthier and that the less wealthy will be faced with higher premiums that may preclude them from purchasing private health insurance. He also predicts increased administrative costs and higher prices for medical services as the wealthy, assisted by insurance, will be able to demand and pay for the best of care. He suggests that the inflationary pressures of private insurance can already be seen in the increased cost of drugs that are purchased under existing health insurance policies in Canada. He also predicts that the interests of insurance companies and providers of health services will prevent attempts to regulate or remove private insurance once it has become established.

Tracey Epps and David Schneiderman of the University of Toronto argue that the Supreme Court ignored the effects of international trade agreements when it decided *Chaoulli* and that NAFTA in particular will restrain the ability of Canadian governments to respond to *Chaoulli*. Quebec and other provinces will have to allow American insurance firms to compete on the same terms as Canadian firms because private health insurance will not fall until the NAFTA reservation for a social service established or maintained for a public purpose. Attempts by Canadian governments to restrict or end private insurance once it has been introduced will be subject to the expropriation provisions of Article 1110 of NAFTA that requires the Canadian government to pay compensation. They argue that NAFTA may inhibit the ability of governments to turn the clock back and decide that experiments with increased private funding and private delivery of health services were a mistake because of the costs of compensating American investors.

Possible Governmental Responses to *Chaoulli*

The next section contains a number of essays that explores a variety of ways that Canadian governments can, should and likely will respond to *Chaoulli*. These essays also demonstrate that each province may take a different tack in responding to *Chaoulli* and that some provinces including Saskatchewan, Canada's pioneer in Medicare, already allow private insurance for services covered in the public system.

Claude E. Forget draws on his long experience with the Quebec health care system, including as a former Minister of Health, to explore the appropriate response to *Chaoulli* in that province. Although he originally supported complete governmental control over the health system when Medicare was developed in Quebec, he now accepts that private health insurance must play an increased role. For him, the majority judgment in *Chaoulli* has made clear that individuals are paying too great a price for seemingly intractable inefficiencies and lack of capacity in the public health system. He argues that the dissenting judgment is based on a serious ethical flaw, namely the idea that social benefits can prevail over individual suffering on a utilitarian calculus. On a more practical level, he notes that while substantial progress has been made to reduce waiting times in Quebec over the last two years, that province still lacks central management of waiting lists. He argues that queue jumping through private insurance would not be fundamentally different than the queue jumping that now tacitly occurs by changing doctors or hospitals or the preference given to patients whose costs are paid by workers' compensation.

Timothy Caulfield and Nola M. Ries of the University of Alberta examine possible reactions to *Chaoulli* in Alberta, the jurisdiction most likely in Canada to embrace a larger role for private financing and insurance. They contrast the reaction in the rest of Canada which focused on minimizing the impact of *Chaoulli* to Premier Ralph Klein's enthusiastic acceptance of the case as affirming the right of individuals to buy the health care that they need. They argue that Alberta's likely use of *Chaoulli* to increase the privatization of the Alberta health system is ironic given the government's previous unhappiness with judicial activism; the satisfaction of most Albertans with their health systems;

and Alberta's large budget surplus that could be used to enhance its health system. They also suggest that the result of a Charter challenge to Alberta's prohibition on private medical insurance for public services might be different in Quebec because of initiatives taken in Alberta with respect to waiting lists and the ability of Albertans on waiting listings to be compensated for treatment outside of the province. They caution, however, that only 34 of 100 such requests were approved in 2004–05. They express worry that *Chaoulli* may create a perverse incentive for the Klein government to under-resource the public system to satisfy its ideological desire for increased privatization.

Gregory P. Marchildon of the University of Regina examines the history of Medicare in the western province for clues about how they may react to Chaoulli. He draws analogies between Premier Klein's enthusiastic acceptance of *Chaoulli* and Ernst Manning's opposition to a single payer medicare system as incompatible with the rights and responsibilities inherent in a free and democratic society. Manning's government subsidized private health insurance schemes within the province until 1969 when private health insurance was prohibited so that Alberta could receive federal funds for Medicare. Marchildon predicts the British Columbia may follow the Alberta lead and notes that private insurance was only prohibited in that province by a NDP government in 1992. Marchildon explains how as a result of the famous doctors' strike of 1962, Saskatchewan continues to allow private medical insurance. At the same time, Saskatchewan dampens demand for private health insurance through others means and still sees itself as Canada's pioneer of single payer universal medicare insurance. This essay suggests that *Chaoulli* may present the most direct challenge to Medicare in Manitoba where private health insurance has been prohibited since 1958. Marchildon's account demonstrates the great range of nuanced policy responses that governments have and will continue to take when formulating health care policy and helps to place private health insurance into a larger policy context. His paper also highlights the enormous political challenges that were overcome by those seeking to establish one-tier Medicine in Canada and, building on the concerns of Lemmens and Archibald regarding the Canadian Medical Association's support of the Chaoulli decision, the history of opposition to single-tier Medicare on the part of organized medicine within Canada.

Terrence Sullivan and his colleagues at Cancer Care Ontario examine methods to shorten and rationalize waiting lists. After a crisis in 1999 and 2000 in which 1,500 Ontario Cancer patients had to be sent to the

United States for treatment, waiting times for cancer treatment in Ontario have now stabilized. They warn, however, that cancer rates will rise and that already 25% of cancer patients that should receive radiation therapy are not receiving it. They urge prevention strategies, but warn that progress on this front takes time that may not fit into either electoral cycles or the pressures of Charter litigation. They argue that waiting times are inevitable in any health care system, but can be made more rational through the use of public targets and data, standard triage tools (as used in the Western Canada Waiting List Project), provincial wide central management (as done in Saskatchewan and soon to be introduced in Ontario) and by system redesigns and experimentation where appropriate. They conclude that seeking an easy fix to the problem of waiting lists through the development of two-tier insurance that would allow some to jump queues is, in the words of Robert Evans, akin to the search for powdered unicorn horn. But whilst Sullivan and his colleagues disagree with the idea of duplicate private insurance for medically necessary hospital and physician services that would allow queue-jumping, they nonetheless stress there is must always be a role for private insurance and the private sector at the boundaries of the public system. In this regard, they examine the development of private clinics in Ontario to provide intravenous cancer drugs, a development that was previously mentioned by Charles Wright in his essay. The great challenge ahead in terms of drawing lines between public and private insurance, or private pay, is the development of new drugs and therapies that may not be sufficiently cost-effective to fund in the public sector. Presently, cancer drugs that have some benefit but are not considered cost-effective to be publicly funded cannot be provided to patients within a public hospital. Sullivan and colleagues raise the question of whether or not patients in public hospitals should be able to pay for drugs that are not considered 'medically necessary' but still may have some benefit.

Caroline Pitfield and Colleen M. Flood of the University of Toronto address the extent to which provinces may be able to defend themselves against a Chaoulli-style challenge to legislation prohibiting a two-tier system by improving safety valves or administrative appeal mechanism. Although the judges on the Court differed on whether Quebec's safety valves were adequate, they all seemed to agree that the adequacy of appeal mechanisms could affect the constitutionality of the health system. Pitfield and Flood examine Ontario's Health Services Appeal and Review Board and although it more independent and has a more specific mandate to deal with long wait times than other provincial boards they nonetheless still find that it would fall short of what is required in order to respond to waiting times and to protect the Ontario system from constitutional challenges. In particular, they find that the Board has no mandate to respond to instances where the psychological stress of waiting is acute. They argue that the Board has to have this mandate in order for the Ontario system to be able to resist a s. 7 challenge to its provision. They discuss the possibility of implementation of a wait time guarantee that could include within the formulation of those maximum wait times an acknowledgment of how long is too long to wait both from a clinical and a psychological perspective. They also discuss granting the Board the discretion to do justice in individual cases where the psychological effects of waiting are of such magnitude that s. 7 rights are engaged. Accessibility to the Board is also a problem and Flood and Wright make a variety of recommendations in particular relating to improving the speed with which the Board makes decisions so that applicants have relief in the face of long wait times not just in theory but in practice.

Chaoulli **and the Future of Medicare in Canada**

This collection concludes with two very important but different visions of both the *Chaoulli* case and its impact on the future of Canadian Medicare. They provide an interesting and accessible contrast for citizens to decide what they think about the *Chaoulli* case.

Stanley H. Hartt Q.C., who acted as counsel for Senator Kirby and other Senators in their intervention before the Supreme Court, defends *Chaoulli* as 'constitutional bright line in the sand' with respect to waiting lists. He defends the underlying philosophy of the majority's judgment as one that that requires 'social policy engineering' to give way to 'individual rights.' Hartt argues that the *Chaoulli* case can improve Medicare in Canada including the arbitrary nature of waiting lists. He also expresses hope that the *Chaoulli* case will prompt governments to adopt the Kirby's Committee proposed health care guarantee to give every patient access to treatment elsewhere if services cannot be supplied within standard wait times. He defends the health care guarantee as a 'self-regulating remedy' that is preferable to case by case adjudication either before administrative boards or the courts. He observes that the health care guarantee is neutral on the question of whether health care services are delivered publicly, privately or through some mixture.

Hartt concludes that the introduction of the health guarantee is a practical and urgent necessity because of *Chaoulli* and that the decision cannot be wished away.

The Hon. Roy Romanow draws on both his experience in negotiating the Canadian Charter and as the chair of the federal Commission of the Future of Health Care in Canada to provide a critique of *Chaoulli* and to warn of its threats to Medicare. He traces the history of s.7 of the Canadian Charter and expresses surprise that three judges on the Supreme Court would interpret it to be violated by laws that prohibit private health insurance. He questions the underlying philosophy of the case and expresses concerns that personal consumer preference may prevail over social need and the need to respond equitably to human need and suffering. With respect to health care policies, Romanow cites the United States as an example of the inefficiency of departures from the single payer system of medicare, noting that paper work costs about $1000 a year per person in the United States compared to about $300 a year in Canada. He acknowledges the need for health care reform, but suggests that the wait list problem that the Court focused on should be put into a larger value-based context and the evidence about the inefficiencies of departures from the single payer model.

Although it would be unrealistic and unwise to expect agreement on divisive topics such as the appropriate role of courts, the effects of private insurance, or the best response to waiting lists, our hope is that the different contributions in this volume contribute to a more informed debate. Whatever one's view about *Chaoulli* or its effects on Medicare, it is a decision that demands attention from governments and health policy-makers and full and frank discussion by citizens.

Notes

1 2005 SCC 35. An edited·extract of this lengthy judgment is contained in appendix C of this volume.
2 2000 R.J.Q. 786. An edited and translated extract of this lengthy judgment is contained in Appendix A of this volume.
3 [2002] R.J.Q. 105. See Appendix B in this volume.
4 *Auton v. British Columbia* [2004] 3 S.C.R. 657.
5 [1986] 1 S.C.R. 103.
6 R. S. Q. c. C-12 s.9.1.
7 198 U.S. 45 (1905).

8 [1988] 1 S.C.R. 3.

9 *Chaoulli v. Quebec* [2005] SCC 35 at paras 138, 85.

10 [1990] 2 S.C.R. 1199.

11 *Gosselin v. Quebec* [2002] 4 S.C.R. 429; *Auton v. British Columbia* [2004] 3
   S.C.R. 657.

12 *Chaoulli v. Quebec* at para 64

ACCESS TO CARE, ACCESS TO JUSTICE

What Did the Court Decide in *Chaoulli*?

Chaoulli: The Political versus the Legal Life of a Judicial Decision

PETER H.RUSSELL

Major decisions of high courts in constitutional democracies have a double life. The existence we readily recognize is the one at the legal level – what the judges actually wrote, their arguments and holdings and how judges and lawyers subsequently interpret and use the judges' words. But high court decisions on matters of great public interest and controversy live at another level – at the political level, in the public discourse and debate of the political community.[1] At this political level, such decisions take on virtually a mythic quality and their significance depends not on what the judges actually said but on what they are alleged to have said – and to have meant – by their supporters and detractors. What the decision comes to mean in the political life of the country may differ – indeed may differ wildly – from what the judges actually decided. This is so because the decision's political meaning is shaped by journalists, publicists, politicians and academics whose interpretation of the decision's significance has only the most tenuous relationship with the judges' words.

Chaoulli v. Quebec,[2] is surely a case with the potential of living such a double life. Undoubtedly it touched on one of the most contentious policy issues in Canada today – the extent to which Canada's public system should be privatized. On June 10, 2005, the day after the Supreme Court rendered its decision, front-page headlines heralded it as a policy bombshell. 'The new face of medicare,' trumpeted *The Globe and Mail*.[3] 'Timely health care a basic right, Supreme Court says,' screamed the *Toronto Star*.[4] The stories under these headlines, written by the papers' leading columnists, proclaimed the decision as a policy revolution. In the *Globe*, Jeffrey Simpson began his story with the pronouncement that, 'Canadian medicare will never be the same.' Tom Walkon writing on the *Star's* front page was equally dramatic: 'The Supreme Court has delivered a hammer-blow to medicare.' Though my sample of news coverage is very limited, I would venture a guess that the first wave of news coverage was much the same throughout the country and *Chaoulli* began its political life as a decision in which the Supreme Court of Canada had executed a policy revolution that would convert Canadian medicare from a single-tier public system to a public/private two-tier system.

Unlike the journalists, I did not have to meet a deadline and had the luxury of being able to read the judgment carefully before saying anything about it. Nor in what I said – and eventually wrote – did I have to do anything to increase newspaper proprietors' profits or improve news-show ratings. I could be careful and measured. I could make eyes glaze over. And when I had read and re-read the three opinions offered by the judges and began to ruminate on them, I was struck by just how narrow the decision really was. In its own terms, it neither changed the face of medicare nor established a Charter right to timely health care – nor ushered in a two-tier system of health care. As Bernard Dickens suggests in this volume 'there is less than meets the eye'[5] in the decision, and I might add 'less than meets the ear.' I decided that if I wrote anything about *Chaoulli*, it would focus on the difference between the decision's legal and political meanings.

What the Supreme Court decided

The Supreme Court actually decided – four judges to three – that sections of two Quebec statutes that prohibit private insurance for health care services available in the public system violate the right to personal 'inviolability' in section 1 of the *Quebec Charter of human rights and freedoms*. That is all that the Supreme Court majority in this case decided. The Court did not decide that the prohibition against private insurance for services available through the public plan violates the *Canadian Charter of Rights and Freedoms*. On that question the justices split – three to three. The opinion co-authored by Chief Justice McLachlin and Justice Major and concurred in by Justice Bastarache found that the Quebec legislation as well as contravening section 1 of the Quebec Charter, also violated section 7 of the Canadian Charter and could not be saved by section 1, the reasonable limits clause. The opinion co-authored by Justices Binnie and LeBel and concurred in by Justice Fish held that the legislation violates neither the Quebec nor the Canadian

Charter. The decisive opinion in the case was written by Justice Deschamps who found that the Quebec legislation violated the Quebec Charter. Justice Deschamps declined to address the question of whether the legislation contravened the Canadian Charter.

In declining to consider the constitutionality of the Quebec legislation under the *Canadian Charter of Rights and Freedoms*, Justice Deschamps was following a strategy set out by Justice Jean Beetz in the early days of the Charter. In 1985, in the *Singh* case[6] involving a challenge to federal immigration procedures, Beetz turned first to the question of whether the legislation was inconsistent with the statutory *Canadian Bill of Rights*. Only if he found that the legislation met the requirements of the *Bill of Rights* would he consider its consistency with the *Charter of Rights and Freedoms*. The thinking behind this strategy was one of judicial restraint. Statutory codes of rights such as the *Bill of Rights* and the various provincial charters often contain clauses that define rights differently – indeed often more broadly – than the Canadian Charter. Judges should first endeavour to give full effect to these 'quasi-constitutional' instruments and only go on to consider the weightier constitutional issues under the Canadian Charter if they find the impugned legislation does not infringe a statutory bill or charter. These statutory instruments, Beetz argued 'are susceptible of producing cumulative results for the better protection of rights and freedoms,' results that 'will be lost if these instruments fall into neglect.'[7] To this rationale, Justice Deschamps adds the consideration that 'the Quebec Charter is the product of the legislative will of Quebec's National Assembly.'[8] This deference to Quebec's constitution, as we shall see and as Jean-Francois Gaudreault-DesBiens and Charles-Maxime Panaccio show in their chapter,[9] is soon offset by Justice Dechamps' inclination to use the jurisprudence of the Canadian Charter to interpret the Quebec Charter.

Justice Deschamps points to significant differences between section 1 of the Quebec Charter and section 7 of the Canadian Charter. Whereas the right not to be deprived of the right to life, liberty and security of the person' in section 7 of the Charter is qualified by the words 'except in accordance with principles of fundamental justice,' section 1 of the Quebec Charter simply states that 'Every human being has a right to life, and to personal security, inviolability and freedom' with no qualification. She also notes that the Quebec Charter lacks a general limitation clause similar to section 1 of the Canadian Charter. Instead its section 9.1 states that 'In exercising his fundamental freedoms and rights, a person shall maintain a proper regard for democratic values, public order and the general well-being of the citizens of Quebec.' The differences noted above indicate that the right in section 1 of the Quebec Charter is less qualified than section 7 of the Charter.

There is the additional difference that 'inviolability' is not mentioned in section 7 of the Canadian Charter – and it is the right to personal inviolability on which Justice Deschamps anchors her judgment. Although I have always thought of 'inviolability' as referring to protection against the most severe and abusive assault on a person (and that is how the English dictionaries I consulted treat it) and therefore a narrower concept than personal security, Justice Deschamps considers the right to personal inviolability to be 'broader' than the right to 'security of the person' in section 7 of the Charter. She does not refer to any definition of the concept but makes the somewhat circular observation that when personal inviolability is used in civil liability cases in Quebec it 'includes both physical and mental or psychological inviolability.'[10] But this, of course, refers only to aspects of 'inviolability' not to the substance of inviolability itself. To justify her finding that long delays experienced by Quebec citizens who could not afford to pay for private medical services infringed the right to inviolability of the person, Justice Deschamps refers to Chief Justice Dickson's opinion in the *Morgentaler* case that delays in waiting for therapeutic abortions could deprive a person of the right to security of the person in section 7 of the Charter. Her reasoning is that since the protection of personal inviolability is a broader right than 'security of the person' it must include at least what is protected under the latter. So in an odd way, Justice Deschamps brings in the jurisprudence of the Canadian Charter to interpret the meaning of the Quebec Charter.

She does much the same with section 9.1 of the Quebec Charter. Although it appears to be a limitation on how citizens should exercise their rights, she treats is as being analogous to the Canadian Charter's section 1 setting out the conditions under which legislation might legitimately limit a right. Thus she invokes the jurisprudence of the Canadian Charter's section 1 under which the onus is on government to prove that a right-infringing law encroaches on a right no more than is necessary to achieve an important public purpose. In the case at hand, Quebec had not proved that in order to prevent an exodus of doctors to private medicine it was necessary to prohibit private insurance for services covered by medicare. The Chief Justice, Justices Major and Bastarache concurred with all of this, but instead of following the Beetz judicial strategy went on to deal with the Canadian Charter issues.

Justices Binnie, LeBel and Fish did not accept Justice Deschamps' application of the Quebec Charter. On the substantive question about waiting lists and personal security or inviolability, they did not accept her dismissal of the trial judge's finding of insufficient evidence linking the prohibition of private insurance to long life-threatening waiting lists. And they treated the Quebec Charter's section 9.1 on its own terms, holding that a successful effort to defeat the prohibition against private insurance 'would not show 'the proper regard for democratic values' or 'public order' required by section 9.1, 'as the future of a publicly supported and financed single-tier health plan should be in the hands of elected representatives.'[11]

So far from delivering a hammer-blow to Canadian medicare, the Court's decision in *Chaoulli* affects only Quebec and even does this in a rather mild manner. The Supreme Court's ruling does not render Quebec's legislative prohibition of private health insurance constitutionally invalid. The Quebec's National Assembly can re-assert its prohibition against private health insurance simply by re-enacting the legislation with a statement that it stands notwithstanding s.1 of the Quebec Charter. By using the Canadian Charter's notwithstanding clause, the National Assembly could do that too if the majority had based its decision on section 7 of the Canadian Charter. Quebec is one province whose political leaders have not been afraid to invoke the Canadian Charter's override clause to protect matters of vital interest to the province. The Court has suspended the application of its decision until June 2006.[12] Whether Quebec uses that time to improve its management of waiting lists and satisfy the Supreme Court majority, or abandons its prohibition of private insurance or keeps the prohibition by using the nowithstanding device will be decided by politicians. In Quebec, and in every other jurisdiction including those that, like Quebec, prohibit private health insurance, the future of medicare will be decided by politicians not judges.

What the Court did not decide in *Chaoulli*

The major issue of constitutional law on which the Supreme Court split down the middle and therefore did not decide in *Chaoulli* is the scope of the Canadian Charter's section 7 and the meaning of its crucial qualifying phrase 'except in accordance with the principles of fundamental justice.' On no other Charter section has the Supreme Court of Canada departed so blatantly from the intentions of the Charter's framers. It did so in one of its earliest decisions on the Charter, *Reference re BC Motor Vehicle Act*.[13] In that decision, Justice Lamer, speaking for a unanimous court, held that 'principles of fundamental justice' referred not only to procedural fairness but also to substantive considerations – despite evidence that in 1981 the Special Joint Parliamentary Committee on the Constitution was assured by the Minister of Justice and other justice officials that section 7 was drafted to cover only procedural matters. Justice Lamer tried to assuage fears of the Court becoming a 'super-legislature' by stating that the judges would find the 'principles of fundamental justice' not in the 'realm of general public policy' but in the basic tenets of our legal system ... the inherent domain of the judiciary ...'[14] However, in subsequent decisions, it did not back away from applying section 7 and 'principles of fundamental justice' to major issues of public policy, such as abortion,[15] assisted suicide,[16] child welfare[17] and the death penalty.[18]

The big Charter issue in *Chaoulli* was not whether section 7 covered only procedural justice or applied only to the operation of the legal system. The Court had already pushed section 7 well beyond those boundaries. But now, if Chief Justice McLachlin and her two colleagues had their way, section 7 would be pushed a significant step closer to becoming a platform for Canada's judiciary to assume the role of a 'super- legislature.' The key difference between the two trios of justices who applied the Canadian Charter to the prohibition of private health insurance for services available under medicare was not over whether the right to security of the person might be infringed by long waiting periods for medical services. Binnie, LeBel and Fish agreed with the trial judge that 'in *some* circumstances *some* Quebecers may have their life or 'security of person' put at risk by the prohibition against private health insurance.'[19] The two groups of justices differed over whether threats to security of the person arose from laws that observed 'principles of fundamental justice.' McLachlin, Major and Bastarache held that the Quebec legislation prohibiting private insurance did not observe these principles because it was 'arbitrary.' Binnie, LeBel and Fish agreed that 'arbitrary' laws would violate 'principles of fundamental justice' but that the Quebec laws were not arbitrary. Whether the Supreme Court will significantly increase the judiciary's role in reviewing Canadian public policy depends very much on how the judicial tie in *Chaoulli* over what constitutes unconstitutional arbitrariness is eventually settled.

In *Morgentaler*, the Supreme Court majority's ruling that the provisions of the Criminal Code governing therapeutic abortions were not in accordance with principles of fundamental justice was based on a number of technical and procedural deficiencies in the law and as well as on the way it was administered. Chief Justice Dickson who wrote one of the majority decisions found that the lack of an adequate standard to guide hospital abortion committees and the failure to establish such committees in many parts of the country meant that a defence in the criminal code was not available on a consistent basis throughout the country and that this was 'manifestly unfair.' Justice Beetz who wrote the other majority opinion also found that certain features of the law were 'manifestly unfair' because they imposed requirements – that therapeutic abortions be performed only in eligible hospitals and that doctors who perform abortions be excluded from the committees – that did not serve the purpose of the law and in that sense were 'unnecessary.'

In *Chaoulli*, McLachlin, Major and Bastarache take this notion of manifest unfairness in the way the criminal law is written and administered and expand it into a general concept of arbitrariness. Citing Justice McLachlin's words from her dissenting judgment in *Rodriquez*, they say that 'A law is arbitrary where "it bears no relation to, or is inconsistent with, the objective that lies behind (it)."'[20] The objective of the Quebec laws prohibiting private health insurance is to prevent a diversion of resources from the public system that would ultimately reduce the quality of care available through the public system. The rights claimants bear the burden of showing that the impugned Quebec laws are arbitrary in that they bear no relation to or are inconsistent with that purpose. In the opinion of the Chief Justice and her two colleagues, the rights claimants have made such a demonstration by showing that in a number of foreign countries, namely Sweden, Germany and the United Kingdom, that allow private insurance, only a small percentage of the population purchase this insurance and the great majority continue to rely on the public system. Their discussion of this evidence did not deal with the quality of public health care as compared with private health care in these countries nor with how the medical insurance laws of these countries interacted with their social and economic contexts. Neither did they comment on the conclusion of the Romanow Royal Commission that there was no evidence that adoption of private health care system would produce a more efficient, affordable or efficient system. On the other hand, they were impressed by submissions to the Senate Committee chaired by Michael Kirby and Kirby's conclusion that private contributions, including insurance for some services, can improve the breadth and quality of health care for all citizens. They conclude that this evidence – the quantitative evidence from Europe plus Kirby – 'stands as the best guide with respect to the question of whether a ban on private insurance is necessary and relevant to the goal of providing quality public health care.'[21]

Binnie, LeBel and Fish accept McLachlin's definition of what makes a law arbitrary but disagree vigorously with the inflation of these words by the McLachlin trio in the present case. Substitution of the word 'unnecessary' for 'inconsistent' in the definition, they argue, substantially alters the meaning of 'arbitrary': '"Inconsistent" means that the law logically contradicts its objectives, whereas "unnecessary" means that the objective could be met by other means.' This inflation of 'arbitrary' as a test of what constitutes unconstitutional arbitrariness would significantly expand the scope of judicial review:

> If a court were to declare unconstitutional every law impacting 'security of the person' that the court considers unnecessary, there would be much greater scope for intervention under s.7 than has previously been considered by this Court to be acceptable ... The courts might find themselves constantly second-guessing the validity of governments' public policy objectives based on subjective views of the *necessity* of particular means used to advance legitimate government action as opposed to other means which critics might prefer.[22]

In essence, the Binnie trio reject the McLachlin trio's treatment of 'the principles of fundamental justice' as it would do exactly what Justice Lamer warned against when, in *Reference re BC Motor Vehicle Act*, he wrote that the Court must 'secure for persons 'the full benefit of the Charter's protections' ... while avoiding adjudication of the merits of public policy.'[23]

Binnie, LeBel and Fish consider the evidence submitted at trial and sections of both the Romanow and Kirby reports that deal with the risk of an expanded private health system diverting resources from the public system. In their view, concern about this danger is directly relevant to the purpose of legislation banning private insurance. Applying the Chief Justice's original definition of 'arbitrary,' they conclude that the legislation is not inconsistent with its purpose of maintaining a strong public health system and therefore 'would not violate any *legal* principle of fundamental justice ...'[24]

The Supreme Court's fiercest anti-activist critics may make light of the difference in *Chaoulli* between the two trios of justices on section 7 of the Charter. In their mind the Court has already interpreted the Charter's terms so liberally and applied it so vigorously that adoption of a wider view of section 7 can be of little consequence. However, I think the position taken by the McLachlin trio would significantly widen the scope for successful section 7 challenges to legislation. Granted the right to liberty in section 7 has been narrowed by the Court to exclude use of the Charter to provide protection against economic regulation[25] – and it was to protect the right to liberty in the 14th Amendment of that country's Constitution that the US Supreme Court fashioned its substantive due process doctrine. Still, 'security of the person' is a broad concept that could attract many challenges from individuals who believe that their personal security is undermined by laws they deem to be unnecessary. This would be particularly the case if judges can be as easily convinced that a law is unnecessary as the Chief Justice and her colleagues were in *Chaoulli*. If the Supreme Court's majority endorses the McLachlin trio's view of unconstitutional arbitrariness it will substantially increase judicial activism in Canada. Indeed, as Sujit Choudhry points out in his chapter, if the McLachlin/Major doctrine of constitutional arbitrariness were to be adopted by a majority on the Court, it would invite the Canadian judiciary to take on an even greater legislative role than that opened up by the substantive due process introduced into American constitutional law by the United States Supreme Court in the *Lochner* case.[26]

The future of judicial activism and medicare

Unlike the future of medicare, the future of judicial activism is entirely in the hands of the judges. The imminent retirement of Justice Major who reaches age 75 in 2006 leaves just two justices – the Chief Justice and Justice Bastarache – on record as supporting the expanded view of the principles of fundamental justice in section 7. The robust nature of the Binnie trio's rejection of that position suggests that those three justices are not about to be won over to the expanded view. Thus the future of *Chaoulli*'s legal life depends on Justices Deschamps, the two newly appointed justices, Abella and Charron, who did not take part in the decision, and Justice Major's replacement. Three of these four will have to be won over to the McLachlin trio's view if it is to prevail as constitutional law in Canada.

I think it would be wrong to predict that Justice Deschamps will support the wider treatment of section 7 simply because in *Chaoulli* she came down on the side of those challenging the Quebec legislation. Her judgment, as we have seen, did not deal at all with Canadian Charter arguments against the legislation. It is possible that she confined her judgment to the Quebec Charter because she was not comfortable with the position McLachlin and Major were developing on the Canadian Charter. As for Abella and Charron, on the basis of their records as members of the Ontario Court of Appeal as well as their professional activities off the bench, Abella is thought to be on the activist side of the judicial spectrum and Charron on the more cautious and restrained side. But even if Justice Abella is inclined to take a generous and liberal view of some Charter rights (for example equality rights), she may not be attracted to the wider view of section 7 advanced by the Chief Justice and her colleagues in *Chaoulli*. Not only are there the social democratic values inherent in upholding legislation aimed at preserving a single-tier public health system, but there is also the warning issued by former Chief Justice Dickson in *Edwards Books* in 1986, a warning with which Binnie, LeBel and Fish conclude their judgment in *Chaoulli*:

> In interpreting and applying the *Charter* I believe the courts must be cautious that it does not simply become an instrument of better situated individuals to roll back legislation which has as its object the improvement of the conditions of less advantaged individuals.[27]

Justice Abella is likely to take that warning to heart and to be mindful of that period in American constitutional law, also mentioned in the Binnie trio's opinion,[28] when 'substantive due process' was used by the United States Supreme Court to strike down legislation bringing on the welfare state. If Abella is by no means a sure bet for supporting the expansive view of section 7, Charron, who is a very careful and cautious jurist, is even less likely to be won over to that side. Thus, it seems unlikely to me that the Chief Justice's treatment of section 7 will win the support of all three of the sitting members of her Court who have yet to be been heard from on the matter.

This underlines the importance of the new member of the Court who will be appointed to fill the vacancy created by Justice Major's retirement. It also draws attention to the Martin government's latest proposal for reforming the process of Supreme Court appointments.[29] Under this proposal, the Minister of Justice will submit a list of up to eight candidates to a nine-person Advisory Committee made up of MPs from the four parties recognized by the House of Commons, a retired judge chosen by the Canadian Judicial Council, a provincial government representative chosen by the governments of the region from which, by convention, Justice Major's replacement must come (Alberta, Saskatchewan and Manitoba), a lawyer chosen by the Law Societies of that region and two lay persons 'of integrity and distinction' from the region who will be chosen by the Minister of Justice. In assessing the candidates, the Advisory Committee is to consult widely but cannot interview the candidates *in camera* or in public. In the end it will provide the Justice Minister with an unranked list of three candidates with a commentary on the strengths and weaknesses of each. The Prime Minister will make the final selection from this list. Although committee members will not be able to question candidates directly about their views on *Chaoulli*, that decision will surely be on the minds of some members of the committee – in particular the MPs with strong views on both judicial activism and medicare. That said, however, I very much doubt that a consensus will form on the committee either on what to look for in their consultations or on what has been found. I also doubt that candidates' orientation on *Chaoulli* will be a factor in the Prime Minister's final selection. So the new justice will likely assume his or her position on the Court as an unknown quantity with respect to *Chaoulli*. The legal life of *Chaoulli* – whether or not it raises the Court's Charter activism a notch – will remain firmly in the hands of the judges.

The future of medicare, on the other hand, will be determined not by judges but by politics and economics – though the mythic political life of *Chaoulli* may well be part of the politics. Since the decision was rendered in early July, 2005, there have been signs of increasing momentum to expand the already large private sector of Canada's health system. These include the failure of a motion to endorse a one-tier public system at a meeting of the Canadian Medical Association and the opening of a new private cancer clinic in Toronto.[30] Of course it is impossible to know whether the Supreme Court's decision contributed to these developments. Still, for those who favour expanding the private sector of the health system, *Chaoulli*, with its media aura of giving judicial approval to privatization, probably adds some political strength to their cause. The more benign political effect of *Chaoulli* may be, as several contributors to this book argue,[31] to serve as a catalyst for improving the management of waiting times for critically important medical services not only in Quebec but throughout Canada. The political reach of a judicial decision on a major public policy issue usually much exceeds its legal bight.

Up to now, as Guy Giorno has argued,[32] it has been economics much more than law that has held back the growth of private health insurance. The *Canada Health Act* does not prohibit private insurance for services covered by the public plan. However private insurance has not flourished in the four provinces that permit it, presumably because it is hard for private insurers to compete with a non-profit public system that provides reasonably good service. But, as Giorno points out, there must surely come a point at which long and unpredictable waiting times for vitally needed services create a market for private insurers. Such a market is much more likely to exist in large and relatively affluent provinces like Alberta, British Columbia and Ontario which (along with Manitoba and Prince Edward Island) prohibit private insurance for services covered by medicare. *Chaoulli*, in its political guise, may well add to the pressure on governments of these provinces to remove the private insurance ban.

If we do see the introduction of private insurance for basic medical services in these provinces, it will likely be as a result of decisions made by provincial governments and legislatures, not by the courts. The political reverberations of *Chaoulli* may well be a factor in the politics of expanding the private sector of the Canadian health care system, but not nearly as important a factor as law professors would have you believe. Of course it is possible that in a province whose government chooses to continue its prohibition of private insurance, the courts will come back into play. If they do, the challenge to the prohibition will be based on the Canadian Charter and we will find out how the Supreme Court decides the major constitutional issue about the principles of fundamental justice which it opened up, but did not decide, in *Chaoulli*.

In the meantime, while the legal life of *Chaoulli* is basically in abeyance, its political life, now totally detached from what the judges actually said and did, rolls on in the public life of the country. The conference that gave rise to this book is a good example. In the *Toronto Star*'s front page report on the conference under the headline 'Romanow fears "end of medicare"'[33] we can see Romanow and the *Star* using *Chaoulli* to rally support for the single-payer system. At this point there is no way of knowing who will make the most of *Chaoulli* – its supporters or its opponents. We can only be sure that the political dividends and deficits it yields have little to do with what the Court actually decided.

Notes

1 I have presented a fuller elaboration of this idea, in Peter H. Russell, *Recognizing Aboriginal Title: The Mabo Case and Indigenous Resistance to English-Settler Colonialism,* (Toronto: University of Toronto Press, 2005), p. 248.

2 2005 SCC 35

3 *The Globe and Mail,* Friday, June 10, 2005, p. A1

4 *Toronto Star,* Friday, June 10, 2005, p. A1

5 See Bernard Dickens in this volume.

6 *Singh v. Minister of Employment and Immigration,* [1985] 1 S.C.R. 177

7 *Ibid,* at p. 224.

8 *Chaoulli v. Quebec,* at para 25.

9 See Gaudreault-DesBiens and Panaccio in this volume

10 *Chaoulli v. Quebec* at para 41.

11 *Ibid.* at para 273.

12 See chapter by Kent Roach in this volume for discussion of the Court's decision on August 4, 2005 to suspend its judgment until June 9, 2006.

13 [1985] 2 S.C.R. 486.

14 *Ibid.* at 503.

15 *Morgentaler v. The Queen,* [1988] 1 S.C.R. 30.

16 *Rodriquez v. British Columbia,* [1993] 3 S.C.R. 519.

17 *New Brunswick v. G.(J.),* [1999] 3 S.C.R. 46.

18 *USA v. Burns and Rafay* [2001] 1 S.C.R.283

19 *Chaoulli,* at para 191.

20 *Ibid.* at para 130.

21 *Ibid.* at para 150.

22 *Ibid.* at para 234.

23 [1985] 2 S.C.R 486, at para 21.

24 *Chaoulli* at para 265.

25 The key case is *Irwin Toy v. Quebec* [1989] 1 S.C.R. 927 at 1004.

26 See chapter by Sujit Choudhry

27 *Chaoulli* at para 274.

28 *Ibid* at para 201.

29 Department of Justice, *Proposal to Reform the Supreme Court of Canada Appointments Process* April 2005 at http://canada.justice.gc.ca/en/dept/pub/scc/index.html

30 Carolyn Abraham, 'Cancer clinic opens the door to private care,' *Globe and Mail,* Auguest 23, 2005, p. A1. For a discussion of the CMA resolution see Lemmens and Archibald in this volume and for a discussion of the new private cancer clinic see Terry Sullivan et al in this volume.

31 See chapters by Stanley Hart and Terry Sullivan in this volume.

32 Guy Giorno, 'Supreme Court or no Supreme Court, the Canada Health Act is not what's stopping private health insurance,' *Globe and Mail*, June 20, 2005, p. A19.

33 *Toronto Star*, September 17, 2005, p. A1

The Chaoulli Judgment: Less Than Meets the Eye – or More

BERNARD M. DICKENS

Introduction

The meaning of judicial decisions, like beauty, is often in the eye of the beholder. Different beholders of the June 9, 2005 decision of the Supreme Court of Canada's seven-judge panel in *Chaoulli v. Québec*[1] see meanings spanning a spectrum of contrasts. Some see the judgment as marking the end of Canada's primarily publicly-funded nationally-structured health service, usually described, with a different scope from the word's roots in the U.S., as Medicare. At the other extreme, some see only judicial condemnation of a failing of Québec's provincial health care service to satisfy requirement of Québec law, with no necessary implications elsewhere. Indeed, since the Supreme Court on August 4, 2005 granted a motion by the Attorney General of Québec for a partial rehearing of the case and stayed the June 9 judgment for twelve months, the judgment may prove to have only limited implications for Québec itself.[2] It is widely agreed, however, that the four-to-three judicial majority, which reversed the lower courts' dismissal of Chaoulli's claim, has fired a shot across the bows of floundering provincial health care systems, with the threat to sink them if inadequacies, evidenced in lengthy waiting lists for necessary care, persist.

The *Chaoulli* Decision

Mr. Zeliotis, who complained of suffering pain and discomfort during the year he had waited for hip replacement surgery, joined with Dr. Chaoulli, who wanted to establish a private hospital service, to challenge Québec's law. Québec's Health Insurance Act[3] prohibitively provided that no person shall make an insurance contract, or a payment under a contract, that covers a service insured under Québec's health care plan. Similarly, the provincial Hospital Insurance Act[4] provided that no one shall make a contract, or a payment under a contract, under which a provincial resident is to be provided with, or to be reimbursed for, a hospital service insured under the provincial plan. The plaintiffs sued the Attorney-General of Québec and the Attorney General of Canada for a declaratory judgment that these provisions violated Québec's provincial Charter of Human Rights and Freedoms, (the Québec Charter)[5] and the Canadian Charter of Rights and Freedoms (the Canadian Charter)[6] respectively.

Section 1 of the Québec Charter provides that '[e]very human being has a right to life, and to personal security, inviolability and freedom.' Under Section 9.1, freedoms and rights, and their exercise, may be legally limited, since 'a person shall maintain a proper regard for democratic values, public order and the general well-being of the citizens of Québec.' Four of the seven Supreme Court justices reversed the lower courts, and rejected the public policy reasoning advanced by the provincial Attorney General. In a judgment written by Madam Justice Deschamps, they found that denials of the patient's rights to purchase privately more speedy medical care than the provincial health care system could provide, and of Dr. Chaoulli's right to provide such care, violated patients' rights to security under section 1, and were not justifiable under section 9.1. Accordingly, the prohibitive provisions of the provincial Health Insurance Act and Hospital Insurance Act were to be struck down. Although two of the three Supreme Court justices from Québec dissented from this view, the Court's majority opened a legal possibility for private insurance of services to be provided in addition to those insured under the public health service plan.

Section 7 of the Canadian Charter provides that '[e]veryone has the right to life, liberty and security of the person and the right not to be deprived thereof except in accordance with the principles of fundamental justice.' Under section 1, Charter rights and freedoms are guaranteed, 'subject only to such reasonable limits prescribed by law as can be demonstrably justified in a free and democratic society.' The three dissenting justices who voted to uphold the provisions challenged under the Québec Charter voted to uphold them equally under the Canadian Charter. Three of the four majority justices who found the challenged provisions to violate the Québec Charter found them in violation of the rights to security of the person under section 7 of the Canadian Charter, and not saved by section 1. They drew upon international experience to find the limiting provisions of the Québec laws not justifiable in Canada's free and democratic society.

The fourth majority justice, Madam Justice Deschamps, being prepared to strike down the challenged laws for violation of the Québec Charter, found it unnecessary to consider and rule on whether these laws were or were not valid under the Canadian Charter. Accordingly, the Supreme Court reached no decision under the Canadian Charter, since the judges who addressed the issue split 3:3 on whether Québec's restrictions violated section 7 of the Charter.

Issues

Key to the majority and dissenting judgments was judicial assessment of evidence on the impact of privately insured services on the provincially-supported public system of health care. The majority considered that evidence of harm to the integrity of the public system was not sufficiently persuasive to justify the complete prohibition of private insurance and supply of parallel (or 'two-tier') services. They found that the Québec government's insistence on absolute prohibition was 'arbitrary' and therefore in breach of provisions of the Québec Charter. Three of the majority judges considered this in addition to violate the Canadian Charter. In contrast, the minority found that the government of Québec had reached a reasonable conclusion that the growth of private sector delivery of health services insured under the public sector system would have a harmful effect on supply of and access to public services, and would prejudice the egalitarian goal of supplying services on the basis of medical need, by privileging access on the basis of wealth or status. The minority found the government's assessment to be evidence-based, non-arbitrary, and a decision better reached by publicly accountable government agencies than by judges. How far judges may superimpose their views over those of governments and legislatures is now often expressed in language of 'judicial activism.'[7]

The issue was not the legality of privately-insured health services as such. Many health care services are covered by private insurance because they fall outside those provincially insured health care services eligible for federal government partial reimbursement under the Canada Health Act (CHA),[8] sometimes described as 'core' services. Such health services may fall outside the scope of core services and not be provincially funded, or be provincially funded with no entitlement to federal reimbursement. It is estimated that nearly 30% of Canadian health expenditures are for privately-insured or non-core services.[9]

The concept of core services that provincial health funding should cover under provincial health service legislation designed to attract federal reimbursement under the CHA was addressed in the *Auton* case.[10] The CHA requires coverage of medically necessary services provided by hospitals or physicians. The *Auton* claim failed in the Supreme Court of Canada because the services that parents of autistic children required, which the province refused to fund, were not delivered by hospitals or delivered or recommended by physicians, and the Court was not satisfied that they were medically necessary in light of possible alternative treatments. In *Chaoulli*, however, the hip replacement surgery was medically necessary and could be undertaken only in hospital under a physician's care; Dr. Chaoulli, who was not the physician treating his co-plaintiff, proposed to establish a hospital. The case therefore clearly concerned services that provincial health care systems operating under the CHA are expected to cover.

The *Auton* case was first decided by the British Columbia trial court in 2000[11] in favour of the claimants for public funding of care for their autistic children. The British Columbia Court of Appeal upheld this decision in 2002,[12] over the defendant government's assertion that its funding arrangements for care of autistic children did not constitute discrimination on grounds of disability, contrary to section 15(1) of the Canadian Charter. The government further contended that, if a section 15(1) violation was found, it was demonstrably justified, and therefore permissible under section 1 of that Charter, because the allocation of scarce health care resources to limitless demands is a government matter, expenditures of taxpayers' monies are a parliamentary matter, and the courts should defer to governmental and parliamentary authorities on both.

When in November 2004, the Supreme Court of Canada reversed the British Columbia trial and appeal courts, finding that the treatment claimed was not a core service and that accordingly there was no discrimination in the provincial government's failure to allocate adequate funding to such services, critical and media attention was directed to private insurance of non-core services, and to the related issue of the potential for private insurance of core services provincial health care systems can supply only subject to health- and life-endangering delays.

This judicial background may explain, at least in part, the overwrought reactions of newsmedia and other commentators to the Supreme Court's *Chaoulli* decision that Professor Peter Russell has noted in his chapter.[13] *Chaoulli* is in some ways more portentous than *Auton*, because the Supreme Court in *Auton* reversed two successful challenges to provincial governmental decisions on health service funding and upheld governmental arguments, whereas in *Chaoulli* the Supreme Court reversed two failed attempts to challenge provincial legislation that upheld governmentally-favoured exclusive insurance of medical and hospital services, and seemed to open entitlements to private insurance parallel to governmental insurance for core health care services. It must be asked, however, whether the *Chaoulli* judgment will bear the precedental value that some commentators have ascribed to it.

The Doctrine of Precedent

The Supreme Court of Canada is not bound by its own decisions, but they are legal precedents for all lower courts. The direct effect of the Supreme Court's decision is that the prohibition of private purchase, sale and insurance of publicly insured health services in the province of Québec can be unlawful. The Attorney General of Québec has been granted leave, however, for a partial rehearing of the case, and the Court has suspended enforcement of its judgment for at least twelve months. The provincial government can therefore formulate its response to the reasoning of the June 9, 2005 majority judgment, and perhaps present additional evidence. The response might include expanded funding for health care services, perhaps with increased federal payments under CHA. If waiting times for medically necessary care were to be eliminated or substantially reduced, the province might claim that, since patients' rights to security under section 1 of the Québec Charter would no longer be violated, the restrictions of the challenged laws would not need to be rendered inoperative. Unless the Supreme Court's majority judgment means that any waiting time will violate the Québec and perhaps the Canadian Charters, a response that waiting times will be eliminated, or confined to maximum limits, might be satisfactory, since the majority's primary goal was not to provide for private health care insurance in itself, but to protect Québec citizens' rights to security through their access to timely necessary medical care.

Madam Justice Deschamps declined to cast her swing vote on whether the challenged Québec legislation violated the Canadian Charter, but in order to interpret the right to 'security' under the Québec Charter, she invoked the *Morgentaler* decision[14] of the Supreme Court,[15] which interpreted 'the right to life, liberty and security of the person' under section 7 of the Canadian Charter. In this landmark decision, the Court struck down the restrictive criminal abortion law on the ground that it violated women's security of the person, because its effect was to delay medically indicated treatment. This closely parallels her concern in *Chaoulli*, that delay exposed the patient to physical pain and psychological suffering. It may therefore be speculated that Madam Justice Deschamps would have found a violation of the right to security of the person under the Canadian Charter, and that, as in *Morgentaler*, it was not justifiable under section 1.

Although the dissenting justices attempted to distinguish the legal relevance of the 1988 *Morgentaler* decision on access to abortion care by reference to its grounding in criminal law, it was a powerful influence on the majority justices in *Chaoulli* on legal and factual grounds. Delays in women's access to therapeutic abortion services when their lives or health were endangered by continuation of pregnancy were ruled to violate their security of the person, guaranteed in law by section 7 of the Canadian Charter, because 'any unnecessary delay can have profound consequences on the woman's physical and emotional well-being.'[16] Delays due to legal provisions on access to care were found 'manifestly unfair'[17] on the basis of the detailed research and evidence provided in the Badgley Report.[18] Principal findings in the Report were that delays in treatment were common, considerably increasing medical risks of procedures and aggravating psychological stress on patients, and that services were inequitably available since 'the procedure provided ... for obtaining therapeutic abortion is in practice illusory for many Canadian women.'[19]

The significance of the Badgley Report to the *Chaoulli* majority justices was that its findings of health-endangering delays in access to medically indicated treatment were submitted to Parliament and distributed to provincial health ministries in January 1977, but when the trial of Dr. Morgentaler began about ten years later, little had been done to reduce delay. Chief Justice Dickson in fact observed that 'even though the Badgley Report was issued 10 years ago, the relevant statistics do not appear to be out of date. Indeed, Statistics Canada reported that in 1982 the number of hospitals with therapeutic abortion committees had actually fallen.'[20] The failure of provincial health ministries and health service agencies, and of the federal government, to address this well-publicized dysfunction in provision of care, and their apparent indifference to the Badgley Committee finding that 'The procedures set out for the operation of the Abortion Law are not working equitably across Canada,'[21] reduced credibility of claims in *Chaoulli* that provincial delays in provision of care would or could be remedied. The abortion issue is sociopolitically contentious, of course, but Justice Deschamps relied upon *Morgentaler* to justify her judicial approach. Addressing more recent committee and commission reports, and the risk of political paralysis, she observed that 'Governments have promised on numerous occasions to find a solution to the problem of waiting lists. Given the tendency to focus the debate on a sociopolitical philosophy, it seems that governments have lost sight of the urgency of taking concrete action. The courts are therefore the last line of defence for citizens.'[22]

Chief Justice McLachin and Justice Major similarly invoked the *Morgentaler* majority judgment that section 7 of the Canadian Charter is violated when delays in access to care due to legal barriers mean 'that the state has intervened in such a manner as to create an additional risk to health, and consequently this intervention constitutes a violation of ... security of the person,'[23] not justifiable under section 1. They closely analogized the 'delays in treatment giving rise to psychological and physical suffering'[24] shown in *Morgentaler* to those in *Chaoulli*, leading to the same conclusion of a Charter violation requiring that the legislation seen to cause the delays be struck down.

The three-to-three division of the *Chaoulli* court left the challenge under the Canadian Charter unresolved, but it would not necessarily have been more clearly resolved had Madam Justice Deschamps made her decision. The Supreme Court normally sits as a full bench of nine justices. Accordingly, a ruling on law of four justices might be reversed by a majority of five. The Supreme Court's rulings on the Canadian Charter govern all lower courts throughout Canada. Its decisions under the Québec Charter are decisive within that province, of course, but the absence of a ruling under the Canadian Charter affords the *Chaoulli* judgment no clear legal consequences elsewhere in Canada. In this sense, there may be less to the judgment than meets the eye. This has been no barrier, however, to political speculation and newsmedia commentary about what the judgment means nationwide.

Expansion Beyond the Limits

Despite the uncertain jurisprudential status of the *Chaoulli* judgment within Québec and its inconclusive status outside, the judgment has triggered a series of timely Canadian debates concerning health service funding. Such significant events as publication of the Kirby Report and the Romanow Report had already focused public and governmental attention on the issue of waiting lists for necessary medical care, but the realization that the judicial branch of government could add momentum to the movement for improved performance added a dimension of apparent urgency to policy-making. Debates extend beyond striking a balance between federal and provincial governmental and private insurance funding of health care services, to the interaction of clinical care and public health preventive and related care, and the international trade implications of private health insurance and services, particularly under the North American Free Trade Agreement (NAFTA) as discussed by Epps and Schneiderman in this volume.

A simplistic approach to the competing claims about the impact of privately insured, two-tier health care on publicly-funded services concerns whether such care would assist or at least not harm public services, or compromise them. The former view was advanced by reference to European experience, which was claimed to show that public services are relieved by some patients eligible to receive them opting instead for private-sector care, expanding the overall supply of services and leaving the public sector no different from, and perhaps improved over, its former level of performance. The Supreme Court majority found this evidence persuasive.

The countering view is that siphoning off scarce medical specialists and resources into delivery of luxury care for the privileged few would inequitably impoverish public sector care. The inequity might be multidimensional in that the compromise of public sector services, indicated by aggravated or prolonged waiting times for necessary care, might induce Canadian authorities to seek to recruit medical and related personnel from other countries. Expanded immigration of service providers into Canadian public sector services would risk depleting the quality of health services in the countries from which the immigrants were recruited, which may have funded their education and training. The Court's decision in favour of the *Chaoulli* applicants might therefore add to global inequity in access to medical personnel and necessary medical services. The migration of health service personnel from resource-poor to wealthier countries is a continuing challenge in the struggle for international health care equity.

The migration of health workers, for instance from the Indian subcontinent, the Caribbean and sub-Saharan Africa to developed countries has been described as reaching crisis proportions. It has been observed, for instance, that 'many African-trained doctors and nurses are seeking and finding employment and postgraduate opportunities in developed countries, such as the USA, Canada, and the UK.'[25] A criticism has been that 'to poach and rely on highly skilled foreign workers from poor countries in the public sector is akin to the crime of theft,'[26] and the same applies to recruitment into private sector, or second tier, services. Governmental action and international collaboration are required to resist continuation of '[a] 'medical carousel' around which doctors continuously rotate ... Thus, Tanzanian, Kenyan, or Nigerian doctors [once] moved to South Africa, South African doctors moved to the UK, British doctors moved to Canada and the USA, and Canadian doctors migrated to the USA.'[27] Emergence of two-tier health services in Canada would risk aggravation of global health care inequity.[28]

Further, strategies to deter physicians from directing their public-sector patients into private-sector services in which they have financial interests, such as by conflict of interest sanctions or prohibiting public-sector personnel from ownership of or service in private-sector facilities, raise legal enforcement concerns and issues of practitioners' Charter rights. The UK Department of Health updated its voluntary *Code of Practice for NHS [National Health Service] employers involved in the international recruitment of health care professionals,* most recently in December 2004, to take account of evolving trends. Comparable strategies might be required in Canada to address inter-provincial and international migration particularly of doctors, but Charter-protected mobility rights and international free-trade agreements might affect attempted controls by direct billing, direct prohibition, indirect disincentive and other techniques.[29] Responses to the *Chaoulli* judgment will have to address the capacity of public sector services to limit waiting times, and the impact on the supply of skilled personnel of emergence of second-tier private health services.[30]

Much of the debate concerning public-sector treatment waiting times addresses means to improve provincial and federal levels of public funding of clinical services. However, as long ago as 1974, the Lalonde Report[31] proposed to relieve the burden of individual illness by promotion of preventive health care. Preventive care has now been enhanced in Canada by speedy implementation of a central recommendation of the Naylor Committee Report.[32] Triggered by the severe acute respiratory syndrome (SARS) outbreak in Toronto in the Spring and Summer of 2003, the Naylor Report urged establishment of what in 2004 became the Public Health Agency of Canada, fashioned from what had been the Population and Public Health Branch of Health Canada. As the Naylor Report observed:

> Among the functions of public health are health protection (e.g., food and water safety, basic sanitation), disease and injury prevention (including vaccinations and outbreak management), population health assessment; disease and risk factor surveillance; and health promotion. The public health system tends to operate in the background unless there is an unexpected outbreak of disease ... An effective pubic health system is essential to preserve and enhance the health status of Canadians, to reduce health disparities, and to reduce the costs of curative health services.[33]

Accordingly, at least part of a response to the challenge of unacceptably long waiting times posed by the *Chaoulli* judgment may be channeled through investments in public health rather than clinical care services. It is an issue of political judgment, however, whether such investments would have sufficient visibility to produce political rewards, and reassure a court that a government is taking positive steps to address demands for clinical care.

Even if the Supreme Court rejects further argument it may have allowed the government of Québec to present through its August 4, 2005 statement that 'The motion for a partial rehearing is granted,' and reinstates all or part of its June 2005 judgment, it is not evident that Québec or any other province except Alberta is going to make efforts actively to encourage private health insurance coverage parallel to publicly insured services. Were a province to take or allow steps in this direction, however, provisions of international trade law on delivery of services across national boundaries might come into force. Neither the North American Free Trade Agreement (NAFTA) nor World Trade Organization (WTO) agreements specifically address health care issues to any penetrating effect.[34] Nevertheless, such agreements would have to be seriously considered, since services may be so broadly defined, for instance under NAFTA, as to encompass them. Both federal and provincial governments should in principle ensure that their health care legislation, regulations and practices comply with NAFTA and WTO agreements. This might open the way to American health service providers and insurers securing a bridgehead into Canada. It is a commercial judgment whether Québec's population of about eight million, or Ontario's of over ten million, presents an attractive market. In the

United States an estimated 46 million people lack health insurance, and millions more are underinsured, because private insurers offer to fund only services they find to be profitable to their investors.[35] The Supreme Court has held that, when provincial governments delegate their health care responsibilities to private agents such as hospitals, the Canadian Charter is applicable.[36] However, private insurers and facilities acting independently may have to satisfy the terms of provincial human rights codes, perhaps on non-discrimination on grounds of mental or physical disability.[37] Further, U.S. insurers' administrative costs are considerably greater than the costs of maintaining Canadian provincial health insurance agencies.[38]

Canada's NAFTA obligation to treat nationals of the U.S. and Mexico as favourably as Canadians may be subject to lawful exceptions. In entering NAFTA, the Canadian government was aware of the differences in health care provision and insurance among NAFTA partners. Much Canadian opposition to entry raised fears of Americanization of health care in Canada, which the federal government attempted to allay. However, under the Canadian constitution, provinces enjoy extensive jurisdiction over management of health care facilities and personnel. They are not necessarily constrained by prohibitions or mandates of the federal government. Provincial action might therefore trigger a national breach of NAFTA or WTO agreements. Were a province to exclude an American or Mexican interest from enjoyment of its NAFTA or WTO entitlements, that interest might sue the provincial and/or federal government for compensation, in a Canadian, American or Mexican Court or before an available international trade tribunal.[39]

In the *Chaoulli* case before the Supreme Court, the governments of Ontario, New Brunswick and Saskatchewan were represented in addition to the governments of Quebec and of Canada. In subsequent litigation, the federal government could explain to the Court the implications for the Canadian health care system of a legal requirement that private health insurance for publicly-funded core services be available, presenting their arguments in the NAFTA and international free trade environments of competition, and payment of compensation for denial of opportunities to compete in trade.

Conclusion

What the Supreme Court justices said in *Chaoulli* can be read in the law report and in an appendix to this book, but what their words mean in practice has yet to be clarified. The position that will be established in

June 2006 should shed significant light on a judgment that so far has generated mainly heat. Nevertheless, Canada has a short breathing space to consider whether or how a two-tier health care system might serve to advance the goal to which the country is wedded, to provide all Canadians with equitable access to medically necessary health care services. The suspended judgment will serve Canadians well if it focuses political and public minds and determination on meeting the challenge of delays in access to necessary care.

Notes

1 Chaoulli v. Quebec (Attorney General), [2005] S.C.C. 35.
2 See Kent Roach in this volume on the significance of the twelve month suspension of the June 9 judgment.
3 R.S.Q., c. A-29, section 15.
4 R.S.Q., c. A-28, section 11.
5 R.S.Q., c. C-12.
6 R.S.C. 1985, Appendix II, No. 44. Schedule B.
7 This term is explored in the chapters by Roach, Manfredi, and Choudhry.
8 R.S.C. 1985, c. C-6.
9 Canadian Institute for Health Information, Public and Private Shares of Total Health Expenditure, by Use of Funds, 2001.
10 *Auton (Guardian ad litem o v. British Columbia (Attorney Genel)* (2004), 245 D.L.R.(4th) 1 (Supreme Court of Canada).
11 (2000), 78 B.C.L.R.(3d) 55; see also additional reasons at (2001), 84 B.C.L.R.(3d) 259.
12 (2002), 220 D.L.R.(4th) 411.
13 See Peter H. Russell in this volume.
14 *R. v. Morgentaler* (1988), 44 D.L.R.(4th) 385 (Supreme Court of Canada).
15 (2005), S.C.C. 35, para. 43.
16 *R. v. Morgentaler* per Dickson C.J.C. at 402.
17 Ibid, per Beetz, J. at 452.
18 Report of the (Badgley) Committee on the Operation of the Abortion Law. (Ottawa: Minister of Supply and Services Canada, 1977.)
19 Ibid. at 141.
20 *R. v. Morgentaler* at 410.
21 Badgley Committee at 17.
22 *Chaoulli* at para. 96.
23 Ibid. para 118.

24 Ibid. para 119.
25 Editorial. Migration of health workers: an unmanaged crisis. The *Lancet* 2005; 365:1825.
26 Ibid.
27 Eastwood J.B., Conroy R.E., Naicker S., West P.A., Tutt R.C., Plange-Rhule J. Loss of health professionals from sub-Saharan Africa: the pivotal role of the UK. The *Lancet* 2005, 365: 1893–1900.
28 Editorial. Medical migration and inequity of health care. The *Lancet* 2000; 356:177.
29 See Flood C.M, Archibald T. The illegality of private health care in Canada. Can. Med. Assoc. J. 2001; 164: 825–30.
30 See Colleen Flood, Mark Stabile and Sasha Kontic in this volume.
31 Lalonde, M. *A New Perspective on the Health of Canadians*, Ottawa: Health and Welfare Canada, 1974.
32 National Advisory Committee on SARS and Public Health, *Learning from SARS: Renewal of Public Health in Canada*, (Ottawa: Health Canada, 2003.)
33 Ibid at 2.
34 Gold E.R. Health care reform and international trade. In Caulfield T.A., von Tigerstrom B., *Health Reform and the Law in Canada: Meeting the Challenge*. (Edmonton, Alta: University of Alberta Press, 2002) at 223–244.
35 See Geyman J. *Falling Through the Safety Net: Americans Without Health Insurance*. (Munroe, Me., Common Courage Press, 2005) ; Sered S.S., Fernandopulle R. *Uninsured in America: Life and Death in the Land of Opportunity* (Berkeley, University of California Press, 2005)
36 *Eldrid v. British Columbia (Attorney-General)* (1997) 151 D.L.R. (4th) 577 (S.C.C.).
37 But see the Supreme Court's generous accommodation of commercial insurance companies in *Zurich Insurance Co.* v. *Ontario Human Rights Commission* (1992), 93 D.L.R. (4th) 346.
38 Woolhandler S., Campbell T., Himmelstein D.U. Costs of health care administration in the United States and Canada. New England J. Medicine 2003; 349; 768–75.
39 See Epps and Schneiderman, in this volume.

Chaoulli and Quebec's *Charter of Human Rights and Freedoms*: The Ambiguities of Distinctness

JEAN-FRANÇOIS GAUDREAULT-DESBIENS AND
CHARLES-MAXIME PANACCIO

Introduction

The *Charter of Human Rights and Freedoms*[1] is undeniably one of the founding stones of the Quebec legal order. Because of the role it plays, this Charter can rightly claim a constitutional status, at least if this word is understood in a functional perspective.[2] This extraordinary status is not only confirmed in the Charter through its primacy clause,[3] but also in the preliminary provision of the province's *Civil Code*, which states, *inter alia*, that '[t]he Civil Code of Québec, *in harmony with the Charter of Human Rights and Freedoms* and the general principles of law, governs persons, relations between persons, and property.'[4]

The *Quebec Charter* bears a striking resemblance to some of the best known international rights-protection instruments: it is wide-ranging as to the set of rights and liberties it guarantees and as to its scope of application, it provides effective remedies, and, most importantly, its tone is solemn and aspirational. In that, it simply cannot be compared to other anti-discrimination statutes, even though they have also been characterized, largely due to their particular object, as having a special, 'quasi constitutional,' nature.[5] Because of its breadth, its status, the aspirations it enshrines, its enactment prior to the *Canadian Charter* and, last but not least, the relative absence in Quebec of the kind of constitutional patriotism the *Canadian Charter* has triggered elsewhere in Canada, Quebeckers have developed a kind of special relationship with their *Charter of Human Rights and Freedoms*. Arguably, it can be characterized as playing a part in their identity reference alongside the *Civil Code*, the *Charter of French Language*, or even the provincial powers set out in s. 92 of the *Constitution Act 1867* – not unlike the role the *Canadian Charter* itself or the *Canada Health Act* play in English-speaking Canada's own identity reference.[6] The *Canadian Charter*, the enactment of which in 1982 had awakened the ghost of a marginalization or trivialization of the *Quebec Charter*,[7] prompted several jurists to reaffirm the latter's unique place in the province's legal landscape. Paradoxically, it may very well have been the *Canadian Charter* itself that ended up being symbolically marginalized not only as a result of the *Quebec Charter*'s preeminent status in Quebec's legal psyche but also as a result of the omnibus override of the *Canadian Charter* by the Lévesque government immediately after its enactment.

While it would be inaccurate to say that such a marginalization occurred, the distinctness of the *Quebec Charter* is not always easy to handle from a judicial standpoint.[8] This is most evident in *Chaoulli* v. *Quebec*,[9] which highlights the somewhat paradoxical treatment reserved to that Charter by the Supreme Court of Canada. As regards the *Quebec Charter*, the main actors in the Supreme Court's *Chaoulli* tragicomedy are, first, Madam Justice Marie Deschamps whose reasons stand out because of their author's exclusive reliance on this instrument,[10] and, second, Justices Ian Binnie and Louis LeBel, whose reasons explicitly speak to the interpretation of that Charter. Chief Justice McLachlin and Major J, supported by Bastarache J., concurred with Deschamps J.'s conclusions as to the application of the Charter to the case, while Fish J. concurred with the minority judgment of his colleagues Binnie and LeBel. The major part of this paper will revolve around the segment of Deschamps J.'s opinion that deals with the interpretation to be given to s. 9.1, the *Quebec Charter*'s limitation clause, as this interpretation reveals the ambiguous legal consequences flowing from that Charter's alleged distinctness. We see such an ambiguity because while Justice Deschamps is at pains to emphasize the distinctness of the *Quebec Charter* in the first part of her judgment, later on she crudely – and, in our view, mistakenly – assimilates the analysis to be undertaken under s. 9.1 of that Charter to that used pursuant to s. 1 under the *Canadian Charter*.[11]

That being said, the *Quebec Charter*'s distinctness and the special type of relationship Quebeckers have with it, instead of with the *Canadian Charter*, fundamentally speaks to the distinctiveness of Quebec itself. Thus, in the last part of the paper we will see that this loaded word in the post-Meech era nevertheless describes a tangible reality whenever one considers attitudes in Quebec vis-à-vis the privatization of health insurance.

The Ambiguities of Distinctness?

Two visions of the appropriate role of the judiciary

Early on in her opinion, Deschamps J. notes that, due to its human rights connection, the *Quebec Charter* is distinct from other Quebec statutes.[12] From a positive law angle, this is hardly a novelty, because provincial human rights codes have been characterized for quite some time by the Supreme Court as 'quasi- constitutional' in nature. She even goes on to argue that whenever a Quebec statute is challenged, 'it is appropriate to look first to the rules that apply specifically in Quebec before turning to the *Canadian Charter*, especially where the provisions of the two charters are susceptible of producing cumulative effects, but where the rules are not identical.'[13] That statement alone – which some-how affirms the analytical but also, in all likelihood, the remedial prior-ity of the *Quebec Charter* over the *Canadian Charter* – could provide the basis for another paper given the important questions of constitutional theory that it raises. Suffice it to say here that Justice Deschamps finds support for her proposition in Beetz J.'s opinion in *Singh v. Minister of Employment and Immigration*,[14] where the late judge argued that human rights legislation, whether provincial or federal, should not be entirely eclipsed by the *Canadian Charter*, since allowing such instruments to become obsolete would inevitably lead to losing their cumulative pro-tective effects.

After noting some similarities between the Quebec and Canadian Charters, Deschamps J. states that, faced with such similarities, '[i]t is ... appropriate to consider the two together. Distinctions must be made, however, and I believe that it is important to begin by considering the specific protection afforded by the *Quebec Charter* for the reason that it is not identical to the protection afforded by the *Canadian Charter*.'[15] She further notices the differences between s. 1 of the *Quebec Charter* and s. 7 of the *Canadian Charter*. Section 7 requires the claimant to demonstrate not only a violation of either one of his rights to life, liberty or security of the person, but also that this violation was not made in accordance with the principles of fundamental justice. In contrast, s. 1 of the *Quebec Charter* only requires the claimant to demonstrate a violation of either the 'right to life, and to personal security, inviolability and freedom.'[16]

Deschamps J. then stresses in broader terms the importance of affirm-ing the Quebec Charter's distinctness, arguing that deciding *Chaoulli* on the basis of this quasi-constitutional legislation would 'enhanc[e] an instrument that is specific to Quebec.'[17] In all likelihood, Deschamps J. does not refer here to the mere fact that this particular legislation is distinct to Quebec because it was enacted by that province's National Assembly, a comment which would be outrageously banal. It is arguable instead that she highlights the distinctness of the Charter because of the distinctness of Quebec society itself within Canada. This interpretation is *a contrario* comforted by another statement of hers, to the effect that 'Quebec *society* is no different from Canadian society when it comes to respect [the fundamental rights to life and liberty].'[18] At the very least, this seems to indicate that her understanding of the interplay between the Quebec and Canadian Charters may have been forged as much in response to Quebec society's claim of distinctness as in response to the *Quebec Charter*'s inherent textual distinctness itself.

If this is indeed the case, then Deschamps J.'s opinion on s. 9.1 (the *Quebec Charter*'s limitation clause) is all the more puzzling. Indeed, after having affirmed, as will be seen, the specificity and priority of the *Quebec Charter* and emphasized the need to draw normative implications from the textual differences between s. 1 of the *Quebec Charter* and its *Canadian Charter* equivalent, s. 7, she then collapses the analysis of the *Quebec Charter*'s limitation clause with that of the *Canadian Charter*'s s. 1 despite obvious textual differences. Given Deschamps J.'s prior reliance on Justice Jean Beetz's prudential remark in *Singh* to the effect that quasi-constitutional, rights-protecting, instruments should not automatically be subsumed into the *Canadian Charter* and that due consideration should thus be given to the textual differences between these instruments and the *Canadian Charter*, her conflation of s. 9.1 of the *Quebec Charter* and of s. 1 of the *Canadian Charter* is rather surprising. In contrast, the dissenting judges (Binnie, LeBel and Fish) manage to *consistently* give meaning to the textual differences between the Quebec and Canadian Charters, without ever solemnly affirming the abstract priority of one over the other. As we will demonstrate, their approach allows for a more rigorous management of the ambiguities of distinctness.

Before we begin examining both sets of reasons in more details, it is appropriate to set out the relevant limitations clauses. Section 1 of the *Canadian Charter* states that '[t]he Canadian Charter of Rights and Freedoms guarantees the rights and freedoms set out in it subject only to such reasonable limits prescribed by law as can be demonstrably justified in a free and democratic society.' For its part, s. 9.1 of the *Quebec Charter* provides that '[i]n exercising his fundamental freedoms and rights, a person shall maintain a proper regard for democratic values, public order and the general well-being of the citizens of Quebec. In this respect, the scope of the freedoms and rights, and limits to their exercise, may be fixed by law.'

Justice Deschamps quickly assimilates the analysis to be undertaken under s. 9.1 of the *Quebec Charter* to that to be undertaken under s. 1 of the *Canadian Charter*. We suggest that this is a dubious proposition and that there are compelling reasons to be more attuned to the differences between these two provisions. Although we are of the view that even the application of the more demanding s. 1 should have led to the conclusion that the two anti-private insurance provisions were justified, we believe that this conclusion should *a fortiori* have been reached under s. 9.1. Of course, especially when it comes to constitutional (or quasi-constitutional) matters, one should not be overly literal. The issues are often deeply controversial and interpretation is a complex exercise. But text remains an important part of the equation, and there are obvious textual hints in s. 9.1 which speak to the distinctiveness of the *Quebec Charter* and which should make one weary of assimilating it to s. 1. Unless some form of super-eminent principle can be relied upon to justify a *contra legem* interpretation disregarding the text or part of it, its interpretation should strive to make sense of all of its features.

As is well-known, section 1 has initially been interpreted by the Supreme Court as mandating a rather strong form of judicial review. However, the Court's early confidence in its powers of intervention has quickly abated and it has since oscillated between stringency and deference.[19] Even when interpreted most stringently, however, section 1 had rarely (if ever) been used to reach such radically interventionist results as were reached in *Chaoulli*.[20] Hence, our point is that if the stringent interpretation of the more demanding s. 1 could not entirely be sustained, it makes even less sense to invoke s. 9.1 in support of stark interventionist results. Section. 9.1 leaves much more space for judicial deference, as well as for more 'utilitarian' and 'communitarian' forms of reasoning, and thus more space for the successful justification of legislative limits to guaranteed rights. Indeed, as we shall argue later, this section's explicit imposition upon claimants of an obligation to exercise their fundamental freedoms and rights with 'proper regard for democratic values, public order and the general well-being of the citizens of Quebec' also warrants such a conclusion. While the minority judges took s. 9.1's textual hints and acknowledged this difference, the majority judges, unfortunately, did not. With respect, this constitutes a clear interpretive mistake, which, moreover, is at odds with the Supreme Court's own recent case law dealing with the margin of appreciation to be afforded to governments in dealing with complex problems in the field of health care.[21]

That said, following a rather cursory analysis, Justice Deschamps concluded that the rights to life, personal security and inviolability guaranteed by s. 1 of the *Quebec Charter* had been infringed[22] by the combination of health care delays and prohibitions on private insurance, and moved to an application of s. 9.1. She boldly assimilated the application of s. 9.1 to that of s. 1 by relying on statements made by the Court in *Ford*[23] and applied quite an unforgiving version of the *Oakes* test ¯reminiscent of the early years of the *Charter*. She found that while there were pressing and substantial objectives and that the means used were rationally connected to these objectives, the legislative means failed at the minimal impairment stage. In her view, the evidence suggested that the threat posed to the public system by private insurance was remote and avoidable. Thus, it had not been shown that the rights-infringing prohibition was *necessary* and hence minimally impairing.[24]

Then, invoking a popular conception of the division of labour between the judiciary and the legislature (the former would be in charge of rights-protection while the latter would be in charge of policy-making), she rejected any calls for judicial deference. Once all the evidence is before the court, she said, 'there is nothing that would justify [the judiciary] in refusing to perform its role on the ground that it should merely defer to the government's position.'[25]

This is as though the judiciary's role may not *require* deferring in some circumstances. Of course, 'the ground' for deference is not *merely* that the judiciary should defer. That would amount to a preposterous tautology. There must be good reasons for deference, which there undoubtedly were in this case.[26] One may in addition point out that it is also part of the judiciary's role to apply *the law*, and yet Justice Deschamps never examines the contents of s. 9.1 in any detail. As alluded to above, disregarding the text of an enactment, whatever it is, is not necessarily inconceivable. But with this comes a higher burden of justification that Deschamps J. did not fully discharge in her reasons.

The minority's reasons were distinctly more nuanced. Justices Binnie and LeBel aptly noted that while the *Quebec Charter* often covers the same ground as the *Canadian Charter*, it remains distinct in its drafting and methodology. They also observed that s. 9.1 has the added feature of placing *on the claimant* the obligation to exercise *Quebec Charter* rights with 'proper' regard for 'democratic values, public order and the general well-being of the citizens of Quebec.'[27] However, in their view, the exercise by the appellants of their claimed *Quebec Charter* rights in order to defeat the prohibition against private insurance did not show 'proper regard for democratic values' or 'public order,' notably because the future of health care should be in the hands of elected representatives. Moreover, they linked the prohibitions to the value of equality (or, if one prefers, fairness) by noting that those who seek to have access to private insurance are the more advantaged members of society.[28] They thus seem to be suggesting that there is no good reason why one should have better access to health care simply because one can afford it. And the anti-private insurance provisions are a rational part of a scheme which aims at preventing a state of affairs where money would trump need.[29]

In Justices Binnie and LeBel's view, the evidence amply supported the prohibition on private insurance contracts. The objectives were compelling and the means were rationally connected to them. As to minimal impairment, they stressed the need to leave the legislature a margin of appreciation in controversial questions of social and economic policy. These questions, they said, are not for the courts to decide. The legislative provisions concerned all citizens of Quebec and addressed concerns shared by all, as well as rights belonging to everyone. The legislature attempted to find a solution that would be acceptable to everyone in the spirit of the preamble of the *Quebec Charter*, which stresses justice, the equal worth and dignity of human beings, as well as the need to respect the rights and freedoms of others and the common well-being. In short, their view was that the issue of whether one had a right to resort to private insurance or not raised deep philosophical and practical issues, to which the legislature had given a reasonable answer in the circumstances.

Decoupling s. 9.1 of the Quebec Charter and s. 1 of the Canadian Charter

There is a strong case for decoupling the analysis under s. 1 of the *Canadian Charter* from that under s. 9.1 of the *Quebec Charter*.

First, it must be noted that the genealogies of s. 1 and s. 9.1 are somewhat different. Section 1 of the *Canadian Charter* was inspired from certain provisions of the *International Covenant on Civil and Political Rights*,[30] while s. 9.1 of the *Quebec Charter* is closer to article 29(2) of the

Universal Declaration of Human Rights.[31] Second, many had noticed that s. 9.1 seems more favourable to the State than s. 1 in terms of deference, burden and potential lines of justification.[32] Some even clearly expressed the view that it would be *wrong* to apply the early stringency of *Oakes* to s. 9.1.[33] The late Professor Morel suggested that while the State's measures would have to avoid arbitrariness and would generally have to be proportional, they would not necessarily have to be minimally impairing. That was a bit of an odd argument since minimal impairment is an aspect of proportionality; but we can all understand that he meant that the State should be given more latitude in order to achieve valid goals.[34] And in *Ford*, as we shall see later, the representatives of the Attorney General of Quebec had submitted that s. 9.1 only conferred judicial control of the ends of the law and not of the means chosen to attain these ends. This was also an odd way to translate the presence a more forgiving standard of review; but, again, we can understand that what was meant was that once the law was shown to be a rational way of attaining an end that complied with the limitations grounds of s. 9.1., courts should show some deference to the State.[35]

All these considerations were, however, ignored by Justice Deschamps who relied entirely on statements made by the Supreme Court in *Ford* for the proposition that s. 9.1 is, for all intents and purposes, equivalent to s. 1, requires the same approach and leads to the same results. The problem is that this proposition simply does not follow from what was said in *Ford* and from the doctrinal authorities referred to in that case. A closer look at what the Court said in *Ford* thus seems in order. For the record, it said the following:

> It was suggested in argument that because of its quite different wording s. 9.1 was not a justificatory provision similar to s. 1 but merely a provision indicating that the fundamental freedoms and rights guaranteed by the Quebec *Charter* are not absolute but relative and must be construed and exercised in a manner consistent with the values, interests and considerations indicated in s. 9.1 – 'democratic values, public order and the general well-being of the citizens of Québec.' In the case at bar the Superior Court and the Court of Appeal held that s. 9.1 was a justificatory provision corresponding to s. 1 of the Canadian *Charter* and that it was subject, in its application, to *a similar test of rational connection and proportionality*. This Court agrees with that conclusion. The first paragraph of s. 9.1 speaks of the manner in which a *person* must *exercise* his fundamental freedoms and rights. That is not a limit on the authority of government but rather does

suggest the manner in which the scope of the fundamental freedoms and rights is to be interpreted. The second paragraph of s. 9.1, however [...] does refer to legislative authority to impose limits on the fundamental freedoms and rights [...] That was the view taken of s. 9.1 in both the Superior Court and the Court of Appeal. As for the applicable test under s. 9.1, Boudreault J. in the Superior Court quoted with approval from a paper delivered by Raynold Langlois, Q.C., entitled 'Les clauses limitatives des Chartes canadienne et québécoise des droits et libertés et le fardeau de la preuve,' and published in *Perspectives canadiennes et européennes des droits de la personne* (1986), in which the author expressed the view that under s. 9.1 the government must show that the restrictive law is *neither irrational nor arbitrary and that the means chosen are proportionate to the end to be served.*

In the Court of Appeal, *Bisson J.A. adopted essentially the same test. He said that under s. 9.1 the government has the onus of demonstrating on a balance of probabilities that the impugned means are proportional to the object sought. He also spoke of the necessity that the government show the absence of an irrational or arbitrary character in the limit imposed by law and that there is a rational link between the means and the end pursued. We are in general agreement with this approach.* The Attorney General of Quebec submitted that s. 9.1 left more scope to the legislature than s. 1 and only conferred judicial control of 'la *finalité des lois,'* which this Court understands to mean the purposes or objects of the law limiting a guaranteed freedom or right, and not the means chosen to attain the purpose or object. What this would mean is that it would be a sufficient justification if the purpose or object of legislation limiting a fundamental freedom or right fell within the general description provided by the words 'democratic values, public order and the general well-being of the citizens of Québec.' It cannot have been intended that s. 9.1 should confer such a broad and virtually unrestricted legislative authority to limit fundamental freedoms and rights. Rather, *it is an implication of the requirement that a limit serve one of these ends that the limit should be rationally connected to the legislative purpose and that the legislative means be proportionate to the end to be served.* That is implicit in a provision that prescribes that certain values or legislative purposes may prevail in particular circumstances over a fundamental freedom or right. *That necessarily implies a balancing exercise and the appropriate test for such balancing is one of rational connection and proportionality* (the emphasis is ours).[36]

The Court's statements in *Ford* can therefore be encapsulated in the following propositions: (i) s. 9.1 is a justificatory limitations provision which applies to the State, therefore (ii) it must imply tests of rationality and proportionality,[37] (iii) the burden of justification must be put on the State and, thus, (iv) *Oakes* should be applied. That is all. There is no discussion of the particular formula and limiting grounds used in 9.1, no discussion of how rationality and proportionality presuppose underlying substantive values which must be explicated and balanced, and no mention of institutional considerations. Surely, it does not follow from the fact that both s. 1 and s. 9.1 require a rationality analysis and some kind of proportionality test that they should in every case yield the same result. Contrary to what the Court seems to be assuming, there is ample conceptual space between merely testing the purported ends of a law and applying the full rigours of the *Oakes* test at its most stringent.

Furthermore, one can apply *Oakes'* analytical grid under s. 9.1 and, *at the same time*, consciously show a higher degree of deference toward the legislature as a result of that legislature's clear indication to that effect. Indeed, the application of that grid, which revolves around the legitimacy of the governmental objective pursued and the proportionality analysis, hardly dictates any particular level of judicial deference. As the Supreme Court's post-*Oakes* case law itself demonstrates, criteria such as 'pressing and substantial objectives,' 'rational connection,' 'minimal impairment,' etc., are standards that can be applied more or less rigorously depending on the circumstances of each case and, *a fortiori*, on explicit legislative instructions.[38] As will be expounded later, the wording of s. 1 of the *Canadian Charter* hints that the appropriate level of deference should be measured on the basis of consideration first and foremost pertaining to fairness (the just, to borrow from Paul Ricoeur[39]), whilst the *Quebec Charter's* s. 9.1 entertains that the same can also be evaluated on the basis of considerations pertaining to the good.

Raynold Langlois himself, in the very paper that judges in *Ford* and *Chaoulli* have quoted in favour of their assimilation of s. 9.1 to s. 1, was of the opinion that whereas s. 1 required a full-on justificatory analysis (*contrôle d'opportunité*), s. 9.1 imposed more of a test of rationality or reasonableness (*contrôle de rationalité*). Thus, in his view, while 9.1 was comparable to s. 1, it remained less demanding:

> 'The text of s. 9.1 is not as explicit as section 1 of the Canadian Charter. The reasons of text which, among other things, justify that the courts impose a test of opportunity and reject the traditional tests of reasonableness and rationality for laws limiting the Canadian Charter, do not exist for the

Quebec Charter. Thus we can believe that the test of irrationality and arbitrariness traditionally applied in reviewing the validity of laws, applies to laws restricting rights conferred by the Quebec Charter.'[40]

Therefore, calling for tests of rationality and proportionality did not amount to saying much. *Of course*, for any kind of limitation on a right to be justified it must be rationally connected to valid aims. Otherwise it negatively affects right-protected interests for absolutely no reason. A limit on a right must also create benefits which are broadly proportional to the inconvenience. These are mere requirements of rationality, which are a necessary part of all justificatory endeavours. But this is simply to state the obvious. It avoids all the hard questions of substance and value, as well as the textual, historical and philosophical differences between s. 1 of the *Canadian Charter* and s. 9.1 of the *Quebec Charter*. For instance, s. 9.1's allocation of justificatory burdens is much less clear than s. 1's. Indeed, section 9.1 imposes a burden *on the citizen* to exercise his rights within certain limits, which is certainly a hint of the kind of philosophy which is conveyed by the provision and by the Charter generally. It effectively tells citizens not to stand abusively on their individual rights. Such an approach is also mandated by the particular grounds of limitations, as explained below. Most importantly, it seems particularly plausible in the context of Quebec, a mixed jurisdiction where the civilian doctrine of abuse of rights, which seeks to target unreasonable exercises of one's rights, is recognized and applied. For instance, article 6 of the *Civil Code of Quebec* provides that '[e]very person is bound to exercise his civil rights in good faith,' and article 7 states that '[n]o right may be exercised with the intent of injuring another or in an excessive and unreasonable manner which is contrary to the requirements of good faith.'[41] Justice Binnie put the same idea a little differently in his dissent in *Syndicat Northcrest v. Amselem*, when he said that '[t]he Quebec *Charter* is concerned not only with rights and freedoms but with a citizen's *responsibilities* to other citizens in the *exercise* of those rights and freedoms.'[42] Be that as it may, following *Ford*, Justice Deschamps concluded that the analytical approach developed in *Oakes* had to be followed, but failed to make the required distinction between the analytical approach to be followed, on one hand, and the level of judicial deference to be granted to legislative choices, on the other.[43]

Had she not blinded herself to the explicit text of s. 9.1, accepting the state's justification would have been made even more imperative. There is obviously no textual silver bullet, since the grounds of limitations have furry edges, but the expressions 'democratic values,' public order (*ordre public*) and general well-being of the citizens certainly suggest that the burden of justification imposed on government is at least lighter than the one required under s. 1. Let us briefly consider them in turn.

First, what about 'democratic values,' which is where the wording of s. 9.1 comes closest to that of s. 1? 'Democracy' is undeniably a controversial concept, but there is a strong argument for believing that 'respect for democratic values' at least means some level of respect (and thus deference) for representative institutions' decisions on matters of social controversy, especially when the evidence is complex and largely inconclusive. If it refers to what is 'just,' it does so in a way that representative institutions are given considerable leeway in evaluating what belongs or not to that sphere.

'Public order,' for its part, is also a furry-edged notion. As a term of art, however, *ordre public* (like the English term *public policy*) refers to a mix of positive and critical moralities,[44] including economic and social moralities.[45] What is clear, in any event, is that *ordre public*, as a source of limits to be imposed on rights, is quite vast and, in the Canadian context, certainly includes measures which are connected to the maintenance of a single-tier public medicare system, as long as it would not be utterly irrational to do so in the circumstances.

'General well-being of the citizens' is another rather vague expression. Nevertheless, the expression seems to be pointing towards a morality of the good, of which there are various sorts. On the one hand, it could suggest a utilitarian calculus. Hence, limits to rights would be justified when the State's measure maximizes the good of utility.[46] As it has often been pointed out, whatever notion of utility one uses, it is never easy to tell which of two competing measures would create optimal levels of it.[47] But legislatures are better placed than courts when it comes to such an evaluation.

On the other hand, 'general well-being' can also be taken a little differently, as encompassing non-utilitarian moralities of the good, which often invoke the classical notion of 'the common good.'[48] Taken in that sense, it could quite straightforwardly be argued that a reasonably efficient single tier public medicare system which treats everyone equally on the basis of need is an intricate part of a society's search for justice and the common good, as it is grounded in the values of community, solidarity, health, life and equality/fairness, all to be enjoyed in common. This is indeed something that was noted by the minority in *Chaoulli*.[49]

In sum, under the guise of democratic values, s. 9.1 arguably refers to moralities which emphasize the just, while it refers more specifically to the good through references to public order and the general well-being of the citizens. By and large, this would call for more and not less judicial deference to legislative choices, as it opens up further justificative vistas. Very likely, in a context such as that of health policy and the delivery of services in complex situations, a more lenient justificatory process relating to considerations based on the good of the measure should prevail, thereby leaving the anti-private insurance provisions standing.

This could be true even under the more stringent standard posited in s. 1 of the *Canadian Charter*. As noted, the *Oakes* 'test' itself carries very little substantive guidance. It simply mandates a balancing exercise, and has been applied in widely divergent ways. In the early days of the *Charter* what, loosely following Ronald Dworkin, we may call a 'Taking Rights Seriously' attitude to s. 1 was prevalent. For instance, in *Singh*, it was said that mere utilitarian considerations would generally not be enough to justify the infringement of a right; and in *Oakes* it was said that any *prima facie* infringement of a Charter rights-provision amounted to a 'violation of constitutionally protected rights,' that the burden of proof on the government was a steep one, etc.[50] This attitude, of course, has been mollified as early as in *Edwards Books*,[51] but it regularly comes back and the Court has constantly oscillated between the 'Taking Rights Seriously' interpretation and a more deferential one based notably on institutional and democratic considerations.

The 'Taking Rights Seriously' interpretation is a contentious one, but it is one that fits rather well the text of s. 1, which states that rights are guaranteed and that they can *only* be subject to limits that are *reasonable and demonstrably justified in a free and democratic society*. But even under such a test, there are many reasons to believe that in the present case the limits should have been found to be reasonably justified, particularly on a straight liberal-egalitarian interpretation of s. 1.[52] In fact, the only coherent political philosophy that could be plausibly invoked in order to sustain the result reached by the Court is American style right-libertarianism.[53]

Reactions in Quebec

Right-libertarianism is not exactly a widespread ideology in Quebec. As we will later see, it may very well be that it is a reluctance to embrace this ideology and the atomistic individualism it implies that may explain the moderately negative reactions of a majority of Quebeckers to *Chaoulli*. However, another line of inquiry is also worth exploring. For that purpose, it first bears noting that Justice Deschamps has observed in her reasons that the principles of public health care set forth in the *Canada Health Act* 'have become the hallmarks of Canadian identity,'[54] and that that this Act has acquired such an iconic status that any attempt at questioning its principles triggers emotional reactions. If this is indeed the case, any attempt at structurally reforming this statutory framework is doomed to fail as a result of the transformation of public health care into a taboo subject. An interesting question is whether such a taboo exists in Quebec, from where the *Chaoulli* case emanates. Although it is beyond the scope of this paper to canvass all the reactions triggered by this judgment in Quebec, suffice it to say that these reactions have been mixed, but generally moderate.

On the legal front, two well-known constitutional law professors opined that questions relating to access to quality health services are a matter of public policy rather than law and thus deplored the lack of deference shown by the majority judges in respect of Quebec's legislative choices. They further argued that resort to the Quebec and Canadian Charters' notwithstanding clauses would be legitimate in such a case.[55] Another law professor, adopting what could be termed a 'rights are rights are rights' approach, denounced abstract criticism against 'judicial activism' as well as systematic calls for judicial deference when fundamental rights are at stake, even when complex social choices are involved.[56] Last, a health law expert observed that both the majority and the minority judges were equally interventionist, in that each group got involved into the political process simply as a result of characterizing policy choices for legal purposes. He added that the manicheanism that tends to inform debates over health care in Quebec and Canada actually obscures a phenomenon of public-private hybridization that has been going on for a while, especially in Quebec.[57] Neither the public sector nor the private sector can claim any kind of ontological monopoly over the good or the bad.

A similar rejection of manicheanism, as well as a denunciation of the hypocrisy of governments posturing themselves as the orthodox defenders of a purely public system while practically facilitating such hybridization, probably best characterize the reactions of a majority of non-jurists. For example, according to Michel Clair, the author of a well-known report on health care, we should resist presenting private solutions to the problems of health care as a panacea, but we should also refrain from demonizing any change leading to some private sector involvement in this area on the basis of an idealized, but inaccurate, image of the virtues of the current model. Like many other pundits in Quebec, he reads *Chaoulli* not so much as a Trojan horse that will inevitably lead to the demise of Quebec's public health care regime, but as an element in the collective reflection on a system that is in dire need of structural reforms.[58]

Opinion polls on the reform of this regime also reflect the 'principled pragmatism' that characterizes the approach of a majority of Quebeckers on health care. A Léger Marketing poll conducted after *Chaoulli*'s release revealed that 54% of the respondents supported the Supreme Court's conclusion while 41% were against it.[59] In the same vein, a CROP poll found that 62% of its respondents supported that conclusion.[60] These figures are consistent with the results of previous polls which showed that of all Canadians, Quebeckers tend to be the most favorable to some private sector involvement in the health care system.[61] What bears noting, however, is that the last two polls contained an important caveat. Indeed, both evoked a private sector involvement at the condition of maintaining either 'the integrity of the public system' or 'free and universal medical care.' This essentially means that while a majority of Quebeckers reject a two-tier system where financial means trump medical needs, they are not per se opposed to resorting to the private sector if this leads to a reduction of the inefficiencies of the public system. What distinguishes their attitudes from those of many of their fellow Canadians is that they do not seem to equate a 'public' system with the necessary exclusion of the private sector. Thus, their approach is principled in that they are not ready to compromise on equity and accessibility, but it is also pragmatic in that they are ready to consider the private sector as a means by which these objectives can be achieved. Even a center-left think-tank such as the *Institut du Nouveau Monde* is open to some private sector involvement if and only if 1) proof is made that this might 'contribute to improving the organization and access, or the quality of services, by harnessing an expertise, or technological equipments and resources that would otherwise not be available,' and 2) 'the State closely monitors the quality of the services so provided.'[62] The recent Ménard report on the sustainability of the health care and social services system also opens the door to an increased reliance on the private sector in the health care system, which is seen as inevitable given the aging of the population and the pressures that this will put on the public regime.[63]

This relative openness to some private sector involvement in the public health care system possibly points to a more than trivial difference between Quebeckers and other Canadians. Indeed, the former tend to privilege a functional rather than a symbolic stance toward that system and its evolution, while it is the exactly the opposite for a large number of the latter.[64] For Quebeckers, the public health care system is not an identity marker, and a majority of them support it not so much because they view a public system as a central feature of Canadian identity – an identity, it must be recalled, to which a significant number of them are at best indifferent – but first and foremost because they are committed to social-democratic ideals. It is possibly this fact that accounts for the rather lukewarm reception reserved to arguments in favor of the use of the Charters' notwithstanding clauses to protect the pre-*Chaoulli status quo*.[65] Since Quebeckers have generally failed to adhere to the 'myth of the sacred' triggered by *Canadian Charter* since its enactment,[66] one would think that they would be less reluctant to support the use of notwithstanding clauses in a case such as *Chaoulli*. But the absence of public health care in their identity reference probably explains why it is not the case. Unlike questions pertaining, for example, to the French language and its status, it is as if public health care was simply not fundamental enough to them to warrant such a muscular intervention. Undeniably, it may be a hallmark of Canadian identity, to use Madam Justice Deschamps' language, it may even be an intrinsic component of the fabled 'Quebec model,' but it is not a founding stone of Quebec identity, which explains why even a ruling viewed by many as a beacon of neo-liberalism is accepted with a significant dose of calm[67] or with a sense of fatality.[68]

Conclusion

Irrespective of whether or not one supports the involvement of the private sector in the delivery of health care services in Canada, we are of the view that, as a matter of law, the minority's reasons in *Chaoulli* are by far more convincing than those of the majority, especially regarding the interpretation to be given to the *Quebec Charter*. On this front, while refraining from making declarations about the need to enhance this Charter's distinctness and possibly that of Quebec society as well, they actually manage to give a tangible say to both. Indeed, not only are they practically giving meaning to the explicit differences between the Canadian and Quebec Charters, they also concretely allow space for the expression of the National Assembly of Quebec's policy choices. This approach starkly contrasts with that of Madam Justice Deschamps who, in spite of a formal pledge to enhance the said Charter's distinctness, does not hesitate in *Chaoulli* to refer to a feature of the Canadian identity which is hardly recognized or valued as such by a majority of Quebeckers while practically obliterating the most striking specificities of the *Quebec Charter*. All things considered, maybe the ambiguities of distinctness are indeed more satisfyingly addressed and managed through informality and pragmatism rather than through formality and solemn declarations ...[69]

Notes

1 R.S.Q. c. C-12.
2 See: A.-F. Bisson, 'La Charte québécoise des droits et libertés de la personne et le dogme de l'interprétation spécifique des textes constitutionnels,' (1986) 1 *R.D.U.S.* 19, at 21, footnote 1. A functional perspective would not conflate an instrument's 'constitutional status' with its formal 'entrenchment' in the constitution.
3 S. 52.
4 S.Q., 1991, c. 64
5 See, for provincial human rights codes: *Winnipeg School Division No. 1* v. *Craton*, [1985] 2 S.C.R. 150. For a similar characterization in respect of the Canadian Bill of Rights, R.S.C. 1970, app. III, and the Canadian Human Rights Act, S.C. 1976-77, c. 33, see, respectively, *Singh* v. *Minister of Employment and Immigration*, [1985] 1 S.C.R. 177, and *Robichaud* v. *R.* [1987] 2 S.C.R. 84.
6 On the concept of 'identity reference,' see: F. Dumont, *Genèse de la société québécoise*, (Montréal : Boréal, 1993).
7 The ghost metaphor is borrowed from G. Otis, 'Le spectre d'une marginalisation des voies de recours découlant de la Charte québécoise,' (1991) 51 *R. du B. 561*. In the same vein, see also: A. Morel, 'La coexistence des Chartes canadienne et québécoise: problèmes d'interaction,' (1986) 17

R.D.U.S. 47; A. Morel, 'L'originalité de la Charte québécoise en péril,' in: Barreau du Québec, *Développements récents en droit administratif (1993),* (Cowansville : Éditions Yvon Blais, 1993), p. 65.

8 For instance, leaving aside the interplay between the Quebec and Canadian Charters, it bears noting that the Supreme Court has rejected the argument that the particular civil remedies provided for by the *Quebec Charter* for rights violations formed a regime of liability distinct from the ordinary civil law regime of extra-contractual liability. Thus, the right violation that constitutes a fault at civil law must be proven to have caused damages according to ordinary rules to justify a claim for damages. See: *Béliveau St-Jacques* v. *Fédération des employées et employés de services publics Inc.*, [1996] 2 S.C.R. 345; *Aubry* v. *Éditions Vice-Versa Inc.*, [1998] 1 S.C.R. 591. There might have been compelling reasons for deciding in that way and we do not wish to take position on this question here. However, it does illustrate the gap that may sometimes exist between the abstract wish of enhancing that Charter's distinctness and the practical difficulty of doing it.

9 2005 SCC 35. Unless otherwise stated, all paragraph references refer to this decision.

10 At par. 11 Justice Deschamps states that the arguments based on the *Quebec Charter* were mentioned in the notice of appeal and in Delisle J.A.'s statement of the grounds of appeal, but that none of the Court of Appeal judges addressed them. This is untrue, since at par. 49 and 50 of his reasons Justice Delisle says that Quebec's anti-private insurance provisions do not infringe ss. 1, 4, 5, or 6 of the *Quebec Charter*. The two other judges agreed with Justice Delisle's reasons in this regard.

11 As noted by Peter Russell in his contribution to the present volume,' Justice Deschamps used the *Canadian Charter* as an interpretive guide to the *Quebec Charter* also in relation to the relevant rights provisions, as she construed the *Quebec Charter*'s s. 1's reference to 'inviolability' as having *at least* the same breadth as the reference to 'security of the person' in s. 7 of the *Canadian Charter*. But at the stage of rights-definition, the broader wording of the *Quebec Charter* worked to her advantage so there was no danger in distinguishing both provisions. This was not the case when it came to rights-limitations, since then the broader wording of s. 9.1 (as compared with section 1 of the *Canadian Charter*) worked against her position.

12 *Chaoulli at* para. 25.

13 Ibid at para 26.

14 *Singh* at 224 (Beetz J. wrote his opinion on his own behalf and on that of Estey and McIntyre JJs.)

15 *Chaoulli* at Para. 28
16 Ibid at Para. 37-41.
17 Ibid at Para. 31.
18 Ibid at Para. 38. Our italics.
19 On that evolution, see: R.M. Elliot, 'The Supreme Court of Canada and Section 1 ˉErosion of the Common Front,' (1987) 12 *Queen's L.J.* 277; A.Lokan, 'The Rise and Fall of Doctrine Under Section 1 of the Charter,' (1992) 24 *Ott. L.R.* 163; C.M. Dassios & C.P. Prophet, 'Charter Section 1: The Decline of Grand Unified Theory and the Trend Towards Deference in the Supreme Court of Canada,' (1993) 15 *Advocates Q.* 289.
20 See generally S. Choudry's contribution to this volume.
21 This was noted by the minority in reference to *Auton (Guardian ad litem of) v. British Columbia (Attorney General)*, [2004] 3 S.C.R. 657, which is all but ignored by the majority.
22 And perhaps the right to freedom protected by that same provision, but it is not as clear that she concludes to such an infringement.
23 *Chaoulli* at para. 47. This unsurprising but unfortunate finding is somewhat contradicted when she notes, at the stage of the minimal impairment test (par. 59) that the trial judge's approach in that respect 'was not appropriate to s. 9.1 of the Quebec Charter.'
24 Ibid at Para. 74. This emphasis on a test of necessity was noticed by Professor Henri Brun who, reflecting on the majority reasons in *Chaoulli*, argued that 'Charters of rights do not demand that the measures adopted by elected legislatures for the common good be necessary, they just ask that they be reasonable, as limits imposed on individual rights.' See: H. Brun, « En toute légitimité, le Parlement doit avoir le dernier mot », Québec City, *Le Soleil*, June 10, 2005, at A15. (Our translation); see also S. Choudry's in this volume.
25 *Chaoulli* at Para. 87
26 Ibid
27 Ibid at Para. 269-70
28 Ibid at Para. 273-4
29 Indeed, it seems undisputed that when it comes to the distribution of health care within a modern society, need is the most appropriate criterion, and wealth a very inappropriate one. See, for instance, M. Walzer, *Spheres of Justice, A Defense of Pluralism and Equality*, (New York: Basic Books, 1983), at 86-91; B. Williams, 'The Idea of Equality,' in *Problems of the Self*, (Cambridge: Cambridge University Press, 1973), at 240.
30 Articles 18, 19, 21, 22. For instance, article 22(2) provides that « [n]o restrictions may be placed on the exercise of [the right to freedom of association]

other than those which are prescribed by law and which are necessary in a democratic society in the interests of national security or public safety, public order (ordre public), the protection of public health or morals or the protection of the rights and freedoms of others.

31 Section 29 provides:
   (1) Everyone has duties to the community in which alone the free and full development of his personality is possible.
   (2) In the exercise of his rights and freedoms, everyone shall be subject only to such limitations as are determined by law solely for the purpose of securing due recognition and respect for the rights and freedoms of others and of meeting the just requirements of morality, public order and the general welfare in a democratic society.
   (3) These rights and freedoms may in no case be exercised contrary to the purposes and principles of the United Nations.

32 E.g. R. Cadieux, «Charte des droits et libertés de la personne, ... articles 9.1., 49 et 52 : développements récents» *in Développements récents en droit administratif (1993)*, Cowansville, Yvon Blais, 1993, 1 at pp. 3-5. The differences between the two limitations clauses were also an object of debate at the National Assembly at the time of adoption of 9.1. Mr. Herbert Marx, a former constitutional law professor at the University of Montreal who was then the Official Opposition's justice critique denounced the fact that s. 9.1 was more lax than s. 1 of the *Canadian Charter*. It was nonetheless adopted as it was. See Assemblée Nationale du Québec, Journal des Débats, 3ème session, 32ème legislature, Vol. 26, No 91, at pp. 6299-6300, No 93 at pp. 6436, 6449-6450, No 105 at pp. 7504-7505, 7507-7508, 7510 and 7513.

33 Morel,, 'L'originalité de la Charte québécoise en péril,' in: Barreau du Québec, *Développements récents en droit administratif (1993)*, at p. 70

34 *Ibid.*, at 72.

35 Generally the determination of the end of a law will be made while having in mind its instrumental potential. In other words, it will not be made in a vacuum, without looking at what the law is capable of accomplishing. Yet it is possible to have a law which is incapable of attaining its purported ends, a law that is thus completely irrational from an instrumental point of view.

36 *Ford v. Quebec (Attorney General)* [1988] 2 S.C.R. 712. at pp. 769-71. The approach was also followed in *Irwin Toy Ltd. v. Quebec (Attorney General)* [1989] 1 S.C.R. 927, at p. 980 and *Godbout v. Longueuil (City)* [1997] 3 S.C.R. 844.

37 In fact, in choosing for or against a particular course of action, proportionality is an aspect of rationality.

38 Again, see S. Choudry in the present volume.

39 P. Ricoeur, *Le Juste*, (Paris: Esprit, 1995).

40 R. Langlois, 'Les clauses limitatives des Chartes canadienne et québécoise des droits et libertés et le fardeau de la preuve,' in D. Turp & G.-A. Beaudoin (dir.), *Perspectives canadiennes et européennes des droits de la personne*, (Cowansville: Éditions Yvon Blais, 1986), 159, at 174-5 & 179. (our translation)

41 This doctrine was applied by courts even before its formal codification in the Civil Code of Quebec. For an illustration of its application in the contractual sphere, see: *Houle* v. *Canadian National Bank*, [1990] 3 S.C.R. 122.

42 [2004] 2 S.C.R. 551, at par. 186.

43 *Chaoulli* at Para. 48

44 We borrow this terminology from H.L.A. Hart, *Law, Liberty and Morality* (Oxford: Oxford University Press, 1963), at 20: Positive morality is 'the morality actually accepted and shared by a given social group' and critical morality refers to 'the general moral principles used in the criticism of actual social institutions including positive morality.' In the same vein, Ronald Dworkin distinguishes between morality in 'an anthropological sense' and morality 'in a discriminatory sense.' See: R. Dworkin, 'Liberty and Moralism,' in *Taking Rights Seriously, Taking Rights Seriously*, (London: Duckworth, 1977), at 248.

45 Quebec Research Centre of Private and Comparative Law, *The Private Law Dictionary*, 2nd ed. (Cowansville: Éditions Yvon Blais, 1991), at 348, defines 'public order' (*ordre public*) as:

Global conception of a society expressed in its basic institutions, its general principles and its imperative norms, the purpose of which is to protect and promote the basic values of the community.

Black's Law Dictionary, 8th ed., St Paul. Thomson, 2004, at p. 1267, defines 'public policy' (which is the common law equivalent of public order), as:

1. Broadly, principles and standards regarded by the legislature or by the courts as being of fundamental concern to the state and the whole of society [...] 2. More narrowly, the principle that a person should not be allowed to do anything that would injure the public at large.

46 Within utilitarianism, rights themselves are protected because they tend to increase utility in the long run.

47 In his contribution to this volume Claude Forget claims that single-payer medicare is being defended though some form of utilitarianism. But even a non-utilitarian such as Rawls accepts the inevitability of prioritizing some cases over others in the delivery of health care and observes in that

respect that it is at the legislative level that conflicts between the two basic principles informing his theory – equal liberty and the difference principle – should be resolved, because the practical application of these principles depends on prior information being available on the frequency and the gravity of the illnesses encountered, the frequency and causes of accidents, and many other factors. See: J. Rawls, *Justice as Fairness: A Restatement* (Cambridge Mass., Harvard University Press, 2001) no. 51.6, at 173-174.

48 For an example of such a conception, see J. Finnis, *Natural Law and Natural Rights,* (Oxford: Oxford University Press, 1980), esp. at Chapters IV (The Other Basic Values) and VI (Community, Communities, and Common Good). Hence, at pp. 155-56, Finnis defines one sense of 'common good' as 'a set of conditions which enables the members of a community to attain for themselves reasonable objectives, or to realize reasonably for themselves the value(s) for the sake of which they have reason to collaborate with each other (positively and/or negatively) in a community.' He then adds: 'The common good in this sense is a frequent or at least a justified meaning of the phrases "the general welfare" or "the public interest."'

49 *Chaoulli* at Para. 223

50 *R. v. Oakes* [1986] 1 S.C.R. 103. This attitude had indeed some broad affinities with some statements made by Ronald Dworkin (although it amounted to a rather rough and ready application of them). R. Dworkin, *Taking Rights Seriously* esp. ch 4 (Hard Cases) and 7 (Taking Rights Seriously).

51 *R v. Edwards Books and Art Ltd.* [1986] 2 S.C.R. 713.

52 Following, for instance, the liberal-egalitarianism of Rawls or Dworkin. J. Rawls, *A Theory of Justice,* Cambridge, Mass, Harvard University Press, 1971; R. Dworkin, *Sovereign Virtue. The Theory and Practice of Equality,* (Cambridge, Mass.: Harvard University Press, 2000). It is certainly not fanciful to believe that the Supreme Court's conception of what is justified in a free and democratic society loosely followed such forms of liberal egalitarianism. In *Oakes,* for instance, Chief Justice Dickson stated that in interpreting s. 1, '[...t]he Court must be guided by the values and principles essential to a free and democratic society [... such as] respect for the inherent dignity of the human person, commitment to social justice and equality, accommodation of a wide variety of beliefs, respect for cultural and group identity, and faith in social and political institutions which enhance the participation of individuals and groups in society.' *Oakes,* at p. 136.

53 On this point see S. Choudry's contribution to the present volume, at the section 'Economic Libertarianism.'

54   *Chaoulli* supra at Para. 16.

55   H. Brun, « En toute légitimité, le Parlement doit avoir le dernier mot »,
Québec City, *Le Soleil*, June 10, 2005, at A15; P. Garant, « Recours justifié à
la clause dérogatoire si le gouvernement en a le courage », Québec City,
Le Soleil, June 10 2005, at A15. The Quebec Charter's «notwithstanding
clause» is found at s. 52, which provides that 'no provision of any Act,
even subsequent to the Charter, may derogate from sections 1 to 38, except
so far as provided by those sections, *unless such Act expressly states that it
applies despite the Charter*.' (our emphasis)

56   F. Bachand, « Une critique troublante », Montreal, *La Presse*, June 15, 2005,
at A25.

57   P. Molinari, « Les paradoxes de la société distincte », Montreal, *La Presse*,
June 10, 2005, at A15.

58   M. Clair, « Il faut se ressaisir. Le jugement de la Cour suprême doit donner
une nouvelle impulsion à notre système de santé », *La Presse*, June 11, 2005,
at A24.

59   Institut économique de Montréal, *Opinion des Québécois à l'égard du
jugement de la Cour suprême du Canada relatif à l'interdiction aux citoyens de
payer pour des soins de santé déjà couverts par le gouvernement*, June 22, 2005.

60   D. Lessard, « Les Québécois favorables au privé », Montreal, *La Presse*,
June 30, 2005, p. A4.

61   A. Duchesne, « Les Québécois ouverts au privé », Montreal, *La Presse*, June
2, 2004, p. A14.

62   Institut du Nouveau Monde, *Recueil des propositions adoptées. Rendez-vous
stratégique sur la santé de l'Institut du Nouveau Monde*, Montréal, June 2005,
at 9, available on line : www.inm.qc.ca. Our translation.

63   Comité sur la pérennité du système de santé et de services sociaux du
Québec (L.J. Ménard, pres.), *Pour sortir de l'impasse : la solidarité entre nos
générations*, (Québec : Ministère de la Santé et des Services sociaux 2005),
available on line: www.solidaritedesgenerations.qc.ca.

64   We indeed see the public medicare system as constituting an almost
untouchable aspect of Canadian identity in the rest of Canada. A good
example of such «medicare nationalism» is the Romanow Report: Commission on the Future of Health Care in Canada, Final Report, November
2002. www.hc-sc.gc.ca/english/ pdf/romanow/pdfs/
HCC_Final_Report.pdf

65   In addition to the suggestions made by Professors Brun and Garant, *supra*,
that resort to the notwithstanding clause could be conceivable in the
instant case, the official opposition formed by the Parti québécois has also
called for the use of that clause, as well as some other actors of the health

care system. See: T. Chouinard, « Le PQ réclame la clause dérogatoire », Montreal, *La Presse*, June 10, 2005, p. A6; A. Boivin, « Un jugement à se réapproprier », Montreal, *Le Devoir*, June 21, 2005, p. A7; B. Dubuc et al., « Nous ne voulons pas nous retrouver à la merci des assureurs privés », Quebec City, *Le Soleil*, July 2, 2005, p. A22.

66 The expression 'myth of the sacred' comes from : P. James, D.E. Abelson & M. Lusztig, 'Introduction: The Myth of the Sacred in the Canadian Constitutional Order,' in: P. James, D.E. Abelson & M. Lusztig, eds., *The Myth of the Sacred. The Charter, the Courts, and the Politics of the Constitution in Canada*, (Montreal & Kingston: McGill-Queen's University Press, 2002), p. 3.

67 See : J.-R. Sansfaçon, « Des assurances, et après? », Montreal, *Le Devoir*, June 30, 2005, p. A6.

68 See : A. Dubuc, « Le début de la fin », Montreal, *La Presse*, August 20, 2005, p. A24.

69 For a remarkable examination of explicit and implicit approaches to the recognition and management of distinctness, see : R.A. Macdonald, 'The Design of Constitutions to Accommodate Linguistic, Cultural and Ethnic Diversity: The Canadian Experiment' in: K. Kulcsar & D. Szabo, eds., *Dual Images. Multiculturalism on Two Sides of the Atlantic*, (Budapest: Institute for Political Science of the Hunagrian Academy of Sciences & Royal Society of Canada, 1996), p. 52.

Charter Perspectives on *Chaoulli*: The Body and the Body Politic

LORRAINE E. WEINRIB*

Introduction

The Supreme Court of Canada's *Chaoulli* decision brought together two of the most revered structural elements of Canadian life – constitutional rights and one tier public medicine.[1] The unexpected ruling pinpointed Quebec's legislated prohibition against private medical insurance as the material cause of unacceptable waiting periods for access to health care and then declared the offending provisions invalid. The stay of the invalidation order for one year, granted upon the request of the Attorney General of Quebec, provides a window of opportunity to examine the judgment for its legal, political and social policy implications. Such examination is warranted because *Chaoulli* revealed deep division on the Court as to the methodology for *Charter* analysis, the relationship between law and policy and, perhaps most importantly, the judicial role within rights-based democracy.

This paper relates the methodological elements of the *Chaoulli* judgment to the more abstract questions. The general argument is that the judiciary has both the constitutional duty and the institutional capacity to evaluate claims of *Charter* infringement even within the most policy-laden regulatory context. The legitimacy of this extraordinary authority rests on the legal character of its exercise, however. The more particular argument is that the two judgments that apply the *Charter* stray from this narrow pathway, albeit in different ways.[2] Critics, this time on the left, have once again challenged not merely the controversial ruling, but the legitimacy of the whole *Charter* enterprise.[3]

Both judgments identify but regrettably do not offer guidance on the *Charter* infraction identified by all the judges: the human cost of waiting lists within the public system. Reluctant to impose financial burdens on government, the judges fail to identify the important social and economic costs resulting from delayed health care. After analyzing the strengths and weaknesses of the two *Charter* judgments, the paper concludes with a brief outline of the message that policy makers should take from the *Chaoulli* judgment in their long delayed redesign of the public medical system to accord with the strictures of the *Charter*.

The Supreme Court's Ruling

The ruling in favour of *Charter* infringement is relatively straightforward and may be considered the authoritative set of reasons for the purposes of this essay. While only three of the seven judges rendering judgment supported this ruling, Justice Deschamps' separate ruling, based on the parallel protections in Quebec's statutory *Charter*, is in full sympathy with this judgment.[4] The reasons for judgment of Chief Justice McLachlin and Justice Major, with the support of Justice Bastarache, can thus be said to enjoy Justice Deschamps' implicit approval.[5] Accordingly, my reference to this judgment will describe it as the 'majority opinion.'

The bottom line of the majority opinion may be clearly stated. Quebec's prohibition of private healthcare insurance restricted access to private health care to all but the very rich. Everyone else had to endure the risks to life and health attendant to the delays in the public healthcare system. These delays amounted to an unjustified breach of s. 7 of the *Charter*. To correct this situation, the majority removed what it considered the impediment to timely private health care by nullifying the statutory impediment to private health insurance.

The majority had to rule on a number of sequential questions to assess the validity of the *Charter* claim and to design the appropriate remedial order. The doctrinal tests for the threshold breach of s. 7 are clear and stable. Therefore, the cogency of the claim to breach of the 'right to life, liberty and security of the person' set down in s. 7 was fairly obvious: the delay in access to health care within the public system posed a considerable risk to life or health. Indeed, the Court was unanimous on this one point.

The next step was much more contentious: determination whether the breach conformed to 'the principles of fundamental justice.' This element of *Charter* methodology remains so unsettled that it provides the obvious juncture at which the majority and the dissent might part company. Having decided this question against the government of Quebec, the majority took the argument one step further, to consider whether the breach of s. 7 might be justified under s. 1 of the *Charter*, which permits governments to justify rights infringements according to a complicated evaluation of proportionality of the breach to important state policies. Again, the majority decided against the government.

The dissenting judgment, by Justices Binnie and Lebel, with the concurrence of Justice Fish, acknowledged the legal parameters of the *Charter* claim and agreed that the delays posed a risk to life and security of the person. It restricted this finding to 'some people' on 'some occasions,' however, – an early signal perhaps that it was less dissatisfied with the delivery system for public health care.[6] The full force of the disagreement between the majority and the dissent became apparent in the consideration of the 'principles of fundamental justice.' The dissent's delineation of the appropriate tests and its examination of the argumentation and supporting evidence focused less on the Court's special obligation to protect constitutional rights than on the legitimacy and desirability of a public health care system, whatever its operative performance. This defence of the public system reflected strong concern that the majority's analysis and remedy favoured the wealthy, who can pay for private insurance, at the expense of the less fortunate, in terms of material wealth and health, who may find themselves trapped within an eroding public system. The dissent might have, but did not, work these values into persuasive legal argumentation.

Before turning to a more detailed examination of the reasoning, the next section examines the constitutional framework that delineates and legitimates the roles of courts and legislatures under the *Charter*.

The Body and the Body Politic

Bodily autonomy is one of the oldest precepts of liberal theory. It is also one of the primary components of the concept of human dignity, which stands as a foundational principle within modern, rights-based democracy. Human dignity, as a constitutional principle, shapes the interpretation of all rights guarantees by stipulating that each person must be regarded as possessing inherent and innate human dignity. For that reason the state must treat each person as an end in herself, rather than a means to the well-being or advantage of others – regardless of wealth or power. Governments with limited temporal and policy mandates will not, on their own, meet this standard in the design and impact of every exercise of public authority.[7] In any event, legislatures cannot be the final arbiter of their own fidelity to this foundational principle. Independent review is necessary. Such review can be provided by government, but the final authority on constitutional guarantees must emanate from the courts, because the Constitution has the status of supreme law.

The Canadian *Charter*, like many other rights-protecting instruments at the national and supra-national level, crystallizes the general idea of respect for human dignity into a guarantee of personal integrity. Thus, section 7 of the *Charter* protects the individual's life, liberty and security of the person against the state. This protection is not absolute, but it does command considerable respect in the formation of public policy. It prevails unless and until dislodged by public policy possessing exceptional characteristics. Ordinary political preferences do not suffice. Modern rights-protecting instruments, like the *Charter*, were put in place to dislodge precisely this arrangement. Their purpose was to effect the transition from legislative democracy to rights-based democracy.[8]

Charter rights should not be regarded as restricting or usurping the prerogative of sovereign law-making bodies. While this understanding may reflect the historical development of constitutional rights-protection in Canada, it is conceptually unsound. It sets up an inappropriately antagonistic relationship between courts and legislatures as well as between law and policy.

Within rights-based democracy, the authority of legislatures is circumscribed by the constitution's guarantee of a range of rights and freedoms that delineate, together, the inherent and equal human dignity of all persons within the ordering of society. Fundamental rights and freedoms, in other words, are neither the gift of the legislature nor the residue that remains when the policy-making function is spent. Rather, legislatures are creatures of the constitution. Accordingly, they must operate within the constitutional framework of rights protection.

The protection accorded under s. 7 of the *Charter* reflects this constitutional structure. It sets out the standards by which the state may exercise its constitutional authority. The right to life, liberty and security of the person protects against state encroachment on the security of one's personal physical integrity as well as one's personal autonomy. Case law has established that the zone of protection includes the physical and psychological well-being not of a deracinated individual, but of a person with priorities and aspirations and as well as given and chosen relationships that carry responsibility.[9] Delayed access to medical care encroaches on one's ability to take care of oneself, to support oneself and to fulfil one's obligations.

Encroachments must conform to the 'principles of fundamental justice' to pass *Charter* review. These words have confounded attempts at definition, but have delineated content nonetheless. They encompass the basic understandings of justice within the operation of administrative law and criminal law, in particular, procedural justice.[10] Testing compliance with such standards is well within the traditional role and institutional competence of the judiciary. Violation of the principles of fundamental justice can result from state action and inaction, in the structural and operational interstices of government administration or in the failure by government to provide administrative arrangements deemed constitutionally necessary.[11]

The *Charter* applies an extra layer of constitutional framing to all *Charter* guarantees. Section 1 of the *Charter*, as noted, allows the state to justify encroachments on *Charter* guarantees when such encroachments are 'prescribed by law' and 'justified.' This formulation is derived from parallel formulations in the text or interpretation of other modern rights-protecting instruments at the national and international level. Canadian courts have adapted the doctrinal tests developed in these instruments to *Charter* review. Since s. 7 already allows deprivation of the threshold protections afforded – life, liberty and security of the person – when the state conforms to principles of fundamental justice, there is little room for s. 1 to operate to save a breach of s. 7. The Canadian courts have acknowledged this fact by suggesting that s. 1 analysis might apply to s. 7 only in times of emergency.[12]

The relationship between the *Charter*'s guarantees, as individual entitlements crystallizing inherent, equal human dignity, on the one hand, and its formulations such as 'principles of fundamental justice' and 'justified limitations' upon rights, is not obvious. The basic question is this: do these latter formulations further elaborate the fundamental concepts that inform the protection of the guaranteed rights and freedoms or do they introduce concepts that compete with, weaken or even negate these guarantees? In the context of access to health care, one can formulate this distinction in more concrete terms: where does one draw the line between the body, as the corporeal manifestation of the individual's personal sovereignty, protected by constitutional directives informing judicial review, and the body politic, as the collective that actualizes majority preferences, forwarding the common good according to standards of consensus and reasonableness?

Academic commentary and judicial pronouncements on this perennial question take a particular shape. They stake out different positions as to when, how and to what extent one works within the conceptual framework of inherent and equal human dignity, justice and fundamental principle, to invoke some of the standard vocabulary that collects at one end of the spectrum, or within the operational framework of balancing, reasonableness, consensus and public policy, i.e., considerations that collect at the other end of the spectrum.

Chaoulli provides an opportunity to situate access to health care on this spectrum. Health care concerns fall fully within the zone of individual autonomy. Leaving legislation and the *Charter* aside for the moment, it is clear that one can seek and give fully informed consent to beneficial care to cure illness and alleviate injury. The state may intervene in a number of ways, however. It may legislate to regulate private health care, for example on the basis of morality (consistent with inherent human dignity) and safety, including professional training and accreditation and the provision and regulation of hospitals. It may choose to regulate the business of private health care insurance. It may intervene more intrusively, e.g., to provide a public health care system, supported by insurance premiums or by general taxation. It may then determine whether private health care will co-exist with public health care or yield to it.

The configuration under examination in the *Chaoulli* case combined a publicly funded health care monopoly with a ban that extended to private health insurance, but not to private health care. Such a scheme coerces through taxation a transfer of wealth in return for state provision of care. *Chaoulli* raises but does not determine important questions at the interface of public policy and *Charter* guarantees: to what extent may the state create a virtual monopoly in health care services that does not apply basic principles of fairness to its delivery? Can such a monopoly operate without transparency, accountability and quality standards in respect to waiting lists when delay poses risks to life and health?

Some commentators insist that health care delivery is pure politics and the exclusive preserve of the elected and accountable legislature.[13] But does this describe the constitutional universe in which Canadians live? Can the state, in the *Charter* era, collect our money and run the system in such a way as to offer no basis on which to ascertain its failings, the condition precedent to calling government to political account? Can the millions of decisions that ultimately determine the time of treatment be free of requirements to report, meet clinical standards and submit to procedures for independent review? One can imagine that governments might consider it advantageous not to generate the statistical data that would inform public opinion on the state of the public health care system. Informed citizens might withdraw political support from governments that continuously delivered health care with such delays as to undermine health and, in extreme cases, life.

The Judgments

a) The Judicial Role

The majority judgment affirms a generous scope for the *Charter's* protection of fundamental rights and freedoms against state policy preferences, affirming that the judiciary must enforce constitutional constraints upon legislatures, as creatures of the Constitution.[14] Accordingly, naked policy choices can neither delineate nor circumscribe the responsibilities that governments shoulder under the Constitution.[15] Similarly, the influence that government-sponsored reports enjoy in the policy arena does not extend to constitutional questions.[16] While the government may argue that public health services must be so lean as to have built-in delays, a court applying *Charter* strictures must differentiate between accessing health care and accessing a waiting list.[17] The former supports life and health; the latter may pose risks to life and health.

While the dissent makes the same determination as to judicial authority, it deploys weaker language and formulations. Health care is characterized as social policy, not as a right-laden regulatory system. It stresses that preference for single- or two-tier medicine must be the product of legislative deliberation, supported by democratic mandates and public debate.[18] The petitioners, in other words, have mistakenly claimed territory as the domain for bodily autonomy that belongs to the domain of the body politic. The dissent, perhaps reacting to the majority, sets out to save the public system rather than restricting its attention to the more judicial task of assessing the quality of health care delivery within the public system on *Charter* standards.

b) The Right to Life, Liberty and Security of the Person

The majority sets out the claim submitted by the petitioners, Dr. Chaoulli and George Zeliotis. They were not interested in establishing a freestanding right to health care from the state, more money for the public system generally or even a reduction in waiting times. Their demand was to invalidate Quebec's prohibition against private insurance, to open up wider access to private health care. Their prize was a *Charter* ticket to exit the public system.

The majority agreed that the prohibition of private insurance violated s. 7 of the *Charter* in creating delays in the public system that increased the risk of pain, psychological suffering and even death. The next step involved a leap of logic: the systemic infringement would not materialize if 'ordinary Canadians' could access private health care, where providers operate under strong incentives to serve their market without delay.[19] Such access, however, is barred by its prohibitive expense to all but the 'very rich,' who can pay for private health services as needed or self-insure.[20] To end the state's encroachment on *Charter*-protected interests, i.e., life and security of the person, required removal of the statutory impediment to immediate access to health care in the private arena.[21]

It is worth drawing attention here to two specific elements of the reasoning. First, the majority does not identify as the problematic impediment to access to health care the delay produced by waiting lists in the public system, which blocks access to the *public* system's health services. Rather, the operative impediment to which the systemic failure of access is attributed is the statutory ban on private insurance, even though its purpose and effect is to block access to pooled insurance funds that would secure access to *private* health care services.

Second, we know that the claimants before the court were strong supporters of two tier health care and fashioned their argumentation accordingly. In Dr. Chaoulli's factum, for instance, the primary s. 7 interest violated was the patient's liberty interest to arrange for his health care as best suited him, with the life and security interests playing the secondary role of establishing that the relevant liberty interest is not a merely economic interest.[22] Why did the majority accept this characterization of the access problem, given that it regarded the relevant s. 7 interests as life and security of the person, not liberty?[23] Perhaps the answer to that question lies in the delineation of the operation of the ban on private health insurance. To the majority it disadvantaged 'ordinary Canadians,' but left the 'very rich' with the best of both systems. Such extensive encroachment on individual fundamental interests might have seemed beyond repair. As we shall see, the dissent constructed this social divide in very different terms.

The dissent joined the majority in finding a threat to s. 7 guarantees of life and security of the person, but unlike the majority it did not recognize widespread erosion of s. 7 rights. Rather, it acknowledged that in *some* circumstances, *some* Quebeckers might have their lives or security of the person put at risk by the insurance ban.[24] Denial of life-saving care would certainly signal such an encroachment, but would be the rare case.[25]

At this stage of the argument, the developing chasm between the majority and dissent becomes apparent. In the next stage, any common ground disappears. The majority maintains its focus on the right-holder's claim to individual autonomy, as it should, but extended this claim excessively to include entitlement to access a private market in medical services. The dissent, repelled at what it considers the danger to one tier medicine posed by rights-based analysis, seeks to situate public health care within a rights-free domain of social policy, majoritarian preferences, consensus and standards of reasonableness and balancing.

c) Principles of Fundamental Justice

The majority took up the test of arbitrariness as the applicable standard for compliance with the 'principles of fundamental justice.' It asked, did the state policy 'bear no relation to' or stand 'as inconsistent with' its objective?[26] The Quebec government argued that its ban on private health insurance was necessary to the provision of effective health care. Without the ban, the private system would undermine and compete with the public system.[27] The claimants denied this assertion, suggesting that the public system did not need the ban to provide medical services; rather, it needed more resources and better management.[28] The majority rejected the government's position as unproven.[29] It observed that the comparably better operation of health care systems in other Western democracies did not rest on a public monopoly.[30]

The dissent, committed to shielding one tier medicine from *Charter* strictures, delineated the principles of fundamental justice in deferential terms such as reasonableness, balancing and consensus– considerations that congregate at the public policy end of the spectrum of argumentation, as noted earlier. Although it noted that s. 7 analysis must pertain to the 'basic tenets' of the legal system, the standard applied was neither substantive nor related to justice in any obvious way. Instead, it appealed to popular opinion. The principles of fundamental principles of justice were those principles accepted by reasonable people as encompassing what was 'vital to the notion of justice.'[31] Accordingly, they became the substance of public policy rather than a template by which to evaluate the fundamental fairness of public policy.

Having determined that 'fundamental justice' meant public notions of justice, the dissent went on to describe the waiting lists within the public system as a necessary and acceptable mode of 'rationing.' No definition of this term was provided; no description or analysis of the 'rationing' system supported its positive characterization. Mr. Zeliotis' personal circumstances purportedly supported this proposition. The various elements of his health condition, including depression, and the desire for a second diagnostic opinion had, after all, contributed to delay in his case. These elements of his personal case seemed sufficiently strong to weigh against the earlier findings as to the deleterious impact of delay on life and well-being in a significant number of cases.[32] The dissent made no mention of the obvious connection between illness, immobility, pain and isolation on mental health. Turning to other evidence, the dissent seemed to take comfort in statistics that indicated that 33% of patients on waiting lists were not actually waiting for care, without regard for the impact of delay on the other 67%, some number of whom must fall within the group earlier identified as suffering deterioration of health or higher risk of death.[33]

The dissent noted that there is no consensus on the question of waiting list administration and no set of national standards for timely treatment. It also noted the absence of adequate data for the application of such standards.[34] One might have thought that these findings would be fatal to any affirmation of the fundamental fairness of the system. Instead, the dissent made the best of the waiting list phenomenon by pronouncing that a public health system without 'rationing' would not have engaged in a correct balance of (unidentified) competing interests, i.e., it would be 'overbuilt.'[35]

This line of thinking precluded any state obligation to investigate and oversee the administration of the waiting lists or to expand capacity in the public system if that turned out to be the underlying problem. Moreover, opening up access to the private system to those who could afford insurance, but not direct payment for private health care as needed, would simply amount to favouring the wealthy and those with social status without reason.[36]

Perhaps the oddest element in this analysis is the reference to Quebec's provision of a 'safety valve,' in the form of reimbursement for the cost of insured services rendered outside Quebec or outside Canada for services unavailable at home.[37] This possibility seemed to cure other (unconceded) defects in the system, even though there was no evidence of the effectiveness of this 'safety valve' in the medical history of the two claimants before the Court. On the contrary, the litigation record indicated that this exception was rarely available, that its administration suffered from 'lapses in judgment' and 'on occasion,' unlawful action. Justice Deschamps is more forthcoming; she notes that the voluminous record in this case reveals no administrative arrangements for accessing this funding.[38]

There was no mention of the fact that having a serious medical intervention far from home is likely to add to the considerable stress and anxiety related to the need for immediate medical treatment. Indeed, the Supreme Court of Canada has noted the personal, social and economic burdens that accessing remote health care can entail.[39] Moreover, one of the reasons that the petitioners had secured public interest standing to bring the case had been that persons in need of urgent medical care should not have to go through legal proceedings to access health care.[40]

The dissent's analysis shifted focus away from each and every individual right-holder's full physical integrity. Having just described the operative flaws of this 'safety valve,' the dissent affirms it as an 'an important element of flexibility, if administered properly.' These words jump out from the page. If the whole system worked according to basic standards of fairness, the violation of s.7 would not have been proved in the first place. The dissent's lack of concern for the operation of the public system may be driven by its strong desire to protect one-tier medicine from the majority's analysis and remedy.

Why doesn't this judgment, based on a voluminous factual record, tell us how the system actually works?[41] On what basis is it appropriate to assume that the 'rationing' that produces the delays in the public system, identified as encroachments on the right to life and security of the person in one part of the judgment, can operate as evidence of praiseworthy avoidance of an 'overbuilt' system in another part of the judgment?

d) Section 1

The majority proceeds to s. 1 justification, which the dissent did not consider having found no violation of s. 7. The majority must confront a familiar *Charter* conundrum: can state action that fails to conform to the principles of fundamental justice satisfy the justification tests under s. 1? The majority addresses this point directly, noting that where the arbitrariness standard has not been met under s. 7, it is very unlikely that s. 1 justification tests could be satisfied.[42] By definition, arbitrariness would seem to imply a lack of rational connection. Nonetheless, the majority engages in a full limitation analysis, rather than resting on the lack of rational connection, which would suffice. It concludes by noting that the government's submissions would also fail the minimal impairment test as well as the balancing of beneficial and deleterious effects test.

e) Remedy

It is remarkable that so little attention is paid to the remedy granted by the majority. The link between the risks to the right to life and security of the person and the waiting lists is obvious. The link between the insurance ban and these risks, however, is not, either in terms of infringement or remedy. As the dissent emphasized, the expert and comparative evidence before the Court, as well as expert predictions of what would follow from invalidating the insurance ban, demonstrated complexity that the majority either ignored or dismissed too easily. There were too many variables in play, including how the government would circumscribe the private medical system once it was opened up to private health insurance.[43] A parallel private system might even aggravate rather than alleviate delays in the public system.[44] The majority insisted that when one looks to evidence instead of mere assumptions, 'the connection between prohibiting private insurance and maintaining quality public health care vanishes.'[45]

What does *Chaoulli* stand for?

The *Chaoulli* judgment makes clear that the state is bound by the *Charter* when it establishes and administers a public health care system. At a minimum, the state must deliver health care in a way that does not seriously breach the right to life, liberty and security of the person. It is unlikely that this will happen if private ordering prevails, as apparently it does in the administration of waiting lists that apparently remain the preserve of individual doctors.[46]

One must therefore assume, until compelling evidence to the contrary comes forward, that it is the absence of systematic administration of the waiting lists according to public values that has produced an unacceptable degree of delay. In any event, it is impossible to reach any informed opinion on the causes and effects of waiting lists until there is adequate statistical data. Thus, the state's obligation at this time must be to create the requisite data, apply the requisite analytic techniques to that data, pinpoint problem areas, and develop a good administrative plan to reduce waiting lists according to clinical standards. This type of system can be defended as conforming to the basic tenets of fundamental justice.

It is not clear, at this time, whether it is possible to bring the public health system into *Charter* compliance. We do not know whether savings can be found in eliminating waste and inefficiency. It may be that much more money is necessary to administer an efficient and responsive system. It is necessary, however, to accept the fact that rights cost money. The *Charter* does inform the policy choices and priorities of government. It is also necessary to recognize, at least in the context of health care, that denying rights also costs money. The social and economic loss produced by the long waiting periods for some forms of medical care should not be ignored. It is common sense that many people on the waiting lists become unemployed, lose businesses, cannot finance their children's education, etc.

The great contribution of the litigation to the public good in Canada lies in the light that it has shed on the way in which our political representatives and our executive governments have failed to analyze and correct the failings in the delivery of health care. To consider this neglect as the justification for radical judicial surgery upon the body politic, as does the majority, is as unfortunate as the dissent's description of rationing medical care as acceptable and appropriate because the general public, which has been deprived of the information necessary to consider the shortcomings of the system, considers it just.

Below the surface of the *Chaoulli* judgments we can discern the basis for principled and operational standards that would accord with the principles of fundamental justice. Such standards must include the criteria to prioritize the caseload by setting standards of clinical need and making provision to deal with exceptional cases on an individual basis.[47] These standards must resonate with the *Charter*'s directive that the state must not discriminate on the basis of disability.

One can imagine the possibility of circumstances in which *Charter* infractions might be so serious that the courts would have to think of alternatives to the public system as remedial orders. That point has not come. The weaknesses of the majority's analysis and its treatment of the evidence put forward make that fact clear.

The fate of our public health care system lies where it should lie, in the hands of our representative, accountable legislatures and the executives that guide their agenda. The judiciary cannot run the country. But judges can, and should, make clear when the occasion arises that public authority has failed to heed the most basic precept that informs the provision of health care: do no harm.

Notes

* Faculty of Law, University of Toronto

1 The author acknowledges the assistance of Ian Bell in the preparation of this paper. *Chaoulli v. Quebec (Attorney General)*, 2005 SCC 35, delivered June 9, 2005 [*Chaoulli*].

2 Kent Roach, 'Too Much Judicial Activism or Too Little,' in this volume.

3 In this volume, see Sujit Choudhry, 'Worse than *Lochner*,' Andrew Petter, 'Wealthcare: The Politics of *Charter* Revisited,' Allan Hutchinson, 'Condition Critical: Health Care and Constitutional Rights.'

4 *The Charter of Human Rights and Freedoms*, R.S.Q., c. C-12 ['the Quebec *Charter*'].

5 Peter Russell, '*Chaoulli*: The Political vs. the Legal Life of a Judicial Decision,' in this volume, takes a different view on this point.

6 *Chaoulli, supra* note at 200.

7 Lorraine E. Weinrib, 'Dignity as a Rights Protecting Principle,' (2004), 17 *National Journal of Constitutional Law* 235.

8 Lorraine E. Weinrib, 'Canada's Rights Revolution: From Legislative to Constitutional State,' (1999), 33 Israel L. Rev. 1.

9 *R. v. Morgentaler*, [1988] 1 S.C.R. 30, *Rodriguez v. British Columbia*, [1993] 3 S.C.R. 519, *New Brunswick (Minister of Health and Community Services) v. G. (J.)*, [1999] 3 S.C.R. 46, *Blencoe v. British Columbia (Human Rights Commission)*, [2000] 2 S.C.R. 307 [*Blencoe*].

10 See the judgments cited in the previous note, and Lorraine E. Weinrib, 'The *Morgentaler* Judgment: A Study in Constitutional Rights, Legislative Intention, and Institutional Design,' (1992), 42 University of Toronto L. J. 22, Lorraine E. Weinrib, 'The Body and the Body Politic: Assisted Suicide under the *Canadian Charter of Rights and Freedoms*,' (1994), 39 McGill L. J. 618.

11 *Reference re Provincial Court Judges,* [1997] 3 S.C.R. 3, *Reference re Secession of Quebec,* [1998] 2 S.C.R. 217, *Blencoe, supra* note .
12 *Reference re. Section 94(2) of the Motor Vehicle Act (B. C.),* [1985] 2 S.C.R. 486
13 Christopher Manfredi, 'Déjà Vu All Over Again: *Chaoulli* and the Limits of Judicial Policymaking,' in this volume.
14 *Chaoulli, supra* note 1 at para 107.
15 *Ibid.,* at para. 108
16 *Ibid.,* at para. 151.
17 *Ibid.,* at para. 123.
18 *Ibid.,* at paras. 161, 166–170, 183–185.
19 *Ibid.,* at para. 124.
20 *Ibid.,* at paras. 111, 106.
21 *Ibid.,* at paras. 111, 124.
22 Factum of the appellant Chaoulli, paras. 141–155. Para. 155: 'Pour démontrer une atteinte au droit de la liberté, l'appelant soumet respectueusement qu'il lui suffisait de prouver, comme il l'a fait, que dans bien des cas, dans le secteur public, des services ne sont pas rendus selon des modalités qui lui conviennent.'
23 *Chaoulli, supra* note 1 at para. 124.
24 *Ibid.,* at para. 191.
25 *Ibid.,* at para. 203.
26 *Ibid.,* at paras. 130–131.
27 *Ibid.,* at para. 135.
28 *Ibid.,* at para. 137.
29 *Ibid.,* at para. 138.
30 *Ibid.,* at para. 140. See [need cites here] for strong criticism of the majority's comparative analysis.
31 *Ibid.,* at paras. 208–209.
32 *Ibid.,* at para 211. Here we see some conflation of the public and private litigant.
33 *Ibid.,* at para 219.
34 *Ibid.,* at paras. 211, 217.
35 *Ibid.,* at para. 236.
36 *Ibid.,* at paras. 223, 236.
37 *Ibid.,* at para. 224.
38 *Ibid.,* at para. 44.
39 *Morgentaler, supra* note 9 at para. 49.
40 Colleen Flood and Caroline Pitfield, 'Possible Governmental Responses and Establishment of Robust Appeal Mechanisms,' in this volume, describe the slow workings of Ontario's safety valve. That may be the reason

that it deals primarily with claims to after the fact reimbursement. It is likely that those who cannot pay up front for health care elsewhere cannot avail themselves of the benefit of this safety valve.

41 Terry Sullivan, 'A Just Measure of Patience: Managing Waiting Times for Cancer Care in Ontario,' and Charles Wright, 'Different Interpretations of 'Evidence' and Implications for the Canadian Healthcare System' (both in this volume), provide some insight to the working of the waiting lists and the efforts in Ontario to manage them better. Mr. Wright reports that evidence on the absence of data, proper administration and evaluation of the waiting list phenomenon was before the trial court in *Chaoulli*.

42 *Chaoulli, supra* note 1 at para. 155.

43 *Ibid.,* at paras. 243–247.

44 *Ibid.,* at paras. 243–244.

45 *Ibid.,* at para. 152.

46 [cite to another commentary in the volume here?]

47 *Chaoulli, supra* note 1 at paras. 221, 223.

Chaoulli and the Proper Role of the Courts
in a Democracy

Worse than *Lochner*?

SUJIT CHOUDHRY*

Ripstein's E-mail

On the morning that *Chaoulli*[1] came down, I received an e-mail from my colleague Arthur Ripstein asking: 'What do you think of the Supreme Court's *Lochner* decision?'

At first blush, this way of gauging my reaction was deeply puzzling, because the cases appear to have little in common. *Lochner* was a judgment of the United States Supreme Court, finding unconstitutional an obscure New York statute that set maximum hours of work in bakeries and which affected perhaps a few thousand workers.[2] *Chaoulli* struck down Quebec's ban on private health care insurance, a core design feature of Canada's most cherished social program, Medicare, and could fundamentally reshape health care delivery to tens of millions. But the differences do not stop there. *Chaoulli* was decided a few weeks ago, whereas *Lochner* is now a century old. Finally, the judgments involved the interpretation of two distinct constitutional documents, the United States' *Bill of Rights* and Canada's *Charter*. Although those documents share striking similarities, they also differ fundamentally in many respects.[3]

But despite these differences, approaching *Chaoulli* through the lens of *Lochner* yields a number of critical insights. To understand why, we need only look at how Ripstein posed his question. *Lochner* was invoked as an implicit benchmark for evaluation, without any introduction or explanation for why it may be relevant to constitutional analysis in Canada. *Lochner*'s meaning was assumed to be so obvious that its mere mention would be immediately understood, even though it is from another country and another century. And in assessing *Chaoulli* through the lens of *Lochner*, Ripstein is not alone. Of the nine facta filed in *Chaoulli* in opposition to the constitutional challenge, *at least four* cited *Lochner* to buttress their submissions, without any sense that this reference was eccentric or incomprehensible.[4]

The invocation of *Lochner* by counsel in *Chaoulli* speaks volumes about the character of Canadian constitutional argument. It has often been said that our constitutional culture is inherently comparative in orientation. Throughout our history, comparative experience has been looked to as a source of models to be adopted and adapted, but also of lessons to be learned and dangers to be avoided. As we have grappled with the decisions of whether to adopt a constitutional bill of rights, how to draft it, and how to interpret it, the American constitutional experience has figured prominently in the Canadian constitutional consciousness. One recurrent theme has been the repeated invocation of *Lochner* and the era of American constitutional jurisprudence to which it gives its name.[5] Over the last four decades of Canadian constitutional development, the *Lochner* era has lurked as a spectre over the drafting and interpretation of the *Charter*, relied on by politicians, civil servants, academics, and legal counsel as a negative, anti-model of comparative experience to be avoided at all costs.

So Ripstein's use of *Lochner* as a negative frame of reference in *Chaoulli* is part of a much older constitutional practice. If we want to understand *Chaoulli* better, it would pay dividends to grapple in more detail with the *Lochner* metaphor. And since *Lochner* has multiple and divergent meanings – standing for judicial activism and economic libertarianism – the real issue is not why *Lochner* matters, but *how* it matters. Some of *Lochner*'s meanings are more apposite than others in shedding light on *Chaoulli*. But taken together, they should give us considerable pause for concern.

To equate a case with *Lochner* is about the worst insult a constitutional lawyer can make. As we shall see, *Chaoulli* may be even worse than that thoroughly discredited judgment.

Judicial Activism?

When constitutional scholars refer to *Lochner*, they are in fact referring to the *Lochner* era, a forty-year period of American constitutional jurisprudence that began in 1897. During the *Lochner* era, the U.S. Supreme Court struck down close to two hundred state and federal laws regulating American economic life. The most infamous judgments found unconstitutional laws establishing conditions of work, such as minimum wage laws. The *Lochner* era came to an end in 1937, when the Court rejected much, if not all, of its *Lochner*-era jurisprudence.

Although *Lochner* is now part of America's constitutional past – its 'Constitution in Exile,' as Randy Barnett has termed it[6] – it is still the topic of intense academic interest. American constitutional theorists have sought to come to terms with *Lochner*'s ongoing significance for the American constitutional project. With some notable exceptions, they take the wrongness of *Lochner* as a fixed point, and feel compelled to explain why exactly *Lochner* was in error. And so the answer to this question tells American courts how they must *not* engage in constitutional interpretation today.

If we sift through American constitutional discourse, we find that *Lochner* entails at least three different kinds of mistakes. First and foremost, *Lochner* is synonymous with judicial activism. On this account, the sin of the *Lochner* court was that it imposed its own policy preferences on democratically elected legislatures, while maintaining the pretence of engaging in constitutional interpretation. The *Lochner* court made two sets of doctrinal moves that gave rise to this suspicion. First, it set limits on the range of permissible ends of governmental regulation, ruling some government objectives off-limits. In *Lochner* itself, for example, the Court held that redressing inequality of bargaining power was an illegitimate end for state law, because it was inherently paternalistic. Second, the Court demanded a 'real and substantial' connection between legislative ends and the means chosen to vindicate them. As Michael Perry has explained, this entailed the courts' second-guessing legislative assessments of costs and benefits, as well as the failure to opt for regulatory means less intrusive of freedom of contract.[7]

According to the dissenting judgments in *Lochner*, this approach to constitutional adjudication was tantamount to turning the court into a super-legislature. Legal reasoning was rhetorical cover for the reality that the Court struck down policies simply because it disagreed with them, pretending all the while that it was engaged in the objective enterprise of applying the constitution. The hero for opponents of *Lochner*'s alleged activism was Justice Holmes, who argued in dissent that 'the accident of *our* finding certain opinions natural and familiar or novel and even shocking ought not to conclude *our* judgment upon the question of whether statutes embodying them conflict with the Constitution.'[8] For *Lochner*'s critics, the Court's jurisprudence was driven by personal allegiances of class, which led it systematically to favour capital in its struggles with labour.

This scathing critique naturally raised the question of what sort of judicial review would *not* be open to this charge. Fortunately, Justice Harlan's dissent in *Lochner* points the way forward to an alternative conception of the judicial role. Justice Harlan began by suggesting that there would have been little legal controversy if New York had set a maximum work day of 18 hours, as opposed to 10. The question then became at what point state legislation would be too intrusive, and hence unconstitutional. In a key passage, Justice Harlan argued that:[9]

> [w]hat is the true ground for the state to take between legitimate protection by legislation, of the public health and liberty of contract is not a question easily solved, nor one in respect of which there is or can be absolute certainty. ... 'The manner, occasion, and degree in which the state may interfere with the industrial freedom of its citizens is one of the most debatable and difficult questions of social science.'

To expect the legislature to prove definitely that a 10 hour work day was scientifically justified was impossible. In such a situation, the issue was whether 'the question is one about which there is room for debate and for an honest difference of opinion,' or whether 'the state has acted without reason.'[10] On the basis of the extensive factual record tendered before the Court, this test was easily met.

Justice Harlan laid the seeds for a jurisprudence of self-doubt. This is an attitude or a mindset of judicial modesty, flowing from the courts' own awareness of the limits of their institutional competence, relative to that of legislatures, in marshalling and digesting reams of social science evidence. It counsels self-imposed judicial deference when confronted with a challenge to legislation whose factual basis is itself subject to debate and dispute among 'those having special knowledge' of the policy area at hand. Because courts lack the expertise and the experience to second-guess these judgments, the preferable policy is judicial non-intervention, always subject to the limiting case of public policy without any factual foundation whatsoever. Judicial self-doubt also entails accepting most, if not all governmental objectives as legitimate.

Fast forward a century to *Chaoulli*. In the debate over whether governments should allow a parallel private system to deliver medically necessary services, there are two types of disagreements. The first is a disagreement at the level of principle, over whether individuals should be able to purchase faster and/or higher quality care on the private market. The second is the empirical disagreement over the impact of a parallel private system on Medicare. Quebec had defended the ban on private insurance on the basis that so doing was necessary to preserve the integrity of the public system. This claim was the key point of disagreement between the majority and the dissenting judges, and, indeed, was the focus of extensive expert testimony at trial. Health services researchers testified that a parallel private system would reduce public support for the public plan because of the possibility of exit. Indeed, those most likely to exit – the wealthy – also have the greatest power to protect the public system, because they are disproportionately powerful politically. The trial court also heard testimony that a private sector would lead to the bleeding of human resources from the public sector, either if physicians leave Medicare entirely, or if physicians practicing in both sectors prioritize their private patients. Finally, because private insurers would cherry-pick the healthiest and wealthiest patients, public health insurance would be left holding the bag for the sickest and the poorest, without the ability to pool risk across the entire population.

But there was evidence on the other side. An expert witness, and an interim report prepared by the Standing Senate Committee on Social Affairs, Science and Technology pointed to the co-existence of public and private sectors in a number of OECD countries (e.g. the United Kingdom and New Zealand) to dispute Quebec's claim that a ban on private insurance and a public monopoly were necessary to maintaining quality of care in the public sector.

The trial judge made a definitive finding of fact that Quebec's fears were well-founded: 'We cannot act like ostriches. The result of creating a parallel private health care system would be to threaten the integrity, sound operation and viability of the public system.'[11] The dissenters in the Supreme Court argued that absent a palpable error, the trial judge's findings of fact could not be disturbed, and was equally certain in its conclusions: 'Failure to stop the few people with ready cash does not pose a structural threat to the Quebec health plan. Failure to stop private health insurance will, as the trial judge found, do so.'[12]

But the majority strenuously disagreed. Justice Deschamps, writing for herself, stated that the trial judgment was 'based solely on the 'fear' of an erosion of services,'[13] and that 'no study was produced or discussed'[14] which substantiated this claim. Chief Justice McLachlin was even harsher, characterizing the empirical arguments both for and against Quebec's ban on private health care as 'competing but unproven 'common sense' arguments, amounting to little more than assertions of belief.'[15] 'We are in the realm of theory,' she wrote.[16] The tie-breaker was the evidence from OECD countries, which 'refutes the government's theoretical contention that a prohibition on private insurance is linked to maintaining quality public health care.'[17]

Underlying this factual disagreement, though, was a remarkable degree of agreement on the nature of the judicial role. Chief Justice McLachlin was clearest, stating that the courts' task in *Charter* challenges to government policies 'is to evaluate the issue in the light, not just of common sense or theory, but of the evidence.' Testable, provable facts drive adjudication; judges must 'look to the evidence rather than to assumptions.'[18] And for the most part, the dissenting judges defined their task as producing firm conclusions grounded in evidence, which pointed in the opposite direction. Thus, the trial judge's definitive findings of fact merited deference from the Supreme Court. And the majority's treatment of OECD data was dismissed as amateur public policy tourism. The dissenting judges' assumption through most of its reasons, like the majority's, appeared to be that governments had to meet a stringent test of justification; they only differed on whether that test had been met.

But in an important sense, setting up the nature of judicial review in this way misconceived the character of the problem. The trial judge was too definitive in concluding that private health care posed an unequivocal threat to the viability of the public system, and so too was the majority's position that there was an absence of evidence on the issue. In reality, the Court was presented with a case in which the evidence was inconclusive or conflicting. Consider the two most comprehensive studies of health care reform in recent years, the Romanow Commission and the Kirby Committee. On the impact of a parallel private system on public health care, both are equivocal. Thus, the Romanow Commission states that 'Private facilities ... *may* actually make the situation worse for other patients because much-needed resources are diverted from the public health care system to private facilities.'[19] The Kirby Committee is likewise qualified in its conclusions, suggesting that: 'allowing a parallel private system ... *may* even make the public waiting lines worse.'[20] The regulation of private health care, then, is not dissimilar from the problem which faced the court in *Lochner*, in which experts disagreed on the extent of the threat posed to the health of bakers by long working hours. It would have been more honest for both the majority and dissenting judges to acknowledge that public policy in this area is based on approximations and extrapolations from the available evidence, inferences from comparative data, and, on occasion, educated guesses. Absent a large-scale policy experiment, this is all the evidence that is likely to be available. Former Justice LaForest offered an apt observation in another *Charter* case which rings true in the current context: '[d]ecisions on such matters must inevitably be the product of a mix of conjecture, fragmentary knowledge, general experience and knowledge of the needs, aspirations and resources of society.'[21]

In *Charter* adjudication, the two provisions which focus the judicial mind on these questions are s. 1, which authorizes 'reasonable limits' on *Charter* rights if they are 'demonstrably justified in a free and democratic society,' and s. 7, which grants everyone the right not to be deprived of life, liberty, and security of the person except in accordance with 'the principles of fundamental justice.' The two provisions have a complicated relationship, since the principles of fundamental justice are an internal limit on the scope of s. 7 which in theory could do some of the work of s. 1. The Court recently sought to differentiate the two provisions in *Malmo-Levine*, suggesting that

> ... for a rule or principle to constitute a principle of fundamental justice for the purposes of s. 7, it must be a legal principle about which there is significant societal consensus that it is fundamental to the way in which the legal system ought fairly to operate, and it must be identified with sufficient precision to yield a manageable standard against which to measure deprivations of life, liberty or security of the person.[22]

By contrast, the inquiry under s. 1 is different. In its first decision interpreting s. 1, *Oakes*,[23] the Supreme Court laid down a now-familiar test to determine if a limit on a *Charter* right is justified. The rights-limiting measure must pursue a 'pressing and substantial objective,' and the means chosen to achieve this objective must meet a test of 'proportionality' – i.e. that there be a rational connection between the infringing measure and the objective behind it, that the measure minimally impair the right in question, and that the salutary effects of the measure outweigh the deleterious effects of the rights-infringement.

Unfortunately, the Court has not entirely succeeded in minimizing the overlap between the two provisions. The key problem is that the Court has held s. 7 protects individuals from 'arbitrary' deprivations of life, liberty and security of the person, where arbitrary is defined as a deprivation that 'it bears no relation to, or is inconsistent with, the objective that lies behind [it].'[24] This replicates the 'rational connection' analysis of the *Oakes* test, albeit in a very deferential fashion. Chief Justice McLachlin's reasons in *Chaoulli* further run the two provisions together by interpreting arbitrariness as connoting necessity – exactly the sort of inquiry mandated by *Oakes*. This move makes directly relevant to the interpretation of the principles of fundamental justice under s. 7 the case-law under s. 1 subsequent to *Oakes*.

As is well known, *Oakes* sets up a stringent test of justification; however, what has largely escaped observation is that empirics are central to every stage of the *Oakes* test. The leading proponent of this view on the Court has been Chief Justice McLachlin, a fact that goes a long way to explaining the tone of her reasons in *Chaoulli*. As she explained in *RJR MacDonald*, the *Oakes* test sets up a process of 'reasoned demonstration,' as opposed to simply accepting the say-so of governments.[25] By this, she means that '[t]he s. 1 inquiry is by its very nature a fact-specific inquiry.'[26] As she continued:

> In determining whether the objective of the law is sufficiently important to be capable of overriding a guaranteed right, the court must examine the *actual objective* of the law. In determining proportionality, it must determine the *actual connection* between the objective and what the law *will in fact achieve*; the *actual degree* to which it impairs the right; and whether the *actual benefit* which the law is calculated to achieve outweighs the *actual seriousness* of the limitation of the right. In short, s. 1 is an exercise based on the facts of the law at issue and the proof offered of its justification, not on abstractions.[27]

Later on, in *Sauvé*, Chief Justice McLachlin built upon these themes.[28] She held that governments seeking to justify the denial of the right to vote to prisoners under s. 1 cannot rely on 'vague and symbolic objectives,' such as inculcating respect for the rule of law.[29] Rather, rights can only be justifiably limited in response to concrete, precise and real problems or harms whose existence can be demonstrated to the satisfaction of a court through the normal trial process.

In other words, disputes over justifiable limits on *Charter* rights have in many important cases – like *Chaoulli* – been *factual* disputes about the nature of social problems, and the effectiveness of government policy instruments in combating them. This approach to interpreting s. 1 has created a major institutional dilemma for the Court, given the practical reality that public policy is often made on the basis of incomplete knowledge. This problem has given rise to an extensive jurisprudence. Although it has never been framed in this way, the basic question in these cases is the same: Who should bear the risk of empirical uncertainty with respect to government activity that infringes *Charter* rights? This has become one of the unarticulated yet central questions in *Charter* litigation.

One answer would be that in a constitutional, rights-based regime, in which rights are the rule and of presumptive importance, limitations on rights are the exception, and governments bear the onus of justification in upholding rights-infringing measures, the state bears the risk of empirical uncertainty. But to set such a high bar for governments may be to ask too much of them. It may simply be impossible to prove with scientific certainty that the means chosen to combat the problem actually will do so, and that other, less intrusive means to tackle the problem are equally effective. As Justice LaForest wrote in his dissenting judgment in *RJR MacDonald*, to require governments to bear the risk of empirical uncertainty 'could have the effect of virtually paralyzing the operation of government ... it will be impossible to govern ... it would not be possible to make difficult but sometimes necessary legislative choices. There would be conferred on the courts a supervisory role over a state itself essentially inactive.'[30]

The Court has struck a compromise between these two extremes, creating its own jurisprudence of self-doubt that is largely identical to Justice Harlan's dissent in *Lochner*. In cases where there is conflicting or inconclusive social science evidence, the question is whether the government has a 'reasonable basis' for concluding that an actual problem exists, that the means chosen would address it, and that the means chosen infringes the right as little as possible.[31] This standard is understood as expecting something less of governments than definitive, scientific proof. But as with Justice Harlan's dissent in *Lochner*, an absolute lack of evidence is unacceptable; there must be some factual basis for the public policy.

A pair of examples explains how these principles have operated in practice. In *Irwin Toy*, the Court upheld a Quebec statute prohibiting advertising directed at children under 13 years of age, on the basis that children were unable to distinguish fact from fiction and were susceptible to manipulation. The evidence before the Court clearly demonstrated that children between 2 and 6 could not distinguish fact from fiction, whereas expert opinion was divided on at what point between 7 and 13 'children generally develop the cognitive ability to recognize the persuasive nature of advertising.' However, this evidence, albeit inconclusive, was enough for the Court. As it said, the cut off age of 13 was made 'without access to complete knowledge,' but as long as 'the legislature has made a reasonable assessment as to where the line is most properly drawn, especially if that assessment involves weighing conflicting scientific evidence ... it is not for the court to second guess. That would only substitute one estimate for another.' Conversely, in *Tétrault-Gadoury*,[32] the Court found unconstitutional a cut off age of 65 for the receipt of unemployment insurance benefits. One reason offered in defense of the cut off was to prevent abuse by individuals who no longer intended to seek employment. In finding the cut off unconstitutional, the Court noted that the federal government had not adduced any evidence to substantiate this claim.

To get a handle on where *Chaoulli* fits into the Court's larger jurisprudence of self-doubt and empirical uncertainty, we need to briefly explore the contours of the case-law. The 'reasonable basis' test has largely been worked out in the context of cases on freedom of expression. The Court has rejected conventional morality as an acceptable justification for limiting free speech, opting instead for the principle that speech can only be limited if it is harmful. This interpretive choice has had the unanticipated effect of locking the Court into a search for evidence of the real, concrete harms of prohibited speech. The difficulties this has created for the Court have come home in a set of cases concerning laws prohibiting pornography and hate speech.[33] Unable to rely on morality-based justifications for these laws, the Court has been confronted with the absence of definitive evidence demonstrating that these forms of speech are harmful. In three of its pornography decisions (*Butler, Sharpe, Little Sisters*) the Court has been able to point to *some* social science evidence, which satisfies the reasonable basis test. But in cases on hate speech (*Keegstra, Ross*), where such evidence was entirely absent, the Court has relied on 'experience and common sense'[34] and 'reason or logic'[35] to bridge the empirical gap. Moreover, common sense and logic were relied on in two of the pornography decisions (*Butler, Sharpe*) as additional supports for those judgments. Interestingly, Chief Justice McLachlin has explicitly endorsed this approach, in *Sharpe*.

Taken together, the Court terms this approach the 'reasonable apprehension of harm' test. But although the Court has been unanimous in accepting the reasonable basis test to assess inconclusive social science evidence, and in permitting governments to rely on common sense or logic to surmount evidentiary gaps, there have been significant disagreements in recent cases over the boundaries of these doctrines. In some cases, the disagreement has centred on what kinds of *inferences* governments are entitled to draw from inconclusive evidence. The most famous clash occurred in *RJR MacDonald*, and centred on the link between tobacco advertising and consumption, given the absence of definitive evidence linking the two. The Court divided on whether governments were entitled to infer from the widespread use of 'brand preference' and 'informational' advertising by tobacco companies that such a link existed. Four dissenting judges (led by Justice LaForest) were willing to infer that by convincing smokers not to quit, these advertisements had the effect of sustaining levels of consumption, while three judges in the majority (led by then Justice McLachlin) refused to do so.[36]

And the Court has also split on the circumstances in which it is appropriate to apply 'logic' or 'common sense' to surmount an absence of evidence. The Court, concerned that too broad an approach could undermine entirely the idea that governments can only justifiably limit constitutional rights to respond to real problems, has attempted to set some limits on when it could accept the existence of harm without evidence. It suggested in *Thomson Newspapers* that its common sense or logic approach to the existence of harm applied to hate speech and pornography because 'the possibility of harm is within the everyday knowledge and experience of Canadians, or where factual determination and value judgments overlap.'[37] Thus, the Court refused to infer from the fact that opinion polls influence voter choice in election campaigns that inaccurate polls mislead large numbers of voters and have a significant impact on the outcome of an election, 'without more specific and conclusive evidence to that effect.'[38] The message was that pornography and hate speech were in a special and narrow category.

But then in *Harper*, a divided Court disregarded this self-imposed limitation, and upheld restrictions on third party expenditures during election campaigns on the eve of the last federal vote.[39] The justifications for the restrictions were to further the value of political equality (to equalize participation in political debate, to protect the outcome of an election from being distorted by third party expenditures, and to safeguard the public's confidence in the electoral process) and to protect the integrity of spending limits for candidates and political parties. The majority openly acknowledged that both the alleged harm and the efficacy of legislative responses to it were 'difficult, if not possible, to measure scientifically,'[40] but nonetheless was willing to reason that both the harm existed and the cure was effective. The dissent, led by Chief Justice McLachlin, argued that in the absence of evidence, '[t]he dangers posited are entirely hypothetical' and 'unproven and speculative' and 'the legislation is an overreaction to a non-existent problem,' and was completely unwilling to entertain the common sense argument.[41]

Against this backdrop, *Chaoulli* is merely the latest episode in an ongoing story in which the Court has struggled to come to terms with the institutional task it set itself in *Oakes*. In response to the question of who bears the risk of empirical uncertainty with respect to government activity that infringes *Charter* rights, the rights-claimant or the government, the answer has been, in effect, both. But even though the Court has agreed on this compromise, deep disagreements persist along its ragged edges.

Given that Chief Justice McLachlin has figured prominently in Canada's jurisprudence of self-doubt and empirical uncertainty, and given the direct and significant relevance of this jurisprudence to *Chaoulli*, one would have expected this material to be front and centre in her judgment. Astonishingly, however, she does not even mention, let along engage with, these cases. And it is equally surprising that these cases only make a cameo appearance in the dissent.[42]

The Court's complete failure to cite, follow, or even attempt to distinguish its own precedents led it to make a fundamental legal error: it posed the wrong question. The question was *not* whether Quebec had convincingly demonstrated that a ban on private insurance was necessary to maintain the integrity of public health insurance. Rather, the question was whether Quebec had a 'reasoned apprehension of harm' that opening the door to private insurance would pose this threat. To return to *Lochner*, the Court spoke in the voice of Chief Justice Peckham, when in fact it should have spoken in the voice of Justice Harlan's dissent. Instead of proceeding with Peckham's cocksure certainty to repeat the institutional error of the *Lochner* court, the Court should have approached the constitutional challenge with Justice Harlan's self-doubt and judicial modesty. The empirically complex question of what disincentives best protect the public monopoly over health care financing, is, to repeat Justice Harlan, 'one about which there is room for debate and for an honest difference of opinion.' Mere disagreement with the Quebec government was not enough. The standard was whether the Quebec government lacked a 'reasonable basis' upon which to proceed, and the materials put into evidence more than met this attenuated standard. The Court's disregard for this evidence is nothing short of astonishing.

Even if the evidence were insufficient, perhaps common sense and logic could have bridged the gap. Ironically, an excellent model of how the Court could have reached that conclusion is offered by then Justice McLachlin's concurring judgment in *Adler*.[43] That case involved an unsuccessful constitutional challenge to the selective funding of Roman Catholic schools in Ontario. The government claimed that if public funding were extended to private religious schools, it would lead parents to remove their children from the public system, which would diminish the diversity of the student body, and, in turn, undermine the ability of public schools to promote mutual tolerance in a diverse polity. Justice McLachlin accepted this argument on the basis of common sense and logic. But if she were willing to infer the willingness of parents to exit public schools in response to financial incentives, and the threat this would pose to the goals of public education, why was she so unwilling to infer the willingness of health care providers to exit public health care in response to financial incentives, and the threat this would pose to the integrity of Medicare?

Economic Libertarianism?

Let us now turn to *Lochner*'s second meaning: economic libertarianism. This line of criticism posits that the doctrinal categories employed by the *Lochner* court reflected a normative commitment to the principles of freedom of contract and property, and to strict limits on the scope of state intervention in the economy. To reject *Lochner* is to fight for the ability of the state to redress the inequities and exploitation that arise from the unregulated marketplace. The principal villain is the so-called doctrine of 'substantive due process.' Under the American *Bill of Rights*, individuals enjoy the right not to be deprived of life, liberty or property except by 'due process of law.' Under substantive due process, the *Lochner* court read this clause in two ways that created constitutional roadblocks for the welfare state. Liberty was interpreted to encompass liberty of contract, thereby bringing any law regulating the market under constitutional scrutiny. Then the Court construed 'due process' to impose substantive limits on legislation depriving persons of contractual freedom, such as the law restricting bakers' hours in *Lochner*. It was substantive due process and the libertarianism of *Lochner* that presented significant constitutional obstacles to Roosevelt's New Deal. And the post-*Lochner* constitutional settlement in the United States has entailed the decisive and explicit repudiation of the aggressive protection of economic rights, so that socioeconomic legislation almost always passes constitutional muster.

The claim here is subtly different from the activist critique of the *Lochner* court. This group of critics accepts that the *Lochner* court did not merely impose its personal policy preferences on democratic legislatures. Rather, they argue that the judgments of that Court flowed from larger political ideologies, and that a substantive value choice by the judiciary is not only desirable, but an inescapable feature of constitutional interpretation. Thus, the problem with *Lochner* was not in its appeal to a political theory of the relationship of the state and market, but in its appeal to the wrong political theory.[45]

As I have explored in depth, the libertarian reading of *Lochner* was an important theme in the drafting of the *Charter*. The concern was that a *Charter* worded identically to the American *Bill of Rights* would invite successful constitutional challenges against the Canadian welfare state. The focus of engagement was the Canadian version of the American due process clauses, section 7 of the *Charter*. To pre-empt a libertarian reading of the *Charter*, two important drafting choices were made. First, while the American due process clauses protect 'life, liberty, and property,' the *Charter* protects life and liberty but deliberately omits protection for property, to prevent property rights-based constitutional challenges. Second, property was replaced with 'security of the person,' to send a cue to the courts that they should not interpret liberty like the *Lochner* court to encompass economic liberty and freedom of contract, but rather, to encompass corporeal interests such as bodily integrity and physical liberty.

Notwithstanding these clear textual choices, for the past twenty years, parties have attempted to argue that s. 7 protects freedom of contract.[46] In large part, this litigation has been made possible by the *Charter*'s protection of 'liberty,' a term broad enough to encompass economic freedom. And so liberty has been described by litigants as encompassing the right of a retailer to sell goods (*Edwards Books*), the right to advertise (*Irwin Toy*), the right of a prostitute to contract for her services (*Prostitution Reference*), the right to practice a profession (*Pearlman, Walker*), and even the right to operate video lottery terminals (*Siemens*)! These claims have been consistently rejected by the Court. Indeed,

Lochner has been relied on by the Court as the reason to *not* accept these claims.[47] Perhaps since hope springs eternal, this did not stop Dr. Chaoulli from framing his challenge to the prohibition on private insurance as based on the right to enter into contracts for medical services. And, not surprisingly, this version of Chaoulli's constitutional claim was unanimously rejected by the Court.

In the face of the text of the *Charter* and the Court's jurisprudence, the oft-repeated claim made by left-wing critics of the *Charter*, such as Andrew Petter and Alan Hutchinson in their contributions to this volume, that constitutional adjudication could launch a Canadian *Lochner* era and the rollback of the Canadian welfare state would appear to be a histrionic exaggeration.[48] But there is actually much more to the link between *Lochner*'s libertarianism and the *Charter*, which should give us considerable pause for concern. To understand why, we need to turn to the early history of the *Charter*, a history which I fear the Court has forgotten.[49] Notwithstanding that the *Charter* is a human rights document, many early *Charter* challenges were brought by corporations, and created the fear that powerful economic interests would hijack the *Charter* to pursue a deregulatory agenda. Notwithstanding the absence of property and contractual rights in the *Charter*, it was feared that the courts would interpret other *Charter* rights to protect economic interests indirectly. Thus, the first case on freedom of religion was brought by a corporate defendant who challenged the constitutionality of a Sunday closing law on the ground that it compelled the observance of the Christian Sabbath. Without irony, the Court articulated the interests underlying freedom of religion exclusively by reference to human beings, yet granted corporations, which could not hold that right themselves, standing to raise the rights of third parties in defence to criminal prosecutions. The effect of the successful challenge was to permit retail businesses to operate seven days a week. Pending challenges to laws asserting that the right to contract fell within the scope of the *Charter*'s right to freedom of association raised the same concerns.

Against this backdrop, the stringent interpretation of s. 1 given by *Oakes* amplified these concerns. Critics suggested that *Oakes* would prevent s. 1 from saving legislation which infringed constitutional rights in many circumstances. This possibility was illustrated by *Oakes* itself. That case involved a constitutional challenge to an evidentiary rule in a federal narcotics control statute, that if the fact of possession was proven, the intention to traffic was inferred unless the accused provided to the contrary. The Court held that the rule contravened the *Charter*'s presumption of innocence, and was not justified under s. 1. The law failed the rational connection branch of the *Oakes* test because of the possibility of erroneous convictions for trafficking where an innocent individual could not adduce enough evidence to rebut the presumption. Critics quickly pointed out that the Court's reasoning demanded an impossibly high degree of fit between legislative ends and means.

Oakes purported to lay down a uniform standard for limitation analysis, which did not vary according to policy context. To apply such an exacting standard to laws regulating economic activity is fraught with problems. Because problems of imperfect information, and the need to limit enforcement costs, most of these laws rely on statistical generalizations that do not hold true in every situation but are convenient to administer. But *Oakes* suggested that laws which produced false positives were for that reason irrational and unconstitutional.

Consider the blanket ban on private insurance in *Chaoulli*. On the Court's reasoning, such a law is irrational because it prohibits private insurance in every case, including those where Medicare cannot provide access to care within a reasonable time. But the 'rational' alternative, the right to exit the public system in the event that care within a reasonable time is not available, is not immune from the possibility of error either. Because a wait-time standard is a statistical generalization based on population-level data, it will not be accurate in every case. And so if error is the gravamen of *Oakes*, no law would pass the muster of s. 1.

Taken together, the incidental protection of economic liberties through rights such as freedom of religion and association and the restrictive approach to justifiable limits on *Charter* rights in *Oakes* threatened to introduce *Lochner*'s laissez-faire constitutionalism into Canada through the back door. But less than ten months after *Oakes* was handed down, the Court responded to these criticisms with an astonishing shift in direction, in a case involving the regulation of economic activity. *Edwards Books* was the second constitutional challenge brought to a Sunday closing law by a corporate defendant. The Court found that the law infringed the *Charter*'s guarantee of freedom of religion, but was justified under s. 1. The critical feature of the judgment was a decisive shift in tone from the language of stringent justification to the language of deference.

The goal behind the legislation was to protect the rights of retail employees, by granting them the right to a common pause day which is shared with most members of the community. One argument pressed before the Court was that a policy alternative to achieve this goal that would be less restrictive of the rights of retailers would be to give employees the right to not work on Sundays, while permitting retailers to remain open. The Court rejected this suggestion, because the choice granted to employees by such a law would be more illusory than real. The Court noted that '[t]hese employees do not constitute a powerful group in society,'[50] because they were 'older, more likely to be female, ... low-skilled, non-union and poorly educated employees whose continued earnings are critical for family support, people who have the least mobility in terms of job alternatives and are least capable of expressing themselves to redress their grievances.' And from this specific conclusion, the Court set out a more general interpretive principle that was a decisive repudiation of *Lochner* era libertarianism:[51]

> In interpreting and applying the *Charter* I believe the courts must be cautious to ensure that it does not simply become an instrument of better situated individuals to roll back legislation which has as its object the improvement of the condition of less advantaged persons.

Accepting the *Charter* challenge in this case, in other words, would have expanded the freedom of relatively advantaged retailers while contracting the freedom of relatively disadvantaged retail employees. The clear message from the Court was that when legislatures intervene in the market to enhance the interests of the vulnerable, the court should defer.

Edwards Books is an important part of the *Charter*'s early history against which one must interpret *Chaoulli*. Although *Edwards Books* concerned s. 1 of the *Charter*, *Chaoulli*'s approach to the interpretation of s. 7 – reading the 'principles of fundamental justice' to incorporate an *Oakes*-style proportionality analysis – made *Edwards Books* directly relevant. Significantly, however, *Edwards Books* was not cited or discussed by the majority judgments. Indeed, Chief Justice McLachlin made no reference at all to the massive jurisprudence, or even to the very possibility that courts should defer in some *Charter* cases. But the dissent did cite *Edwards Books* with good reason, because it was of direct relevance. Canadian Medicare combines a regime of public financing with private delivery for medically necessary hospital and physician services. Its principal beneficiaries are the poor, who would otherwise be unavailable to afford a comparable level of care in an unregulated marketplace, and who lack the means to purchase private insurance. Conversely, those who would benefit from the right to exit Medicare and purchase private insurance are the middle and upper classes. The majority did not come right out and say this. Chief Justice McLachlin suggested that 'the vast majority of Canadians (middle-income and low-income earners)' would be able to purchase private health insurance,[52] although she cited no evidence for this claim. Justice Deschamps was more honest. She suggested that 'people with average incomes'[53] would be able to purchase private insurance – which by implication means persons with below average incomes would be unable to do so. If one accepts the factual premise that the government had a reasonable basis to conclude that permitting the relatively well off to exit the system would work to the detriment of those left behind, then the design of Medicare as a universal social program is clearly a case where governments are legislating to protecting the vulnerable – in this case, the poor. This is exactly kind of situation referred to in *Edwards Books* as one where the Court should defer.

Now the majority in *Chaoulli* could conceivably attempt to distinguish *Edwards Books*, on the basis that *Edwards Books* was merely about leisure time spent with family and friends, while *Chaoulli* was about waiting lists that threaten individuals' health and even their lives. However, to describe both cases in this way would miss an important dimension of the character of the dilemma facing the Court. In *Edwards Books*, the principal beneficiaries of the Sunday closing law were retail workers who observed Sunday as a religiously-mandated day of prayer and rest. Likewise, in *Chaoulli*, Medicare protects the security of the person and the lives of the poor who would be unable to afford care of comparable quality on the private market. So in both *Edwards Books* and *Chaoulli*, *Charter* rights are on *both* sides of the equation, a fact that further warrants judicial deference. The dissent is mistaken when it says that the debate over the design of Medicare is 'about social values' and 'not about constitutional law.'[54] The institutional question for the Court is who should make the choice of how to balance competing constitutional rights. The lesson from *Edwards Books* may be that when the state legislates to ensure that constitutional rights have equal value, courts should be reluctant to intervene.

Worse than *Lochner*?

Not only does *Chaoulli* repeat many of the judicial mistakes closely identified with the *Lochner* court; it may in fact be worse. In recent years, American legal historians have generated a large body of work which casts the *Lochner* court in a different light. '*Lochner* revisionists' claim that the *Lochner* court was acting not to further class preferences, but on the basis of a full-blown constitutional theory with deep roots in the American constitutional tradition. Howard Gillman has best described this tradition as being based on a distinction between legislation promoting the interests of narrow interest groups, and laws directed at promoting the public welfare.[55] Thus understood, *Lochner* was premised on a commitment to neutrality or equality before the law.[56] Although perhaps rightly criticized today, legal historians now say that *Lochner* should be judged in context, and that it was right for its time.

It is very hard to say the same about *Chaoulli*, for it is very difficult to reconcile *Chaoulli* with two of the Court's recent decisions – so much so that a cynic could suggest that the principal explanation for the resulting pattern of judgments is a class bias.

First compare *Chaoulli* with *Auton*,[57] in which a unanimous Court rejected a *Charter* challenge to British Columbia's refusal to fund therapy for autistic children. The claimant's argument, that the denial of therapy constituted discrimination on the basis of disability, and hence was a violation of the *Charter*'s equality rights guarantee, s. 15, was fairly straightforward. Although the Court dismissed the claim – not itself surprising – what was unexpected was how it did so. The Court found no violation of s. 15, and, indeed, suggested that that the funding of non-core health care services was within the discretion of provincial governments and did not engage the *Charter*. This reasoning is so difficult to defend that the only way to read *Auton* as having created a political questions doctrine around the scope of the Medicare envelope. The clear message from the Court was that the Court did not wish judges to be drawn into adjudicating upon the design of Medicare on a case-by-case basis, a task for which they are poorly qualified. Indeed, the dissenting judges in *Chaoulli* suggested that this was the rationale for *Auton*.[58]

But in *Chaoulli*, the Court has held that Quebec's ban on private insurance is unconstitutional because it applies even in circumstances where wait times are unreasonably long. So the judgment has, astonishingly, set up the courts as the arbiters of reasonable wait times on a case-by-case basis – an institutional quagmire, a constitutional quicksand that will severely test the lower courts. And as the dissenting judges in *Chaoulli* point out, the Court's refusal in *Auton* to define 'reasonable health services' is inconsistent with its willingness in *Chaoulli* to define reasonable wait times.[59] These two questions are not different in any relevant legal respect. But what *is* different, of course, is who the winners and losers are in the two judgments. In *Auton*, at least one parent could not afford private care. In *Chaoulli*, the beneficiaries are likely to be those Canadians who can afford private health care. The net result is that those who can afford private health care have won the right to exit the system, while those trapped in the system without the means to exit get no help at all.

Now compare *Chaoulli* with *Gosselin*,[60] a constitutional challenge to Quebec's now repealed workfare program. Under the scheme, welfare recipients under 30 received a fraction of the benefit available those over 30. However, most of the difference would be paid to those who participated in on-the-job training, community work, or remedial education. Two critical factual issues were the actual availability of these opportunities, and the impact on welfare recipients of being unable to enrol in these programs. Experts had testified at trial that a very small percentage of welfare recipients under 30 were actually enrolled in these programs, and the total number of welfare recipients was far larger than the number of available positions. The argument was that the legislature had essentially abandoned young welfare recipients. The only first-hand testimony regarding the difficulties of accessing these programs and the impact of not securing access was provided by one welfare recipient. The trial judge found that this testimony was insufficient to make out the case against the government. Chief Justice McLachlin agreed, stating that it was 'utterly implausible ... to find the Quebec government guilty of discrimination [against] ... tens of thousands of unidentified people, based on the testimony of a single affected individual.'[61] Since the claimant had been able to enroll in these programs, Chief Justice McLachlin suggested that 'participation was a real possibility,' and that the claimant had dropped out of programs because of 'personal problems, which included psychological and substance abuse components, rather than to flaws in the programs themselves.'[62] And like the trial judge, Chief Justice McLachlin dismissed the expert testimony, and noted that 'it was not open to this Court to revisit the trial judge's conclusions absent demonstrated error.'[63]

But in *Chaoulli*, the majority was willing to rely on the testimony of one patient to impugn the constitutionality of the public health care system of an entire province that serves not tens of thousands, but millions. The trial judge had found that the patient's delay in receiving joint replacement (which he ultimately received) was ultimately 'caused not by excessive waiting lists but by a number of other factors, including his pre-existing depression and his indecision and unfounded medical complaints.'[64] Yet, the majority disregarded this finding of fact, with

Justice Deschamps simply stating that 'Zeliotis is a patient who has suffered as a result of waiting lists.'[65] And the evidence at trial demonstrating that wait lists across Quebec's health care system as a whole posed a risk to human health and life largely came from practicing physicians, none of them experts on waiting lists, who provided evidence that was anecdotal and vague. Nevertheless, the majority was willing to conclude that waiting lists were a system-wide problem in Quebec. The inconsistencies in the treatment of individual and expert testimony are not tied to any real difference between the issues in *Chaoulli* and *Gosselin*. But again, what was different is whose interests were at stake: welfare recipients, or the relatively advantaged.

It is impossible to say whether a class bias, unconscious or otherwise, is at work.[66] But, as they say in politics, the optics are bad.

Could *Chaoulli* have been motivated by the Court's desire to shape the politics of Medicare? Consider the following remarkable passages from Justice Deschamps concurring judgment:[67]

> The government had plenty of time to act. Numerous commissions have been established ... and special or independent committees have published reports ... Governments have promised on numerous occasions to find a solution to the problem of waiting lists. Given the tendency to focus the debate on a socio-political philosophy, it seems that governments have lost sight of the urgency of taking concrete action. The courts are therefore the last line of defence for citizens. ... While the government has the power to decide what measures to adopt, it cannot choose to do nothing in the face of the violation of Quebeckers' right to security. The government has not given reasons for its failure to act. Inertia cannot be used as an argument to justify deference.

Justice Deschamps' sense of frustration leaps off the page. Perhaps the real explanation for the judgment is the Court's sense that the political process has failed to address the problem of waiting lists. And so the Court took it upon itself to force governments to act.

But if that is the true reason for the Court's otherwise indefensible ruling, it is a flimsy one indeed. To be sure, the idea that judicial review should redress the inadequacies of democratic politics is one of the principal justifications for the *Charter*. But it is important to carefully define the circumstances under which one can honestly say that politics systematically and unfairly disadvantages certain interests. One strand of the post-*Lochner* approach to constitutional adjudication in the United States was that courts should selectively intervene to protect 'discrete and insular minorities' whose interests are likely to be systematically disregarded in majoritarian politics.[68] This idea makes sense of an aggressive approach to constitutional adjudication in the defence of the rights of gays and lesbians, criminal accused, and aboriginal peoples.

But *Chaoulli* was exactly the opposite sort of case. It was a challenge to a *universal* social program. And the design feature of the program at issue – the legal and practical inability to opt out of waiting lists – potentially affects everyone at some stage of their lives. The persons on wait lists are not a small minority of Canadians lacking in political power. They are our mothers and fathers, our brothers and sisters, our friends and co-workers, and, indeed, ourselves. To be sure, politics can be difficult and slow. But this was an easy case for the Court to leave to the political process, instead of attempting to save Canada from itself.

The Court should have never heard this case.[69]

Notes

* Sujit Choudhry is an Associate Professor at Faculty of Law, University of Toronto. He is cross-appointed to the Department of Health Policy, Management and Evaluation in the Faculty of Medicine, and the Department of Political Science in the Faculty of Arts and Science. Professor Choudhry is also a member of University of Toronto Joint Centre for Bioethics, and a Senior Fellow at Massey College. Professor Choudhry holds law degrees from Oxford, Toronto, and Harvard, was a Rhodes Scholar, and served as Law Clerk to Chief Justice Antonio Lamer of the Supreme Court of Canada. Professor Choudhry has written widely in both constitutional law and health law. He has published approximately 40 articles, book chapters, and reports. His articles have appeared in the *New England Journal*, *Health Affairs, Social Science and Medicine*, the *Journal of Political Philosophy*, the *International Journal of Constitutional Law*, the *Canadian Journal of Law and Jurisprudence*, and many other journals. He is the editor of two forthcoming volumes, *The Migration of Constitutional Ideas* (Cambridge University of Press) and *Dilemmas of Solidarity: Rethinking Redistribution in the Canadian Federation* (University of Toronto Press) (with Jean-François Gaudreault-Desbiens and Lorne Sossin), and is currently writing a book, *Multinational Federations and Constitutional Failure: The Case of Quebec Secession*. Professor Choudhry's op-eds have appeared in the *Globe and Mail*, the *Toronto Star*, the *Montreal Gazette*, and the *Ottawa Citizen*. Professor Choudhry was a consultant to the Royal Commission on the Future of Health Care in Canada (the Romanow Commission), the National Advisory Committee on SARS and Public Health (the Naylor Committee), and the World Bank Institute at the World Bank. He currently serves on the Academic Advisory Committee to the Province of Ontario's Democratic Renewal Secretariat, and is a member of the Governing Toronto panel which is re-examining the structure of municipal government in Toronto.

Thanks to Arthur Ripstein for his e-mail, Bob Charney, Colleen Flood, Ira Parghi and Kent Roach for helpful comments, Sasha Kontic for research assistance, and Jaya Parghi Choudhry for providing some valuable perspective. © Sujit Choudhry, 2005

1 *Chaoulli v. Quebec (Attorney General)*, 2005 SCC 35 [Chaoulli].

2 *Lochner v. New York*, 198 U.S. 45 (1905).

3 For example, unlike its American counterpart, the *Charter* lacks express constitutional protection for rights of property and contract, so as to not fetter the ability of governments to regulate the economy. Moreover, in contrast to the individualistic overtones of the *Bill of Rights*, the *Charter* explicitly authorizes affirmative action and justifiable limitations on rights, and protects not only rights for all individuals but also for members of Canada's linguistic minorities and aboriginal peoples. Most famously, the *Charter* permits legislatures to override selected *Charter* rights for renewable five year periods, in contrast to American-style judicial supremacy.

4 Factum of the Respondent, Attorney General of Quebec at para. 101; Factum of the Respondent, Attorney General of Canada at para. 48; Factum of Intervener, Attorney General of Ontario at para. 27; Factum of Intervener, Canadian Labour Congress at para. 8.

5 For a detailed examination, see S. Choudhry, 'The Lochner era and comparative constitutionalism' (2004) 2:1 International Journal of Constitutional Law 1.

6 Randy E. Barnett, *Restoring the Lost Constitution: The Presumption of Liberty* (Princeton: Princeton University Press, 2004).

7 The *Lochner* court made these moves through its interpretation of 'due process' to encompass substantive limits on government policies depriving individuals of life, liberty, or property. For further discussion see Michael Perry, *The Constitution in the Courts: Law or Politics?* (Oxford: Oxford University Press, 1994) at 162–64. Thus, in *Lochner*, when faced with the argument that New York's law was justified to protect the health of bakers, Chief Justice Peckham found 'that the trade of the baker ... is not an unhealthy one *to the degree* which would authorize the legislature to interfere with ... the right of free contract on the part of the individual' (*Lochner* at 59), presumably meaning that if some threshold were passed, state regulation of hours of work would be justified. And if health concerns were valid, Chief Justice Peckham suggested that other means were

at the state's disposal short of limiting hours of work, such as setting workplace health and safety standards.

8 *Lochner* at 76.

9 *Ibid.* at 72.

10 *Ibid.* at 73.

11 *Chaoulli c. Québec (Procureure Générale)*, [2000] J.Q. 479 at para. 263 (Q.L.).

12 *Chaoulli*, at para. 181.

13 *Ibid.* at para. 68.

14 *Ibid.* at para. 64.

15 *Ibid.* at para. 138.

16 *Ibid.*

17 *Ibid.* at para. 149.

18 *Ibid.* at para. 152.

19 Canada, Commission on the Future of Health Care in Canada, *Building on Values: The Future of Health Care in Canada – Final Report* (Saskatoon: Commission on the Future of Health Care in Canada, 2002) (Commissioner: Roy J. Romanow, Q.C.) at 139 [italics added], online: Commission on the Future of Health Care in Canada <http://www.hc-sc.gc.ca/english/care/romanow/hcc0086.html>.

20 Canada, The Standing Senate Committee on Social Affairs, Science and Technology, *The Health of Canadians – The Federal Role, Vol. 6: Issues and Options* (Ottawa: Sentate Standing Committee on Social Affairs, Science and Technology, 2002) (Chair: The Honourable Michael J.L. Kirby) at 42 [italics added], online: Commission on the Future of Health Care in Canada < http://www.hc-sc.gc.ca/english/care/romanow/hcc0362.html>.

21 *McKinney v. University of Guelph* [1990] 3 S.C.R. 229 at 304.

22 *R. v. Malmo-Levine*, 2003 SCC 74 at para. 113 [Malmo-Levine].

23 *R. v. Oakes* [1986] 1 S.C.R. 103 at 105–06 [Oakes].

24 *Rodriguez v. British Columbia (Attorney General)*, [1993] 3 S.C.R. 519 at 594–95, 619–20; *Malmo-Levine*, at para. 135; *Chaoulli*, at para. 130.

25 *RJR-MacDonald Inc. v. Canada (Attorney General)*, [1995] S.C.J. No. 68 at para. 129 (QL) [*RJR*].

26 *Ibid.* at para. 133.

27 *Ibid.* [emphasis added]

28 *Sauvé v. Canada (Chief Electoral Officer)*, 2002 SCC 68.

29 *Ibid.* at para. 21–22.

30 *RJR* at para 67.

31 *Irwin Toy Ltd. v. Quebec (Attorney General)*, [1989] 1 S.C.R. 927 at 994.

32 *Tétreault-Gadoury v. Canada (Employment and Immigration Commission)*, [1991] 2 S.C.R. 22.

33 *R. v. Keegstra*, [1990] 3 S.C.R. 697 [*Keegstra*]; *R. v. Butler*, [1992] 1 S.C.R. 452

[*Butler*]; *Ross v. New Brunswick School District No. 15*, [1996] 1 S.C.R. 825 [*Ross*]; *Little Sisters Book and Art Emporium v. Canada (Minister of Justice)*, 2000 SCC 69 [*Little Sisters*]; *R. v. Sharpe*, 2001 SCC 2 [*Sharpe*].

34 *Sharpe, Ibid.* at para. 94.

35 *RJR*, at para 154.

36 In my view, that decision was largely driven by the refusal of the Attorney-General of Canada to disclose to the Court a study examining the comparative effectiveness of a partial and complete advertising ban on tobacco advertising, which led the court in effect to draw an adverse inference (as emphasized in a separate concurring judgment by Chief Justice Lamer and Justice Iacobucci).

37 *Thomson Newspapers Co. v. Canada (Attorney General)*, [1998] 1 S.C.R. 877 at para. 116.

38 *Ibid.* at para. 117.

39 *Harper v. Canada (Attorney General)*, 2004 SCC 33.

40 *Ibid.* at para. 79.

41 *Ibid.* at para. 34; *Ibid.* at para. 41; *Ibid.* at para. 34.

42 *Chaoulli* at para. 176.

43 *Adler v. Canada*, [1996] 3 S.C.R. 609.

44 Although expert evidence was tendered by counsel for the Attorney-General of Ontario at trial, and was referred in the trial judgment, 9 O.R. (3d) 676 at 703-705. I thank Bob Charney for bringing this point to my attention.

45 Ronald Dworkin, for example, argued that *Lochner* was mistaken because it endorsed a libertarian, as opposed to an egalitarian conception of liberalism which views the regulatory and redistributive state as an important vehicle for individual freedom. Ronald Dworkin, *'Freedom's Law: The Moral Reading of the American Constitution'* (Boston: Harvard Univ. Press, 1996) at 82.

46 *R. v. Edwards Books and Art Ltd.*, [1986] 2 S.C.R. 713 [*Edwards Books*]; *Irwin Toy, supra* note 31; *Reference re ss. 193 and 195.1(1)(C) of the Criminal Code (Man.)*, [1990] 1 S.C.R. 1123 [*Prostitution Reference*]; *Pearlman v. Manitoba Law Society Judicial Committee*, [1991] 2 S.C.R. 869 [*Pearlman*]; *Walker v. Prince Edward Island*, [1995] 2 S.C.R. 407 [*Walker*]; *Siemens v. Manitoba (Attorney General)*, 2003 SCC 3 [*Siemens*].

47 *Prostitution Reference*, at 1164–66.

48 See the essays by both Alan Hutchison and Andrew Petter in this volume. See also Allan Hutchison, *Waiting For Coraf: A Critique Of Rights* (Toronto: University of Toronto Press, 1995); Joel Bakan, *Just Words: Constitutional Rights and Social Wrongs* (Toronto: University of Toronto Press, 1997); Michael Mandel, *The Charter of Rights and the Legalization of Politics in*

Canada, 2d. ed. (Toronto: Thompson Educational Publishing, 1994); Harry Arthurs, 'Constitutional Courage' (2004) 49 McGill L.J. 1.

49 For important contemporaneous academic analysis, see Andrew Petter, 'The Politics of the Charter' (1986) 8 Supreme Court L.R. 472; Patrick J. Monahan & Andrew Petter, 'Developments in Constitutional Law: The 1985–86 Term' (1987) 9 Supreme Court L.R. 69; Andrew Petter, 'Immaculate Deception: The Charter's Hidden Agenda' (1987) 45 Advocate 857; and Andrew Petter & Patrick J. Monahan, 'Developments in Constitutional Law: The 1986–87 Term' (1988) 10 Supreme Court L.R. 61.

50 *Edwards Books,* at 778.

51 *Ibid.* at 779.

52 *Chaoulli* at para. 137.

53 *Ibid.* at para. 55.

54 *Ibid* at para. 166.

55 Howard Gillman, *The Constitution Besieged: The Rise and Demise of Lochner Era Police Powers Jurisprudence* (Durham: Duke University Press, 1993).

56 *Lochner* revisionism has given rise to vigorous debate in the American legal academy. For recent examples, see David E. Bernstein, '*Lochner* Era Revisionism, Revised: *Lochner* and the Origins of Fundamental Rights Constitutionalism' (2003) 92:1 Georgetown L.J. 1; David E. Bernstein, '*Lochner's* Feminist Legacy' (2003) 101 Michigan L.R. 1960; David Strauss, 'Why Was *Lochner* Wrong?' (2003) 70 U. Chi. L. Rev. 373; Cass R. Sunstein, '*Lochnering*' (2003) 82:1 Texas L.R. 65; David E. Bernstein, '*Lochner's Legacy's* Legacy' (2003) 82 Texas L.R. 1; Randy E. Barnett, *Restoring the Lost Constitution: The Presumption of Liberty.*

57 *Auton (Guardian ad litem of) v. British Columbia (Attorney General)*, 2004 SCC 78.

58 *Chaoulli* at para. 163.

59 *Ibid.*

60 *Gosselin v. Quebec (Attorney General)*, 2002 SCC 84.

61 *Ibid.* at para. 47.

62 *Ibid.* at para. 48.

63 *Ibid.* at para. 50.

64 *Chaoulli* at para. 211.

65 *Ibid.* at para. 35.

66 Andrew Petter and Allan Hutchison no doubt think that there is. See their essays in this volume.

67 *Chaoulli* at paras. 96 and 97.

68 This suggestion was made in footnote 4 of *United States v. Carolene Products Co.*, 304 U.S. 144 (1938).

69 As Kent Roach argues in this volume.

'Condition Critical': The Constitution and Health Care

ALLAN C. HUTCHINSON*

TOLD YOU SO![1]

Most constitutional commentators took one of two approaches to this so-called Charter-bashing. Some dismissed (and, no doubt, still will) it as alarmist and mere scare-mongering; the Charter was a jewel in the constitutional crown and should not be derided as mere indulgent bauble. Others patronised such critics by suggesting that they had something useful to say by way of caution, but that they over-sold themselves and under-stated the positive effects of the Charter. Nevertheless, this ranting had some impact because the Supreme Court did modify and mollify its approach in light of these criticisms, especially in its approach to equality (abandoning the old Bill of rights approach) and to the reach of the Charter under s.32 (rejecting unsustainable distinctions). Moreover, the general thrust of the law-is-politics critique was heeded to the limited extent that the courts backed off from a transparent and discredited version of 'legal formalism' which pretended that constitutional law was simply a matter of interpretive conformity that had no connection to wider debates about national values and social policies. The Supreme Court sought to nurture a less legalistic and more pragmatic approach to their constitutional duties. Ironically, these very efforts to bolster their democratic legitimacy by relying upon an apparently more overt mode of democratic justification revealed even more starkly how un-democratic the judges' involvement judicial review under the Charter; see A. Petter, 'Twenty Years of Charter Justification: From Liberal Legalism to Dubious Dialogue' (2003) 52 U.N.B.L.J. 187 and Kent Roach, 'Too Much Judicial Activism or Too Little?' in this volume. However, the subsequent turn to 'dialogue theory' not only failed to legitimize judicial review, but also served to facilitate the kind of reactionary politics which informs *Chaoulli*.

Cautioning that judges are not free to go wherever their personal political preferences take them, the general thrust of the dialogue theory was that, because the legislature possess the final word on Charter matters by virtue of the s.33 override power, the courts can proceed to engage in a more overt balancing of political values under the s.1 'reasonable limits' provision. The claim and hope is that the courts and the legislature will engage in an institutional conversation about the Charter and how it can be used to advance shared democratic goals in particular and pressing issues of the day; see *Bell Express Vu Limited Partnership v. R.*, [2002] 2 SCR 559 and K. Roach, *The Supreme Court on Trial: Judicial Activism or Democratic Dialogue* (Toronto: Irwin Law 2001). See also *Vriend v. Alberta*, [1998] 1 SCR 493 and *Corbiere v. Canada (Minister of Indian and Northern Affairs)*, [1999] 2 SCR 203. While this resort to 'democratic dialogue' goes beyond a discredited legal formalism, it lets the political cat out of the judicial bag without any plan for getting it back in or keeping it suitably leashed; see *Doucet-Boudreau* v. *Nova Scotia (Minister of Education)*, [2003] SCC 62 at 19, 20 and 25, Iacobucci and Arbour JJ. Indeed, an uncommitted observer might be forgiven for thinking that, on the question of whether 'law is politics,' the Court has given up the ghost rather than exorcise the wraith of judicial activism. And this is exactly what *Chaoulli* reveals. Rather than calm fears that the courts are undisciplined and unlimited in their powers, it manages to reinforce that perception and gives judges almost free rein to legislate their own preferences in the guise of institutional restraint and political modesty. Presenting judicial review as part and parcel of a democratic dialogue merely underlines the extent to which democracy has been turned into a pathetic and enfeebled caricature of itself.

The first temptation to be resisted is that of trying to explain away the *Chaoulli* decision as somehow aberrational or exceptional. The whirlwind of *Chaoulli* is the wretched harvest to be reaped from the bad seeds that were sown in *RJR-Macdonald*, *Gosselin*, *Auton* and a whole lot more Supreme Court judgments. Moreover, the roots of the privatised vision of social justice which came to bloom in *Chaoulli* can be found even in those decisions, like *Morgentaler*, which are hailed as the highpoints of Charter doctrine. Looking back, it is hard to imagine that it could have been otherwise. However, Charter-enthusiasts will point to a variety of factors to explain away *Chaoulli* and keep alive their roseate vision of the Charter's redemptive qualities – there were only seven judges involved; one of the majority is retiring at the end of the year; there will be a minimum of three new judges when a similar issue comes back to the Court; the three dissenting judges will likely still be on the court at that time; only three judges found the Charter to be implicated in the decision; and there was no agreed opinion among the four judges in the majority. But to highlight such 'technicalities' and to postulate that it might be different next time around with a slightly different Court and a slightly different set of facts is to bolster hope where none exists and to perpetuate the liberal myth of the Charter; see Bernard Dickens, 'The Chaoulli Decision – Less than Meets the Eye or More?' this volume and Peter H. Russell, '*Chaoulli*: The Political vs the Legal Life of a Judicial Decision,' this volume.

When Alexander Pope versed that 'hope springs eternal in the human breast;/Man never Is, but always To be blest,' A. Pope, *An Essay on Man* Epistle I, Frank Brady, ed. (New York: MacMillan 1988), he obviously never anticipated the Canadian Charter of Rights. For all those who lauded the Charter as a harbinger of all that is good and true in the democratic scheme of things, the Supreme Court's decision in *Chaoulli* must be considered to be the end of the line. After *Chaoulli*, it is surely self-delusional rather than merely hopeful to pretend that the Supreme Court and the Charter can be relied upon to breathe some progressive life into the Canadian body politic; see in this volume Lorne Sossin, 'Towards a Two-Tier Constitution: The Poverty of Health Rights,' Kent Roach 'Too Much Judicial Activism or Too Little?' and Stanley Hartt, 'Arbitrariness, Randomness and the Principles of Fundamental Justice: Wait Time Guarantees,' this volume. Indeed, for anyone who still possesses the remotest prospect of an open mind, there can be little doubt now that the proverbial woman of larger girth has brought the curtain down on the Charter Soap-Opera. Not only has she finished her song and left the stage, but she has left the constitutional building entirely. The dream – for that was what it was – of the Charter of Rights as something that would be interpreted generously to protect and advance the interests of ordinary Canadians is revealed as little more than, well, a dream and a fantastical one at that. At best, it was an indulgent reverie by the chattering classes and, at worst, a more suspicious exercise in political deception by Canada's elite. The 'large and liberal' rendition of the Charter which was promised has been fully realised only if 'liberal' is understood to represent the laissez-faire musings of 'progressive conservatives' and other oxymoronic heirs of the Lockean tradition. Any notion of a public or social good has been eclipsed by a privatised vision of social justice in which the privileges of the haves hold the have-nots hostage to their own economic freedom. Quite simply, the decision in *Chaoulli* confirms that the Charter has allowed the political right to hijack democracy in the name of constitutional justice.

The top and bottom line is that the Supreme Court is open to libertarian arguments from the political far Right. And let there be no doubt that Chaoulli's and Zéliotis' was a far right position. In their submissions to the trial court, Dr. Chaoulli submitted that 'Marxist-Leninist dogmas led to the egalitarian ideology that now exist' and counsel for George Zéliotis argued that the case was about 'the right of more affluent people to have access to parallel health services'; see *Chaoulli and Zéliotis v. Attorney-General of Quebec*, [2000] J.Q. no 479 (Que. Sup. Ct.), Piché J. at paras 7–8. Moreover, soon after the judgment, in a speech at the Heritage foundation, a decidedly and overtly conservative American organisation, Dr. Chaoulli reveled in the Court's decision. He crowed that 'this Canadian Supreme Court ruling was like the fall of a second Berlin Wall ... [because] it opens up a unique opportunity ... to counter, what is called in the United States 'liberal' and what I call 'socialist,' lobbies that are pushing their agenda for socialized medicine.' Indeed, he refers to the 'terrifying opinion' of the dissenting judges; see Jacques Chaoulli, 'A Victory for Freedom: The Canadian Supreme Court's Ruling on Private Health Care' (Paper presented to the Heritage Foundation, July 2005) 892 The Heritage Lectures 1 at 2–3 and 4, available online: The Heritage Foundation, <http://www.heritage.org/Research/HealthCare/hl892.cfm>; and Christopher Manfredi, 'Déjà Vu All Over Again: *Chaoulli* and the Limits of Judicial Policymaking,' this volume.

The willingness of the Court to go along with this extremist rhetoric is both an astonishing recognition of its own ideological commitments and a slap in the face for Canadian democratic politics generally. The stand-out feature of such politics has been the unwavering commitment to making health care available to all Canadians on the basis of medical need, not status, connections or ability to pay. It is exactly the kind of regressive politics peddled by Chaoulli and Zéliotis that the great bulk of Canadian citizens and politicians have consistently opposed and sought to overcome in the last fifty years. In sabotaging that deep-seated and established commitment to universal health care, the Supreme Court has revealed the incontestable reactionary and partial underpinnings of its Charter jurisprudence. While the Supreme Court will still be prepared to accept some progressive arguments, it will only do so insofar as they do not jeopardise or threaten the underlying conservative ideology of the Charter. When push comes to shove, the Supreme Court will prefer libertarian positions to more progressive ones. Furthermore, when the Court does make a future decision (as it will) that sits more comfortably with progressive values, the usual claque of Charter cheerleaders will breathe a collective sigh of relief and announce that the Supreme Court judges and the Charter are back on track – the mistake that was *Chaoulli* will be conveniently forgotten or downplayed and the liberal march of the Charter will be restored. This is a chilling prospect which ought to be denounced by all those who claim to be supporters of democracy.

For all the Supreme Courts' formal and subtle qualities, the constitutional game is (or ought to be) about the substance of what is decided; 'conceptual coherence' seems to come a very poor second to the substantive justice of constitutional arrangements. If the same-sex marriage saga puts in question the Supreme Court's legitimate role in a democracy, other decisions serve to underline the particular and partial cut of the judiciary's substantive politics. In terms of winners and losers, it can now be safely conclude that we have managed to craft for ourselves (or, at least, the courts and its apologists have) a screwed-up constitution. The promise of a 'People's Charter' is now only a fleeting memory. The Charter is supposed to enshrine those values which Canadians believe are so fundamental to their society that they should be beyond the vagaries and vanities of the immediate political process. While those exact commitments are never beyond controversy, most agree that these values are intended to be *constitutive* of a 'free and democratic society.' That being the case, how did the courts manage to give constitutional recognition to the advertising freedoms of RJR-MacDonald, but turn aside the claims of welfare recipients and funding pleas of autistic children's parents? These questions and answers deserve a full and rigorous accounting.

Of course, when these contrasting series of decisions are approached separately, they both have a modicum of sense and justification to them, at least in lawyers' internalised frames of doctrinal reference. In the Charter's earlier days, the Supreme Court decided, without much debate, that corporations count as an 'everyone' in the constitutional rush to legislative judgment; they could claim basic rights and freedoms. Having made this fateful step, they completed the rest of the march in the mid-1990s when it upheld the tobacco companies challenge to legislative efforts to curb their 'freedom of expression' by demanding explicit warnings on their products; see *RJR-Macdonald*, [1995] 3 SCR 199. The basic rationale was that 'expression' was such a fundamental activity in a democracy that it must be protected even in dubious circumstances. Why this applied to so-called commercial speech as much as political expression was left largely unexplained. In short, despite much soul-searching, the Supreme Court seemed to feel that the cost of constitutionally-protected advertising was the price of democratic justice.

Fast forward several years to 2002. *Gosselin* involved whether a Quebec regulation providing for reduced welfare benefits for individuals under 30 not participating in training or work experience employment programs infringed, among other things, welfare recipients' s.7 right to security of the person; see [2002] 4 SCR 429. The majority of the court held that s.7 does not place positive obligations on the government to guarantee adequate living support, but simply restricts the state's ability to deprive people of their right to life, liberty and security of the person. Although it is not too difficult to demonstrate that the difference between 'support' and 'deprivation' is not as air-tight or different as the Court suggests, *Gosselin* is not wholly objectionable and reprehensible on its own terms; for a desperate effort to build a defence of the Charter around Arbour and L'Heureux-Dube's dissents, see Lorne Sossin, 'Towards a Two-Tier Constitution: The Poverty of Health Rights,' in this volume. However, when it is put together with *RJR-Macdonald*, the full ideological thrust of the Charter and Supreme Court's approach to s.7 begins to take a more sinister shape. While the welfare recipients are told to pursue their interests unaided in the political arena, tobacco companies are given the considerable leverage of constitutional benefit in their continuing (and well-funded) efforts to negotiate with government. By virtue of its decisions, the Supreme Court has managed to exacerbate the already large imbalance between the political clout of the haves and have-nots. For many, this is a travesty, not a triumph of constitutional justice.

This deeply troubling approach was brought further home with a vengeance a couple of years later. In *Auton*, [2004] 3 SCR 657, the Supreme Court decided that autistic children had no constitutional right to require British Columbia to fund expensive therapy for them. The Court was very sympathetic to the children and their parents (and hoped that the province would reconsider their decision to deny funding), but held that health policy was not part of the Constitution. The Court determined, following the logic of *Gosselin*, that it was a matter for fiscal calculation by politicians, not constitutional principle by law-yers. Such a decision sounds not entirely unreasonable on its own terms. That is, until it is viewed against the Court's findings in the tobacco advertising cases. By what frame of reference or set of values can it be argued that the commercial opportunities of tobacco compa-nies are more deserving of constitutional protection than the well-being of autistic children? Reliance will no doubt be placed by judicial apolo-gists on the fact that the former is about keeping government's intru-sive tendencies in check, whereas the latter demands that government dig into its own pockets to finance such measures at the courts' behest. Ironically, however, the cost of the children's requested therapy is de-cidedly meagre compared to the truly huge social cost of coping with smoking-related illnesses. At the end of the day, both decisions have significant resource implications for society: it is simply that one is more direct than the other.

Mindful that it is possible to make legal arguments to support almost any political position (as the litigants and interveners in *Chaoulli* amply demonstrate), it is not difficult to draw fine distinctions between basic legal principles and established constitutional categorizations; see Lorraine Weinrib, 'Charter Perspectives on Chaoulli – the Body and the Body Politic,' in this volume. But the essential point is that, regardless of fancy legal argument and subtle rationalisations, autistic children and welfare recipients are seen to simply count for less than tobacco companies in the constitutional scheme of things. And, therefore, they count for less in the calibrations of democratic decision-making. Such legal posturing is surely not the sole measure or crowning glory of a noble constitutional scheme – legalistic formulations do not for social justice make. As if to add insult to injury, the courts come to this pass, not as a conclusion of contested political judgment, but as a purported constitutional fact of the matter. This is a lamentable state of affairs that should deeply trouble all Canadians. However, as the Danes have a habit of saying, 'bad is never good until worse happens.' And *Chaoulli* was worse. If *Gosselin* and *Auton* were disappointing and debilitating, then *Chaoulli* is the stuff of nightmares.

As it should be, the contemporary debate on health care is vigorous and engaged. Canadians hold a variety of views on how health care should be funded and organised. Yet there is an emerging consensus that the Canadian system of health care is ailing. The basic facts not only support that popular sentiment, but suggest that things might be worse than generally appreciated. Although Canada is 10th on a global scale in the total amount it spends per capita on health care, the returns on that investment are weak – Canada ranks 26th in physicians per capita, 22nd in infant mortality, 15th in access to health technology and 21st in public spending. These are sobering figures and indicate that the Canadian health care system is in need of considerable renovation; see Canadian Medical Association, *2005 Report Card: General Population* 9 (August 2005). Yet, whatever agreement there is on the system's present condition, there is no firm or shared understanding on what to do about it. There are widely divergent views about how to remedy the situation. Although there are many different approaches, the central tension is between those who maintain that increased public funding and re-structuring of the present system is necessary and those who hold that greater opportunities for private intervention must be allowed. The present debate is sharply joined over whether individuals should be able to purchase privately those medical services which are exclusively available under the public scheme. There are no easy answers here and none that transcend entirely contested ideological commitments. As much as many strive to deny it, health care is inevitably and unavoid-ably a political matter; see in this volume, Andrew Petter, 'Wealthcare: The Politics of Charter Revisited' and Christopher Manfredi, 'Déjà Vu All Over Again: *Chaoulli* and the Limits of Judicial Policymaking.'

In a democracy (of which Canada holds itself out to be a leading exemplar), the most pressing issue is often as much about *who* gets to decide divisive matters as it is about *what* gets decided. Of course, while these two issues are not entirely separate, they each raise different questions of validity and legitimacy. By most democratic lights, the objective is less about getting it right in some absolute sense and more about arriving at decisions which engage public opinion and respect. The value of democratic decisions is measured by their enabling proce-dures as well as by their resulting content: democracy is about organisational form as well as substantive enactments; see A. Hutchinson, *The Companies We Keep: Corporate Governance for a Demo-cratic Age* (Toronto: Irwin Law) [forthcoming in 2005]. Health care is perhaps the most compelling illustration of this democratic conun-drum. Moreover, because the subject-matter is so contested and its resolution is so contingent, it is important to ensure that the decisions of one generation do not bind entirely the options of the next generation. Indeed, the evolving history of health care in Canada can be under-stood as one indicator of Canada's emergence to maturity as a devel-oped and democratic country. However, *Chaoulli* challenges the very nature of both Canadian health care and Canadian democracy. In its monumental decision, the Supreme Court has barged into the political fray and taken a decidedly partial stance in the debate over health care. In the process, the courts have undermined not only the debate on health care, but also the democratic foundations of the Canadian polity. As such, the *Chaoulli* decision is an abomination of the most debilitating kind; it threatens not only the personal, but also the political health of all Canadians.

In the starkest terms, *Chaoulli* obliges all Charter-watchers to accept for good or bad that Charter adjudication is energised by a political ideology which emphasises, among other things, that individual entitlements are much more important than social responsibilities, that negative liberty is to be promoted at the expense of positive liberty, that people's capacity to exercise their rights is a matter of choice rather than circumstance, and that legislatures are not only not to be trusted, but are the breeding grounds of capricious and arbitrary decision-making. None of these underpinnings are new (nor is the critical illumination of them original), but *Chaoulli* combines them and lays them bare in an arresting and fresh way. As such, these planks in the Charter's conservative platform deserve to be carefully identified and exposed for what they are.

A central and basic tension in modern constitutionalism is between the orientation of rights around the notions of civil claims and social entitlements. Civil rights are traditionally thought to encompass life, liberty and security of the person, cruel and unusual punishment, arbitrary arrest, fair trial, movement, speech, conscience, religion, peaceful assembly, and voting. In contrast, social rights are most often used to include work, social security, leisure, standard of living, health, education and housing. In contrast to the civil rights advocates who concentrate on the political liberty of individuals from government abuse, the social rights proponents rely on a notion of collective responsibility that expects the state to intervene actively to ensure an equitable distribution of opportunities and resources. While these disparate ideologies often overlap in their concerns, they suggest a very different approach to the interpretation and ambit of their shared rights. Most importantly, a glance at the Charter's language and the court's jurisprudence over the last 20 years leaves little doubt that civil claims have prospered as social entitlements have simply been passed over. This balance is nothing new, but the fact that it has been confirmed as a matter of constitutional law as opposed to democratic politics is highly significant. Prior to 1982, the balance was a matter of general political debate. However, since 1982, whereas civil claims have been entrenched as 'fundamental' and, therefore, beyond political re-evaluation, social entitlements have been relegated to distinct second-best status and must always defer to the primacy of civil claims.

This political vision which has prevailed is highly individualistic and anti-state. The legitimate role of the state is limited to facilitating freedom by imposing a minimum of formal and equal constraints upon people's activities. People are treated as rational and private individuals who share little more than an abstract humanity. By treating everyone as the same and equally placed to exercise rights, this political approach ignores the very different material and social conditions in which people live. It depicts a just society as one in which the achievement of personal liberty and social justice can be effected without concern for serious economic equality. Indeed, rather than the courts being 'the last line of defence for citizens' (para.96) as Deschamps J presumes, her decision instead reveals that they are the last line of defence for the affluent and the privileged. When Deschamps J. contends that 'the question is whether Quebeckers who are prepared to spend money to get access to health care that is, in practice, not accessible in the public sector because of waiting lists may be validly prevented from doing so by the state' (*Chaoulli*, para.4), she conveniently fails to mention that it is not simply whether one is 'prepared to spend money,' but whether one has money to spend. Emphasising that shifting the design of Canada's health system to the courts is not a wise or desirable idea, the dissenting opinions of Binnie and LeBel JJ. hit the nail squarely on the head:

'Those who seek private health insurance are those who can afford it and can qualify for it. They will be the more advantaged members of society. They are differentiated from the general population, not by their health problems, which are found in every group in society, but by their income status. We share the view of Dickson CJ that the Charter should not become an instrument to be used by the wealthy to 'roll back' the benefits of a legislative scheme that helps the poorer members of society. He observed in *Edwards Books*, at p. 779: 'In interpreting and applying the Charter I believe that the courts must be cautious to ensure that it does not simply become an instrument of better situated individuals to roll back legislation which has as its object the improvement of the condition of less advantaged persons.' (Para.274)

Indeed, *Chaoulli* confirms that the extent of a person's wealth and resources remains the real measure of citizenship; the ability to participate and take advantage of one's civil claims is limited by and proportionate to one's material status. The Supreme Court has again missed entirely the irony of Anatole France's praise for 'the majestic equality of the laws, which forbid rich and poor alike to sleep under the bridges, to beg in the streets, and steal bread.' A. France, *The Red Lily*, trans. by W. Stephens (1970) 91. What is the 'progressive' notion on health care is not open-and-shut, but it would surely give considerable weight to the commitment that a system which provides a certain and similar level of care for all is to be preferred to a system which allows some to buy a level of care which is better or higher than for others. Equality of opportunity demands more than the dismantling of formal barriers to participation, it also requires substantive and affirmative measures to actualise those opportunities and possibilities. The holding in *Chaoulli* strengthens rather than dismantles those barriers. According to the Supreme Court, while the Chaoullis of the world must not be prevented from spending their resources and wealth on obtaining health care, those without such resources and wealth have no corresponding social and affirmative right to health care. In light of *Gosselin*, it would seem that, if government decided to opt for an entirely or mostly private system of health care, the Supreme Court would not recognise a duty on government to provide services for those who could not afford a decent level of health care. While this scenario is unlikely (at least in the near future?), it does reveal the cut and consequences of a *Chaoulli*-style approach to constitutional law and health care; see Lorne Sossin, 'Towards a Two-Tier Constitution: The Poverty of Health Rights,' this volume.

As such, *Chaoulli* persists in the absurd notion that the true basis of individual freedom is the absence of collective constraint and state interference – individuals are most free when they are left entirely to their own devices and desires. Yet the roots of this belief run deep in the law. Even some of the more progressively-inclined decisions of the Supreme Court, such as the recognition of gay rights and abortion rights, build on this flawed and discredited foundation. For instance, in *Morgentaler*, even Wilson J. grounded her more expansive interpretation of s.7 in order to protect pregnant women's freedom on a negative and solitary concept of personhood. She perpetuated and gave comfort to the conservative claim that the state that governs best is the state that governs least: 'the rights guaranteed in the Charter erect around each individual, metaphorically speaking, an invisible fence over which the state will not be allowed to trespass.' *R. v. Morgentaler*, [1988] 1 SCR 161 at 164. In effect, Wilson's adoption of an individualistic ideology leaves women to their own devices and stymies the struggle to encourage government to fulfil its progressive and affirmative obligations to provide appropriate health facilities and services. Sadly, any progressive spin of *Morgentaler* is curtailed by its conservative underpinnings and *Chaoulli* is the fruit of such a poisoned tree.

However, notwithstanding the Supreme Court's affirmation of a regressive constitutional ideology, the most outrageous and unconscionable feature of *Chaoulli* is the majority's conclusion that restrictions on private health care are 'arbitrary': 'a law is arbitrary where 'it bears no relation to, or is inconsistent with, the objective that lies behind [it]"; see McLachlin CJ and Major J (para.130). The claim that there is no rational basis whatsoever for the established policy that the best way to preserve universal health care is by curtailing the operation and availability of private health insurance is an affront to Canadian democratic history and politics. It is one thing for the majority to disagree with the political appeal and rightness of a scheme of socialised medicine, but it is another thing entirely to dismiss such a view as 'arbitrary.' Universal and non-private health care may not be the best scheme in some reasonable people's eyes, but how can it be capricious or despotic as 'arbitrary' implies – is the explanation that the Quebec and federal legislature did this for the sheer hell of it with no purpose in mind or only an oppressive one? Such a conclusion grossly misrepresents and condemns the past half century of political struggle and governmental policy in Canada. It may be that the majority believe that allocating health care on the basis of status or wealth rather than need is preferable, but it is simply insulting to declare any other view to be not only wrong-headed, but also arbitrary. This is a breathtaking piece of judicial hubris.

Deschamps J. has it entirely backwards when she states that the courts are 'an appropriate forum for a serious and complete debate' and that 'it must be possible to base the criteria for judicial intervention on legal principles and not on a socio-political discourse that is disconnected from reality' (para.86 and 87). It is the courts and not the legislators who are 'disconnected from reality.' Her claim that 'the courts have a duty to rise above political debate' (para.89) is much more honoured by her (and her colleagues) in the breach than the observance. Not only is there no such fabled place outside of 'socio-political discourse,' but her judgment is the best evidence that she has failed to meet her own earnest standards; 'legal principle' is revealed as simply one very transparent and partial kind of 'socio-political discourse.' As Binnie and LeBel JJ in their scathing dissent assert, 'the debate is about *social* values; it is not about constitutional law' (para.166). Or, perhaps, more accurately, a constitutional law which entrenches the social values represented in the majority's reasoning is bad constitutional law. Notwithstanding Binnie and LeBel JJ., constitutional law is always about social values; the only issue is whose social values.

Of course, I would have been delighted to have been proved wrong in mine and others' dire warnings about the Charter's likely growth and judicial development. However, the basic set-up and structure of Charter adjudication always made that a very long shot. Indeed, the effort by Charter supporters and sceptics to make the best of a bad job has only tended to make matters worse. So committed are the bulk of constitutional lawyers to the overall jurisprudential enterprise whatever their political beliefs, it is now commonly believed that the Charter is here to stay and that the courts' performances are to be criticised, but the overall process is to be salvaged. This is a depressing state of affairs. It is simply mistaken, as many Canadian (and American) commentators seem to think and hope, that the challenge of constitutional law and theory is best understood and confronted as little more than a series of problems in institutional design. This way of thinking is an ignoble effort to finesse the real difficulties of constitutional justice and to pass off genuine questions of substantive entitlement as only formal calculations.

The fact is that the Charter and its judicial enforcement are deeply incompatible with and often antagonistic to progressive notions of justice. On balance, they do much more harm than good to the democratic cause and we would be well rid of it; see Robin West, 'Constitutional Scepticism' (1992) 72 B.U. L. Rev. 765. Nonetheless, getting rid of the Charter or its judicial enforcement is not on the cards. In the meantime, it will be vital to maintain an implacable critical expose of the courts. At the same time, efforts can be made along at least three fronts. One is to multiply the number of sites at which 'constitutional review' takes place in the hope that this will place responsibility on all actors in the system and not simply defer to the last-say power of courts; see M. Tushnet, *Taking the Constitution Away from the Courts* (Princeton: Princeton University Press 1999) and 'Non-Judicial Review' (2003) 40 Harv. J. on Legis. 453. Another is to make courts more representative and accountable by making serious (as opposed to superficial and lame) efforts to democratise the appointments process; see Allan Hutchinson, 'Judges and Politics: An Essay From Canada' (2004) 24 L.S. 275. And another is to encourage governments to overcome their reticence to use s.33's override provisions; it is as much a part of the Charter as any other and its possible use is actually relied on by the courts to legitimise their own role and functioning. While this will be a definite second-best set of strategies to abandoning the Charter, they do offer some chance to reduce the pernicious impact of *Chaoulli*-style constitutional adjudication.

A few years ago, Justice McLachlin (as she then was) urged a more engaged and democratic approach to constitutional law. She stated that 'the elected legislators, the executive and the courts all have their role to play. Each must play that role in a spirit of profound respect for the other. We are not adversaries. We are all in the justice business, together.' Beverley McLachlin, 'Charter Myths' (1999) 33 U.B.C. L. Rev. 23 at 36. If *Chaoulli* is anything to go by, this is some justice and some cooperation. The idea that there is any kind of dialogic cooperation between courts and legislatures is offensive. Indeed, what occurs is neither just nor respectful. Or, perhaps to put it more accurately, it is a brand of justice which shows no respect for democracy and which equates justice with business. Unless Canadians want to turn health care over to business, they had better act quickly and decisively. Like it or not, Canadians are now 'in the justice *business* together' – **told you so!**

Notes

* Osgoode Hall Law School, York University, Toronto. I am grateful to Derek Morgan, Joan Gilmour, Paul Saguil, Lorne Sossin and especially Andrew Petter for their critical comments and helpful suggestions.

1 See A. Hutchinson, *Waiting for Coraf: A Critique of Rights* (Toronto: University of Toronto Press 1995). This is not said with a resounding triumphalism or smug complacency, but with a deep and genuine regret. After almost 25 years of Charter experience, it can now be reported that almost all the worst fears of the early Charter critics have come to pass – judicial review under the Charter of Rights and Freedoms operates as an institutional device to curb democratic politics and to entrench a conservative ideology. The Charter is indeed a potent political weapon, but one that has been and continues to be used to benefit vested interests in society and to weaken further the relative powerlessness of the disadvantaged and

under-privileged. See, for example, J. Bakan, *Just Words: Constitutional Rights and Social Wrongs* (Toronto: University of Toronto Press 1997,); A. Petter, 'The Politics of The Charter' (1986) 8 Sup. Ct. L. Rev. 473; M. Mandel, *The Charter of Rights and the Legalisation of Politics in Canada* 2nd ed. (Toronto: Thompson Educational Publications, 1994); and A. Petter, 'Wealthcare: The Politics of Charter Revisited,' this volume. Whether or not that was the intention of its proponents and drafters is beside the point. As is the lingering and still widely-held belief that it is possible in constitutional matters to make a silk purse of social justice out of the pig's ear of the Charter. The fact is that Charter adjudication is in a 'critical condition' and, more to the point, is not worth saving. It would be best to let it die in peace rather than engage in extensive efforts to resuscitate it.

Understood in such light, the recent decision of the Supreme Court in *Chaoulli* is simply the death rattle of a constitutional progeny. It brings home in the most clear and compelling way the particular politics of constitutional law and adjudication – when the stakes are sufficiently high, the entitlements of affluent and privileged Canadians are important enough to permit the claims of 'ordinary Canadians' to be set aside. Of course, there have been victories along the way for a more progressive vision of democratic constitutionalism, but these have been few and far between. Moreover, those successes, like gay rights and electoral reform, have been less a rejection of a conservative politics than an incidental corollary of its more individual and institutional commitments. From the initial first fumblings of the courts, the Charter was utilised by corporate and established groups to protect and often advance their own agenda of interests, even if some benefits did accrue to the less advantaged and privileged.

Wealthcare: The politics of the *Charter* Revisited

ANDREW PETTER*

> Every man for himself said the elephant as he danced among the chickens.
> –Tommy Douglas

Of Health and Wealth

'Health is wealth' is one of my Irish mother-in-law's favourite sayings. In *Chaoulli v. Quebec (A.G.)*,[1] however, the Supreme Court of Canada turned this aphorism on its head. In a four-to-three decision, the Court held that, given the failure of the Quebec government to provide timely access to Medicare services, Quebeckers have a constitutional or quasi-constitutional[2] right to purchase private health insurance to access corresponding services from commercial health care providers.

What would be the implications of this decision if it were implemented and applied across the country? One implication is that Canadians who can afford private health insurance would have access to better medical care than those who cannot. Another implication is that those who exercise their right to buy private health insurance would have a weaker stake in ensuring that the Medicare system provides timely and effective medical services. Indeed, where the private and the public systems competed for the same health care professionals, those with private insurance would have an interest in the most qualified of these being diverted into the private system where their services could be accessed on a preferred basis.

What about the implications for the public health care system? Would the introduction of private health insurance, in addition to improving the quality of health care for those who can afford it, compromise the quality of health care for those who cannot? Many believe that the answer to this question is 'yes.' They argue that a two-tier system of health care would siphon resources from and weaken support for Medicare, making it more difficult to manage the public system effectively. Others disagree. They argue that expanding private medical services would increase the overall capacity of the health care system and thereby reduce pressure on the public system. Still others argue that the risk to Medicare from private health insurance is uncertain but, insofar as it exists, the more prudent strategy for reducing wait times is not to expand private medical services for the few, but to improve public medical services for all.[3]

Debate over the relative merits of a one-tier or two-tier health care system has been at the heart of Canadian politics for almost forty years. This debate has engaged Canadians at all levels. It has prompted countless community groups, professional bodies and public interest organisations to hold forums, to undertake studies and to produce position papers. It has been the subject of numerous public commissions, and has played a part in virtually every federal and provincial election campaign since the mid 1960s. Moreover the debate has been about values and ideology as much as it has been about costs and benefits. In many ways, it has been a debate about the fundamental nature of Canada. Do we want a country in which health care is viewed as a market commodity, with access determined by one's economic status? Or do we want a country in which health care is viewed as a public good, with access determined by one's medical needs? Or we do we think that it's somehow possible to have both?

Since the introduction of our national Medicare plan almost forty years ago, the position that has prevailed in this debate has been the one favouring retention of a single-payer model of public health insurance for core medical services. This has remained true despite the considerable stress experienced by the public health care system in recent years. Thus the 2002 Romanow Report[4] and the subsequent health care accord reached by Canada's first ministers[5] rejected private health insurance in favour of improving medical services in the public system. Indeed, to say that the single-payer model has prevailed understates the reality. Canada's commitment to a universal public health care system is widely regarded by citizens as a core social value and a defining national achievement. This too was reaffirmed last year when Tommy Douglas, best known as the father of Medicare, was voted the greatest Canadian is a nation-wide competition undertaken by the CBC.[6]

Now a majority of judges on the Supreme Court of Canada has told us in *Chaoulli* that they know better. In the majority's eyes, the single-payer payer model of health insurance and its goal of providing equal health care services for all, far from embodying this country's commitment to social justice, violates the rights of those who could gain access to medical services more quickly by purchasing private health insurance. Moreover, according to the Court, there is no evidence to suggest that the introduction of private health insurance would compromise the quality of Canadian health care. Never mind the trial judge's finding that the 'effect of establishing a parallel private health care system would be to threaten the integrity, proper functioning and viability of the public system.'[7] Never mind the recommendations of various public commissions that the single-payer model should be retained. Never mind the decisions of different governments over the years that have rejected two-tier health care. All of this can be ignored in *Charterland*, where judges get to decide what qualifies as evidence and what can be cast aside as mere 'assertions of belief'[8] or 'socio-political discourse that is disconnected from reality.'[9]

Thus, with the benefit of a one day hearing, three of four majority judges were able to conclude that prohibiting private health insurance 'is not necessary or even related to the provision of quality public health care'[10] – a conclusion they based on a review of second-hand information concerning the health care experience of other western democracies. The efficiency and apparent dependability of this methodology makes one wonder why the federal government allowed the Romanow Commission to hold months of hearings, gather hundreds of submissions, and spend $15 million before releasing its recommendations on the future of Canada's health care system. Apparently the job could have been done much more quickly, cheaply and reliably simply by putting a reference to the Supreme Court.

Given the complex and contentious nature of the issues raised by *Chaoulli*, many expected that this would be a case in which the Court would be reluctant to substitute its opinion for that of the legislature. In past *Charter* cases involving complex issues and conflicting claims, Supreme Court judges have sometimes shown great deference to legislative choices, particularly where a statutory regime purports to protect the interests of vulnerable groups.[11] Apparently these considerations do not apply, however, when it comes to evaluating the intricacies and impacts of competing health care schemes. Notwithstanding testimony from experts and representations from anti-poverty and public health care advocacy organisations that two-tier health care would hurt the economically disadvantaged, who are more likely to suffer from poor health and who cannot afford private insurance,[12] three of the majority judges held that they had sufficient evidence to conclude that the legislation was 'arbitrary' and therefore contrary to 'the principles of fundamental justice.'[13] Ironically, these are the words of a Chief Justice who has previously maintained that the value judgments made by courts under the *Charter* are themselves 'essentially arbitrary,' and has urged judges to seek guidance in 'the dominant views being expressed in society at large on the question in issue.'[14]

What about the remedy adopted by the Court? If the Court's objective was to secure citizens' rights to access health care services, why did it not order the Quebec government to provide such access within the public system as suggested in the factum of the Charter Committee on Poverty Issues and the Canadian Health Coalition?[15] This remedy would have preserved the single-payer model and its principle of equal access to health care based on one's medical need rather than one's personal wealth. It therefore would have enabled the Court to avoid the appearance that it was more concerned about protecting the rights of those with money than of those in need of medical care. Yet the Court shied away from this remedy, presumably because it would have required judges to assume responsibility for directing the public health care system. And managing government services, unlike dismantling them, is something that even activist judges are not prepared to do.

Some have suggested that the Court's judgment was intended as a 'wake up call' to governments about the need to fix Medicare by reducing wait times for medically necessary procedures.[16] If this indeed was the motivation, the judges were playing a dangerous game based on questionable assumptions and with little regard for the consequences. First, there has in recent years been no lack of political pressure or commitment regarding the need to reduce wait times. This issue was a key component of the agreement reached last fall amongst federal and provincial governments to pump an additional $41 billion into the public health system over the next 10 years.[17] Under that agreement, the Health Council of Canada was charged with developing benchmarks for reasonable wait times, and the provinces committed to reporting on their success in meeting those benchmarks.[18] Thus this 'wake up call' came at a time when no one seems to have been asleep. Second, by deciding that access to private health insurance is a *Charter* right, the Court has given constitutional legitimacy to those advocating a two-tier health care system for Canada, unleashing political forces that may be difficult to contain.[19] There are many ways to arouse people from their slumbers. By tearing down a central pillar of Canada's Medicare system, the Court opted for a wrecking ball over an alarm clock. Finally the Court appears to have acted with disregard for the trade implications of its decision, ignoring the Romanow Report's admonitions that, to be protected as 'public services' under such agreements, health care services must be 'universally accessible on the basis of need rather than the ability to pay' and must be 'financed out of public revenues.'[20] By requiring governments to allow private insurers to fund core medical services in commercial health care facilities, the Court's ruling threatens Canada's trade position.[21] In doing so, it could well limit the capacity of governments to set future directions on health care policy, including making it difficult, if not impossible, to restore a universal, single-payer system. In short, this is one wake-up call from which Canadians may never be allowed to get back to sleep.

If all of this sounds disturbing, it should. If it seems to suggest that the Court is engaging in political decision-making, it does. If, on the other hand, it comes as a shock, it ought not to do so. The path trodden by the Court in *Chaoulli* is shaped by ideological norms and assumptions that have been part and parcel of the *Charter* enterprise from its inception; and the power invoked by the Court has been nurtured by Canadian politicians and scholars over the same period of time. This does not mean that the outcome in *Chaoulli* was inevitable – the strong dissenting judgment of the minority demonstrates that it was not – but it does mean that *Chaoulli* was a *Charter* calamity waiting to happen.

The Politics of the *Charter* Revisited

In the mid 1980s, as the Supreme Court of Canada was issuing its first decisions under the *Canadian Charter of Rights and Freedoms*, a vigorous debate took place amongst Canadian legal academics about the political nature and consequences of the *Charter*. In that debate I and other progressive *Charter* sceptics argued that, beyond the confines of the criminal law, the *Charter* was more likely to serve the interests of the economically privileged than those of ordinary and disadvantaged Canadians.[22] The reason for this, we contended, was that *Charter* rights are grounded in an ideology of liberal legalism that holds that the main enemy of freedom is not disparities in wealth or concentrations of private power, but the state. This ideology finds expression in the fact that the rights set out in the *Charter* are predominantly negative in nature, with little in the way of positive economic or social entitlements. It is further animated by a belief that existing distributions of property are products of private initiative rather than state power, and that when courts protect these distributions through the application of the common law rules, they act as 'neutral arbiters' rather than as state actors.[23] Such property distributions are therefore regarded as the 'natural foundation' upon which *Charter* rights are bestowed and against which the constitutionality of state action is judged.

The ideology of liberal legalism, we maintained, removes from *Charter* scrutiny the major source of inequality in our society – the unequal distribution of property entitlements among private parties – and directs the restraining force of the *Charter* against the arms of the state best equipped to redress such inequality – the ostensibly democratic arms consisting of the legislature and the executive.[24] In doing so, it gives political meaning to the *Charter*'s open-ended provisions. For example, shaped by this ideology, equality rights do not guarantee citizens a right to be made substantively equal, but rather a right to be treated equally by government. Thus section 15 of the *Charter* places no positive duties upon the state; it is satisfied by 'equal' inaction as much as it is by 'equal' action. Similarly, the right to security of the person in section 7, according to this ideology, does not require governments to implement measures to make people secure. In the *Charter* scheme of things, courts are to disregard threats to personal security emanating from the market and common law property rights. It is only when the 'normalcy' of the market is disrupted by legislative or executive action that section 7 rights are engaged.

Our conclusion was that the *Charter* shares much the same reverence for private markets and individual autonomy, and the same hostility to legislative and executive action, that animated the common law. This did not mean that the entire legislative regime of social entitlements and economic regulation put in place in Canada following the Second World War would suddenly be dismantled under the *Charter*. Even if courts were so inclined, the political costs of doing so, thankfully, were too great for them to contemplate. What the *Charter* was more likely to do was 'to enable judiciary to chisel away at certain aspects of the regime, and to erect barriers to future innovation.'[25] Nor did it mean that there would be no progressive *Charter* decisions. There would be some, 'though most would involve courts upholding legislation – in other words, doing nothing.'[26] In addition, there would be exceptional 'instances in which the *Charter* is used to expand the protection afforded by a particular regulatory scheme (subject to the right of legislatures to dismantle the scheme altogether).' [27] Thus our view on the overall political impact of the *Charter* could be summed up as follows:

> At best, the *Charter* will divert progressive energies, inhibit market regulation, and legitimize prevailing inequalities in wealth and power. At worst, it will undermine existing programmes and block future reforms.[28]

These arguments caused something of a stir at the time, though this must have been due to the pungency of our prose rather than the novelty of our ideas. Certainly the positions we advanced were unique neither to us nor to Canada. A number of scholars in this country had previously raised similar concerns.[29] In England, John Griffith's well-known treatise, *The Politics of the Judiciary*, had critiqued the British legal system along the same lines.[30] And in the United States, John Hart Ely among others had written of the 'systematic bias' embedded in the system of rights favoured by the 'upper middle-class, professional class from which most lawyers and judges, and for that matter most moral philosophers are drawn.'[31] These people, Ely argued, see their social and economic status most threatened by the regulatory and redistributive powers of the modern state. Thus no one should be surprised that they regard as 'fundamental' those values that afford them protection from such state powers; '[b]ut watch most fundamental-rights theorists start edging toward the door when someone mentions jobs, food, or housing: these are important, sure, but they aren't *fundamental.*'[32]

Probably the most convincing exposé of liberal legalism's ideological hold on the *Charter*, however, came not in the form of academic writings, but in the Supreme Court of Canada's own 1986 decision in *Dolphin Delivery*.[33] In a judgment that offended progressive proponents of the *Charter* more than it did sceptics, the Court unanimously held that a common law injunction prohibiting unionized workers from picketing a private corporation did not constitute state action, and was therefore not reviewable as a breach of the *Charter* right to freedom of expression. It is hard to imagine a more blatant illustration of the privileged position that the *Charter* accords property rights and the institutions that protect them. Not surprisingly, the decision provoked a barrage of indignation from progressive academics of all *Charter* persuasions. *Charter* proponents excoriated the Court for renouncing the *Charter*'s progressive possibilities;[34] *Charter* critics lamented the politics of the decision, but welcomed its candid acknowledgement of the *Charter*'s regressive propensities.[35]

The Politics of the *Charter* Refined

In the wake of the critical commentary concerning *Dolphin Delivery* and other early *Charter* decisions, judges who were troubled by the political dimensions of their *Charter* role sought to moderate the *Charter*'s regressive tendencies. This they did in two ways. First, they found reasons to defer to legislative choices where statutes provided protection to vulnerable groups,[36] where equality rights were invoked by those who were not socially disadvantaged,[37] or where there was a lack of conclusive social science evidence.[38] Second, they developed techniques that increased the *Charter*'s progressive potential. One such technique was simply to be receptive to negative and formal rights claims that were directed against legislative provisions that were inequitable and outdated, such as those that restricted a woman's right to abortion[39] or that, on their face discriminated against gays and lesbians.[40] Another technique was to develop equality rights doctrines requiring governments to ameliorate the adverse impacts of their policies upon disadvantaged groups[41] and allowing judges to extend rather than strike down under-inclusive statutory benefits.[42] A third technique was to apply *Charter* rights to legislation that withdrew statutory protections, thereby imposing obligations on the state to reinstate some such protections in limited circumstances.[43] In addition, judges interpreting the common law increasingly took *Charter* values into account, despite their continued insistence that the *Charter* did not directly apply.[44]

These techniques enabled judges to counter the regressive pull of the *Charter* on a case-by-case basis. By operating as qualifications and exceptions, however, their effect was to ameliorate rather than alter the *Charter*'s regressive tendencies: constraining the legislative and executive arms of the state remained the central mission of the *Charter* enterprise. The major impact of these techniques, therefore, was to allow the courts to be more selective in their use of *Charter* rights and to opt for legislative refinements over invalidity, though almost always on the understanding that invalidity remained the default *Charter* position.[45]

Moreover, these techniques left it to individual judges to decide, according their own beliefs and inclinations, when the *Charter*'s underlying ideology would be given full expression and when it would be held in check:

- In some cases judges decided that the *Charter* does not permit powerful interests to strike down legislation aimed at protecting vulnerable groups;[46] in other cases they reached the opposite conclusion.[47]
- In some cases, judges deferred to legislative choices in the absence of conclusive social science evidence;[48] in other cases they did not.[49]
- In some cases judges invoked formal equality rights to strike down laws directed against gays and lesbians;[50] it other cases they found reasons to avoid doing so.[51]
- In some cases judges emphasized that equality rights are intended to protect the socially disadvantaged;[52] in other cases they emphasised that equality rights are available to members of advantaged groups.[53]
- In some cases judges were prepared to remedy a *Charter* breach by extending legislative benefits;[54] in other cases they were not.[55]
- In some cases judges held that withdrawing legislative protections violated the *Charter*;[56] in other cases they found that such withdrawals were justified.[57]
- In some cases judges invoked the *Charter* to modify the common law;[58] in other cases they declined to do so.[59]

Thus, in the process of moderating *Charter* decision-making, the Court has developed its own constrained version of palm tree justice.

Judges have been encouraged in this process by the rise of dialogue theory and its effort to legitimize judicial review based not on the ability of judges to find right answers, but rather upon the contention that *Charter* decision-making engages judges in a democratic dialogue with legislatures. Dialogue theorists make two claims as to why this dialogue is democratic: first, they assume that the deliberations of judges in *Charter* cases will improve the quality of legislative decision-making; second they assert that, under the *Charter*, it is legislatures not the courts that usually get the final say.[60] I have explained elsewhere why I find these propositions unpersuasive,[61] and I will consider their contribution to *Chaoulli* later in this paper. Their significance for this purpose, however, is that neither provides a normative vision of rights to guide or constrain the courts in their enterprise.[62] On the contrary, by accepting that there are no right answers when it comes to *Charter* decision-making, dialogue theorists provide no metewand with which to evaluate the appropriateness of judicial action; they essentially authorize judges to do whatever they want within the bounds that liberal legalism allows. Is it any wonder that the Court embraced this theory within months of it being committed to paper?

The Politics of the *Charter* Reaffirmed

Armed with a *Charter*, whose underlying structure and political assumptions remained intact, and fortified with a theory of judicial review that authorises courts to do what they want, it was only a matter of time before there emerged a majority of Supreme Court of Canada judges who were less resistant to the *Charter's* underlying ideology. This is what appears to have happened in recent years. With the departure of some judges and the arrival of others,[63] the Court has shown itself more willing to succumb to the *Charter's* regressive tendencies. This trend is evident in four contentious cases decided in the past four years: *Gosselin v. Québec (A.G.)*,[64] *Trociuk v. British Columbia (A.G.)*,[65] *Auton (Guardian ad litem of) v. British Columbia (A.G.)*,[66] and now *Chaoulli*.

In *Trociuk* and *Auton*, the Court drew on the *Charter's* negative conception of rights to strengthen section 15's commitment to formal equality. In *Trociuk*, an 'estranged' biological father sought a declaration that legislation granting mothers control over the process of registering the births and names of their children violated his equality rights and was constitutionally invalid. The Court unanimously granted the declaration, rejecting the decision of the court below that the legislation was justified as a means of protecting the well being of mothers and their children. In doing so, the judges embraced a conception of equality that presumed that genetic fathers have the same stake as genetic mothers in the process of registering births and naming children. This formal vision of equality was reinforced by the Court's willingness to see *Charter* equality rights used by a member of an historically advantaged group to challenge legislation that benefits those who have historically been disadvantaged. According to the Court, an absence of historical disadvantage is not a compelling factor against a finding of discrimination.

Trociuk involved a claim made on behalf of an historically advantaged group to gain greater influence in relation to government's birth registration and naming practices. *Auton*, on the other hand, involved a claim brought on behalf of a disadvantaged group to extend government health care benefits to better meet their medical needs. In the latter case, parents of autistic children maintained that government, by refusing to fund certain autism therapies, had denied their children equal benefit of the law without discrimination, thus breaching section 15 of the *Charter*. The Court dismissed this claim, holding that the denial of funding resulted from the procedures not being provided by designated 'medical practitioners' rather than from their being directed at persons with autism. According to the Court, the denial was therefore not discriminatory. In reaching this conclusion, the Court rejected arguments that government had a duty under section 15 to ensure that its definition of funded services did not have adverse impacts upon those with autism and, if it did, to ameliorate these impacts. Invoking the hollow logic of formal equality, the judges held that the duty to ameliorate went no further than requiring governments to provide equal access to procedures that were already funded; it did not require government to fund new procedures.[67]

While *Trociuk* and *Auton* mark a reaffirmation of liberal legalism in relation to section 15, *Gosselin* and *Chaoulli* do the same in relation to section 7. These latter cases, however, more explicitly expose the ideological assumptions and political workings of the *Charter*, in much the same way that *Dolphin Delivery* did almost twenty years ago. Louise Gosselin was a Quebec woman whose social assistance benefits had been cut by legislation reducing benefits for all persons under 30. These cuts, she maintained, had left her in a position of abject poverty, thereby denying her *Charter* right to security of the person. The Court rejected this claim, a majority of judges holding that section 7 did not place positive obligations on the state to ensure that Gosselin enjoyed security of the person, only negative obligations not to deprive her of such security. And, as the judges saw it, '[s]uch a deprivation does not exist in the case at bar.'[68] In reaching this conclusion, the Court, much like its predecessor in *Dolphin Delivery*, simply assumed that the state is not implicated in the distribution and protection of property entitlements in our society. Here, as there, one is expected to accept that such entitlements, and the whole regime of laws and institutions that helped to create and preserve them, are pre-political and not subject to *Charter* review. Thus the *Charter* guarantees personal security not to individuals who 'naturally' *lack* such entitlements, but only to individuals who 'naturally' *enjoy* such entitlements and wish to resist government efforts to take them away or restrict their use.

Louise Gosselin represented individuals on one side of this line. George Zeliotis and Jacques Chaoulli represented those on the other. Zeliotis was a retired businessman who had become frustrated with wait times in the Quebec health care system; Chaoulli was a physician who wished to provide private health care services to patients in the province. They both resented the fact that Quebec legislation prevented individuals from purchasing private health insurance for the kind of medical services provided through the public system. They maintained that this prohibition deprived Quebeckers of their rights to life and to personal security in section 1 of the *Quebec Charter* and to life and security of the person in section 7 of the *Canadian Charter*. A majority of the Supreme Court agreed,[69] holding that the legislation violated such rights by denying those who had money timely access to medically necessary services. In doing so, the majority rejected the holding of the trial judge and the claims of experts, governments and public interest groups that allowing private health insurance would drain resources from and otherwise jeopardise the public Medicare system. The majority was equally unpersuaded by arguments that such a move would weaken public solidarity and commitment to Medicare, and would promote social inequality by allowing more health care services to be allocated based on wealth rather than need.

The political message and meaning of *Gosselin* and *Chaoulli* become even clearer when these cases are considered together. Despite the *Charter's* fine words, the social rights it confers do not speak to the security of all Canadians, nor to their actual equality. In *Charterland*, persons who lack property enjoy few meaningful social entitlements no matter how much suffering they endure. On the one hand, the *Charter* places no positive obligation on the state to provide them with the basic necessities of life; on the other hand, they have little to gain from the negative rights that the *Charter* confers on those with property to prevent the state from restricting that property's use for constitutionally protected ends. Thus while the *Charter* provides Louise Gosselin no right to call upon the state to provide her with food, clothing or shelter, it provides her the right to purchase private health insurance in the marketplace – if only she had the money to do so. Like champagne and lobster tails, *Charter* rights are only valuable to those who can afford them.

Indeed the situation for disadvantaged Canadians is worse than this. As cases like *Trociuk* and *Chaoulli* demonstrate, not only do the disadvantaged have little to gain in the way of social benefits from the *Charter*, they have much to lose. The reason, of course, is that rights are not commodities to be given away, but rather entitlements governing the relationships amongst individuals within a society. The extent to which the socially advantaged make gains in *Charter* rights, therefore, is often the same extent to which the socially disadvantaged incur losses in statutory rights – like a mother's right to register the birth and name of her child and the right of poor Canadians to a universal system of pubic health care. Moreover, in the *Charter* scheme of things, constitutional rights are to be accorded presumptive priority over statutory rights. Once a *Charter* right is made out, the onus shifts to the state to satisfy a court based on convincing evidence that the statutory right is required to achieve an important social purpose. If the court is not satisfied, the *Charter* right prevails, regardless of how important or well established the statutory right is perceived to be. For those who take *Charter* rights seriously, there is no room for applying a precautionary principle, even in relation to a single-payer Medicare system that has been nurtured and cherished for almost forty years, and upon which so many Canadians depend.

The Politics of Dialogue Theory

The decisions of the Court in *Chaoulli* and in the other three cases discussed above provide strong evidence that the political assessment of the *Charter* that I and other sceptics offered twenty years ago continues to hold true. The *Charter* today remains animated by a negative conception of rights and a formal vision of equality that favours those with property and market power. Yet it is also the case that the Court over the past twenty years has shown that it has the ability to resist the *Charter's* regressive tendencies when it chooses, both by being strategic in deciding when to defer to legislative choices and by developing creative mechanisms to moderate the impact of the *Charter* within the limits allowed by liberal legalism. Thus while the incidence of poverty and the gap between rich and poor in this country have grown in the past twenty years,[70] it would seem far-fetched to suggest that the *Charter* has contributed significantly to these trends. The *Charter's* greater influence has likely been to legitimize governments that have pursued regressive policies such as privatisation, program cuts, and weakening progressive tax regimes, and to condition Canadians to accept such policies and their results as a legitimate feature of a 'free and democratic society.'   What is remarkable about *Chaoulli*, therefore, is not what it discloses about the politics of the *Charter*, but what it discloses about the politics of the Court, or at least of four of its current judges. By relying on the *Canadian* and *Quebec Charters* to pull down a key pillar of

Medicare – a program that lies at the heart of Canada's commitment to social justice – these judges have displayed a degree of judicial activism that caught many legal scholars, including this one, by surprise. What accounts for this development? There are many possible factors, but one that should not be overlooked is the contribution of dialogue theory. I have already referred to the basic elements of this theory and its justification of judicial decision-making based on the claim that, in the *Charter* interplay between courts and legislatures, it is the latter that usually gets the final say. I have also noted that dialogue theorists concede that *Charter* decision-making discloses no right answers, and that they provide no normative vision to guide or constrain the *Charter* enterprise.

Dialogue theory has had a number of impacts on *Charter* decision-making since it emerged in the academic literature and was embraced by the Court in the late 1990s. Most obviously, the theory has provided judges with a new academically accredited justification for their decisions. And the beauty of the theory from a judicial point of view is that it can be used to justify virtually any decision that the courts choose to make. This, in turn, has allowed judges who have sought to moderate the *Charter*'s regressive tendencies to rely upon the theory to explain their use of creative remedies, such as extending under-inclusive legislation rather than striking it down.[71] In this way, dialogue theory has helped courts to appear more nuanced and progressive in their *Charter* decision-making, thereby further enhancing the image and legitimacy of the *Charter* in the eyes of lawyers, scholars and the community at large.

Another significant impact of dialogue theory on *Charter* decision-making results from the reassurance it provides to judges that their judgments are transitory, and that legislatures can remedy or reverse any problems that arise from their *Charter* decisions. I believe that this reassurance is misguided in that it underestimates the influence of courts and overestimates the capacity of governments.[72] In particular, it hugely discounts both the political force of *Charter* decisions and the constraints placed on governments by market forces and globalisation. Misguided or not, however, it has encouraged judges to see their *Charter* role as being advocates rather than arbiters, and their judgments as being missives directed at government rather than verdicts directed at society.[73]

By bolstering the *Charter*'s ostensible legitimacy, increasing public support for *Charter* decision-making and encouraging judges to perceive their *Charter* role as advocates rather than arbiters, dialogue theory has emboldened judges, including those who are prepared to give full expression to the *Charter's* underlying ideology and regressive tendencies, to be more activist in their *Charter* decisions. This may not be what scholars who advanced the theory intended, but like those who ride to power on the back of a tiger, such scholars ought not to be surprised when they end up inside.[74] This metaphor is perhaps most aptly applied to dialogue theorists who support judicial activism. Kent Roach, for example, has characterized minimalist definitions of rights as unfortunate, and has argued that dialogue theory, by freeing judges from the anxiety that they have the final say, gives them licence to 'err on the side of more robust approaches to judicial review.'[75] I suspect that the decision in Chaoulli does not represent the kind of 'robust approach' that Professor Roach had in mind. But, since he provides no grounds for preferring one kind of judicial activism over another, he has no basis for protesting the fact that the majority in *Chaoulli* relied upon his views to support its decision.[76]

Other scholars have argued that dialogue theory militates in favour of judicial restraint. The leading proponent of this view is Patrick Monahan who has maintained that the theory is best served by judges making 'minimalist rulings' that leave 'the greatest scope possible for potential responses by the legislative and executive branches.'[77] It might be argued that this version of dialogue theory, which was not referenced by the Court in *Chaoulli*, does not place its academic adherents on the back of the *Charter* tiger alongside their activist counterparts. This argument would have greater force were it not for the fact that Dean Monahan has recently voiced support, both as a scholar and as an advocate, for employing the *Charter* to challenge legislative restrictions on access to private health care.[78] By encouraging this degree of judicial activism, he has signalled that his earlier advocacy of 'minimalist rulings' can be disregarded or can be reconciled with this result. Either way, it appears that he has avoided the back of the *Chaoulli* tiger only insofar as he has preferred to occupy its mouth.

Having helped to cultivate the conditions for the Court's judgment in *Chaoulli*, it will be interesting to see what dialogue theorists, especially those who advocate judicial activism, now have to say in response. Will they, for example, argue that the Court was not activist enough, and that all would be well if only the judges, instead of providing access to private health insurance, had ordered government to make improvements to the public health care system? This seems to be the position advanced by Professor Roach in this volume; however it is a position that suffers from two major weaknesses. First, without a normative vision of rights to back them up, dialogue theorists offer no constitutional basis for preferring their remedy to the one embraced by the Court.[79] Second, it is a position that fails to account for the *Charter's* underlying ideology. While activist dialogue theorists may place no constraints on judicial decision-making, liberal legalism and the institutional limits of courts most assuredly do. Thus while judges have been able to moderate the *Charter's* regressive tendencies when it has suited their purpose, they have done so within an ideological paradigm and judicial structure that restricts their creative capacity. It is no coincidence therefore that most judges have balked at imposing major expenditures upon governments[80] or directing the delivery of government programs.[81] Such remedies smack too much of positive rights and political decision-making for even dialogue loving judges.[82]

Conclusion

In rising to new heights of judicial activism, the Supreme Court of Canada in *Chaoulli* has exposed the depths of the *Charter's* regressive vision of rights. More frighteningly, it has embraced this vision to undermine a program that lies at the core of Canada's commitment to social justice, and has done so at a time when that program is already under severe stress from the pressures exerted upon it by market forces and globalisation. It is entirely possible, indeed likely, that the majority was acting out of the very best of intentions, perhaps believing that its decision would prod governments to address the deficiencies in the public health care system. But even judges ought to be mindful of where a road that is paved with good intentions can lead – particularly when it is a road that is strewn with hazards, and with which they have limited familiarity and navigational expertise. While judges may well have believed that their decision would help improve health care for Canadians, therefore, it is far more likely that it will have the opposite effect. By handing the imprimatur of constitutional rights to advocates of private medicine and two-tier health care, the Court has dealt a serious blow to the legitimacy of the single-payer model of health insurance, and the values of collective responsibility and social equality that it seeks to uphold.

What can be done to counter this? While I am tempted to suggest that the notwithstanding clauses of the *Quebec* and *Canadian Charters* [83]should be invoked to overcome the decision in *Chaoulli* and to prevent future use of the *Canadian Charter* to attack single-payer health insurance, I believe that the culture of constitutional rights that has built up in this country over the past twenty years, and the resulting constraints it has placed on the political process, make this unlikely. Moreover, use of these clauses would leave the Court's ruling on rights unchallenged, and could be construed by some as a legislative acknowledgement of a *Charter* violation. In light of these considerations, a more productive strategy, though one that would still require a significant degree of political resolve, would be for the Quebec National Assembly to amend the *Quebec Charter* to stipulate that single-payer health insurance is consistent with its rights guarantees,[84] and for the federal government to put a reference question to the Supreme Court seeking a conclusive decision on the *Canadian Charter* issue.[85] The hope with respect to the reference would be that, with three new judges sitting on the Court,[86] at least two of these would concur with the three minority judges in *Chaoulli* to create a majority against there being a *Canadian Charter* violation.

I started this paper by referring to the views of judges on our health care system, and I will end it by doing the same. What follows are the words of a judge whose opinions were shaped not by a one-day judicial hearing consisting of lawyers' arguments, but rather by an eighteen month commission in which he and other commissioners spoke with hundreds of people and received 1500 submissions. The *British Columbia Royal Commission on Health Care and Costs* completed its work in November of 1991,[87] and here is what its chair, Mr. Justice Peter Seaton, had to say to the graduating class of the University of Victoria when he received an honorary degree in June of the following year:

> We Canadians take a lot for granted. I do not propose that we have a flag raising ceremony every morning. I do propose that we, as individuals, stop now and then, and recognize what a decent society we live in. Professor Evans [another Commissioner] said of another society that, 'they do not mind throwing people overboard as long as they cannot hear the splash.' Most Canadians listen for the splash and they do care ...

> The key is, we do not have one system for the rich and another for the poor. When people in authority are making decisions about health care, they are dealing with the health care of themselves and their families. So long as that is the case, we will have a good system.

If we move to a scheme in which those who can afford it have better care, it will follow that those who have not got money will get poorer care, and it will get poorer and poorer. Those in charge will not be alarmed. It will be the health of 'other people' and 'other people's children' that is threatened ...[88]

Mr. Justice Seaton, sadly, is no longer with us. His views on health care, however, remain as relevant today as they ever were. As someone noted for his compassion and humility, he was a judge who understood that rights in a free and democratic society are best served when everyone has a stake in their protection, and that allowing those with money to buy their way out of collective responsibilities undermines the rights of all. Like most other Canadians, he listened for the splash. And I imagine that he would be saddened to learn that its sound has apparently been drowned out by *Charter* chatter in at least some chambers of the Supreme Court of Canada.

Notes

* Faculty of Law, University of Victoria. I am grateful to Joel Bakan, Benjamin Berger, Hamar Foster, Martha Jackman, Hester Lessard, Murray Rankin, David Schneiderman and Jeremy Webber for their helpful comments and suggestions, and to Jennifer Bond for her invaluable research assistance. © Andrew Petter, 2005.
1 [2005] SCC 35 [*Chaoulli*].
2 Justice Deschamps based her decision solely upon the *Quebec Charter of human rights and freedoms*. However her reasoning, while distinguishable on the basis of the different wording of the two *Charters*, is highly sympathetic to that of the other three majority judges who also found a violation of the *Canadian Charter*.
3 For discussion of these positions see Commission on the Future of Health Care in Canada, *Building on Values: The Future of Health Care in Canada – Final Report* (Saskatoon: Commission on the Future of Health Care in Canada, 2002) (Chair: Roy Romanow) [Romanow Report].
4 Ibid.
5 Office of the Prime Minister, 'A 10-year plan to strengthen health care' (16 September 2004), online: <http://www.pm.gc.ca/eng/news.asp?id=260> ['10-year plan'].

6 CBC News, 'Tommy Douglas crowned 'Greatest Canadian" (30 November 2004), online: <http://www.cbc.ca/story/arts/national/2004/11/29/Arts/TommyDouglasGreatestCanadian041129.html>.

7 As cited in *Chaoulli, supra* note 1 at para. 242.

8 *Ibid.*at para. 138.

9 *Ibid.* at para. 85.

10 *Ibid* at para. 140.

11 See *e.g. R. v. Edwards Books and Art Ltd.,* [1986] 2 S.C.R. 713 and *Irwin Toy v. Quebec (Attorney General),* [1989] 1 S.C.R. 927 [*Irwin Toy*].

12 *Chaoulli, supra* note 1 (Factum of the Charter Committee on Poverty Issues and the Canadian Health Coalition, Intervener at para. 48 [Coalition & CCPI Factum]).

13 *Chaoulli, supra* note 1 at para. 128.

14 Madame Justice B.M. McLachlin, 'The Charter: A New Role for the Judiciary?' (1991) 29 Alta L. Rev. 540 at 545-47.

15 *Chaoulli, supra* note 1 (Coalition & CCPI Factum, *supra* note 12 at para. 48).

16 See *e.g.* The Toronto Star, 'Editorial: Medicare ruling a wake-up call' (June 10, 2005), online: http://www.thestar.com/NASApp/cs/ContentServer?pagename=thestar/Layout Article_Type1&c=Article&cid=1118353812238&call_pageid=968256290204&col=968350116795; and comments by Health Minister Ujjal Dosanjh, as cited in Cristin Schmitz, 'Ruling may Reshape Medicare: But Gov't Insists System Won't be Undermined' (June 10, 2005), online:The StarPhoenix <http://osgoode.yorku.ca/media2.nsf/0/649135adf0264c4c8525701c004efc33/$FILE/RulingMayReshape.pdf>.

17 Government of Canada, 'FMM 2004 Investments for Health and New Funding Levels (10-Year),' online: <http://www.pm.gc.ca/grfx/docs/tables1_e.pdf>.

18 '10-year plan,' *supra* note 5.

19 Anyone who doubts the political significance of this decision need only consult Dr. Chaoulli's speech at a recent Heritage Lecture in the United States: Jacques Chaoulli, M.D., 'A Victory for Freedom: The Canadian Supreme Court's Ruling on Private Health Care' Heritage Lecture #892 (July 22, 2005), online: <http://www.heritage.org/Research/HealthCare/hl892.cfm>. The judgment also influenced the Canadian Medical Association's recent endorsement of private-sector health services: See Trudo Lemmens and Tom Archibald, 'The CMA's *Chaoulli* Motion: Evidence-Based Policy-Making?' in this volume.

20 Romanow Report, *supra* note 3 at 242.

21 See Tracey Epps and David Schneiderman, 'Opening Medicare to Our Neighbours or Closing the Door on a Public System? International Trade Law Implications of *Chaoulli v. Quebec*' in this volume.

22 This view was expressed in different forms by scholars such as Allan Hutchinson, Judy Fudge, Joel Bakan, Harry Glasbeek and Michael Mandel, although the variant set out here derives from my own writings, particularly: A. Petter, 'The Politics of the Charter' (1986) 8 Sup. Ct. L. Rev. 473; A.C. Hutchinson & A. Petter, 'Private Rights/Public Wrongs: The Liberal Lie of the Charter' (1988) 38 U.T.L.J. 278 [Petter and Hutchinson, 'Private Rights/Public Wrongs']; and A. Petter, 'Canada's Charter Flight: Soaring Backwards into the Future' (1989) 16 J.L. & Soc'y 151 [Petter, 'Charter Flight']. For Professor Hutchinson's variant see "Condition Critical': The Constitution's Death Rattle?' in this volume.

23 *Retail, Wholesale and Department Store Union, Local 580 [R.W.D.S.U.] v. Dolphin Delivery Ltd.*, [1986] 2 S.C.R. 573 at 36 [*Dolphin Delivery*].

24 For a discussion of the democratic shortcomings of these arms of the state, see A Petter, 'Look Who's Talking Now: Dialogue Theory and the Return to Democracy' in Richard Bauman and Tsvi Kahana, eds., *The Role of Legislatures in the Constitutional State* (Cambridge: Cambridge University Press, forthcoming).

25 Petter, 'Charter Flight,' *supra* note 22 at 154.

26 *Ibid.* at 155.

27 *Ibid.*

28 *Ibid.* at 161.

29 See *e.g.* D. Schmeiser, 'Disadvantages of an Entrenched Canadian Bill of Rights' (1968) 33 Sask. Law Rev. 249; D. Smiley, 'The Case against the Canadian Charter of Human Rights' (1969) 2 Can. J. of Political Science 277; R.A. Macdonald, 'Postscript and Prelude—The Jurisprudence of the Charter: Eight Theses' (1982) 4 Sup. Ct. L. Rev. 321; and P. Russell, 'The Political Purposes of the Canadian Charter of Rights and Freedoms' (1983) 61 Can. Bar Rev. 30.

30 J.A.G. Griffith, *The Politics of the Judiciary*, (Manchester: Manchester University Press, 1977).

31 J.H. Ely, *Democracy and Distrust: A Theory of Judicial Review*, (Cambridge: Harvard University Press, 1980) at 59.

32 *Ibid.*

33 *Dolphin Delivery, supra* note 23.

34 See *e.g.* David Beatty, 'Constitutional Conceits: The Coercive Authority of Courts' (1987) 37 U.T.L.J. 83.

35 See *e.g.* Petter and Hutchinson, 'Private Rights/Public Wrongs,' *supra* note 22.

36 See *e.g. Irwin Toy, supra* note 11.

37 See *e.g. R. v. Turpin*, [1989] 1 S.C.R. 1296 [*Turpin*].

38 See *e.g. R. v. Sharpe* [2001] 1 S.C.R. 45 [*Sharpe*]. The Court's approach in

such cases is discussed at length in Sujit Choudhry, 'Worse than *Lochner?'*
in this volume.

39 *R. v. Morgentaler*, [1988] 1 S.C.R. 30.

40 *M. v. H.*, [1999] 2 S.C.R. 3.

41 See *e.g. Eldridge v. British Columbia (Attorney General)*, [1997] 3 S.C.R. 624.

42 This strategy was adopted in *Vriend v. Alberta* ([1998] 1 S.C.R. 493 [*Vriend*])
where the Court extended prohibitions on discrimination in Alberta
human rights legislation to include discrimination on the basis of sexual
orientation, rather than declare such prohibitions constitutionally invalid.

43 In *Dunmore v. Ontario (Attorney General)* ([2001] 3 S.C.R. 1016 [*Dunmore*]),
for example, the Court found that legislation excluding agricultural
workers from Ontario's labour relations regime violated their freedom of
association, though the Court made clear that the *Charter* did not require
them to be provided the same protection afforded to other workers.

44 See *e.g. R.W.D.S.U., Local 558 v. Pepsi-Cola Canada Beverages (West) Ltd.*,
[2002] 1 S.C.R. 156 [*Pepsi-Cola*].

45 One possible exception is *Dunmore* (*supra* note 43) in which the Court held
that government had a positive obligation to reinstate some measure of
legislative protection for agricultural workers. Even here, however, the
degree of protection required by the Court appears to have been more
symbolic than real.

46 See *e.g. Irwin Toy*, *supra* note 11.

47 See *e.g. RJR-MacDonald Inc. v. Canada (Attorney General)*, [1995] 3 S.C.R. 199.

48 See *e.g. Sharpe*, *supra* note 38.

49 See *e.g. Thomson Newspapers Co. v. Canada*, [1998] 1 S.C.R. 877.

50 See *e.g. M. v. H.*, *supra* note 40.

51 See *e.g. Egan v. Canada*, [1995] 2 S.C.R. 513.

52 See *e.g. Turpin*, *supra* note 37.

53 See *e.g. Law v. Canada*, [1999] 1 S.C.R. 497.

54 See *e.g. Nova Scotia (Workers' Compensation Board) v. Martin; Nova Scotia
(Workers' Compensation Board) v. Laseur*, [2003] 2 S.C.R. 504.

55 See *e.g. Schachter v. Canada*, [1992] 2 S.C.R. 679 [*Schachter*].

56 See *e.g. Dunmore*, *supra* note 43.

57 See *e.g. Newfoundland (Treasury Board) v. Newfoundland and Labrador Assn. of
Public Employees (N.A.P.E.)*, [2004] 3 S.C.R. 381 [*Newfoundland Pay Equity*].

58 See *e.g. Pepsi Cola*, *supra* note 44.

59 See *e.g. Hill v. Church of Scientology of Toronto*, [1995] 2 S.C.R. 1130.

60 See *e.g.* P.W. Hogg and A.A. Bushell, 'The *Charter* Dialogue Between
Courts and Legislatures (or Perhaps the *Charter of Rights* Isn't Such a Bad
Thing After All)' (1997) 35 Osgoode Hall L.J. 75 and Kent Roach, *The*

Supreme Court on Trial: Judicial Activism or Democratic Dialogue (Toronto: Irwin Law, 2001).

61 A. Petter, 'Twenty years of Charter Justification: From Liberalism to Dubious Dialogue' (2003) 52 U.N.B.L.J. 187 [Petter, 'Charter Justification'].

62 Professor Roach concedes as much in a recent article when he states that 'dialogue is not a theory of judicial review that will tell judges how to decide hard cases,' and then seeks to justify the judicial role in Charter dialogues by reference to a 'legal process tradition' that is no less devoid of normative content: K. Roach, 'Dialogic Judicial Review and its Critics' (2004) 23 Sup. Ct. L. Rev. 49 [Roach, 'Dialogic Judicial Review'].

63 The past five years have seen the departure of Justices Arbour, Iacobucci, Gonthier, L'Heureux Dube, and Cory, and the arrival of Justices LeBel, Deschamps, Fish, Abella, and Charron, although the latter two were not appointed until after *Chaoulli* was heard, and thus did not take part in *Chaoulli* or the other three decisions discussed in this section.

64 [2002] 4 S.C.R. 429 [*Gosselin*].

65 [2003] 1 S.C.R. 835 [*Trociuk*].

66 [2004] 3 S.C.R. 657 [*Auton*].

67 See Benjamin L. Berger, 'Using the Charter to Cure Health Care: Panacea or Placebo?' (2003) 8 Review of Constitutional Studies 20.

68 *Gosselin, supra* note 64 at para. 81.

69 Deschamps J on the basis of the *Quebec Charter,* and three other judges on the basis of the *Canadian Charter.*

70 K. Scott and R. Lessard, 'Income Inequality as a Determinant of Health' (November 2002), online: Public Health Agency of Canada < http:// www.phac-aspc.gc.ca/ph-sp/phdd/overview_implications/02_income .html>.

71 See *e.g. Vriend, supra* note 42.

72 See Petter, 'Charter Justification,' *supra* note 61.

73 One prominent dialogue theorist, for example, refers to the courts' involvement in *Charter* dialogues as 'contributions to political debates, and not judicial supremacy.' (Roach, 'Dialogic Judicial Review,' *supra* note 62 at 52).

74 This allusion is borrowed from John F. Kennedy (Inaugural Address, 20 January 1961).

75 Roach, 'Dialogic Judicial Review,' *supra* note 62 at 72. It is worth noting however that, in the wake of *Chaoulli*, Professor Roach now allows that constitutional minimalism may not be such a bad thing after all in relation to section 7 cases: Roach, 'The Courts and Medicare: Too Much or Too Little Judicial Activism' in this volume [Roach, 'The Courts and Medicare].

76 *Chaoulli, supra* note 1 at para. 89, citing Roach, 'Dialogic Judicial Review,' *ibid.* It is more than a little ironic that the passage that the Court quotes comes from a section of this article in which Professor Roach is trying to counter arguments that his justification of dialogue theory lacks normative foundation.

77 P. Monahan, 'The Supreme Court of Canada in the 21st Century' (2001) 80 Can. Bar Rev. 374 at 392.

78 See S. Hartt and P. Monahan, 'The Charter and Health Care: Guaranteeing Timely Access to Health Care for Canadians,' C.D. Howe Institute, Commentary, No. 164, May 2002. Dean Monahan also served as counsel for Senator Kirby *et al.* in the *Chaoulli* case.

79 There is no clearer evidence of this than the fact that the majority in *Chaoulli* relied on Professor Roach's characterisation of the judicial role within his version of dialogue theory to support their: *Chaoulli, supra* note 1 at para. 89.

80 See *e.g. Newfoundland Pay Equity, supra* note 57.

81 See *e.g. Auton, supra* note 66.

82 Professor Roach comes close to conceding this point in his contribution to this volume when he acknowledges that, 'it is doubtful that judges will be eager to supervise the public system to ensure the adequacy of its performance.' (Roach, 'The Courts and Medicare,' *supra* note 75 at 17).

83 *Quebec Charter of Human Rights and Freedoms*, R.S.Q. c. C-12, s. 52; *Canadian Charter of Rights and Freedoms*, s. 33.

84 I am indebted to Martha Jackman for this suggestion.

85 Given that Justice Deschamps based her decision solely on the *Quebec Charter*, the obvious rationale for a reference would be to end the legal uncertainty created by the 3-3 split on the *Canadian Charter* issue.

86 Justices Abella and Charron and the replacement for Justice Major who is due to retire later this year.

87 British Columbia Royal Commission on Health Care and Costs, *Closer to Home: The Report of the British Columbia Royal Commission on Health Care and Costs* (Victoria, 1991).

88 From an unpublished address to the graduating class of 1992 by the late Justice Peter Seaton, excerpted in a letter to the editor by my colleague, Professor Hamar Foster, that will appear in the September 2005 issue of the Advocate (BC).

Déjà Vu All Over Again: *Chaoulli* and the Limits of Judicial Policymaking[1]

CHRISTOPHER P. MANFREDI

On June 9, 2005 the Supreme Court of Canada arguably provided its conservative critics with the best of all possible decisions. Not only does the judgment in *Chaoulli v. Québec (Attorney General)*[2] open the door to their preferred policy outcome, it confirmed many of their warnings about non-interpretive, results-oriented judicial activism. *Chaoulli* as much as any other decision illustrates the fact that the Supreme Court is a political, rather than legal, institution. It makes policy not simply as an accidental byproduct of performing its ordinary adjudicative function, but because it exercises power on the basis of judgments about which legal rules will produce the most socially beneficial results.[3] Paraphrasing John Hart Ely, one can easily characterize the outcome in *Chaoulli* as: 'We like Kirby, you like Romanow. We win, 4–3. Statutory provision invalidated.'[4] How otherwise to explain the fact that references to the Kirby Report outnumber references to the Romanow Report by thirteen to three in the two controlling judgments? By contrast, twelve paragraphs of the dissenting judgment contain references to the Romanow Report, and its references to the Kirby Report are there only to refute the majority's interpretation of the Senate Committee's findings.

Although the Charter is not responsible for the Court's status as a political institution, it has increased judicial policymaking power by expanding the range of social and political issues subject to the Court's jurisdiction. For a while Canadians appeared to have resolved the debate about the wisdom of this power in favour of courts. There is perhaps no better illustration of this than the tactical maneuvering that accompanied a Conservative party motion in 2003 to reaffirm the traditional definition of marriage and direct 'Parliament [to] take all necessary steps within the jurisdiction of the Parliament of Canada to preserve this definition of marriage in Canada.' The motion presented members of the governing Liberal party with a dilemma. Most of them, including key cabinet ministers, had supported an almost identical motion in 1999, but the government's new policy was that the definition of marriage should be changed to include same-sex unions. Then Prime Minister Chrétien suggested that those members could vote differently in 2003 in good conscience because a vote for the Conservative motion would be a vote *against* the Charter. Why? Because 'all necessary steps' might include invoking the notwithstanding clause, and to invoke the notwithstanding clause would be to undermine the Charter. The Charter's growing authority as the final word in political debate was clearly evident in the buttons that youth delegates to the 2005 Liberal party convention wore to support same-sex rights: 'It's the Charter, stupid!'

Chaoulli is an outlier only with respect to its political orientation. Otherwise, it is the entirely predictable consequence of a process in which the Court has progressively liberated itself from the ideas that there are fixed limits to its decision making capacity and that the Charter has any meaning independent of what judges give it through 'broad and purposive' interpretation. Having brought into conflict Canada's two most cherished contemporary national symbols – the Charter and publicly-funded health care – *Chaoulli* provides an important opportunity to revisit the reasons why some observers remain unconvinced that Charter review is unconditionally good for Canadian democracy. The source of this skepticism about rights-based judicial policymaking is both normative and empirical. In normative terms, the fact that final courts of appeal are political institutions generates a paradox for modern liberal constitutionalism: if judicial review evolves such that political power in its judicial form is limited only by a constitution whose meaning courts alone define, then judicial power itself is no longer constrained by constitutional limits. In empirical terms, complex policy issues – like health care – involve multiple stakeholders, constantly changing facts and evidence, and predictive assessments about the future impact of decisions for which the adversarial system of adjudication may not be well-suited. In the pages that follow I explore both sets of issues in the specific context of *Chaoulli*. I begin with an overview of the *Chaoulli* litigation and the Court's judgments, and then turn more specifically to the ongoing normative and empirical concerns reflected in the case.

Health Care on Trial

The *Chaoulli* judgment had its origins in two separate constitutional complaints about the organization of Quebec's health care system that coincided with the most difficult years of cutbacks to the provincial health care system. In 1993, George Zeliotis, then 61, suffered several medical problems, including depression and a heart attack. In 1994, he began having recurring hip problems; he was operated on his left hip in 1995 and, in 1997, after some delay, he was operated on his right hip. During his year-long wait in 1996, Zeliotis investigated whether he could pay privately for surgery and discovered that the terms of Quebec's health care laws prohibited him from either obtaining private insurance or paying directly for services provided by a physician in a public hospital. He pleaded his case with administrators, politicians and the local media, without success.

Although it was Zeliotis's condition and waiting time for surgery that led to the eventual court case, the key protagonist in the judicial battle was Dr. Jacques Chaoulli. Trained in France and Quebec, Chaoulli received his license to practice medicine in Quebec in 1986. He soon became well-known in medical circles through his attempts to set up a home-based, 24–hour practice for doctors making house calls in Montreal's South Shore region. After intense lobbying of government officials and the refusal of the regional board to recognize his practice in 1996, Chaoulli undertook a three week hunger strike to draw attention to the situation. He then decided to become a 'non-participating' doctor in the public health care system, but soon realized, like Zeliotis, that the disincentives for opting out of the system are very high. Few patients are able to pay directly for medical services without insurance coverage, and non-participating physicians are effectively barred from caring for their patients within publicly-funded hospitals.

Contrary to many popular accounts, Chaoulli was never Zeliotis's physician, but they effectively combined resources for a legal challenge before the Quebec Superior Court in 1997. Together, they claimed that Article 15 of the *Quebec Health Insurance Act*, which proscribes private insurers from covering publicly-funded services, and Article 11 of the *Quebec Hospital Insurance Act*, which prevents non-participating physicians from contracting for services in publicly-funded hospitals, were unconstitutional under the terms of the Canadian Charter of Rights and Freedoms. In addition to Chaoulli (who, exceptionally, represented himself) and Philippe Trudel (representing Zeliotis), the case involved a host of expert witnesses, most of whom argued that the plaintiffs' claims would jeopardize the integrity of the public health care system. In her judgment rendered in February 2000, Justice Ginette Piché echoed these arguments, and was severe in her criticism of the plaintiffs.[5]

Justice Piché ruled that access to health care is, indeed, a right but also pointed out that there exists no right to determine the source of that care. She also affirmed that existing limits on private insurance coverage might be in violation of these same rights because they could limit an individual's timely access to care, but that such limitations would only contravene life, liberty and security of the person if the public system could not guarantee access to similar care. Justice Piché went further to argue that limitations on private insurance that impeded individual rights were legitimate as a way of protecting the collective rights of the rest of the population. Chaoulli appealed to the Quebec Court of Appeal in November 2001, to no avail. All three appellate court judges upheld Justice Piché's decision in judgments delivered in April 2002.[6]

Chaoulli then turned his efforts toward the Supreme Court, his ultimate objective at the start of the legal battle. Zeliotis once again joined the effort, with his counsel Philippe Trudel providing his services *pro bono* for the high-profile case. The Supreme Court granted leave to appeal in May 2003. By this time, the case had moved from a lone crusade to a public debate about private health care in Canada. Five other provinces (Ontario, Manitoba, British Columbia, New Brunswick and Saskatchewan) signed on as third party interveners with Quebec and Canada, as did high-profile interest groups committed to protecting the public health care system (e.g. the Canadian Labour Congress, the Canadian Health Coalition, and the Charter Committee on Poverty Issues). Meanwhile, organizations and businesses with a direct economic stake in the Supreme Court's decision sided with the plaintiffs.

In addition, the case attracted a highly unusual third party intervener in the form of a group of ten federal Senators who had signed the Senate Standing Committee on Social Affairs, Science and Technology report on health care reform. Known as the Kirby Report (after its chairman, Liberal Michael Kirby), it contained some controversial suggestions about the mix of public and private delivery of health care in Canada, including a 'Care Guarantee' to establish a maximum waiting time for each treatment or procedure, after which time the provincial government would have to make that service available by other means (such as funding treatment provided elsewhere).

A full year after oral arguments in *Chaoulli*, a divided Supreme Court – seven justices rendered three separate judgments – invalidated Quebec's prohibition against private insurance for publicly-provided services by a one vote margin. According to Justice Marie Deschamps, the existence of lengthy waiting lists for certain surgical procedures affected the rights to life and personal inviolability protected under s.1 of the Quebec Charter of Rights and Freedoms (which has quasi-constitutional status) in a way that could not be justified under s.9.1 of the same document (which operates similarly to s.1 of the Canadian Charter). Justice Deschamps rejected both the alleged micro- and macro-level consequences of eliminating the public monopoly on health care provision. She indicated that 'no study produced or discussed' at trial supported the conclusion that the availability of private insurance would have perverse consequences on individual behavior in the system;[7] nor did she find adequate evidence that private insurance would lead to increased costs or a general deterioration of the public system.[8] To the contrary, she cited the experience of other OECD countries as evidence that 'a number of measures are available…to protect the integrity of Quebec's health care plan' even with private insurance.[9] In choosing to base her decision on the Quebec, rather than the Canadian Charter, Justice Deschamps departed significantly from the issues that engaged the attention of the judges below her, as well as the parties before the Court. None of the lower court judgments had discussed the Quebec Charter; none of the twelve constitutional questions formulated by Justice Major for the Court on August 15, 2003 dealt with the Quebec Charter; and, contrary to the impression given by Justice Deschamps,[10] only four brief paragraphs of the Zeliotis factum raised arguments based on the Quebec Charter.

Chief Justice McLachlin, with Justices Major and Bastarache, concurred with Justice Deschamps's Quebec Charter analysis, but went further in declaring that the prohibition was also invalid under s.7 of the Canadian Charter. According to the Chief Justice, 'access to a waiting list is not access to health care,' so that 'prohibiting health insurance that would permit ordinary Canadians to access health care, in circumstances where the government is failing to deliver health care in a reasonable manner, thereby increasing the risk of complications and death, interferes with life and security of the person as protected by s. 7 of the *Charter*.'[11] Moreover, she found the prohibition 'arbitrary,' and therefore contrary to the principles of fundamental justice.[12]

Like Justice Piché in the trial court, Justices Binnie and Lebel, writing in dissent with Justice Fish, argued that the question at issue in *Chaoulli* was not one that could 'be resolved as a matter of law by judges.'[13] In their view, there is no 'constitutionally manageable standard' for determining what constitutes 'reasonable' access to health care services.[14] Moreover, even if such standards did exist, the dissenting justices saw no reason, either as a matter of fact or law, to reverse the lower court decisions. On the factual question, they accepted the lower court finding that broad access to private insurance would promote a two-tier health care system that 'would likely have a negative impact on the integrity, functioning and viability of the public system.'[15] On the legal issue, although recognizing that the meaning of s.7 of the Canadian Charter has been expanded, they noted that this challenge did not 'arise out of an adjudicative context or one involving the administration of justice.'[16] Therefore, it did not engage even a broad interpretation of s.7.

The result of these judgments was that Quebec's ban on private insurance for publicly insured services was invalidated by a four-to-three margin. Since a majority of the Court did not reach this outcome on Canadian Charter grounds, the decision did not have any immediate legal impact outside of Quebec. In fact, until at least June 9, 2006 the decision will not have any legal impact even inside Quebec, since the Court granted the province's subsequent motion for a partial rehearing and stay of its judgment for twelve months (retroactive to June 9, 2005) on August 4, 2005. However, the political impact of the case is already being felt. Political leaders in Quebec have remained tight-lipped but the political stakes for the Quebec Liberal government, suffering in public opinion polls as never before, could not be greater. On the one hand, the decision could be an unmitigated disaster, proving to Quebecers the incapacity of their provincial government to protect their collective rights to public health care against incursions from a federal institution. On the other hand, the popular Quebec Minister of Health and Social Services, Dr. Philippe Couillard, could emerge as a champion of Quebec's health care system. And in some circles, a silver lining is that *Chaoulli* may give Premier Jean Charest the ammunition he needs to move forward in his quest to reform Quebec's public programs. Just weeks after the court ruling, his hand-picked working group on the continuity of the health care system, led by Bank of Montreal executive Jacques Ménard, cited *Chaoulli* in proposing the extension of private clinics in Quebec.

As Chief Justice McLachlin noted near the end of her judgment, 'the import' of the various reports analyzing health care in Canada and other countries 'is a matter of some debate.'[17] By citing the Kirby Report in ten separate paragraphs, compared to only one citation of the Romanow Report, she clearly indicated which side of the debate she found more persuasive. At one level, I agree with the Chief Justice's analysis. The debate over health policy has increasingly degenerated into a demagogic contest between 'Canadian values' and 'American-style, two tier, medicine for profit,' which is the unfortunate trap into which the dissenting justices fall.[18] If I were a legislator I would vote to repeal any prohibition against private health insurance on the grounds that individuals should have the widest possible freedom to make decisions concerning something as important to their well-being as health care, especially if that freedom is already limited by compulsory taxation to support a public system.[19]

However, it is profoundly problematic to claim that the Charter of Rights and Freedoms, through the Supreme Court, speaks to the kind of health care regime that Canada should have. Yet this is precisely what *Chaoulli* signifies. Consider, for example, Justice Deschamps justification for judicial intervention in this case. 'Courts,' she argued, 'have all the necessary tools…to find a solution to the problem of waiting lists' and respond to 'the urgency of taking concrete action' in the face of a 'situation that continues to deteriorate.' Governments 'cannot choose to do nothing,' and when they do, 'courts are the last line of defence for citizens.'[20] Implicit in her justification is the assumption that constitutional adjudication can authoritatively resolve apparently intractable policy disagreements. In this sense, *Chaoulli* is a good illustration of the dynamic of judicial policymaking: identify a policy problem (waiting lists), assert jurisdiction over the problem through a broad interpretation of particular rights, and then specify a solution to the problem (access to private health insurance).

For critics of the Court, this dynamic raises several normative and empirical concerns. One normative concern is the basic legitimacy of rights-based judicial review in democratic regimes that place a premium on decision making accountability. Having unelected, virtually life-tenured judges reviewing the decisions of elected legislators poses a special dilemma for democratic theory. A second normative issue concerns the scope of judicial review once its basic legitimacy is established. There are degrees of judicial review, the most extensive of which permits courts to nullify legislation on broad substantive grounds. The principal empirical issue is that certain 'attributes of adjudication,' which flow from its traditional structure' and give judicial policymaking 'its own habits of analysis' and 'repertoire of solutions,' constrain the Court's institutional policymaking capacity.[21] The result is a process that is passive, incremental, focused on rights and remedies, concerned with historical rather than social facts, and poorly suited to measuring the behavioural impact of decisions. There is, in other words, a tension between the type of analysis required to solve complex and multi-faceted social problems and the techniques used by the judicial process to gather, process and evaluate information. In the next two sections of the paper I examine these normative and empirical issues.

Normative Issues

Much of the normative debate about judicial policymaking under the Charter has concerned the meaning and extent of 'judicial activism.' Sujit Choudhry and Claire Hunter have argued that this is 'a notoriously slippery term, which variously means the departure from well-established precedent, adjudication based on judicial preferences, or the judicial reallocation of institutional roles between the courts and other branches of government, depending on who is employing it and in what context.'[22] In order to overcome definitional ambiguities, they define activism exclusively in terms of *Charter*-based challenges to 'majoritarian' acts (i.e. federal and provincial legislation, and municipal by-laws), but exclude non-*Charter* cases and *Charter* challenges to common law rules, secondary legislation and official action.[23] In a response to their article, James Kelly and I offered a broader, yet equally measurable, definition of judicial activism as the willingness of courts to impose constitutional limits on government action.[24] As we argued there, a completely restrained court would never do this, and a completely activist one would do it at every opportunity. However, in the real world no court's behaviour reflects either extreme, with every court exercising a mixture of restraint and activism. Fortunately for this discussion, *Chaoulli* fits both the Choudhry-Hunter and Manfredi-Kelly definitions of judicial activism.

That judicial activism should be a feature of the post-Charter Court should not come as a surprise: it is an inevitable and intentional product of the Charter's design. There is no doubt that section 52(1) of the *Constitution Act, 1982* and section 24(1) of the *Charter* explicitly establish a political regime of constitutional supremacy in which limits on political power are enforced through judicial review of statutes, regulations, and official conduct. There is, therefore, little room for debate in Canada about whether such judicial review is legitimate, or even about whether courts should be activist by interfering with decisions by other political institutions when they exceed their constitutional authority. Indeed, to question the basic legitimacy of judicial review would be to question one of the fundamental tenets of liberal constitutionalism, which is that checks and balances are necessary to keep political power within constitutional boundaries. There *is* room for normative debate, however, about the proper scope of judicial review under the Charter. More precisely, the Court can be criticized for gradually eliminating the structural constraints on its power that flow from traditional jurisdictional rules and conventions of interpretation.

Take, for example, the Court's treatment of the doctrines of standing, mootness, and political questions. The traditional purpose of these doctrines was to exclude certain questions from judicial review on the grounds that there are fixed limits to adjudicative decision making capacity. One point of criticism, therefore, is that the Court has gradually replaced quasi-categorical rules of standing and mootness with entirely discretionary criteria, while absolutely rejecting the political questions doctrine in Charter cases and adopting value-enforcing, noninterpretive judicial review. For example, prior to 1975 standing to challenge legislation in ordinary law suits was governed by a relatively clear rule: only individuals directly harmed in a concrete way by government action had a legal right to challenge it. By 1981, the Court had given itself the discretion to grant standing to anyone who could demonstrate 'a genuine interest in the validity of the legislation' where 'there is no other reasonable and effective manner in which the issue may be brought before the Court.'[25] The significance of this is that liberalizing access to standing is 'directly related to the expansion of judicial power.'[26] Indeed, under traditional rules it is arguable that neither Zeliotis nor Chaoulli would have had standing to challenge the Quebec law.[27] Nevertheless, even the *Chaoulli* dissenters could not resist granting the two men *Borowski*-derived 'public interest standing' to challenge the law, simply because they are Quebec citizens raising serious questions about Quebec's health plan that might not otherwise be brought before a court.[28] Yet, the principle underlying the traditional standing doctrine is precisely that some questions are unsuitable for judicial resolution, no matter how serious.

The same principle underlies the mootness doctrine, which has also been transformed into a discretionary rule. In 1989, the Court properly dismissed a pro-life challenge to Canada's abortion law as moot because it had already nullified the law in question (albeit for different reasons).[29] However, the Court indicated that mootness need not constitute an absolute barrier to consideration on the merits: If the Court is faced with an issue of high public importance, fully argued by engaged adversaries, it *may* be beneficial to mobilize scarce judicial resources and establish legal rules even where a case is technically moot. Ten years later, in *M. v. H.*,[30] the Court illustrated the significance of a discretionary mootness doctrine. Although the original parties had voluntarily resolved their dispute about responsibility for paying support in the aftermath of a relationship breakdown, the Ontario government still disagreed with lower court judgments about the constitutionality of the definition of 'spouse' in its Family Law Act. According to Justice Peter Cory, this was sufficient to make the controversy live rather than moot. Nevertheless, he argued that 'even if the appeal were moot, it would be appropriate for the Court to exercise its discretion in order to decide these important issues. The social cost of leaving this matter undecided would be significant.'[31] While this last statement may be true, it is not obvious why the *Court* should be the institution to decide the issue. As with the doctrine of standing, the Court's treatment of mootness is now driven by the conviction that no issue is in principle beyond the Court's competence to decide.[32]

Although the self-aggrandizement of policymaking authority evident in the Court's treatment of standing and mootness is an important part of the background to *Chaoulli*, its seeds were sown in two early s.7 decisions: the *B.C. Motor Vehicle Reference* and *Operation Dismantle*.[33] In the *Motor Vehicle Reference*, Justice Antonio Lamer held that a 'broad, purposive analysis' of s.7 required that the 'principles of fundamental justice' not be constrained by any meaning the Charter's drafters might have attached to them. To interpret s.7 according to its intended meaning, Justice Lamer argued, would cause Charter rights to be 'frozen in time to the moment of adoption with little or no possibility of growth, development and adjustment to changing societal needs.'[34] 'If the newly planted 'living tree' which is the Charter is to have the possibility of growth and adjustment over time,' he continued, 'care must be taken to ensure that historical materials...do not stunt its growth.'[35] The practical consequence of this approach was to attach a substantive meaning to the principles of fundamental justice. The Charter's framers had sought to avoid this because it had permitted the US Supreme Court to declare laws unconstitutional simply because they 'arbitrarily' interfered with protected rights.[36] It is hardly surprising, then, that two decades later,

Chief Justice McLachlin could rely on a substantive principle of 'arbitrariness' to invalidate Quebec's prohibition against private health insurance.

Operation Dismantle's contribution to *Chaoulli* was to extend s.7 beyond matters concerning the administration of justice and to reject the political questions doctrine as a limit on Charter review. At issue in the case was the federal cabinet's decision to allow cruise missile testing. A coalition of disarmament groups challenged the decision on the grounds that, by increasing the risk of nuclear conflict, it infringed the rights to life and security of the person. Rather than dismiss the claim outright as non-justiciable, or at least as unrelated to the purposes of s.7, the Court declared that 'disputes of a political or foreign policy nature may be properly cognizable by the courts.'[37] Once this policy area was included within Charter review, then every policy – including, eventually, health care – had to be included. Indeed, even the *Chaoulli* dissenters, who expressed doubts about the institutional competence of courts to adjudicate health policy disputes, were unwilling to exclude the issue from justiciability altogether.[38] My point here is not that the Court *will* decide every broad policy issue that comes before it – both *Auton v. British Columbia* and *Gosselin v. Quebec* attest to the selectivity of judicial intervention – but that there is now an established principle that there is *no* policy dispute that the Court cannot resolve if it chooses to do so.[39]

In general terms, the Court has carved out a set of jurisdictional rules and conventions of interpretation that encourage it to 'enforce norms that cannot be discovered within the four corners' of the Charter.[40] The normative problem in this approach is where, precisely, the Court should find these norms. According to one view, judges should, and do, take their cues from 'widely held principle[s] of social morality.'[41] While this standard makes judicial determination of social desirability seemingly less arbitrary, it is problematic for at least two reasons. First, it does not address the question 'Widely held *by whom*?' This is particularly problematic in a federal system, where policy autonomy is granted to sub-national political units precisely to allow for the implementation of divergent social moralities. Second, the emphasis on '*widely held* social morality' (emphasis added) is inconsistent with one of the important rationales for rights-based judicial review, which is to provide counter-majoritarian protection for minority rights. Yet if judicial policymaking exists merely to implement what is already a 'widely held' belief, then one could argue that it is unnecessary except as an acceleration mechanism.

As Ely argued, discovering the fundamental values implicitly protected by constitutions is a problematic enterprise. The central difficulty is that each of the available alternatives – natural law, reason, tradition, consensus, and 'neutral principles' – ultimately collapses into some version of judicial policy preference.[42] Moreover, very few Charter cases actually involve disputes about fundamental rights. This is apparent in the Court's increasingly common practice of temporarily suspending declarations of invalidity, which has been praised as a remedial alternative that respects institutional boundaries and promotes democracy. The Court has (belatedly) adopted this remedy in *Chaoulli*, but if Quebec's prohibition against private insurance is an arbitrary and unreasonable denial of fundamental rights, then it seems unjustified to allow the practice to continue. Either Charter review is a question of fundamental rights – in which case violations should not be tolerated even temporarily – or it's really about policy micro-management.

Empirical Issues

Much of the empirical criticism of judicial policymaking concerns the differences between deciding particular cases and formulating general policies.[43] Developed to decide particular cases, the adversarial system is generally bipolar, depends on historical facts about events that transpired between disputing parties, and seeks to implement retrospective remedies. By contrast, policy formation is multi-polar, relies on social facts about ongoing phenomena, and seeks to regulate social relations prospectively. As an institution with enhanced policymaking authority under the Charter, the Court has attempted to deal with these differences by relying on interveners to represent better the range of social interests implicated by its decisions, relying on extrinsic evidence for social facts, and exploring novel uses of its remedial powers. It is unclear, however, whether these measures satisfactorily address the inherent limitations of adjudication as a general policymaking process. The Court's use of extrinsic evidence, in particular, has been problematic.

Take, for example, the role of social facts in *R. v. Morgentaler*.[44] In this decision, the Court relied extensively on the Badgley Report for its understanding of the practical operation of Canada's abortion law.[45] The Court found two of the Report's findings especially relevant to its s.7 evaluation of the abortion law. The first was that, under the existing regulations, there was an average interval of eight weeks between a woman's first medical consultation and the performance of an induced abortion. What caught the Court's attention was the relationship between this delay and complication rates for therapeutic abortions, which meant that the law infringed s.7 by posing a real risk to physical health. The second finding was that forty-five percent of the Canadian population was not served by hospitals with therapeutic abortion committees. Moreover, access to these hospitals varied among provinces and regions. The Report thus concluded that 'the procedure provided in the Criminal Code for obtaining therapeutic abortion[s] is in practice illusory for many Canadian women.'[46] To the Court, this violated the principles of fundamental justice.

On the surface, the Report's findings, and the government's failure to act on them, support the desirability (and even necessity) of judicial action in the abortion field. On closer analysis, however, the picture is less clear.[47] For example, the Report made it clear from the outset that it was not the abortion law itself that produced operational inequities and disparities in obtaining therapeutic abortions, but rather 'the Canadian people, their health institutions and the medical profession.' Furthermore, it reported significant improvement over the pre-1969 abortion regime in terms of both access and safety. For example, it reported that, with only two exceptions, the rate of legal, therapeutic abortions increased every year between 1970 and 1974 in every province and territory. At the same time, the number of criminal charges and convictions for induced abortions decreased dramatically. Indeed, an alternative interpretation of the Badgley Report is that the impugned law provided a historically superior, if not flawless, abortion regime whose imperfections were the result of factors that could not be easily overcome by simply nullifying the law as unconstitutional. Indeed, as recently as 2003, the Canadian Abortion Rights Action League continued to find barriers to access to abortion.[48]

An even more egregious example of the Court's limited capacity to process extrinsic evidence of social facts is its attempt to formulate a general policy on unreasonable trial delays. At issue in *R. v. Askov*[49] was a relatively straightforward question: had there been an unreasonable delay in bringing the accused to trial? According to Justice Peter Cory, the answer to this question depended on several historical facts: the length of the delay, the specific reasons for the delay, whether the right to be tried in a reasonable time had been waived, and the degree of prejudice caused by the delay. Applying these factors to the particular case before him, Justice Cory determined that the two-year delay between preliminary hearing and trial was clearly excessive, and he stayed the proceedings against Askov.

Justice Cory was not content, however, to leave matters there. Among the evidence submitted on behalf of Askov was an affidavit by Carl Baar about three court delay studies he had conducted. Baar's studies indicated that the jurisdiction from which *Askov* had originated experienced significantly longer institutional delays than comparable jurisdictions. Although the affidavit had a narrow purpose – to demonstrate the unreasonableness of trial delays in a specific case and jurisdiction – Justice Cory read it as a broader analysis of the general problem of trial delay. Based on the affidavit, as well as his own inquiries, Cory identified delays of six to eight months as the outside limit of reasonableness and confidently predicted that this would only 'infrequently' result in stays of proceedings.

As it turned out, *Askov* led to dismissals, stays or withdrawals of almost 52,000 criminal charges involving more than 27,000 cases in Ontario alone between October 1990 and November 1991.[50] In unprecedented public comments about the unanticipated consequences of *Askov*, Cory expressed the Court's 'shock' at the impact of the decision.[51] According to Baar himself, the unintended negative consequences of *Askov* were an entirely predictable result of the Court's extremely flawed use of extrinsic evidence. In trying to formulate general policy, rather than decide a particular case, 'the Supreme Court went beyond the facts in *Askov*, and beyond the material presented in both affidavits, to establish principles of law not necessary for the decision in the case, principles founded on incomplete and incorrect analysis of the material before it.'[52] The Court tried to repair the damage in *R. v. Morin* (1992) by indicating that it had only intended to articulate general guidelines in *Askov*, and by changing the outer limits of 'unreasonable delay' from eight to fourteen months.[53] Finally, in *R. v. Bennet* the Court apparently gave up altogether trying to understand the social science of court delay.[54] Given these difficulties in formulating policy for the administration of justice, where judicial expertise is presumably high, the Court's foray into the health policy debate is particularly problematic.[55]

At issue in *Chaoulli* was the relationship between two indisputable facts: waiting lists exist for certain services in the Quebec health care system, and Quebec law prohibits private insurance for services provided by the public system. If there is any advantage to exploring issues like this through litigation, it is that concrete cases may reveal how a law actually operates. In this case, not even the historical facts of the two complaints shed light on the relationship between waiting lists and the prohibition against private insurance. There was no evidence that Zeliotis himself would have been better off without the prohibition, or even that he had not received 'health care services' that were 'reasonable as to both quality and timeliness.'[56] Chaoulli's complaint was not really even about waiting lists, but about his philosophical opposition to state interference with the freedom to practice medicine as he wished. Zeliotis had no evidence of actual harm (thus no standing), but a plausible and sympathetic s.7 claim; Chaoulli had standing by virtue of receiving administrative penalties, but an implausible and unpalatable s.7 claim (freedom of contract). The very combination of these two complaints as a pretext for judicial intervention is itself illustrative of overreaching.

In the absence of concrete evidence about the relationship between waiting lists and private insurance in Quebec, Chief Justice McLachlin turned to the Kirby Report, whose findings she summarized in ten sound-bite paragraphs.[57] In her words, the existence of waiting lists indicated that Quebec was 'failing to provide public health care of a reasonable standard within a reasonable time,' thereby 'creating circumstances that trigger the application of s. 7.'[58] Under these circumstances, a measure that 'subjects people to long waiting lists' by limiting access to 'alternative medical care' is unconstitutional.[59] Therefore, the prohibition against private health insurance infringes s. 7. According to the Chief Justice, removing this prohibition would improve individual health care outcomes without adversely affecting collective access to public health care.

As an exercise in general policy formation, *Chaoulli* resembles *Askov* in its questionable use of expert evidence and prediction of benefits without long-term costs. As such, it also risks repeating some of the worst features of *Askov*: (1) a confident prediction of limited impact that proves to be terribly inaccurate; (2) denial of judicial responsibility for the consequences; and (3) a follow-up judgment designed to clarify and ameliorate matters. The empirical critique of judicial policymaking holds that there are systematic barriers to the proper use of such evidence and the ability of courts to predict the consequences of their decisions.[60] Information is presented in a way that detracts from its comprehensiveness; promotes unrealistic simplification; exaggerates its authoritativeness; and confuses hypotheticals with axiomatic statements.

However, the problem with the Court's reliance on the Kirby and Romanow reports goes beyond even these systematic barriers, since both reports entered the decision making process during the final stage of proceedings. Both the Romanow Commission and Kirby Committee issued their final reports in 2002, approximately four years after the trial proceedings in *Chaoulli* and two years after Justice Piché's decision. Consequently, to the extent that the adversary process can provide an effective critical review of competing social facts, the Court did not even have the benefit of that process for the two reports. Its only opportunity for external assessment of them came during a four hour hearing.

There are measures that could improve judicial capacity to obtain, process and interpret social facts.[61] However, adopting these devices would further erode the institutional differences between courts and other political institutions that justify judicial review in the first place. Indeed, we accept judicial review of majoritarian institutions precisely because courts presumably reach decisions on a different basis than legislatures and executives. A second paradox of modern judicial review, therefore, is that it may be possible to enhance institutional capacity only at the expense of reducing normative legitimacy.

Conclusion

The traditional sources of judicial authority are impartiality and expertise. The *Chaoulli* decision is only the most recent illustration of why critics continue to raise fundamental questions about these two characteristics as they apply to the Supreme Court.[62] Although the justices are not partial in the sense of having personal interests at stake in the outcomes of specific cases, they do have distinctive visions of the good society that they can advance through their discretionary control over rules of procedure and conventions of interpretation. Moreover, the issues on which most Charter decisions turn are outside the traditional boundaries of judicial expertise and depend on subjective assessments of often conflicting social science evidence. In the final analysis, there is no compelling reason to grant authoritative status to the Court's judgments in Charter cases.

The question of what kind of health care system Canada should have is simply not amenable to resolution through the language of legal rights. Indeed, 'rights talk' may be counterproductive because it narrows the scope of policy discussion by equating legally enforceable rights with a single, 'correct' policy choice. However, in the culture of omnipotence that now surrounds the Supreme Court's approach to the Charter, these limitations and dangers of the judicial process are brushed aside. *Chaoulli* teaches us two important lessons. One is about how badly Canadian democratic institutions have deteriorated when ten senators have more impact on public policy as intervenors before the Supreme Court than as parliamentarians. The second is that we should not be surprised that a Charter and judicial process powerful enough to force fundamental change in a long-standing social institution like marriage might also be powerful enough to force fundamental change in a health care policy barely two generations old.

Notes

1 I wish to acknowledge the financial support of the Canadian Institutes for Health Research. I also thank my colleague and research collaborator, Antonia Maioni, for her input, particularly on details about the litigation in Quebec. Jim Kelly and Grant Huscroft also provided valuable comments on earlier drafts of the paper. Of course, none of these individuals bears any responsibility for the paper's content.
2 *Chaoulli v. Québec (Attorney General)* 2005 SCC 35.
3 Malcolm Feeley & Edward L. Rubin, *Judicial Policy Making and the Modern State* (Cambridge: Cambridge University Press, 1998) 5.
4 John Hart Ely, *Democracy and Distrust* (Cambridge: Harvard University Press, 1980) 58.
5 *Chaoulli c. Québec (Procureur générale)*, [2000] R.J.Q. 786.
6 *Chaoulli c. Québec (Procureur générale)*, [2002] R.J.Q. 1205.
7 *Chaoulli, supra* note 2 at para. 62,
8 *Ibid.* at para. 66.
9 *Ibid.* at para. 84.
10 *Ibid.* at para. 12.
11 *Ibid.* at paras. 123–124.
12 *Ibid.* at para. 153.
13 *Ibid.* at para. 161.
14 *Ibid.* at para. 163.
15 *Ibid.* at para. 181.
16 *Ibid.* at para. 195.
17 *Ibid.* at para. 151.
18 *Ibid.* at paras. 223, 251–255.

19 I should emphasize that this is a point on which my research collaborator, Antonia Maioni, and I disagree.

20 *Chaoulli, supra* note 2 at paras. 96–97.

21 Donald L. Horowitz, *The Courts and Social Policy* (Washington: Brookings Institution, 1977) 33–56.

22 Sujit Choudhry & Claire E. Hunter, 'Measuring Judicial Activism on the Supreme Court of Canada: A Comment on *Newfoundland (Treasury Board) v. NAPE*,' (2003) 48 McGill L.J. 525 at 531.

23 *Ibid.* at 539–541.

24 Christopher Manfredi & James B. Kelly, 'Misrepresenting the Supreme Court's Record? A Comment on Sujit Choudhry & Claire E. Hunter, "Measuring Judicial Activism on the Supreme Court of Canada,"' (2004) McGill L.J. 741 at 746.

25 *Minister of Justice of Canada v. Borowski*, [1981] 2 S.C.R. 575, 598.

26 *United States v. Richardson*, 418 U.S. 166, 188 (1974) Powell J., concurring.

27 For a similar criticism of the Court's decision to grant standing, see Kent Roach, 'The Courts and Medicare: Too Much or Too Little Judicial Activism?,' in this volume.

28 *Chaoulli, supra* note 2 at para. 188.

29 *Borowski v. A.-G. Canada*, [1989] 1 S.C.R. 342.

30 [1999] 2 S.C.R. 3.

31 *Ibid.* at para. 44.

32 There is perhaps no more striking example of this than *Reference re Secession of Quebec*, [1998] 2 S.C.R. 217.

33 [1985] 2 S.C.R. 486; [1985] 1 S.C.R. 441.

34 [1985] 2 S.C.R. 554.

35 *Ibid.,* 554–55.

36 *Lochner v. New York*, 198 U.S. 45 (1905).

37 [1985] 1 S.C.R. 441, at 459. For more on the similarities of *Chaoulli* to *Lochner*, see Sujit Choudhry, 'Worse Than Lochner?,' in this volume.

38 *Chaoulli, supra* note 2 at para. 183.

39 *Auton v. British Columbia*, [2004] 3 S.C.R. 657; *Gosselin v. Quebec*, [2002] 4 S.C.R. 429. For a discussion of the *Auton* litigation, see Christopher Manfredi, & Antonia Maioni, 'Reversal of Fortune: Litigating Health Care Reform in *Auton v. British Columbia*, (2005) 29 S.C.L.R. (2d) [forthcoming].

40 Ely, *supra* note 4 at 1.

41 Feeley & Rubin, *supra* note 3 at 161.

42 Ely, *supra* note 4 at 43–72.

43 Horowitz, *supra* note 8 at 45, 47.

44 *R. v. Morgentaler*, [1988] 1 S.C.R. 30.

45 Committee on the Operation of the Abortion Law. *Report of the Committee on the Operation of the Abortion Law* (Ottawa: Supply and Services Canada, 1977).

46 *Ibid.* at 141.

47 *Ibid.* at 17, 66, 57, 68.

48 CARAL, *Protecting Abortion Rights in Canada.* Ottawa, 2003.

49

50 Carl Baar, 'Criminal Court Delay and the Charter: The Use and Misuse of Social Facts in Judicial Policy Making,' (1993) 72 Can. Bar Rev. 305 at 314.

51 *The Globe and Mail* (17 July 1991) A5.

52 Baar, *supra* note 34 at 316–317, 314.

53 *R. v. Morin*, [1992] 1 S.C.R. 771.

54 [1992] 2 S.C.R. 168.

55 See, e.g., Colleen Flood 'Finding Health Policy 'Arbitrary': The Evidence on Waiting, Dying, and Public vs. Private Insurance,' in this volume and Charles Wright, 'Perspective of an Expert Witness: Beguiling differences in the Interpretation of "Evidence,"' in this volume.

56 *Chaoulli, supra* note 2 at para. 158.

57 *Ibid.* at paras. 140–149.

58 *Ibid.* at para. 105.

59 *Ibid.* at paras. 137, 152.

60 Christopher P.Manfredi & Antonia Maioni, 'Courts and Health Policy: Judicial Policy Making and Publicly Funded Health Care in Canada' (2002) 27 J. Health Pol. Pol'y L. 211 at 218–219.

61 ChristopherManfredi, *Extrinsic Evidence, Social Science and Constitutional Adjudication in the United States: Implications for Litigation under the Charter of Rights and Freedoms.* (Ottawa: Department of Justice, Corporate Policy and Programs Sector, Research Section, 1992).

62 See, e.g., the contributions to this volume by Peter Russell, Andrew Petter, Lorne Sossin, and Allan Hutchinson.

Chaoulli and Prospects for Increased Access to Justice and Care

'Towards a Two-Tier Constitution? The Poverty of Health Rights'

LORNE SOSSIN[1]

The debate about the effectiveness of public health care has become an emotional one. The Romanow Report stated that the *Canada Health Act* has achieved an iconic status that makes it untouchable by politicians ... The tone adopted by my colleagues Binnie and Lebel JJ. is indicative of this type of emotional reaction. It leads them to characterize the debate as pitting rich against poor when the case is really about determining whether a specific measure is justified under either the *Quebec Charter* or the *Canadian Charter*.

Deschamps J. from *Chaoulli*[2]

Those who seek private health insurance are those who can afford it and qualify for it. They will be the more advantaged members of society. They are differentiated from the general population, not by their health problems, which are found in every group in society, but by their income status. We share the view of Dickson C.J. that the *Charter* should not become an instrument to be used by the wealthy to 'roll back' the benefits of a legislative scheme that helps the poorer members of society ...

Binnie and Lebel JJ. from *Chaoulli*[3]

Introduction

Where you sit often has a significant impact on where you stand on issues of rights. Every individual at some point in her life will come into contact with the health care system. Not everyone will experience poverty, and consequently dependence on the state for income support. Rights do not exist in the abstract. They take on meaning through social, economic, political, historical and personal contexts. In this chapter, I suggest there is a disjuncture between how the Supreme Court has approached access to basic minimum levels of sustenance as a matter of social policy and access to private health insurance.

Other contributors to this volume focus on the politics of the courts' constitutional decision-making, but I wish to focus on the implications of a more basic question – when are the subjects of constitutional litigation 'them' and when are they 'us'? I consider this question in relation to two significant social rights settings – *Gosselin v. Quebec*,[4] dealing with a right to public social assistance and *Chaoulli v. Quebec*,[5] dealing with a right to private health insurance. Both cases concern Quebec government policies in relation to the welfare state, and in both cases there is a challenge under s.7 of the *Charter of Rights and Freedoms*[6] (as well as a related claim under the Quebec *Charter of Human Rights and Freedoms*).[7] In my view, these cases, together with related s.7 jurisprudence on social rights, reveal what threatens to become a two-tier constitutional discourse that favours the rich over the poor.

The rights at issue in *Chaoulli,* including the right of self-reliant individuals to obtain health care in the market where the public system is unable to meet minimum standards, represent the upper-tier of constitutional goods. Accessing health care is seen as a matter of 'life,' 'security of the person' or 'personal inviolability.' In this world, the state must justify its intervention in the sphere of private choice and market relations. This is a world inhabited by many affluent Canadians, including judges. How many have waited the agonizing months for an MRI for themselves or their loved ones? How many have turned to private clinics in Montreal or traveled to Buffalo or Seattle for an elective procedure? As Deschamps J. notes at the outset of her reasons in *Chaoulli,* health care is 'a constant concern.'[8] Poverty rights, by contrast, constitute the lower-tier of constitutional discourse. There is no right to welfare recognized in Canada, nor any right to adequate health care for those dependent on the public health system, and few limitations on how governments choose to structure social benefits. If you are unhappy with inadequate resources for housing or the threat of violence, there is nowhere to turn. In light of current judicial salaries, this is a world no sitting judges inhabit and one with which no more than a handful have had personal experience.

Accepting the premise that the Court is engaged in policy-making in such cases,[9] or at least in a dialogue about policy-making,[10] the critical question is *why* the Court adopts particular policy preferences. Why refrain from intervening in policy choices involving scarce resources in *Gosselin*, but intervene in those choices in the context of health care in *Chaoulli*? Should such preferences be seen as expressions of ideological convictions as Allan Hutchinson and Andrew Petter suggest in this volume,[11] or as expressions of personal values as suggested by Peter Russell?[12] I argue both perspectives inexorably shape judicial decision-making in the context of social rights. Because people seek heath care and are willing to pay for it, a public system of health care may involve interfering with these preferences. Consequently, the right to access health care differs from poverty rights. To assert poverty rights necessarily presumes entanglement in a public scheme of benefits to which there is no private alternative. I conclude that the time is ripe for the Court to recognize social rights and public obligations based on the state's response to those in need and that, notwithstanding flaws in both the majority and dissenting judgments in *Chaoulli*, that case may yet serve as a catalyst for progressive change.

This discussion is divided into two parts. The first part canvasses the Court's treatment of poverty rights and health rights, particularly under s.7 of the *Charter*. This part features an analysis of the Supreme Court's decisions in *Gosselin and Chaoulli*, in order to illustrate the Court's growing two-tier approach to constitutional rights. The second part explores three barriers which must be surmounted in order to pave the way for a more coherent approach to social rights and a more socially just constitutional system: these include the dichotomy of positive/negative rights, the paradigm of choice and moral responsibility, and the need for judicial empathy.

Part One: Toward a Two-Tier Constitution?

Social assistance, or social welfare, refers to a series of income supports provided by the state. These supports typically vary across provinces and across several categories. Families with children usually receive greater amounts than individuals. Disabled people usually receive more than able-bodied people. Benefits now increasingly come with conditions, including time limitations on the receipt of benefits and workfare provisions which require able-bodied recipients to be actively seeking employment, engage in state provided employment or job training.

Section 7 of the *Charter* protects life, liberty and the security of the person and the right not to be deprived thereof except in accordance with the principles of fundamental justice. The Supreme Court has read

s. 7 as protecting interests fundamentally related to human life, liberty, personal security, physical and psychological integrity, dignity and autonomy. It has held that these interests are protected because they are intrinsically concerned with the well-being of the living person 'based upon respect for the intrinsic value of human life and on the inherent dignity of every human being.'[13]

While certain statutory social benefit schemes have been held by courts to give rise to certain rights enjoyed by recipients, courts have rejected the claim that the *Charter* or any other constitutional principle created a 'right to welfare.'[14] This is said to fall into the category of 'economic rights' (like the right to contract or the right to work) and to have been expressly excluded from s.7 of the *Charter* so as to avoid recreating a *Lochner*-era role for courts.[15]

The Supreme Court deferred and avoided any opportunity to address the question of social rights under the *Charter* for low-income groups. Famously, in *Irwin Toy*,[16] Dickson C.J., for the majority, left open the question of whether the *Charter* could operate to protect 'economic rights fundamental to human ... survival.'[17] While this obiter phrase is oft repeated, courts have been reluctant actually to extend section 7 rights to such settings. David Wiseman summarizes the track record as follows:

> Claims that have been rejected include a claim to protection against a no-grounds eviction from public housing; a claim for access to expensive and only partially publicly subsidized HIV/AIDS medication; a claim to protection against inadequate care for extended-care residents of nursing homes; a claim to an additional allowance for provision of full-time health-care services in the home, rather than as an in-patient; a claim to protection against withdrawal of social assistance prior to any hearing of an allegation of having resumed living with a spouse; a claim to protection against discontinuance of electricity service, when not in arrears, for failure to pay a security deposit; and claims to protection from a significant reduction in levels of social assistance.[18] [footnotes omitted]

While some judges have offered comments on s.7 of the *Charter* (usually in dissent or in decisions overturned on appeal) which stoked the embers of a regime of poverty rights in Canada, there has been little to encourage poverty rights activists in *Charter* jurisprudence, particularly under s.7.[19] The Supreme Court did not directly confront the issue of poverty rights until its judgment in *Gosselin v. Quebec.*[20]

Louise Gosselin ('Gosselin') had her social assistance benefits cut in the late 1980s after failing to participate in a mandatory job training program for recipients under the age of 30. As part of the province's welfare reform initiative, those people under the age of 30 who did not participate in the training program had their benefits reduced from $424 per month to $173 per month.

The majority of the Court in *Gosselin* concluded that the Government of Quebec did not violate the *Charter* in penalizing Louise Gosselin and providing her assistance at a level well below the minimum level which the Government itself deemed necessary to provide for the basic necessaries of life.[21] The Court split on the s.15 issue of whether the scheme discriminated on the basis of age as it applied only to those under 30. This equality rights challenge was dismissed by a 5:4 majority. The Court also dismissed the s.7 *Charter* challenge by a 7:2 majority. Finally, the Court dismissed a challenge pursuant to s.45 of the *Quebec Charter* by a 8:1 majority. In essence, the various majorities added up to a ruling that whether Louise Gosselin, and the approximately 75,000 member class she represented in the litigation, were provided with sufficient support to survive or not was a matter of governmental policy preference, not a matter of constitutional law.

For the purposes of this analysis, the reasons of the Court under s.7 *Charter* and under s.45 of the *Quebec Charter* analysis are the most relevant aspects of the case. With respect to whether this reduction in benefits constituted a violation of substantive guarantees under s.7, McLachlin C.J., writing for the majority, held that it did not. In so doing, like Dickson C.J. in *Irwin Toy*, McLachlin C.J. left open the possibility that substantive rights might be recognized in the future,

> One day s. 7 may be interpreted to include positive obligations. To evoke Lord Sankey's celebrated phrase in *Edwards v. Attorney-General for Canada*, [1930] AC 124, the *Canadian Charter* must be viewed as a 'living tree capable of growth and expansion within its natural limits': see *Reference Re Provincial Electoral Boundaries (Sask.)*, [1991] 2 S.C.R. 158, at p. 180, *per* McLachlin J. It would be a mistake to regard s. 7 as frozen, or its content as having been exhaustively defined in previous cases. ... *I leave open the possibility that a positive obligation to sustain life, liberty, or security of person may be made out in special circumstances.* However, this is not such a case. The impugned program contained compensatory 'workfare' provisions and the evidence of actual hardship is wanting. The frail platform provided by the facts of this case cannot support the weight of a positive state obligation of citizen support.[22] [Emphasis added.]

Two separate dissents from Justices Arbour and L'Heureux-Dubé concluded that the scheme did violate section 7 of the *Charter* and could not be saved by s.1.

The Court in *Gosselin* also considered whether s.45 of the Quebec *Charter of Human Rights and Freedoms* created a right to a minimum level of social assistance. That section provides:

> 45. Every person in need has a right, for himself and his family, to measures of financial assistance and to social measures provided for by law, susceptible of ensuring such person an acceptable standard of living.

The Court (with only L'Heureux-Dubé J. dissenting) concluded that while the affirmation of a right to income support by the state was clearly contemplated under this provision, it was beyond the purview of the Courts to dictate how government fulfilled this mandate.

Notwithstanding the negative outcome, *Gosselin* did not stymie claims asserting poverty rights under the *Charter*. As Margot Young has written, 'In the current political climate, there are scarce other options to address the very obvious, disturbing and seemingly intractable injustices that surround us.'[23] Some of this continuing litigious approach has borne fruit. In *Falkiner v. Ontario,* for example, the Ontario Court of Appeal held that an Ontario Regulation which deemed spousal recognition in circumstances which discriminated against specific women on the basis of sex, marital status and the newly recognized analogous ground of 'receipt of social assistance.'[24]

Shortly after *Gosselin,* in cases such as *Auton*[25] and now *Chaoulli,* the focus of social rights has shifted from social welfare to health care. At first glance, the Court's approach to a right to health care in Canada closely resembles the approach outlined above to poverty rights. For example, just as the Court has rejected the idea that the state owes a constitutional obligation to ensure a minimum level of sustenance, it has also rejected the idea that the state owes a constitutional obligation to ensure a minimum level of health care. The jurisprudence on health related rights under the *Charter* has been explored elsewhere in detail. Colleen Flood, in a recent survey of the jurisprudence on health care rights in Canada, concludes that courts have not been proactive in this field and until *Chaoulli,* approached medicare issues with overt reticence and deference to government choices.[26]

Until *Chaoulli,* the courts in Canada responded with caution to claims which sought to compel provincial governments to fund particular health benefits,[27] and to claims which sought to compel the federal government to enforce the conditions of the *Canada Health Act*.[28] Where litigants found some success was in the context of some s.15 equality constraints on health care expenditures. In *Eldridge*, for example, the Court held that a B.C. health care facility's failure to provide translation services to a deaf woman violated her s.15 rights.[29]

Eldridge was viewed as a significant breakthrough in *Charter* jurisprudence and judicial activism at the time. The Court appeared to recognize an obligation on the part of government to expend public funds to ensure adequate translation services for users of the public health care system. This case, far from setting the trend, appears in retrospect as the high-water mark of judicial intervention in health care funding, even though only relatively small amounts of funding were involved.[30] More typical of recent approaches to the complex and contested domain of health care expenditures is *Auton (Guardian ad litem of) v. British Columbia (Attorney General)*.[31] *Auton* involved a challenge to the British Columbia government's policy against funding certain forms of early intensive behavioural intervention ('IBI') for children with autism. The British Columbia Court of Appeal, following the *Eldridge* framework, upheld the enabling legislation but issued a declaration that the policy violated *Charter* rights, and ordered the provincial government to deliver IBI services to all autistic children.[32]

In reversing the Court of Appeal's decision, the Supreme Court of Canada relied almost entirely on the source of the policy in order to show that it did not give rise to a benefit in law within the meaning of section 15 of the *Charter*.[33] Because the province had a discretion whether to fund what are termed 'non-core' medical services and because it had chosen not to fund the IBI services, the claimants, in the eyes of the Court, could not make out a claim that they had been denied a benefit. . In this way, Chief Justice McLachlin distinguished *Auton* from *Eldridge*, observing, '*Eldridge*... was concerned with unequal access to a benefit that the law conferred and with *applying* a benefit-granting law in a non-discriminatory fashion. By contrast, this case is concerned with access to a benefit that the law has not conferred.'[34] Some have argued that *Auton* should be viewed narrowly within the context of the Court's commitment to defer to political decision-making over funding new or experimental medical techniques.[35] Nevertheless, it is significant that the Court concluded in the alternative that even if the requested service could be characterized as a benefit, the test to demonstrate discrimination under section 15 had not been met.

Chaoulli, the subject of this volume, represents an important departure from this line of social rights jurisprudence and deservedly has attracted intense scrutiny. The facts and circumstances of the case have been analyzed in the first section of this collection and need not be rehearsed again here. In brief, a 4:3 majority of the Supreme Court held that legislative provisions prohibiting individuals from contracting for private health insurance to pay for medical services infringes the *Quebec Charter.* The Court split 3:3 on the issue of whether these provisions also violate s.7 of the *Charter.* The three judges of the Court who found such a violation, held that it could not be saved under s.1 of the *Charter.*

Both Deschamps J. writing for herself on the Quebec *Charter* challenge, and McLachlin C.J. and Major J., writing for themselves and Bastarache J. on the s.7 *Charter* challenge, conclude that the significant wait times for critical procedures which patients in the public health system in Quebec must endure endanger their well-being and may be life-threatening. Pursuant to s.1 of the *Quebec Charter,* Deschamps J. held that prohibiting individuals who wish to seek private health insurance to meet their health care needs violates their 'personal inviolability' and further that such a measure cannot be justified under s.9.1, which provides a scheme for limiting rights analogous to s.1 of the *Charter.* McLachlin C.J. and Major J. concur with Deschamps J. on the *Quebec Charter* challenge, and further conclude that the measure violates the right to life and security of person of those affected and that because the measure is 'arbitrary,' it is not in accordance with the principles of fundamental justice under s.7. They further hold that the violation cannot be saved under s.1. Finally, Binnie and Lebel JJ., writing dissenting reasons for themselves and Fish J., concluded that the provisions do not trigger a s.7 *Charter* violation, and that it is not the proper role of the Court to be interfering with policy choices on health care.

The distinctions between *Chaoulli* and *Gosselin* are revealing. In *Chaoulli,* for example, McLachlin C.J. and Major J. characterize the prohibition on private health insurance as an arbitrary measure with no demonstrable impact on strengthening the public health system. In *Gosselin,* by contrast, the majority decision (also authored by McLachlin C.J.) accepts the connection between depriving social assistance recipients of benefits and encouraging them to seek self-reliance through seeking private employment.

Can the Supreme Court's approach to social rights in *Chaoulli* and *Gosselin* be reconciled? The traditional analysis would seek to distinguish the two on the basis of negative and positive rights. In *Chaoulli*, the applicants seek to invalidate a government prohibition, and in so doing, assert the kind of negative liberty which has come to characterize *Charter* protections. In *Gosselin*, by contrast, the applicants sought to enforce a positive obligation on the part of government to provide adequate social assistance. One might also distinguish the two settings for social rights on the basis of a paradigm of choice and responsibility. In *Chaoulli*, the applicants are seeking to exercise choice and take responsibility for their own well-being but cannot do so by virtue of state intervention. In *Gosselin*, the applicant is penalized for failing to take responsibility for her well-being and for poor choices. One can distinguish the two cases based on the judicial identification with the claims at issue. The *Chaoulli* scenario is likely a familiar one to judges who experience health care needs of their own. The *Gosselin* scenario, again by contrast, is utterly foreign to most judges, who are more likely to identify with the state's interest in inculcating values of self-reliance and market skills in social assistance recipients than with the plight of the recipients themselves. While both judgments reflect a liberal, individual-rights oriented approach to the *Charter* which has provided succor to the critics such as Allan Hutchinson and Andrew Petter in this volume who argue *Charter* jurisprudence is necessarily conservative and regressive,[36] in my view the link in *Chaoulli* between essential needs and fundamental rights is significant and has progressive potential. Below, I explore these distinctions and their implications for a two-tier constitutional system in greater detail.

The Poverty of Health Rights

Poverty rights and health rights are related in significant ways. Health care and social assistance both relate to the essential necessaries of life. Socioeconomic status continues to be one of the most important indicators of health needs and the lack of adequate health care can increase risks of poverty and dependence on social assistance.[37] While health care spending is up across the country, spending on social assistance in those same jurisdictions has either been cut or failed to keep up with inflation. Indeed, as Martha Jackman has pointed out, cuts to social assistance send many people into the health care system, where addressing their needs is a far more expensive proposition.[38] The lack of adequate shelter, for example, often leaves individuals more prone to a host of preventable disease. The lack of adequate nutrition can lead to costly and chronic long term health issues. Given their reliance on the public health system and the inaccessibility of private insurance schemes, low-income groups arguably have the most to lose from the move to private health care funding and a two-tier health care system.

If a two-tier system of constitutional rights is to be avoided, there are in my view three conceptual barriers which must be addressed: first, the artificial dichotomy of positive/negative rights, second, the paradigm of choice and moral responsibility as a determinant of constitutional rights, and third, the absence of judicial empathy with the plight of the poor. I discuss each of these barriers briefly below.

The Dichotomy of Positive/Negative Rights

The Supreme Court has been as resistant to the idea of a right to health care as it has been to a right to social assistance. The basis for this reticence is often characterized as the Court's aversion to positive rights and its preference for negative liberties, particularly under s.7 of the *Charter.*

The Chief Justice's reference to 'positive obligations' in *Gosselin*, highlighted above, is telling. As Justice Arbour observed in her dissenting reasons in *Gosselin*, 'This is a view that is commonly expressed but rarely examined.'[39] The right to be free from state interference (for example, through being searched or imprisoned by the police) is characterized as a negative right. The right to sustenance by the state or to adequate housing or health care, is by contrast characterized as a positive obligation. On this view, state action is subject to constitutional constraint but not state inaction. Constraints on state action are a question of law; while state inaction, by contrast, is a question of policy.

McLachlin C.J. and Major J. in *Chaoulli* state authoritatively that 'The *Charter* does not confer a freestanding constitutional right to health care.'[40] Rather, where the government chooses to establish a health care scheme, that scheme must comply with the *Charter.*

Even many poverty rights advocates accept this distinction and argue that such positive obligations are appropriate under the *Charter,* especially in light of the fact that Canada is a signatory to the *Covenant on Economic, Social and Cultural Rights.*[41] Arbour J. went a step further in her dissenting reasons in *Gosselin*, suggesting that positive rights are compelled by the wording of section 7 of the *Charter.*[42]

I suggest that the better view is that the positive/negative rights distinction itself is pernicious. It assumes a world of rights-bearing autonomous individuals which is foreign to most low-income people. As Martha Jackman has observed, 'To be in a position to complain about state interference with rights, one has to exercise and enjoy them. But without access to adequate food, clothing, income, education, housing and medical care, it is impossible to benefit from most traditional human rights guarantees.'[43] This is not to say the state should somehow be held constitutionally responsible for poverty. The constitutional concern derives not from the fact of individuals in need (whether due to market conditions, personal frailties, tragedies, addictions or victimization of one kind or another), but from the state response (or lack of response) to that need.[44]

For Mr. Chaoulli ('Chaoulli') and Mr. Zeliotis ('Zeliotis'), the issue may appear one of negative liberty. They wish to enter into private arrangements for the provision of health care and the Government of Quebec, by the terms of health insurance legislation, prohibit this activity. It may well be the case that for Zeliotis, or others with a host of acute and chronic ailments, waitlists may prove life-threatening. However, for those dependent on the state, for whom such private arrangements are out of reach (which may, ironically, include Zeliotis himself if the nature of his condition and his age were to make him an unattractive candidate for private insurers), it is state inaction which jeopardizes patients' lives and well-being in the context of wait-lists. The distinction between state action and state inaction in the context of people dependent for their well-being on state assistance of one kind or another cannot be sustained. Whether the state provides Louise Gosselin with no assistance, with $158 per month, or with assistance sufficient to meet her basic needs, it does not alter the fact that these are all decisions which reflect specific policy preferences, political values and trade-offs respecting scarce resources.

If one fishes out the red herring of positive and negative rights, one is left with a starker and more relevant question: should the Courts recognize and enforce an obligation on governments not to ignore and not to sustain serious harm to the social well-being of those who depend on them? I do not see how the *Charter* or the *Quebec Charter* could be construed as relieving the Courts of this role.

Those who caution against such a role for the Court raise the dizzying prospect of the Court's micromanaging the complexities of the welfare state. As the dissenting justices in *Chaoulli* lament,

The Court recently held in *Auton (Guardian ad litem of) v. British Columbia (Attorney General)*, [2004] 3 S.C.R. 657, 2004 SCC 78, that the government was not required to fund the treatment of autistic children. It did not on that occasion address in constitutional terms the scope and nature of 'reasonable' health services. Courts will now have to make that determination. What, then, are constitutionally required 'reasonable health services'? What is treatment 'within a reasonable time'? What are the benchmarks? How short a waiting list is short enough? How many MRIs does the Constitution require? The majority does not tell us. The majority lays down no manageable constitutional standard. The public cannot know, nor can judges or governments know, how much health care is 'reasonable' enough to satisfy s. 7 of the Canadian Charter of Rights and Freedoms ('Canadian Charter') and s. 1 of the Charter of Human Rights and Freedoms, R.S.Q. c. C-12 ('Quebec Charter'). It is to be hoped that we will know it when we see it.[45]

This concern is another red herring. The Court's intervention, beyond declaratory affirmation that recipients of social assistance, like recipients of health care, are rights holders, can be limited to settings where the state has either caused, permitted or failed to prevent living conditions which are unreasonable and unjustified, and as a result, 'shock the conscience' of Canadians.[46] This is no different than when the Court asks how much delay in holding a hearing is unconstitutional.[47] The Court can provide guidelines or tests or criteria that ensure compliance with the *Charter* without running public programs. In this way, the courts may contribute to the legitimate policy-making process without preempting the legitimate scope for governments of differing political convictions to pursue their own agenda.[48]

As Arbour J. intimates in *Gosselin*, a more robust approach to social rights under s.7 would likely require a robust approach to the relationship between s.1 and s.7 of the *Charter* (and, presumably, between s.1 and s.9 of the Quebec *Charter*). A government may have legitimate and overriding reasons for failing to meet minimum standards of health care. For example, consider the SARS crisis which struck Toronto in the summer of 2003. In order to address that crisis, many hospitals were closed, surgeries cancelled and needed health services not provided. The public health system arguably failed to discharge the kind of s.7 obligations discussed herein. However, the government would have a compelling s.1 argument as to why that constituted a justifiable and reasonable limit on s.7 rights. Further, and more controversially, the

Court's decision in *Newfoundland v. N.A.P.E* suggests that budgetary crises might also justify reduced services.[49] As the scope of s.7 social rights is better articulated, the relationship between those rights and s.1 of the *Charter* will also be subject to renewed attention.

Both in *Irwin Toy* and again in *Gosselin*, the Supreme Court was careful to leave undecided the nature and scope of the relationship between social rights and the *Charter*. In the wake of *Chaoulli*, it is entirely likely that the Court will soon be asked to rule on the question of a right to adequate health care in the public sector. Not only would such a right be consistent with s.7, but also would bring *Charter* jurisprudence in line with s.36 of the *Constitution Act, 1982*,[50] and with Canada's commitment to international human rights instruments which recognize the right to adequate social services. If the Court declines to recognize such a right based on the positive/negative rights dichotomy, it will have traveled even further down the road of a two-tier Constitutional system.

Choice and Moral Responsibility

Should Canadians such as Chaoulli and Zeliotis have the choice to opt for private health insurance if they wish? Should the government be able to interfere with this freedom? Could *Gosselin* have avoided reduced social assistance by being more responsible for herself or making better choices? Should the *Charter* be used to thwart governmental attempts to instill self-reliance and responsibility among those who are dependent on social benefits? The discourse of choice and responsibility is a powerful constitutional norm in the *Charter* era.

Those who are poor, by and large, do not choose to be poor any more than those who are sick choose to be sick. The invidious dichotomy of the deserving and the undeserving poor has animated the law of social assistance since the inception of the welfare state (and beyond, back to the poorhouses of England).[51]

In *Gosselin*, the Chief Justice pointed out that Louise Gosselin was the author of at least some of her own misfortune:

> She ended up dropping out of virtually every program she started, apparently because of her own personal problems and personality traits. The testimony from one social worker, particularly as his clinic was attached to a psychiatric hospital and therefore received a disproportionate number of welfare recipients who also had serious psychological problems,

does not give us a better or more accurate picture of the situation of the other class members, or of the relationship between Ms. Gosselin's personal difficulties and the structure of the welfare program.[52]

The perspective of Gosselin as a 'drop-out' with personal difficulties does not do justice to the circumstances to which inadequate benefits had compelled her. According to her testimony, she relied on charities for food, often went hungry and under-clothed, and suffered from a lack of education, training and low self-esteem.[53] Whether her choices led to her deprivation or her deprivation led to her choices seems a particularly unhelpful and unresolvable line of inquiry.

While governments structure social benefits programs on the premise of morally worthy or unworthy recipients, this view need not and should not be validated by the Courts in the course of its constitutional interpretation. As the Charter Committee on Poverty Issues asserted in its intervenor's factum in *Gosselin*,

> With respect to deference accorded policy choices 'based on some fundamental conception of morality' the Respondent underscores the value of workforce participation. However, depriving people of food, clothing and housing as a means of pursuing this end cannot be characterized as a shared or morally acceptable value. As noted above, the evidence suggests that such deprivation actually increased marginalization from the workforce. To the extent that the conception of morality underlying the Regulation relies on a stereotype of 'morally undeserving' young social assistance recipients, prone to avoiding work, such a consideration is clearly discriminatory in its assumptions and contrary to the 'moral obligation of inclusion that informs the spirit of our *Charter*.'[54]

Morality, law and poverty are intertwined in various ways. For example, welfare fraud is often treated as a moral transgression warranting serious penalties. It is a form of cheating innocent taxpayers of their hard-earned contributions to the public purse. Tax evasion, on the other hand, is often treated as a minor regulatory matter. It is a form of cheating the government, which in any event cannot be trusted with the hard-earned contributions of taxpayers. In surveys, taxpayers consider tax evasion unfair not because it is a fraud on the public purse but because they believe only the rich have the opportunity to take advantage of it.[55]

A similar dynamic may be seen in the context of health care services. Those people with the means to go out of the country or to private clinics for services are not seen as betrayers of a public health system but rather as people doing what all of us would if we could afford it. Who wouldn't go to Buffalo for same-day MRI service if they could afford to? To the extent that *Chaoulli* reinforces this stratification, between the fortunate who have a constitutional right to access private health care and the unfortunate who will be unable ever to exercise such a right, the Court contributes to the normative force of the deserving and the undeserving rights-holder, between the self-reliant and the dependent, between those who succeed in the market economy and those who have failed. It is not only that a paradigm of choice will lead to a two-tier health care system but that it also underpins a two-tier system of constitutional rights.

The Need for Judicial Empathy

The positive/negative rights dichotomy and the paradigm of choice and moral responsibility are not frameworks compelled by the language of the constitution. They are expressions of judicial preference. It should neither surprise nor concern us to learn that judicial decision-making is influenced by the particular facts of a case and the particular circumstances and life histories of particular judges. Nor is it simply a question of personal experience or background. Although such experience and background may legitimately inform judicial instincts when it comes to issues of credibility,[56] should it also shape issues of constitutional doctrine? Given that issues of constitutional doctrine do not take shape in the abstract, especially where fundamental rights are concerned, then perhaps the question is not whether but where judicial empathy should be directed.[57]

The Court has developed an activist tradition in defending the rights of the criminally accused under the *Charter* even though few if any of the judges involved have had personal experience as subjects of the criminal justice system. It is clear that the sense of injustice on the part of judges when confronted with wrongful convictions or improperly imprisoned individuals is palpable. Should a similar sense of injustice arise when confronted with an individual left to subsist on a fraction of the poverty line or to languish on a life-threatening wait-list?

As critics have observed in the context of *Gosselin*, the majority reasons of McLachlin C.J. reflect an attitude of paternalism towards Louise Gosselin and others in her situation. Writing in the context of the s.15 equality analysis, she stated:

> We must decide this case on the evidence before us, not on hypotheticals, or on what we think the evidence ought to show. My assessment of the evidence leads me to conclude that, notwithstanding its possible short-term negative impact on the economic circumstances of some welfare recipients under 30 as compared to those 30 and over, *the thrust of the program was to improve the situation of people in this group, and to enhance their dignity and capacity for long-term self-reliance. The nature and scope of the interests affected point not to discrimination but to concern for the situation of welfare recipients under 30.*[58] [Emphasis added.]

While the lack of judicial empathy with the applicant characterized *Gosselin*, the presence of judicial empathy is a telling feature of the *Chaoulli* decision. The divide in the Court with respect to constitutional doctrine was mirrored by the division of approach to the subject group of the challenge. For the majority, the subject group was those who wished to obtain health care privately but were prevented by the state from doing so. For the dissenting justices, however, the subject group was all citizens of Quebec (and especially those unable to obtain health care privately due to their income or health conditions and so who in effect would have to rely exclusively on a diminished public health care system if the applicants claim was sustained).

I began this paper by suggesting that where you sit has much to do with where you stand on rights. I do not subscribe to the view, however, that because judges typically come from advantaged circumstances, they are unable to identify with the plight of the disadvantaged. I fully accept that Supreme Court judgments are about politics. To say that the Supreme Court is embroiled in politics when it weighs into areas of social rights is to say that judicial decision-making is more complex than we think, not that it is a simple knee-jerk ideological equation, as suggested by Allan Hutchinson and Andrew Petter, among others.[59] Judgment is an expression of humanity and the capacity for empathy across social, economic, ethnic and cultural divides is substantial. The Court's jurisprudence in areas of criminal procedure rights, for example, reflects this capacity. In areas as diverse as police racial profiling and aboriginal youth justice, judicial decisions have been the catalyst for social reform which governments have otherwise been unwilling to undertake.

While expressions of empathy with low-income groups have been rare (in part because of concerns over the choices of those affected), empathy with those receiving inadequate health care is likely to be both deeper and broader. The effect of *Chaoulli*, at least in Quebec, will be to allow a certain portion of the population to opt out of the public health system. The basis for this finding is that the public health system subjects all people in Quebec to wait times for health care which so endanger their well-being as to violate their right to 'personal inviolability' under the *Quebec Charter*. There is little evidence that the departure of Zeliotis and others in his position will improve wait times, and a growing body of empirical evidence to suggest that the departure of middle and high-income groups may well cause the public health system to deteriorate further.[60] The next question to face the courts will be, what of the right to 'personal inviolability' or, in the context of s.7, the right to 'life, liberty and security of the person' of those who have no choice but to rely on the public health system? It is my hope that in answering these questions, the Court will view this constitutional puzzle alive to social and economic realities and to the perspective of those with the most on the line.

While the majority in *Chaoulli* pays too little attention to the needs and interests of those dependent on the public health system, their approach reflects the universal appeal of the right to health. In part because we have a public health system, health rights are not seen as marginal as are poverty rights. There is a greater likelihood of judicial empathy in such settings and less likelihood of the Court viewing recipients of health care through the paradigm of choice and moral responsibility. Generally, those who need medical treatment are not seen as undeserving. In this sense, we can expect to see more judicial activism with respect to health care and as the link between fundamental rights and essential human needs grows, so does the likelihood that judicial activism will finally trickle down to benefit the poor.

Conclusion

The role of a judge in constitutional interpretation ought to be to walk in the shoes of those most in need, whether discriminated minorities, the criminal accused or those dependent on the state for care and sustenance. By recognizing that the *Charter* is triggered by the state's response to need (whether its response is to create a social benefit or to turn a blind eye), the formulaic debate over what is and is not 'an economic right' or a 'positive obligation,' what is and is not 'self-reliance' and a matter of 'choice,' should give way to a principled debate over the constitutional limits of social rights in the welfare state.

In order to avoid a two-tier approach to constitutional rights, the right to opt out of public health care and contract for private health insurance in the interests of better addressing basic health care needs should not be unhinged from the broader right to basic health care rights for all Canadians. In order to ensure a universal and coherent approach to social rights, we need to surmount dichotomies of positive and negative rights (and remedies), and paradigms of choice and responsibility. This evolution of constitutional interpretation will require a judiciary alive to the needs and the life circumstances of the most vulnerable and disenfranchised members of society. This will require increased judicial empathy and a conscious attempt by judges to walk in the shoes of those less fortunate than themselves.

The decision is *Chaoulli* is described by several observers in this collection as a step backwards and as an illustration of the regressive impact of the *Charter* on social and economic relations.[61] I disagree with key aspects of the majority and minority positions, but I nevertheless believe the decision may yet have a surprisingly progressive influence on *Charter* jurisprudence. By establishing the connection between deprivations of the basic necessaries of life and fundamental rights, *Chaoulli* may well be the first step through the doors left open in *Irwin Toy* and *Gosselin* toward constitutional protections for those dependent on the state for their survival. If state obligations to those in need are not foreclosed under the Constitution, as these obiter remarks suggest they are not, then it is hard to imagine more compelling settings for elaborating such obligations than in the basic need for health care and sustenance of those dependent on state support. In this context, the debate over the two-tier health system may turn out to be a catalyst for a far broader debate on the two-tier constitutional system. Such a debate is welcome and overdue.

Notes

1   Faculty of Law, University of Toronto. I wish to thank Zimra Yetnikoff for her dedicated and excellent research assistance on short notice for this paper. I am grateful to Kent Roach for his comments on this paper. I also am grateful to Grant Huscroft, Andrew Petter, Christopher Manfredi and

Allan Hutchinson for their questions and comments regarding my argument during the Access to Care, Access to Justice conference.

2   *Chaoulli v. Quebec (Attorney General)* 2005 SCC 35 at para. 16 [*Chaoulli*].
3   *Ibid.* at para. 274.
4   *Gosselin v. Quebec* 2003 SCC 84.
5   *Chaoulli, supra* note 2.
6   *Canadian Charter of Rights and Freedoms,* Part I of the *Constitution Act, 1982,* being Schedule B to the *Canada Act 1982* (U.K.), 1982, c.11 ['*Charter*' or '*Canadian Charter*'].
7   *Quebec Charter of Human Rights and Freedoms*, R.S.Q. c. C-12 ['*Quebec Charter*'].
8   *Chaoulli, supra* note 2 at para. 2
9   See Christopher Manfredi, 'Déjà Vu All Over Again: *Chaoulli* and the Limits of Judicial Policymaking,' this volume.
10   See Kent Roach, 'Too Much Judicial Activism or Too Little?' this volume.
11   See in this volume Allan Hutchinson, 'Condition Critical: Health Care and Constitutional Rights' and Andrew Petter, 'Wealthcare: The Politics of Charter Revisited.'
12   See Peter H. Russell, '*Chaoulli*: The Political vs the Legal Life of a Judicial Decision,' this volume.
13   *Rodriguez v. B.C. (A.G.)*, [1993] 3 S.C.R. 519 at 585, Sopinka J.
14   See, for example, *Masse v. Ontario* [1996] O.J. No. 363 (Div. Ct.).
15   On the exclusion of 'economic liberty,' see Peter Hogg, *Constitutional Law of Canada* (3rd ed.) (Toronto: Carswell, 1997) 44.7(b). On the link to *Lochner v. New York* (1905) 198 U.S. 45, see Sujit Choudhry, 'Worse than Lochner,' this volume.
16   *Irwin Toy Ltd. v. Quebec (Attorney General)*, [1989] 1 S.C.R. 927.
17   *Ibid.* at p.1003. Section 7 provides that everyone has the 'right to life, liberty and security of the person and the right not to be deprived thereof except in accordance with the principles of fundamental justice.'
18   David Wiseman, 'The Charter and Poverty: Beyond Injusticiability' (2001) 51 U.T.L.J. 425 at 437.
19   While s.15 claims have also featured prominently in the quest for 'welfare rights' under the *Charter*, the focus of this analysis will be on s.7, which addresses substantive social rights directly. For a review of the literature and case law prior to *Gosselin*, see Martha Jackman, 'What's Wrong with Social and Economic Rights' 11 (2000) N.J.C.L. 235; M. Farrel, 'Social and Economic Rights in Canada: Why Class Matters' (2000) 11 N.J.C.L. 225; Bruce Porter, 'ReWriting the Charter at 20 or Reading it Right: The Challenge of Poverty and Homelessness in Canada' (Paper presented to the

Canadian Bar Association, April 2001), available online: CERA <http://
www.equalityrights.org/cera/docs/charter20.rtf>; Lynn A. Iding, 'In a
Poor State: The Long Road to Human Rights Protection on the Basis of
Social Condition' (2003) 41 Alta. L. Rev. 513; D. Wiseman, 'The Charter and
Poverty: Beyond Injusticiability (2001) 51 U.T.L.J. 425; T. Scassa, 'Social
Welfare and Section 7 of the Charter: *Conrad v. Halifax (County of)*' (1994) 17
Dal. L.J. 187; I. Morrison, 'Security of the Person and the Person in Need:
Section 7 of the Charter and the Right to Welfare' (1988) 4 J.L. & Social
Pol'y 1; I. Johnstone, 'Section 7 of the Charter and the Right to Welfare'
(1988) 46 U.T. Fac. L. Rev. 1; and M. Jackman, 'The Protection of Welfare
Rights Under the Charter' (1988) 20 Ottawa L. Rev. 257.

20   2004 SCC 84; for analysis of the issues in the case and lower court judgments, see N. Kim & T. Piper, '*Gosselin v. Quebec*' (2003) 48 McGill L.J. 750.
The Court did recognize a kind of welfare right in *Finlay v. Canada*, [1993]
1 S.C.R. 1080, which concerned the issue of whether a welfare recipient
could compel the federal government to enforce obligations which provinces owed to provide for basic needs pursuant to the Canada Assistance
Plan ('CAP') funding arrangement. However, in 1995, when the Canada
Health and Social Transfer replaced CAP, the obligations owed by the
provinces relating to substantive benefits were repealed. For discussion,
see Lorne Sossin, 'Salvaging the Welfare State?: The Prospects for Judicial
Review of the Canada Health & Social Transfer,' (1998) 21 Dal. L.J. 1
['Salvaging the Welfare State?'].

21   The scheme provided her with an amount that was approximately 20%
of the poverty level for a single person in an urban area, set at $914.00 in
1987. The Chief Justice summed up the philosophy behind the scheme in
the following terms: 'Long-term dependence on welfare was neither
socially desirable nor, realistically speaking, economically feasible'
(para. 7).

22   *Gosselin, supra* note 4 at paras. 82–3.

23   M. Young, 'Why Rights Now: Law and Desperation' (Paper presented to
the University of Toronto, Faculty of Law, Law & Feminism Series, October 2004) [unpublished] at 3.

24   *Falkiner v. Ontario* [2002] O.J. No. 1771 (C.A.), 59 O.R. (3d) 481). Leave to
appeal to the Supreme Court of Canada was granted in March of 2003. In
the Fall of 2004, the Ontario Government abandoned its appeal of this
decision.

25   *Infra* note 32.

26   See, for a recent example, Colleen Flood, 'Just Medicare: The Role of
Canadian Courts in Determining Health Care Rights and Access' in

Colleen Flood, ed., *Just Medicare: What's In, What's Out, Who Decides* (Toronto: University of Toronto Press) [forthcoming in 2006]. For an exception to this deferential stance, see *Doe et al. v. Manitoba*, [2004] M.J. No. 456 (Q.B.).

27 *Ibid.* which reference above is this referring to?

28 See *Brown v. British Columbia (Minister of Health)*, [1990] B.C.J. No. 151 (holding that the B.C. government had not violated the rights of AZT drug users by requiring that they pay a portion of the cost unless); Sujit Choudhry, 'The Enforcement of the Canada Health Act' (1996) 41 McGill L.J. 461. See also Sossin, 'Salvaging the Welfare State?' *supra* note.20

29 *Eldridge v. British Columbia (Attorney General)*, [1997] 3 S.C.R. 624.

30 On *Eldridge* and its cost implications, see Christopher Manfredi & Antonia Maioni, 'Courts and Health Policy: Judicial Policy-Making and Publicly Funded Health Care in Canada' (2002) 27 J. Health Pol. 213.

31 2004 SCC 78.

32 *Auton (Guardian ad litem of) v. British Columbia (Attorney General)* (2002), 220 D.L.R. (4th) 411, 2002 BCCA 538 [*Auton*].

33 For a discussion of the Court's formalistic approach to the application of the *Charter* in *Auton*, see L. Pottie & L. Sossin, 'Demystifying the Boundaries of Public Law: Policy, Discretion and Social Welfare' (2005) U.B.C. Law Rev. 147.

34 *Auton, supra* note 32 at para. 38 [emphasis in original].

35 See Donna Greschner & Steven Lewis, '*Auton* and Evidence-Based Decision Making: Medicare in the Courts' (2003) 82 Can. Bar Rev. 501. Even that reading of the decision may be unduly broad. In *Wynberg v. Ontario*, (2005) 252 D.L.R. (4th) 10 (Sup. Ct.), Kiteley J. distinguished *Auton* on its facts in finding the Ontario Government liable for autism funding for those over six years of age on equality grounds. This decision is currently under appeal.

36 See in this volume Allan Hutchinson 'Condition Critical: Health Care and Constitutional Rights' and Andrew Petter, 'Wealthcare: The Politics of Charter Revisited.'

37 See Martha Jackman, 'Misdiagnosis or Cure? Charter Review of the Health Care System' in *Just Medicare: What's In, What's Out, Who Decides* (Toronto: University of Toronto Press) [forthcoming in 2006].

38 *Ibid.* at 15.

39 *Supra* note 4 at para. 319.

40 *Chaoulli, supra* note 2 at para. 104.

41 Article 11 of the Covenant contains a minimum right to an 'adequate standard of living,' 16 December 1966, 993 U.N.T., s.3. Similarly, Article 22

of the Universal Declaration of Human Rights, GA Res. 217(III), UN GAO, 3d. Sess., Supp. No. 13, UN Doc. A/810 (1948) provides that 'Everyone has a right to a standard of living adequate for the health and well-being of himself and of his family, including food, clothing, housing and medical care and necessary social services...' For discussion of this covenant and its influence (and lack of influence) over Charter interpretation, see Bruce Porter, 'Judging Poverty Rights: Using International Human Rights Law to Refine Scope of Charter Rights (2000) 15 J.L. & Soc. Pol'y 117, available online: CERA <http://www.equalityrights.org/cera/docs/poverty.htm>.

42   *Gosselin, supra* note 4 at para. 309.

43   Martha Jackman, 'What's Wrong with Social and Economic Rights?' *supra* note 19 at 243.

44   See the discussion of this point in Arbour J.'s dissent in *Gosselin*, where she states that, '...government accountability in the context of claims of underinclusion is to be understood simply in terms of the existence of a positive state obligation for which the state may or may not be causally responsible' (para. 381). See also *Dunmore v. Ontario (Attorney General)*, [2001] 3 S.C.R. 1016, in which the Court refers to a constitutional violation where the state sustains a violation of fundamental freedoms even where the state did not initiate the violation (at para. 36).

45   *Chaoulli, supra* note 2 at para. 163.

46   For a discussion of this term in the context of the s.7 *Charter* standard, see *Suresh v. Canada (Minister of Citizenship and Immigration)* 2002 SCC 1 at para. 49 .

47   See, for example, *Blencoe v. British Columbia*, [2000] 2 S.C.R. 307.

48   For discussion (and an argument for constitutionally required wait time guarantees, see Stanley Hartt and Patrick Monahan, *The Charter and Health Care: Guaranteeing Timely Access to Health Care for Canadians* (Toronto: CD Howe Institute Commentary, No. 164, 2002) and Stanley Hartt, 'Arbitrariness, Randomness and the Principles of Fundamental Justice: Wait Time Guarantees,' this volume. This is analogous to the approach to social rights under the new South African constitution, where courts apply a reasonableness test to the attempt to address social needs by the state. For a discussion of this approach, see D. M. Davis, P. Macklem and G. Mundlak, 'Social Rights, Social Citizenship, and Transformative Constitutionalism: A Comparative Assessment' in Joanne Conaghan et al., *Labour Law in an Era of Globalization* (Oxford: Oxford University Press, 2002) 511–34.

49   2004 SCC 66 (where the Court held that the Newfoundland government's decision not to satisfy a pay equity award violated s.15 of the *Charter* but was a reasonable limit in light of the province's fiscal situation).

50 Section 36 commits governments, *inter alia*, to providing 'essential public service of reasonable quality to all Canadians.'

51 See Michael Katz, *The Undeserving Poor: From the War on the Poverty to the War on Welfare* (New York: Pantheon, 1989).

52 *Gosselin, supra* note 4 at para. 8.

53 Testimony of L. Gosselin, Vol. 1 at 102, 104, 111, 130, 137, 146, cited in the factum of the Charter Committee on Poverty Issues, http://www.povertyissues.org/gossellin/gosselinfactum.htm at para. 38

54 *Ibid* at para. 57.

55 See L. Sossin, 'Welfare State Crime: The Politics of Tax Evasion in the 1980s' (1992) 12 Windsor Y.B. Access Just. 98.

56 See *R. v. R.D.S.*, [1997] 3 S.C.R. 484.

57 For a discussion of empathy in this context, see Toni Massaro, 'Empathy, Legal Storytelling and the Rule of Law: New Words, Old Wounds' (1989) 87 Mich. L. Rev. 2099.

58 *Supra*, note 4 at para. 66.

59 See in this volume Allan Hutchinson 'Condition Critical: Health Care and Constitutional Rights' and Andrew Petter, 'Wealthcare: The Politics of Charter Revisited.'

60 See in this volume Alan Maynard, 'How to Defend a Public Health Care System: Lessons from Abroad' and Colleen M. Flood, 'Finding Health Policy 'Arbitrary': The Evidence on Waiting, Dying and Public vs. Private Insurance.'

61 See in this volume Allan Hutchinson 'Condition Critical: Health Care and Constitutional Rights' and Andrew Petter, 'Wealthcare: The Politics of Charter Revisited.'

The Courts and Medicare: Too Much or Too Little Judicial Activism?

KENT ROACH

The boldness of the Supreme Court's decision in *Chaoulli v. Quebec (Attorney General)*[1] caught many by surprise. Few expected that a Court that had recently rejected equality claims that autistic children should receive intensive treatment[2] would hold that Quebec's prohibition on private health insurance and private payments for services covered in the public system was fundamentally unjust. The decision was even more surprising because the Court had refused under s.7 of the Charter to examine the adequacy of social assistance or to require that the criminal law should only be used to prevent harm or that it should respect the best interests of children.[3] Like the gay marriage cases, *Chaoulli* raised the spectre of judicial activism, but in a way that could personally affect all Canadians depending on whether private markets for health insurance flourish and their effects on the public system.

Chaoulli raises concerns on all definitions of judicial activism. A number of essays in this volume address the question of whether the Court made radical new law and allowed individual rights to trump collective interests.[4] In this chapter, I will focus on two other aspects of judicial activism, first whether the Court went out of its way to decide this case and second whether it imposed a private funding remedy for medicare in a manner that precludes continued dialogue. [5]The issues examined in this chapter involve questions of legal procedure that are easy to miss and dismiss. Even the Supreme Court itself did not spend much time on them. It took the judges only a few paragraphs to decide that the applicants had public interest standing to challenge the Quebec law even though they were not on a waiting list. After considering extensive supplementary submissions from the parties and the intervenors, the Court did not even bother to give reasons when it subsequently suspended its judgment until June, 2006.[6] Decisions about standing- who is entitled to litigate- are connected with issues of remedies- who should benefit from the court's decision. Much about *Chaoulli* and the future role of the courts in medicare can be revealed by examining these neglected issues.

My thesis is that the majority of the Court in *Chaoulli* avoided many of the complexities of judicial intervention in the health care field because they granted standing to self-appointed critics of the public system and advocates of private health care as opposed to those who were actually on a waiting list or otherwise denied needed and urgent medical treatment. The Court failed to grapple with seemingly intractable problems of waiting lists and limited capacity and instead relied on a controversial prediction that increasing the role of the private sector would improve the health care system. In addition, the Court considered only the case for an easy remedy- a simple, one-shot negative remedy of holding Quebec's legislative restrictions on private health insurance inoperative- as opposed to more difficult and positive remedies that would give an affected person needed medical treatment or address systemic flaws in the delivery of health care. Despite the willingness of the majority to intervene in *Chaoulli,* courts may be reluctant to issue more complex remedies that attempt to achieve systemic reforms of the public system even though such remedies may be necessary to ensure that the promise of *Chaoulli* is realized for all Canadians especially those who will be unable to purchase private health insurance. This makes it even more important that Canadian governments do not take *Chaoulli* as the last word on medicare reform.

My examination of the legal details of the case should interest Canadians because it suggests that despite the dramatic and unexpected decision in *Chaoulli,* the courts may continue to be reluctant to intervene in health care to assist those who suffer on public waiting lists that could become longer should doctors and facilities be diverted to the private sector as a result of the decision.[7] In this sense, the message of *Chaoulli* could be truly and cruelly ironic. Judges who were prepared to hold Quebec's restrictions on private health insurance inoperative in a case brought by those not on any waiting list may not be prepared to intervene to require the government to provide potentially life saving treatment to those languishing on a wait list. In contrast, the minority of the Court who refused to strike down the Quebec laws, rightly in my view, left open the possibility that courts could in the future 'supervise enforcement on the rights of those patients who are directed affected...on a case-by-case basis...rejection of the appellants' global challenges to Quebec's health plan would not foreclose individual patients from seeking individual relief tailored to their individual circumstances.'[8] The majority of the Court may have simply opened the system to more private health insurance that may benefit those who can afford it while doing nothing for the less advantaged who must rely on the public system. From the vantage point of those who cannot or do not contract out of the public system in the new world created by *Chaoulli*, the problem may actually be too little judicial activism.

The Perils of Public Interest Standing

Who are Jacques Chaoulli and George Zeliotis and why did the courts even consider their challenge to Quebec's restrictions on private health insurance? The Supreme Court's judgments reveal little about the litigants in this landmark case. The trial judge did not doubt the sincerity of Mr. Zeliotis's belief that he would have had better access to hip replacement surgery in a private system, but she expressed doubts about its accuracy. The trial judge examined Dr. Chaoulli's attempts to establish a private house call and ambulance service, concluding that he 'obstinately insisted on practising medicine as he pleased...Dr. Chaoulli never testified that he had received inadequate care or that the system had not responded to his personal health care needs.'[9] Despite these findings, the Supreme Court unanimously held that both men had standing not as individuals directly affected by waiting lists, but as representatives of the public interest.

Justice Deschamps dismissed the standing issue in a paragraph concluding that 'the question is not whether the appellants are able to show they are personally affected by an infringement,' but rather whether they had a genuine interest as citizens in the constitutionality of the legislation, raised a serious issue and whether there was 'no other effective means available to them.'[10] Justice Binnie and LeBel in their dissent also granted the two men public interest standing as citizens. They reasoned that the applicants' arguments against the ban on private insurance were 'not limited to a case-by-case consideration' and that 'it would be unreasonable to expect a seriously ailing person to bring a systemic challenge to the whole health plan, as was done here.'[11] Nevertheless, they eventually held that the abstract and debatable nature of the applicants' public interest claims were fatal to their success while leaving themselves open to case by case claims that could presumably be brought by the directly affected.

The decision to grant public interest standing follows an expansion of standing since the 1970's that has recognized the rights of opponents of bilingualism and legalized abortions to claim that laws violated the Constitution. In many ways, public interest standing is a good thing that increases access to justice and recognizes that sometimes no one is directly affected by a law and sometimes those who are directly affected by the law cannot be expected to challenge it in court. At the same time, however, public interest standing can allow cases to go before the court in an abstract manner without facts that add flesh and blood to the case. The absence of concrete adjudicative facts may be more of a problem in some cases than others. For example, the absence of such facts were not a problem when courts rejected abstract claims that bilingualism or legalized abortions were unconstitutional. On the other hand, facts may be needed to help the court make contextual judgments and balance competing interests when the court is prepared to recognize legal rights.

The Court in *Chaoulli* applied its 1981 precedent that allowed anti-abortion activist Joseph Borowski to challenge the legalization of abortion under the Criminal Code.[12] The grant of standing and the lack of specific facts in that case was not a problem if the court was prepared to hold, as it eventually did, that the fetus did not have legally enforceable rights, but it would have been a problem had the court recognized such rights. In such a case, the court would need a factual background in order to reconcile and balance fetal rights with the competing rights of women who carry the fetus. A limited decision on the facts of the case could then be revised and refined in subsequent litigation. The grant of public interest standing in *Chaoulli* to those not directly affected by a waiting list meant that the judgment focused entirely on dynamic policy predictions and did not deal with the concrete facts of any individual case. The Attorney General Quebec made this point strongly in the oral hearing of the case, arguing that the appellants put forth 'an inadequate and highly hypothetical factual context' that asked the court to accept that someone in Quebec would be denied access to medically required treatment because of the prohibition on medical insurance 'without anyone knowing, notably the nature of health services which would be required, the availability of such services, the causes of an eventual delay…'[13] The lack of specific facts meant that Quebec had to justify every possible waiting list and every possible hypothetical.

In prior cases, the Court had been cautious about deciding constitutional issues in the absence of concrete facts.[14] In 1992, it denied standing to the Canadian Council of Churches to challenge new procedures for determining refugee status on the basis that individual refugee applicants were more directly affected.[15] In 1993, Justice Major denied standing to two corporations to challenge a holiday closing law reasoning that 'in the absence of facts specific to the appellants, both the court's ability to ensure that it hears from the most directly affected and that Charter issues are decided in a proper factual context are compromised.' He relied on an earlier case that would seem to apply to *Chaoulli:* 'Charter decisions should not and must not be made in a factual vacuum. To attempt to do so would trivialize the Charter and inevitably result in ill-considered opinions. The presentation of facts is not...a mere technicality; rather, it is essential to a proper consideration of Charter issues....Charter decisions cannot be based upon the unsupported hypotheses of enthusiastic counsel.'[16] The procedural decision to hear the case affected its substance. The neglect of the facts of the individual case before the court make the judgments read more like briefs to a legislative committee than an ordinary judicial decision. *Chaoulli* was framed as a sweeping and abstract private reference case and the Court's answer to the case was not surprisingly just as sweeping and abstract.

In the absence of any concrete adjudicative facts, all of the Court's judgment revolved around dynamic and contentious predictions about the effects of Quebec's legislation or what Sujit Choudhry calls 'educated guesses.'[17] Legislative or policy 'facts' are a moving and elusive target and indeed much of Quebec's request that the Court suspend it judgment focused on the numerous improvements that Quebec has made to its health system since the trial judge heard the evidence. Although courts at times, and particularly under s.1 of the Charter, have to grapple with policy issues, the core of their expertise, as well as their institutional advantage over legislatures, lies in deciding legal issues based on the concrete adjudicative facts of individual cases. Although many argue a weakness of the courts is their focus on the particular case[18], it also gives them an institutional advantage over legislatures and non-adjudicative executive bodies who may lose sight of the plight of individuals in their focus on fiscal management. To this extent, judicial intervention has the potential to add value and sharpen debates about medicare. The Court in *Chaoulli,* however, did not work the institutional advantage of courts.

Although the majority of the Court stressed that it had no choice but to decide the case, it could have avoided the issue. The three judges who granted leave to appeal (all of whom ended up part of the majority judgment) could have refused to hear the case given the unanimous decisions of the courts below.[19] Even after leave was granted, the Court could have refused to grant public interest standing and have waited for litigation by directly affected individuals. *Chaoulli* is an activist decision in the sense that it dealt with an issue that the court could have legitimately declined to have decided.

A Case that Should Not Been Decided: Passive Virtues and Constitutionalism Minimalism

The Court's bold decision raises the issue of whether Canadian courts should engage in what Alexander Bickel has defended as the passive virtues of avoiding constitutional judgment until absolutely necessary and what Cass Sunstein has defended as constitutional minimalism which limits constitutional judgment to the facts of the case. Bickel argued that a particular virtue of the courts was their ability 'to relate a legislative policy to the flesh and blood facts of an actual case.'[20] Sunstein similarly argued that minimalism allowed judges 'like sailors on an unfamiliar sea-or a government attempting to regulate a shifting labor market...[to] take small, reversible steps, allowing itself to accommodate unexpected developments.' [21]Both Bickel and Sunstein were concerned that unnecessary judicial pronouncements would aggravate the counter-majoritarian difficulty of unelected courts in a democracy, as well the likelihood of courts making mistakes as they ventured beyond the concrete facts of the case before them.

Although I embrace Bickel's understanding of judicial review as part of a dialogue with legislatures and society, I have in the past argued that Canadian courts need not be attracted to passive virtues and constitutional minimalism because of the ability of Canadian legislatures to limit and override rights under the Charter.[22] *Chaoulli*, combined with the Court's approach to s.7 of the Charter, however causes me to qualify my previous views. The case for what Patrick Monahan has defended as 'particularistic court decisions that are fact-sensitive and context specific' and that 'leave more room for dialogue with the legislature than would a court decision announcing a broad or sweeping new rule that went far beyond the facts of the case'[23] is stronger in s.7 cases such as *Chaoulli* because the Court has effectively read s.1 out of s.7 by holding that limits on s.7 rights could only be justified under s.1 in emergencies. In doing so, the Court has undermined the dialogic structure of the Charter which is designed to give governments ample opportunity to justify limitations on Charter rights. In many cases, the result has been that the Court has been cautious, often too cautious, in recognizing rights under s.7. [24]Alas not in *Chaoulli*.

The case for crafting a minimal judgment is also stronger because the Court was faced only with contentious policy predictions that increased privatization would either improve or harm the efficiency of the health care system as opposed to a proven injustice. Although the majority of the Court made strong arguments about the unique contributions and responsibilities of courts in this case, their judgment ignored the judiciary's most distinctive feature: its ability to consider claims of injustice based on the concrete effects of government policies on particular individuals and groups.

Medicare Litigation by those Directly Affected by Waiting Lists?

The Court claims to be justified in granting public interest standing because it would be unrealistic to expect litigation by a directly affected individual awaiting medical treatment. There is, however, precedent for health care litigation by the directly affected. In the 1997 case of *Eldridge v. British Columbia*[25], the Court decided a moot case because the hearing impaired applicants had already endured medical procedures without the communication provided by the interpretation service. If courts are to decide health care cases on the facts of individual cases, it may be necessary for them to decide cases even though the medical crisis that prompted the case has passed. The facts of these moot cases may give the courts a better factual platform on which to make their decisions.[26]

Show Me the Money: Damage Claims

In addition to deciding moot cases, courts could decide damage claims made by those who are denied timely treatment. In 2004, a Quebec Court authorized a class action brought on behalf of about 10,000 women who had since 1997 had to wait more than 8 weeks for radiotherapy for breast cancer. Healthcare class actions have the potential to command the attention of governments.[27] Nevertheless, the courts may be cautious. For example, the Supreme Court rejected a class action damage claim brought by those on social assistance in Quebec on the basis that social economic rights under the Quebec Charter should only be enforced by way of a declaration. The Court was also concerned about the difficulties of calculating such damages and their impact on the government's finances.[28] The double standard between health care and social assistance litigation that Lorne Sossin observes in his chapter might be increased if class actions flourished in the health care context.[29]

Individuals may also sue for damages caused by the lack of health care. The trial judge in *Auton* only awarded the parents $20,000 symbolic damages for violation of the Charter, but an Ontario judge in *Wynberg* awarded larger damages to compensate for the cost of past and future autism treatment and defended damages as a traditional remedy that does not interfere with governmental decision-making.[30] Contingency fees may make damage litigation more accessible, but many people will be unable to pay disbursements or adverse cost awards. Damage awards can create distributional inequities. Some with the ability to litigate will receive damages but many others will receive no damages. It is also not clear that damage awards will require governments to improve health services. It may only increase their defensive measures such as warnings about the dangers of waiting lists or the development of wait lists for wait lists. Sporadic and protracted civil litigation is unlikely to require governments to reduce waiting times especially compared to administrative schemes such as the health care guarantee proposed by the Kirby Committee and advocated by Stanley Hartt in his contribution to this volume. [31]

The Legal Emergency Room: Interlocutory Injunctions and Administrative Appeals

Another way health care litigation can be brought by the directly affected is to allow litigants to enter the legal equivalent of the emergency room by applying for a pre-trial or interlocutory injunction. In order to obtain such an interim remedy, applicants must demonstrate that they risk irreparable harm; that they have a serious legal case; and that the balance of convenience, including the public interest, favours granting an interim remedy before it is possible to have a full trial on the merits. In cases involving medically required treatment, it may be quite easy for applicants to satisfy the irreparable harm requirement. It is less clear, however, whether they can demonstrate a serious legal issue. It will not be enough to show that their rights to life, liberty or security of the person are affected, but also that the impugned government policy may violate the principles of fundamental justice. In *Chaoulli*, the three judges who held that there was a s.7 violation based their decision on the arbitrariness of the complete ban on private medical insurance in terms of protecting the public health care system. It may be more difficult for other Charter applicants to prove that less absolute measures or a particular waiting list is arbitrary especially if the government can demonstrate that it acted reasonably in making difficult trade-offs and triage decisions. At the same time, waiting lists could be held to be arbitrary if they continue to be based on the ability of particular doctors to do operations in specific hospitals as opposed to rational provincial wide criteria as have been developed in Saskatchewan and are planned in Ontario.[32] Litigation may place increased and beneficial pressure on provinces to increase the rationality of waiting lists.

Even if a court accepts that a patient risks irreparable harm and has a serious Charter case, it will still have to find that the balance of convenience and the public interest favours granting the interim injunction requiring treatment. Applicants will argue that exemptions from waiting lists will cause only limited harm to the public system, but governments will argue that court-ordered queue jumping will harm the public interest and the integrity of waiting lists. Much will depend on how individual judges exercise their remedial discretion.

Requests for interlocutory injunctions to obtain medical treatment may increase in the wake of *Chaoulli*. Already in Ontario, a number of such injunctions have been obtained to prevent the withdrawal of treatment for autistic children.[33] The success of those cases may be of limited value to litigants who challenge waiting lists or who seek to expand or improve the coverage of the public health system. The Ontario cases can perhaps be explained by a desire to preserve the status quo of providing intensive therapy for autistic children, as well as the separate issue of whether age cut offs for that therapy are discriminatory. In any event, an interlocutory injunction is probably the most effective and least expensive legal remedy for those harmed by the public system. By focusing on the flesh and blood of the individual case, interlocutory injunction cases may result in the courts doing justice in some compelling individual cases. Indeed, this may be what Justice Binnie and LeBel contemplated in their dissent when they stressed that they would not preclude case by case adjudication and remedies in individual cases. At the same time, however, interlocutory injunctions will likely only have a limited effect on the health care system. Although much cheaper and faster than a full trial, a motion for an interlocutory injunction is still beyond the means of most Canadians. The judicial role can be defended for its focus on the merits of the individual case, but court-ordered queue jumping may be unfair to similarly situated individuals who have not engaged in expensive litigation.

Interlocutory injunctions may be inferior to administrative mechanisms that have the potential to be quicker, less costly and more systemic than court ordered remedies. Unfortunately, as Colleen Flood and Caroline Pitfield demonstrate in this volume, administrative appeals need much improvement in terms of access, speed and transparency.[34] The best legal emergency room for those unreasonably placed on waiting lists may not be the expensive superior courts, but reformed administrative procedures such as a combination of health care guarantees and accessible administrative appeals.

The Ease of Simple and Negative Remedies

Why did the Court venture into the medicare debate despite its previous caution and deference on matters of public policy including the scope of the public medicare system? The simplicity of the remedy requested by the Charter applicants made their substantive claims attractive to the majority. Indeed, in the second paragraph of their reasons, Chief Justice McLachlin and Justice Major happily noted that 'the appellants do not seek an order that the government spend more money on health care, nor do they seek an order that waiting times for treatment under the public health care scheme be reduced. They only seek a remedy that because delays in the public system place their health and safety at risk, they should be allowed to take insurance to permit them to access private services.' They underlined the limited nature of their ruling by adding that 'the Charter does not confer a freestanding constitutional right to health care.'[35]

The applicants in this case asked for a simple, traditional and easy to enforce remedy. They did not ask the court to declare that governments had to provide new health care services, as in *Eldridge* and *Auton*, let alone to retain jurisdiction to ensure systemic compliance with the Charter, as in *Doucet-Boudreau v. Nova Scotia*. Justice Deschamps recognized the limits of the negative remedy when she stated that the 'relief sought by the appellants does not necessarily provide a complete response to the complex problem of waiting lists.' She quickly added, however that 'it was not up to the appellants to find a way to remedy a problem that has persisted for a number of years and for which the solution must come from the state itself.'[36] The negative remedy granted by the Court followed the argument proposed by Stanley Hartt and Patrick Monahan that courts should use the Charter to strike down restrictions on private health care, including penalties that the federal government might assess against provinces.[37] Unfortunately, this approach does not offer any hope for those who cannot purchase private health care and who may look to the courts for more complex and positive remedies to improve the public system.

The Difficulties of Positive and Systemic Remedies

Although it was tactically wise for the litigants in *Chaoulli* to request a negative remedy, it would be wrong to conclude that the courts are restricted to ordering negative remedies. As discussed above, interlocutory injunctions and damages can be awarded in individual cases. Declarations and structural injunctions are also available as systemic remedies and they may be of crucial importance if, as many have predicted, an increase in services purchased in the private sector makes it more difficult to find the trained personnel and perhaps facilities needed to provide services in the public system. In Quebec, some of these remedies could be granted in the first instance through human rights commissions.

The Supreme Court's only case dealing with positive remedies to ensure the provision of medical treatment was its decision in *Eldridge* to issue a declaration that British Columbia was required under s.15 of the Charter to provide sign language interpretation to deaf patients for medically necessary treatments. The Court reasoned that a 'declaration, as opposed to some kind of injunctive relief, is the appropriate remedy in this case because there are myriad options available to the government that may rectify the unconstitutionality of the current system. It is not this Court's role to dictate how this is to be accomplished.'[38] The Court also suspended the declaration for six months in order to give the government time to establish a system of interpretation. Although the British Columbia government set up such systems by this time, there is evidence that other governments not directly bound by the case failed to do so and claims continue to be heard by human rights commissions concerning translation issues.[39] A complaint to a human rights commission is, of course, far less expensive than Charter litigation. *Eldridge* suggests that courts may in appropriate cases issue declarations of entitlement to medically required treatment while also giving governments time to comply with such directions.

The limits of declarations, however, became more obvious in the subsequent *Little Sisters* litigation. Although the majority of the Court relied upon a declaration that customs officials had violated the Charter by targeting imports from a gay and lesbian bookstore, Justice Iacobucci argued in a strong dissent that declarations were not appropriate in cases where governments were unable to comply with the Charter, where subsequent litigation was likely, and where there was a need for ongoing monitoring of the government's compliance with the Charter.[40] Little Sisters has subsequently gone to the great expense of commencing new litigation because of its continued conflicts with customs.[41]

The Court's subsequent decision in *Doucet-Boudreau v. Nova Scotia* [42]affirmed that courts could issue stronger remedies than declarations to ensure systemic compliance with the Charter. The majority of the Court upheld the trial judge's retention of jurisdiction and his requirement that the government submit progress reports on the construction of new minority language educational facilities. A similar approach could be required with respect to public health care reform given its complex and dynamic nature. *Doucet-Boudreau* was, however, a bitterly divided 5:4 decision with four judges in a strongly worded dissent arguing that retention of jurisdiction was procedurally unfair to the government; that it violated the separation of powers; and that it allowed the judge to act in an illegitimate political fashion by putting pressure on the government to make long overdue systemic reforms. In the wake of this controversy, trial judges may think twice before they exercise their powers to retain jurisdiction in a health care case to ensure that the public system satisfies Charter standards.[43] Nevertheless, such strong remedies may be necessary should the public system become worse.

The Case for Delay

The Court's original judgment in *Chaoulli* ignored the issue of remedy even though it was discussed in the factums and during the hearing. Dr. Chaoulli requested an immediate declaration of invalidity on the basis that any delay would be too long for those facing a potential threat to their life or security of the person, but the members of the Senate Committee and the Canadian Medical Association both asked for an unprecedented 36 month delay of their requested remedy of striking down Quebec's restrictions. Despite these competing arguments and the potentially destabilizing nature of its decision, the Supreme Court remarkably and recklessly ignored the issue of remedy in its original judgment. The actual remedy granted by the Court is far from clear. The four judges in the majority only agreed that the restrictions violated the Quebec and not the Canadian Charter. Hence, the majority could not strike the law down under the Canadian Charter, but only hold it inoperative under the Quebec Charter.

The Quebec government responded to the ruling by asking the Court for a partial re-hearing and an 18 month suspension of its judgment. Quebec warned that allowing the judgment to have immediate effect might disrupt efforts to integrate the provision of health services and have implications under free trade agreements. It argued that 18 months were required to allow a multidisciplinary committee with health, finance, legal, intergovernmental affairs and insurance experts to conduct a study to be followed by public consultation and new legislation. [44]Dr. Chaoulli, as well as a coalition of British Columbia private health clinics, argued that the case did not satisfy the three categories for suspending a declaration of invalidity under the Canadian Charter as outlined in *Schachter v. Canada* [45]: namely that an immediate declaration would threaten the rule of law, public safety or deprive someone of an existing benefit. The Ontario Court of Appeal had relied on such a categorical approach when it refused to follow lower courts and suspend its declaration that the traditional definition of marriage was unconstitutional.[46] The result of that decision was that facts on the grounds -same sex marriages- were created that restrained the ability of governments to respond with either a compromise position of civil unions or with the notwithstanding clause which cannot be used retroactively.[47] An immediate remedy in *Chaoulli* might similarly have created facts on the ground- insurance contracts and American insurance companies who would claim rights under free trade agreements.

The Supreme Court's August 4 decision to suspend its judgment for 12 months retroactive to its first judgment should be welcomed even though the case, at least as understood by the majority of the Court, does not fit easily into the restrictive *Schachter* categories and does not involve a declaration of invalidity under the Canadian Charter. Nevertheless, a suspension of a judgment under the Quebec Charter is analogous to a suspended declaration of invalidity under the Canadian Charter. As I have argued elsewhere, delayed or suspended declarations of invalidity can and should serve as instruments of dialogue.[48] In addition, the Supreme Court has recognized that a suspension may be necessary to prevent the development of prescriptive rights that might fetter the government's range of responses.[49] The reduction of Quebec's request from 18 to 12 months, however, seems suspect given that Justice Bastarache had previously reasoned that an 18 month delay was justified because of the 'large sums of money spent by the legislature on social assistance programs...and the complexity of the programs at issue, a court should not intrude too deeply into the role of the legislature in this field.'[50] Medicare is even more complex and expensive that social assistance and it remains to be seen whether Quebec will be able to devise a comprehensive response by June, 2006. It will be important for Quebec to have adequate regulation of insurance in place by that time because after that time, as suggested by Tracey Epps and David Schneiderman in this volume, American insurance companies will be able to bring claims under NAFTA should Quebec later decide to prohibit or restrict their private services. [51]

Suspended judgments fit into a public law model of litigation started with *Brown v. Board of Education* [52]in which courts recognize that delay is inevitable because of the positive obligations that rights place on the state. The Charter Coalition on Poverty requested in its supplementary submissions on remedy that the court consider 'an effective and systemic remedy for all, not just for the more advantaged' and suggested that Quebec be required to report back to the court on steps taken to comply with its judgment to ensure that Quebec's response did not discriminate against the poor.[53] Time will tell whether the Court's rejection of this request reflects a more general remedial conservatism demonstrated by the minority in *Doucet-Boudreau*. Two judges, Justices Iacobucci and Arbour, who formed part of the more activist majority in *Doucet-Boudreau* have retired. Much may depend on how Justices Abella and Charron and Justice Major's successor decide not only the substantive Charter issues, but also the related remedial issues.

The 12 month suspension of the judgment means that Dr. Chaoulli and Mr. Zeliotis do not receive the automatic and immediate remedy that has traditionally followed from a court victory. This seems appropriate given the Court's findings that they were not directly affected by the unconstitutional law.[54] Stanley Hartt raises a more serious concern, namely the danger that people may die or suffer on waiting lists during the delay.[55] Such concerns need to be taken seriously, but also assume that a person on a waiting list has no remedies. There is no principled reason why courts should not be able to respond to emergencies even while governments are given time to respond to their decisions. Unfortunately, a recent case suggests that a suspended declaration of invalidity under s.52(1) of the *Constitution Act* may preclude any remedy for affected individuals under s.24(1) of the Charter during the period of delay.[56] In *Chaoulli*, however, the Court could only agree on a remedy under the Quebec Charter and the precise effects of suspending its judgment until June, 2006 are not clear and it remains to be seen whether individuals can take advantage of the judgment in Quebec while it is suspended or whether Quebec will ask the Court for more time.

The Case for Dialogue Between Courts and Legislatures About Medicare

Andrew Petter in his contribution to this volume has blamed dialogue theory for the judicial activism of *Chaoulli*. In his view, the idea that Charter decisions are not the final word has turned judges into 'advocates rather than arbiters' who see their judgments are 'missives directed at government rather than verdicts directed at society.' [57]It is difficult to know for certain what motivates judicial decisions, but it is not clear that dialogue theory motivated Chief Justice McLachlin and Justice Major who offer no comment on the ability of governments to limit or override Charter rights or about the appropriate remedy, all fundamental features of dialogue theory. Dialogue theory may have motivated the Court's subsequent decision to suspend its judgment for 12 months, but given the lack of reasons for this decision, it is difficult to know for certain.

Even if dialogue theory did motivate the Court, Dean Petter's hostility to it seems somewhat misplaced given that dialogue theory gives governments more reply options than rights- based theories that assume judicial supremacy. Indeed, dialogue theory suggests that Quebec need not accept *Chaoulli* as the last word or a privatization solution for medicare. Quebec could, consistent with the idea of a robust dialogue, re-enact the ban on private insurance notwithstanding the Quebec Charter thus ensuring that private insurance for services covered by the public system remained illegal. Quebec could also use the s.33 override under the Canadian Charter. The Court's suspension of its judgment preserves this option because, unlike the gay marriage cases, it prevents facts on the grounds from developing that would be immune from a retroactive use of the override. The fact the override is unlikely is related more to Quebecers's dissatisfaction with their health care system than the idea that the override itself is illegitimate.[58] Dialogue theory is notable in its acceptance of the override.

There are many other options open to Quebec short of the override. They include intensive regulation of health insurance providers to ensure that they do not discriminate, for example, on the basis of age or disability. This may require amendment of s.20.1 of the Quebec Charter that deems actuarial decisions based on sex, age, civil status and health to be non-discriminatory. Other options include the creation of wait list guarantees with public funding to assist those who cannot access private health insurance[59] and the improvement of administrative appeal mechanisms so that governments can demonstrate that individual claims will be taken seriously within the existing system.[60] Another option is to amend the Quebec Charter to help ensure that those who cannot purchase private health insurance do not suffer discrimination as compared to the more advantaged groups who can purchase such insurance. Positive governmental action could make up for any reluctance of courts to order positive and systemic remedies to assist those who must rely on the public health care system. There are also options to mitigate some of anticipated adverse effects of private health insurance. Regulations can be targeted at doctors and facilities in an attempt to regulate queue jumping by those with private insurance or to attempt to ensure that private services augment rather than divert existing capacity in the health care system.[61] To be sure, Charter decisions can impose transactions costs on governments, but they do not paralyze governments. Indeed, the burden of legislative inertia in *Chaoulli* is reduced because the majority only decides the case under the Quebec and not the Canadian Charter.

Quebec can and should canvass all available options before the *Chaoulli* judgment takes effect in June 2006. Although some governments such as Alberta may respond to *Chaoulli* by encouraging more privatization, most will likely only increase the efforts to improve the public system by decreasing the length of waiting lists and increasing their rationality. As Peter Russell argues in this volume the fate of medicare will ultimately be decided by politicians not judges.[62]

Dean Petter criticizes dialogue theory for providing no normative content to justify further judicial activism to protect those who must continue to rely on the public health care system. Contrary to his suggestions, however, the courts' commitment to listening to actual claims of injustice is not devoid of normative content. By having an institutional role to consider claims of injustice independently of the legislature, the executive and conventional wisdom[63], the courts stand for the normative proposition that individuals matter and that they matter equally. Judges who act as judges have an obligation to ensure that Charter rights are enjoyed equally and they have broad remedial powers to accomplish this task. A commitment to scrutinizing the effects of governmental policies on individuals and to the equal enjoyment of basic rights are arguably the two most important moral lessons of the last century. In contrast, the normative premises of those who oppose taking the claims of individuals seriously in the name of an absolutist defence of democracy, medicare or a critique of the Charter are not clear. If, as argued by both Claude Forget and Stanley Hartt in their contributions to this volume[64], the normative premises are utilitarianism, they are suspect for their willingness to sacrifice individuals to the collective good. If, as I suspect, they are based on a more benign sense that Canadians should trust their elected governments to do the right thing, they discount the failures of the existing medicare system and exhibit a faith in governments that is for most only a nostalgic memory.

Conclusion

The problem with *Chaoulli* is not that the Court intervened in the health care field, but that its reliance on public interest standing and negative remedies suggests that it may be reluctant to assist those directly affected by waiting lists with more positive and systemic remedies. *Chaoulli* could amount to pleasing judicial activism for those who can sell and purchase medical insurance, but not nearly enough judicial activism to assist those who suffer in the public health care system.

Another problem is that some neo-liberal governments may become less invested in the public system if advantaged classes can exit from the public system as a result of *Chaoulli*. At the same time, *Chaoulli* has the potential to encourage other governments to be more responsive to individuals who suffer on waiting lists and whose pleas might not otherwise be heard. This may require increased judicial activism to protect those who suffer in the public system and the majority in *Chaoulli* should accept the minority's willingness to consider the case for individual remedies under s.24(1) of the Charter. Under a dialogic bill of rights like the Charter, however, taking rights seriously does not mean that individual rights always will prevail. Governments have an opportunity to justify limits and overrides on individual rights. They also have an opportunity to demonstrate that administrative mechanisms are a justified and reasonable response to the plight of those suffering on waiting lists. Legislative and administrative activism can respond to and head off judicial activism. Consistent with the dialogue model, the fate of medicare ultimately remains with elected governments and with Canadians.

Notes

I thank Sujit Choudhry, Colleen Flood, Judith Keene, Warren Newman, Andrew Petter, Bruce Ryder and Lorne Sossin for helpful comments on earlier drafts. Mistakes and responsibility remain my own.

1 2005 SCC 35 (henceforth *Chaoulli*)
2 *Auton v. British Columbia* [2004] 3 S.C.R. 657.
3 *Gosselin v.* Quebec [2002] 4 S.C.R. 429; *R. v. Malmo-Levine* [2003] 3 S.C.R. 571; *Canadian Foundation for Children v. Canada* [2004] 1 S.C.R. 76. For an overview of s.7 jurisprudence which concludes that the decision *Chaoulli* is a 'striking departure from the Court's consistent deference to legislative judgment on broad policy issues such as the criminalization of marijuana, the proper approach to the correction of children and whether social welfare benefits were adequate.' Sharpe and Roach *The Canadian Charter of Rights and Freedoms* 3rd ed (Toronto: Irwin Law, 2005) at 210–11.
4 See for example Choudhry and Petter in this volume.
5 This follows my definition of judicial activism in Roach *The Supreme Court on Trial: Judicial Activism or Democratic Dialogue* (Toronto: Irwin Law, 2001) at 104–111. For other definitions see Christopher Manfredi in this volume.
6 On August 4, 2005, the Court released the following ruling: 'The motion for a partial rehearing is granted. The Court's judgment is stayed for a period of 12 months from the date such judgment was issued, namely June 9, 2005.' Supreme Court Bulletin August 12, 2005.
7 For such an argument based on comparative experience see Flood, Stabile and Kontic in this volume.
8 *Chaoulli v. Quebec* at para 264.
9 Ibid at para 187.
10 Ibid at para 35.
11 ibid at para 189.
12 *Borowski v. Canada* [1981] 2 S.C.R. 575.
13 Translated Transcript of Oral Hearing at http://www.law.utoronto.ca/visitors_content.asp?itemPath=5/5/0/0/0&contentId=1109
14 *Borowski v. Canada* [1989] 1 S.C.R. 342; *Daigle v. Tremblay* [1989] 2 S.C.R. 530
15 *Canadian Council of Churches v. Canada* [1992] 1 S.C.R. 236
16 *Hy and Zels v. Ontario* [1993] 3 S.C.R. 675 at 694–5 quoting *Mackay v. Manitoba* [1989] 2 S.C.R. 357 at 361–2.
17 Choudhry in this volume.
18 See for example Manfredi in this volume.
19 Supreme Court Bulletin May 9, 2003 leave granted by Chief Justice

McLachlin and Justices Bastarache and Deschamps. On the Court's discretionary power to set its own agenda see Roy Flemming *Tournament of Appeals* (Vancouver, University of British Columbia Press, 2004).

20 Bickel *The Least Dangerous Branch 2nd ed* (New Haven: Yale University Press, 1986) at 115–116.

21 Sunstein *One Case at a Time* (Cambridge: Harvard University Press, 1999) at 259.

22 Roach *The Supreme Court on Trial* ch. 8.

23 Monahan 'The Supreme Court of Canada in the 21st Century' (2001) 80 Can. Bar Rev. 374 at 391.

24 Courts could be more expansive in their interpretation of s.7, if they were more willing to consider justifications for limiting s.7 rights under s.1 see Roach 'Common Law Bills of Rights as Dialogue Between Courts and Legislatures' (2005) 55 U.T.L.J. 733 at 761ff. As Lorne Sossin suggests in this volume, courts could be more active with respect to social welfare rights under s.7. The applicable section 1 standard would have to depend on the context with a more rigourous standard applying to protect the rights of unpopular minorities and a more deferential standard applying in other cases. See Choudhry in this volume.

25 [1997] 3 S.C.R. 674.

26 But for arguments that the Court in *Eldridge* underestimated the costs of providing provincial-wide systems see Manfredi and Maioni 'Courts and Health Policy' (2002) 27 J. of Health Politics, Policy and Law 213.

27 *Cilinger v. Centre Hospitalier de Chicoutmi* at www.law.utoronto.ca/faculty_content.asp?itemPath=1/13/0/0/0&contentId=1109. See also *Williams v. Ontario* 2005 O.J. 3508 (Sup.Ct.).

28 *Gosselin v. Quebec* supra at para 97 per McLachlin C.J. and at paras 295–296 per Bastarache J.

29 See Lorne Sossin in this volume.

30 *Auton v. British Columbia* (2001) 197 D.L.R.(4th) 165 aff'd (2003) 220 D.L.R.(4th) 411 rev'd [2004] 3 S.C.R. 657; *Wynberg v. Ontario* (2005) 252 D.L.R. (4th) 10 at paras 801–04 (Ont. Sup. Ct.).

31 See Hartt in this volume. See also the Senate Standing Committee on Social Affairs, Science and Technology April 2002 vol. 5 ch. 2 principle 20.

32 On waiting lists see Charles Wright and Terrence Sullivan et al in this volume.

33 *Eisler (Litigation Guardian of) v.* Ontario (2004) 239 D.L.R.(4th) 169 (Ont Sup Ct); *Naccarato (Litigation Guardian of) v. Ontario* 2004 CarswellOnt 3228; *Bettencourt (Litigation Guardian of) v. Ontario* (2005) 74 O.R.(3d) 550 (Ont.

Sup. Ct.); *Kohn v. Ontario (Litigation Guardian of)* [2004] O.J. No. 4112; *Wynberg v. Ontario* [2004] O.J. no. 1066 (Sup.Ct.).

34 Pitfield and Flood in this volume. For a failure of an administrative appeal in Quebec see *Stein v. Tribunal administratif du Quebec* [1999] R.J.Q. 2416.

35 *Chaoulli* at para 103–104.

36 *Chaoulli* at para 100.

37 Hartt and Monahan 'The Charter and Health Care: Guaranteeing Timely Access to Health Care for Canadians (Toronto: C.D. Howe Institute, 2002).

38 *Eldridge v. British Columbia* [1997] 3 S.C.R. 624 at para 96.

39 Roach 'Remedial Consensus and Dialogue under the Charter' (2002) 35 U.B.C.L. Rev. 211.

40 *Little Sisters v. Canada* [2000] 2 S.C.R. 1120.

41 *Little Sisters v. Canada* (2005) 193 C.C.C.(3d) 491 (B.C.C.A.).

42 [2003] 3 S.C.R. 3.

43 In a case involving the supply of drugs to prevent mother to child HIV transmission, the South African Constitutional Court has affirmed the availability of structural injunctions and supervisory jurisdiction. *Minister of Health v. Treatment Action Campaign (No. 2)* 2002 5 SA 721 at 758. For arguments that such remedies may be an appropriate response to both governmental defiance and incompetence in complying with constitutional rights see Roach and Budlender 'Mandatory Relief and Supervisory Jurisdiction'(2005) 5 South African L.J. 327.

44 Supplementary Factum of Quebec Attorney General June 27, 2005.

45 [1992] 2 S.C.R. 679.

46 *Halpern v. Ontario* (2003) 225 D.L.R.(4th) 529 (Ont.C.A.).

47 *Ford v. Quebec* [1988] 2 S.C.R. 712.

48 Roach 'Remedial Consensus and Dialogue under the Charter' supra

49 *R. v. Guignard* [2002] 2 S.C.R. 472.

50 *Gosselin v. Quebec* at para 292. In supplementary submissions, Mr. Zeliotis argued against the delay, but in the alternative asked for a 6 month delay. Did the Court simply split the difference between this request and Quebec's request for 18 months? For a case in which the Court unscientifically dealt with numbers, in that case by doubling the average time for cases to go to trial see *R. v. Askov* [1990] 2 S.C.R. 1199 at 1240.

51 Tracey Epps and David Scheiderman in this volume.

52 Chayes 'The Role of the Judge in Public Law Litigation' (1976) 89 Harv. L.Rev.1281.

53 Supplementary Factum of Charter Committee on Poverty and Canadian Health Coalition at paras 18, 50–51.

54 In contrast see *Wynberg v. Ontario* (2005) 252 D.L.R.(4th) 10 at para 786 (Ont. Sup.Ct.) for an immediate declaration of entitlement to autism therapy in cases involving directly affected persons who also were awarded compensatory damages for the therapy.

55 Hartt in this volume

56 *R. v. Demers* [2004] 2 S.C.R. 489. In prior cases such as *R. v. Bain* [1992] 1 S.C.R. 91, the Court had correctly suggested that during a delay, individual remedies could still be ordered to prevent abuses. For criticism of *Demers* see Roach *Constitutional Remedies in Canada* (Aurora: Canada Law Book, as updated) at 14.1769.1 ff.

57 Andrew Petter in this volume. See also Hutchinson in this volume.

58 Gaudreault-DesBiens and Panaccio in this volume.

59 Hartt in this volume.

60 Flood and Pitfield in this volume.

61 Terrence Sullivan et al in this volume.

62 Peter Russell in this volume

63 Roach 'Dialogic Judicial Review and its Critics' (2004) 23 S.C.L.R.(2d) 49 at 71 as cited in *Chaoulli* at para 89 per Deschamps J.

64 Hartt and Forget in this volume.

Evidence in the *Chaoulli* Case

Implications of *Chaoulli* for Fact-Finding in Constitutional Cases

HAMISH STEWART

The widespread public concern about the Supreme Court of Canada's astounding decision in *Chaoulli*[1] springs largely from the fear that it will, in Roy Romanow's words, signal 'the end of medicare as we know it.'[2] But this fear depends on a contested empirical proposition: that the availability of private health insurance will undermine the public health insurance system. If the public health care system could function properly in the presence of private insurance, then allowing private insurance would not mean the end of medicare as we know it. And to a large extent, the difference between the trial judgment and the Supreme Court of Canada's majority judgment in *Chaoulli* turns on differing assessments of this empirical proposition. The trial judge was satisfied that it was correct; the majority of the Supreme Court was not. The Supreme Court's reversal of the trial judge's factual finding was not only critical to the result in *Chaoulli* itself, but has disturbing implications for the fact finding process in future constitutional cases.

In *Chaoulli*, four judges of the Supreme Court held that provisions of Quebec statutes[3] preventing an individual from purchasing private insurance for services provided by the public health care system the relevant statutes violated s. 1 of the Quebec *Charter of Human Rights and Freedoms* and could not be justified under s. 9.1;[4] three of these judges also held that the statutory provisions infringed s. 7 of the *Canadian Charter of Rights and Freedoms* and could not be justified under s. 1. In the view of the three judges who reached this result under s. 7 of the Canadian Charter, the evidence established that delays in obtaining health services through the public system 'are widespread and have serious, sometimes grave consequences';[5] that these delays could have 'significant adverse psychological effects';[6] and that removing the prohibition on private insurance would not undermine the availability or quality of the public system.[7] Delays in obtaining medical treatment, at least where the physical or psychological impact was 'serious,'[8] engaged the applicants' security of the person under s. 7 of the Canadian Charter. Consequently, the statutory scheme causing the delays had to accord with the principles of fundamental justice. The requirement that 'laws should not be arbitrary' is a well-established principle of fundamental justice.[9] The Quebec scheme was held to be arbitrary, and thus contrary to s. 7, because the prohibition on private insurance was not necessary to preserve the public system.[10] The limit on the applicants' s. 7 right could not be justified under s. 1 because its very arbitrariness meant that it was not rationally connected to its objective.[11]

The finding that prohibiting private insurance is not necessary to preserve the public system was crucial; for if it is the case that prohibiting private insurance is, or may reasonably be regarded as being, necessary for the preservation of the public health insurance system, then the Quebec scheme would not be arbitrary and would not offend s. 7 of the Canadian Charter or s. 1 of the Quebec Charter. That is just what the trial judge found.[12] Three judges of the Supreme Court of Canada agreed.[13] On what basis could the Supreme Court of Canada overturn this factual finding?

The purpose of a trial is to determine disputed facts and the purpose of an appeal is to ensure that the outcome of the trial is not tainted with legal error. Appellate courts are generally reluctant to review factual determinations, and in some proceedings are prohibited from doing so.[14] The Supreme Court of Canada has held in a long line of cases that, in civil proceedings, an appellate court should not overturn a trial court's factual finding unless 'the trial judge is shown to have committed a palpable and overriding error or made findings of fact that are clearly wrong, unreasonable or unsupported by the evidence.'[15] The reasons for this limit on appellate review are familiar. The trial judge is in a better position than an appellate court to make factual findings because of 'his or her extensive exposure to the evidence, the advantage of hearing testimony *viva voce*, and the judge's familiarity with the case as a whole.'[16] While some of the advantages of hearing testimony *viva voce* may be overstated, particularly in the area of making credibility judgments based on demeanour, there is no question that a trial judge who is immersed in the evidence and has heard the examination in chief and, more importantly, the cross-examination of the witnesses is in a much better position to find facts than an appellate court reading a transcript. Moreover, systemic interests in the integrity and finality of the trial process are promoted by limiting appellate review of factual findings.[17] If the parties knew that a trial judge's factual findings could readily be overturned on appeal, their incentive to put forward the best possible case at trial might be significantly weakened.

Now, the nature of the facts at issue in *Chaoulli* is different from the nature of the facts at issue in the usual civil or criminal proceedings. The leading civil cases limiting appellate review of factual determinations are all cases where the trial judge had to decide what had happened, as between the parties, in the past. Similarly, criminal cases always involve determinations of what a particular person did in the past. In *Chaoulli*, the crucial factual question was the effect of the availability of private insurance on the availability and quality of health care under the public system. This is not a question about what happened in the past, but a question about what is likely to happen in the future if the statute in question is invalidated. That is, the facts at issue in *Chaoulli* are not 'adjudicative facts' but 'legislative facts.'[18] They 'involve the use of social and economic data to establish a more general context for policy-making.'[19]

The determination of legislative facts often depends upon social scientific evidence and upon somewhat speculative judgments about human behaviour. Social evidence is rarely unequivocal and is often difficult to assess for those who are not trained in statistical methods, and even for those with such training. Some issues of legislative fact may not be readily capable of proof even where the social science evidence is abundant. For these reasons, when legislative facts are in issue, the Supreme Court has indicated both that an appellate court may show *less* deference to the trial judge, but that all courts (both at trial and on appeal) should show *more* deference to the legislature. In *RJR-MacDonald*, McLachlin J. stated in that 'a lesser degree of deference [to the trial judge's factual findings] may be required where the trial judge has considered social science and other policy oriented evidence' but that the appellate court 'should remain sensitive to the fact that the trial judge has had the advantage of having competing expert testimony firsthand.'[20] Yet as deference to the trial judge decreases in this type of case, deference to the legislature increases. Where Charter issues depend on the resolution of factual issues that in turn depend on contested social scientific evidence, it is settled law that the government need show only a reasoned basis for the legislature's decision. In *Butler*, the government's s. 1 justification for criminalizing obscene forms of expression depended in part on the empirical claim that obscene materials cause certain harms. If this empirical claim were false, then the limit on the right would not be rationally connected to its objective, and the relevant provision of the *Criminal Code*[21] would be constitutionally invalid. Moreover, the government has the burden of proof in a s. 1 justification. So, it would seem, the government should have been required to prove on a balance of probabilities that obscene expression caused the harms alleged. Instead of imposing this difficult task on the state, the court allowed the government to satisfy the rational connection branch of the *Oakes*[22] test by establishing a 'reasoned apprehension' that the claim was true.[23] Similarly, in *Malmo-Levine*, a 'reasonable apprehension' that marijuana could cause harm to a rather small group of Canadians[24] was sufficient to support the conclusion that Parliament's decision to criminalize the possession of marijuana was not arbitrary under s. 7 of the Charter. To demand proof that marijuana could cause more serious harms would, it was said, 'involve the courts in micromanagement of Parliament's agenda.'[25]

Thus, in reviewing the trial judge's factual findings in *Chaoulli*, the judges of the Supreme Court had two choices. They could have applied the deferential 'palpable and overriding error' standard from civil cases and allowed the trial judge's factual findings to stand unless palpable and overriding error was demonstrated; or they could have noted that the facts in issue were legislative facts and, while showing less deference to the trial judge, showed more deference to the National Assembly's policy choices.

In my view, it should not have mattered which of these approaches was followed; in either case, the trial judge's factual findings should have been allowed to stand.[26] If the 'palpable and overriding error' standard were applied, it would be difficult indeed to reverse the trial judge. Although her factual findings are presented briefly, they follow an extensive and careful summary of the evidence of all the experts.[27] There is no suggestion that she misunderstood what the experts said or misrepresented their conclusions on the critical factual issues. There is no 'palpable and overriding error' in her treatment of the expert evidence. If less deference was appropriate on the ground that the facts in issue are legislative and not adjudicative, then the question for the purpose of an arbitrariness analysis under s. 7 should have been whether the Quebec government had a reasoned basis for its conclusion that prohibiting private health insurance would support the public health insurance system. Even if we accept McLachlin C.J.C. and Major J.'s characterization of the expert evidence as supporting 'competing but unproven 'common sense' arguments'[28] concerning legislative facts, it can hardly be said that the evidence provided no reasoned basis for it, and that was all that was required.[29]

These points may be illustrated with reference to the evidence of one of the experts. The trial judge may well have placed considerable weight on the evidence of Professor Theodore R. Marmor of Yale University, called by the government as an expert on health care policy. McLachlin C.J.C. and Major J. do not cite his report directly, but characterize the evidence of government's experts as follows:

> Their conclusions were based on the 'common sense' proposition that the improvement of health services depends on exclusivity ... They did not profess expertise in waiting times for treatment. Nor did they present economic studies or rely on the experience of other countries.[30]

One is tempted to suggest that if a trial judge had characterized Marmor's evidence this way, an appellate court would readily find palpable and overriding error. Marmor directly addressed the critical question: what would be the effects of permitting private health insurance? His answer was that there would be 'a number of undesirable side effects' including decreased public support for the public system, cost pressures, and increased administrative costs. His report (as quoted and summarized by the trial judge[31]) spoke directly to the effects of the availability of private insurance on waiting times in the public system and to the experience of other countries. His qualifications as an expert on health policy issues do not appear to have been challenged, and if those qualifications did not give him 'expertise in waiting times for treatment,' it is hard to know what would. His report was not an exercise in speculative common sense but an exercise of his particular expertise. The trial judge largely accepted it, along with similar conclusions reached by other experts, and noted that only one of the expert witnesses had reached the opposing view. She expressly found that 'L'établissement d'un système de santé parallèle privé aurait pour effet de menacer l'intégrité, le bon fonctionnement ainsi que la viabilité du système publique.'[32] It is impossible to discern any basis for appellate interference with this conclusion.[33]

It may well be that our adversarial trial system is not well-suited for the determination of legislative facts.[34] But, at least for the time being, the adversarial trial system is the system we have for resolving constitutional challenges, including those that involve legislative facts, and we ought to make the best of it. The majority's treatment of the trial judge's factual findings in *Chaoulli* does not even attempt to make the best of it. The majority reverses the trial judge's factual findings without adverting to the test of 'palpable and overriding error,' without adverting to the 'reasonable apprehension' standard that has previously been applied to contested social science issues in Charter adjudication, and without making clear the basis on which, in its view, the trial judge erred in her fact-finding.[35] McLachlin C.J.C. and Major J. embark on a fresh fact-finding process, based largely on evidence that was not before the trial judge and was therefore not tested in an adversarial context.[36] If that is how constitutional cases are decided, the parties – both applicants for Charter relief and governments resisting that relief – will have little reason to invest time, energy, and money in attempting to establish the empirical propositions on which their positions rest at trial, and may prefer, on appeal, to invoke material that has not been tested through cross-examination at trial and to appeal to the 'common sense' of an appellate panel. To decide constitutional cases this way would be to forego the advantages of the adversarial trial process (such as they are) without getting anything in return. The Supreme Court's decision in *Chaoulli* may well be bad for medicare; it is certainly bad for constitutional adjudication in an adversarial trial system.

Notes

1 Chaoulli v. Quebec (Attorney General), 2005 SCC 35 [hereinafter Chaoulli], rev'g Chaoulli c. Québec (Procureur générale), [2002] R.J.Q. 1205 (C.A.), which aff'd Chaoulli c. Québec (Procureur générale), [2000] R.J.Q. 786 (C.S.) [hereinafter Chaoulli [Trial]]. An edited English translation of this judgment is contained in Appendix A of this volume.

2 Tracey Tyler, 'Romanow fears 'end of medicare',' *Toronto Star*, 17 September 2005, p. A1; see also the media reactions cited in Peter Russell's contribution to this volume.

3 *Health Insurance Act*, R.S.Q., c. A-29, s. 15; *Hospital Insurance Act*, R.S.Q., c. A-28, s. 11.

4 Deschamps J. decided the case under the Quebec Charter; McLachlin C.J.C. and Major J., Bastarache J. concurring, decided the case under the

Canadian Charter, but stated that they agreed with Deschamps J.'s analysis und the Quebec Charter.

5 *Ibid.* at para. 112 *per* McLachlin C.J.C. and Major J., Bastarache J. concurring.

6 *Ibid.* at para. 116.

7 *Ibid.* at para. 140; compare *ibid.* at paras. 41–5 *per* Deschamps J. (holding that treatment delays infringed the right to personal inviolability under s. 1 of the Quebec Charter).

8 *Ibid.* at para. 123; compare *ibid.* at paras. 37–45 *per* Deschamps J. (holding that the statutory scheme infringed the applicants' right to personal inviolability under s. 1 of the Quebec Charter).

9 *Ibid.* at para. 130; see also *R. v. Malmo-Levine* (2003), 179 C.C.C. (3d) 417 (S.C.C.); *Rodriguez v. British Columbia (Attorney General)* (1993), 107 D.L.R. (4th) 342 (S.C.C.); *R. v. Morgentaler* (1988), 44 D.L.R. (4th) 385 (S.C.C.).

10 *Chaoulli*, at paras. 152–3; compare *ibid.* at paras. 59–98 *per* Deschamps J. (holding that the statutory scheme did not minimally impair the applicants' rights and so could not be justified under s. 9.1 of the Quebec Charter).

11 *Ibid.* at para. 155.

12 *Chaoulli [Trial.]* at p. 827.

13 Binnie, LeBel, and Fish JJ.

14 In proceedings by way of indictment, the Crown's right to appeal from an acquittal is limited to grounds involving 'a question of law alone': *Criminal Code*, R.S.C. 1985, c. C-46, s. 676(1)(a).

15 *L.(H.) v. Canada (Attorney General)* (2005), 251 D.L.R. (4th) 604 (S.C.C.) at para. 4, emphasis removed. See also *Housen v. Nikolaisen* (2002), 211 D.L.R. (4th) 577 (S.C.C.) at para. 10; *Lensen v. Lensen* (1987), 44 D.L.R. (4th) 1 (S.C.C.) at p. 9; *Stein v. The Ship 'Kathy K.'* (1976), 62 D.L.R. (3d) 1 (S.C.C.) at p. 5. Even commentators who are critical of 'palpable and overriding error' as a standard of review agree with the rationales that motivate it; see, for instance, R.D. Gibbens, 'Appellate Review of Findings of Fact' (1992), 13 Adv.Q. 445; Paul M. Perell, 'The Standard of Appellate Review and the Ironies of *Housen v. Nikolaisen*' (2004), 28 Adv.Q. 40.

16 *Housen*, at para. 18.

17 *Housen*, at paras. 16–17; see also Charles Alan Wright, 'The Doubtful Omniscience of Appellate Courts' (1957) 41 Minn.L.Rev. 751 at pp. 778–82.

18 See also Christopher Manfredi's and Sujit Choudhry's contributions to this volume. The distinction between adjudicative and legislative facts appears to have originated in Kenneth Davis, 'An Approach to Problems of Evi-

dence in the Administrative Process' (1942), 55 Harv.L.Rev. 364 at pp. 402–
3, and is widely employed by courts and commentators; see, for instance,
Danson v. Ontario (Attorney General), [1990] 2 S.C.R. 1086 at p. 1099; Peter
W. Hogg, 'Proof of Facts in Constitutional Cases' (1976) 26 U.T.L.J. 386 at
pp. 394–5.

19 John Hagan, 'Social Science Evidence in Constitutional Litigation' in
Robert J. Sharpe, ed., *Charter Litigation* (Toronto: Butterworths, 1987) 213 at
p. 215.

20 *RJR-MacDonald Inc. v. Canada (Attorney General)*, [1995] 3 S.C.R. 199 at para.
141. The factual questions in *RJR-MacDonald* concerned the effects of
tobacco advertising on tobacco consumption. The court did not accept the
trial judge's finding that a ban on advertising was not rationally connected
to the objective of reducing consumption, but ultimately agreed with him
that the government had not justified the ban on tobacco advertising.

21 *Criminal Code*, s. 163(8) (defining 'obscene').

22 *R. v. Oakes*, [1986] 1 S.C.R. 103.

23 *R. v. Butler*, [1992] 1 S.C.R. 452 at pp. 501–4. Other cases where a 'reasoned
apprehension of harm' was sufficient to satisfy a factual element of a s. 1
justification include *R. v. Sharpe* (2001), 194 D.L.R. (4th) 1 (S.C.C.) and
Harper v. Canada (Attorney General) (2004), 239 D.L.R. (4th) 193 (S.C.C.).

24 *Malmo-Levine*, at para. 136.

25 *Ibid.* at para. 133.

26 The dissenters in *Chaoulli* suggest that the more deferential standard was
applicable: *Chaoulli*, at para. 235 *per* Binnie and LeBel JJ. dissenting.
Deschamps J. appears to articulate a new, even less deferential, standard:
'a court must show deference where the evidence established that the
government has assigned proper weight to each of the competing interests.' *Ibid.* at para. 95. It is hard to see what work the word 'deference' does
in this standard.

27 *Chaoulli [Trial.]* at pp. 796–808.

28 *Chaoulli*, at para. 138; compare *ibid.* at para. 63 *per* Deschamps J.

29 See also *Chaoulli*, at para. 176 *per* Binnie and LeBel JJ. dissenting. Or, as
Sujit Choudhry puts it in his contribution to this volume, '[t]he standard
was whether the Quebec government lacked a 'reasonable basis' on which
to proceed, and the materials put into evidence more than met this attenuated standard.'

30 *Chaoulli*, at para. 136.

31 *Chaoulli [Trial.]* at pp. 805–9; see also *Chaoulli*, at paras. 214–223 *per* Binnie
and LeBel JJ. dissenting.

32 *Chaoulli [Trial]* at p. 827, emphasis removed.

33 Compare *Chaoulli*, at paras. 214–6 *per* Binnie and LeBel JJ. dissenting.
34 As suggested by Christopher Manfredi in his contribution to this volume.
35 Deschamps J. holds that the trial judge's analysis has to be 'adapted' for the purposes of the Quebec Charter because, having dealt with the matter under the Canadian Charter, she placed the burden of proof on the applicants rather than on the state: *Chaoulli*, at paras. 60, 67, 88. However, it is not enough to observe that the burden of proof is in the wrong place; it must also be asked whether this error would have affected the outcome. Would the trial judge have reached a different conclusion, on the evidence, absent the alleged error? Her factual findings suggest that she would not.
36 *Chaoulli*, at paras. 140–9; at para. 229, Binnie and LeBel JJ. argue that such evidence should, at least, 'be filtered and analysed at trial through an expert witness.'

Experts and Evidence: New Challenges in Knowledge Translation

MORRIS BARER

The Supreme Court decision in *Jacques Chaoulli and George Zeliotis versus the Attorney Generals of Quebec and Canada*[1] has raised some critical questions regarding the future course of health care financing in Canada. One gauge of the importance of an issue or event is the number of conferences that are organized around it, and the rapidity with which this occurs. Including the conference from which the papers in this volume are drawn, at least three nationally-advertised conferences have materialized in the past few months.[2] The focus of each is some combination of the legal and policy ramifications of, and potential economic opportunities pried open by, the Chaoulli case.

But the judgement also poses some new challenges for the health services research community in Canada. That community includes a number of the world's most respected thinkers on methods for, and the keys to, successful knowledge translation–the application of research evidence in clinical and health care system decision-making. Virtually all of their work has focused on the interface between research evidence and the decision making of the system's policy- and decision-makers such as politicians, senior bureaucrats, program managers, regional CEOs, and clinicians. We have a growing understanding about the keys to successful knowledge translation, so long as we believe that those do, in fact, represent the decision-makers in the system.

The *Chaoulli* case may have changed the nature of the health systems and services knowledge translation challenge, at least in Canada, and perhaps forever. For the research community now must use the *Chaoulli* case, and others such as the recent *Auton*[3] case, to try to determine what adjustments need to be made in our understanding of effective knowledge translation, when the decision-maker is a Supreme Court judge rather than a deputy minister, a regional CEO, or a program manager. For those (researchers, system decision-makers *and* research funding agencies with knowledge translation mandates) interested in knowledge translation, one of the most unsettling aspects of the *Chaoulli* decision was the misuse, and ignorance, of evidence.

This raises huge new challenges. Are there generalizable trends evident in the types of evidence the courts do and do not take into account in rendering their judgements, or does it depend on the predilections of the judges and the day of the week? Are critical syntheses of evidence a useful tool with this audience? And if they are, how does one go about generating 'trust and credibility in both the people doing the syntheses and the processes they use,' given that 'co-production processes' are not an option?[4] Are particular types of 'evidence' (e.g. methods, or discipline-bases) more convincing before a judge than other types? What makes a compelling 'expert witness' in the eyes of the courts? Do we need to provide researchers with 'expert witness' training? What possible substitute strategies can be brought to bear when researchers do not have the opportunity to establish long-term relationships with a decision maker? Are there ways of turning the courts' love for the compelling anecdote or story into a knowledge translation strategy? Can we design effective 'crap detection' programs to help judges who may be 'substantively ignorant,'[5] sift the evidence wheat from the chaffe? Even if we can, would they sign up?

This last question is of far more than rhetorical interest. For if the answer to the former is 'no' or, more likely, the answer to the former 'yes' but to the latter 'no,' then we run a serious risk of seeing the courts becoming servants of the health policy zombie masters.[6] A zombie, in this context, is a seemingly sensible idea about the health care system that easily meets the test of surface plausibility but that, when viewed through a critical evidence lens turns out to have no basis in fact. What makes it a zombie is that it cannot be permanently killed, no matter how compelling the evidence.[7] Zombies can be suppressed for a time, but they periodically re-emerge to stalk the land and strike terror into the hearts of well-meaning health care policy analysts. Zombie masters, then, are those individuals, groups or organizations that perpetuate the life of a zombie, either because it fits with their economic interests, or philosophy, or both.[8] When judges choose to ignore, or misinterpret, research evidence, they become servants of the health policy zombie masters.

There were more than enough zombie ideas in the *Chaoulli* decision to keep the zombie hunters busy for quite a while.[9] Predominant here, of course, were the ideas about the putative benefits of private health insurance for core medical services. Claims about the wonders of private insurance have been around for half a century at least, and have repeatedly been shown to be specious. Yet they persist, they are promoted, and the Supreme Court justices, or at least enough of them, bought the story, hook, line and sinker, and evidence be damned.

It gets worse. What was particularly dismaying is that the judges who wrote the decision for the majority showed no evidence that they understood the implications of opening up Canada to private insurance for core services, in a world increasingly dominated by voracious international trade agreements. As colleagues and I have noted elsewhere,[10] and as Epps and Schneiderman note in their paper in this collection, this is a one-way street. It is likely to be practically, or financially, impossible to reverse direction, once one starts down this road. In this, the majority were simply irresponsible. But they will not be held accountable for their failure to do their homework. It is the rest of us who will pay, and pay, and pay....

And so the Chaoulli decision has left us with a combination of evidence misinterpreted and evidence ignored. Therein lie the challenges for those of us, either organizationally, or individually, whose project it is to increase the relevance and application of health policy research evidence in the continuous, positive, evolution of Canada's health care system.

Notes

1 2005 SCC 35.
2 Osgoode Hall Law School, York University, Toronto (October 26, 2005), *'Chaoulli and the Restructuring of Health Care in Canada'*; Canadian Independent Medical Clinics Association, Vancouver (November 11–12, 2005), *'Saving Medicare: Strategies and Solutions.'*
3 [2004] 3 S.C.R. 657.
4 Lomas, J., 'Using Research to Inform Healthcare Managers' And Policy Makers' Questions: From Summative to Interpretive Synthesis,' *Healthcare Policy* 1(1):55–71
5 Evans, Robert G., 'Baneful Legacy: Medicare and Mr. Trudeau,' *Healthcare Policy* 1(1):20–25

6 Hutchinson, this volume, covers some of the reasons why we should not be surprised to find this happening.

7 Barer, M.L., R.G. Evans, C. Hertzman, and M. Johri (1998), *Lies, Damned Lies, and Health Care Zombies: Discredited Ideas That Will Not Die*, Houston, TX: Health Policy Institute Discussion Paper #10, University of Texas (Houston) Health Science Center

8 Evans, R.G., M.L. Barer, G.L. Stoddart and V. Bhatia *Who Are the Zombie Masters, and What Do They Want?*, (Toronto, Ont.: Ontario Premier's Council on Health, Well-being and Social Justice, 1994).

9 Examples can be found elsewhere in this volume; see, e.g., the papers by Flood et al., Wright, and Evans.

10 Evans, R.G., M.L. Barer, S. Lewis, M. Rachlis, and G.L. Stoddart (2000), *Private Highway, One-way Street: The Decline and Fall of Canadian Medicare?*, HPRU 2000:3D, Vancouver, B.C.: Centre for Health Services and Policy Research, U.B.C.

Different Interpretations of 'Evidence' and Implications for the Canadian Healthcare System

CHARLES J. WRIGHT

Introduction

The majority decision of the Supreme Court in *Chaoulli v. Quebec (Attorney General)*[1] provides an excellent illustration of the two different meanings that exist for the word 'evidence.' On one hand evidence is proof or convincing grounds for believing something, and on the other evidence is what a person says under oath in court. They are not mutually exclusive, but it is understandable that scientists and lawyers may weigh their relative importance differently.

This paper will focus on the evidence presented both at the Quebec Superior Court and the Supreme Court of Canada trials of the *Chaoulli* case, as it relates to the issues of waiting lists and the potential effects on the Canadian health care system. I shall examine the Courts' decisions from the point of view of differing interpretations of what constitutes evidence. In this paper there will be no discussion of the many legal issues that are so ably covered in other contributions to this volume.

It seems clear from the judgment that the majority decision depended to a very large extent on the perception that current waiting times for surgical services are excessive, that this causes serious consequences for patients, and that governments are choosing not to deal with the problem adequately. In this light, the Supreme Court's decision can and should be used as a call to long overdue action on the part of governments and health authorities. The nature of the required action will be described.

Finally, the more serious resource problems about to confront the Canadian health care system in relation to the principle of equity will be discussed in the context of the Supreme Court's decision.

The Potential Effect of Private Healthcare Insurance on the Canadian Public Healthcare System

The evidence from the medical literature that had been submitted to the trial judge on this question was summarily dismissed in the majority opinion of the Supreme Court. The complete documents containing this evidence and all the relevant references are in the records of the Quebec Superior Court trial. First, I will discuss the evidence considered by the Quebec Superior Court and, in turn, rejected by the Supreme Court. I will then move to consider the evidence that appears to have convinced the Supreme Court majority to permit the remedy of private health insurance.

Potential effect on waiting lists

Two articles in prestigious journals, one monograph, one in-depth national report and one investigative documentary were cited in the Quebec Superior Court. The Audit Commission of the National Health Service in the UK reported on the activities of hospital doctors in England and Wales in 1995 with a damning indictment of the arrangement that permits surgeons to work both in the private and public systems.[2] The report noted that surgeons, on average, do one third to one half as many operations for large private fees as they do in the publicly funded system, and that they deliberately spend less time than they are contracted for working in the public system in order to conduct private practice. There was systematic evidence that British surgeons and anesthetists were short-changing patients and the National Health Service in favour of their private practices.

In an analysis of the situation in Israel, where physicians are also permitted to work in both private and public health care, it was noted that some of the physicians set up duplicate private clinics, creating the incentive to maintain queues in the same clinics in the public system.[3]

A study of waiting lists for cataract surgery in Manitoba found that patients attending surgeons who also work in private clinics waited far longer than patents whose surgeons worked only in the public system. The median wait for a public system patient whose surgeon also worked privately was 23 weeks, compared with ten weeks for the patients with surgeons working only in the public system.[4]

A national study of Australia's surgical workforce commissioned by the Federal Department of Human Services and Health concluded that delays in elective surgery in the public hospital system are caused largely by surgeons' reluctance to work in public hospitals and the fact that they encouraged their patients to use the private system preferentially.[5]

An investigative report commissioned in 1995 by the Joseph Rowntree Foundation (UK) for social policy research and development, examined the regular activities of physicians working in the public system and also part time in private practice. There was a strong tendency for physicians progressively to favour the private system and divert their commitment away from the public system. Patients faced waits of up to a year for elective surgery in the public system by a specialist but almost immediate 'private' treatment by the same specialist for those prepared to pay. Commenting on these findings, an editorial news report in the British Medical Journal stated, 'There is a danger that some doctors are allowing their greed to distort healthcare in Britain. Either we as a profession accept this (as in the United States) or we put a stop to it from within the profession.'[6]

It should not be surprising that physicians and surgeons are driven by the normal incentives that are well known to drive human behaviour. The problem is not that they are behaving unprofessionally or performing inappropriate services but the presence of systematic incentives towards behaving in this way. The fact that this incentive does not exist within the present Canadian system is a fundamental strength, not a weakness to be eliminated.

The evidence presented at the trial Court also dealt with the concern that public waiting lists would be affected adversely by the well known tendency of private health insurers to be selective in accepting clients. This is known as 'cream skimming' in the insurance business, where some occupations are black-listed and high risk patients are often completely refused coverage. In a hybrid system the costs associated with the higher risk patients would, of course, be borne selectively by the public sector. In jurisdictions where there is no legal impediment to access to public or private systems, the private hospitals are definitely not the preferred place of treatment for complex, risky surgery or serious illness.[7] These facilities rarely have students or residents nor do they have a full range of complex supporting services. In another analysis, it was noted that for-profit hospitals do not provide care any more efficiently or with greater public benefit than do non-profit institutions, but they do distort service delivery patterns. They siphon off high revenue patients and vigorously try to avoid providing care to patient populations who are a financial risk.[8] Dr. Arnold Relman, editor of the New England Journal of Medicine, commented that the private for-profit hospitals in the USA do not benefit the public system: 'In fact, by seeking to maximize revenues and avoid uninsured patients, they contributed to the problems of cost and access our healthcare system now faces.'[9] There is no question that expansion of private health care insurance in Canada would inevitably lead to creation of an investment-owned hospital industry.

The Supreme Court Response to the Evidence Presented at the Quebec Superior Court

In the majority judgment of the Supreme Court, the evidence on the potential effect of private health care on waiting lists in the public system received scant attention and was inexplicably dismissed as 'human reactions.'[10] The quote that follows must surely be the most bizarre comment in the entire judgment, given the various studies and reports that were put before the Court and discussed earlier:

> It is apparent from this summary that for each threat mentioned, no study was produced or discussed in the Superior Court. While it is true that scientific or empirical evidence is not always necessary, witnesses in a case in which the arguments are supposedly based on logic or common sense should be able to cite specific facts in support of their conclusions.[11]

I find this utterly inexplicable as the evidence in question, consisting of the published results of specific studies, statements from respected leaders in medicine, and research in prestigious medical journals, convinced the Quebec Superior Court to reject Chaoulli's arguments. Unfortunately, the March 2005 edition of the Canadian Health Services Research Foundation's 'Mythbusters' series entitled 'Myth: A parallel private system would reduce waiting times in the public system' was not available at the time of the Supreme Court's deliberations. The paper updates the evidence with multiple references and concludes:

> The mountain of evidence against parallel private healthcare underscores some logical flaws in arguments for it. First, since healthcare practitioners can't be in more than one place at the same time, creating a parallel private system simply takes badly needed doctors and nurses out of our public hospitals. Given that most people believe we already have a shortage of

both, it's hard to see how removing them from the public system will help alleviate public waits. Second, since doctors earn more in the private sector, they have what economists call a perverse incentive to keep public waiting lists long, to encourage patients to pay for private care. A parallel private system can provide faster care–to those with deeper pockets. However, it seriously compromises access to those waiting for care in the public system, and contradicts one of the features of public healthcare of which Canadians are most proud: that citizens should receive care based on their need, not on their ability to pay.[12]

On reading the majority judges' decision it is apparent that the evidence they found most compelling was that related to the suffering and death of patients on waiting lists, the governments' apparent unwillingness to take the steps that would be necessary to improve the situation, and the fact that a public medical system and private health insurance co-exist in various forms in many other countries. McLachlin C.J. and Major J. (on behalf of themselves and Bastarache J.) write with respect to the suffering and death caused by waiting lists:

> Delays in the public system are widespread and have serious, sometimes grave, consequences…Inevitably, where patients have life-threatening conditions, some will die because of undue delay in awaiting surgery…In addition to threatening the life and the physical security of the person, waiting for critical care may have significant adverse psychological effects.[13]

The decision then goes on to consider the *Canadian Charter of Rights and Freedoms*:[14]

> Where lack of timely healthcare can result in death, the s. 7 protection of life is engaged; where it can result in serious psychological and physical suffering, the s. 7 protection of security of the person is triggered. In this case, the government has prohibited private health insurance that would permit ordinary Quebecers to access private health care while failing to deliver healthcare in a reasonable manner, thereby increasing the risk of complications and death.[15]

In her decision, Deschamps J., who ruled that the prohibition against private insurance violated the Quebec *Charter of human rights and free-*

doms,[16] but who declined to rule on the issue of the *Canadian Charter*, stated:

> The government had plenty of time to act. Numerous commissions have been established…governments have promised on numerous occasions to find a solution to the problem of waiting lists…it seems that governments have lost sight of the urgency of taking concrete action.[17]

While acknowledging that utilizing private health insurance would not provide a complete solution to the problem of waiting lists, Deschamps J. stated that the appellants' only burden was 'to prove that their right to life and to personal inviolability had been infringed. They have succeeded in proving this.'[18]

The central issue in the *Chaoulli* case

If I may take the liberty of paraphrasing the Court's decision into simple language, it would look like this:

- Provinces have the right to infringe *Charter* rights if connected to the greater good.
- This infringement is not necessary in order to maintain a healthy public system.
- Surgical waiting lists cause serious suffering and inappropriate death.
- The public healthcare system in general, and the federal and provincial governments in particular, have failed to solve the waiting list problem.
- Private healthcare insurance is a necessary (although not sufficient) redress for the situation in healthcare in Canada today.

I recognize that this commentary does not even touch on any of the complex legal issues involved, but I believe that this simplification is essential to focus attention on the overriding issue that must be addressed now throughout the country, namely waiting lists for surgical services. It is obvious that if waiting lists were either absent or within reasonable bounds the *Chaoulli* appeal would have failed.

The reality is that it succeeded, and I would argue that it is now more important to deal with the core issue highlighted by the Court's decision, namely inappropriate waiting lists, rather than to expend much energy on how to overcome the further legal challenges that could follow. The most appropriate and highest priority course of action now is to definitively address the waiting list problem.

The Current Lack of Management of Waiting Lists in Canada

Waiting lists are the key issue in the *Chaoulli* judgment. It is impossible to deny that current wait times for some surgical services are inappropriately long in many areas in the country. However, some important facts tend to be lost in the media hype and public anxiety about waiting lists.

This may come as a major surprise to readers, but with few exceptions there is no systematic management of waiting lists for surgical services in Canada.[19] Evidence to this effect was presented to the Supreme Court,[20] and cited in the dissenting decision written by Binnie and LeBel JJ.[21] The fact is that in the vast majority of jurisdictions, hospitals and health authorities do not even have validated compiled information on waiting lists, let alone any organized interest in managing the flow of patients within them. Waiting lists are kept by individual surgeons or groups of surgeons in individual offices. In some cases hospitals have taken the initiative to insist that all patients waiting for surgery should be 'booked' into a central booking office, but even this small step towards management of the lists is absent in most hospitals throughout the country. This lack of basic information and the laissez-faire attitude towards surgeons' lists permits significant disparities and sometimes gross exaggeration of the problem for vested interest reasons.

Nobody questions the surgeon's primary role in making the decision that a patient should have surgery, but firm and fair management of hospital and operating resources in relation to patients' levels of urgency is required, rather than individual surgeons, departments and hospitals operating entirely independently of each other. What is required in jurisdictions throughout the country is a systematic collaborative multi-disciplinary approach to waiting list management. In Canada, this approach was pioneered by the Cardiac Care Network in Ontario[22] and is underway in a similar fashion now in Saskatchewan[23] and in the Cancer Care Ontario organization.[24]

Prioritization of patients on waiting lists for surgery is another important issue that was addressed in depth by the Western Canada

Waiting List Project.[25] The results demonstrated that it is possible for surgeons to agree upon reasonable criteria on which decisions can be made concerning relative priority of different patients on waiting lists.

Yet another more contentious issue is the appropriateness of the decision that the patient requires surgery in the first place. There is abundant literature showing wide variations in the rates of surgery for the same elective procedure in different communities.[26] Reviews of the appropriateness of indications for surgery are another piece of ideal waiting list management which is not yet significantly implemented in any area of practice in Canada.

Established wait list statistics may also be misleading.[27] Patients on long waiting lists may be booked on more than one list, have already been called for surgery and declined, have died of unrelated causes, may choose to be waiting for a convenient time or particular provider, or surgery may no longer be required on the basis of careful reassessment.

Finally, systematic registration and management of waiting lists could yield accurate information on actual waiting times, and any deterioration or death occurring during the wait for surgery. Currently there is an astonishing lack of valid information on this throughout the country. On several occasions the judgment refers to the problem of death occurring on waiting lists with the implication that the death is caused by the underlying condition for which treatment is being withheld. As discussed below, the only waiting list in which this may happen is that for cardiac surgery. To maintain perspective it is necessary to consider the patients with the diseases where the waiting lists tend to be the longest, namely hip or knee arthritis and cataract. There is no question that many patients waiting for long periods of time continue to suffer pain and disability, but it would be far-fetched to attribute the cause of any deaths to the arthritis or cataract.

In the case of heart surgery the situation is particularly interesting. Current rates of cardiac surgery are declining markedly as more and more of the problems that used to require open surgery are now being dealt with by less invasive methods. The result is that waiting lists for open heart surgery are now largely within reasonable bounds, and not only in Ontario where the Cardiac Care Network (CCN) has been in operation for years. Cardiac surgery is the one area where lack of prompt treatment could cause death, and the data on this are very interesting indeed. In the most recent information from the Ontario CCN (issued May 2005)[28] it can be seen that the great majority of open heart operations are being performed within the recommended maximum wait times that were set (85%, 86% and 92% for the emergency and urgent, semi-urgent and elective categories respectively). In the last complete year studied, the death rate in patients on the waiting list was one in 210 patients but it is unknown how many of these patients would have died in any case with what is, after all, a frequently lethal condition. This statistic must be pondered beside the fact that one in 40 patients having open heart surgery die as a direct result of the surgery or its complications.

Setting 'recommended maximum wait times' is difficult as there is little hard evidence on which to base decisions, especially in elective surgery that has more to do with lifestyle and symptoms than mortality. However, the Federal government has recently launched an important initiative to bring reasonable national standards to bear on the issue.[29] The development of these standards would then permit local jurisdictions to use them uniformly if and when they begin to get involved in waiting list management.

The 'evidence' about patients suffering and dying on waiting lists that clearly impressed the Supreme Court judges may have been somewhat exaggerated, but waiting lists now command attention as they have become the focus of the public's disaffection with the Canadian health care system.

Call to Action

There is little doubt that the achievements of the Ontario CCN in improving the waiting list situation could be replicated for most of the surgical procedures currently involving long waits, even with the present and recently promised level of resources. It is astonishing that so little has been done in the country as a whole in the management of waiting lists and that the Supreme Court of Canada had to cite the inaction of governments on this issue as a reason for deciding that patients' *Quebec Charter* or *Canadian Charter* rights were violated, leading to the decision permitting private health care insurance. More resources may be required but there are already enormous resources in our health care system (around 30–40% now of provinces' budgets plus the federal contribution) and the recent federal-provincial health accords have promised much more.

It is already the case that very little use is made of private health insurance in those provinces where it is permitted and there is little doubt that the source of the demand for private care would be reduced to a small group of vested interests if the steps discussed above were taken by provincial governments, health authorities and hospitals to manage surgical waiting lists appropriately. The research, knowledge and means already exist to do this. What is now needed is the will to engage on the part of governments, health authorities and hospitals and to cooperate on the part of physicians and other health providers.

Insatiable Demand for Healthcare Services and the Limits of Public Funding

The issue of ever-increasing demand for health care and the limits of public funding is difficult, sensitive and distasteful but must be addressed in any debate surrounding healthcare in Canada. This is particularly so in the context of a debate over the limits of public insurance and the appropriate role for private insurance. Currently there is such profound reluctance on the part of politicians to engage the issue that it has almost been accorded taboo status. No matter how efficiently the healthcare system is run, no matter how well we may succeed in managing and improving the situation for those on surgical waiting lists as discussed above, the gap between the demands on the healthcare system and the resources that can be made available for it will continue to grow.

Is there a person in Canada who genuinely believes that any healthcare system can provide any potentially beneficial service to anyone who needs or wants it at any time, without any delay, regardless of how small the potential benefit or how great the cost? This is surely a rhetorical question. It is obvious that there will never be an end to the development of drugs, health services and interventions that will advance our ability, however small, to fight disease and postpone death. This is the whole point in our substantial investment in health research. Many of these advances will be rapidly absorbed into regular medical practice at reasonable cost, often replacing previous and less effective treatments. However, in many fields of healthcare the benefit of a new drug or intervention to patients may be so marginal and the cost so enormous that a reasonable, objective assessment of the cost-effectiveness ratio is likely to deem it unsupportable in terms of the public basket of services.

There are some powerful looming examples of this, demanding rational policy rather than emotional outbursts in the media. The Supreme Court recently dealt with the example of autism in the *Auton* case,[30] remarkably but unsurprisingly deciding that it was not discriminatory of the provincial government to deny funding for the extremely expensive treatment program now available for autistic children, as they also deny funding to other 'experimental' therapies. But what happens when a new treatment that is marginally beneficial at huge cost is no longer experimental?

In many jurisdictions public pressure has already forced ministries of health to fund Herceptin® to reduce (not eliminate) the risk of recurrence of breast cancer at a cost of $50,000 per patient. Approximately 3000 women annually in Canada would be eligible, and the drug only benefits one in seven patients taking it. Herceptin® has already doubled the entire new drug program budget of Cancer Care Ontario.[31] Research evidence shows that Avastin®, a newly developed drug for colon cancer, could potentially give an additional three months of life to 5000 patients each year at a cost of at least $60,000 per patient. Many more such drugs are under investigation.

If not with these examples then certainly with others to follow, every society must make difficult decisions on where the boundaries of public healthcare funding will lie, including decisions about how much we are prepared to impoverish infrastructure development, education, culture and all other societal programs. These decisions would be easier if the benefit to be gained from the enormous expense were more substantial, but even there the ability of the public system to pay must eventually reach the wall.

At this point in the discussion the focus shifts onto the issue of equity. Although equity is not one of the five widely quoted tenets of the *Canada Health Act*[32] it was clearly an important, perhaps the most important, underlying principle in the development of the current Canadian healthcare system. Equity in the health care system remains an important principle for the majority of Canadians as has been repeatedly confirmed in nation-wide studies,[33] and this has significant implications for the health policy that must be developed. The statement in the *Canada Health Act* that 'medically necessary' services are insured[34] must be seen in the context of its time and place and needs to be reworded now as more and more marginal-benefit/huge-cost drugs and services become available. Decisions in this arena are and always will be unpalatable but no reasonable alternative is apparent.

It is ironic that the principle of equity becomes a double edged sword in the arena of medical ethics. It cuts sharply through attempts to make private healthcare available for the full range of usual health services and it cuts equally sharply into the selective provision of any service that is deemed unaffordable for the system to provide to all. There is inexorable logic pointing to the next step, namely a decision that some such services must be deemed uninsured in the public system, thereby rendering private payment or insurance for them lawful even under current federal and provincial legislation.

Summary and Conclusion

The evidence about the potential effects of private health care on the public system that led the lower Court to reject Chaoulli's application received little attention in the Supreme Court. The Supreme Court majority in *Chaoulli* chose to focus on the long waiting lists for surgical services, the resulting suffering and death of patients and the governments' unwillingness to respond appropriately, constituting violation of the appellants' *Quebec Charter* right to life and personal inviolability. As a result it allowed that private health insurance is an appropriate remedy. This chapter has emphasized the need to address the central issue that the judges found so compelling, whether the judgment seems balanced to us as health care 'experts' or not. The urgent need is for provincial ministries of health, health authorities and hospitals to step up to the waiting list challenge using policies and management strategies that are well-known and available, but widely ignored in the present system. Finally, the reality of the gap between the infinite potential demand for health care services and the resources that can be made available in a public system must be addressed rather than studiously ignored by politicians and health care leaders. Decisions about what can and cannot be funded must become subject to carefully developed policy on the basis of cost-effectiveness rather than the pleadings of vested interests and pressure groups.

Notes

1 2005 SCC 35, rev'g [2002] R.J.Q. 1205 (C.A.) and [2000] R.J.Q. 786 (C.S.) [*Chaoulli*].
2 D. Light, 'Betrayal by the Surgeons' (1996) 347 Lancet 812.
3 M.L. Barer *et al.*, 'Accommodating Rapid Growth in Physician Supply: Lessons from Israel, Warnings for Canada' (1989) 19 Int. J. Health Serv. 95.
4 Manitoba Centre for Health Policy and Evaluation, *Surgical Waiting Times*

in Manitoba (Winnipeg: Manitoba Centre for Health Policy and Evaluation, 1998), online: Manitoba Centre for Health Policy <http://www.umanitoba .ca/centres/mchp/reports/pdfs/surgwait.pdf>.

5 P.E. Baume, *A cutting edge: Australia's surgical workforce 1994. Report of the Inquiry into supply of, and requirements for, medical specialist services in Australia* (Canberra: Commonwealth Department of Human Services and Health, 1994) and S. Chapman, 'Australian's Surgeons Savaged by Cutting Report' (1994) 309 Br. Med. J. 1254.

6 Christopher Bulstrode, 'Embarrassing Greed?' (1995) 310 Br. Med. J. 199.

7 H.J. Aaron & W.B. Schwartz, *The Painful Prescription* (Washington, D.C.: The Brookings Institution, 1984) at 22.

8 R. Sutherland & J. Fulton, *Spending Smarter and Spending Less* (Ottawa: Health Group, 1994) at 77.

9 A. Relman, 'Shattuck Lecture–The Health Care Industry: Where is it taking us?' (1991) 325 N. Engl. J. Med. 855.

10 *Supra* note 1 at para. 62.

11 *Supra* note 1 at para. 64.

12 Canadian Health Services Research Foundation, 'Mythbusters, Myth: A parallel private system would reduce waiting times in the public system' (March 2005) at 2, online: Canadian Health Services Research Foundation <http://www.chsrf.ca/mythbusters/pdf/myth17_e.pdf>.

13 *Supra* note 1 at paras. 112–116.

14 Part I of the *Constitution Act, 1982*, being Schedule B to the *Canada Act 1982* (U.K.), 1982, c. 11 [*Canadian Charter*].

15 *Supra* note 1 at summary.

16 R.S.Q. c. C-12 [*Quebec Charter*].

17 *Supra* note 1 at para. 96.

18 *Supra* note 1 at para. 100.

19 Canadian Health Services Research Foundation, 'Evidence Boost: Manage waiting lists centrally for better efficiency' (March 2005), online: Canadian Health Services Research Foundation <http://www.chsrf.ca/ mythbusters/pdf/boost1_e.pdf>.

20 Steven Lewis *et al.*, 'Ending waiting-list mismanagement: principles and practice' (2000) 162 CMAJ 1297.

21 *Supra* note 1 at para. 212.

22 B. Monaghan *et al.*, 'Through the looking glass: the Cardiac Care Network of Ontario 10 years later' (2001) 4 Hospital Q. 30.

23 A.J. Ehman, 'Saskatchewan's new system tracks surgical waits' (2004) 171 CMAJ 1158.

24 Farrah Schwartz *et al.*, *A Four-Point Strategy to Reduce Waiting Times in*

Ontario (Toronto: Cancer Care Ontario, 2004), online: Cancer Care Ontario <http://www.cancercare.on.ca/documents CQCOfourpointstrategy.pdf>.

25 T.W. Noseworthy *et al.*, 'Waiting for scheduled services in Canada: development of priority-setting scoring systems' (2003) 9 J. Eval. Clin. Pract. 23.

26 The evidence is summarized and referenced in C.J. Wright, G.K. Chambers & Y. Robens-Paradise, 'Evaluation of indications for and outcomes of elective surgery' (2002) 167 CMAJ 461.

27 See *e.g.* B. Sobolev, P. Brown & D. Zelt, 'Potential for bias in waiting time studies: events between enrolment and admission' (2001) 55 J. Epidemiol. Community Health 891 and Health Council of Canada, *Health Care Renewal in Canada: Accelerating Change* (Toronto: Health Council of Canada, 2005) at 30, online: Health Council of Canada <http://hcc-ccs.com/ report/Annual_Report/Accelerating_Change_HCC_2005.pdf>.

28 Cardiac Care Network of Ontario, 'Patient Access to Care' online: Cardiac Care Network of Ontario <http://www.ccn.on.ca/access.html>.

29 Dr. Brian Postl, CEO of Winnipeg Health Sciences Centre, has been appointed to lead a national task force to achieve this.

30 *Auton (Guardian ad litem of) v. British Columbia (Attorney General)*, [2004] S.C.R. 657.

31 Personal communication with Dr. Brent Zanke, Head of Systematic Therapy, Cancer Care Ontario (September 2005)[unpublished].

32 R.S.C. 1983, c. C-6, s. 7.

33 Canada, National Forum on Health, *Canada Health Action: Building on the Legacy* (1997), online: Health Canada <http://www.hc-sc.gc.ca/hcs-sss/ com/nfh-fns/index_e.html> and Canada, Commission on the Future of Health Care in Canada, *Building on Values: The Future of Health Care in Canada, Final Report* (Ottawa: National Library of Canada, 2002), online: Health Canada <http://www.hc-sc.gc.ca/english/care/romanow/ index1.html>.

34 *Supra* note 32, ss. 2, 7 and 9.

Comparative Evidence About Private Health Insurance

How to Defend a Public Health Care System: Lessons from Abroad

Introduction

The *Chaoulli* decision is a 'wake up' call for those Canadians interested in securing an efficient and equitable health care system. As many have noted over the decades, health care systems public (e.g. Canada and the UK) and private (e.g. the USA) are always in a state of 'crisis'[2] This notion of crisis is an inevitable product of two certainties: firstly that we are all suffering from a terminal, sexually transmitted disease called life, and secondly that resources always and everywhere are scarce and have to be rationed. The result inevitably is that some folk are denied care from which they would benefit and which they would like to consume.

Given these certainties, the pertinent policy challenge for all policy makers is who shall live in what degree of pain and discomfort, when all must die? Or, to be less direct and emotional, what principle of equity should determine access to health care? In Canada, Western Europe and Australasia and increasingly in the Pacific Rim countries, the answer to this question involves repudiation of market principles of willingness and ability to pay in favour of the allocation of health care on the basis of need. This is nicely demonstrated by data from the Organisation for Economic Cooperation and Development which shows that the public sector dominates in health care delivery and finance in most affluent countries. For instance many affluent countries, as diverse as Japan and Spain have over 70 per cent of their total health care funded from public sources (Canada has 69.9 per cent) and with the exception of the USA, these countries usually fund 80 per cent and more of inpatient care from public funds (Canada 86.6 per cent).[3]

This paper seeks to address the issue of equity and then to review the poor guardianship of Medicare and other public health care systems by many of its advocates and defenders in terms of the efficient use of tax payers' funds. The *Chaoulli* decision requires that these folk reform Medicare by improving its transparency, accountability and efficiency, challenges which are dealt with in the second section. There is an obvious risk that Federal and Provisional Governments in Canada will duck this obligation to the voter and instead elect for the easy option of permitting private insurance. This is likely to compound the inefficiencies evidenced in Medicare with new inefficiencies in an expanded private sector. Furthermore it will undermine equality of access as expressed in Medicare legislation and practice. The concluding section seeks to remind us all that the defence of equity principles inherent in public health care systems has to be continuous. Those with different ideological beliefs will continue to challenge Medicare and NHS type health care systems because they will make money and gain power from the pursuit of their individualistic values.

Remember those equity goals?

Health care reformers like Bismarck in Germany and Lloyd George in Britain were politicians who responded to threats similar to those now facing the architects of Canadian Medicare. The 'market solution' then and now (e.g. in the US) involved both the denial of care and the bankruptcy of follow citizens as a result of their misfortune and genetic susceptibility. Government intervention was, and is, needed to create financial protection for citizens.

The political risks faced by the early health care reformers included concern about having a fit labour force to man the armed forces and staff industry during times of great economic development. Thus Lloyd George's campaign to introduce welfare state redistributive policies in 1911 in the UK was influenced by the high levels of rejection due to illness and disability of potential recruits to fight in the Boer War at the beginning of the 20th Century.

Underpinning these motives were related political and public health concerns. For instance, a failure to ensure vaccination, immunisation and other preventive interventions can lead to low levels of take up by the poor. Diseases amongst such groups can affect the middle classes, thereby creating a rationale for redistribution: caring for the poor benefits the well off!

However, in Germany, Britain, Canada and other welfare states, the drive for collective action is basically political. Then, as now, Government action to redistribute and protect the disadvantaged has political and social benefits. A nice present day example of this is China. Since the adoption of a 'capitalist path' in China, economic growth has created large inequalities in the distribution of income and wealth, particularly between urban and rural areas. Furthermore, the Maoist system of public health with efficient monitoring of disease and the provision of basic programmes of prevention and care ensured both the control of infectious diseases and a reduction in relative and absolute mortality rates. Come economic liberalisation since 1989 in China, come the collapse of this system and the development of major public health challenges (e.g. SARS, HIV-AIDS and TB) and inequalities in health care provision that challenge the survival of the Communist Party. This challenge is now being met by redistributive policies to restore rural health care, improve public health surveillance and control and mitigate the political consequence of gross inequality.

Underlying these political issues are ideological or value issues related to the type of society Canada or any other country wants. These values are in part the products of the 'real politic' outlined above, but are also related to more general cultural values.

The description of the rival ideologies has been discussed for decades.[4] The competing camps are essentially libertarian and egalitarian. For the former, the primary goal is freedom – and in health care this means freedom of choice, based on individuals' willingness and ability to pay.

Libertarians believe that individuals are the best judges of their own welfare and if this leads to unequal or no health care protection for the poor, so be it! These folk prefer under-regulated, or even better, unregulated markets as the means of delivering diversity, inequality and the protection of individual freedom.

Egalitarians place equality of opportunity above freedom and other values. They believe that all members of society have equal rights to basic goals, of which health care may be one. In societies like these in Canada, Western Europe and elsewhere, a consensus has emerged that health care is a basic good and that in the absence of equality of opportunity, there is a moral obligation to compensate those deprived of health care by creating public financed provision. Such intervention creates financial protection for those in need. Health care is provided **not** on the basis of willingness and ability to pay but **on the basis of**

need, where need is defined as the patient's capacity to benefit from health care per unit of cost (the cost effectiveness rule).

The libertarian position is nicely supported by conventional economic analysis, which assumes that the consumer is king and the market should be competitive so as to service his wishes with the minimum of government intervention. This market approach, as an end rather than a means, protects inequality, rewards achievement and punishes under achievement. It provides incentives for innovation, for instance encouraging physicians to develop private practice and pursue personal profit even though this may create inappropriate and inefficient health care provision[5] as well as facilitating reductions in public sector waiting times.

Outcomes such as these require careful regulation, something opposed by libertarians, even though capitalists are always the enemies of capitalism, as Adam Smith, the 18th century political economist argued:

> People of the same trade seldom meet together, even for merriment and diversion, but the conversation ends in a conspiracy against the public, or in some contrivance to raise prices. It is impossible indeed to prevent such meetings, by any law which either could be executed, or would be consistent with liberty and justice. But though the law cannot hinder people of the same trade from sometimes assembling together, it ought to do nothing to facilitate such assemblies, much less to render them necessary.[6]

Whilst these ideological perspectives are always and everywhere in competition with each protagonist claiming the 'failure' of their opponents' 'regime' and the superior potential of their perspective, the choice of approach depends on the national political and social decisions.

What sort of society do Canadians, Brits and others want? Do they want to experiment with the inequality and inefficiency inherent in the diversity and (lack of) choice in the US health care system and risk the consequence that once altered any system is difficult to reverse? Or do they want to adhere to egalitarian principles and defend those principles by improving the efficiency of Medicare by mitigating its failings, such as excessive waiting time and other inefficiencies? Ultimately, such choices are the product of the voting system and the politicians it creates. However, in reaching its decisions, the electorate has to be clear about the implication of its choices. Do Canadians want a better performing egalitarian health care system, allocating care on the basis of need like most other civilised states, or a fragmented and more expensive system that treats its citizenry unequally, perhaps excluding people from protection and imposing potential financial ruin on them, as in the USA?[7]

Improving Health Care Efficiency

The problems of private health insurance

Private insurance does not and cannot mitigate inequalities – that is not its purpose. It may reduce 'inefficiencies' in terms of the waiting times of the relatively affluent but can create expenditure inflation whilst perpetrating the real inefficiencies inherent in all health care systems, public and private.

These problems are epitomised by Australia, where a libertarian administration (and a Prime Minister, John Howard, who has always opposed Australian Medicare) has sought to undermine the public health care system. By providing subsidies (30 per cent tax offsets and other incentives) to purchase private health insurance, the Government has driven up insurance coverage from 30 per cent to 45 per cent of the population. However, the cost of this in terms of reductions in tax revenue amounts to $A2.5 billion, which some argue could, if spent on Medicare, have created more health care activity. The Howard reforms are inequitable in that they subsidise the more affluent who can pay taxes and enhance their claims on health care provision in relation to ability and willingness to pay rather than need.[8]

In the Australian system there is considerable regulation of private health insurance (PHI) and unlike in the USA, premia are community rather than individual rated and the government has to sanction any premium increase.[9] As ever in the PHI industry and as noted in a report of the Organisation for Economic Cooperation and Development,[10] premia rates tend to inflate at rates in excess of increases in the consumer price index (e.g. currently US health insurance premia are rising at about 10 per cent annually). The consequence of premia inflation in Australia is that their growth increases subsidisation and continuously erodes the tax take of government.

Australian policy is inequitable, expenditure-inflationary and does nothing to mitigate the inherent inefficiencies of the health care industry, but it has contributed to Prime Minister Howard's re-election! The deficiencies of this approach are generally inherent internationally in all health care reforms or 'redisorganisations' of both public and private systems of provision.

The motivation for private insurance development

As Stefan Gress explains more fully in this volume there is a distinction to be made between supplementary and complementary (double-cover) systems of private health insurance. For instance, in France there is supplementary private insurance that citizens purchase to meet the cost of the user charges levied by the public French health care system. As in Canada, there is pressure in France for complementary insurance (e.g. by AXA one of the largest international insurance companies).[11]

In the UK, New Zealand and Australia there is complementary or double-cover private health insurance (PHI), which is sometimes subsidised by the State (as in Australia) and sometimes required to be independent of Government support (as in the UK). The prosperity of these sectors is a product of quality and waiting times in local public health care systems and related motivations. Thus in the UK, employers purchase PHI as a fringe benefit for their executives. This is partly a product of labour market competition and partly a self-interested policy to ensure that executives are kept fit to work. The individual PHI market has declined steadily as for many self-pay is more economical.

Another powerful factor in the creation and survival of private insurance is the pecuniary self-interest of physicians: the private sector generally pays well. The Conservative Minister of Health in the UK in the late 1960s, Enoch Powell noted:

> 'The universal discovery every Minister of Health makes at or near the
> outset of his term of office is that the only subject he is ever destined to
> discuss with the medical profession is money.'

This monetary discussion has two related Oliver Twist-like strands: more money for the payment of practitioners, and more money for the development of their services. The consequence of removing the cash limitations of the public health service by the introduction of PHI is that these twin forces can be unleashed. Unsurprisingly post- *Chaoulli*, Canadian medical groups, as discussed by Trudo Lemmens and Tom Archibald, have supported private insurance as this frees them from the 'shackles' of the public sector and gives them access to more resources to enhance their income and to develop services, some of proven cost effectiveness where citizens wait in the public sector (e.g. hip replacement) and some of little cost-effectiveness (e.g. cosmetic surgery) which are highly remunerative for practitioners. When public health care systems are seen to be inefficient and failing to deliver services of proven cost effectiveness in a timely fashion, the solution is not to throw out the baby with the bathwater but to manage better medical practices which produce in an affluent society like Canada, avoidable waiting times and other service delivery problems.

What appears to be the reasoned advocacy of PHI by distinguished medical practitioners should be seen for what it often is: self-interested advocacy of depriving Canadian households of further resources to fund health care expenditure which creates incomes and jobs for themselves. With health care systems public and private being observably inefficient in their use of society's resources (see next section), the challenge is not to spend more but to spend what is available more efficiently. Unfortunately self-interested politicians competing for votes might find the complementary PHI route much easier to adopt than policies which hold providers, be they practitioners, hospitals or pharmaceutical 'drug dealers' to account! But as Chalmers, the architect of the Cochrane Collaborative argued:

> 'Because professionals sometimes do more harm than good when they intervene in the lives of other people, their policies and practices should be informed by rigorous, transparent, up to date evaluations'[12]

Health care market failures

Sadly such good sense is not the basis of public or private policy making in health care. Regardless of the public-private mix in the finance and provision of care and regardless of the GDP of countries, there are common failures in the provision of health care to populations. These failures in public health care systems can reinforce ideologically driven criticism. Thus waiting times in Canada, Australia and the UK generate libertarian advocacy of complementary (i.e. duplicate) private health insurance. The reluctance of public policy makers to manage their resources efficiently creates an opportunity for antipathetic ideology advocacy.

There are four common failures in all health care markets public and private, and one failure that is a continuing problem in many public health care systems:

a. There are large variations in the provision of care to similar populations and hence considerable scope for rationalisation, economy
   and the redeployment of resources.
b. All countries, regardless of their income and health care systems,
   fail to deliver cheap, evidence-based programmes for the management of chronic illnesses in particular, thus imposing on their citizenry avoidable morbidity and mortality. Furthermore, insult is
   added to injury by evidence that on some occasions where care is
   given, it is inappropriate, offering patients little or no improvement
   in health, whilst exposing them to the risks of the procedure and
   infections in the hospitals.
c. The management of medical errors in all health care systems is
   poor, with a reluctance to generate data and deploy safety-engineer-
   ing techniques to learn from the 'good' performers and improve or
   curtail the performance of 'bad' providers.
d. There is generally an absence of measures of 'success' or improvements in patient reported quality of life. Outcomes measurement
   where it exists focuses on failures, in particular mortality, complications and readmissions. Whilst such data are important, they reflect
   the fate of a small minority of unfortunate patients. Most patients
   survive hospital interventions, but no health care organisation
   systematically measures the relative degrees of success of clinicians
   in terms of improving patient functioning (physical, social and
   psychological).
e. In addition to these four generic health care problems, there is the
   problem of waiting times inherent in many public health care
   systems due to a combination of poor management of the four
   preceding failures and at the margin some funding problems.

Without reform of incentive structures and the development of the
quantitative management techniques (e.g. six sigma safety engineering
approaches[13]) needed to inform health care choices, the inefficiency
inherent in public and private health care systems will continue and be
used by ideological opponents as evidence of system 'failure' and the
need to change the policy approach.

Elaborating on each of these issues, it is evident that they have a good
evidence base, are generally known by the research, policy and practitioner communities but ignored by reformers and the clinical and non
clinical managers of health care, public and private. The inefficiencies
inherent in Canadian Medicare and UK-NHS threaten their existence

and waste taxpayers' money. To complement them with PHI failures, in particular enhanced expenditure inflation will create additional economic burdens on the Canadian economy, increased inefficiency as frivolous inefficient new procedures are developed and marketed and increased inequality to access and utilisation of health care particular by the old, the sick and the poor, who are major health care users, is unwise unless Canadian governments are prepared to regulate both sectors, and their interactions, with a rigour absent in all countries.

Jack Wennberg and his colleagues at Dartmouth College, USA, have produced the best example of evidence of variations in medical practice over three decades. The focus of their work has been the analysis of practice variations in US-Medicare, a federally funded programme, providing benefits for the American elderly. A nice review of this literature can be found in Health Affairs.[14]

The most recent large-scale analysis of US Medicare practice variations showed significant differences in the volume and cost of care provided to similar patients across the USA.

> Twofold differences among regions in per capita Medicare spending have long been recognized. After adjustment for age, sex, and race, per capita Medicare spending in 2000 was $10,550 in Manhattan, New York, for example, but only $4,823 in Portland, Oregon. The differences in spending are largely unrelated to differences in illness or price. Rather, they are due to differences in patterns of practice, which are more inpatient-based and specialist-oriented in regions with high per capita expenditures. As compared with similar enrolees in Portland, Medicare enrolees in Manhattan spent more than twice as much time in the hospital and had twice as many visits to physicians per year. During their last six months of life, Manhattan Medicare enrolees were three times as likely as Portland enrolees to spend a week or more in an intensive care unit and had five times as many visits to a medical specialist.[15]

The causes of these variations and their inherent waste are numerous, but a primary issue is the failure to manage the physician (or induce self management in the profession).[16]

> 'The substantial variation from area to area in the consumption of medical care and in its per capita cost is sustained by the policies of hospital boards and administrators, regulatory agencies and providers of medical insurance. The policies seldom take into account the existing level of health

care in a community; a common result is an increase in medical services in areas that already have high rates of consumption. When such inequities develop, the people receiving the greater number of medical and surgical procedures do not necessarily benefit, particularly when the procedures entail substantial risk.'

'The amount and cost of hospital treatment in a community has more to do with the number of physicians, their medical specialties and the procedures they prefer, than the health of their residents.'

The provision of appropriate care for the chronically ill could be funded by the removal of inappropriate care. The work of the American physician Robert Brook and others has chronicled how by setting practice standards in relation both to the evidence base and expert opinion and analysing clinical practice retrospectively, much unnecessary and sometimes harmful 'care' can be identified and removed.[17] Thus an Anglo-American study of cardiac surgery interventions in a UK-NHS region concluded:

'Inappropriate care even in the face of waiting lists, is a significant problem in Trent. In particular, by the standards of the UK panel, one half of the coronary angiographs were performed for equivocal or inappropriate reasons, and two fifths of the CABGs were performed for similar reasons. Even by the more liberal US criteria, the ratings were 29% equivocal or inappropriate for coronary angiograph and 33% equivocal or inappropriate for CABGs.'[18] (Bernstein et al 1993) (15)

Whilst a significant number of clinical interventions have sparse or absent evidence bases, there are others where therapies are known to be clinically and cost effective but are not implemented, resulting in significant levels of avoidable morbidity and mortality. The identification, monitoring and management of chronically ill patients with diseases such as hypertension, diabetes, chronic obstructive pulmonary disease, asthma and mental illness can be done cheaply with considerable patient benefits. The Rand Corporation concluded that only 55 per cent of Americans received appropriate care[19] and similar outcomes have been found in other US studies:[20] US health care systems fail to deliver simple cost effective procedures that would reduce mortality and morbidity.

Similar problems in delivering evidence based care for the chronically ill is evident everywhere from Kyrgyzstan to China to Europe and North America. A British response to this has been to put in place incentives for GPs to provide a 'quality outcome framework' (QOF), which includes monitored achievement of the delivery of cost effective care to the chronically ill.[21] By paying British doctors for what they should provide anyway, the Government has had success in reducing the deficiencies of practices but at a significant cost to the taxpayer!

Individual countries report varying levels of medical errors, e.g. from 3 per cent (some US work) to 16 per cent (Australia) of hospital admissions.[22] Any such estimates are subject to wide ranges of error due to reporting difficulties and the human desire to avoid criticism. However, whatever the rate, the causes are quite well chronicled with often simple, cost effective remedies being often ignored, e.g. infection and hand hygiene. Medication errors, surgical errors and similar problems are usually the product of poor data collection combined with individual and corporate willingness to ignore problems. Reducing errors (never removing them, as this would not be efficient!) requires real time data collection and incentives for managerial performance, for instance, three standard deviations from the average. Such practices are evolving, slowly!

Over 150 years ago the English nurse Florence Nightingale (who was the first female member of the Royal Statistical Society) advocated the management of the success of a hospital in terms of whether patients were 'dead, relieved or unrelieved.' No Canadian, British or other hospital has an outcome measurement system of such sophistication in 2005!

Nightingale argued:

'I am fain to sum up with an urgent appeal for adopting this or some uniform system of publishing the statistical records of hospitals. There is a growing conviction that in all hospitals, even in those which are best conducted, there is a great and unnecessary waste of life ... In attempting to arrive at the truth, I have applied everywhere for information, but in scarcely an instance have I been able to obtain hospital records fit for any purpose of comparison. If they could be obtained, they would enable us to decide many other questions besides the ones alluded to. They would show subscribers how their money was being spent, what amount of good was really being done with it, or whether the money was doing mischief rather than good.'[23]

During the last 30 years, researchers have developed generic quality of life measures such as Short Form 36[24] and EQ%D.[25] These have been translated into dozens of languages and used in thousands of clinical trials. However, they have not been used in routine health care. These instruments can be used to get patient views on their physical and mental functioning before and after treatment so that 'value added' (if any!) can be identified. Furthermore, such data can also be used to appraise the comparative performance of physicians in restoring patient health.

The fifth 'failure' issue that dominates the debate about public health care systems is waiting time. This has been a particular problem in the UK NHS but can be seen also in countries as diverse as Australia, Chile, Denmark, New Zealand and Spain. The usual view of this phenomenon is that waiting times create a secondary and private market for the service of physicians, and one where the pay tends to be superior to that of the public sector. When the UK NHS was created in 1948, the Government yielded to medical pressure and permitted the continuance of private practice in the hospital sector in order to acquire the profession's agreement to the creation of a public health care system. He is alleged to have described this as 'stuffing their mouths with gold' to drown out their opposition to the creation of the NHS!

The nature and causes of waiting lists are complex. They have been described as 'random numbers assembled by civil servants.'[26] Typically these data are not kept up to date and thus patients allegedly on waiting lists may be dead or treated as well as still waiting! Even where the data are accurate, and hospital administrators are not 'cheating' in their construction and management to attract additional resources to their organisations, their causes may be diverse.

For instance waiting in a public system may be the result of 'bottlenecks' in local public hospitals, which, because they are poorly managed disadvantage patients, leaving them in pain and discomfort and waiting cost effective procedures that could be delivered after a little targeted investment and better management.[27] However even more malign may be the self-interest of physicians who can perceive a financial gain in terms of income generation from private sector activity. This may manifest itself in a variety of ways from low levels of activity in public facilities to reluctance to adopt new techniques (in particular day case surgery) that would speed up patient through put. Such behaviours are often the product of weak public sector management that does not define and enforce contracts efficiently. It seems likely that this may be contributing to current Canadian waiting time issues. However as Yates emphasised waiting lists appear in providers that appear to be efficient and amongst those that appear to be inefficient.[28] There is not one explanation of waiting in the UK NHS that fits all hospitals. Each has particular and often unique explanations for its waiting characteristics. Each list needs its own 'surgical remedies' to cut waiting, using data and providing incentives for change with sometimes only marginal increases needed in expenditure.

The recent investment in the NHS by the Blair Government is reducing waiting times sharply with nearly 95 per cent of patients treated within six months and waiting times (from referral to inpatient care) planned to fall to 12 weeks maximum by 2008. This policy has been based on investment in additional capacity, public and private. In addition Blair has sought to get the NHS to 'act smarter' in its utilisation of capacity with an array of radical, untested and ill-coordinated policies aimed at creating 'contestability' as an instrument to root out inefficient practices. These policies include a new consultant contract that makes NHS obligations better defined and better remunerated, and private practice less attractive. With the decline of waiting times due to Government policy, the future of the private health insurance (PHI) sector is less certain. Whilst employers are continuing to offer PHI as a fringe benefit, the market is growing in competitiveness as carriers seek to control expenditure inflation to retain market share. Evidence of reduction in the volume of PHI is not as yet apparent but could follow as the 2008 waiting time target and the enhancement of NHS facilities progresses.

If private practice is augmented by private health insurance in Canada, this typically will be not for emergency care but for diagnostic and elective care. Given the nature of this market, the impact of supplier induced demand for care may result in the provision of inappropriate care to create income. There is evidence in the public and private sector of unnecessary surgery. For instance criticism of the appropriateness of tonsillectomy in the 1970s led to major reductions in activity. As specialists reduced their activity in this area they increased activity for myringotomies (or in the UK what was called 'glue ear'). This in turn has been shown to be inappropriate as it gives few benefits to most patients.[29] Other examples of areas of unnecessary surgery include cataract removal and hysterectomy.[30]

The existence of a two tier health care system creates the potential for health care activity and quality to be reduced in the public sector. In the UK the process of care in the private sector is generally regarded as superior with physicians wearing 'private sector suits' and having a

more bedside manner. Furthermore facilities, in terms of patients' crea-
ture comforts (e.g. TV, single room etc) are superior. With specialists
'diverted' to the private sector by money, more junior practitioners may
treat public patients. However whether this produces inferior outcomes
is a matter of conjecture rather than something with an evidence base
and again it is a product of public sector management inefficiency in
not enforcing public sector employment contracts. The natural propensity of politicians is to leave public sector restrictive trade practices
unreformed. In part this is part of the ethos of trusting professionals
and in part it is a product of the difficulty of enforcing contracts in a
market where evidence is often weak and professional judgement dominates. Klein asserted that in the UK, there was an implicit contract
between the medical profession and Government whereby the medics
did not question funding, provided Government did not question clinical practice.[31] Thatcher and her desire for 'value for money' breached
this 'entente cordiale' and Blair who demands that the NHS and its
workers 'act smarter' is continuing her reforms, even more radically.

The debate about the role of the private sector in the NHS is complicated by recent evidence that shows that those NHS physicians practicing in the private sector may have higher public sector activity rates
than those publicly employed physicians who are full time employees
of the NHS.[32] This finding highlights the gulf between rhetoric and
evidence in this debate. There are many factors that influence the effect
of private practice on the functioning of a public health care system in
particular weak public sector management and a failure to regulate the
fees and clinical governance practices of private sector providers. With
poor management and poor regulation of private suppliers there is
potential for a two-tier care to damage the public system. However
when such effects are alleged they are poorly quantified in most countries and are often the product of political and managerial weaknesses
in managing the excesses of physicians and their trade unions. Furthermore if such weaknesses were reduced, waiting times would be reduced and the political clamour around this market failure and the
desire for private alternatives would be absent.

Instead of focusing public debate solely on funding, waiting time and
activity levels, it is timely to complement these with investment in
evaluation of experiments using outcome measures in routine clinical
practice. Such data would be useful complements to 'failure' measures
and assist more efficient use of society's scarce resources. However it is
important to grapple with the possibility, even the certainty that the

current Canadian 'crisis' over waiting times and private insurance is an inevitable product of weak political and managerial control of a potentially fine health care system built on egalitarian principles where practice remains inefficient[33] and in so doing creates the potential for private sector development and with it the potential for damage to public sector provision.

Overview

Private health insurance (PHI) based on international experience offers no remedies for the market failures outlined here and is generally designed to worsen equity. If PHI were to emerge in Canada, Federal and Provincial administrations would have to regulate it vigorously to avoid both 'cream skimming' policies that challenge Medicare finance and equity policies and the inefficient provision of care, e.g. failure to deliver appropriate care and the propensity to deliver care of little clinical benefit to patients. Whichever ideological path is chosen, these well documented and generally ignored problems of inefficiency in the use of society's resources will have to be mitigated. Once the path of duplicated public and private health is chosen, it will be very difficult to reverse the system as the consumer and provider benefits will make electoral change costly as demonstrated by Labour's acceptance of Howard's PHI reforms in the last Australian election.

Conclusions

What are the lessons of international health care reform?

  i. In most industrialised and wealthy countries health care is largely funded and often provided by Government or its agencies (e.g. social insurance schemes).
 ii. This structure is the product of agreed social values of an egalitarian nature.
iii. Libertarian opponents who, for example, question 'sustainability' and highlight system deficiencies regularly challenge these values. These groups prefer greater inequality, more rapid expenditure inflation and inefficiency that benefit their supporters, particularly medical practitioners and the pharmaceutical industry.
 iv. Public health care provision, like its private counterpart is often

inefficient. Governments' failure to mitigate these inefficiencies fuels opposition to Medicare and the NHS, as they produce unnecessary and unacceptable waiting times and media opposition hype. If the egalitarian perspective is to survive, there needs to be not just political consensus about ideological values but also agreed radical reform of the public health care systems to improve their efficiency.

v. In the absence of the reform of Medicare, waiting time challenges will continue to divert managers and policy makers and induce a wasteful debate about the impact of a two tier health care system on the quality and availability of publicly provided care rather than on remedying the deficiencies of the public system.

vi. A reform programme targeting inefficiencies in clinical practices (variations, errors, inappropriate care, failure to deliver appropriate care and the reluctance to measure and manage success (improvements in patient reported quality of life) in conjunction with failure (avoidable mortality and morbidity) will be opposed by public and private providers as it will redistribute their income and power.

vii. Sad myopia that leads to assertions that private providers, private insurance and 'market' mechanisms are 'solutions' to vague notions of public sector failure (which are usually ideologically based) are unfortunate but are an unavoidable fact of political life. Where libertarian goals overcome egalitarian goals, the markets they create tend to monopolisation and, because capitalists are the enemies of capitalism, have to be regulated rigorously and at considerable cost by Government.

viii. Over ten years ago, some economists offered some advice to Chinese policy makers[34]

   a. Established market economies do not use the market mechanism to govern their health care sectors. Market forces are enlisted here and there where it is safe to do so. But the important decisions regarding the allocation of resources are NOT left to the market in any Western country, even the United States.

   b. 'Competition' and 'markets' should be means to an end, but not ends in themselves. In this seminar, 'competition' and 'markets' have often been treated as if they were ends in themselves. If they are treated as ends, the objectives of efficiency, equity and cost containment will NOT be achieved.

c. Better health is the major objective of health systems. Despite the great gains that China (Canada and the UK!) has made in achieving good health at low cost, the burden due to PRE-VENTABLE deaths and illnesses is still enormous. To remedy the situation and avoid losing previous gains, there is a continuing need for strong government actions.

d. One reform of the Chinese health system (and all others) that would be most destructive of its proper objective would be to allow the development of COMMERCIAL health insurance. Western countries that use health insurance to finance their health sectors do so either through public insurance or very tightly REGULATED, NONCOMMERCIAL social insurance. The only exception, the United States, is desperately trying to escape from the negative consequences of commercial insurance.[35]

These lessons from international experience of health reform are as relevant to Canada (and the UK!) in 2005 as they were in 1995 and are now for China. Courts may overturn legislation with evidence free views but the ultimate challenge for Canada is what sort of health care system do you want? Canadian policy makers and managers, like their counterparts in the UK and elsewhere have failed to manage their public health care systems efficiently. To leap from these failures to a PHI duplicate system 'cure' is naive at best and stupid at worst. Without rigorous regulation and evaluation, such evidence free reforms may damage the health of both the Canadian economy and its population. Do Canadians want one based on egalitarian principles or the greater inequality and cost inflation inherent in the libertarian market solution? The choice imposed by the Courts, if it cannot be reversed requires a dynamic public sector response whereby Medicare is better managed and private health insurance if it is to emerge is carefully and rigorously regulated by the Governments of Canada. Whatever choice you make requires you to manage much more effectively the public health care system you have. The defects of this system have been emphasised by local researchers such as Esmail and Walker,[36] who diagnose the problem correctly but offer treatment that is clearly neither cost effective nor consistent with equity goals. As ever the failure to manage efficiently public health care systems, feeds the rhetoric of libertarian would-be reformers such as the Fraser Institute and creates the potential for the erosion and destruction of public systems of health care

aimed at providing care in a more equitable manner. Such false proph-
ets should be reminded, corrupting Mencken that for every complex
problem they have identified, their solution is simple, direct and wrong!

Notes

1 Alan Maynard is Professor of Health Economics, University of York,
   England and Chair of the York NHS Hospitals Trust.
2 See for example R.G. Evans, 'Political Wolves and Economic Sheep: the
   sustainability of public health insurance in Canada' in A. Maynard, ed.,
   The Public-Private Mix for Health (London: Radcliffe Medical Press, 2005)
   ['Political Wolves'] and A. Maynard, ed., *The Public-Private Mix for Health*
   (London: Radcliffe Medical Press, 2005) [*Public-Private*].
3 OECD (2002).
4 See for example A. Maynard & A. Williams, 'Privatisation and the National Health Service' in J. Le Grand & R. Robinson, eds., *Privatisation and
   the Welfare State* (London: George Allen & Unwin, 1984) and A. Williams,
   'The Pervasive Role of Ideology in the Optimisation of the Public-Private
   Mix in Public Healthcare Systems' in A. Maynard, ed., *The Public-Private
   Mix for Health* (London: Radcliffe Medical Press, 2005).
5 A.S. Relman, 'Shattuck Lecture - the Nation's Health Care Industry: where
   is it taking us? (1991) 325 (12) New Eng. J. Med. 854.
6 Adam Smith, *An Inquiry into the Nature and Causes of the Wealth of Nations*,
   vol. 1 (Oxford: Oxford University Press, 1976) at 145.
7 D.L. Bartlett & J.D. Steele, *Critical Condition: How Health Care in America
   Became Big Business—and Bad Medicine* (New York: Doubleday, 2004) and A.
   Maynard, *Public- Private, supra* note 2.
8 J. Hall & A. Maynard, 'Healthcare Lessons from Australia: what can
   Michael Howard learn from John Howard?' (2005) 330 British Medical
   Journal 357.
9 *Ibid.*
10 F. Columbo & N. Tapay, *Private Health Insurance in OECD Countries: the
   Benefits and Costs for Individuals and Health Systems.* Working Paper No. 15,
   (Paris: OECD, 2004).
11 See L. Rochaix & L. Hartmann, 'The Public-Private Mix for Health in
   France' in A. Maynard, ed., *The Public-Private Mix for Health* (London:
   Radcliffe Press, 2005) and M.M. Bellanger & P.R. Mosse, 'The Search for
   the Holy Grail: combining decentralised planning and contracting mechanisms in the French health care system' 14 (S1) Health Economics S119.

12 I. Chalmers, 'Trying to do More Good than Harm in Policy and Practice: the role of rigorous, transparent, up-to-date evaluations. (2004) 589 Annals of the American Academy of Political and Social Science, 22.

13 Online: <http://www.sixsigma.org>.

14 Web Supplement October, 2004.

15 E.S. Fisher et al., 'The Implications of Regional Variations in Medicare Spending. Part 2: health outcomes and satisfaction with care' (2003) 138 (4) Ann Intern Med. 288.

16 J. Wennberg & A. Gittelsohn, 'Variations in Medical Care Among Small Areas' (1982) 246 (4) Sci Am 120.

17 R. Brook, 'Appropriateness: the next frontier' (January 1994) British Medical Journal 218.

18 S.J. Bernstein et al., 'The Appropriateness of the Use of Cardiovascular Procedures: British versus U.S. perspectives' (1993) 9 Int J Technol Assess Health Care 3.

19 E. Kerr et al., 'Profiling the Quality of Care in Twelve Communities: results from the CQI study (2004) 23 (3) Quality of Care 247.

20 H.H. Pham et al., 'Delivery of Preventive Services to Older Adults by Primary Care Physicians' (2005) 294 JAMA 473.

21 A. Maynard & K. Bloor, 'Do Those Who Pay the Piper Call the Tune? (2003) 8 Health Policy Matters, available online: <http://www.york.ac.uk/depts/hstd/pubs/hpmindex.htm>.

22 L.T. Kohn et al., *To Err is Human: building a safer health care system* (Washington DC: National Academy Press, 2000) and R.M. Wilson et al., 'The Quality of Australian Health Care Study' (1995) 163 Australia Medical Journal 458.

23 F. Nightingale, *Some Notes on Hospitals*, 3rd ed. (London: Longmans, 1863).

24 <http://www.sf36.0rg>.

25 <http://www.euroqol.org>.

26 M. O'Donnell, *A Sceptic's Medical Dictionary* (London: BMJ Publishing Group, 1997).

27 J. Yates, *Why Are We Waiting?* (Oxford: Oxford University Press, 1987).

28 *Ibid.*

29 NHS Centre for Reviews and Dissemination, University of York 'The Treatment of Persistent Glue Ear in Children' (1995) 1 (4) Effective Health Care.

30 A consumer-orientated review of these problems can be found at <http://www.quackwatch.org/consumereducation/crhsurgery.html> and at Pub Med of the US, online: <http://www.ncbi.nlm.nih.gov>. The National Library of Medicare currently cites 1776 papers about unnecessary surgery.

31 R. Klein, *The New Politics of the National Health Service* (New York: Prentice Hall, 2001).

32 K. Bloor et al., 'Variation in Activity Rates of Consultant Surgeons and the Influence of Reward Structures in the English NHS' (2004) 9 (2) Journal of Health Services Research and Policy 76.

33 N. Esmail & M. Walker, 'How Good is Canadian Health Care? 2005 report, an international comparison of health care systems (Vancouver: The Fraser Institute, 2005).

34 R.G. Evans. 'Political Wolves' *supra* note 2.

35 For a recent reform proposal for the US health care system, see E.J. Emanuel & V.R. Fuchs, 'Health Care Vouchers – A Proposal for Universal Coverage' (2005) 352 New Eng. J. Med.1255.

36 *Supra* note 33.

Blending Private and Social Health Insurance in the Netherlands: Challenges Posed by the EU

ANDRÉ DEN EXTER

1. Introduction

In *Chaoulli v. Quebec*, the Canadian Supreme Court has opened the floodgates to a two-tier healthcare system.[1] In reaching their conclusion that Quebec laws were in breach of s.7 of the Canadian *Charter*, Chief Justice McLachlin and Justice Major referred favourably to the coexistence of public (or social) insurance with private insurance in a number of jurisdictions within Europe. But at the same time as the justices of the Supreme Court allowed the introduction of private insurance in Quebec, within the Netherlands the health care system was moving to integrate social and private insurance. The new Dutch Health Insurance Bill is aimed to guarantee equal access to basic healthcare through the introduction of a universal health insurance scheme that will abolish the social and private health insurance-split in curative care, and at the same time improve efficiency by introducing competitive elements to the social health insurance system.

This 'marketization' of social health insurance is unique in Europe and challenges European Community (EC) law. 'Revitalisation' of the underlying solidarity notion, by introducing market principles in the field of public services, makes it extremely vulnerable to the free movement and competition rules of the common market. So far, the European Court of Justice (ECJ) has shielded solidarity-based institutions from the full brunt of competition. However, there are serious concerns that the ECJ will deny further antitrust immunity when the solidarity elements become blurred or subordinated due to the introduction of competitive elements into healthcare. Although the Dutch and Canadian health insurance systems seem now to be on different tangents with the former expressing a stronger commitment to access on the basis of need and not ability to pay, there are still lessons for the Canadian system from the Dutch experience. Both countries share the (potential) consequences of international binding trade rules when liberalising public (social security) services unilaterally.

2. Health Insurance in the Netherlands

2.1 Social and Private Health Insurance

Presently the Dutch health insurance system can be characterised as a dual system of social (compulsory) and private or voluntary health insurance. Those who are excluded from the social insurance scheme are free to purchase private health insurance. Social insurance is based on the 'solidarity' principle and regulated by statutory law. In healthcare, the 'solidarity' principle means that there is no relationship between the premium paid and access to the insurance entitlements. Unlike the ancient and Christian *caritas* concept, solidarity is institutionalized by means of social security legislation, and therefore has been accomplished by (legitimized) force. This concept of compulsory solidarity leads to political choices, such as the redistribution of resources in order to guarantee equal access to healthcare. Its redistributive effect shows that solidarity is based on the notion of social justice.

The underlying legal source of social health insurance can be found in the Dutch Constitution, Article 22(1), stipulating that 'the authorities shall take steps to promote public health.' This provision has been generally interpreted as a 'mere' obligation of the government to be concerned with setting up health facilities and facilitating access to necessary healthcare. This obligation has been effectuated by a health insurance system that can be divided into three programs.

The first program covers exceptional medical expenses associated with long term care or high-cost treatment, covered by the so-called Exceptional Medical Expenses Act (AWBZ-scheme). This insurance scheme is mandatory for all and covers both residents and non-residents, meeting the criteria set by the law.

The second program is largely administered by sickness funds under the Health Insurance Act ('*Ziekenfondswet*'), establishing a statutory insurance scheme for curative care. Sickness funds are private law entities operating on a non-profit basis (associations and foundations) who contract with health care providers that deliver the insured care. Sixty-five percent of the population are covered for curative care by

Sickness Funds (all those earning below 32,000 Euros in 2005). A further five percent of the population is covered by a health insurance scheme for public servants. Dutch citizens earning above 32,000 Euros (thirty percent) are free to purchase private insurance for curative care .

The 'Ziekenfondswet' defines the nature of care for those covered by sickness funds in terms of entitlements (e.g., general practitioner care, paramedical care, specialist medical care, obstetric care, etc.).[2] More specific details of benefit provision are regulated by the Health Insurance (Treatment and Services) Decree and associated ministerial regulations and by the specific policies of sickness fund. In principle, the insured may claim the types of care as benefit-in-kind entitlements provided by contracted health providers. The insured have free choice of provider, but that is restricted to contracted providers only. In exceptional cases, however, the insured may opt for a (foreign) non-contracted provider, for instance in case of waiting lists, and will receive cash benefits to pay for the cost of care (reimbursement model).

The statute requires that sickness funds guarantee access to medical care specified in the insurance scheme. This end result obligation forms the essence of the benefit-in-kind healthcare system, for which the insurer is accountable and can be held liable in case of non compliance. As benefit-in-kind insurers, sickness funds must purchase sufficient care in and/or outside its area of activity. Except for *force majeure*, the sickness fund cannot be released from its obligation to provide access to healthcare. Given the benefit-in-kind system and its obligation of result, an appeal against insufficiently contracted care has never been accepted by the judiciary because it is considered a normal business risk. The same holds for insufficient hospital budgets, agreed to and provided by the sickness fund.[3]

The nature and scope of the packages covered by private medical insurance are largely identical to those required to be provided by the sickness funds pursuant to the 'Ziekenfondswet.' Private medical insurance policies are, however, more flexible, allowing for free choice of provider, and permitting cash benefits instead of benefit-in-kind entitlements. In order to prevent the exclusion of certain risk groups that rely on private health insurance, the Health Insurance Access Act 1998 guarantees the availability of health insurance for these groups (e.g., the elderly).[4] Under this regime, access to health insurance has been guaranteed by introducing a standard policy that health insurance companies are obliged to offer to these risk groups upon request, and a premium set by the government.

Although the nature and scope of entitlements of the different packages for curative care covered by sickness funds and private insurers are more or less identical, this does not necessarily mean that the insured share equal rights to health services. Due to the statutory regime, administrative courts rule sickness fund litigation procedures, whereas civil courts adjudicate private insurance disputes using civil law principles. Civil courts have proved more willing to recognize patients' reimbursement claims with reference to these general contractual norms (i.e., reasonableness and fairness). Administrative courts, on the other hand, are inclined to reject patients' claims on the basis of their reading of rights and health care benefits as contained by public law, including protocols and guidelines.[5] The divergence in judicial interpretation is one of the reasons given by government for reforming this sector and eliminating the distinction between sickness funds and private insurers (this reform is discussed further below).

From a Canadian perspective, however, it is important to note that regardless of whether or not one is covered by a private insurer or by a sickness fund will not affect how long one has to wait for treatment. In other words, having private insurance does not allow those insured to jump queues for treatment since treatment is based on objective medical criteria (medical necessity), irrespective of ones insurance status. Also, since hospitals charge similar tariffs for public/privately insured, there is no incentive to treat patients differently.

Finally, the third sector covers all kinds of supplementary care regarded as being less necessary. Supplementary (private) insurance can be taken out to cover the costs of these kinds of care, which are not included in the first or second sector. This is a voluntary health insurance scheme where the insurers – both sickness funds and private health insurance companies – themselves determine the content and scope of the package and the conditions under which this type of insurance can be taken out. They also set the premiums. Supplementary insurance may cover dental care, eyeglasses, a higher standard of hospital accommodation, and alternative medicines.

2.2 Health Insurance Reform, January 2006

In January 2006, the health insurance system will change drastically, abolishing the social-private insurance split and introducing a basic health insurance scheme in the second sector. In the past, health care reform in the Netherlands has oscillated between either efforts to unite the different coexisting schemes into one or retain the existing schemes.[6] With the introduction of the new Health Insurance Act, the 'Zorgver-

zekeringswet,' the government has finally chosen for a single insurance scheme.[7] The '*Zorgverzekeringswet'* introduces a compulsory health insurance scheme for the entire population. Although services will be provided by competing (for-profit) insurance companies, the scheme will still very much continue to pursue the objective of solidarity, i.e. that care will be provided on the basis of need and not ability to pay. By introducing a competitive market for both providers and insurers within the framework of solidarity, the new scheme is aimed to cure healthcare problems such as uncontrolled rising costs, lack of efficiency, and poor quality of health care (including waiting lists).

In brief, the new Health Insurance Act will legislate that all insured will have coverage for essential curative care. What is essential will be tested against the criteria of proven efficacy, cost effectiveness, and the need for collective financing. The new Act will replace the current schemes in the existing curative care insurance sector (sickness funds and regulated private insurers). Private (supplementary) insurance will remain as it is and may become more important as it is possible that several entitlements will be stripped from the present array of covered entitlements (or in the Canadian rhetoric 'delisted').

To cope with excessive waiting times, the new act introduces more flexibility. This means that the insured may select from several schemes (benefit-in-kind, cash benefits or a combination of both schemes), strengthening freedom of choice. However, in the case of cash benefits, reimbursement is maximized to certain limits defined by law. Also, due to the jurisprudence of the European Court of Justice on patient mobility, the new Law has incorporated 'maximum waiting times' for specific medical interventions.[8] Consequently, patients can claim for treatment abroad as well as for full reimbursement in cases exceeding the medically accepted waiting time. In exceptional cases, when the state of health requires urgent medical intervention, the sickness funds can even be forced to reimburse the costs of treatment in a country outside of the European Union. However, as a rule, the treatment provided should be recognised by national (i.e. Dutch) law.

Instead of a public law scheme the government has with this new legislation opted for a health insurance scheme based on private law. The goal is to stimulate for-profit insurance companies to compete with sickness funds and each other in the market for curative care. That choice is driven by a market ideology, i.e., maximizing consumer welfare where consumers make their own consumption decisions based on good information, clear preferences, and appropriate incentives.

The fate of the healthcare market as a free market has been tempered by restrictive measures such as requiring open enrolment (i.e., insurers must accept anyone who wishes to join, regardless of age, sex, health status), prohibiting 'risk-rate' tactics that insurers use in unregulated free markets, and eliminating premium rate restrictions by setting a flat rate premium (€ 1,100 a person yearly). Upholding the solidarity principle, those with low incomes will be partly compensated for the flat rate premium by a so-called income related 'health care allowance.' Furthermore, a risk equalization system (RES) will be introduced to protect those health insurers with whom a disproportionate number of high-risk individuals choose to enrol. Finally, the new law will require insurers to offer a minimum package of essential services, meaning that all insurance contracts must provide coverage for essential curative care tested against the criteria of proven efficacy, cost effectiveness, and the need for collective financing.[9] The insured package follows from the coverage provided under the former Health Insurance Act. These measures should guarantee access to health care for all citizens.In the meantime, market elements such as free choice of provider and insurer, competition between providers and insurers (both on tariff, premium[10] and quality), more flexible standard policy arrangements (including choice of a benefit-in-kind or reimbursement model, or a mixture of these policy arrangements) and (voluntary) out-of-pocket arrangements will stimulate insurers to purchase more efficiently and also improve citizens' accountability for claiming healthcare.

Although the health insurance scheme is derived from previous plans introducing regulated competition in healthcare, the main difference is the introduction of a for-profit arrangement in social health insurance. This form of 'privatizing' social health insurance, i.e. for-profit insurers performing a public task, is not unique and can be observed in other EU countries, as well in other social security schemes such as old-age pensions, invalidity and occupational health benefits.[11] Despite such developments, however, the for-profit insurance arrangement has raised serious questions about whether or not the 'Zorgverzekeringswet' is 'Europroof.'[12]

3. European Community law and health insurance reforms

By emphasizing the need for competitive markets within the social health insurance scheme, the Dutch healthcare reforms have challenged European Community/European Union law, potentially threatening the view that social health insurance is part and parcel of social security. These reforms consequently affect member states' discretionary authority in this field.

The most problematic reforms are the free movement principles and competition law rules, including secondary Treaty rules and the relevant jurisprudence of the European Court of Justice interpreting these rules. In order to understand the potential European threats, I will now turn to discuss the relevant legal principles of Community law.[13]

3.1 The New Health Insurance Law: Exempted under the Third Non-Life Insurance Directive?

The Insurance Directives
In several Member States, private health insurance serves as a partial or complete alternative to the health coverage provided for by the social security system (for example, Ireland, Germany and the Netherlands). In order to simplify the free movement of private insurance services within the EU, 'Insurance Directives' were introduced that are based on the free movement of services provision (Art 49 EC). Establishing an internal market for insurance, the Directives created a single system for the authorization and financial supervision of insurers by the Member State in which they have their head office. Such authorization, issued by the home Member State, enables insurers to carry out their insurance business anywhere in the EU. The Directives also require Member States to abolish controls on premium prices and prior notification of policy conditions in the case of private insurers entering the insurance market outside the country of origin.

The main impact of the single license regime laid down by the Insurance Directives has been an increase of competition within different national markets. The abolition of prior approval of policy conditions and tariffs by supervisory authorities, which was the rule in many Member States before the adoption of the Insurance Directives, was intended to encourage insurers to enter new markets, and thus increase competition within those markets. The Insurance Directives also allow individuals and businesses to buy insurance in another Member State. As such, the Insurance Directives have had a liberalizing influence on insurance markets.

The Third Non-life Insurance Directive
Private health insurance falls within the scope of the Third Non-life Insurance Directive (Directive 92/49/EEC).[14] Article 2(1) of the Directive clearly excludes social health insurance schemes. This is relevant not merely for social security organizations but also for private insurers that are performing a public service, such as providing social health

insurance. However, in the case where insurance funds or companies operate a social security scheme (i.e. workplace accidents at the *'organizations's own risk,'* then the Directive is still applicable. This is a result of the European Court of Justice' ruling in *Commission v. Belgium,* in which the Court concluded that the Directive applies where the insurance is offered by organisations operating at their own risk.[15]

The 'organization's own risk' element in the Belgian case was not challenged, and therefore the Court did not elaborate upon what was meant by this. It leaves open the possibility that the Directive could be interpreted narrowly, meaning that it will apply to companies operating a voluntary scheme at their own insurance risk, or in the alternative more broadly, speaking to any 'economic activity.' In the case of the latter, it is settled case law that on a (competitive) market of demand and supply, where services are being provided according to a certain price, the activity will be considered an 'economic' instead of a 'social activity.' If the broad interpretation is accepted then a substantial part of social insurance activities will fall under the scope of the Insurance Directive, which will have a dramatic impact on the Member States' abilities to manage their respective social health insurance schemes. This means that in order to determine the applicability of the Directive, it is relevant to know whether or not the insurance is offered at the organization's own risk and the scheme in question pursues an economic or a social activity.

If the Directive is applicable then this basically means that governments will not be allowed to control the prices and conditions of insurance products. However, an insurance scheme can still be exempted from the Directive by Article 54 for reasons of the 'general good.'[16] According to that provision, legal restrictions can be justified to protect the general good in cases where private health insurance schemes 'completely or partially' replace the social security system.[17] This is the case for instance in Ireland and the Netherlands. Such restrictions may include a requirement for open enrolment, rating on a uniform basis, lifetime cover, and offering standard policies in line with social security schemes and in combination with participation in risk or loss equalization schemes (RES).

Among (Dutch) lawyers, the interpretation of 'completely or in part' has caused some controversy. A strict interpretation would result in a finding that private health insurance schemes may only co-exist with statutory health insurance schemes and cannot supplant them in order to qualify for the exception. This is due to the wording of 'may replace' used in Article 54. A more generous interpretation would find that a 'private' (i.e competing for profit insurers within a rubric of governmental regulation) health insurance scheme can replace a statutory scheme over time, without the requirement of co-existence.[18] The European Commission takes the view that article 54 (partial or complete alternative) encompasses the situation in which a Member State decides to entirely assign the cover of statutory social health insurance to private insurance enterprises which must conduct such activity at their own risk, following insurance techniques and on the basis of contractual relationships governed by private law.[19]

In the latter case, private health insurance schemes could comply with article 54 but only if the Court considers the disputed measures (i.e. governmental regulations providing for premium rating and open enrolment in combination with a loss compensation scheme) as objectively necessary and proportionate to the objective pursued. This means that national measures, in order to be found to be aimed at achieving the important objective of serving the general good, must satisfy the following requirements: they must be applied in a non-discriminatory manner; they must be justified by imperative requirements in the general interest; they must be suitable for securing the attainment of the objective which they pursue; and they must not go beyond what is necessary in order to attain it.[20]

With respect to the reformed Dutch health insurance, there are serious doubts as to whether the new scheme will satisfy the ECJ's necessity and proportionality test. That test prescribes that if restrictive measures go further than is necessary to perform the assigned tasks under the same conditions, the restrictive measures cannot be exempted as being necessary and proportionate. Since there are less intrusive alternatives available, such as the Health Insurance Access Act, which provides full compensation insurance for high-risks, one may question whether the ECJ will accept the Commission's opinion. If not, should the ECJ deny the new Health Insurance Act based on the proportionality test, then it will question the legal sustainability of the new scheme.

3.2 Social Health Insurance excluded from EC Competition Law?

Within the European Union, competition policy is designed to ensure the functioning of the common market as required by the Treaty's free movement provisions. Community competition rules pursue the promotion of competition among undertakings and aim to remove distortions of such competition (e.g., price or market agreements). Two crucial provisions on competition in the EC-Treaty are Articles 81 and 82, which, respectively, prohibit agreements that distort intra-community trade and the abuse of a dominant position.[21] These provisions also affect the health sector, and are most problematic in their application to the health insurance market.

Attempts within Europe to introduce market forces into health care systems have raised the question of whether EC competition principles are applicable to traditional public law activities, such as social health insurance. The central issue here is whether the Treaty concept of 'undertaking' is applicable to social health insurance funds, such as sickness funds.[22] The ECJ has defined the concept of an 'undertaking' to encompass 'every entity engaged in an economic activity, irrespective of the legal status of the entity and the way in which it is financed.'[23] Without doubt private for-profit companies competing in the new Dutch health insurance scheme will fall within the definition of economic activity and therefore within the competition law. Still, as I will discuss hereafter, a separate antitrust exception under article 86(2) EC might apply. But will the Treaty apply in the case of sickness funds, or private not-for-profit entities performing a social task? To answer this question, the *Poucet and Pistre*[24] ruling is crucial.

In the *Poucet and Pistre* case, the ECJ made it clear that the concept of undertaking does not include organizations pursuing a social objective and who have been charged with the management of certain compulsory social security schemes based on the principle of solidarity. The solidarity principle requires the following: that insurance benefits be identical for all who receive them; that financial contributions be proportional to the income; that sick and healthy persons share the cost of sickness; and that contributions for insurance be compulsory and not risk-rated. Another characteristic that should be taken into account is the fact that the social security entities act as agents of the state, meaning that they perform insurance activities under the supervision of the state, operate on a not-for-profit basis and do not determine either the amount of the contributions they require or the scope of benefits they offer.[25] As a rule, social security schemes fulfilling these conditions, generally are not considered to be performing an 'economic activity' and, therefore, fall outside the scope of article 81 and 82 EC. In principle, all conditions should be met, but because the weight or importance of the conditions may differ, it is difficult to predict when a social security activity will not be subject to European competition rules.

What has become clear from *Poucet and Pistre,* as well as from subsequent cases, is that the social purpose of an organization is not in itself sufficient to except its activities from being classified as involving an economic activity for the purposes of the competition rules.[26] What seems to be decisive is how the entity's activities relate to the solidarity principle.

This conclusion can be drawn from the *FFSA* case, which ruled that a social security entity, offering an optional old-age scheme that operated on a capitalization (or equivalence) basis[27] with limited elements of solidarity, was engaged in an economic activity.[28] The principles established in *FFSA* were confirmed in three parallel judgments, in which a pension fund providing supplementary old-age pensions to medical specialists was classified as an economic undertaking.[29] The Court emphasized the fact that the funds themselves determined the amount of contributions and benefits and that they operated in accordance with the capitalization principle, under which the amount of the benefits depended on the financial results of the investments made. The social purpose of the funds, the body's non-profit status, and the restrictive rules under which it operated made the scheme less exposed to competition rules, but did not prevent the organizations' activities from being classified as undertakings.[30]

These rulings indicate that, when elements of the capitalization principle are added to solidarity-based health insurance schemes and premiums are risk-rated, the legal status of the scheme becomes increasingly blurred and the scheme even can assume the features of private insurance under the scope of EC competition rules. Under the new 'Zorgverzekeringswet,' capitalization elements are being introduced that may threaten the notion of solidarity.[31] This will harm solidarity elements, such as the risk equalization scheme, because the health care allowances will become subordinated due to the introduction of competitive (i.e. capitalization) elements into healthcare and because sickness funds' services will loose their social character and their immunity from competition laws. To prevent sickness funds from being subjected to such laws it is crucial to underscore the solidarity principle. Without doubt, the so-called income related 'health-care allowance' – which should prevent certain insured categories from being subject to excessive premium burdens – reflects such a solidarity element. However, whether this measure is sufficient to satisfy the requirements of article 81 and 82, and ergo, to guarantee solidarity in the long term remains to be seen.

An analysis of the Court's jurisprudence has identified several elements that tend to demonstrate that an insurance scheme applies the solidarity principle, and thus is not engaged in economic activity and not subject to the competition law. The *Poucet and Pistre* criteria have been further developed in the *Cisal* case.[32] There the Court concluded that solidarity exists between better and less well paid workers if there is no direct link between the contributions paid and the benefits granted. Compulsory membership in the plan is also required for solidarity to exist. Moreover, solidarity is present when social security activities are subject to supervision of the State and the nature and level of benefits and the amount of contributions are, in the last resort, fixed by the State. An insurance entity that thus transfers risk between members regardless of the level of contribution fulfils an exclusive social function, and therefore does not carry out an economic activity.[33]

Although statutory supervision is important, the solidarity element seems to be decisive in determining whether an insurer is performing an economic undertaking. In *AOK Bundesverband*, the Court held that the solidarity principle was fulfilled by an equalization of costs and risks among the German sickness funds.[34] Because of risk equalization, sickness funds are not in competition with each other or with private institutions with respect to providing statutory pharmaceutical benefits. Even the latitude that the sickness funds have for setting their contribution rates and their limited freedom to compete with each other (in order to attract members), does not call the non-economic nature of their activity into question. Indeed, the Court considered some competition with regard to contributions to be in accordance with the principles of sound management (efficiency) and in the interest of the proper functioning of the social security scheme. As long as a sickness fund is pursuing a specific interest inseparable from or integrally connected with its exclusive social objectives, the fund does not act as an economic undertaking and therefore, EU competition rules do not apply. Under the new Dutch Health Insurance Act, this reasoning might preserve the sickness funds solidarity-based character, as long as the solidarity elements remain dominant. But it is uncertain, because the Dutch sickness funds operate differently from the German Krankenkassen in terms of competition, organization's own risk and discretionary power in purchasing health services.

Should the Court conclude that sickness funds perform an economic activity in terms of the competition rules, the funds may still be exempted pursuant to article 86(2) EC.[35] This provision offers special immunity from the general competition rules for certain undertakings that perform a task of 'general economic interest.' It is clear that sickness funds have been entrusted with carrying out such a service of general economic interest, namely the provision of a solidarity-based health insurance system.

3.3 Hindering of Competition by Diagnosis Treatment Combinations (DBCs)

What will become particularly problematic for ensuring solidarity, in terms of competition law, are the recent price-setting rules and determination of diagnosis treatment combinations (DBCs) (the Dutch equivalent of Diagnostic Related Group-based administrated prices (DRGs)). Based on the ECJ's jurisprudence on competition law, member states are not allowed to invite, stimulate or sanction any entrepreneurial behaviour, which in itself would be a cartel or an abuse of dominant position. Such measures would violate the Treaty.[36] The process of defining DCBs can be characterised by cooperation, consultation and mutual consent between relevant actors in the Dutch health policy field, excluding foreign providers. Since the determination of DBCs will be based on Dutch norms exclusively, this may create a competitive advantage for Dutch insurance companies when contracting health providers according to Dutch prices. Foreign insurers and providers, offering similar services according to competitive prices, are not invited in the DCB definition process, which makes the system extremely vulnerable to the anti-cartel provision.

3.4 Will the Levelling System Be Considered State Aid?

The new Health Insurance Act, coming into force in January 2006, provides for the principle of open enrolment and for premium rate restrictions. The new Act will alsoprohibit (for-profit) insurers from rejecting potential purchasers who are high risk, at least for curative care services. To compensate the insurers for the financial losses due to an unequal distribution of the insurance risks, a risk equalization (levelling) system (RES) between the insurers will be introduced. What is particularly problematic in this context are the competition rules governing state aid. One effect of such a statutory compensation measure is that it grants cross-subsidies to certain health insurance funds (those who have enrolled higher risks) through charges imposed on other private insurance undertakings and government contributions.

The issue of whether such a risk equalisation system is tantamount to state aid has been already been debated in the context of Ireland in 1994. Questions arose there over the issue of whether Ireland's voluntary health insurance (VHI) scheme, including a levelling system, was in conformity with European state aid rules. The Irish health insurance scheme provides insurance for hospitalisation and is operated by a governmental agency.

The European Commission concluded that the Irish RES, due to the financial transfers between insurers made under the RES to the VHI agency, was in principle 'state aid' pursuant to article 87(1) EC.[37] According to the Commission, however, the Irish RES was justified as being *compensation* for public service obligations imposed on all health insurance companies in Ireland (including open enrolment, lifetime cover, and community rating). This decision is being disputed by the British insurer BUPA in a case pending before the European Court of First Instance.[38]

The Dutch government, defending its RES in Parliament, referred to the *BUPA* case and argued that it concerns a justified measure that is necessary to compensate insurers for the additional costs incurred by a disproportionate level of high-risk profiles. But unlike the (Irish State Aid?)*BUPA* case, the Commission concluded that the Dutch RES did not apply only to the additional costs.[39] Therefore, the financial support provided as part of the RES constitutes, in the view of the Commission, 'state aid' within the meaning of Article 87 EC and the Dutch government must consequently submit the restrictive measure to the Commission in order to be approved. However, the Commission went on to conclude that the RES could be exempted from competition rules since it was a justified obligation given to undertakings charged with a 'service of general economic interest' ('SGEI,' Art. 86(2) EC), i.e. providing private health insurance which is open to everybody on similar conditions at an affordable price.

Whether or not the RES is a necessary and proportionate measure to maintain solidarity and the affordability of private health insurance remains to be seen, particularly since a recent study has shown that the proposed risk compensation scheme, combined with premium rate restrictions and open enrolment, do not fulfil the necessity and proportionality-test.[40] Ultimately, the ECJ has to decide whether the Dutch RES will be accepted as being an undertaking charged with a SGEI, and that the Dutch RES is both necessary and proportionate. Until then, the levelling system's conformity with EU competition rules and the Insurance Directive remains in serious question. In the case of a negative answer, where the Dutch RES fails the proportionality test and is not considered to be charged with a SGEI, then the current levelling system and thus solidarity is under threat. Then the Dutch government will be forced to change the RES in line with competition law. A more drastic but 'EC proof' alternative would be the exclusion of private insurance companies from the new health insurance scheme. Then sickness funds will remain being the only institutions allowed to guarantee solidarity, since they are likely be excluded from EC competition law.

4. Final remarks

Recent health insurance reforms in the Netherlands have been characterised by efforts to mimic market-like behaviour, but (subject to some caveats) still remain within the parameters of a redistributive system where access to care is assured on the basis of need and not ability to pay. This approach to reform, however, has made the system extremely vulnerable to EC free trade and competition rules. Although the ECJ has approved certain market elements in social security schemes in order to maintain solidarity and financial sustainability, it has not provided member states a carte blanche when reforming their social security system. The emphasis on incorporating direct insurance principles, such as competition, insurers' financial risk, (indirect) selection of risks, capitalization elements such as no risk-related premium and medical saving accounts threaten the traditional solidarity notion underlying social security and puts into question the social security exemption under free trade and competition rules.

Such a strategy appears to be based predominantly on Treaty exceptions, to be interpreted and assessed by the ECJ on a case by case-basis. Given the Court's activist reputation this may not be a very wise strategy to pursue. Instead of asking the Court to show mercy towards the liberalization of social health insurance, a less hazardous approach (from an EU perspective) would be to either create a fully private (for-profit) system, thus abandoning the solidarity principle, or an entirely public (not-for-profit) model of health insurance. But it cannot be overlooked that true solidarity, solidarity amongst strangers as understood by Habermas, is ultimately found in the public model.[41]

5. Relevance to Canada

Unlike the Netherlands, Canada is not an EU member state. Both countries, however, share supranational binding trade rules arising from either the European Union, or the World Trade Organisation (WTO). Consequently, the challenges posed by the EC treaty when liberalizing the Dutch social insurance scheme, may - mutatis mutandis - also occur when opening the Canadian public services to complete or partial private health insurance (the applicability of the General Agreement on Trade in Services (GATS) on Medicare). Although this is not the place to discuss the impact of GATS-law extensively, one should not underestimate the consequences of the (partial) liberalisation of public (social security) services. Public services may fall under the scope of the agreement, particularly when provided 'in competition with one or more service suppliers' (Art 1: 3(c) GATS).[42]

However, should Medicare fall within the scope of GATS, the Canadian government can exclude or limit the impact of specific GATS obligations (e.g., the market access and national treatment obligation) that may affect trade in that service. This approach should provide the authorities with some room to manoeuvre in order to regulate Medicare services, although it requires a careful scheduling of specific limitations. Nonetheless, a strategy of drafted limitations or non-commitments can be submitted to dispute settlement and may come under pressure in future trade rounds.[43]

As such, the potential 'marketization' of Medicare shows several similarities with the Dutch health insurance reforms. The liberalisation of the social security scheme may bring it under the regime of international trade law, making it difficult to regulate. Furthermore, public health insurance protection is based on treaty-exceptions, and it is unclear how the solidarity exceptions will develop given the absence of GATS rulings on competition in the public services sector.

As in the Dutch case, one may question whether such a competitive market approach is in the interests of patients. On a competitive health insurance market, the solidarity principle is under constant pressure since risk-bearing insurers have to break even on each contract. Despite the open enrolment option, investing in subtle (implicit) selection mechanisms might be even more profitable for insurers than being compensated by a highly complex and administrative levelling system. In a way, this is what Medicare may face when the resources to invest in cost-reducing activities are limited, and it has to compete with private insurers. Competition on a parallel health services market may end in poor services and threaten equal access to health care. Therefore, blending Medicare with private health insurance should be avoided. In order to safeguard the values that Medicare stands for, a partial insurance alternative that does not compete with the public system is preferred. At the same time, the partial insurance alternative will help the public system in cope with waiting lists by simplifying patient mobility.

Notes

1 *Chaoulli v. Quebec (Attorney General)*, [2005] SCC 35.
2 Sickness Fund Act of 15 October 1964, Staatsblad (Official journal of state), 392.
3 Appeal court 's Hertogenbosch 2 July 1990, *RZA* 1990, 127.
4 Health Insurance Access Act of 27 March 1986, Staatsblad (Official journal of state), 123.
5 Herbert Hermans & André den Exter, 'Priorities and Priority-setting in Healthcare in the Netherlands' (1998) 39: 3 Croat Med J 345 at 353–354.
6 See Ministry of Health (MoH), *Structuurnota Gezondheidszorg (restructuring healthcare)* (Leidschendam: Ministry of Public Health and the Environment,1974);; W. Dekker, *Report of the Government Committee on the structure and financing of health care*(Rijswijk: Ministry of Welfare, Health and Cultural Affairs, 1988); MoH, *Working for patients* (Rijswijk: Ministry of Welfare, Health and Cultural Affairs, 1990); A.J. Dunning, *Keuzen in de Zorg (Report of the Government Committee on Choices in Healthcare)* (Rijswijk: Ministry of Welfare, Health and Cultural Affairs, 1991).
7 The 'Zorgverzekeringswet' (Zvw) was approved by Parliament on June 14, 2005 and will come into force on January 1, 2006; Official Journal of the State 2005, 358.
8 *Geraets-Smits v. Stichting and Peerbooms v. Stichting*, C-157/99 [2001] E.C.R. I-5473 [*Smits/Peerbooms*]. At para. 103 the ECJ accepted the notion of maximum waiting times, referring to 'undue delay.' 'Undue delay' should be determined as the period within which medical treatment is necessary with respect to the patient's medical condition and history.
9 Like the National Institute for Clinical Excellence (NICE) in the UK, the Dutch (WHICH COMMITTEE?) will follow a similar approach to review research evidence on the clinical effectiveness and cost-effectiveness of pharmaceuticals and medical procedures, as well as provide recommendations as to which drugs should (or should not) be made available to insured patients.
10 Despite the flat rate premium, insurers can compete by lowering premiums on combined supplementary health insurance policies and divergent (voluntary) out-of-pocket arrangements.

11 Nonetheless, the German equivalent of the 'Zorgverzekeringswet,' the so-
called 'Bürgerversicherung' as introduced by the *Rürup* Commission, is
based on the elimination of private and social health insurance categories
while still offering coverage to a majority of the population. The German
'Bürgerversicherung' proposal has been criticized by, among others, the
Federal Constitutional Court Chairwoman Helga Sodan, because it introduces compulsory admission to public health insurance bodies that will
violate the constitutional principal of autonomy. For more details see H.
Sodan, 'Die Bürgerversicherung als Bürgerzwangsversicherung' (2004)
37:7 Zeitschrift für Rechtspolitik 217. Furthermore, Ireland has already
introduced a voluntary health insurance scheme providing insurance for
hospitalisation, which is operated under a governmental agency known as
the Voluntary Health Insurance Board. In the mid-1990s, the private health
insurance market was opened to competition under the provisions of the
Health Insurance Act 1994 [HIA 1994]. Besides providing basic rules for
health insurance operators, the HIA 1994 enshrined the basic principles of
community rating (i.e., charging the same premium rate for a given level
of service), lifetime coverage, open enrolment, and minimum benefit
policies. In this respect see various contributions in: A. den Exter, ed.,
Social Competitive Health Insurance Yearbook 2004 (Rotterdam: Erasmus
University Press, 2005).

12 E.g., A. den Exter, 'De Europese kwetsbaarheid van de Zorgverzekeringswet (the New Health Insurance Act and EC law)' (2005) 80:2 *NJB*
(Dutch Law Journal) 87.

13 Although the European Union is the successor of the European Community, here the emphasis is on the EU's 'first pillar' of activities, i.e. internal
market law. Technically speaking however, this is 'Community law,' and
therefore EC law is the term used in this paper.

14 EC, *Council Directive 92/49 of 18 June 1992 amending Directives 73/239/EEC
and 88/357/EEC as regards the co-ordination of laws, regulations and administrative provisions related to direct insurance other than life assurance,* [1992]
O.L.J. 228/1.

15 Case C-206/98, [2000] E.C.R. I-3509.

16 The concept of the general good is based on both the Treaty (article 28 EC)
and the Court's jurisprudence. Here, the focus is on the Court's interpretation of the general good exemption. It was developed first in the context of
the free movement of services and goods and was subsequently applied to
the right of establishment. The Court requires that a national provision
must satisfy the following cumulative requirements in order to validly
obstruct or limit exercise of the right of establishment and the freedom to

provide services: it must come within a field which has not been harmonised; it must pursue an objective of the general good; it must not be discriminatory; it must be objectively necessary; it must be proportionate to the objective pursued, and it must also be necessary for the general good. The objective of the general good exception is to prevent a provider of services from being safeguarded by rules to which the provider is already subject to in the Member States where he is established. In its interpretative communication, the Commission has applied these principles to the insurance sector. See EC, Commission Interpretative Communication, *Freedom to Provide Services and the General Good in the Insurance Sector,* [2000] O.J. C. 43/3 at 22 and 27–28.

17 Art 54(1) reads: 'Notwithstanding any provision to the contrary, a Member State in which contracts covering the risks [...] may serve as a partial or complete alternative to health cover provided by the statutory social security system may require that those contracts comply with the specific legal provisions adopted by that Member State to protect the general good [...].

18 J.W. Gronden van de, 'Zorg tussen lidstaat en interne markt (Health care and the internal market), Wetenschappelijk instituut voor het CDA (2003) at 55, at <http://www.zorgaanzet.nl/Resources/ZorgAanZet/Documentatie/Rapporten/KantelingenWI112003.pdf>.

19 Letter from Commissioner Frits Bolkestein (on behalf of the Commission) to the Dutch Minister of Health, Welfare and Sport, Mr Hans Hoogervorst (25 November 2003) Brussels, CAB/PvB/D (03) 0848, page 2 in which the Commission gives a formal opinion on the draft of future health insurance legislation.

20 *Gebhard v. Consiglio dell'Ordine degli Avvocati e Procuratori di Milano,* C-55/94, [1995] E.C.R. I-4165.

21 These provisions forbid 'all agreements between undertakings, decisions by associations of undertakings and concerted practices which may affect trade between Member States and which have as their object or effect the prevention, restriction or distortion of competition within the common market' (art. 81) and stipulate that 'any abuse [...] of a dominant position within the common market or in a substantial part of it shall be prohibited as incompatible with the common market insofar as it may affect trade between Member States' (art. 82).

22 'Undertaking,' as used in the Treaty, is the equivalent of 'enterprise.'

23 *Höfner and Elser v. Macrotron GmbH,* C-41/90, [1991] E.C.R. I-1979 at para. 21.

24 Joined Cases C-159/91 and C-160/91, [1993] ECR I-637 at paras. 10–15.

25 *Ibid.*; also see *Fédération Francaise des Sociétés d'Assurance (FFSA) and others v. Ministere de l'Agriculture et de la Peche,* C-244/94, [1995] E.C.R. I-4013 at para. 14 [*FFSA*].

26 *Cisal di Battistello Venanzio & C. Sas v. INAIL,* C-218/00, [2002] E.C.R. I-691 at para. 37 [*Cisal*].

27 In this case entitlements depended solely on the amount of contributions paid by the recipient and the financial results of the investments made by the managing organization. Payments were not made on a redistributive basis and contributions were not solely dependent on income and limited by a ceiling.

28 *FFSA, supra* note 25 at paras. 17–19.

29 *Albany International BV v. Stichting Bedrijfspensioenfonds Textielindustrie,* C-67/96, *Brentjens' Handelsonderneming BV v. Stichting Bedrijfspensioenfonds voor de Handel in Bouwmaterialen,* C-115/97, C-116/97 and C-117/97, and *BV Maatschappij Drijvende Bokken v. Stichting Pensioenfonds voor de Vervoer-en Havenbedrijven,* C-219/97, [1999] E.C.R. I-6025 and in the subsequent judgment *Pavel Pavlov and Others v. Stichting Pensioenfonds Medische Specialisten,* Joined Cases C-180/98 to C-184/98, [2000] E.C.R. I-6451.

30 Although the *FFSA* case did not concern a health insurance scheme, it is relevant to the health sector because the Court referred to the *Poucet and Pistre* case.

31 e.g., a flat-rate premium, a no-claim refund arrangement providing a premium reduction when the costs of insured care remain below a certain limit voluntary co-payments in exchange of lower set premiums.

32 *Cisal, supra* note 26.

33 *Freskot AE v. Elliniko Dimosio,* C-355/00, [2003] E.C.R. I-5263 at paras. 78–79.

34 *AOK Bundesverband and others v. Ichthyol Gesellschaft Cordes and others,* joined cases C-264/01, C-306/01, C-354/01 and C-355/01, [2004] E.C.R. I-2493 at para. 53.

35 Article 86 states: 'Undertakings entrusted with the operation of services of general economic interest […] shall be subject to the rules contained in this Treaty, in particular to the rules on competition, insofar as the application of such rules does not obstruct the performance […] of the particular tasks assigned to them. […].' See also a recent publication by the Commission that clarifies this concept and the Community legal regime relevant to it: EC, Commission, *Green Paper on Services of General Interest,* COM(2003) 270 Final (Brussels: Commission of the European Communities, 2003), online: European Commission <http://europa.eu.int/eur-lex/en/com/gpr/2003/com2003_0270en01.pdf>.

36 E.g., *van Eycke v. Aspa*, c-267/86, [1998] E.C.R. I-4769; *Commission v. Italy (customs agents)*, C-35/96, [1998] E.C.R. I-3851; *Carlo Bagnasco and others v. BPN and others*, C-215/96 and C-216/96, [1999] E.C.R. I-135.

37 EC, Commission State Aid Decision N 46/2003 of 23 January 2003 concerning Ireland – Risk Equalisation Scheme in the Irish Health Insurance Market, C(2003)1322 Final, online: European Commission <http://europa.eu.int/comm/secretariat_general/sgb/state_aids/comp-2003/n046–03.pdf>.

38 Case lodged before the Court of First Instance T-289/03 *BUPA v. Commission*.

39 EC, Press Release, IP/05/531, 'State Aid: Commission endorses public funding for new Dutch health insurance scheme' 3 May 2005), online: European Commission http://europa.eu.int/rapid/pressReleasesAction .do?reference=IP/05 531&format=HTML&aged=0&language= EN&guiLanguage=en.

40 F. Paolucci, A. den Exter & W. van de Ven, 'Solidarity in social health insurance markets' (Paper presented to the European Conference on Health Economics, London, September 2004) [unpublished]. Available online: <http://www.lse.ac.uk/collections/LSEHealthAndSocialCare/pdf/EHPGFILES/EHPGPAPERS/E HPG1PaoluccidenExtervandeVen.pdf>.

41 J. Habermas, *Faktizität unde Geltung: Beiträge zur Diskurstheorie des Rechts und des demokratischen Rechtsstaats* (Frankfurt: Suhrkamp, 1993) at 655.

42 Markus Krajewski, 'Public Services and Trade Liberalisation: Mapping the Legal Framework' (2003) 6:2 *J International Economic Law* 341 at 353, 359.

43 *Ibid*, at 55.

The Role of Private Health Insurance in Social Health Insurance Countries – Implications for Canada

STEFAN GREß

1 Introduction

Private health insurance serves three distinct functions in Western European social health insurance systems.[1] The first is as an *alternative* for mandatory (statutory) social health insurance arrangements. In Germany, a part of the population may chose between joining private health insurance and remaining in social health insurance. The second function is to *supplement* basic health insurance, providing coverage for services not covered by social insurance or to cover the financial risks of co-payments and coinsurance. A third function of private insurance is to provide what can be termed *complementary or double-cover* coverage, in which insured purchase additional private insurance even while they have to participate in existing social schemes.[2] Double-cover private health insurance is rather rare in social health insurance countries.[3] Double-cover private health insurance, however, would be allowed in Quebec post the Supreme Court of Canada's decision in *Chaoulli.*

Health policy makers face several key challenges when regulating private health insurance markets, depending on the function private health insurance fulfils. The need for regulation usually is much higher for alternative private health insurance than for supplementary private health insurance.[4] If private health insurance is to be compatible with prevalent solidarity-based value systems, regulation has to ensure access to private insurance cover for bad risks such as the chronically ill. At the same time, premiums have to be affordable especially for ageing policy holders. Section 2 of this chapter reviews how regulation in the Netherlands and in Germany has sought to solve these problems for alternative private health insurance.[5]

The market for supplementary health insurance depends very much on the extent of the basic benefits package in social health insurance. If benefits of social health insurance are rather comprehensive and of good quality and if co-payments are low, supplementary private health insurance typically covers what could be called luxury goods (e.g. more comfortable board and lodging in hospitals). As a consequence, a smaller degree of regulation for supplementary private health insurance than for alternative private health insurance is justifiable in terms of social acceptability. Section 3 reviews supplementary private health insurance in social health insurance countries paying close attention to access problems resulting from supplementary private health insurance. Finally, section 4 summarizes the findings of the previous sections and discusses the implications of these findings for Canada in light of the *Chaoulli* decision.[6]

2 Alternative Private Health Insurance

In both Germany and the Netherlands, governments regulate alternative private health insurance quite extensively in order to assure access and affordable premiums for bad risks. Both governments require private health insurers to offer standard contracts and regulate market activities in many other ways. Before considering these regulations and their effect, it is useful to describe the manner of premium calculation in private health insurance as opposed to calculation of contributions in social health insurance.

2.1 Calculation of Premiums in Private Health Insurance vs. Calculation of Contributions in Social Health Insurance

One of the most important differences between social and private health insurance is the setting of premiums (private health insurers) and contributions (social health insurers). *Income-related contributions* are not related to individual health risks but to the income of the insured. A certain percentage of income is paid as contribution to the social health insurer. Higher income people therefore pay higher amounts than lower income people. As a consequence, income-related contributions lead to income solidarity. There is also risk solidarity, as contributions do not depend on health status. Social health insurers in Germany calculate income-related premiums. *Community-rated* premiums or contributions are the same for all insured of one health insurer. This method realises risk solidarity because it leads to redistribution between the healthy and the sick. However, it does not achieve income solidarity, as the poor pay a higher share of their income for health insurance than those with high income. Social health insurers in the Netherlands calculate a mix of income-related and community-rated contributions. *Risk-related* premium calculation typically is applied by private health insurers. Individuals pay a premium according to individual risk: people with high health risks (typically, the old, the sick and the chronically ill) pay high premiums, people with low health risks (typically, the young and healthy) pay low premiums – neither risk solidarity nor income solidarity is therefore achieved. Private health insurers in Germany and in the Netherlands calculate risk-related premiums. However, in both countries private health insurers are influenced by society's and consequently government's view on solidarity and thus have to offer standard contracts with community rating (Netherlands) or limited risk rating (Germany). As the premium of those standard contracts, on average, do not cover all health expenditure of the insured, all other private insured face an additional premium to pool excess costs.

2.2 Markets for Alternative Private Health Insurance

Although Germany and the Netherlands share some common characteristics of alternative private health insurance, there are also some important differences. This section reviews common characteristics as well as differences with regard to the extent of the market for alternative private health insurance, the determination of premiums and benefits in non-standard as well as in standard contracts and the relationship of alternative private health insurance to providers.

2.2.1 Market Structure

In the *Netherlands,* most higher-income residents who are not eligible for sickness fund insurance opt to take out private health insurance with one of the 40 or so private health insurance companies. Less than one percent of Dutch residents do not have any health insurance at all, consisting mostly of illegal residents and groups refusing insurance due to religious reasons. In the last decade, private health insurers have strengthened their collaboration with sickness funds (social health insurers) for several reasons. Although obliged to keep separate legal entities due to different supervisory regimes, they have joined forces under the umbrella of larger financial banking and insurance conglomerates. In doing so, they have gained access to the addresses of the sickness fund insured to whom they can offer other insurance. They also benefit from the long experience of sickness funds in local and regional contracting with health care providers. Similarly, sickness funds have benefited from the administrative experience of private health insurance companies. They have expanded traditional health insurance to a wider range of collective insurance and employee benefits packages, both for the sickness fund insured and privately insured, under the umbrella of the larger conglomerates. Such packages have gained importance in the Dutch market, in particular after recent changes in other social insurance legislation shifted some of the financial risks for sickness and disability from social insurance to the employers, who in turn started seeking insurance coverage for their risks.

In *Germany*, the border between social and private health insurance has been stable from the early 1970s until now. While about 90 percent of the population is socially insured, around eight percent are covered by alternative private health insurance. They consist of three major groups: the self-employed, civil servants and those employees above an income threshold. There is a major difference to the situation in the Netherlands – in Germany all three groups can choose to stay as voluntary members in social health insurance or to opt for private health insurance when they become self-employed, civil servants or their income surpasses the income ceiling. Once they opt for private insurance, they are more or less prohibited from returning to a social insurer in the future. Private and social insurers both compete for all three groups who can choose between the two systems.

2.2.2 Premiums and Coverage

In both the *Netherlands and Germany*, private insurers can decide to accept or decline applicants, set financial conditions, determine their range of benefits and adjust their premiums according to the risk structure of the insured. They offer a wide range of insurance policies, with varying coverage, deductibles and eligibility criteria. In general, the coverage is at least as wide as that of the social health insurance and includes medical care, hospital stay, drugs and medical aids and some other services. As there is no standardised package of entitlements, coverage varies. Furthermore, private health insurers can exclude preexisting conditions from coverage. However, this is only true for market contracts and not for standard contracts (see next section)

Dutch private health insurers have never charged fully risk-related premiums.[7] Until the 1970s, most if not all companies charged community based premiums for all of their insured. In the early 1970s, one of the private companies started to offer cheap policies to students. Other companies followed, and then charged higher rates to elderly insured. They also started to refuse high risk groups, or to exclude pre-existing conditions from coverage. This triggered a spiral of premium differentiation and risk selection. After the private insurers failed to implement an informal agreement to solve these problems, the Dutch government felt obliged to step in and to take measures to counteract the newly created access barriers to private health insurance.[8]

In *Germany*, premium calculation of alternative private health insurance is also risk related. However, government regulation restricts the degree of risk rating. The insurer assesses the risk of the insured once, at the beginning of the insurance contract in a process called *underwriting*. However, insurers are not allowed to re-assess the health risk during the insurance contract or to cancel the contract. Consequently, changes in health risk after the start of the contract can not lead to changes in the premiums to be paid by the insured.

Since high income employees, self-employed and civil servants can leave social health insurance and opt for alternative private health insurance (whereas average and low income employees must remain in the statutory system), there is adverse selection against social health insurance: People in poor health normally do not leave social health insurance, since they would have to pay higher premiums in alternative private health insurance. It is also unattractive to switch to alternative private health insurance if there are several children and a non-working spouse in the family, since the latter are covered for free in social health insurance, while private health insurers calculates a separate premium for each person insured. Less than a quarter of persons with earnings above the income ceiling actually switch to private insurance. Still, on average persons holding alternative private health insurance have higher incomes than persons with social health insurance. Half of the individuals who opt for alternative private health insurance are young, single, high earners or married couples with double incomes, and half are civil servants.

2.2.3 *Standard Contracts*

Since there is no legal obligation to accept anyone seeking private health insurance, private health insurers may refuse individuals trying to get coverage, charge higher premiums to high risk groups or exclude pre-existing conditions altogether. Insurers also offer collective contracts to certain groups they see as attractive, e.g. white collar office workers. Thus, the elderly and other persons perceived as high risk because of genetic disposition, family history of chronic illness or past experience, face access barriers in seeking alternative health insurance. In the *Netherlands* private insurers have engaged in selection activities, but they also have shown restraint in this regard, realising that such practice is viewed unfavourably in egalitarian Dutch society. Reflecting this public perspective, the Dutch government has passed regulation concerning standard contracts with private insurers.[9] As a consequence, government determines coverage and cost-sharing arrangements of the WTZ (*Wet op de Toegang tot Ziektekostenverzekering*, Health Insurance Access Act) standard contract scheme. Benefits are almost identical to the sickness fund insurance coverage. Illustrating the importance of the WTZ as a risk pooling mechanism for high risk groups in the private market, the share of private health insurance expenditure financed under the standard contract was approximately 30 percent in 2003 while the share of insured was only 13 percent.

Persons covered by standard contracts pay government-controlled premiums. As this premium does not fully cover the average cost of the WTZ-insured, all other persons with private health insurance participate in a mandatory cost-sharing system by paying an additional premium each year. The government adjusts the premium each year by looking at the average costs over a moving three year average, but may deviate from this adjustment because of other financial considerations. As a consequence of mandatory cost-sharing, private health insurers do not have any incentives to improve cost-effectiveness of health care provision for standard contracts. For a substantial part of their customers they have become purely administrative bodies – even more so than social health insurers.

In *Germany*, private health insurers are not obliged to offer standard contracts by law. However, they only are eligible to receive half of the premium for employees by their respective employers if they do offer standard contracts. Deficits incurred by standard contracts are compensated across all private health insurers. Benefits of the standard policy have to be comparable to the standard package of social health insurance. They are quite similar and uniform across all private health insurers. At the end of the year 2003, only 0.14 percent of all persons with alternative private health insurance held standard contracts. The small number market share of standard contracts can be explained by the fact that the maximum premium for the standard policy is pegged to the average maximum contribution to social health insurance and therefore is quite high.

2.2.4 Relationship with Providers

Private insurers in the *Netherlands,* unlike sickness funds, are not obliged to contract with providers. Traditionally, privately insured themselves pay their general practitioner, medical specialists and other health care services by fee for service, handing in their bills to their insurer for reimbursement. In recent years, private health insurers in the Netherlands increasingly have arranged to pay providers directly. The fees for the medical specialists for treating patients with private health insurance are the same as for treating patients with social health insurance.

In *Germany,* private health insurers do not have contractual relationships with health care providers. Privately insured patients can choose a provider without the need for approval of the health insurer. Private health insurers do not negotiate with providers about tariffs and prices. Instead, the Ministry of Health regulates the maximum tariff physicians or dentists may charge for the treatment of privately insured persons. This maximum amount is higher than the payments health care professionals receive from social health insurers.[10] In hospital, charges are required by law to be the same for standard treatment, but extra charges have to be paid for private room and for seeing the chief medical officer privately. Prices for prescription drugs for persons with alternative private health insurance are higher, too. Pharmaceutical companies and retailers are obliged to give rebates to social health insurers but not to private health insurers.

2.3 Market Outcome of Alternative Private Health Insurance

This section assesses the market outcome of alternative private health insurance. It focuses on equity in finance as well as in delivery of health care services. It also considers effects on cost containment.

2.3.1 Effects on Fairness in Health Care Finance

Persons with private health insurance pay risk-related premiums that have a regressive effect. There is no income solidarity and little if any risk solidarity. In Germany, self-employed and high-income insured in poor health who have chosen to stay in social health insurance may be subsidised by those average and low income employees who are insured in social insurance and cannot switch to private insurance.[11] It is likely that those who profit individually from opting out are the young and healthy, thus increasing the burden of high costs groups for the social insurance. In terms of fairness and social justice, the consequences of this situation are undesirable.[12] In the Netherlands it is also clear that forcing all high income employees to leave social health insurance has redistributive consequences as the risk pooling of social insurance is limited to lower income groups.

2.3.2 Effects on Equity in Health Care Delivery

In the Netherlands, actual health services are identical for persons with social health insurance and persons with alternative private health insurance. Dutch society values equality very highly.[13] In the second half of the 1990s, there has been a quite heated discussion about preferential access to health care facilities for employees. Employers were facing increased financial risks of absenteeism of disabled and sick workers. As a consequence, they were seeking ways to circumvent waiting lists for specialist care and for some elective procedures in hospitals.[14] In some cases, the cost of such priority access was covered by the wider employee benefit schemes offered by the health insurance conglomerates.

Although there is no clear evidence available, persons covered by alternative private health insurance in *Germany* appear to receive more comprehensible and faster treatment than persons with social health insurance. This is due to the fact that in Germany there are tight budgets for ambulatory and hospital care financed by sickness funds. Providers have substantial incentives to treat privately insured patients preferentially since they can charge higher prices and this additional income does not decrease their budget. Of course, the behaviour of health care professionals is not determined by economic incentives only. However, several surveys point out that privately insured persons feel that their relationship with providers is less determined by economic constraints than persons with social health insurance do.[15]

2.3.3 Effects on Cost Containment

It is not uncommon in countries with a large private health care sector that providers charge higher prices for persons with private health insurance in order to compensate for lower prices in the public sector. However, this is not common practice in the Netherlands. Payment of providers by private health insurers is regulated by government and private insurers are not allowed to pay higher fees. As also discussed by Andre den Exter and Colleen Flood and colleagues in this volume, this reduces the incentives for preferential treatment of persons with private health insurance.

In Germany, cost containment of social health insurers is affected by the existence of alternative private health insurance in several ways. However, the net effect is unclear. Private health insurers are quite successful in picking good risks while the bad risks remain in social health insurance. As mostly the young and healthy with higher incomes above the income ceiling opt out of the public scheme, loss of income for social health insurers is quite substantial. People who switch on average are less expensive than persons who do not. Social health insurers have to cover the remaining bad risks. Consequently, the financial situation of social health insurers would improve substantially if all people above the income ceiling had to remain in social health insurance.

However, there are several factors counteracting this tendency. First, health care providers are reimbursed by private health insurance on a much higher level than by social health insurers. This leads to cross-subsidies back to social health insurance, as many ambulatory care providers would be hard pressed financially if they had only patients covered by social health insurers.[16] Second, standard contracts and severe restrictions on returning to social health insurance in older age increase the share of older persons in private health insurance. Unfortunately, there are no reliable calculations whether the existence of alternative private health insurance in Germany leads to higher or to lower contribution rates for social health insurers.

It is clear, however, that alternative private health insurance in Germany in the given legal framework is less effective with regard to cost containment than social health insurance, especially in ambulatory care. This is in line with the findings of Robert Evans in this book. The reasons for this disparate development seem to be quite clear – higher prices for services and less budgetary restraints in alternative private health insurance. Moreover, administrative and marketing costs for private health insurance (11 to 13 percent of income) are higher than in social health insurance (4 to 5 percent).[17]

3 Supplementary Private Health Insurance

Whereas alternative private health insurance is available only in some countries, supplementary private health insurance is available in any social health insurance system. This section consists of two parts. First, it summarises the way supplementary private health insurance is organised in Belgium, France, Germany, the Netherlands and Switzerland. Second, it assesses the effects of supplementary private health insurance.

3.1 Markets for Supplementary Private Health Insurance

Expenditure of supplementary private health insurance as a share of social health insurance expenditures are rather small in Belgium, Germany (both 2 percent), the Netherlands (6.5 percent) and rather high in France (13 percent) and in Switzerland (23 percent).[18] Market shares are increasing over time, complementary to the decreasing size of the standardized benefits package and to the increase of co-payments in social health insurance.

In all countries, both for-profit and not-for-profit insurers offer supplementary private health insurance. There is no general tendency as to market behaviour of for-profit-insurers and not-for-profit insurers. In France, non-profit mutual insurance companies (*mutuelles*) existed long before the social security scheme was created in 1945 and their traditional market was partially taken away from them at that time. They claim to be less inclined toward risk selection. They do not exclude potential applicants and do not calculate risk-related premiums.[19] For-profit insurers came into the market only in the 1980s. They position themselves as risk managers and, indeed, their premiums seem to vary more with risk than those of the *mutuelles*.[20] The situation is very similar in Belgium: *Mutuelles* (sickness funds) in Belgium usually apply the same principles in supplementary private health insurance as in social health insurance (community-rated premiums, acceptance of all applicants) whereas for-profit insurers calculate risk-related premiums and offer individual or collective contracts. In Germany and the Netherlands, there are no significant differences in market behaviour of for-profit and not-for-profit insurers in the supplementary private health insurance market.

Public regulation in EU-countries differs significantly from non-EU-countries. The third non-life directive of the European Union allows only financial regulation in supplementary private health insurance.[21] Most countries have adapted national regulation, although the French government has been quite reluctant to let go of tax exceptions for not-for-profit insurers (*mutuelles*) and the requirement for the notification of new policies. In contrast, non-EU Switzerland requires even the approval of new policies. Usually private health insurers calculate risk-related premiums for supplementary private health insurance. They offer a large variety of arrangements for co-payments and deductibles.

Benefits in supplementary private health insurance differ widely and mostly depend on the extent of coverage in social health insurance. The most common benefit is upgraded hospital accommodation which is prevalent to a different degree in all countries. Benefits for dental care that are not part of the social health insurance benefits package in Switzerland or are only partly covered (Germany, France, the Netherlands) are very common, too. With the exception of France and Belgium, the market for supplementary private health insurance to cover co-payments is not substantial. Switzerland even prohibits coverage of co-payments in social health insurance by supplementary private health insurance. Similar initatives also have been adopted by countries without social health insurance, e. g. Australia with respect to the Medicare benefit for physician services. Increases in social health insurance cost sharing which were implemented in the hope of curbing consumption and expenditures have stimulated growth of supplementary private health insurance in France.[22] However, if supplementary private health insurance covers user charger consumption of health care service is unlikely to decrease. As a consequence, the same is true for expenditures in the public system.

3.2 Market Outcome of Supplementary Private Health Insurance

In this section effects of supplementary private health insurance on equity in health care delivery, consumer mobility in social health insurance and cost containment in social health insurance are discussed.

3.2.1 Effects on Access to Health Care

Access problems to supplementary private health insurance are common in France.[23] Access to supplementary private health insurance varies according to income and social class. Low-income-groups comprise 63 percent of the uninsured (only supplementary insurance) and only 13 percent of them have access to high-coverage supplementary insurance for dental care. As a consequence, consumption of ambulatory care, dental care and glasses is much smaller in low-income-groups. The French system also appears to discriminate against foreigners, young people aged between 20 and 24, and those over 70 years old, all of whom are less likely to be covered by supplementary health insurance. While 59 percent of unskilled workers have little or no supplementary private health insurance, the same is true for only 24 percent of all executives.[24]

In response to these access problems, the French government in 2000 introduced a means-tested, public supplementary insurance program called CMU (*Couverture maladie universelle*) to ensure access to health care for the poor. For those whose income is below a certain threshold (about 10 percent of the population is eligible), this insurance covers all public co-payments and offers lumps-sum reimbursements for glasses and dental prostheses. Health professionals are not allowed to charge more than the public tariff or the lump-sum for CMU beneficiaries. Thus, at least in theory, access to health care is free of charge for CMU-beneficiaries. Patients with supplementary private health insurance in France do not enjoy preferential treatment, as seems to have been assumed by the majority of the court in the *Chaoulli* decision. They see the same providers. Moreover, remuneration does not differ. The benefit of holding supplementary private coverage consists solely of reducing co-payments.

A market solution to mitigate access problems and to increase pooling is the establishment of group contracts. The exclusionary effects of risk-related premiums and underwriting procedures for individual contracts in supplementary private health insurance are mitigated to a considerable degree when insurance is sold to employment-related groups with community-rated premiums. The risks of the individuals concerned are pooled. Moreover, the average risk structure of employees is better than that of non-employees so that employment-based group contracts are attractive for private health insurers.

3.2.2 Effects on Cost Containment in Social Health Insurance

The effects of supplementary private health insurance on cost containment in social health insurance are difficult to measure. Existing evidence is rather ambiguous. On the one hand, governments increasingly rely on supplementary private health insurance to fill gaps left by the decreasing size of benefits packages in social health insurance. Further, supplementary private health insurance generates additional revenues for providers who face tight budgets and thus decreases opposition from providers towards governments' cost-containment policies in social health insurance. On the other hand, due to cost containment measures it sometimes takes a long time before new drugs, treatments or a new technology are included in social health insurance. Supplementary private health insurance puts pressure on social health insurers to include innovative therapies in their coverage. This tendency may in fact act as a cost driver in social health insurance. Moreover, the coverage of co-payments by supplementary private health insurance counteracts the intention of reducing expenditure in the social health insurance sector in France and Belgium. The prime motivation behind the increase of co-payments was to curb public health expenditures. Moreover, government argued that co-payments were intended to make patients consume more responsibly. However, as supplementary private health insurance increasingly covers public co-payments, any impact these measures may have had will be counteracted and, more specifically, borne mainly by the poor if the regulator does not intervene.[25]

4 Conclusions and Implications for Canada

The need for regulating alternative private health insurance is particularly large since an unregulated market might not safeguard access to adequate health insurance for persons without access to social health insurance. Accordingly, governments in Germany and the Netherlands regulate alternative private health insurance extensively. The higher degree of regulation in the Netherlands does reflect the fact that a larger share of the population does not have access to social health insurance – while in Germany there is only an option to exit social health insurance. Moreover, the clear separation between alternative private health insurance and social health insurance in the Netherlands prevents some of the market outcomes of alternative private health insurance in Germany. Private health insurers in the Netherlands are unable to attract primarily persons from social health insurance with good health and high income – as German private health insurers are able to do. Moreover, there are no indirect subsidies of alternative private health insurance to social health insurance in the Netherlands via provider remuneration. Equal remuneration schemes for to a certain degree prevent preferential treatment for patients holding alternative private health insurance.

In regulating alternative private health insurance, there is a trade-off between autonomy of consumers and degree of regulation. Regulation seems to follow a progression – beginning with restrictions on pre-existing conditions exclusion clauses or minimal coverage mandates through community ratings requirements or other bans on risk underwriting and ending up with high risk pooling between insurers. The potential benefits of private health insurance – its flexibility and potential for innovation – are constrained as governments increasingly dictate the terms of insurance contracts. To their already considerable administrative costs, private health insurers now must add regulatory compliance costs. Moreover, the more regulated alternative private health insurance becomes, to safeguard access and to attain cost-effective care, and the less regulated social health insurance becomes, to make it more cost-effective without jeopardising access, the less distinguishable the two types of insurance become. This is true more so in the Netherlands than in Germany and is reflected in the persistent – and finally successful – attempts of the Dutch government to integrate social health insurance and alternative private health insurance as more fully discussed by Andre den Exter in this volume.

In both alternative and supplementary private health insurance, the link between the legal status of insurers (for-profit or not-for-profit) and market outcomes is surprisingly low. While the market behaviour of sickness funds may mitigate access problems – for example by increasing risk pooling in group contracts – it may also counteract policy measures in social health insurance – e.g. by covering user charges.

Regulation for supplementary private health insurance – at least outside the European Union – can increase access, e.g. by banning pre-existing conditions exclusion clauses, requiring minimal coverage mandates through community ratings requirements, prohibiting risk underwriting and increasing risk pooling by increasing incentives for group contracts. As a consequence, supplementary private health insurance becomes more similar to social health insurance.

Implications for Canada

Double-cover or complementary private health insurance in Canada is different from alternative private health insurance in Germany or the Netherlands and from supplementary health insurance Belgium, France,

Germany, the Netherlands and Switzerland. As Colleen Flood and colleagues point out in this volume the majority of the Supreme Court failed to grasp this distinction. Nonetheless, there are important lessons for Canada from the European experience.

First, theoretically private health insurers charge risk-related premiums.[26] If they do so, there is neither risk solidarity nor income solidarity. As a consequence, sick people and poor people are less likely to be covered by private health insurance. If a country places a lot of weight on a financing mechanism that provides risk solidarity as well as income solidarity, this might not be socially acceptable.

Second, there are several instruments to increase risk solidarity and access in private health insurance. The regulator can introduce standard contracts similar to those in the Netherlands or Germany. Tax incentives may increase incentives for employers to offer group contracts and increase pooling. Pre-existing conditions clauses can be banned, premium rate restrictions can be introduced. In the end, if private health insurance is regulated extensively to increase risk solidarity it might look very similar to a public programme. If this is the case it is probably more efficient from a policy point of view to introduce a public programme right away and save on regulation costs and administrative costs.

Third, experience in social health insurance countries shows that preferential treatment of patients with private health insurance coverage depends very much on provider remuneration. If there are two parallel insurance systems and providers gain more from treating private patients than from treating public patients, preferential treatment for the former will follow.

Finally, experience in social health insurance countries also shows that preferential treatment of persons with private health insurance will only occur if something is amiss in the public system – such as waiting lists in the Netherlands and very tight budgetary constraints in Germany. Strong demand for private health insurance is a good indicator for policy makers to solve the problems in the public programmes.

Notes

1 It is important to note that historically social and private health insurance have similar roots in the income protection schemes of the medieval guilds and the 18th and 19th friendly societies and mutual funds.

2 This terminology is not standardized. Sometimes the term *substitute* private health insurance is used instead of *alternative* private health insurance (see for example Mossialos, Elias / Thomson, Sarah (2001): *Voluntary health insurance in the European Union*. London: London School of Economics, Discussion Paper No 19) and the term *complementary* private health insurance is sometimes used instead of *supplementary* private health insurance (see for example Colombo, Francesca / Tapay, Nicole (2004): *Private Health Insurance in OECD Countries: The Benefits and Costs for Individuals and Health Systems*. Paris: OECD Health Working Paper No. 15).

3 As a rule budgetary constraints – especially with regard to capacity planning (number of physicians, number of hospitals, etc.) – are less severe in social health insurance countries than in tax-financed countries. The Netherlands are an exception to this rule. If waiting times are not a severe problem, there is no demand for double-cover private health insurance (see Osterkamp, Rigmar (2002): 'Warten auf Operationen - ein internationaler Vergleich.' ifo-schnelldienst **55**(10): 14–21).

4 See for example Jost, Timothy Stoltzfus (2001): 'Private or public approaches to insuring the uninsured: lessons from international experience with private insurance.' New York University Law Review **76**(2): 419–93.

5 This refers the private health insurance in the Netherlands up to the year 2005. For a more comprehensive and up-to-date overview of private health insurance in the Netherlands see Tapay, Nicole / Colombo, Francesca (2004): *Private Health Insurance in the Netherlands. A Case Study*. Paris: OECD Health Working Papers No. 18. For the consequences of the 2006 health insurance reform see the chapter by den Exter in this book.

6 Sections 2 and 3 is mostly based on a shortened and updated version of Wasem, Jürgen /Greß, Stefan / Okma, Kieke G.H. (2004): The role of private health insurance in social health insurance countries. Social health insurance in Western Europe. Saltman, Richard / Busse, Reinhard / Figueras, Josep. London, Open University Press: 227–247.

7 This is due to due three main factors. First, private health insurer were keen to deprive government of arguments to expand the scope of statutory social health insurance. Second, for-profit non-specialist health insurers preferred a quiet market in order to focus on more profitable lines of business – private health insurance for them mainly is a means to sell other products. Finally and maybe most importantly, private health insurers founded by sickness funds have a significant market share in alternative private health insurance and refrain from applying strict risk rating and underwriting. See chapter 4 of Schut, F.T. (1995): *Competition in the Dutch health care sector*. Ridderkerk: Ridderprint.

8 See Okma, K. (1997): *Studies on Dutch health politics, policies and law.* Utrecht: Ph. D. thesis.

9 For an in-depth analysis for the process leading to the implementation of this regulation see chapter 5 of Okma, K. (1997): *Studies on Dutch health politics, policies and law.* Utrecht: Ph. D. thesis.

10 Prices in ambulatory care can be up to three times as high for privately insured as for socially insured (by law this not possible for insured with a standard policy).

11 Due to a lack of data, this can not be proven clearly.

12 See Jacobs, Klaus / Schulze, Sabine (2004): 'Systemwettbewerb zwischen gesetzlicher und privater Krankenversicherung: Idealbild oder Schimäre?' Gesundheit und Gesellschaft Wissenschaft 4(1): 7–18.

13 From an economic point of view, there are some incentives for preferential treatment of patients with private private health insurance by general practitioners due to differences in remuneration (fee-for-service for alternative private health insurance, capitation for social health insurance). However, there are no incentives for preferential treatment by specialists, since the same fee-for-service tariffs apply for both groups.

14 See Brouwer, Werner /Exel, Job van /Hermans, Bert / Stoop, Arjen (2003): 'Should I stay or should I go? Waiting lists and cross-border care in the Netherlands.' Health Policy **63**: 289–298.

15 See Braun, Bernard (2000): *Rationierung und Vertrauensverlust im Gesundheitswesen - Folgen eines fahrlässigen Umgangs mit budgetierten Mitteln?* St. Augustin: Asgard.

16 About 8 percent of the population holds alternative private health insurance. In ambulatory care, these persons account for 13 percent of health care expenditures.

17 See Burger, Stephan /Hollenberg, Frank / Männel, Beate (2002): 'Diskussion um Verwaltungskosten ist ein Ablenkungsmanöver.' Die BKK(12): 517–521 for social health insurance and Verband der privaten Krankenversicherung e. V. (2004): *Die private Krankenversicherung – Zahlenbericht 2003/2004.* Köln: Verband der privaten Krankenversicherung e. V. for private health insurance.

18 See Paolucci, Francesco /Schut, Erik /Beck, Konstantin /Van de Voorde, Carine /Greß, Stefan / Zmora, Irith (2005): *Supplementary health insurance as a tool for risk-selection in mandatory health insurance markets: a five countries' comparison:* iHEA 5th World Congress: Investing in Health. Barcelona, Spain. July 10 - July 13 2005.

19 See Buchmueller, Thomas /Coufinhal, Agnes /Grignon, Michel / Per-

ronnin, Marc (2004): 'Access to physician services: does supplemental insurance matter? Evicence from France.' Health Economics **13**(7): 669–687.

20 See Couffinhal, Agnès / Paris, Valérie (2001): *Utilization Fees imposed on Public Health Care Systems Users in France.* Paris: Credes.

21 See the chapter by den Exter in this book.

22 See Imai, Yukata /Jacobzone, Stéphane / Lenain, Patrick (2000): *The changing health system in France.* Economics Department Working Papers No. 269. Paris: OECD.

23 See Turquet, Pascale (2004): 'A stonger role for the private sector in France's health insurance?' International Social Security Review **57**(4): 67–90

24 See Bocognano, Agnès /Couffinhal, Agnès /Dumesnil, Sylvie / Grignon, Michel (2000): *Which Coverage for Whom? Equity of Access to Health Insurance in France.* Paris: Presentation at the European Public Health Association Congress, Paris Dec 14–16 2000.

25 See Buchmueller, Thomas /Coufinhal, Agnes /Grignon, Michel / Perronnin, Marc (2004): 'Access to physician services: does supplemental insurance matter? Evicence from France.' Health Economics **13**(7): 669–687

26 Robert Evans in this volume correctly points out that this is not always true in practice.

Finding Health Policy 'Arbitrary': The Evidence on Waiting, Dying, and Two-Tier Systems

COLLEEN M. FLOOD, MARK STABILE
AND SASHA KONTIC

Introduction

The majority of the Supreme Court in the *Chaoulli* decision decided that the Quebec health care system must be 'two-tier' to be constitutional.[1] In other words, in order to comply with the Quebec Charter, residents of Quebec must be allowed to purchase private insurance so that they may avoid waiting for care in the public system. The court, however, was evenly split 3:3 on whether or not s. 7 of the Canadian *Charter* was breached and thus split on the application of this ruling to the rest of Canadian medicare. Because Justice Deschamps did not rule on the Canadian Charter but only on the Quebec Charter, this decision technically affects only Quebec. Three justices (McLachlin C.J. and Major J. writing on behalf of themselves and Bastarache J.) found Quebec laws banning private insurance to be in breach of s.7 and concluded that the laws were not in accordance with the principles of fundamental justice because they were 'arbitrary.' This judgment will provide strength to *Charter* challenges to legislation in other provinces that prevents the flourishing of a second-tier, such as provisions that prevent physicians from working in both the public sector and the private sector. Three other justices (Binnie J. and Lebel J. writing on behalf of themselves and Fish J.) found the Quebec laws prohibiting private health insurance did not breach the Quebec Charter or the Canadian *Charter*.

The significance of this decision cannot be overstated. Medicare is the only universal program of entitlements in Canada in which rich and poor are treated equally, that is not means-tested, and where those with means cannot 'opt' out to a privately-funded sector (as they can with public schools). The *Chaoulli* decision portends the fall of one-tier medicare, the most cherished social program in Canadian history.[2]

Here we will explore the court's treatment of health economics and health policy and its comparative analysis of health care systems in other countries. We will argue that the majority decision with respect to the Quebec Charter and the decision written by McLachlin C.J. and Major J. with respect to the Canadian *Charter* each reveal a flawed understanding of the dynamics of public and private financing in health care. In particular, we review the conclusion in the McLachlin/Major judgment that laws banning the purchase of private health care insurance are 'arbitrary', by examining closely the evidence of the dynamics of public and private insurance in a number of countries. We believe it may be one thing to question the evidence supporting a ban on private insurance, but quite another altogether to describe the policy as 'arbitrary.'

We analyze four conclusions reached by the majority (on the Quebec Charter) (written by Deschamps J.) or in the McLachlin/Major judgment. They are as follows:

1. the 'public sector monopoly' in Canada causes waiting lists;
2. the freedom to purchase private insurance will reduce the burden on the public system because the public system will no longer have to treat those people who are privately insured;
3. the freedom to purchase private insurance will allow many residents to avoid delays in treatment in the public sector; and
4. that the ability to purchase private insurance will have no detrimental effect on the public system as evidenced by the experience of other jurisdictions in which there are two-tier systems.

We also address, in particular, McLachlin/Major's unwillingness to value equality as a worthy governmental objective. Obviously equality cannot trump all other factors, for equality in misery is not worthwhile. But if Chief Justice McLachlin and Justices Major and Bastarache had put some value on aspiring to achieve equality in allocating health care (and to acknowledge the difficult policy constraints and choices that must be made to achieve that goal), this may have tempered their bullish approach.

False Conclusion 1: The Public Sector Monopoly Causes Waiting Lists

The majority concludes that waiting lists are caused by the public sector monopoly over hospital and doctors' services. McLachlin C.J.

and Major J. write: 'The result is a virtual monopoly for the public health scheme...[t]his virtual monopoly, on the evidence, results in delays in treatment that adversely affect the citizen's security of the person.'[3]

But the majority's solution to this problem is not consistent with experience in other jurisdictions. A recent review of waiting times in OECD countries irrefutably demonstrates that many countries with two-tier systems (in which their citizens may purchase private insurance to cover essential hospital and physician services) *also struggle with waiting lists*. Other countries within which waiting lists are a significant policy concern are Australia, Denmark, Finland, Ireland, Italy, the Netherlands, New Zealand, Norway, Spain, Sweden and the UK.[4] Countries that do not record waiting lists (or at least do not acknowledge them as a political problem) include the US, Switzerland, Luxembourg, Japan, Germany, France, Belgium and Austria. Notably, a number of these latter countries limit access to care through a range of user fees and, in the case of the US, report a significant portion of their population as uninsured.[5]

A complicated range of factors is necessary to explain why one group of countries experiences problems with waiting lists and another does not. Clearly the difference is *not* due to the inability to purchase private insurance and thus *not* due to the 'virtual monopoly' in the public health scheme. Only within Canada are there (in some provinces) express prohibitions on private insurance for essential hospital and physician services (creating a 'public monopoly'). But it is clear that Canada is not alone in struggling with waiting lists. Indeed, compared to countries such as the UK and New Zealand, where there are two-tier systems, Canada has much shorter waiting lists and times.

The ability to spend in a public system is constrained by the tax capacity of the country and its other priorities. As a consequence, systems that have a greater proportion of private financing may not experience such resource constraints and thus waiting list problems. But other, more fundamental access problems manifest themselves because people either cannot afford to buy private insurance or private care and/or do not qualify for private insurance because of their health needs. The US, for example, does not have a political problem of waiting lists, but some 45.8 million Americans do not have any insurance coverage at all and thus may wait infinitely long for care unless it is provided as an act of charity. As a second example, France has high user charges or out-of-pocket payments at the point of service; therefore many people may not get into the system in the first instance to be counted as 'waiting'. The court did not consider these negative features of foreign systems seemingly desirable by virtue of their lack of waiting times and ignored the even more fundamental problem of barriers on access to care.

Waiting lists are an extremely complex phenomenon. They are caused by a variety of interacting factors including supply in terms of number of physicians and other health professionals, capacity within hospitals, and differing incentives both for through-put and for productivity (salary, fee-for-service, capitation, etc.) Waiting may occur in any system, be it public or private, that attempts to limit to some extent the level of capacity in the system in order to control total spending; it is a form of rationing. Measurement and the management of supply and capacity relate to sustainability. In the absence of such measures there is a presumption of shortage and, in the public system (all other things being equal) taxes must rise to provide more money and/or other areas of spending must be cut, for example education or welfare. In the private sector, (all other things being equal) premiums must rise and/or high-risk individuals or costly treatments must be excluded from coverage. It is wrong to assume that within the private sector waiting does not occur at all; for example, currently in Regina couples may wait up to a year for privately-financed infertility services.[6]

False Conclusion 2: Freedom to purchase private insurance will reduce the burden on the public system because the public system will no longer have to treat privately insured patients

Justice Deschamps, for the majority of the Court on the Quebec Charter writes: 'because the public plan already handles all the serious cases, I do not see how the situation could be exacerbated if that plan were relieved of the clientele with less serious health problems.'[7] The unspoken assumption is that in a two-tier system, waiting times would go down. This is the policy argument most frequently advanced by those in favor of greater privatization; a resilient argument because it accords with the intuition of many about what would be the effect of introducing a private tier of hospital and doctors' services. For example, the factum of one of the intervenors (a collaboration of private clinics) states, 'moreover, it is counterintuitive to suppose that the ability to access private health services could do anything other than reduce the pressures on the public system.'[8]

Intuition in the case of health care markets though is often wrong. In any event, intuition should not dictate legal reasoning.

Why won't pressure on the public sector be reduced by the creation of a private-tier? The key assumption made by the intervenor quoted above is that providers will be performing treatments in the private sector using resources and time that are not currently being exploited in the public system. But the Canadian system, as in many other OECD systems, is characterized by a limited supply of physicians and other skilled medical personnel. That, together with bed capacity, is the principal argument advanced to claim that the public system is 'underfunded.' In other words, limited capacity/supply is a critical component of waiting times.

A recent OECD study of the factors causing waiting lists showed empirically that '[t]he availability of doctors is the most significant association with waiting times.'[9] 'Econometric estimates suggest that a marginal increase of 0.1 practicing physicians and specialists (per 1,000 population) is associated respectively with a marginal reduction of mean waiting times of 8.3 and 6.4 days (at the sample mean) and a marginal reduction of median waiting times of 7.6 and 8.9 days, across all procedures included in the study. Analogously, an increase in total health expenditure per capita of $100 is associated with a reduction of mean waiting times of 6.6 days and of median waiting times of 6.1 days.'[10]

Such results clearly indicate the dangers of fostering a privately-funded tier that would attract capacity (particularly time spent working by specialists and other physicians) away from the public system. Fewer physicians within the public sector or fewer physician hours spent in the public sector is likely to be associated with longer waiting times. To demonstrate this we attempt, below, to calculate the impact on waiting times if some of the existing physician capacity is diverted to a private-pay tier in Ontario.

The Supreme Court (and the analysis of limited capacity above) assumes that medical need will stay the same and will simply be transferred from the public to the private sector (and ignores the supply/capacity issue referred to above). However, it is likely the case that the private sector will expand the concept of 'need' for those who have private insurance and will meet those needs using physicians and nurses that could otherwise have been working in the public system to treat more urgent and higher priority needs. In essence, wait times could be exacerbated by an increase in demand fuelled by both consumers and producers; in effect resulting in the increased 'medicalization' of relatively minor complaints.

The demand for health care and determinations of medical necessity are highly subjective and dependent upon the decision-making of individual clinicians who respond to a variety of economic and other factors in determining 'need' and in advising upon what treatments are required to meet those 'needs.' Thus, for example, an anxious patient who demands an MRI in the event of a headache may well have this 'need' met in the private sector given the economic incentives there are to respond to such need. This patient would probably not have been prescribed an MRI examination in the public sector, but will now be using the time of a physician and technician that could have been used to treat public sector patients. In New Zealand, for example, which has a two-tier system, a survey of private insurers revealed, 'evidence for efficacy and cost-effectiveness is seldom explicitly sought' in determining what services are insured; insurers seldom look beyond the professional opinion of the doctor recommending the intervention.[11]

It is often claimed that allowing a two-tier system will introduce an element of competition into a moribund health care system. A public sector monopoly often suffers from not being as nimble as successful actors in private markets. But a façade of competition is created through the establishment of duplicate insurance or two-tier system.[12] Allowing people to purchase private insurance for services meant to be covered in the public system does not inject a competitive element into the health care system. Unlike the shoe salesman who will feel the monetary pinch as her customers depart to a new shoe store down the road, the departure of those able to afford private insurance into a privately-funded sector will have few, if any, financial consequences for the hospitals and specialists remaining in the public sector. Perversely, there will be less incentive to improve productivity and reduce waiting times; this would be particularly so as the more vocal, wealthy and politically-connected move to the forefront of the exodus to the privately-funded tier.

As noted previously, countries that have two-tier systems (where private insurers cover services that are available in the public system) often struggle with long wait times. In New Zealand, approximately 35-37% of the population has private insurance, but spending by private insurers accounts for just 6.5% of total spending.[13] Most of the difficult and expensive cases are not covered by the private sector. And, moreover, there are very long waiting lists in the public sector for services that are covered by private insurance, such as hip and knee replacements.

Has support for the public system been eroded by private insurance? This is, of course, virtually impossible to prove one way or another because of a variety of factors that influence support, and the difficulty of demonstrating 'support one way or another'. A survey showing rising concern over falling public spending on health care is unsurprising given that the vast majority of the population in two-tier systems like those in the UK and New Zealand do not hold private insurance and thus are still completely dependent on the public system.[14] The only way to answer this question would be to survey individuals pre and post purchase of private insurance to see if their views on spending to alleviate waiting lists in the public system had changed.

Within New Zealand there is certainly some indirect evidence of a loss of political support for public spending, particularly on those services that are covered by private insurance (e.g. elective surgery.) For example, the New Zealand government legislated to provide for a 'booking system' to manage waiting lists for the 65% of the population without private insurance. This means that individuals are not placed on a waiting list for service through the public system unless and until the system can meet their needs within 6 months; those not placed on a waiting list are referred back to their family physician to 'manage' their care. This practice creates de facto waiting lists for waiting lists, but those are now not recorded centrally (and thus cannot be used to criticize government performance). Those who hold private insurance do not have to put up with such harsh rationing techniques[15] and their political support for this booking system probably would be less if they too were subjected to it. It demonstrates that is often easier to be tougher about resource allocation decisions that affect someone else. [16]

False Conclusion 3: Freedom to purchase private insurance will allow many ordinary residents to avoid delays in treatment in the public sector

It is manifestly clear from a *policy* perspective that if one agrees that equitable access is an important goal, the answers to reducing waiting times lie within improving the capacity and productivity of the public system. But the majority of the Supreme Court does not ask itself this larger policy question. Rather, it starts from a different place. As McLachlin C.J. and Major J. note: 'The appellants do not seek an order....that waiting times for treatment under the public health care scheme be reduced. They only seek a ruling that because delays in the public system place their health and security at risk, they should be allowed to take out insurance to permit them to access private services.'[17] Even though the Court ignores the question of whether the public system can be reformed, they still contend that '[t]he question in this case, however, is not whether single-tier health care is preferable to two-tier health care.'[18]

They go on to note: 'the appellants have established that *many* Quebec residents face delays in treatment that adversely affect their security of the person and *that they would not sustain but for the prohibition on medical insurance*. It is common ground that the effect of the prohibition on private insurance is to allow only the very rich, who do not need insurance, to secure private health care in order to avoid the delays in the public system.' [19] (emphasis added)

A key empirical question in light of this statement is how many Quebeckers or Canadians generally would benefit from the introduction of a two-tier hospital and doctors' care insurance system. Nowhere in any of the factums presented nor in the lower courts was this issue directly addressed. Despite this absence of evidence, McLachlin C.J. and Major J. nevertheless conclude that the appellants have established that 'many' Quebec residents would not have their security jeopardized if indeed private health insurance were available. They also conclude that 'ordinary' Quebeckers could avoid suffering if the ban on private insurance were not in place.[20]

Having concluded that 'many' and 'ordinary' Quebeckers would benefit from private insurance, McLachlin and Major then examine the experiences of other jurisdictions and note, contradictorily, that only a relatively small percentage of the populations in these systems have private insurance. They state that in Sweden only a 'small minority of the population' purchase private insurance, that in Germany 'only' 9% of the population purchase private insurance, and that in the UK just 11.5% of citizens buy private insurance. They use these statistics as partial justification to dismiss the Quebec government's claim that it is necessary to ban private insurance to protect public medicare and to conclude that governmental policy in this regard is 'arbitrary.'

They cannot have it both ways. If only a small percentage of the population is likely to be covered by private insurance (thus eliminating concerns that the public sector will be imperiled) then this seriously qualifies their conclusion that 'many' Quebeckers would benefit. If indeed 'many' Quebeckers would benefit and buy private insurance, then they should not so readily dismiss concerns that the sustainability (politically and financially) of the public sector will be imperiled.

The empirical evidence on *who* benefits from private health insurance indicates that those with high or above-average incomes are more likely to have private coverage than those in lower income brackets. In the United Kingdom for example, where privately insured health care exists as a parallel alternative to the publicly funded system, about 12% of the population have private insurance;[21] that coverage is strongly related to income. A 2001 study reveals that 40 percent of people in the wealthiest ten percent of the population are privately insured, whereas only 5 percent of people in the bottom forty percent have private insurance.[22] Overall, 44 percent of those with above-average income have private coverage, as compared to 10 percent with below-average income.[23]

Greater numbers of people have private coverage in other countries such as Australia and New Zealand, where patient cost-sharing (or out-of-pocket payment) is required within the basic public system. For example, in New Zealand most people have to pay the full out-of-pocket cost of a visit to a family doctor, which ranges between $50 and $60 per visit. Similar to the UK, the likelihood of having private insurance is significantly associated with income. In New Zealand, approximately 37 percent of the total population has private coverage.[24] About 60 percent of people with above-average incomes have private coverage, as compared to only 24 percent of people with below-average incomes.[25] More detailed results from the 1996/97 New Zealand Health Survey show that 13.3 percent of those with an income of $10,000 or less and 14.2 percent of people with income between $10,001 to $20,000 have private insurance, compared to 60.9 percent with incomes over $50,001.[26] A study from the New Zealand Ministry of Health also indicates that health status does not correlate with health insurance, and that 'people had health insurance because they could afford to, and not because of poor health'.[27]

Australian data from 1998 shows that only 20% of people with an annual income of less than $20,000 had private coverage compared to 76% of people with an annual income of $100,000 or more.[28] After the introduction of a tax rebate scheme in 1998 (a regressive form of financing), private insurance purchasing did increase; about 42 percent of the Australian population currently has some type of private insurance cover. However, a Commonwealth study conducted in 2001 found that despite the rebates, 68% of people with above-average incomes have private coverage, whereas only 33% of people with below average incomes do.[29] The main reason that Australians do not purchase private insurance is because they consider it too expensive.[30]

So much for the argument that access to privately-funded hospital and doctors insurance would benefit 'ordinary' Quebecers.

There is nothing to suggest that private insurance for essential hospital and physician services would be distributed any more fairly in Canadian society. Income related disparities connected to private insurance are obvious now in Canada *vis-à-vis* prescription drug, dental, home care, long-term care, rehabilitation, and many other health services that are not protected by the *Canada Health Act* (and thus for which private insurance/private payment is allowed). The 2001 Commonwealth survey shows that about 79 percent of Canadians in above-average income brackets have supplementary health insurance, as compared to only 36 percent of people with lower incomes.[31] Results from the survey also show that 22% of people questioned did not fill prescriptions and that 42% did not access needed dental care because of the cost involved.

So what to conclude from all of this with respect to the majority reasoning in *Chaoulli*? There are two possibilities:

a. either the majority was not aware of the income-disparities associated with private insurance or at least the magnitude of these disparities; or
b. the majority was cognizant but considered that if wealthier Canadians would benefit and there was insufficient evidence that poorer Canadians would suffer any more than they do now (enduring long waiting lists in the public system) then a two-tier system should be allowed.

False Conclusion 4: Allowing A Two-Tier System Will Have No Detrimental Effect On The Public System.

Given long wait times, what effect will abolishing the ban on private insurance have on the public health care sector? It is difficult to answer that question from comparative data because every country's system is a product of its own history; there is also the difficulty of reaching firm conclusions using social science methodologies and qualitative evidence.

Canada is the only country in which private hospital and doctors' services insurance is banned. Because health and insurance are provincial matters, the restriction does not apply evenly across Canada. Six provinces - British Columbia, Alberta, Manitoba, Ontario, Quebec and Prince Edward Island - prohibit private insurance coverage for medically necessary hospital and physician services.[32] Yet even in provinces where private health insurance is allowed, such coverage is basically non-existent because of status and price disincentive policies that discourage physicians from working in both the public and the private sector. Every province, except for Newfoundland, has implemented some form of disincentive strategy to dissuade private delivery of medically necessary services.[33]

No other country provides a valid comparator when considering what the implications are of allowing a two-tier system. Nevertheless, with caveats, one can attempt to predict the effect of private insurance on waiting times on the basis of the evidence in other jurisdictions, filtered through Canada's history, laws, interest groups, political economy, and international obligations under free trade and human rights agreements.

The Quebec government defends itself by arguing that a ban on private insurance is necessary to protect the public system, an argument rejected by the majority of the court. The burden of proof is upon the applicant to demonstrate that the violation is not in accordance with the principles of fundamental justice. But it does not seem that the applicants in the *Chaoulli* decision had to do more to satisfy this burden than refute the evidence of the government witnesses called to satisfy the majority.

One of the most concerning aspects of the judgment is the majority's cavalier treatment of evidence presented by social scientists, including that of Charles Wright, a contributor to this volume. All the social scientists but one testified to the detrimental effects of allowing a two-tier system. The majority dismissed all of their testimony in the harshest of terms; they were condemned for making arguments based on 'common sense' rather than grounded in economic studies or upon the experience of other countries.[34] Indeed McLachlin C.J. and Major J. conclude in the context of their s.7 analysis that governmental policy was 'arbitrary' given the lack of evidence supporting the contention that to allow parallel private insurance would undermine the operation of publicly-funded medicare.[35] As the dissenters point out, the majority prefers the evidence of just one physician called by the appellants and dismisses the conclusions reached by the trial judge's assessment of the credibility and reliability of six other expert witnesses called.[36]

As Sujit Choudhry points out in this volume, however, what links the majority and minority decisions is the demand for a high degree of evidence on the part of government to justify the deprivation of a s.7 right although those on both sides disagree on whether that evidentiary burden has been satisfied.

Another disturbing aspect of the majority judgment is the court's ability to understand and translate experiences from other jurisdictions. McLachlin C.J. and Major J. accept the appellants' evidence that the experience of other developed countries suggests 'that there is no real connection in fact between prohibition of (private) health insurance and the goal of a quality public health system.'[37] What was the evidence that the Court relied on?

In reviewing the experiences of other jurisdictions, Deschamps J. glides over the health care systems in Austria, Germany, the Netherlands, the UK, New Zealand, Australia and Sweden. Drawing on the Kirby report, McLachlin CJ and Major J provide a quick tour of the purported benefits of the health care systems of Sweden, Germany, and the UK. There is also passing reference to Australia, Singapore and the U.S. They conclude: 'that many western democracies that do not impose a monopoly on the delivery of health care have successfully delivered to their citizens medical services that are superior to and more affordable than the services that are presently available in Canada.'[38] But they provide no justification or explanation of the measures or variables considered to reach their sweeping conclusion that the health care systems discussed are 'superior' to or more affordable than that of Canada's.

On the latter front it is important to note that merely comparing Canada unfavorably to other countries who spend less as a percentage of GDP spent on health does not reveal much. The assumption usually is that there is waste or inefficiency in the system. But percentage of GDP spent is simply an accounting tool for total spending, not a measure of how well the money is spent. The vast majority of total health care spending, for example, is for the salaries and remuneration that we pay our doctors and nurses. Canada pays its labour higher rates than some other jurisdictions. Indeed many feel that we do not pay these professionals enough. Thus the fact that we spend more on health in Canada than, for example, the UK or New Zealand, does not mean per se that the money is wasted (or at least no more than in any other system for as Alan Maynard points out in this volume there are vast inefficiencies in both public and private health insurance systems).

Through their comparative analysis of health care systems the majority amply demonstrates why courts should be extremely cautious of wading into these difficult policy areas. The fundamental error that the majority makes is to conflate all health care systems with some role for private insurance into one group - which they consider to be 'two-tier' in nature. In fact there are at least four distinct ways of financing health care[39] and European countries such as the Netherlands and Germany are better classified not as two-tier (which allow parallel or duplicate private coverage for services ostensibly covered by the public system) but group-based. In group-based systems, as are discussed by Stefan Gress in this volume, private insurers **do not** perform a duplicate role as would be allowed by the *Chaoulli* decision, allowing people to jump queues for treatment. Instead private insurance is required to provide full coverage for certain segments of the population.

For example, in the Netherlands an individual earning less than Euros 33,000 (Canadian $48,886) must contribute to and is eligible for social (publicly funded) insurance (similar to Canadian medicare as it is progressively financed). All others are free to purchase private insurance that does not 'top-up' coverage in the public system; the insurance must cover all the needs of those who elect it to buy it.[40] Moreover, as also discussed by Andre den Exter in this volume, physicians do not have an incentive in the Netherlands to give priority to patients with private insurance over those with social insurance because the fees or tariffs paid are the same; indeed, it is part of the ethical code of physicians not to treat patients with social insurance or private insurance differently.[41] In Germany, wealthier patients can opt to stay in the social insurance scheme or take out private insurance; but as in the Netherlands, private insurance must cover all their needs (i.e. it does not 'top-up' coverage by the social insurance scheme). Furthermore, one cannot easily opt back into the social insurance scheme once having opted out.

These systems are very different from what the majority envisaged to be the case in *Chaoulli*, where the universal public system would stay in place, but citizens may buy private insurance that duplicates coverage in the public system. Moreover, private insurers in Europe are often heavily regulated to stop them from cream-skimming (that is selecting only the healthy for coverage) and risk-rating (that is charging premiums that reflect the risk of individuals to ill-health). To be clear, this kind of system will *not* evolve in Quebec as a result of a striking down the ban on private health insurance for services that are now exclusively insured by medicare. The entire funding base of medicare – involving a shift from tax-funded to social insurance premiums – would have to occur in order to mimic the European model touted by the majority as superior to the Canadian system.

Two-tier systems similar to those mandated by *Chaoulli* include New Zealand and the U.K. In these countries private insurance **duplicates** coverage of services that are publicly insured. Physicians work in both the public and private sectors, with specialists often 'topping-up' their public sector incomes in the more lucrative private sector. Consideration of the specific experiences of these jurisdictions shows that historically, both countries have wrestled with waiting lists that are much longer than those currently within Canada.[42] The length of waiting times in these two-tier systems strongly refutes the linkage made by the majority between long waiting lists and Canada's public monopoly on healthcare insurance. But the majority does not consider evidence of long waiting times in New Zealand and the U.K.

The majority of the court describes as merely 'theoretical' the concern that private-pay insurance and providers will undermine the public system. But the experiences of other jurisdictions demonstrate this is a concern through the various measures they take to counteract it. For example, McLachlin C.J. and Major J. discuss the small amount of private insurance in Sweden, but fail to mention that physicians there are prevented from working both in the public and the private sectors. Swedish physicians must choose one or the other and the inability to operate largely in the public system with a top-up from the private sector provides a brake on the extent to which the private sector can develop at the expense of the public system. Similar measures are taken in other two-tier systems, namely Luxembourg, Greece and Italy.[43] This prohibition is applied in every province (except for Newfoundland) in Canada as well.[44]

Are *all* these governments misguided as to the problems of a parallel private sector? Are they all 'arbitrary' in their policy choices? If not, then is it 'arbitrary' to take the next step and simply ban private insurance for essential hospital and physician services?

Limited Capacity

As mentioned earlier, in our view, capacity is the key problem with respect to the introduction of a two-tier healthcare insurance system.

Where will the specialists and physicians come from to staff a privately paid tier if not from the public sector? The majority does not address this fundamental question.

In the short run, the capacity of the system is limited. It takes six years to train a family doctor; it takes nine years to train a medical oncologist (eleven years for a surgical oncologist). Even assuming a huge influx of capital from the private sector it is simply not feasible to bring on stream a whole new wave of Canadian-trained physicians. In 1994 it cost, on average, $950,459.00 to train a family doctor and $ 2,303,304 to train a subspecialist;[45] undoubtedly it costs far more now.[46] Currently, the cost of tuition in medicine is but a small fraction of the public cost of educating medical undergraduates and does not apply to the training of postgraduates in family medicine, the specialties and sub-specialties. The high cost to the public can be justified by the benefit that flows from the services they provide to the publicly-insured system under medi-care. Were they to practice in a parallel, privately-insured tier, the case would be strengthened to recover from them a far greater proportion of that cost in the form of higher retrospective tuition payments.

Apart from the significant lag there would be in bringing on-stream a considerable increase in the number trained physicians, there is the possibility of recruiting physicians from other jurisdictions were we to offer higher rates of payment and/or better conditions here. But once again there are significant barriers to entry imposed by the various colleges of physician and surgeons in each province. Some marginal increase in capacity might be possible in the short run as some Cana-dian trained physicians may be lured back from higher-paid positions in the US or other countries (although a recent study already shows that there are more physicians returning to Canada than leaving presum-ably because they value other aspects of their working and personal lives more than higher remuneration).[47] It is also likely that existing physicians in the public sector would be able to be more productive if there was more private sector capacity in terms of private hospital beds and private nursing staff – although to what extent is unknown.

But let us make the opposite assumption to that assumed by the Supreme Court, namely that capacity is constant.[48] What then would be the effect on the development of a private-pay tier? The majority as-sumes no negative effect on the public system. We use cross country evidence compiled by the OECD to evaluate what the upper bound of the ramifications would be on waiting times in Ontario from introduc-ing a two-tier system that would see some capacity diverted from the publicly funded tier to the privately funded tier. It is difficult to know where in this range the true effect would lie. It would, among other things, depend on our assumptions on the following three factors: First, physicians who leave the public system will take some patients out of the system with them for treatment. However, these physicians would presumably take less than their share of the total waitlist of patients in order to offer improved wait times in the private tier. Second, the patients who purchase private insurance, and therefore leave the public system, are likely to be wealthier (as noted above this has been the experience in other jurisdictions) and therefore healthier. As such, the health utilization, a priori, of the patients who use the private tier, is likely to be lower than of those in the public tier. Finally, and importantly, an increase in demand or 'need' is likely to result from the introduction of a private tier, therefore crowding out the shifting of utilization from the public to the private tier. All three of these factors will contribute to the effect of a shift in physician capacity presented below.

Our evaluation draws on research by Siciliani and Hurst, who use data from eight OECD countries to model the effects of physician supply on waiting lists for surgical procedures.[49] We take their estimates[50], together with published wait times and physician capacity data, to compute wait-time elasticities that we then use to illustrate an upper bound on the effects of introducing a private, second tier in Canada. Wait times data in Canada are available for only a select group of procedures and provinces, [51] and clearly better data would be preferable, but we can only use what is available. We calculate that the wait-time elasticity with respect to changes in the supply of specialist physicians is 0.9 using mean wait-times and 1.6 using median wait times. Elasticity in this context means the responsiveness of wait-times to changes in physician capacity. That is, a 10% decrease in the population of specialists serving the public system would result in up to a 9% increase in mean waiting times, and up to a 16% increase in median waiting times. Wait time data for Canada are reported using median waiting times. Assuming that 10% of specialist capacity is diverted from the public to the private sector, we estimate that median wait times for hip replacements in the public sector would increase from 126 days to up to 146 days. Wait times for knee replacements would increase from 177 days to up to 205 days. Wait times for cataract surgery in the public sector would increase from 80 days to up to 93 days, and wait times for CABG would increase from 17 days to up to 20 days.

These are estimated national averages and any single province's experience may deviate from this estimate. Manitoba's knee replacement wait list is considerably shorter than the average, for example, and wait times would be predicted to increase from 105 days to up to 122 days. Nevertheless, the basic point remains: assuming a constant number of specialists working a set number of hours across both public and private sectors, diverting resources from the public sector to the private sector results in an increase in wait-times in the public sector. The larger the privately funded sector, the greater the increase in wait times in the publicly funded sector. It is of concern that the majority of the court gave no credence to this factor at all. Seemingly they were reassured that the integrity of medicare would not be affected by the mere existence of public or social insurance in tandem with private insurance in European countries. They did not explore to any extent waiting times in countries with two-tier systems, the various measures that countries take who value solidarity to suppress the negative effects of private financing, or the access and other quality problems inherent in systems with more private financing.

Individual Rights vs. Collective Rights

The majority does not consider that the goal of ensuring access to health care on the basis of need as opposed to ability to pay is worthy of concern. The majority seemed either unwilling or unable to conceptualize the collective good in this regard (that what medical resources we have should be directed to those most in need and not those most able to pay) and to balance it against individual rights. Justice Deschamps says that no one questions the need for the public system as a 'safety-net',[52] but of course, medicare aspired to be much more than a mere safety net. Justice Deschamps seems to view medicare as fulfilling the same role as social assistance or workers compensation; much more in keeping with the vision of health care as played out in the United States than historically has been the vision of medicare in Canada. McLachlin C.J. and Major J. accept that individual rights to life, liberty and security are violated by having to wait for treatment in the public system when *some* may have avoided waiting by purchasing private insurance. But if life, liberty and security interests of individuals are engaged when suffering on long waiting lists, than if there is a prospect that their suffering may be *worsened* by introducing a second tier, then surely the court should tread even more cautiously as they, in the words of Lorne

Sossin in his chapter, risk trading off the rights of some for the rights of others.

Conclusion

In the aftermath of *Chaoulli* the key question will be the extent to which provincial governments will be allowed to ensure the integrity of their respective health care programs. In Manitoba, Ontario and Nova Scotia, physicians are prohibited from charging more in the privately funded sector than they are able to charge under the provincial publicly funded insurance plan.[53] This discourages physicians from opting out of publicly-funded medicare and thus preserves and protects limited human resources (capacity). In all provinces except Newfoundland, physicians are prevented from working both in the public system and in the private system – they have to opt in or out. Will such provisions in the wake of *Chaoulli* be the subjects of a *Charter* challenge?

Prior to *Chaoulli* one may have thought that administrative provisions or sanctions could not be the subject of a s.7 challenge, but the McLachlin/Major judgment suggests otherwise.[54] This raises the possibility that other laws passed to prevent the flourishing of a two-tier. system and to protect the integrity of publicly-funded care – for example, those preventing doctors from charging privately funded insurance plans more per service than they can for the publicly funded plan or preventing doctors from working in both the public and the private sectors – may also be struck down on the basis that they too result in a "system" that leaves an individual no choice but to leave the country for care.

In any subsequent litigation a newly constituted Supreme Court should revisit its conclusions about the dynamics between public and private health insurance and the inter-relationship between these different modes of finance and waiting lists/times. As we have attempted to demonstrate in this paper, the core issues are those of equality of access and of capacity, the available evidence on which the majority of the Court did not consider adequately.

With respect to equality of access, we presented figures on the socioeconomic status of those who hold private insurance in a number of different countries. The numbers clearly demonstrate that private health insurance is the prerogative of the wealthy and effectively available to a much smaller percentage of the poor. As Robert Evans also points out in this volume, where private insurance is available in a country it is often heavily publicly subsidized. This results in even greater inequities as public dollars that could have been spent on ensuring access for those in greatest need are instead spent on assisting the wealthy and the middle-class to obtain preferential access to a second tier through the purchase of private insurance. Australia presents a good example of this inequitable phenomenon

The other key issue is that of capacity. There are only a limited number of doctors and nurses available; increasing their number in short of a decade is impossible unless accreditation problems are eased and more are lured quickly into the country. If some or all of the work of doctors and nurses is shifted from the publicly funded to the privately funded sector, the consequences are obvious for those remaining in the public sector, who most frequently will be our poorest and sickest citizens.

Using calculations from a survey of OECD countries, we calculate that a 10% decrease in the population of specialists serving the public system would result in up to a maximum of a 9% increase in mean waiting times, and a maximum of a 16% increase in median waiting times. Certainly all of these figures are debatable – in particular the percentage of physicians or physician hours that would actually be transferred from the public to the private sector will be key to calculating the impact on waiting lists under medicare. It is also possible that a more lucrative public sector will lure more physicians to Canada and into training. But it takes 6 years to train a family doctor and 11 years to train a subspecialist – and hundreds of thousands of public dollars. Moreover, there are still many professional barriers to entry for foreign-trained physicians (and their own home countries too suffer shortages and will be thinking of ways to attract them to stay or return). As Bernard Dickens notes in this volume, foreign recruitment could contribute to global inequities in health.

In allowing a private-tier, the capacity question and the consequent effect on public sector waiting lists deserved far greater study and consideration on the part of the majority than it was accorded in the *Chaoulli* decision.

Justice Albie Sachs of South Africa's constitutional court has written of how judicial lack of expertise regarding the technical complexities of socioeconomic policy should correspond to judicial modesty. In Sachs' eyes, judges should not 'be philosopher kings and queens who tell government how to function'; but nevertheless, in situations were deprivations go 'to the core of a person's life and dignity', then courts are better equipped to balance competing interests than governments whose bureaucratic and operational concerns demanded compromise.[55]

But as Lorne Sossin notes in this volume, in *Charter* jurisprudence on social welfare and health rights the Supreme Court of Canada has privileged the rights of the wealthy over the rights of the poor. In *Chaoulli*, McLachlin C.J. and Major J., having characterized long waiting lists as being a product of the 'public monopoly' in health insurance (which at a cross-systems level is clearly wrong) then proceed to assume that 'ordinary Quebeckers' could avoid waiting if they were free to buy private insurance. The evidence from other countries clearly demonstrates that 'most' Quebeckers would not benefit from private insurance – and, in fact the majority acknowledges this itself when they speak of the small proportion of the population that hold private insurance in other jurisdictions.

What McLachlin C.J. and Major J. fail to make explicit is that the section 7 rights of Quebeckers are satisfied by the mere *chance* to purchase private insurance and thus a *chance* to jump queues in the public sector. Their decision also completely ignores that these chances will be distributed unequally in society and that it is the most well off who will have a greater opportunity to purchase private health insurance and use it to jump public sector queues.

If challenged the court must surely concede that it considers the section 7 rights of those who cannot afford to buy private insurance to be as significant as those who can. Although strongly declarative that the constitution offers no free-standing right to publicly-funded health care, the *Chaoulli* decision potentially opens up arguments in this regard through its acceptance of the evidence of the threat to life and security of the person represented by public sector wait lists. But apart from the wild-card of opening up arguments to a constitutional right to timely treatment in the public sector, at a minimum if, as the Supreme Court found, section 7 rights are engaged by long waiting times in the public sector, then it should be extremely hesitant to overturn any laws that may exacerbate further threats to these rights. We use the word 'may' here to indicate that a risk of further erosion of section 7 rights, particularly amongst the most vulnerable in society, is something that the court should weigh seriously, although it is beyond the ability of the government to prove the issue conclusively either one way or another. To put it another way, the realization of some Quebecker's s. 7 rights should not be justified if there is a credible threat of worsening the rights of others to life, liberty and security. [56]

Notes

We would like to thank Kent Roach, Duncan Sinclair, and Carolyn Tuohy for their respective comments on this paper. All errors and omissions remain our own.

1 Chaoulli v. Quebec (Attorney General), 2005 SCC 35 [Chaoulli].
2 Many powerful groups support a two-tier system and welcome the Chaoulli decision. See Ralph Klein, 'Alberta moving ahead on private health care' Toronto Star (9 August 2005) A13; André Picard, 'MDs change tactics, refuse to denounce public health care' The Globe and Mail (17 August 2005).
3 *Chaoulli*, at para 106.
4 See Luigi Siciliani & Jeremy Hurst, 'Explaining Waiting Times Variations for Elective Surgery Across OECD Countries' 7 OECD Health Working Papers (2003), online: OECD <http://www.oecd.org/dataoecd/31/10/17256025.pdf>.
5 In 2004, 45.8 million people (15.7% of the population) in the United States did not have some form of health insurance coverage. See Carmen DeNavas-Walt, Bernadette D. Proctor & Cheryl Hill Lee, 'Current Population Reports, P60–229 - Income, Poverty, and Health Insurance Coverage in the United States: 2004' (Washington: U.S. Census Bureau, 2005) at 16, online: U.S. Census Bureau <http://www.census.gov/prod/2005pubs/p60–229.pdf>.
6 Random survey by the authors of private clinics in Regina.
7 *Chaoulli*, at para 66.
8 See the Factum of the Interveners, Cambie Surgeries Corporation, False Creek Surgical Centre Inc., and Others, in the Chaoulli decision. Available online at http://www.law.utoronto.ca/healthlaw/docs/chaoulli/Factum_CambieSurgeries_etal.pdf> [Interveners]. (University of Toronto Law web-site).
9 Luigi Siciliani, supra
10 Ibid.
11 Ashley Bloomfield, 'New Zealand' in Chris Ham and Glen Robert, eds., Reasonable Rationing: International Experience of Priority Setting in Health Care (Maidenhead: Open University Press, 2003) 16 at 37.
12 Colleen M. Flood, International Health Care Reform: A Legal, Economic and Political Analysis (London: Routledge, 1999).
13 Bloomfield, supra.

14 R. J. Blendon, M. Kim & J. M. Benson, 'The Public versus the World
    Health Organization on Health System Performance' (2001) 20 Health
    Affairs 10, cited in C. Tuohy, C. Flood & M. Stabile, 'How Does Private
    Finance Affect Public Health Care Systems? Marshalling the Evidence
    from OECD Nations' (2004) 29:3 Jnl of Health Politics Policy and Law 359
    at 388. The authors note that 'A decline in the public share over the 1987–
    1997 period, in fact, is significantly correlated with higher levels of sup-
    port for public expenditure, although it does not appear to be associated
    with satisfaction with the system as a whole.'
15 A newspaper article reported recently concern on the part of the elderly
    to news that that Canterbury District Health Board planned to cut 7,200
    people from waiting lists and refer them back to their general practitioner
    to manage their care – see Mike Crean, 'Elderly in fear of waiting-list
    letter,' The Press, New Zealand (8 May 2003), copy on file with the au-
    thors.
16 For example, in Oregon the public were surveyed about what list of
    services should be include in the Medicaid program. If all of the public
    surveyed were themselves limited by the choices made, then arguably
    quite a different list would have been compiled.
17 Chaoulli, at para 103.
18 Ibid. at para 108.
19 Ibid. at para 111.
20 Ibid at para. 124.
21 Cathy Schoen & Michelle Doty, 'Inequities In Access to Medical Care in
    Five Countries: Findings from the 2001 Commonwealth Fund Interna-
    tional Health Policy Survey' (2004) 67 Health Policy 309.
22 Carl Emmerson, Christine Frayne & Alissa Goodman, 'Pressure in UK
    Healthcare: Challenges for the NHS' Institute for Fiscal Studies (2000),
    online: <http://www.ifs.org.uk/publications.php?publication_id=1889>.
    Data for the study was compiled from the 1994–95 to 1997–98 British
    Family Resources Survey.
23 Cathy Schoen, supra
24 Ministry of Health, 'Future Funding of Health and Disability Services in
    New Zealand' (2002) at 39, online: http://www.moh.govt.nz/moh.nsf/0/
    8C766E4FF69F86ADCC256F2B007F14A3/$File/futurefundingofhealthand
    disabilityservicesinnewzealand.pdf; Kathy Spencer, 'The New Zealand
    Experience – the approach to private health insurance in New Zealand'
    New Zealand Ministry of Health (2004), copy on file with the authors.
25 Cathy Schoen, supra

26 Sandra Hopkins & Jacqueline Cumming, 'The Impact of Changes in Private Health Expenditure on New Zealand Households' (2001) 58 Health Policy 215.

27 S Triggs, 'Patients in Profile: The Use of Health Care Services in New Zealand' (Wellington: Ministry of Health, 1995), cited in Sandra Hopkins & Jacqueline Cumming, Ibid.

28 Australian Bureau of Statistics, 'Health Insurance Survey' June 1998, online: <http://www.ausstats.abs.gov.au/Ausstats/subscriber.nsf/Lookup/CA25687100069892CA256889000AF9BC/$File/43350_Jun%201998.pdf>.

29 Cathy Schoen, supra .

30 Australian Bureau of Statistics, 'Private Health Insurance' 2003, online: http://www.abs.gov.au/ausstats/abs@.nsf/7884593a92027766ca 2568b5007b8617/be010e1c499d3010ca256db20000c99b!OpenDocument

31 Schoen, supra

32 Colleen M. Flood & Tom Archibald, 'The Illegality of Private Health Care in Canada' (2001) 164:6 Can Med Assoc Jnl. 825 at 828.

33 Ibid.

34 Chaoulli, supra at para 136.

35 Ibid. at paras 130 and 153.

36 Justices Binnie and LeBell JJ. write at para. 214: 'Our colleagues the Chief Justice and Major J. dismiss the experts accepted by the trial judge as relying on little more than 'common sense' (para. 137). Although we agree that the experts offered 'common sense', they offered a good deal more.'

37 Ibid. at para 139.

38 Ibid. at para 140.

39 Carolyn Tuohy, Colleen Flood & Mark Stabile, supra identified four basic models of structuring the relationship between public and private financing; parallel public and private systems; co-payment; group-based; and sectoral.

40 For a discussion see J. Wasem, S. Greß & K. G. H. Okma, 'The Role of Private Health Insurance in Social Health Insurance Countries' in R. Saltman, R. Busse & J. Figueras eds., Social Health Insurance in Western Europe (London: Open University Press, 2004) 227.

41 The Dutch Professional Guidelines for Doctors, found in the Individual Health Care Professions Act states at Article II.2 that doctors have to treat patients equal in equal cases See J.E.M. Akveld and H.E.G.M. Hermans, Health Care in The Netherlands, In: H. Nys ed., International Encyclopedia of Medical Law, (Leuven, Belgium, 1995), p. 1–112.

42 For a discussion see Carolyn Tuohy, Colleen Flood and Mark Stabile, supra

43 Francesca Columbo & Nicole Tapay, 'Private Health Insurance in OECD Countries: The Benefits and Costs for Individuals and Health Systems' OECD Working Papers No. 15 (2004) at 24 FN 38, online: OECD < http://www.oecd.org/dataoecd/34/56/33698043.pdf>.

44 Colleen Flood & Tom Archibald, supra

45 These figures are from 1994. The figures allow for (a) a greater number of educator clinicians required to provide essential education, (b) the cost of essential teaching, research and services of clinical appointees and trainees, (c) a complete accounting of resources regardless of where they are incurred or who pays, (d) higher salaries for professional personnel and (e) patient demands requiring more clinical training under close supervision for both undergraduate and graduate physicians. Please see: Leslie S. Valberg et al., 'Planning the Future Academic Medical Centre' (1994) 151:11 CMAJ 1581 at 1585–86.]

46 Unfortunately, our research reveals that no training cost estimates exist that are more recent than those calculated in the Valberg study. Duncan Sinclair, one of the co-authors of the Valberg study, states that there is a dearth of research on this topic.

47 Over the past five years, Canada has experienced a decrease in the number of physicians leaving the country and an increase in the number of Canadian trained physicians returning to the country. In 2004, 317 physicians returned to Canada, compared to 262 who left the country. See Canadian Institute for Health Information, 'Supply, Distribution and Migration of Canadian Physicians 2004' (2005), online: <http://secure.cihi .ca/cihiwebdispPage.jsp?cw_page=PG_385_E&cw_topic=385&cw_rel= AR_14_E>.

48 Implicit in this assumption is that physician and OR attendant capacity is a constraining factor for waiting lists for Canada. The evidence from the OECD suggests that physician capacity is at least one such factor across the group of countries studied.

49 Luigi Siciliani, supra. The study uses data from eight countries: Australia, Denmark, the UK, Finland, Norway, the Netherlands, Spain and Sweden, and across 10 surgical procedures: hip replacements, knee replacements, cataract surgery, varicose veins, hysterectomy, prostatectomy, cholecystectomy, inguinal and femoral hernia, CABG, and PTCA.

50 It is worth noting the potential limitations of such an exercise. First, we are relying on estimates produced by OECD researchers, and therefore are

subject to any caveats applied to their analysis. Second, we are taking an estimate compiled using data at the country-procedure level, and using it to evaluate a policy change within a particular country. Third, as we argue above, wait-lists are the result of multi-level policy and systems interactions. Using a general model of wait times applicable across the OECD may miss some of the complexities in the Canadian system.

51 Canadian wait-list data are reported by Siciliani and Hurst for hip replacement, knee replacement for BC, Manitoba, and Saskatchewan, for Cataract surgery in BC, and for CABG in Ontario and Saskatchewan. We use these data to formulate our examples.

52 *Chaoulli*, supra at para. 56.

53 Colleen Flood & Tom Archibald, supra at 822. Note that in BC and Alberta, the freedom for opted-out physicians to bill freely is limited by two narrow exceptions.

54 In drawing an analogy between the facts of the *Morgenteler* decision and the case of Chaoulli, McLachlin CJ and Major J note (para 121) 'The sanction by which the mandatory public system was maintained differed: criminal in Morgentaler, "administrative" in the case at bar. Yet the consequences for the individual in both cases are serious. In Morgentaler, as here, the system left the individual facing a lack of critical care with no choice but to travel outside the country to obtain the required medical care at her own expense. It was this constraint on s.7 security, taken from the perspective of the woman facing the health care system, and not the criminal sanction, that drove the majority analysis in Morgentaler.'

55 Justice Albie Sachs, 'Social and economic rights: can they be made justiciable?' (2000) 53 Southern Methodist University Law Review 1381, at 1388-1389.

The Implications of Private Insurance

The CMA's Chaoulli Motion and the Myth of Promoting Fair Access to Health Care*

TRUDO LEMMENS AND TOM ARCHIBALD

Introduction

On August 18, 2005, 64% of delegates at the annual meeting of the Canadian Medical Association endorsed a motion that called for the introduction of private health insurance to pay for health care services 'when timely access to care cannot be provided in the public health care system.'[1] This was just one of many public statements by professional organizations and interest groups that followed the Supreme Court's *Chaoulli* decision. In an interview for CanWest newspapers, the outgoing CMA president, Dr. Albert Schumacher, stated that the CMA's endorsement of this motion 'totally reinforced' the *Chaoulli* decision.[2] The vote followed a clear rejection of another motion a day earlier which called for an explicit endorsement of single tier health care.

For several reasons, this motion merits closer scrutiny and commentary. First of all, the CMA represents the majority of physicians, who are among the key contributors to the health care system. Their voice has to be heard and their concerns have to be taken seriously. Secondly, the CMA is an important and influential contributor to health care policy in this country. Its members participate in various decision-making bodies that shape Canadian health care and its support is crucial for the implementation of many decisions related to the health care system. Clearly, the goal of the CMA in endorsing this motion is to directly influence future decisions made by provincial and federal governments with respect to the health care system. It is using the *Chaoulli* case as an opportunity to express its view of the state of health care in this country and to help bring about fundamental change. Because the CMA motion opens the door to such a fundamental change, and because it is enacted by an organization that is highly influential and explicitly embraces the public interest in its mandate, it calls for public analysis.

We want to discuss two specific aspects of the CMAs position. First, we want to examine how the stance reflected in this motion fits with the ongoing involvement of the CMA in the development and maintenance of a viable health care system. In the first part, we focus on the CMA as an important actor in public policy making. We will discuss in some detail the historical context which precedes this motion, and question whether the motion can easily be reconciled with the CMA's mandate.

The second part examines the consequences of this motion, if implemented, for the ethical commitment of individual physicians towards patients. An important aspect of the CMA's mandate is to help determine professional ethical standards and to promote physicians' commitment towards their patients. This commitment to individual patients is invoked as a key motivating factor for the CMA delegates' endorsement of the motion. In the second part, we sketch some of the potential consequences for physician-patient relations of introducing parallel access to private health care.

By highlighting how parallel private health care will impact on the physician-patient relationship, we want to emphasize how the CMA's motion is also seriously problematic because of what it does not say. While it endorses without rational justification a fundamental shift in Canadian health care policy, it fails to even pay lip service to the need for more stringent regulation and enforcement of ethical standards of physicians in an increasingly commercial health care scene. In our view, the CMAs public endorsement of parallel access, without an explicit and clear recognition of the significant impact of this change on the relations between doctors and patients and without a strong commitment to deal with this impact as a profession, undermines the credibility of the CMA's claim that it is an advocate for the best possible health care system for Canadians. While judges may invoke that the evidence produced in court was either lacking or not well-presented, a public actor directly involved in health care decision making cannot invoke the same excuse.

Part 1: Context

Immediately following the adoption of the CMA's motion, several commentators attributed a high symbolic and political value to the event. CanWest news portrayed the vote of a motion in favour of private health care as an 'historic development;'[3] while André Picard suggested in the *Globe and Mail* that this was the 'first time' that the CMA had opened the door to supporting a parallel private health care system.[4] In short interviews with delegates at the convention, the vote was associated with 'frustration' with the shortcomings of publicly funded health care and its lack of timely delivery of important health care services. Expressions of frustration with the lack of timely access to medical services by physicians are not new. In a speech to the Ontario Medical Association in May 2005, CMA president Dr. Schumacher emphasized that the pain and fear caused by waiting times were even threatening to 'blow up the system as we know it'.[5]

And yet, the CMA has been reluctant to qualify its support for private parallel access as a fundamental departure from the Medicare system. Underlying the CMA position is an assumption that market values can happily coexist with the values of universal Medicare. Indeed, at the same meeting where the Chaoulli motion was adopted, the CMA delegates also endorsed the principle that health care should be provided on the basis of need, and not the ability to pay. Many public statements also demonstrate the belief about the compatibility of parallel insurance and comprehensive health care. In the CanWest interview, Dr. Schumacher emphasized that physicians still strongly endorsed the principle that access to medical care must be based on need and not ability to pay. He defended the CMA vote as a way for physicians to be 'responsible' and emphasized that the delegates had also voted on mandating the board of directors to produce a discussion paper on the appropriate balance between public and private care.

The same dual message also comes through in the factum submitted by the CMA in *Chaoulli*. On one hand, the CMA's position before the Supreme Court was to endorse of private access to services in the absence of timely provision of services within the publicly funded health care system.[6] On the other hand, the factum states that 'the CMA/COA are committed to the fundamental principles of the national system of Medicare – comprehensiveness, universality of coverage, portability of benefits, reasonable access and non-profit administration.'[7] It further refers to Article 31 of the CMA *Code of Ethics* which states that physicians have a responsibility 'to promote fair access to health care resources.'[8] By emphasizing in its public statements the need to be 'responsible' as well as the CMA's continued support of access to medical care on the basis of need, the CMA clearly wants to portray its call for the introduction of parallel private health care as a laudable expression of a commitment to the best possible patient care and as an attempt to save the public system. In fact, the CMA delegates who were interviewed about the CMA motion defended their vote on precisely that basis.

We cannot enter the mind of the CMA delegates, but it should not come as a surprise to them that the motion has evoked many skeptical commentaries.[9] The concerns of individual delegates for patients and frustration about the inherent limitations imposed by limited health care budgets, overcrowded emergency rooms, and excessive waiting lists will likely have been in the mind of some of the motion's supporters. One can sympathize with physicians who, while professionally committed to offering the best possible care to the patient in front of them, have to cross their fingers while their patient is waiting for what they consider urgently needed medical attention. Several of the CMA delegates may have seen this motion not as a call for giving up on the public system, but rather to shock governments into long-overdue action to invest more money in it. But the same delegates should also realize that they have now entered a partnership with others who have never been keen about the – albeit limited – financial limitations imposed on physicians in the context of a single-payer system.

It is worth pointing out here how ironic it is that the CMA, through its intervention in the case and through its motion, is holding hands with Dr. Chaoulli, who seems to personify ardent opposition against any public organization of health care and any social obligation of physicians in a governmentally organized health care system. Indeed, his ongoing struggle with the regional medical authorities over their policies aimed at promoting the availability of medical services in remote regions was invoked by the trial judge, who found his motivations for challenging the Quebec legislation questionable.[10] We can understand how *Chaoulli* created a climate in which genuine frustration could easily be transformed into an enthusiastic embracement of what seems to be an easy way to fix what's going wrong. It is harder to explain, however, how an organization as intimately involved in health care policy making as the CMA can bluntly state that market and public values in health care are entirely compatible; that is, how their proposed private sector can operate with no negative effect on the public system's capacity. Much debate exists on whether a parallel private sector will complement or marginalize the public system. Indeed, the courts in *Chaoulli* confronted this issue. A key issue in *Chaoulli*, at all levels of court, was whether allowing a parallel private sector was a mischief serious enough to render the section 7 infringements fundamentally just. The CMA's motion does not appear to have accounted for this issue anywhere near as much as did the courts in *Chaoulli*.

One should not forget, however, that when the CMA takes a position in the debate about health care, it does so as a representative of its members. The mission of the CMA is '[t]o serve and unite the physicians of Canada and be the national advocate, in partnership with the people of Canada, for the highest standards of health and health care.'[11] While the commitment to the highest standard of health care points to its public role, it is first and foremost committed 'to serve and unite the physicians of Canada.'[12] As a result of the provincial organization of health care, only the provincial member organizations get directly involved in the more clearly partisan negotiations about salary and benefits with the provincial governments. But the CMA nevertheless has a partisan role in the system. On the CMA's website, proud reference is made to the fact that a 2005 survey indicated that 'key decision-makers now consider it the premier lobby group in Ottawa.'[13] It further states that 'the CMA defends the interests of its members and their patients on Parliament Hill, during federal election campaigns and in the media.' Note that the interest of members comes first on the list, as is the case in most professional organizations that are representative of their constituencies. Because of the nature of the profession, and the ethical commitment to patients that is inherently connected to the medical profession, commitment to patients is also seen as part of the CMA mandate; but it does not come first.

There are two contextual factors that must be considered when evaluating the CMA proposal and when determining the political value and weight that the motion should receive. We want to show here briefly how the motion

a) Fits with the historical position of the organization with respect to the health care system; and
b) Will directly benefit at least a part of the members of the CMA without clear evidence of benefit to the patient population.

These factors have largely been ignored and have certainly not been publicly recognized by the CMA, when it argues for the introduction of a parallel private system.

The Historic Compromise: Under Review?

The CMA motion is clearly not as historic as initial media reaction would indicate. On the contrary, it is, in fact, entirely consistent with the CMA's historical stance on Medicare. This stance essentially involved a reluctant concession to single tier Medicare, but – significantly – not a wholesale endorsement of it. During the development of Medicare, physicians in Canada retained clinical autonomy and the fee for service model of payment, but conceded their basic freedom to practice their profession outside the state system. They did so after having strongly maneuvered to block the introduction of universal comprehensive government-sponsored medical care insurance. Indeed, as Carolyn H. Tuohy points out in *Accidental Logics*, the Canadian Medicare program was developed *notwithstanding* opposition by the CMA, and not with its strong support.[14]

When the social-democratic government of Saskatchewan started developing government-sponsored comprehensive health insurance in 1961, the CMA was one of the core contributors to a coalition that lobbied against the plan and that pushed for the introduction of alternative approaches in other provinces. When the federal Conservative government responded to the CMA executive's request to appoint a committee to study the issue, the CMA and its coalition partners did not expect that this commission would recommend a Saskatchewan-style model. Unfortunately for this coalition, the 1964 report of the Royal Commission on Health Services[15], chaired by Mr. Justice Emmett Hall, recommended against a parallel private sector and laid the basis for the legal framework of Medicare. Key among these legal measures at the provincial level was, of course, the ban on private payment challenged in *Chaoulli*. In addition, a private system was choked off from the supply end by requirements in health insurance legislation that physicians opt out of the public plan entirely before they can receive private payment.

The reluctance of the medical organizations to embrace governmentally supported comprehensive health insurance is as apparent from the fact that in 1986, when the Canada Health Act was adopted, its constitutionality was challenged by the Ontario Medical Association.[16] Although the challenge was subsequently dropped, it clearly shows how reluctant medical associations have been in joining the system. Elsewhere in this volume, Gregory Marchildon undertakes a detailed analysis of the formative years of the Medicare model in the four Western provinces.[17] This review showed that, even in the so-called cradle of socialized health care, '...the policy sustainability of the single-payer Medicare model, even after its adoption by all jurisdictions, continued (and continues) to be challenged.'[18] Solidarity, indeed, arose between the CMA and the Canadian Health Insurance Association in resisting – albeit in vain – single-payer Medicare.

Professor Tuohy, in her analysis of the historic developments in health policy in Canada, the U.S., and the U.K., described the Canadian compromise that resulted from the implementation of Medicare as:

> ... a fundamental accommodation between the medical profession and the state, under which physicians retained their status as independent professionals, trading off a degree of entrepreneurial discretion ... in order to retain substantial collective and individual autonomy in clinical matters.[19]

Under this compromise, physicians support for Medicare was contingent – they supported it on the implicit premise that governments would fund and manage the system in ways that met the profession and public's larger interests in maintaining accessibility and quality of patient care.

Over the long term, physicians gained more from this compromise than just clinical autonomy. They also gained significant political voice within the public system. Losses felt privately by Canadian physicians have led governments to share a great deal of regulatory power with physician groups as a kind of compensation. One example is the delegation to provincial physician associations and colleges of physicians of regulatory powers over independent health facilities.[20] More importantly, physician-government bargaining at the provincial level has evolved in many instances into a relationship of joint governance. Fee increases are now but a small (but still important) part of the bargaining agenda between governments and provincial physician associations. In Ontario, Alberta and British Columbia, physician associations play vital roles in determining changes to the content of the public plan: what services are in and what are out.[21] In Ontario, changes to the schedule of benefits continue to originate, but are not finalized, within the provincial medical association.[22]

Thus, governments appear to have paid back to physicians in political voice what they have lost economically. The historic compromise in Canadian Medicare fostered an increased legitimacy for the CMA as a political opinion leader, and positioned physicians, acting collectively, as stewards of the public interest. Now, after *Chaoulli* has undone one part of the legal apparatus of the historic compromise, the CMA seems to seize the moment to recommend revisiting the entire deal. It should recognize, however, that it thereby steps outside the boundaries of a historically evolved compromise, in which it may have given up some liberty, but in which it also has gained legitimacy and influence.

Because of its fundamental commitment to the best patient care, its defense of the principle of fair access on the basis of need, and its important public role and influence within the system, it seems appropriate to ask the CMA for a strong justification of its position. Because of its power and influence, more than other organizations the CMA should be held publicly accountable for its arguments about the need for systemic reform. To use a term that is increasingly popular in medicine, a call for fundamental change should be evidence-based and rationally defensible. The shift proposed by the CMA significantly challenges the status quo and disturbs a system that in a historical perspective has been remarkably successful in providing quality care on the basis of need since it was introduced in the 1960s. In this situation, as before the Supreme Court in *Chaoulli*, it seems reasonable to put the burden of proof on the party proposing change.

To date the evidence suggests, as discussed in the chapter by Colleen Flood,[23] that a parallel private system does not do much at all to solve the problem that was identified in Chaoulli, i.e. the existence of excessive wait times.[24] It is not our task to evaluate here in detail the feasibility of the CMA proposal, but we want to argue that the balance of evidence and political support rest on the parties promoting change. We should expect a more detailed and solid public justification from an organization that has received a public mandate within the Medicare system.

While the he CMA has not provided evidence that its proposal will lead to a reduction of wait times, it also does not address how the public system will suffer significantly from the introduction of a parallel private sector. Although wealthy patients will undoubtedly benefit from such introduction, the CMA's objective of improving the overall provision of health care to Canadians will not be met if it undermines the public system. In the immediate future, patients who have private insurance or who are able to pay privately will benefit from the proposal, but others who depend on a strong public health care system will be prejudiced. Without the 'canary in the coal mine' effect of keeping the wealthy in the public system, fewer checks and balances will exist to ensure that it does not wither on the vine next door to its private twin.[25] If the CMA's concern is for all Canadians, then this scenario should offend it.

In *Chaouilli*, Deschamps J. brushes aside the argument that when influential people are out of the system, pressure to improve the system disappears. The arguments based on potential human reactions to the emergence of a private system, in her words, carry 'little weight' and 'do not appear [...] to be very convincing.'[26] But could the judgment itself be an indicator of this phenomenon? As others in this volume point out,[27] the *Chaoulli* decision seems to contradict so fundamentally its earlier decision in *Auton (Guardian ad litem of) v. British Columbia (Attorney General)*[28] that it is hard to come up with a rational explanation. It is therefore tempting to see the difference between the two cases as one of ease of personal identification with the issues raised.

Recognizing Public and Private Interests of Physicians

Can another motivation also explain the push of the CMA towards privatized health care? At this watershed moment in Canadian health policy, physicians can see an opportunity for emancipation from the public system. After the 1990s, a time of fiscal restraint followed by massive reinfusions of funding and demands for greater efficiency in the system, they feel that the time for *rattrapage* has arrived. If governments will not heed their warnings within the public system, then they will seek their compensation outside the system.

Physician associations can also see potential gains. Professional associations of all kinds have had great difficulty showing gains for their members in the last decade. After so long, the opportunity created by *Chaoulli* is also one that pulls them in opposite directions. Should health care unions and medical associations resist two-tier Medicare, as they have often done on social democratic principles, or should they seize the day, embrace two tier health care, and in the process unshackle their members from the public system? Current conditions in the public system make the second option more tempting from the standpoint of their members' interests. It is also tempting because it may improve the stature of the association in the eyes of its members.

It is worth noting that not all the members agree. Sixty-four per cent is a majority, but not a commanding expression of solidarity. The fact this percentage of delegates voted in favour of the CMA proposal reinforces the existence of serious divisions of opinion within the medical profession itself. That over one third voted against the motion suggests that policy reforms based on it will not meet with applause from all parts of the profession. It should not come as a surprise that some emergency physicians already expressed serious reservations, since emergency services are among those services that are unlikely to be offered through private commercial clinics.[29]

It is understandable that the CMA advances its members' interests, while still defending its commitment to the common good. All associations that represent Canadian health care professionals, be they unions or provincial medical associations, have long been pulled in opposite directions because of their dual public-private functions. In fact, the legislative and regulatory mechanisms that have given health professions a large degree of autonomy are – at least in theory – a public recognition of the fact that their ability to self-regulate and to set professional standards can serve the public interest. In Ontario, this is reflected in regulated health profession legislation which allows the professions to deal with issues that affect not only their professional standing but also their relation with patients and their family members.

For the last four decades, however, the tension between their public role and their private interests has been lessened by the fact that the vast majority of physicians, nurses and other providers have had no alternative but to work in a publicly funded system. In the case of physicians, this has meant that their associations have taken positions within the four corners of the historical concession to Medicare. Among these premises is that, in exchange for conceding to the economic constraints that the single payer system imposes on individual doctors, physician associations gained a stronger voice in the governance of the system itself. As noted above, physician colleges currently play dominant roles in the regulation of private diagnostic facilities in many provinces. Physicians also play a central role in determining what services will be covered by the public plan. In this context, physician associations could both act in publicly-interested ways and advance the interests of their members, because the interests of physicians were already limited by the legal parameters of Medicare.

Against this history, we argue, the CMA's call for a return to private health care should not be seen as the position of a disinterested governing body, but must be understood in the light of the radical structural change it implies, and how it benefits the interests of medical (and other provider) associations that advance it. If Canadian physicians call for a limited two tier health care system, it must at least be recognized that this represents an undoing of the political compromise reached decades ago, and places the CMA and its provincial counterparts in much the same position they were in in the early 1960s when physicians battled so fiercely against single tier Medicare. And it must also be recognized that many physicians who support the introduction of private parallel health care likely do so for the money, and not to improve the system. As one physician stated it in the 1996 Canadian Medical Association Journal, following an earlier CMA debate about privatization of health care: 'Collectively, it seems, we talk a lot more about our incomes and rights than about the patients we serve.'[30]

Part 2: Ethical Implications of Parallel Private Health Care

We mentioned before that the CMA explicitly acknowledges that it has a public mandate. Moreover, as we have argued, physicians and their representative organizations (the CMA, their provincial counterparts and the Colleges of Physicians and Surgeons) have received significant political power throughout the historical development of Medicare. With this power come a public responsibility and a need for public accountability. It seems appropriate to ask from such organizations that they evaluate appropriately the potential impact of their health care proposals on the core professional obligations of its members. In this context, we want to point out some of the potential consequences of the introduction of a parallel private system, based largely on problems already existing within the Canadian health care context and on the more significant experience with commercialized medicine in the U.S. It seems clear to us that the introduction of a more significant system of private parallel health care will affect physicians' ethical obligations towards patients.

If the CMA delegates really believe that private parallel health care offers a solution, they should recognize that this shift has its price. It comes with ethical risks – some of which we are already confronted with at a much lower scale under the current system – that are bound to arise in increasingly commercialized medicine. In our view, if the CMA is going to wage war for a radical change such as a parallel private sector, it better first try to 'win the peace' by offering proactive regulatory solutions to these ethical risks. In the absence of significant regulatory and professional reforms – if ever such reforms can succeed –, the Canadian public will increasingly face the following scenarios:

- Physicians will be put under pressure by more 'empowered' and wealthy patients to recognize that the condition they suffer from is serious and in need of immediate treatment. These patients will be able to jump the public waiting list.
- The most successful private physicians may decide to serve only patients who pay the highest fees and refuse to treat people who cannot pay themselves or do not have a good insurance plan.
- Private physicians and clinics can turn away complex, serious cases requiring urgent treatment, preferring to serve less complex patients.
- Private physicians can turn people to the public system when complications occur and patients require immediate more expensive post-treatment medical care.
- Physicians may make inappropriate referrals to private sector clinics or firms for commercial reasons. This may happen when they have personal interests in these clinics or when they receive financial compensation for referral.
- Commercial interests will drive patients to undergo unnecessary diagnostic procedures such as full body scans. Patients will then exercise pressure to obtain access to potentially more invasive diagnostic services offered in the public system. This may expose them to risks, and will also unnecessarily burden the public system, increasing costs and waiting times.
- Once in the private sector, physicians will be further subject to commercial pressures from insurers and HMOs that may set up in Canada.
- People suffering from long-term illnesses, people with disabilities or people with family histories of disease will be disproportionately excluded from access to private parallel health care.
- Predictive genetic testing will more likely become a cost-effective tool to determine premiums for parallel private health insurance. Access to better health care services for those who are more likely to need health care will become more difficult.[31]

The experience of the United States indicates that these risk scenarios are real. This is not to say that none of these risks currently exist in the Canadian system as it currently exists. The increasing role of private delivery of many publicly-funded services once rendered in hospitals – diagnostic testing, nursing care and therapy services – has already sparked significant controversy. What would be new, under the CMA's proposal, is the extent to which physician services – including specialist and surgical services – will be accessible through privately funded providers.

The first scenario we evoked is associated with the fact that the under the CMA proposal, and the holding in Chaoulli, access to the private sector depends on a kind of need-capacity test. A patient can only access the private sector if the public system does not have the capacity to meet his or her needs in a 'timely' way. This raises a major administrative issue, and our first point of ethical risk. If the CMA proposal allows physicians themselves to be the arbiters of timeliness and need – in other words, to apply the *Chaoulli* 'test' in the clinical context – then the risk of 'diagnostic drift' emerges. Diagnostic drift involves a physician adjusting a diagnosis to allow them to access the private sector. After *Chaoulli* and under the system defended in the CMA motion, physicians would have to decide whether a condition is so severe that the patient cannot wait. For many patients, however, the wait is too long, regardless of the medical view of the physician. They may exert pressure on their physicians to give them access to the private system on the basis of non-medical factors – basic consumer preferences. It is entirely plausible that wealthy patients will be more effective in exercising pressure on their physicians. They are often more vocal, thus combining their financial ability to pay for private care with their political power to push for special treatment.

A related ethical risk arises where physicians working in the private sector turn away complex cases – 'cream skimming' only the simplest and lowest risk cases. This creates a division of labour: the private sector caters to simpler cases, the public to emergencies and costly, high-risk conditions. In addition, the private sector may forward patients to the public when complications occur and thus extra costs of treatment occur. This also negates any potential public benefit from the CMA proposal. If private sector physicians can turn back needy patients on the basis of their ability to pay, then the social benefit is lost. Truly needy persons without private insurance will remain in an overburdened public system.

A similar risk can arise where physicians turn away patients who do not have private insurance coverage. There are several reasons why physicians may turn away patients who do not have private insurance coverage. The most important reason is that the compensation offered in the private system are usually higher. Streamlined payment processes adopted by many private insurers may often seem easier for physicians than the web of rules, procedures, disclosure requirements and government investigative powers contained in health insurance legislation. Those who dream that the administrative burden in a parallel private system will be lower would be in for a surprise, however. The multiplicity of forms and procedures associated with competing private insurance companies in the US creates a logistical nightmare for physicians who serve several insurance companies. The administrative costs associated with this form of health care are phenomenally higher than those associated with our Canadian system.[32]

Once physicians have opted to focus on privately insured patients, likely because of the better payment structures, they are unlikely to contribute further to the public system. As already mentioned, the public system risks being undermined by the fact that in some specialty areas, large numbers of physicians will move to the private parallel system. To counteract this incentive, some countries that allow physicians to work in both systems have regulatory measures in place.[33] In the U.K., the British Medical Association's code of conduct for private practice revolves around four key principles:

- NHS consultants and NHS employing organisations should work on a partnership basis to prevent any conflict of interest between private practice and NHS work; [...]
- The provision of services for private patients should not prejudice the interest of NHS patients or disrupt NHS services;
- With the exception of the need to provide emergency care, agreed NHS commitments should take precedence over private work; and
- NHS facilities, staff and services may only be used for private practice with the prior agreement of the NHS employer.[34]

The code goes on to describe some 'best practices,' which include ensuring that '...private commitments, including on-call duties, are not scheduled during times at which they are scheduled to be working for the NHS,' and that '...private commitments are rearranged where there is regular disruption of this kind to NHS work.'[35]

Some jurisdictions in which private health insurance exist have used other more stringent mechanisms to prevent inequities in access to health care. In some countries, physicians are not at liberty to select patients on the basis of their ability to pay or their insurance coverage. They have to accept patients who present themselves, unless they have professional reasons to refuse them. In the Netherlands, for example, the Code of Conduct of the Medical Profession prescribes that 'the physician shall treat similarly situated patients equally. Discrimination based on religion, philosophical conviction, race, sex, or on any other ground is not permitted.'[36] This prohibition to discriminate covers the prohibition to refuse treatment on economic grounds.[37]

Since the CMA seems so strongly committed to equality of access to care, it seems to us that is should support a comparable ethical commitment of physicians towards all patients, even if private parallel insurance is introduced. This could be done through a clear formulation of the duty to offer care regardless of the source of health care funding in the professional codes of Canadian physicians, or through the expression of this ethical commitment in more stringent regulations. But when such commitment to equal access is implemented, we are no longer dealing with the private parallel system envisaged by the Chaoulli motion. If such measures would be introduced, the effect would be that commercial clinics would not be able to offer faster care to patients who have private health insurance or pay privately than those who do not. Why then even move to an introduction of private health insurance?

Once in the private system, further ethical risks emerge. Experience from the U.S. system is instructive here. Aside from public plans for elderly, disabled and low-income persons, the American 'system' consists of a large and increasingly concentrated group of health maintenance organizations (HMOs). HMOs exert great control over the physicians and institutions within their sweep. As commercial entities, they 'manage' the decisions of physicians not only by setting a wide range of practice parameters, but also by structuring payments in ways that create incentives to adjust clinical decisions in the interests of the HMO. Since HMOs are simply insurance companies seeking to manage costs, there are few reasons to think HMO models will not emerge in Canada as well.

So far in the U.S., experience with HMOs has been somewhat disturbing for physicians. The power of HMOs over U.S. physicians has increased due to mergers and increased concentration in the HMO market. It has begun to spark concerns that commercial considerations are leaking into clinical decisions, even against the wishes of individual physicians. Much commentary on American physicians focuses on the increasing power imbalance between doctors and the HMOs who fund them.[38] Physicians feel they are losing more control over their practices, often to the detriment of patients.

One prominent controversy centres on 'gag clauses.' HMO contracts with physicians contain many rewards and penalties to physicians that are based on clinical decisions, but are not known to the patient. Gag clauses simply make it a term of the contract for the physician *not* to reveal these incentives to patients. Legislation in many U.S. states now bans gag clauses, but the numerous incentives and penalties for utilization, testing and referral choices still remain a strong force constraining physician freedom in the clinical context. Whether from common law or their own ethical code, physicians may be placed in a legal Catch-22: obey their HMOs and violate their duty to disclose, or the reverse.[39]

Incentives take a wide range of forms.[40] HMOs can second guess clinical choices through utilization reviews, either before a patient has received care, or afterward in deciding whether to reimburse for it. Incentives not to question HMO decisions arise structurally as well, by the fact that physicians may lose their place in the HMO's roster of 'productive' physicians if they do so. As well, payment schemes other than fee for service can be imposed by HMOs, schemes that contain their own internal incentive problems. As the CMA has repeatedly noted, shifts away from FFS represent shifts away from complete clinical autonomy for doctors.

In response to HMO pressure, American physicians have begun to organize and confront HMOs, just as their Canadian counterparts are doing to governments here. The American Medical Association has within it a group called Physicians for Responsible Negotiation. PRN does some work with the minority of employed physicians (interns) in U.S. hospitals, but its more prominent advocacy has been on behalf of increasingly vulnerable private practice physicians working under HMO contracts. Among its demands has been federal passage of an antitrust exemption for physicians, which would allow them to bargain collusively (not as a labour union, but as an informal cartel) with HMOs, thus restoring the balance of bargaining power. Many states have already passed physician antitrust exemption legislation for this very reason.[41]

Indeed, perhaps part of the reason why more physicians are now returning to Canada than have moved away is the difficulties encountered by physicians in the commercialized U.S. health care market.[42] The drain of Canadian physicians to the U.S. has been a constant refrain of the CMA and other groups concerned about underfunding and mismanagement of the public system. To the extent mismanagement, clinical interference and bottom-line cost considerations annoy physicians in Canada, they certainly also persist in the U.S.: the only meaningful difference is the source: government or for-profit commercial entity. Furthermore, it is questionable whether commercially driven entities have more respect for the physician-patient relation and for the patients' interest in access to the best possible care than governmental agencies in Canada. As one returning physician, Dr. James Shaw, states it: 'Physicians can evaluate patients and treat them without having to get approval and jump through a million of hoops of HMOs (...) and private insurance companies that try to restrict care.'[43]

Other ethical risks within the private system arise where physicians become entrepreneurs in the private clinics or firms to which they refer insurance-carrying patients. This is already a problem within the Canadian health care system which is insufficiently regulated.

We were reminded of this development when one of us (Lemmens) entered into a conversation on the future of health care with the taxi-driver on the way to the conference on which this book is based. After hearing about the topic of the conference, the driver spontaneously shared a very relevant experience. He was recently told by his physician in one of the Toronto University Hospitals that he had to undergo a gastroscopy, but that there was a waiting time of two years in the public system. He had undergone the same procedure without any significant delay only two years earlier. The physician offered another solution, though: a private clinic at the other side of the road could perform the procedure without any delay for a mere $ 50 fee. The same physician, now wearing a different private hat, served him in the private clinic. With this personal story, the driver captured very well how parallel health care for diagnostic services already exists in Canada, how waiting times are affected by private parallel care – or how they can be manipulated for private gain – and how the existing regulatory framework does not help to curb the conflicts of interest embedded in the system.

The story symbolizes how patients remain bound to their public sector physicians for medical care, but are now seeing more private options for non-physician services such as nursing care, diagnostic procedures, drugs and in Alberta even some kinds of surgery. Privately delivered health services are nothing new in Canada, nor are fears that they will open the way to queue-jumping and to problematic behaviour associated with kick-backs and physician self-referral. Sujit Choudhry, Niteesh K. Choudhry and Adalsteinn D. Brown show in a recent article in the *Canadian Medical Association Journal* in a more systematic way how the problems raised by the taxi-driver's story are already a concern in Canada and how the current regulatory framework in various provinces deals with them.[44]

The fact that we already have these private services is often invoked to argue that, therefore, the integrity of the public system does not depend on a prohibition against private insurance.[45] We would turn it the other way round: the experience we have so far in many of the Canadian provinces with private health care services are a cause for concern. More opportunities for the development of a for-profit private sector increase the possibility of inappropriate self-referral, kickbacks and fee-splitting. And so far, medical organizations have done little to actively curb the abuse resulting from significant conflicts of interest within the system.

To have an idea of what increased private services will bring to us, it is revealing to look at developments in the United States. A recent article by two of the same authors mentioned earlier demonstrates the wide array of responses taken by U.S. federal and state legislators in response to concerns about such incentives and the difficulties the authorities encounter in stamping out questionable practices.[46] The most prominent mechanisms to deal with these practices involve bans on self-referral, and limitations on ownership in private facilities where one practices. In Canada, some provinces have similar provisions in legislation governing independent health facilities. Under such provisions, physicians, for instance, can often not make referrals to any IHF in which they have a personal interest.[47] However, the regulatory framework is insufficient in many of the Canadian provinces and enforcement of existing regulations is weak. For example, in Ontario, physicians can refer patients to a specialized clinic they own if they declare their financial interests. Disclosure to vulnerable patients who trust their physicians to make the right treatment decisions and who are often anxious to receive all possible care offers insufficient protection against the risk that financial interests will affect the public system and will lead to referrals for unnecessary and potentially harmful medical services. To take the example given by the cab driver: are our ethical and policy concerns really solved when physicians tell their patients that they have financial interest in the private clinic to which they refer them?

Given the evidence that private parallel health care creates ethical risks and professional conflicts, the CMA must do more than propose a limited two tier system. When it defends the introduction of such system, it should also immediately recognize its challenges and recommend how they can be dealt with. The CMA itself is not legally capable of implementing such reforms, nor are its provincial counterparts, but they can contribute to the debate. Provincial colleges of physicians will have to take the lead in enforcing existing regulations and in developing more stringent standards. The CMA can set the standards, by proposing new rules in its Code of Ethics. General principles already found in codes of conduct are, in our view, too vague to have regulatory teeth. Specific rules and standards must be promulgated.

Conclusion

In this paper, we analyzed the motion adopted by one of the most important and influential contributors to the Canadian medical system. We recognized that it is among the CMAs important responsibilities to comment publicly on challenges to the health care system. The CMA obviously has the right to push for regulatory reform if its delegates deem this to be required in order to improve the health care system. However, we argued in this paper that the important public role the CMA fulfills also imposes on the organization a duty to provide evidence for its position and to evaluate carefully the consequences of recommended changes. We suggested that no careful process of deliberation and of weighing the benefits and risks of change seems to have preceded the adoption of the motion. The motion seems to be more of the nature of a political statement. Some of the CMA delegates, it seems, have seized the political momentum to argue for the introduction of a system of private health care that may benefit many physicians and some patients, but that little consideration has been given to the serious impact this shift may have on the physician-patient relation in general.

In a first part of our paper, we pointed out that the CMA's support for parallel private health care is not unprecedented, and that it has in the past not been the strong supporter of Medicare it now claims to be. We sketched briefly how the Medicare system as we know it now has evolved overtime and how the CMA has only reluctantly accepted the idea of comprehensive government-sponsored health insurance. We pointed out how the CMA, as other professional organizations, has come up for the interests of its members, and how it has been able to obtain significant benefits for its members under the historically developed compromise of the Medicare system. We suggested that the motion as adopted seems to emanate more from the CMA as an organization which promotes the benefit of its members, and not from the CMA which alleges to promote the best possible health care system.

In the second part of our paper, we sketched some of the possible consequences of changing the health care system in line with the proposed motion. We evoked some of the scenarios that will likely arise as a result of the introduction of parallel private health care. The experience of the US system helps us to imagine the ethical risks that will be created. If the CMA indeed wants to promote the best possible care for patients, as its mission statement reveals, and as its factum in Chaoulli suggests, it also should recognize the significant challenges posed by their proposed changes. It should recognize these risks, and it should start thinking of regulatory and professional reforms that are needed to control the growing conflicts of interests that are already affecting the physician-patient relation.

Perhaps it is not too late for the CMA to reconsider what one of its members proposed back in 1996: 'If the CMA is really committed to exploring the viability of a one-tier comprehensive health service, it should declare a 3-to-5-year moratorium on the privatization issue. ...[I]f the energy we expend on schemes to delist, privatize, define core services and design complex physician-payment schemes were applied to improving the existing system, we could support an excellent one-tier service.'[48] When the CMA does so, it may be more successful in convincing our cab driver that many CMA delegates remain committed to the best possible health care system, and not only – to use his words – to their wallet.[49]

Notes

* We want to thank Colleen Flood and Lorne Sossin for helpful comments on an earlier version of this paper; the driver of a co-op cab for a stimulating conversation on health care related issues; and attendants at the conference for stimulating questions and suggestions. Research for this paper has been supported by a grant from Genome Canada (through the Ontario Genomics Institute) on Health Systems and Insurance Implications of Genetics.

1 Patrick Sullivan, 'Privatization if necessary, not necessarily privatization: CMA' (CMA News Release, August 19, 2005), on line at http://www.cma. ca/index.cfm/ci_id=10028034&la_id=1&topstory=1

2 Mark Kennedy, 'MDs back private option: 65% vote for alternative when timely care lacking' CanWest News service August 18, 2005 [date accessed August 18, 2005]

3 *Ibid.*

4 André Picard, 'MDs change tactics, refuse to denounce private health care' *Globe and Mail* (17 August 2005).

5 Speech to the Ontario Medical Association of May 7, 2005. available at http://www.cma.ca/index.cfm/ci_id/44260/la_id/1.htm [date accessed September 5, 2005]

6 Factum, Chaoulli v. Quebec (Attorney General), 2005 SCC 35 (CanLII) [*Chaoulli*] [Factum of Interveners Canadian Medical Association and the Canadian Orthopaedic Association].

7 *Ibid.* at para. 7.

8 Canadian Medical Association, *Code of Ethics of the Canadian Medical Association* (Ottawa: The Association, 1996) cited in *ibid.*

9 See e.g. Steven Lewis, 'From Hippocrates to Hypocrisy at the CMA' *Winnipeg Free Press*, August 21, 2005; Linda Silas & Steven Lewis, 'The Doctors' Dilemma, and Ours' *Edmonton Journal*, August 15, 2005, A14.

10 See the reference to the trial record by Binnie and Lebel JJ (dissenting) in *Chaoulli supra* note 6 at par. 187.

11 Canadian Medical Association, History, Mission and Vision, http://www.cma.ca/index.cfm/ci_id/44413/la_id/1.htm [date accessed September 14, 2005].

12 *Ibid.*

13 *Ibid.*

14 Carolyn H. Tuohy, *Accidental Logics: The Dynamics of Change in the Health Care Arena in the United States, Britain, and Canada* (New York: Oxford University Press, 1999) at 52–54.

15 Royal Commission on Health Services, *Final Report,* (Ottawa: Queen's Printer, 1964).

16 See M. Mason, 'The *Canada Health Act* and the *Health Care Accessibility Act*: the Legal Challenge' (1989) 56:6 *Ont. Med. Rev.* 20; R.D. Fletcher, 'Perspectives on Deferring the *Canada Health Act* Challenge' (1990) 57:5 *Ont. Med. Rev.* 25, both cited in Sujit Choudhry, 'The Enforcement of the Canada Health Act' (1996) 41 *McGill L.J.*461 at

17 Gregory P. Marchildon, 'Private Insurance for Medicare: Policy History and Trajectory in the Four Western Provinces'

18 *Ibid.* at p. 2 (draft)

19 Tuohy, *supra* note 13 at 30. See esp. pp. 39–47 and Chapter 7, 'Canada:

The Logic of the Single Payer System,' at pp. 203–238. See also Charles D. Naylor, *Private Practice, Public Payment: Canadian Medicine and the Politics of Health Insurance* (Montreal: McGill-Queen's, 1986).

20 Joan N. Gilmour, 'Regulation of free-standing health facilities: an entrée for privatization and for-profit health care' (2003) *Health Law Journal* (Special Issue), 131–152. See also John Lavis *et. al.*; 'Free-standing health care facilities: financial arrangements, quality assurance and a pilot study' (1998) 158:3 *C.M.A.J.* 359.

21 Tom Archibald & Allyson Jeffs, 'Physician Fee Decisions, the Medicare Basket and Budgeting: A Three-Province Survey' (unpublished). Paper submitted to *Defining the Medicare Basket* Project, Faculty of Law, University of Toronto, November 2004. Available on line at http://www.law.utoronto.ca/healthlaw/basket/docs/IRPP30Nov04_ArchibaldJeffs.pdf.

22 Colleen M. Flood & Joanna N. Erdman, 'The Boundaries of Medicare: Tensions in the Dual Role of Ontario's Physician Services Review Committee' Working Paper No. 1, Defining the Medicare Basket Project, Faculty of Law, University of Toronto, March 2004, available on line at http://www.law.utoronto.ca/healthlaw/basket/docs/working1_boundaries.pdf.

23 See Colleen M. Flood, Mark Stabile and Sasha Kontic, 'Finding Health Policy 'Arbitrary': The Evidence on Waiting, Dying, and Two-Tier Systems' in this volume.

24 Carolyn H. Tuohy, Colleen M. Flood & Mark Stabile, 'How Does Private Finance Affect Public Health Care Systems: Marshalling the Evidence from OECD Nations,' (2004) 29: 3 *J. Health Pol.* 359–396. Also available on line at http://www.chass.utoronto.ca/cepa/Private.pdf.

25 A view shared by Andrew Petter in this volume, who writes that, under the model resulting from *Chaoulli* (and the CMA motion), '...those who exercise their right to buy private health insurance would have a weaker stake in ensuring that the Medicare system provides timely and effective medical services.' See Andrew Petter, 'Wealthcare: The Politics of the Charter Revisited' in this volume.

26 *Chaoulli* at para. 64.

27 See Sujit Choudhry, 'Worse than *Lochner*?' in this volume.

28 [2004] 3 S.C.R. 657

29 If the evidence of the development of specialty hospitals in the U.S. is instructive at all, commercialization will less likely benefit physicians working in emergency departments, trauma centers, burn units and other acute and complex care settings. See Sujit Choudhry, Niteesh K. Choudhry & Troyen A. Brennan, 'Specialty Versus Community Hospitals: What Role for the Law?' (2005) (9 August 2005) *Health Affairs* 361 at 363.

30 Cynthia Carver, 'It's time for CMA to put the lid on privatization' (1996) 155:8 *Can. Med. Ass. J.* 1156 at 1157.

31 See in general Trudo Lemmens, 'Selective Justice, Genetic Discrimination, and Insurance: Should We Single Out Genes in Our Laws?' (2000), 45 *McGill L.J.* 347.

32 See, for example, Uwe E. Reinhart *et. al.*, 'U.S. health care spending in an international context.' 23:3 (2004) *Health Affairs* 10–25; Steffie Woolhandler *et. al.*, 'Health care administration in the United States and Canada: micromanagement, macro costs.' (2004) 34:1 (2004) *International Journal of Health Services* 65–78. According to the latter study, the 1999 health administration costs totaled at least $ 294.3 billion (or $ 1,059 per capita), in the United States, compared to only $ 9.4 billion ($ 307 per capita) in Canada.

33 British Medical Association, 'A Code of Conduct for Private Practice: Recommended Standards of Practice for NHS Consultants' (British Medical Association, September 2003), available on line at http://www.bma. org.uk/ap.nsf/Content/CCSCContractprivMS/$file/priv.pdf. See also BMA, 'Focus on...Private Practice' (BMA, June 2004), on line at http:// www.bma.org.uk/ap.nsf/Content/focusprivatepractice0604/$file/ Focusprivprac.pdf.

34 *Ibid.*, Art. 1.4.

35 *Ibid.*, Art. 2.4.

36 See art. II.2 Koninklijke Nederlandsche Maatschappij tot Bevordering van de Geneeskunst, Gedragsregels voor Artsen, 'De arts zal patiënten in gelijke gevallen gelijk behandelen. Discriminatie wegens godsdienst, levensovertuiging, ras, geslacht of op welke grond dan ook, is niet toegestaan' (TL translation); available online: http://knmg.artsennet.nl/ vademecum/files/II.01.html.

37 E-mail communication Professor Herbert Hermans, July 14, 2005.

38 Jennifer L. D'Isidori, 'Stop Gagging Physicians' (1997) 7 *Health Matrix* 187.

39 Stephen R. Latham, 'Regulation of Managed Care Incentive Payments to Physicians' (1996) 22 *Am. J. L. Med.* 399; 1998 Ryan S. Johnson, 'ERISA Doctor in the House?: The Duty to Disclose Physician Incentives to Limit Health Care' (1998) 82 *Minn L.R.* 1631; see also *Weiss v. Cigna Healthcare, Inc.* (1997) 972 F.Supp. 748 (US Dist Court, S.D.N.Y.).

40 Henry T. Greely, 'Direct Financial Incentives in Managed Care: Unanswered Questions' (1996) 6 *Health Matrix* 53

41 Fred J. Hellinger & Gary J. Young, 'An Analysis of Physician Antitrust Exemption Legislation: Adjusting the Balance of Power' (2001) 286:1 *JAMA* 83.

42 Elaine Carey, 'Canadian MDs head home from U.S.: 317 doctors have

returned in past few years.' *Toronto Star*, 25 August 2005. The article
reports on a recent study conducted by the Canadian Institute for Health
Information. See Canadian Institute for Health Information, *Supply, Distribution and Migration of Canadian Physicians* (2004), available online: http://
secure.cihi.ca/cihiweb/dispPage.jsp?cw_page=PG_385_E&cw_ topic=
385&cw_rel=AR_14_E#full [date accessed September 9, 2005]

43 *Ibid.*

44 'Unregulated private markets for health care in Canada? Rules of professional misconduct, physician kickbacs and physician self-referral.' (2004)
    170 *CMAJ* 1115.

45 See e.g. Deschamps J in *Chaoulli supra* note 6 at par. 74.

46 Choudhry, Choudhry & Brennan, *supra* note 29.

47 In Ontario, *General Regulation – Medicine Act*, O. Reg. 114/94, s. 17, and in
    Alberta *By-Laws of the College of Physicians and Surgeons of Alberta*, ss. 47
    and 49. See Choudhry, Choudhry & Brown, *supra* note 27.

48 Carver, *supra* note 30 at 1157.

49 See *supra*.

Preserving Privilege, Promoting Profit: The Payoffs from Private Health Insurance

ROBERT G. EVANS

A majority of the Supreme Court of Canada in the *Chaoulli* decision were convinced that the ability to access private health insurance would result in 'many' Quebeckers being able to avoid unnecessary pain and suffering resulting from long waiting times in publicly-funded Medicare. In this paper, I review the extent to which private insurance is a prevalent form of financing around the world. I argue that private health insurance plays a minimal role worldwide in terms of total expenditures – with the notable exception of the US, and even that very limited role depends on the support of the public sector. The danger is that American rhetoric about the value and role of private insurance will spill over into Canadian society. This danger is a real one – certainly these values and erroneous assumptions about the extent to which private insurance would or could benefit ordinary Quebeckers or Canadians adversely affected the reasoning of the majority in *Chaoulli*.

Insurance basics: Spreading risk and reducing uncertainty

At its most abstract, insurance is very simple. A group of individuals each face some future adverse but uncertain event, such as possible destruction or theft of property, liability for damage to others, illness or injury, or premature death. They each agree to contribute resources, typically but not necessarily money, to a common pool from which some compensation will be paid to (or on behalf of) those participants who do in fact suffer the specified adverse event. The effect is to convert, for each of them, an uncertain future overshadowed by a possible large loss into a certain (or less uncertain) future in which any loss that occurs will be partially or fully compensated – at least financially.

The total cost of adverse events for the group as a whole will not be reduced, indeed to the extent that the process of assigning and collecting contributions, maintaining records and protecting the pooled funds, and assessing and paying compensation requires resources, the total of contributions required from the group will necessarily exceed the total amounts of compensation paid. The process of insurance is costly *per se*, over and above the costs of compensation for the events insured against. What that extra cost buys is relief not so much from the costs imposed by the adverse events themselves – that cost is simply redistributed among the members of the insured group – but from the distress that each participant would otherwise feel in the face of their possible and uncompensated future occurrence.

In principle there is no reason why individuals should not form voluntary associations to provide insurance for each other, and in fact there are numerous historical examples of such associations. But a small association can easily be bankrupted by a large loss or a small miscalculation. The benefits of pooling risks grow as the pool itself grows, but so do the technical demands of estimating variable and complex risks, setting contribution rates, and assessing and paying claims. Accordingly private commercial organizations specializing in these activities – underwriting – long ago took over the field of risk spreading, selling a vast array of diverse insurance contracts to individuals, groups, and other commercial and non-commercial organizations. These contracts, bought by the payment of a 'premium,' entitle the purchaser to receive specified compensatory payments if and only if certain specified adverse events should occur within a specified time period. Insurance coverage is now largely a purely commercial 'product,' bought and sold in private markets.

The elephant in the living room: Health insurance is different – and so is the United States

There is, however, one glaring exception. Insurance against the costs of health care, worldwide, is provided almost entirely outside commercial markets, by governments or quasi-governmental organizations under close public supervision. Amid the rhetorical controversy that surrounds the financing of health care and much increased by the *Chaoulli* court, it is easy to gain the impression that private insurance is a significant source of funds for health care. This impression is false. In high-income industrialized countries the large preponderance of health care financing comes from public sources, and the second largest component is individual out-of-pocket payment. In lower-income, less developed countries these proportions are often reversed. Private insurance, where it exists at all, is a very distant third.

The World Health Report (WHR) provides in its Statistical Appendices estimates of the level and sources of health expenditures for every member country of the World Health Organization. Aggregating across all countries in the 2004 Report (excluding those with populations of less than one million) over half – 55.3% – of health care expenditures are financed in the public sector while another quarter – 24.0% – come out-of-pocket. Private health insurance covers only 16.6% of health care expenditures world-wide. (Another 4.0% comes from other private sources.)[1]

These proportions, however, are distorted by the peculiar example of the United States. Excluding that country, the private insurance share drops to 5.6%. The public and out-of-pocket shares rise to 61.6% and 29.4% respectively. The United States, with 7.1% of world population, accounts for 36.7% of world health expenditure. Private coverage reimburses 35.6% of American health care expenditures, and the American market represents 78.6% of world private health insurance coverage.[2]

In fact, however, these official data overstate the net contribution of private insurance. American governments provide large subsidies to private coverage through the income tax system. If these subsidies are reallocated as indirect public expenditure, private insurance world-wide, even including the United States, covers only 11.0% of health care expenditures. A number of other countries also provide various forms of public subsidy, which if accounted for would bring the private share down still further, but these additional amounts are relatively small.[3]

In Canada, for example, private insurance coverage receives public subsidies similar to those in the United States. Smythe estimated these public subsidies at $2.5 bn. in 1994; expanded in line with growth in private sector spending, this would amount to about $5 bn. CAD in 2004.[4] This compares with an estimated $219 bn. USD subsidy in the United States[5].

Aggregating the individual country data from the WHR into income bands, by reported level of Gross Domestic Product (GDP) per capita in international dollars (and separating the United States from the other countries in the highest income band), yields some very clear differences in financing patterns across country income levels. Averaging within each income band, and counting each country equally, the share of national income spent on health care tends to rise slowly and steadily as national income rises, from around 4% in the lowest income countries to around 8% in the highest. The United States is an obvious outlier at 14%.[6] On average countries spend about 6% of their GDP when each is counted as one or weighted by population, but if countries are weighted by GDP per capita the fact that richer countries spend a larger share – and the heavy influence of the United States – brings the world average proportion up to about 8.5%.

Rising national income is associated with a rising share of health spending from public sources. The relationship is somewhat irregular among the lower income bands, but is approximately monotonic across bands, rising from 40%-50% in the poorest countries to over 70% in the richest. Again the United States is an obvious anomaly, with the highest per capita income yet a reported share of public coverage – 44.4% – similar to that for the world's poorest countries. Adjustment for the public subsidy to private coverage, however, brings the United States close to 60% public payment, slightly above the world average.

The alternative to public coverage is not, however, private coverage. As noted above, outside the United States private insurance covers only 5.6% of world health care expenditures. It is virtually non-existent in countries in the lowest income bands. A cluster of countries in Latin America and a handful in Africa report substantial proportions of private health insurance, and the world leader is in fact not the United States but the Union of South Africa at 42.3% of expenditures reported as covered by private insurance. With these few exceptions, however, private health insurance on any significant scale is overwhelmingly an American phenomenon.

Since the average share of public coverage rises across income bands, it follows that the proportion of out-of-pocket payment falls. But more interestingly, the United States is *not* an outlier in this comparison. The share of health care financed out-of-pocket in the United States, the highest income country in the WHR, is actually slightly lower than the average in the highest-income band of countries excluding the United States. The American anomaly is not the extent of individual, out-of-pocket payment, but the proportion of health care that is collectively financed from private insurance (supported by public subsidy). In other high-income countries nearly all of this would pass through public agencies and be allocated more fairly

Health expenditure data from the individual countries of the Organization for Economic Cooperation and Development (OECD) makes the same point strongly, but with some additional nuances.[7] In almost all high-income countries, public sources cover between 70% and 85% of national health expenditures, the exceptions being the United States, Switzerland, and a couple of more recent and lower income OECD members (Korea, Mexico). Out-of-pocket payments account for most of the remaining expenditure, with private insurance contributing at most about 10% and in a number of countries, virtually nothing.

Powdered unicorn horn: Does *real* private health insurance exist?

It is worth noting, however, that the OECD has over the years struggled with the appropriate categorization of nominally 'private' insurance in its member countries, recognizing that nowhere does such insurance correspond to the standard economic model of a commodity purchased voluntarily by individuals from private, for-profit corporations. Where private insurance exists, it is typically regulated and/or subsidized in order to further particular social purposes that cannot be achieved in a truly competitive private market.[8]

In earlier years the OECD statisticians recognized these interventions by dividing private coverage into 'private social' and 'other' to identify those national systems in which private insurance exists but is provided on a non-profit basis (e.g. France), or is significantly manipulated by governments to generate patterns of costs, benefits, and coverage that would not emerge from a private market (e.g. Australia). This might suggest, by implication, that the remaining private coverage, was purchased voluntarily by individuals in free competitive markets from private, commercial firms – the standard model of the economic theory textbooks. But any such implication would be quite incorrect. The OECD has now abandoned this distinction in tacit recognition that there exist no such truly private markets for health insurance.

The case of the United States focuses the dilemma. The American industry receives – and perhaps survives because of – heavy public subsidies, equal to roughly a third of premium revenue. These are available only to employment-based insurance plans in which group-rated premiums are paid by the employer and individual participation is not voluntary but a condition of employment. American policy-makers are well aware that this tax structure radically distorts the coverage patterns that would emerge in a truly private market, and have largely ignored a generation of calls for 'reform' from free-market advocates. But if the OECD were therefore, quite reasonably, to classify

American private coverage (and similar systems elsewhere) as 'private social insurance,' there would not be much left in the 'other' category. So, at least for now, the OECD has quietly dropped the distinction.

American economists who, somewhat idiosyncratically, view their system as over-insured, have for decades advocated removal of the public subsidy to private insurance as the solution to this perceived problem. It is an open question as to how much private coverage would be left, world-wide, if this commodity were required to find its own customers in free competitive markets, unassisted by public subsidies or regulatory incentives. But it seems undeniable that even its present rather marginal role would be much reduced.

The fundamental point is two-pronged. First, private health insurance, as identified in the WHR and the OECD data system, plays a minimal role in the financing of health care services world-wide. With a handful of exceptions – most prominently the United States and the Union of South Africa – health care is financed almost entirely from either public sector resources or the direct payments of patients. But second, even that very limited role depends on the support of the public sector, through the various forms of subsidies and regulatory incentives in place in a number of countries. If by private health insurance we mean insurance 'products' sold to voluntary purchasers by private, for-profit firms in open competitive markets, unregulated except to assure that contracts will be honoured, then such insurance scarcely exists at all.

This observation raises two inter-related questions.

Why are there no unicorns – and why do we go on debating them?

The first and most obvious question is: 'Why is health insurance so different?' Why do the private commercial firms that dominate the provision of all other forms of insurance, play such a minimal role in the financing of health care? We use the language of 'insurance' against the costs of care for adverse health events, just as we do for accidents, fires, natural disasters or premature death. Yet the mechanisms for determining contributions, and forms and amounts of compensation, could hardly be more different.

Public health 'insurance' finances health care through compulsory levies – taxes or social insurance premiums – that are typically unrelated to individual risk status, but are rather linked to a greater or lesser degree to ability to pay. And public agencies typically fund providers of care directly, rather than reimbursing patients for costs incurred. This pattern, virtually universal and persistent over decades, cannot plausibly be interpreted as the result of a sustained coincidence of policy accidents or mistakes.

The second question, however, arises from the contrast between the limited role of private insurance, and its persisting prominent place in public debates over how to finance care. 'The public-private mix' in health care is a perennially recurring topic, not just in academic conferences of health economists but in broader policy and public discussions as well. Nor have the terms of this debate changed significantly over decades. Despite the considerable accumulation of evidence and refinement of argument, there has been no detectable progress toward agreement on fundamental issues. If private health insurance is relatively unimportant – outside the United States – why do we spend so much time arguing about it?

This latter question has particular significance for Canada. Geographically adjacent to the United States, we come within its very powerful cultural and intellectual influence through the umbrella of its media. And we are increasingly integrated economically, making independent policy-making in many spheres difficult if not impossible. American political, economic and social arrangements are constantly presented to Canadians as the natural order of things.

That natural order of things includes private health insurance. Most Americans view themselves, correctly, as relying primarily on private health insurance. It is easy then to infer, incorrectly, that American health care is primarily financed by private health insurance. (The error arises because a disproportionate share of costs is generated by those private firms will not insure. Unhealthy people are not generally profitable clients.) The fact that in world terms the United States is highly unusual in its reliance on private health insurance, and that nonetheless governments out-spend private insurers by more that two to one, does not register in the American public debates. These then flow across our borders and exert a powerful influence on our perceptions, and on the perceptions of our courts, of what is possible or desirable.

Private coverage in Canada, primarily for dentistry and prescription drugs, is in fact modeled on that in the United States, and receives the same public subsidies. Insurance corporations serve a North American market. Debates about how private insurance operates in various European countries are important for understanding the balance of interests involved, but Canadians do not live on the shores of the Baltic or the

Mediterranean. If private insurance is expanded in Canada, to encompass hospital and medical services, it seems virtually inevitable that it will build on the existing North American framework. Our financing system will converge more toward that of the United States, not, as suggested by the majority in *Chaoulli*, toward the German or the Swedish or other European country.

The public purposes of public health insurance

The short and simple answer to both of these 'Why?' questions is that health insurance is expected to, and to varying degrees does, perform essential social roles that private insurance is by its very nature incapable of performing. When Kenneth Arrow stated: 'The basic function of health insurance is the reduction of uncertainty...' he was wrong on the facts and irrelevant on the principle.[9] Private insurance markets are actually quite good at reducing uncertainty, as indicated by their dominance in non-health markets. But systems of public health insurance, everywhere in the world, do much more.

Simply put, public health insurance is a mechanism to give effect to a pair of particular social or collective choices, decisions first, that access to health care should be based on need for care (usually but not always interpreted as capacity to benefit) rather than on ability to pay, and second, that individual contributions to finance health care should be based on ability to pay rather than use of care. These fundamental principles, that most citizens in most countries appear to support, are very widely articulated as an ideal, though their operationalization requires a degree of organization and affluence that puts them beyond the reach of most lower-income countries. In the industrialized world, however, most citizens express strong and continuing support for these principles, not only in surveys but in political action – and acceptance of associated taxation.

Full implementation implies universal access to 'all medically necessary' services, unimpeded by user fees or other forms of payment linked to use, and financed from taxation based on income or other measures of financial resources. Roughly speaking, this is in fact how most health care services are financed in high-income countries. But such a system requires the healthy and wealthy to subsidize the unhealthy and unwealthy. Some must pay for more than they expect to get – sometimes much more – and some can expect to get more than they could ever pay for – sometimes much more. Moreover the wealthy, when they are unhealthy, do not receive any preference in access to or quality of care despite their greater contributions.

What do you mean, 'We'? Collective principles, individual interests

The implications of the collective principle may be clear, but its implementation is inherently contentious because it sets up an inevitable conflict of economic interests across income classes within the population. Support weakens and resistance builds as one moves up the income distribution. The wealthy are generally better off paying for their own care, and avoiding the taxes necessary to pay for that of others. Thus all real-world health care financing systems draw on a mix of public and private sources, a *de facto* compromise between the broadly held collective objective, and the private interests of those economically most threatened by it. The mix varies across countries depending upon differences in ideology and power structure. How strongly does the population support the collective objective, and how effective is the resistance from the upper end of the income distribution?

Who pays? Conflicts over how we split the bill

The larger the private payment share, whether through direct payments by users or through private insurance premiums, the lighter is the relative burden at the higher end of the income scale and the heavier it is the lower end.[10] Systems with a larger private financing component are highly regressive, requiring people at lower incomes to contribute a larger share of their incomes. Public sources, on the other hand, tend to be proportional or mildly progressive, taking equal or slightly rising shares of incomes at higher income levels.

The regressive nature of charges based on use is fairly obvious, insofar as needs for care are consistently correlated, inversely, with income. The wealthy are healthier. Even if needs for care were on average similar across the income spectrum, however, the costs of care would represent a steadily falling share of rising incomes. But private insurance is equally regressive. Insofar as competitive insurance markets generate premiums that correspond to individuals' risk status, i.e. their *ex ante* expected use of or costs for care, those premiums will on average match the average costs of care in each income class. They will tend to be higher, and *a fortiori* a higher percentage of income, in lower income classes.

The terms of the compromise between collective principles and individual economic interests are always open to challenge, which is why the 'public-private mix' is never permanently settled. The mix of sources can shift over time within countries, depending upon shifts in the larger political balance. Since in high-income countries financing is predominantly public, one observes continuing efforts by the representatives of the wealthy to expand the scope of private financing.[11] In the United States, however, where the extensive private insurance system generates highly unequal access to care and a very regressive distribution of payment burdens, the 'reformers' have been those trying, for decades and unsuccessfully, to establish a universal public system. Unfortunately for Canadians, the propaganda generated in defense of the American insurance industry also influences our public discourse.

It is generally understood, and accepted, that universal access to care on the basis of need necessarily requires a substantial transfer of financial resources from the wealthy and healthy to the unwealthy and unhealthy. But there is room for a great deal of debate about how large a transfer, and from and to which parts of the income distribution. Income taxes typically bear most heavily at the top of the income distribution. Social insurance systems permit the capping of premiums above a certain income level, thus building in a regressive element and reducing the burden on the highest income earners. Sales and other forms of indirect taxation likewise ease the burden at the top end. Private insurance is even more regressive insofar as it entirely decouples contributions from income levels. For a given level of coverage, premium costs depend entirely upon assessed risk, and not at all upon economic resources. And the tax-expenditure subsidies that support private coverage in North America are structured to have their greatest value in the highest tax brackets, creating a further substantial advantage for the better-off.

Who gets to the front of which lines? Conflicts over priority

But the debate over financing sources is not simply about which groups, and particularly which income strata, pay what share of the total health care bill. There is also the question of access to care – on what terms and conditions? Universal, publicly financed care on the basis of need offers, at least in principle, no privileged access for the better-off – no shorter waits or (perceived) higher quality care for those otherwise willing and able to pay providers out of their own pockets, over and above any reimbursement from public programs. But this conflicts directly with the interests both of the better-off themselves, and of those who would provide them, for a price, with more timely access or 'better' care.

In a number of universal, publicly funded health care systems, therefore, one finds 'privilege-preserving mechanisms' that offer more immediate access and/or higher quality services to those higher up the socio-economic spectrum. Where, as in the U.K. and Australia, providers offer services both in the public system, and privately, those willing and able to pay extra can 'jump the public queue' – particularly for access to specialists and to elective surgery – and providers can profit by selling priority along with services. Private insurers can then sell insurance to cover these private fees. The two processes are mutually supporting – without private charges there is nothing for private insurers to cover, and without private insurance, providers might find a smaller market for private care. Private insurers thus have an economic interest in expanding the scope of private charges to patients. This is the kind of system that the majority of the court in *Chaoulli*, considers necessary to uphold Canadians' fundamental rights to life, liberty and security of the person under s. 7 of the Charter.

In some European systems there are also separate insurance programs for the better-off, or for privileged occupational groups, offering access to preferred care at premiums reflecting their generally better health but not their higher incomes. Social insurance systems with multiple insurers facilitate this form of discrimination in favour of the better-off (a good example of this is Germany, which is discussed more fully by Stefan Gress in this volume). The overall financing mix is in consequence more regressive, and the insurance coverage for those with higher incomes may also provide other benefits, such as easier access to specialists.

Primarily tax-based systems may, as in Australia, offer tax concessions or other benefits to those purchasing private insurance to pay for private care. Where they do not, as in the U.K., proposals emerge regularly from the right wing to offer such subsidies. But real public health expenditures have been relatively low in the U.K. for years, and public waiting lists have been unacceptably long. In effect those who pay privately can buy better access for themselves without paying taxes sufficient to provide – through the public sector – a similar standard for everyone else.

These various institutional features to preserve privileged access for the better-off do not represent a major qualification to the predominance of universal, publicly financed health care in high income countries. But they are radically inconsistent with the fundamental principles on which those universal systems are based. They embody, even in a relatively small way, the precisely opposite principle that people should get the care they are willing and able to pay for. The better-off should get better care, on better terms, without being required to support a similar standard for others – in short, exactly what a private market would offer.

Efforts to expand the scope of this market principle to include more user fees, more private delivery and payment, and more public subsidies for private insurance – as Alan Maynard also discusses in this volume – take up a good deal of the public attention and policy discussion that would be better focused on improving the health care system as a whole. Their persistence reflects the political reality, the distribution of power and media access across the income spectrum. The wealthy and otherwise strategically placed are able to command a disproportionate share of public attention for their concerns, ensuring that their privileges are respected and their resources not overtaxed. Where they feel under-privileged and over-taxed, there will be a permanent 'crisis.'

During the apparently endless debate over the 'public-private mix,' a variety of superficially plausible arguments have been developed to claim more general benefits from private financing. On closer examination, however, these all turn out to be spurious. Logic insists, and empirical analysis strongly confirms, that controversies over the health care financing mix are primarily over who pays what share of the health care bill, and whether or not some shall have preferential access to care. But because support for various forms of private financing is rooted not in evidence and argument but in individual and class interests, the recurrent claims of general benefit always survive refutation. They are 'zombies' – ideas that are intellectually dead, but constantly disinterred by those whose interests they serve.

How much will all this cost? Conflicts over system costs and provider incomes

Public-private debates are not, however, entirely about 'Who pays?' and 'Who gets?' There is another important dimension of conflicting economic interests that emerges in a (relatively) small way in the privilege-preserving sectors of the European systems, and is massively present in the United States. There is also a clear conflict of interest between those who pay for care, and those who are paid for it. How much should providers be paid, and for what? The salience of this issue is reflected in by the Canadian Medical Association's response to the *Chaoulli* decision and their support for two-tier medicine. Their stance is no surprise in light of the long opposition of the Canadian medical profession to one-tier medicine, as documented by Greg Marchildon in this volume.

All modern health care systems generate very powerful pressures for cost expansion, and contain no internal mechanisms to mitigate this pressure. Wildavsky summarized this observation as the Law of Medical Money: '... costs will increase to the level of available funds ... that level must be limited to keep costs down.'[12] A principal task of all public financing systems has been to develop mechanisms, within their own institutional and cultural context, for restraining this growth. And all have, more or less, succeeded. The pattern is perhaps clearest in Canada, where the share of national income devoted to health care, previously rising in parallel with the trend in the United States, came to an abrupt stop in 1970 after universal comprehensive coverage of physicians' services had been implemented nation-wide. But a similar pattern is found across the OECD world during the 1970s. The associated institutional changes can be identified country by country.

This process of restraint is inherently very contentious because all health care expenditures are simultaneously and by basic accounting logic someone's income. All cost containment is necessarily income containment. Restraint occurs through some combination of limiting the growth of individual incomes, or restricting the numbers of people earning incomes directly or indirectly from the provision of health care. Despite the considerable political difficulties, however, all public systems have been able to influence, to a considerable degree, the trends in health care expenditures

The one outstanding exception, again, is the United States. Over the last thirty years, health care expenditures in that country (per capita, inflation adjusted) have steadily advanced relative to those in all other countries. As noted above, the share of national income devoted to health care in high income countries averages between eight and nine percent – Canada is currently somewhat above average at ten percent. But the United States is now spending over fifteen percent, and is projected to reach about nineteen percent by 2014. Americans will then be spending a share of their (higher) incomes that is *twice* the average in other high-income countries – all the while leaving a significant portion of their citizenry without insurance

Prior to the mid-1970s costs in the other OECD countries (as a share of GDP) were on average two percentage points below those in the United States, and rising in parallel. But other OECD countries managed to slow their expenditure growth; the United States did not. The gap of two percentage points thirty years ago is now between six and seven percentage points, and growing. These discrepancies are huge. If Americans were now spending only the same share of their incomes as Canadians do, their total costs for health care would be lower by over half a trillion dollars (U.S.) or over $2000 per year for every person in the country.

It's the prices, stupid!

The point is simple and blunt. Private insurance is incapable of containing the expansionary pressures inherent in modern health care systems. If it needed reinforcing, Canadians should note that expenditures on pharmaceuticals in this country, unlike expenditures on hospitals and physicians, are growing very rapidly as a share of our national income – and pharmaceutical insurance in Canada still follows the American model of a mix of public and private insurance and out-of-pocket payment.

Cost containment is not an end in itself. Providers of care have been quick to point out, over the years, that increased expenditure on things that people value and want to buy is a perfectly natural market process – a source for satisfaction, not for concern. And so it would be, if the increased expenditure represented corresponding value for money. But, at least in the American case, it does not.

Recent comparative studies across the OECD have concluded, as critics have long maintained, that 'It's the prices, stupid.' The cost escalation facilitated by private insurance has not bought Americans better health, or even more health care, but merely higher prices.[13] Americans do not get more or better health care than citizens of other countries, they just pay more for what they get. Some, the wealthy and/or well-insured, get care of the highest world standard. Others, the uninsured with minimal private resources, are fortunate to get any care at all, and their health outcomes reflect this. Private insurance preserves radically differentiated access for health care, as for any other market commodity, but not better care overall.

The point has been underlined sharply for Canadians by a recent study of over twelve thousand patients undergoing coronary artery bypass grafting (CABG) in Canada and in the United States.[14] Patient characteristics and outcomes were identified by reviewing individual charts, and costs per case were determined by similar accounting methods. The investigators concluded:

> The in-hospital cost of CABG in the United States is substantially higher than in Canada. This difference is due to higher direct and overhead costs in US hospitals, is not explained by demographic or clinical differences, and does not lead to superior clinical outcomes.[15]

U.S. in-hospital costs per patient were nearly twice those in Canada. 'It's the prices, stupid.'

Private health insurance and cost escalation: Three roads to ruin

The exceptional cost of American health care is directly linked to its exceptional reliance on private insurance. This feeds cost escalation in three distinct ways, none bringing corresponding health benefits for the population served, but all offering higher incomes for the providers and financers of care.

Holding down the loss ratio

First, private insurance generates very substantial overhead or administrative cost[16]– a point originally and strongly emphasized by Justice Hall.[17] All insurance mechanisms, public or private, incur expenses for assessing contributions, collecting and securing revenues, and evaluating and paying claims. Total contributions must exceed claims paid. The ratio of claims paid to contributions collected is in public systems referred to as the 'benefits ratio,' but private insurers call it the 'loss ratio' because it describes the proportion of premium revenue not available for other corporate purposes – including profit. Public insurers strive – and are under pressure from their political masters – to keep the benefit ratio up and limit excessive administrative costs. But private insurers try, as the term implies, to minimize the loss ratio. Public systems typically achieve benefits ratios of 95% or above; private insurers typically hold their loss ratios below 85% and may go much lower.

The difference between premiums and claims is not, of course, all profit. Commercial insurers must assess subscriber risks, design contracts, and determine relative premium structures. They must, in competition with other private insurers, identify and market to groups likely to generate a favourable (low) loss ratio, and avoid those whose claims may exceed the premium revenue they can generate. All this activity is part of the normal business of any commercial insurer, in or out of the health care sector, but it is costly, and must be paid for out of premium revenue.

The costs of preserving inequality – worth it for me!

These overhead costs are incurred in the process of allocating the costs of coverage across the insured population in proportion to their expected losses. Lower premiums are offered to those at lower risk, higher premiums are required from those at higher risk, and excluding those who cannot afford to pay premiums proportionate to their risk status. Commercial markets do not provide products to people who cannot afford them.

This is why private insurance, where it exists, covers a much larger share of the population than of health expenditures. Coverage is differentially offered to the healthy and wealthy, and is limited in terms of what it will cover. The unhealthy and unwealthy are typically priced out of the market, or simply directly excluded. Private firms are not charities, and to survive, must sell only those products, to those persons, from which they can reasonably expect a profit.

All this costly activity serves to link individual or group premium costs, and thus indirectly their contributions to finance health care, more closely to the claims they are expected to generate. This result, however, is in direct contradiction to the principles of care according to need and contributions according to ability to pay. To the extent that the members of a society have accepted these principles, then the normal activities of private insurers are complete waste motion – 'cost without benefit.' Indeed they are worse than waste, because they support the allocation of costs and access in the opposite direction – cost according to need, or at least probability of use, and access according to ability to pay.

Is this patient insured? For what? Headaches in the hospital (and the doctor's office)

The excess overhead costs of private insurers, while substantial, account for only a part of the administrative burden generated by private insurance. Estimates of the excess administrative cost of private insurance in the United States, relative to the costs of a Canadian-style universal system, include the extra costs for providers of having to deal with a multiplicity of insurers, all with a number of different types of contracts with different terms of coverage. Individuals may change coverage frequently, as they change jobs or their employer changes insurers or contract terms. Determining if an individual patient is covered, and if so for what, and then dealing with the insurer to secure reimbursement, has become a major and expensive task for American hospitals and clinics.

On top of these difficulties, insurers are under pressure to control their own costs – reduce the loss ratio – and may therefore contest or simply refuse to pay claims. Given the complexity of the financing environment, this may be a perfectly reasonable response – the provider may indeed be making an inappropriate claim on behalf of the insured. But the process of contesting claims adds further costs.

For 1999 the total of these extra administrative costs in the American health care system, both in the insurance industry itself and in hospitals, clinics, and physicians' offices, had reached an estimated $209 billion.[18] By 2004 a plausible projection would be about $300 billion, or over 17% of total American health care expenditures. This is roughly equal to the *total* health expenditures in each of the next largest systems – Germany and Japan. All of this extra administrative cost – essential activity for each participant but pure waste from the system-wide perspective – is carried forward in the extraordinarily high prices for health services that Americans face.

Who's to stop us? Enforcing Wildavsky's Law of Medical Money

The administrative waste accounts for a substantial share – perhaps as much as half – of the expenditure gap between the United States and other high-income countries. But the third and at least equally important inflationary effect of private coverage is that it provides no effective mechanisms for restraining pure price inflation in the health care sector, or for managing the appropriateness of the care provided. American providers, hospitals and physicians, charge much higher prices for their services than do those anywhere else in the world – because they can.

The mirage of private sector cost control

For years, American policy-makers have clung to the belief that some restructuring of the private insurance system could yield effective mechanisms to limit cost escalation. In the early and mid-1990s, it appeared that 'managed care' was finally working – American cost escalation had leveled off. But by the turn of the century this control had obviously collapsed, and in 2005 Americans have no coherent policy and are increasingly simply looking for ways to push the steadily growing costs onto someone else. *Sauve qui peut*. The relatively effective approaches taken elsewhere in the high-income world depend upon universal public coverage, and this remains blocked by a combination of ideological conviction and economic interest.

It cannot be overemphasized, however, that cost escalation is simultaneously income escalation. Everything that Americans pay (apart from a small adjustment for imports) – becomes the income of some other Americans. Private sector cost containment does not succeed because the people and corporations benefiting from that escalation do not want it to succeed. The administrative waste in the private insurance industry is all paid out in salaries, wages, and corporate profits. This huge market would disappear, and all those incomes with it, if universal public coverage were adopted. Many of the jobs of benefits managers in the public and private sector would go too. Markets for drugs and medical equipment would shrink, revenues of clinics and hospitals, public and private, would drop catastrophically – by over half a trillion dollars – if American health costs fell into line with those in the rest of the high-income world. It will not happen. The 'medical-industrial complex' has sufficient economic and political muscle to block any effective reform – as was amply demonstrated by the defeat of the Clinton plan.

The message for Canadians is that, quite apart from any restrictions imposed by trade agreements, once a private insurance system is embedded, it becomes difficult or impossible to remove. The revenues it generates, both within and outside the insurance industry, become both the reasons for and the means of its defense.

Little America: Pharmaceutical insurance in Canada

Again the example of the Canadian pharmaceutical industry makes the point. A Pharmacare system parallel to Medicare could provide the means, as the National Forum on Health pointed out, to improve the equity of access to prescription drugs and distribute more equitably the burden of their costs.[19] But it could also significantly reduce their over-all costs and improve the appropriateness of prescribing – which is why the pharmaceutical industry bitterly rejected the proposal.

Pharmacare could have been introduced, relatively inexpensively, in the early 1970s. Now the industry has grown so large and so influential politically, not just in Canada but internationally, that the prospects for a Medicare-style Pharmacare are gone, probably forever. Reform of the present inefficient, inequitable, and excessively costly system, supported by an American-style financing system with a large component of private insurance, underpinned by large public subsidies, will be very difficult, perhaps impossible.

No good will come of this? Of course it will – for some

The summary of world experience with private health insurance, then, is that where it exists it functions primarily as a mechanism for providing preferred access to care – shorter waiting times and particularly specialist services – for those with higher incomes. It is also a source of additional income for the providers who serve, and are paid by, that clientele. Private insurance and private billing are mutually supportive; private billing provides a market for private insurance, and private insurance coverage encourages private billing.

Outside the United States, private insurance typically makes little or no significant contribution to the overall financing of health care. While it is sometimes promoted as a way to relieve pressure on public budgets, most private insurance systems depend upon significant public subsidies or other regulatory support that offset much of the supposed benefit. The principal effect of substituting private for pubic payment is to make the mix of health care financing more regressive – increasing the relative burden at lower income levels and reducing it higher up.

Opportunities for increased fees and incomes from private billings also encourage practitioners to expand their private activity and limit their provision of services reimbursed solely through the public system. Far from improving access in public systems, private billings and private insurance tend, for perfectly obvious economic reasons, to reduce general public access.

The United States is the great exception, in which private insurance does support a significant share of health care costs – though only about one quarter after accounting for public subsidies – and public insurance is available only for the elderly and the very poor. Private insurance is the primary source of coverage for the majority of the population – about sixty percent.

Here the effects of private coverage are grotesquely magnified. The opportunities that it offers for providers to increase their incomes through private billings has mushroomed into a system costing (per capita) more than double the OECD median, and roughly fifty percent more than Switzerland – the next most costly. At present this escalation appears totally out of control. Within these costs there is a staggering level of administrative waste directly attributable to the administrative requirements of private insurance.

These massive extra expenditures yield no increased benefits, either in terms of overall health, or even levels of servicing, but only higher prices. Nor does private coverage limit public expenditure; the United States spends as large a share of national income through the public sector as any country in the world. Private expenditures are simply added on top.

What Americans do get for their commitment to private insurance is both the most regressive financing mix in the industrialized world, and the most radically differentiated access. That about forty-five million Americans are uninsured is notorious; but another sixteen million have insurance inadequate to meet their needs. Thirty-five percent of the population aged 19–64 are un- or underinsured.[20] Meanwhile those with either ample private resources or comprehensive insurance coverage have access to some of the finest care in the world. There is no better health system for the healthy and wealthy, and no worse one for the unhealthy and unwealthy.

The question for Canadians, if we are to be forced as a result of the *Chaoulli* decision to accept private coverage for public health care services, is whether this would lead merely to the entrenchment of some extra privileged access for the better-off and increased incomes for those who serve them, or whether it would initiate a slow slide towards what is clearly, and widely recognized as, an American disaster. What else may be forced on us?

There is no question of general benefit – shorter overall waiting lists, for example, or a 'more sustainable' health care system. Such claims are merely part of the marketing campaigns of those who will indeed benefit significantly from the introduction of private coverage. The central question is, how severe will be the damage to the equity, efficiency and effectiveness of the overall system, and to the unhealthy and unwealthy who most depend upon it?

Notes

1 The World Health Organization, *The World Health Report, 2004: Changing History* (Geneva: World Health Organization, 2004).

2 *Ibid.*

3 Organization for Economic Cooperation and Development, *Private Health Insurance in OECD Countries* (Paris: OECD, 2004) Table 3.12.

4 J.G. Smythe 'Tax Subsidization of Employer-Provided Health Care Insurance in Canada: Incidence Analysis' (2001) Edmonton: University of Alberta Department of Economics, Working Paper (August 19, 2001).

5 J. Sheils and R. Haught, 'The Cost Of Tax-Exempt Health Benefits In 2004' (2004) *Health Affairs* Web Exclusive (February 25, 2004) W4:106.

6 The share of national income spent by the United States on health care was over 15% in 2004, and is projected to reach 18.7% in 2014. See S. Heffler *et al.*, 'U.S. Health Spending Projections for 2004–2014' (2005) *Health Affairs* Web Exclusive (February 23, 2005) W5: 74.

7 See, for example, Organization for Economic Cooperation and Development, *OECD Health Data 2005 1st edition* (Paris: OECD, 2005) and Organization for Economic Cooperation and Development, *Private Health Insurance in OECD Countries* (Paris: OECD, 2004).

8 Organization for Economic Cooperation and Development, *Private Health Insurance in OECD Countries* (Paris: OECD, 2004) at 138–42.

9 Kenneth J. Arrow, 'Welfare Analysis of Changes in Health Coinsurance Rates' in R. Rosett, ed. *The Role of Health Insurance in the Health Services Sector* (New York: National Bureau of Economic Research, 1976) 3.

10 A.E. Wagstaff *et al.* 'Equity in the finance of health care in twelve OECD countries' (1999) 18:3 *Journal of Health Economics* 263.

11 For discussion of the role played by the medical profession in lobbying legislators and government, see Trudo Lemmens's paper in this volume.

12 A. Wildavsky, 'Doing Better and Feeling Worse: The Political Pathology of Health Policy' (1977) 106:1 *Daedalus* 105.

13 G.F. Anderson, et al., 'Health Spending In The United States And The Rest

Of The Industrialized World' (2005) 24:4 Health Affairs 903; and G.F. Andersen, *et al.*, 'It's the Prices, Stupid: Why the United States Is So Different from Other Countries,' (2003) 23:3 *Health Affairs* 89.

14 M.J. Eisenberg, *et al.*, 'Outcomes and Cost of Coronary Artery Bypass Graft Surgery in the United States and Canada' (2005) 165:13 *Archives of Internal Medicine* 1506.

15 *Ibid*. at 1506.

16 Organization for Economic Cooperation and Development, *Private Health Insurance in OECD Countries* (Paris: OECD, 2004) Table 2.5.

17 Canada, Royal Commission on Health Services, *Report Volume 1* (Ottawa: The Queen's Printer, 1964) at 732. (Hall Commission)

18 S. Woolhandler, T. Campbell and D.U. Himmelstein, 'Costs of Health Care Administration in the United States and Canada' (2003) 349:8 *New England Journal of Medicine* 768.

19 Canada, National Forum on Health, *Canada Health Action: Building on the Legacy – Volume I – The Final Report* (Ottawa: Health Canada, 1997).

20 C. Schoen, *et al.*, 'Insured But Not Protected: How Many Adults Are Underinsured?' (2005) *Health Affairs* Web Exclusive (June 14, 2005) W5: 289.

Opening Medicare to Our Neighbours or Closing the Door on a Public System? International Trade Law Implications of *Chaoulli v. Quebec*

TRACEY EPPS* AND DAVID SCHNEIDERMAN†

Introduction

With few exceptions, constitutional law in Canada is made with little express regard for the rules and institutions we ordinarily associate with economic globalization.[1] Yet there are important linkages between domestic constitutional systems and bilateral, regional, and transnational commitments undertaken by states around the world. These commitments may mirror, amplify, or conflict with national constitutional commitments. We argue that this is precisely one of the problems with the Supreme Court of Canada's decision in *Chaoulli v. Quebec (Attorney General)* – it is constitutional law made without regard for these instruments and their effects. It is, in other words, constitutional law made in a vacuum.

In the few months since the release by the Supreme Court of its decision in *Chaoulli*, commentators have rushed to offer their prognoses of the decision's long-term impact for medicare.[2] In the wake of the ruling, an old debate has been sparked anew, namely, the merits or otherwise of two-tier health care. The battle lines in the debate are being drawn along now familiar territory, some of which was canvassed by the Supreme Court justices in their decision.[3] But there is one aspect of the debate which did not surface in the Supreme Court's decision, and that is the potential implications of Canada's international trade obligations should steps be taken in the direction of two-tier health care.[4] This is a surprising and indefensible omission given the majority's purported recognition of the need to maintain the integrity of Canada's public medicare plan, premised as it is on delivering the highest possible quality of care irrespective of ability to pay.[5] Although the potential implications of international trade agreements have been canvassed elsewhere[6], it is timely to review them now in the light of the Court's ruling in *Chaoulli* and possible government responses to the Court's directive to open up the public system to private markets.

We consider here the potential implications of the North American Free Trade Agreement (NAFTA), an agreement that came into force in 1994 with the objective of creating a free trade area between the territories of Canada, the US, and Mexico.[7] This paper will examine NAFTA's provisions that are most likely to impact upon Canada's health care system and then consider their implications in light of possible reform options that governments may implement as a result of *Chaoulli*. First, however, a few words will be said about the underlying objectives of international trade and about the fundamental nature of Canada's health care system.

Progressive Liberalization

The key objective of NAFTA is trade liberalization through the reduction of barriers to trade and investment. Liberalization is largely intended to be progressive and to prevent the introduction of new measures that restrict the movement of trade or investment.[8] Existing restrictions (often in the form of 'exceptions' or 'reservations'[9]) are expected to be 'rolled back' over time. Measures to liberalize trade and investment, then, once enacted cannot be reversed but are binding on states far into the future (this is the so-called 'ratcheting' effect).[10] Short of amending negotiated texts, or nullifying these agreements entirely, commitments made are intended to be irreversible.[11]

Irreversibility advances the key presupposition underlying NAFTA (and other trade agreements): that liberalized trade will result in the more efficient allocation of scarce resources, and consequently in improved economic growth and welfare. The success of trade and investment liberalization is dependent on the presence of open markets within each of the trading partners. In an open market, goods and services are allocated on the basis of purchasing power; concerns with equity of distribution are left to other policy instruments. Such is the case with the Canadian health care system where high levels of government intervention seek to achieve goals of distributive justice by providing health care services to all Canadians based on need, regardless of ability to pay.

While popularly described as a 'single-payer public system,' Canada's health care system is in fact characterized by a wide range of public/ private relationships. At the core of the system, 'medically necessary' hospital and 'medically required' physician services are fully publicly *funded*. Outside of this core are numerous important services that are not fully publicly funded, such as prescription drugs used outside of hospitals, home care, dentistry, some vision care, nursing home care and alternative care. While provincial governments provide some of these services (e.g., through publicly funded home care programs), people often have to buy private insurance or pay out of their own pocket for these services.

In terms of *delivery* of health care services, very few publicly funded services are actually delivered by public entities. Rather, publicly funded services are predominantly delivered by private non-profit organizations (e.g., hospitals) or private for-profit professionals (e.g., physicians). This mix of public and private interests on both the financing and delivery sides of the system makes it difficult to draw a sharp distinction between what is public and what is private. As we note below, this causes confusion in applying Canada's reservation to NAFTA which assumes a clear demarcation between public and private.

NAFTA

NAFTA applies to all economic sectors including health, unless there are written exceptions or the parties have made reservations for sectors or parts thereof that they do not wish to be subject to all of NAFTA's provisions. The federal governments of Canada, the US and Mexico are obligated to 'ensure that all necessary measures' are taken in order to give effect to NAFTA's provisions, including their observance by state, provincial and local governments. Thus, the provinces are expected to adhere to NAFTA's rules, though, at bottom, the national governments of each of the NAFTA states are responsible for living up to its obligations.[12]

The NAFTA rules of most relevance to the health care sector are those in Chapter 11 on investment and Chapter 12 on services, in particular the requirement for national treatment and the expropriation provision in Article 1110.[13] National treatment, premised upon the idea of non-discrimination, is the cornerstone of NAFTA. It requires that Canada treat investors, goods and service providers from the US and Mexico no less favourably than it treats its own entities in like circumstances. This means, for example, that if the Quebec government decides to tender for the delivery of cataract surgery, it must give both domestic and US/ Mexican companies the same opportunity to make a bid and be considered for the contract.

The expropriation provision has proven to be NAFTA's most controversial provision. Pursuant to Article 1110, the Canadian government must pay compensation if it nationalizes or expropriates a US or Mexican investment, or takes a measure 'tantamount to nationalization or expropriation.' As a result, a US or Mexican investor could make a claim for compensation in the event that an action by a Canadian government in Canada deprived them of the investment rights they previously held. Investors are empowered to bring claims for compensation before NAFTA arbitral tribunals themselves; they do not need to rely on their national governments to do so on their behalf.

The difficulty with the expropriation rule is that it often is difficult to tell, outside of outright takings of title to property, when a regulation amounts to a compensable expropriation. The provision, not surprisingly, has given rise to a variety of different kinds of claims before international trade tribunals. Panels have found that non-discriminatory regulations may rise to the level of an expropriation under NAFTA so long as the deprivation is 'substantial enough' or 'sufficiently restrictive.'[14] One panel went so far as to find that even 'incidental interference' with an investment which has the effect of depriving owners of a 'significant part' of the 'use or reasonably-to-be-expected economic benefit of property' can give rise to the requirement of compensation under NAFTA.[15] Compensable expropriations, according to another panel, must amount to a 'lasting deprivation of the ability of an owner to make use of its economic rights,' though the deprivation may even be 'partial or temporary.'[16] These standards have proven sufficiently unpredictable that the governments of Canada and the US have modified the standard text used in other trade and investment treaties so as to narrow the range of compensable actions.[17] These modifications can be expected to have no effect on NAFTA's more expansive prohibition on expropriations.

As if following these governmental cues, the tribunal in *Methanex v. United States of America*, more recently, narrowly interpreted the expropriation rule in a case challenging a Californian regulation banning the use of methyl tertiary-butyl ether (MTBE) as a fuel additive in gasoline sold in the state for environmental reasons. The tribunal rejected Methanex's expropriation claim, finding that 'as a matter of general international law, a non-discriminatory regulation for a public purpose, which is enacted in accordance with due process and which affects, inter alia, a foreign investor or investment is not deemed expropriatory and compensable unless specific commitments had been given by the regulating government to the then putative foreign investor contemplating investment that the government would refrain from such regulation.'[18]

While these differing opinions of what constitutes an expropriation do not form binding precedent as do the opinions of high courts, future tribunals likely will look to these decisions for some guidance. [19]

Two key reservations purport to protect Canada's health care sector from the effect of some of NAFTA's provisions, including the national treatment rule in Chapter 12. But these reservations provide no protection from the expropriation provision – expropriations are considered simply beyond the pale. The reservations are set out in the Annexes to NAFTA, with the most critical being contained in Annexes I and II as follows:

- *Annex I*: Protects all NAFTA-inconsistent provincial measures with respect to health that were in place prior to 1 January 1994 and requires that any measures introduced after that date be consistent with NAFTA's provisions.
- *Annex II*: This reservation is important in terms of the future of the health care system as it allows governments to adopt or maintain any measure with respect to health to the extent that it is 'a social service established or maintained for a public purpose.' If hospital services are determined to be social services supplied for a public purpose, for example, the national treatment rule will not apply and access need not be opened to US hospital chains.

The applicability of the Annex II reservation depends largely on the interpretation of the phrase 'for a public purpose.' Regrettably, the meaning of this phrase is not clear. Further, the US has indicated that in the event of a dispute, it would seek a narrower interpretation of the phrase than would Canada. During discussions on the matter after NAFTA was implemented, the US Trade Representative suggested that the phrase only refers to services that are fully government funded *and* publicly delivered.[20] The US interpretation is problematic for Canada as most health care services are privately delivered. The Canadian government, on the other hand, suggested a broad interpretation of the Annex II reservation. It has emphasized 'government intent' as a crucial factor in determining whether a service is provided for a 'public purpose.'

Interpretation is particularly difficult given the mosaic of public and private financing and delivery in Canada's health care system. In the absence of a NAFTA tribunal decision interpreting the reservation, these interpretive difficulties give rise to considerable uncertainty about which services are and are not afforded protection by Annex II. There is a strong indication that the services are being provided for a 'public purpose,' however, as the intent of the government is to provide health care services to all in need. For this reason, we are of the view that the Canadian interpretation of the reservation should prevail and that all publicly funded services should be covered by the reservation.[21]

Reform Options Post-*Chaoulli*

Short of invoking the notwithstanding clause of the Quebec Charter,[22] the government of Quebec must now reconsider the role of private services in the delivery and financing of health care in the province. The government can be expected to take into account not only the *Chaoulli* decision, but also a recent report in the province concerning the sustainability of the health care system. The general theme of the report appears to be that there should be more involvement by the private sector.[23] Similar debates will undoubtedly unfold in other provinces. For example, the Alberta government indicated that it will increase the number of medical services that can be covered by private health insurance and plans to announce a new Health Policy Framework in October 2005. Here we consider some reform options that the Quebec government (as well as other provinces) might consider in the light of *Chaoulli* and assesses the potential NAFTA implications of those options. The options discussed here are those that would have the effect of providing opportunities for foreign insurers or health care providers to enter the Canadian market. To the extent that markets are opened up to US companies, trade and investment law disciplines likely will act to preclude the ability of governments to restore, should they choose to do so at some future date, a fully-publicly funded system. In this way, the principle of progressive liberalization ensures that the changes precipitated by *Chaoulli* will be difficult to reverse.

Private Insurance

The Supreme Court decision appears to require that the Quebec legislation prohibiting private insurance be amended to allow people to purchase private insurance to cover private delivery of services that are currently publicly funded as medically necessary hospital services and medically required physician services.

The first NAFTA-related question would be whether the national treatment rule requires the Quebec government to grant access to American health insurance providers. Unless it can be argued that Canada's reservations protect private insurance from full application of NAFTA's provisions, the answer must be affirmative. Clearly the Annex I reservation provides no assistance since it only protects pre-1994 measures. Any attempt to restrict the market to Canadian insurers would therefore have to rely on the Annex II reservation which allows a NAFTA-inconsistent measure with respect to health to the extent that it is 'a social service established or maintained for a public purpose.' The difficulties in interpreting this phrase have been noted, but the situation being described does not appear to present such difficulties. Private insurance involves people paying out of their own pockets to receive coverage for needed health care services that they wish to obtain from a private provider. There is no 'public purpose' involved in such a system, nor for that matter, any 'social service'; rather, there is a series of private transactions involving the purchase of insurance to cover health care services. Thus, if Quebec allows private insurance to cover publicly-funded services, it will be required, pursuant to NAFTA, to allow US (or Mexican) insurance firms to provide insurance services on the same terms as Canadian firms.

This would be a legally significant extension of the rights of US insurance firms who are presently limited to providing insurance for those services that are not publicly-funded, such as prescription drugs and vision care.[24] The actual significance of this would depend upon a number of factors, most notably the extent of consumer demand for private insurance and the extent of the business opportunities perceived by US insurers. If there was sufficient demand for their services, US insurers that are currently operating in Quebec (for example, those providing coverage for prescription drugs) may well decide to expand their offerings to provide coverage for medically necessary physician and hospital services. As well, other US insurers not presently operating in Quebec would be entitled to offer their services there. The Court, regrettably, was naïve about this possibility. Justice Deschamps maintained, for instance, that 'there is no risk that Quebec public opinion will abandon the plan.'[25]

There are currently a number of US insurance firms operating both in

Quebec and throughout Canada. Of approximately 135 companies selling supplementary health insurance[26] in Canada, about 43 are US companies.[27] In Quebec, in there are 40 US companies selling supplementary insurance out of a total of 112 companies. The services provided by these companies includes non-core health services as well as services that are not completely covered by government plans.[28] Canadians paid a total of $52.7 billion in life and health insurance premiums in 2003.[29] Seventy-five percent of these premiums were paid to Canadian-owned companies, with the remainder going to US, British and European companies.[30] These figures indicate that there is already a market for US companies to provide health insurance services in Quebec and elsewhere in Canada. It remains an open question, however, whether such companies would see any significant benefit in expanding their services and/or presence.[31]

The real impact of NAFTA could be felt, however, not simply in an increase of US insurance companies doing business in Canada, but if the government wanted to reverse its policies in the future. The majority's decision in *Chaoulli* was premised on a finding that waiting lists in Quebec are too long[32] and that the risk to life presented by inordinate wait times for treatment contravenes the guarantee of life, personal security, inviolability and freedom of the person found in the Quebec Charter of Human Rights and Freedoms.[33] The finding that there are long waiting lists was no news to the provinces. It is a problem that has been much discussed in recent years and a variety of initiatives have either been put in place or are being considered in a number of provinces in order to address the problem. In Quebec, for example, the Ministère de la Santé et des Services sociaux is in the process of implementing a software program that will provide physicians and institutions with a computerized service access management system (SGAS) that is designed to assist in managing waiting lists.[34]

It is not at all clear, however, that such initiatives will be successful and further, it is possible that the introduction of a private insurance market would hinder such efforts. Contrary to the majority's finding that the existence of a private insurance market would do no harm to the public system and would assist in the provision of superior health care services, a large number of health economics researchers have found that a private tier would in fact be a detriment to the public system. In particular, Flood and Sullivan have found that there is a tendency for countries with two-tier systems to have longer, not shorter, wait times.[35]

It is conceivable, therefore, that even if the market was opened to private insurance for publicly-funded services in Quebec, waiting lists in the public system would continue to be a problem, perhaps to an even greater degree than they are now. In the case of such an eventuality, litigation may be pursued by a patient suffering on a long waiting list but unable to afford private insurance. Such a patient would reasonably argue that *Chaoulli* ought to be reversed or distinguished. A similar case to *Chaoulli* also could be launched in another province in which the reversal or narrowing of the *Chaoulli* decision could be sought.[36] Governments also would have the opportunity of presenting fresh evidence in support of prohibitions on private insurance. The majority in *Chaoulli*, after all, complained about the lack of government evidence in support of the prohibition.[37] Chief Justice McLachlin and Justice Major described being confronted with 'competing but unproven 'common sense' arguments amounting to little more than assertions of belief.'[38] Indeed, according to dialogue theorists,[39] the structure of analysis under the Canadian Charter (and, one might contend, under the Quebec Charter) invites such reappraisals in cases where governments are able to muster better and more convincing evidence in support of rights infringements. If these litigants were successful at the level of the Supreme Court, it presumably would make redundant the ruling regarding the illegality of the prohibition on private insurance. It equally is conceivable that, given such an outcome, the Quebec government would seek to return to a one-tier system, and re-enact the prohibition that the Supreme Court found illegal in 2005.

This is where NAFTA could show some bite. As noted, the article 1110 expropriation provision has the potential to entrench the investment rights of foreign health insurers by allowing them to claim compensation if a Canadian government nationalizes or expropriates their investment or takes a measure tantamount to nationalization or expropriation. The possible impact of article 1110 in this regard can be explained by considering a hypothetical case in which a US insurance firm, Peace of Mind, Inc., enters the Quebec market to provide insurance for various elective surgical procedures. Within five years, Peace of Mind, Inc. has a significant share of the private insurance market. At the same time, the Quebec government is struggling to contain waiting times in the public sector; doctors and resources have been drained from the public system, leaving those who cannot afford private insurance with worse care and longer lines. With the *Chaoulli* decision having been vitiated, as discussed above, the Quebec government decides to renationalize insurance for all publicly funded services and amends its legislation accordingly. The amended legislation prohibits the purchase of private insurance to cover publicly funded services. Peace of Mind, Inc. finds it has lost access to much of its Quebec market and delivers a notice of intent to submit a claim to arbitration under NAFTA to seek compensation for the indirect expropriation of its investment. The Quebec government now potentially faces a large bill for returning to the system as we know it today.[40]

Private delivery of medically necessary services

As Quebec legislation currently stands, private providers are entitled to offer medically necessary health services. However, due to the inability of consumers to obtain private insurance, there is very little demand for such services. If people were able to obtain private insurance, it is possible that the demand for privately-delivered services would rise. If this were to happen, Quebec would be obliged pursuant to NAFTA's national treatment provision to allow US or Mexican providers to provide services on the same terms as Canadian providers. As with the case of private insurance discussed above, services that are privately funded are highly unlikely to benefit from the protection of the Annex II reservation which only protects social services 'established or maintained for a public purpose.' A service that is both privately financed, privately managed, and privately delivered is not likely to fall within this definition on any plausible interpretation.

There is a strong argument that Quebec would not be obliged to allow US or Mexican providers access to deliver services to people that continue to use the public system (that is, the services that remain publicly funded) as these services would benefit from the protection of the Annex II reservation. It needs to be noted, however, that on the US interpretation of the Annex II reservation, any services delivered by a private entity fall outside the ambit of the reservation, even where they are publicly delivered. Although this interpretation seems extreme, its possible acceptance by a NAFTA arbitral panel cannot be ruled out.

The real impact of NAFTA with regards to private delivery of health care services will depend on how many people actually buy private insurance, and how much of a demand there is for providers of medically necessary physician and hospital services to deliver those services on a private basis. If there is a demand, US providers may see an opportunity and so enter the market. If this was the case, the expropriation provision would apply if the government later wanted to bring these services back into the public fold. The extent of the problem posed for the Quebec government would depend on the extent of the providers' interests there. A hypothetical scenario could unfold as follows. A US corporation, New Lease on Life, Inc. invests substantially in Quebec where it opens clinics in Montreal that provide elective surgery such as hip and knee replacements. As Quebeckers are now able to purchase private insurance to cover these services, New Lease on Life's business is successful and it expands by opening clinics across the province and providing additional services that also can be accessed in the public system.

However, as in the hypothetical situation described in the context of private insurance, the Quebec government decides to renationalize insurance for all publicly funded services and amends its legislation accordingly. The amended legislation prohibits the purchase of private insurance to cover publicly funded services including those provided by New Lease on Life, Inc. and also prevents providers from extra billing or charging user fees for these services. New Lease on Life, Inc. is permitted to continue operations in Quebec, but only under contract to the provincial government. As the government already provided elective surgery services through the province's hospital system, it determines that it has capacity to provide most of the population's needs solely through that system and that it only needs an additional capacity of one clinic in Montreal. It grants a contract to New Lease on Life, Inc. to provide those services. New Lease on Life, Inc. brings a NAFTA claim, arguing that its business interests in Quebec have been expropriated and so claims compensation for lost profits. The company claims that it is unable to bill the government as much as it had billed privately insured patients; in addition, the company claims the loss of its business in those of its clinics that had to be shut down. The government of Canada (on behalf of the government of Quebec) faces a potential damages award against it which adds significantly to the health care budget.[41]

Other Reforms

The implications of NAFTA we have already discussed assume the development of a private tier following repeal of Quebec's prohibition on private insurance. However, as Flood and Sullivan argue, provincial governments can protect the quality of the public sector in other ways besides a formal ban on the sale of private insurance to cover medically necessary services. Provinces across Canada carefully regulate independent health facilities and hospital licenses. These regulatory efforts constrain private coverage further and can be reviewed and strengthened if required. So long as any new measures stress the public purpose for their implementation, they can likely be enacted in a way which would enable them to fall within the NAFTA Annex II reservation. Some provinces – Saskatchewan, New Brunswick, and Newfoundland – do not actually prohibit private insurance but do prohibit physicians from working both within the public and private sectors.[42] Physicians, therefore, must be either in the public system or out of it. Without being able to have a foot in each system, there is only limited scope for private markets.[43] Justice Deschamps referred to these kinds of measures and noted that they are legitimate means for governments to use to protect the public system (as opposed to an explicit ban on private insurance). Given these alternative means, Flood and Sullivan argue that *Chaoulli* is unlikely to deeply compromise medicare.[44]

Yet, as was noted at the beginning of this paper, the Supreme Court has also accelerated the pressures on the Quebec government to do something to improve access to health care (with one year's reprieve before the declaration enters into force). It is therefore relevant to consider the NAFTA implications of other potential reforms that would improve the health care system and at the same time increase opportunities for entry into the Quebec market by foreign companies. A reform that has been given some consideration in Canada is an *internal market model* which involves public funding of services that are provided by private for-profit or non-profit organizations who tender for contracts on a competitive basis with government-appointed bodies such as regional health authorities. Such reform should be undertaken with caution as NAFTA's Article 1110 expropriation provision may result in consequences that were not foreseen as part of the reform model.

As suggested above, we consider it correct to interpret Canada's Annex II NAFTA reservation as covering all publicly funded services, and as a consequence these services should not be subject to NAFTA's national treatment rule. On the other hand, the US interpretation of Annex II implies that even publicly funded services are not covered by the reservation if they are privately delivered; thus, NAFTA should apply. If the US interpretation were to prevail and the national treatment rule found to be applicable, Canadian governments would be required to ensure that US and Mexican providers have the right to be considered on an equal basis for contracts to deliver publicly funded services.

Regardless of the application of the Annex II reservation; however, unintended consequences could flow from the article 1110 expropriation provision if Quebec voluntarily allowed foreign entities to enter its market. For example, contracts might be awarded to foreign entities if they were able to provide services more cost effectively than domestic entities. As discussed above, the potential effect of article 1110 is that where a government allows foreign private entities to operate in a market, it may be forced to pay compensation if it later wishes to remove or restrict their right to operate in that market. Thus, the Quebec government may find that undertaking internal market reform commits it to a course of action that would be costly, if not practically impossible, to reverse at a later date. It is a trite observation that there is a need to allow governments to experiment with different reform initiatives without fear of having to pay compensation in the event of subsequent policy modifications or reverses.

Once again, a hypothetical case will serve to illustrate the potential NAFTA implications. Take a successful new form of gene therapy that is developed to treat cancer. The Quebec government wishes to fund the therapy, yet there are high capital expenses involved in setting up facilities to provide it. Taking into account its ongoing efforts to spend money to improve waiting times, the government determines that it is more feasible to contract out the delivery of such services so that they can be made accessible to all people on the basis of need. There are a number of private enterprises in Canada capable of delivering the services, but US companies are able to offer a more competitive cost structure. Notices to tender are published and contracts are awarded to a US company that will operate facilities in Montreal and Quebec City. The US company performs satisfactorily and the Quebec government renews its contracts for a number of years. Eight years later, however, the government finds that the cost of contracting out has become prohibitive due to factors including exchange rate fluctuations, contract negotiation costs, quality regulation, and monitoring. Given that the cost of providing the therapy has now dropped, the government decides to provide the services out of public hospitals. Accordingly, it gives the US company notice that it will not be re-tendering for contracts when the current contract expires. When it learns that the Quebec government proposes to have publicly funded hospitals provide the services, the US company brings an article 1110 claim based on the expropriation of its profitable business interests in Quebec. The Canadian government is faced with the possibility of having to pay a large sum in compensation if the corporation successfully argues that it has suffered an expropriation of its investment.

It is worth noting here that there has been an increasing amount of private delivery of publicly funded services in many provinces, including private diagnostic laboratories, a handful of user-pay general practice clinics and one 'private' hospital located in Calgary. [45] They provide services such as hernia operations, diagnostic imaging, and orthopaedic, cataract and other surgeries. In British Columbia, four out of five health regions have been contracting out day surgeries to private clinics to manage wait lists. Ontario has a number of private diagnostic laboratories and MRI clinics, although the government has been converting the MRI clinics to non-profit entities, and compensating the owners. For-profit MRI clinics also operate in Nova Scotia and Newfoundland. [46] It appears that the majority of private clinics are operating in Quebec, with one estimate that over 50 private clinics exist in the province. [47] There are approximately 14 for-profit MRI facilities in Quebec[48], at least four of which are located in Montreal[49]. Other clinics in Quebec provide diagnostic tests, cataract surgeries, and orthopaedic procedures. MD-Plus, located in Montreal, is a full private medical clinic. [50] The experience in Ontario provides some anecdotal evidence of the government being able to successfully turn back the clock, so to speak, by converting private for-profit clinics to non-profit entities. This should not be considered precedent that internal reform can be undertaken without any consequences under international trade law; however, as much will depend upon the nationality of the private providers and the profits they stand to lose.

Conclusion

The Supreme Court's decision in *Chaoulli v. Quebec* failed to consider a critical issue in any discussion of health care reform, namely, the implications of Canada's international trade commitments. As this paper has shown, Canada's obligations under NAFTA potentially have significant implications in the light of the *Chaoulli* decision and these demand consideration. *Chaoulli*, together with NAFTA, provides a window of opportunity for US insurers and health care service providers to enter the Quebec market. Once the ban on private insurance for medically necessary health services is removed, such opportunity may arise either from the development of a market for private health insurance as well as for privately delivered services. In addition, opportunities may come out of other reforms (such as internal market reform).[51] Although these implications were neglected by the Supreme Court, it is important that the Quebec government take them into account when assessing its next steps. In addition to thinking long and hard about the consequences of allowing private insurance or service delivery markets to develop post-*Chaoulli*, there are at least two steps the government can take to mitigate the effects of NAFTA. First, to mitigate the effect of the national treatment principle, it should ensure that future policies make explicit that they are in furtherance of a health care system which constitutes 'social services established or maintained for a public purpose.' The clearer its intention in this regard, the more likely that an international trade tribunal or panel will find the sector concerned to be protected and therefore exempt, at least from the national treatment principle under NAFTA.

Second, to mitigate the potential for US health insurers to use the expropriation provision, the government should make clear that any legislative amendments allowing private insurance and/or delivery, are no more than experiments in reform and that they may be reversed in the future. In particular, it should not make any statements that would lead US insurers to believe that the Canadian health sector will be an assured source of future profit for them. While such steps will not guarantee a favourable outcome for Canada in the event of an expropriation claim, they will in our opinion provide a stronger base upon which the government could argue for such a result.

Finally, it must be noted that this is not a problem for Quebec alone. The *Chaoulli* decision will inevitably impact upon other provinces as well. There likely will be pressure for similar cases to be brought in other jurisdictions. Depending on the ideological bent of the government involved, *Chaoulli* will either be a helpful resource to opening markets or a considerable impediment to preserving a fully public system.

Notes

* SJD Candidate, Faculty of Law, University of Toronto
† Associate Professor, Faculty of Law and Department of Political Science, University of Toronto. Many thanks to Michael Trebilcock and Lorne Sossin for comments and to Sasha Kontic for research assistance.
1 Retired Justice La Forest of the Supreme Court of Canada may have been

one of the few Justices on the Court preoccupied with such issues. See, e.g. his ruling in *Hunt* v. *T&N plc* [1993] 4 SCR 289 and Hon. G.V. La Forest, 'The Expanding Role of the Supreme Court of Canada in International Law Issues' (1996) 34 Cndn. Y.B. Intl. 89.

2 Not surprisingly, there is significant variance among these prognoses, from skepticism that the decision will deeply compromise medicare (see Colleen M. Flood & Terrence Sullivan, 'Supreme disagreement: The highest court affirms an empty right' (2005) CMAJ 173(2): 142) to fears that *Chaoulli* will mean the end of medicare as Canadians have known it (see Peter J. Carver, 'Comment on *Chaoulli v. Quebec*' at http://longwoods. com/product.php?productid=17191&page=1 and Gregory Marchildon, 'The Chaoulli case: Two-Tier Magna Carta?' at http://longwoods.com/ product.php?productid=17190&page=1).

3 See for example, in favour of increasing private sector involvement in the health care system: Brett J. Skinner, 'Quebec Health Committee Report: The Glass is Half Empty' (The Fraser Institute, July 30, 2005). On the other side of the battle line, see for example: Roy Romanow, 'Now's the Time to Stand up for Medicare' *The Globe and Mail* (June 10, 2005); Marchildon, supra note 2; Lawrie McFarlane, 'Supreme Court slaps for-sale sign on medicare' (2005) CMAJ 173(3): 269.

4 The issue of international trade obligations was not raised by the parties during the course of the Supreme Court appeal. However, the Quebec government subsequently raised the issue in the context of its application to stay the execution of the judgment, noting that it needed time to examine the implications of Canada's trade obligations. See 'Avis de Requête – À La Cour Pour Nouvelle Audition Partielle de L'Appel; Mémoire de l'intimé le Procureur general du Québec, Exposé des Faits' (para 34) – Cour Suprême du Canada No. 29272, *Chaoulli et Procureur Général du Québec*.

5 See *Chaoulli* at para. 49 (per Deschamps J).

6 See, for example, Tracey Epps & Colleen M. Flood, 'The Implications of the NAFTA and GATS for Canada's Health Care System: Have We Traded Away the Opportunities for Innovative Reform?' (2002) McGill L.J. 47(4): 747; J. Anthony VanDuzer, 'The Canadian Preoccupation with NAFTA's Impact on Health Care Services' (Unpublished, University of Ottawa, December 15, 2003); Heather Heavin, 'A Colloquy on the Romanow Report: The Romanow Report: NAFTA Reservations and Proposed Reform' (2003) 66 Sask. L. Rev. 577; and Jon R. Jonson, 'International Trade Agreements and Canadian Health Care' in G.P. Marchildon, T. McIntosh, and P.-G. Forest, eds., 'The Fiscal Sustainability of Health Care in Canada' (Toronto: University of Toronto Press, 2004) 369.

7 The General Agreement on Trade in Services (GATS) also needs to be taken into account. Our focus, however, is on NAFTA due to space limitations and because, in our view, its provisions have greater potency. For a brief discussion of the implications of the GATS for Canada's health care system, see Tracey Epps, 'Merchants in the Temple? The Implications of the GATS and NAFTA for Canada's Health Care System' (2003) Health Law Review 3. In due course, consideration may also need to be given to the proposed Free Trade Area of the Americas.

8 On progressive liberalization, see Don Wallace Jr. and David B. Bailey, 'The Inevitability of National Treatment of Foreign Direct Investment with Increasingly Few and Narrow Exceptions' (1998) 31 Cornell Int'l. L.J. 615 at 616ff.

9 On reservations and exceptions see Barry Appleton, *Navigating NAFTA: A Concise User's guide to the North American Free Trade Agreement* (Scarborough: Carswell, 1994) c. 21 and UNCTAD, *National Treatment* (New York and Geneva: United Nations, 1999) at 43–50.

10 On NAFTA's ratcheting effects, see Gustavo Vega C. and Gilbert R. Winham, 'The Role of NAFTA Dispute Settlement in the Management of Canadian, Mexican and U.S. Trade and Investment Relations' (2001–02) 28 Ohio N.U.L. Rev. 651 at 676.

11 This is why NAFTA has been described by one of us as having binding, constitution-like features. See, e.g., David Schneiderman, 'Investment Rules and the New Constitutionalism: Interlinkages and Disciplinary Effects' (2000) 25 Law and Social Inquiry 757.

12 NAFTA, Article 1105.

13 Chapter 12 applies to measures relating to cross-border trade in services, while Chapter 11 governs measures relating to US and Mexican investors and their investments in Canada.

14 *Pope & Talbot Inc and the Government of Canada, Interim Award* (2001) 13 World Trade and Arbitration Materials 19 at paras. 96 and 102.

15 *Metalclad Corporation and the United Mexican States* (2001) 13 World Trade and Arbitration Materials 47 at para. 103.

16 *S.D. Myers, Inc.* v. *Government of Canada* (2001) 40 International Legal Materials 1408 at para. 283.

17 On this, see David Schneiderman, 'Congress and Empire: Taking Investment Rules Global' [unpublished] (2005).

18 The Tribunal noted in particular that Methanex, in investing in California, 'entered a political economy in which it was widely known, if not notorious, that governmental environmental and health protection institutions at the federal and state level, operating under the vigilant eyes of the media,

interested corporations, non-governmental organizations and a politically active electorate, continuously monitored the use and impact of chemical compounds and commonly prohibited or restricted the use of some of these compounds for environmental and/or health reasons.' In the Matter of an International Arbitration Under Chapter 11 of the North American Free Trade Agreement and the UNCITRAL Arbitration Rules: *Methanex v. United States of America* (13 August 2005) at Part IV, Chapter D, para. 7 (available online at http://www.state.gov/documents/organization/51052.pdf).

19 As well, tribunals also could have resort to other relevant international arbitration decisions, such as those rendered by the Iran-United States Claims Tribunal. See, e.g., *Ataollah Golpira v. Iran*, Iran Award 32–211–2, 2 IRAN-U.S.C.T.R. 171, Iran-US Claims Tribunal (1983) and *Starrett Housing Corp v. Iran*, Iran Award Itl 32–24–1, 4 IRAN, U.S.C.T.R. 122, Iran-US Claims Tribunal (1983). The range of resources available to dispute panels with which to 'fill in the gaps' of the expropriation rule are canvassed more fully in Rudolf Dolzer, 'Indirect Expropriations: New Developments?' (2002) 11 N.Y.U. Environmental Law Journal 64.

20 The USTR stated that 'the reservation in Annex II (II-U-5) is intended to cover services which are similar to those provided by a government, such as child care or drug treatment programs. *If those services are supplied by a private firm, on a profit or not-for-profit basis, Chapter Eleven and Chapter Twelve apply.*' Draft USTR Guidelines for US States' NAFTA Service Reservations: Guidelines for NAFTA Non-Conforming State Measures (29 November 1995) Inside NAFTA 18.

21 It is also arguable that some services, even though not financed by general taxation revenues, are provided for a public purpose if they are provided by charitable non-profit organizations and made available to Canadians according to need without requiring payment. For a further discussion of this argument, see Epps & Flood, *supra* note 6.

22 As the Court split evenly over whether the ban offended section 7 of the Canadian Charter, there would be no need at this stage to invoke section 33 of the Canadian Charter.

23 Report available at: http://publications.msss.gouv.qc.ca/acrobat/f/documentation/2005/Rapportmenard.pdf.

24 Quebec's current legislation which prohibits private provision of insurance for publicly-funded services is protected from NAFTA's application on two counts. First, it was enacted pre-January 1994 and is therefore not required to be consistent with NAFTA. Secondly, it is strongly arguable insurance for publicly-funded services *is* a 'social service established or

maintained for a public purpose' and that as such, the government is entitled to restrict provision of such services. For the same reasoning, it is strongly arguable that the provision of public insurance (which would continue alongside the introduction of private insurance) would continue to be protected by the Annex I and II reservations and the Quebec government would not therefore be required to outsource its public insurance plan by giving American insurers an opportunity to operate the plan.

25 *Chaoulli* at para. 64.

26 This total comprises life insurers and property and casualty insurers, the majority of which are life insurers.

27 To determine the number of companies providing health insurance in Canada, as well as in Quebec, the following sources were consulted: Canadian Life and Health Insurance Association, Inc., 'Canadian Life and Health Insurance Facts – 2004 Edition (Toronto: Canadian Life and Health Insurance Association Inc., 2000) [hereinafter referred to as 'CLHIA Facts 2004']; Autorité Des Marchés Financiers (Quebec), 'Informations Corporatives et Financières Par Assureur,' online: <http://www.igif.lautorite.qc .ca/ inst_financieres/assurances/informations_par_ assureur.htm>; Insurance Bureau of Canada, 'Directory of IBC Members,' online: <http:// www.ibc.ca/membership_directory.asp>; Autorité Des Marchés Financiers (Quebec), and 'Rapport Annuel sur les Assurances' (2004), online: <http:// www.lautorite.qc.ca/bulletin-publications/publication-institutions-financieres/Rapport_assurance2004_final.pdf>.

28 Extended health and dental plans are the most common types of private insurance coverage and include: prescription drugs/medicines, semi-private or private hospital accommodation, special nursing services, ambulance services, hospital and medical expenses incurred outside of Canada, artificial limbs, prostheses and medical appliances, wheel chairs and other durable equipment, professional services that fall outside of government medical plans such as services from physiotherapists, chiropractors, podiatrists, osteopaths and optometrists, vision care and dental services.

29 A breakdown into premiums paid for life vs. supplementary health insurance is not available. CLHIA Facts 2004, *supra* note 27.

30 A breakdown into the amount of premiums paid to US and other foreign insurers is not available. CLHIA Facts 2004, *supra* note 27.

31 A recent Bloomberg.com report quoted spokespeople for two US health insurers who indicated that they would be assessing what opportunities might exist in Canada as a result of *Chaoulli*. See online at: http://www. pacificresearch.org/press/clip/2005/clip-06-09-05.html. However, a

spokesperson for US insurance interests has noted non-legislative barriers to US insurers in Canada. 'The population is small, and only half of Canadians are in the work force (employers are the biggest purchasers of private health insurance). Also, many Canadians live in small towns all over the country, making it difficult to provide private services in locations other than a few large cities ... furthermore, US companies also would face steep competition from the country's entrenched industry players. Manulife, Great West Life and Sun Life have about 70% of the Canadian benefits market, and all three also operate in the US.' See Council for Affordable Health Insurance, online: http://www.cahi.org/cahi_contents/newsroom/article.asp?id=654.

32 The decision was largely based on waiting list data from 1997. Despite a recent initiative, it is fair to say that since that time, little has been done to address the problem. Tom McIntosh, 'The Taming of the Queue II: Wait Time Measurement, Monitoring and Management,' Colloquium Report (March 31–April 1, 2005), online: <http://www.cprn.com/en/doc.cfm?doc=1274>.

33 RSQ, c. C-12, s.1. Justice Deschamps found the Quebec Charter's guarantee and section 7 of the Canadian Charter, '[w]ith regard to certain aspects,' virtually identical (*Chaoulli*, para. 28).

34 Ministère de la Santé et des Services sociaux, SGAS Project, online: http://www.msss.gouv.qc.ca/en/sujets/organisation/waiting_lists.html (accessed August 18, 2005).

35 Flood & Sullivan, *supra* note 2. See also in this volume: C. M. Flood, 'Finding Health Policy Arbitrary: The Evidence on Waiting, Dying, and Public vs. Private Insurance,' A. Maynard, 'How to Defend a Public Health Care System: Lessons From Abroad,' A. Den Exter, 'Privatizing Social Health Insurance in the Netherlands: Challenge Posed by the EU,' and S. Greß, 'Private Health Insurance in Social Health Insurance Countries – Implications for Canada.'

36 Low, Wakulowsky and Moysa suggest that if the Supreme Court hears the issues raised in *Chaoulli* again, it will likely be in front of the full complement of nine judges, now that Justices Charron and Abella have filled the two vacancies that existed at the time of hearing. It is difficult to predict on which side they may fall. D. Martin Low, Q.C., Lydia Wakulowsky, and Geoff Moysa, 'Failing on the Fundamentals: The Chaoulli Decision,' published online at Longwoods Publishing, http://www.longwoods.com/product.php?printable=Y&productid=17188&page=1.

37 See *Chaoulli*, for example, para. 64 (per Deschamps J.) and paras. 136–37 (per McLachlin CJ and Major J). Of course, it is possible that evidence may also be brought to the opposite effect.

38 *Ibid.* at para. 138.

39 See, e.g., Kent Roach, *The Supreme Court on Trial: Judicial Activism or Democratic Dialogue* (Toronto: Irwin Law, 2001).

40 Of course, whether or not Peace of Mind, Inc brings a claim in the first instance, and the amount of that claim, will depend largely upon the size of their interest in the Quebec market. As to whether the company would succeed, much would depend on whether a tribunal adopted a narrow or expansive view of the expropriation rule. This is precisely the sort of uncertainty that has prodded governments to narrow the scope of the rule in future treaties, as discussed in text associated with note 13, *infra*.

41 Again, it must be noted that such a scenario is only likely in the event that a US investor had a significant investment at stake. Also, as we note in text associated with note 12, *infra*, provinces are not a party to NAFTA and so are not bound to respect its strictures in the same way as are the party states. Party states, however, are responsible under NAFTA for the actions of their sub-national governments. This raises potential federalism questions, beyond the purview of this paper, about the legal and fiscal responsibility of the federal government for actions taken by provinces that are inconsistent with NAFTA.

42 Colleen Flood and Tom Archibald, 'The illegality of private health care in Canada' (2000) CMAJ 164(6): 825.

43 Flood and Sullivan, *supra* note 2.

44 *Ibid.*

45 Loreen Pindera, 'Increasing private delivery of publicly funded services?' (2005) 172:2 CMAJ 167.

46 Loreen Pindera, 'For-profit clinics are legal but "no solution"' (2004) 171:11 CMAJ 1333.

47 *Ibid.*

48 *Ibid.*

49 Susan Pinker, 'Private MRI clinics flourishing in Quebec' (2000) 163:10 CMAJ 1326.

50 *Ibid.*

51 See in this regard, Canada, The Standing Senate Committee on Social Affairs, Science and Technology, *The Health of Canadians – The Federal Role, Vol. 4*, Interim Report (Ottawa: Senate Standing Committee on Social Affairs, Science and Technology, 2001) (Chair: The Honourable Michael J.L. Kirby) at 64–68, online: Commission on the Future of Health Care in Canada <http://www.parl.gc.ca/37/1/parlbus/commbus/senate/com-e/SOCI-E/rep-e/repintsep01-e.htm>.

Possible Governmental Responses to *Chaoulli*

Promises, Promises – Setting Boundaries Between Public and Private

CLAUDE E. FORGET

It has seemed to many philosophers, and it appears to be supported by the convictions of common sense, that we distinguish as a matter of principle between the claims of liberty and right on the one hand and the desirability of increasing aggregate social welfare on the other; and that we give a certain priority, if not absolute weight, to the former. Each member of society is thought to have an inviolability founded on justice or, as some say, on natural right, which even the welfare of everyone else cannot override. The reasoning which balances the gains and losses of different persons as if they were one person is excluded. Therefore in a just society, the basic liberties are taken for granted and the rights secured by justice are not subject to political bargaining or to the calculus of social interests.

John Rawls[1]

The Chaoulli decision requires us to look at the Canadian health system no longer from the perspective of whether is works well or badly but from that of its impact on the country's proclaimed fundamental moral values. This is, after all, the unique role of our court system and it is the foremost responsibility of the Supreme Court to articulate and uphold those values. It is noteworthy that all the judges who had to deal with the case accepted that the evidence showed that individual rights to the integrity of the person had been violated but that only the four judges constituting the Supreme Court's majority in this case felt that the inherent worthiness of the health system could not be allowed to take precedence over individual rights and liberties.

Developed in the 19th century, utilitarianism as a school of moral philosophy has been a dominant feature of the 20th century. There have been countless 'great causes' pursued systematically with only passing concern to the sometimes terrible costs inflicted on individuals. Some of these causes have been at center stage during the past century (like the greater glory of the master race or the dictatorship of the proletariat); some have been pursued more discretely but with an equivalent disregard to the 'collateral damage' (like free trade for manufactured goods and services goods). Utilitarianism views social organization as a great maximizing machine: whose first task is to maximize total utility, aggregate GDP, congruence with God's plan for the human race or whatever and worry about how this total holiness, happiness or wealth is distributed only later. This provides a ready excuse for anyone who wants to believe that the end justifies the means. Economists have contributed to this tendency: get to a Pareto efficient point on the production frontier and engage later in endless and irresolvable debates about whether or not gainers should compensate losers or if it merely is sufficient that they could theoretically do so.[2]

The opening quotation from John Rawls tells us that there must be another way to look at social institutions. His contribution to political philosophy is one of the most significant of the past few centuries. He has returned and injected a new depth to the tradition of Locke and Kant. In his words 'utilitarianism does not take seriously the distinction between persons.'[3]

What the Supreme Court, through the Chaoulli decision is telling us is that, in Canada, a doctrinaire view about the health care system has been pushed so far that some individuals (particularly those on waiting lists) are paying too heavy a cost. It also says, in effect, that the very notion that this cost could be compensated for by the interests of the greatest number cannot and should not even be entertained. I find myself in agreement with this proposition.

This represents for me an overturning of previously held views. Directly involved in policy making and policy implementation at the very time when Medicare was introduced in Quebec, I enthusiastically supported and even moved such things as the induction of community based health and welfare institutions into the public sector, more or less compulsory unionization, forced mergers of institutions, regionalization, the creation of CLSCs (community local services centers) staffed with salaried physicians, fixed income targets for fee earning physicians, capping of medical school enrolments, an early version of a drug plan but, more than anything else, complete government control over all aspects of development in health and social services. Several, perhaps all, of these policies had positive results but over time one could see that they may have been pursued with a perhaps excessive zeal to put in place a 'system' whose rigidity went beyond the need to solve problems. In the 1980s, Ottawa having dropped conditional cost-sharing financing sought to remedy its loss of leverage by adopting the Canada Health Act that transformed very specific cost sharing criteria into hallowed 'principles' pushing further the 'systematic' or more accurately doctrinaire bias in governments' involvement in health services delivery.

However, 'doctrinaire' is too vague a word. 'Socialist' is more specific and more accurate; it is the word that I use, certainly not as a term of disparagement but as the best descriptive word available. The Canadian health system is the product of the times when it was conceived and first put in place: the people who created it were not necessarily socialists but socialist notions were present in the air they breathed. Canadians wear their ideology 'lite'; they do not like to identify themselves as ideologically motivated. However, to paraphrase Keynes, people who think of themselves as the ultimate pragmatists are very often acting upon ideas borrowed from dead economists... but they also prefer not to be reminded of it! Even Canada's sole socialist party prefers to be called by another name. Looking back at the policies espoused thirty years ago, most policy makers of that time probably were not conscious of their ultimately socialist underpinnings. The Canadian health system had a long gestation, going back to the 1920's but it might well have come to naught were it not for the Beveridge Report and the creation of the National Health Services in the UK, by the Labour government elected there just after World War II. Socialist (even communist) ideology and the command and control approach to social organization was at that time at its highest point of popularity, aided by the experience of wartime planning and the inclusion of the USSR among the victors of that war.[4]

While reaffirming the role of the state in regulating health services and ensuring access to health care for our poorest fellow citizens, a sound approach now requires rejecting many of the premises that have supported the particular organization of, and legislation about, health services. The Chaoulli decision makes apparent the basic incompatibility between the legitimate expectations that consumers have in our kind of society and the underlying principles that have governed health care organization and financing. Those principles are totally at variance with the individualistic values that we take for granted in every other aspect of our lives, with opportunities for choice that we deem essential, and with the notion that success in any endeavour should result from performance rather than intent.

This paper addresses three types of issues now present in our health system and attempts to show how present conceptual approaches inhibit rather than help the search for solutions.

First, our governments have approached the problem of the system's performance with an emphasis on what the Romans called 'civic virtue' as opposed to incentives. Structures are endlessly refashioned to create an environment that will, it is hoped, lead to an easier exercise of the 'correct behaviour,' such as shorter LOS, shorter waiting lists etc. Now that our public system has lost the ability to maintain its monopoly it will have to take a deeply critical view of itself and adopt institutional values better attuned to the rest of society

Second, every patient has the right to be treated with respect and enjoy the benefit of pure procedural equality within the public system. However, equality rights have a very restricted meaning in health care and are not consistent with the various prohibitions and exclusions that now exist. The slogan against two-speed health care is very abstract and is contradicted by reality: this clash deserves a close examination.

Third, the Canadian health system makes many promises. One in particular, under the label of 'comprehensiveness' brings the system in conflict not only with today's reality but clashes with any reasonable estimate about the future evolution of costs and financial resources, within the public sector. Because of that commitment, public policy is barred from looking at some vital choices that will ultimately impose themselves.

I – Improved performance cannot come about through ever more rigid bureaucratic controls

The Chaoulli case has been argued and decided on the basis of a widely shared judgement that the system is not working at optimum efficiency and, in particular, that the existence of waiting lists is creating a situation that compromises the life and personal integrity of the person. It can be said that, as there is no constitutional right to publicly funded health care, the courts could go no further to assess the capability and the duty of the system to raise its standards in this regard. Indeed for the judges that rejected the plaintiff's case, namely the opinions of the lower courts as well as the dissenting opinions in the Supreme Court, the role of the court could go no further because of the worthiness of the system's overall objectives. Such a restrictive approach denotes a serious ethical flaw that makes for disturbing reading in the opinion (albeit a dissenting one) from Supreme Court justices. Even if it is true that the health system provides very important benefits to millions of people, there is no acceptable merit in the view that these benefits in some way 'compensate' for inflicting serious avoidable harm even to a few individuals. Such a utilitarian calculus has no ethical standing when the harm in question is forced on these individuals through a government decreed monopoly and when it amounts to compromising the life or security of the person involved.

The decisions made by the parties in this case not to directly challenge the efficiency and quality of the public system is both understandable and regrettable. Federal and provincial laws governing the public health system explicitly state laudable objectives and principles. For instance, section 5 of the *Loi sur les services de santé et les services sociaux*[5] states that Québec residents are entitled to receive health and social services « adéquats sur les plans a la fois scientifique, humain et social, avec continuité et de façon personnalisée et sécuritaire ». Those and similar statements have been regarded as commitments by governments towards Canadian citizens: are these promises not susceptible to judicial interpretations? Have they no more substance than political speeches? Are lawyers overwhelmed by the difficulty of producing and analysing the required evidence or the lack thereof? In my view these remain interesting but unanswered questions.

Be that as it may, unwilling or unable to travel that route, the Supreme Court has decided that, confronted with waiting lists that it considered a threat to an individual's right to life and integrity of the person, that an appropriate remedy was the removal of the de facto monopoly of the public system that was generating these waiting lists. Some provinces, including of course Quebec, enforce such a monopoly through the prohibition of private insurance. It has been an effective tool for this purpose but this is not a necessary condition for the existence of a public monopoly. It remains for possible future judgements to determine whether other means to secure a de facto monopoly are also disallowed.

To sum up, the Chaoulli decision seems to have established a correlation between the maintenance of a de facto monopoly for the public health system, on the one hand, and a level of performance of this system such that it does not result in compromising the life and integrity of the persons that make use of it and have no practical alternative but to use it, on the other hand. This should be seen by those who are responsible for managing the public system as an invitation and a challenge to rapidly narrow the gap between what the system promises and what it can deliver. This can be done (as I shall argue) by acting on both sides of that equation.

At this point, I must add a few words about the argument that, by removing the monopoly, the public health system's ability to deliver results is fundamentally compromised. As we know, the majority opinion in the Supreme Court did not accept that argument. I believe that this opinion is correct. However, as Flood et al. correctly state elsewhere in this book, should private insurance take off in any significant way, much would depend on policies to facilitate the rapid expansion of the health services human resources pool; with a fixed human resources pool any increased demand could only produce inflation for both the public and the private sector. Initially, because of cost containment policies in effect in the public sector there may well be some unused capacity to provide additional services with minimal impact. It should also be said that the more gloomy predictions about the impact of private care emerging as a significant presence, tend to ignore that part of the case load of the public system would also shift.

As for the loss of political support for the public system that might occur where all rich and influential people opt out of the public system, it is based on improbable assumptions. First, as I shall argue later, only a relatively small proportion of the 'health care sector' is privately insurable and total opt out not realistic; second it would assume that a majority of this supposedly influential class opts out which has not happened even in Germany where, if they do, they do not get to pay for the public system; third it assumes that the political support mostly comes from the rich whereas in fact the 'poor' who pay no income tax (some 40% of the population) have far more votes and a greater stake.

A final point must be made again in the context of a discussion about the possible consequences for the public system of the emergence of a 'second tier' consisting of privately financed health care. Proof of some negative impact even if it were produced is not sufficient to clinch the argument. Governments have at their disposal many policy instruments: if no longer allowed to use monopoly, a form of compulsion, to address a problem, it would have to be shown that there is no combination of other policies that could remedy these adverse effects. The paper by Gress in this book illustrates how regulation of private health insurance can powerfully influence its impact on the public system.

For all these reasons I do not believe that the Chaoulli judgement is wrong nor that it will be reversed by some ulterior decision of the Supreme Court. Private insurance for some health services, assuming it does take off (by no means a sure thing), will bring much needed additional financial resources to a sector that badly needs them. It entirely depends on the creative (rather than defensive) response of provincial governments to this fact to ensure that this is matched by allowing a *pari passu* increase in the human resources pool, so that transfers from the public sector are minimized and inflationary pressures are not created. Although, as Hartt correctly states elsewhere in this volume, the judgement does not require Quebec to actually do anything, it would be well advised to use the stay it has obtained to put together such a creative and helpful response. In any case much of the short term scarcity, particularly of medical manpower, is policy induced.

This being said, provincial governments now aware that the public system successfully challenged once could be challenged again, should take a hard look at their objectives and their policies. As Hartt suggests, the issue of waiting time could be revisited by the courts for those who could not afford private insurance and would continue to rely on public health care thus creating an even more direct challenge. In any case, I assume that governments will also want in this newly somewhat more competitive environment, to maintain the market share held by the public system. This carries many implications and later sections of this paper will address some of them. However, I believe there is an overriding consideration that consists in the need to change the institutional culture that has prevailed in our system and that has considerably narrowed the range of policy and managerial options that have been considered as legitimate. The public health system can be improved contrary to the implicit assumption underlying much of the Chaoulli judgement and the debate surrounding it, but that requires a fundamental shake-up.

Over the years, much of the health care policy initiatives have contributed to make health care delivery an ever more tightly regulated monopoly. The 'single payer' character of the system compounded the governmental legislative and regulatory powers to produce over time an increasingly centralized style of management, a rigid, totally unionized context, capped by the enforced mergers of institutions, regionalization of structures and funding resulting in a monopoly position not only in funding but in service delivery. This should surprise no one. This situation has emerged as the natural product of the bureaucratic mindset that enjoys the 'tidiness' of regulated arrangements and dislikes the 'chaos' that accompanies market based solutions. This is the 'command and control' system of socialist economies imported almost absentmindedly into the wider context of a society that places a high value on individual rights, competition as a tool of enforcing performance and personal choice. A clash was bound to come; it has taken over thirty years because the above mentioned trends in public policy took a long time to develop fully and because policy makers have been so wedded to arbitrary ideological principles that normal corrective influences have been inoperative. Courts were fated to intervene sooner or later and indeed they have.

One of those arbitrary ideological premises that policy makers in the health field became wedded to, consisted in their interpretation of the public administration clause of the Canada Health Act. This clause I believe required nothing more than the status of single payer for provincial governments. Without conceding anything in this regard, this status of single payer could have evolved into more open forms of health services delivery, explicitly using competition between health care providers to enhance the performance of the system, encouraging diversity and innovation. Such an option, it is fair to say, was never rejected – it was simply never seriously considered for understandable contextual reasons such as the rather low level of managerial skill found among health institutions when the system was instituted, imitation of the British model of that time and perhaps other reasons. In any case a public administration model has gradually been imposed on health services delivery with the usual problems of deficient performance that is typical of that form of management especially when applied to consumer services. Confronted by the reality of unsatisfactory performance, the typical recourse has been successive waves of structural tinkering and appeals to 'accountability.'

The word 'accountability' has a nice ring to it. In one sense it is mostly an accounting concept: the spending of public funds should be described in detail so that we all know where the money has gone. As a check on the honesty of those who do the spending it is probably a good idea but as an aid in decision making its value is ambiguous. In another and more interesting sense accountability can mean measuring results according to some yardstick as an essential tool to manage a system of reward and punishment. Accountability in this second sense is a non starter in our health system as it is presently organized. The system is a bureaucratic monopoly where managerial responsibly is dispersed between the center and the 'field operators'; attributing responsibility is made almost impossible since in very many instances, and in all really important ones, it is shared. Strong unions and even stronger professional organizations or corporations mean that individual severe lapses from acceptable conduct get sanctioned if ever only after lengthy delays and at a very high institutional cost. Indeed, everything works as though individual positions (for both professionals and non professionals) had become the personal property of those who happen to hold them. In such a system no one ever fails for lack of performance; the same holds largely true for institutions themselves although on occasion trusteeship clauses are triggered leading to sweeping staff changes and reorganization. While penalties are seldom invoked, exceptional performance is rarely rewarded. Incentives are a dirty word in socialist ideology: people should be selfless, dedicated and oblivious to their personal interests; society can endure under-performance but not profit. What we do in the rest of our lives has no relevance in a health field that is treated as a cultural enclave.

Canadian policy makers have shown little interest in exploring different approaches that, in better harmony with the prevailing culture of competition and private initiative, could perhaps exert more leverage on performance. This author in a book published in 1998 suggested the introduction of the concept of 'internal markets' <u>within</u> the ambit of a publicly funded system.[6] The Kirby report has suggested a recasting of the financing rules for hospitals that would make a similar contribution.[7] To my knowledge, nothing like this has been attempted. In both cases, these were tame suggestions. This is why the Supreme Court wake-up call is as timely as it is indispensable.

Most reports that have dealt with the problems of our health care system have indicated that additional funding was required but, at the same time, that those problems were due to more than just lack of money. The Canadian health care system has to discover and exploit the power of competition and incentives to shape behaviour. After some 40 years of trying to find solutions by always moving in the same direction of increased bureaucratization and regulation, the Chaoulli case can hopefully provide the opportunity for a new direction.

II – Health Services as 'Pret a Porter'

The initial explanation given at the time of its inception for the Canadian health system was that it would allow access to health care irrespective of the patient's financial needs and that, as a result, the system would be universal in its application rather than restricted to those who could pay cash or through some private insurance. The obstacle to be overcome was, for some Canadians, the lack of adequate financial resources. In other words, the notion that all health care should be somehow uniform and that strict equality should be enforced through legislation was not a goal. Had it been mentioned at the time, it might have defeated the attempt. An element of relative 'luxury' was recognized in the form of supplements for private rooms and individual responsibility for private duty nursing suggesting that equality was not what the system was trying to install. Those were simpler times, expectations and means to meet them were more modest than they have become.

The notion of equality of all vis-à-vis health services is an intellectual embellishment of later years. The political appeal of forbidding 'two tier' health care is undeniable. After 'command and control' as a principle of organization, 'equality' is the second concept that our health care culture has borrowed from socialist dogma.

In reality, the notion of equality in our health care system has a remarkably narrow meaning. Equal treatment in our system has at most a purely procedural, as opposed to a substantive meaning: individuals should be dealt with according to the same process (albeit with respect for their dignity) without any guarantee that this will translate into equal outcomes

Perhaps because death has long been perceived (erroneously) as the great equalizer, measures to stave off death may by extension be seen to deserve the same role. However, if that belief was taken seriously, health services as presently organized are manifestly inadequate to do away with the observed disparities in life expectancies. Differences related to racial origin, social status, education and income levels still persist and free health care is far from having had the impact that some of the early advocates of our health system hoped for. Beyond the facile slogans against two tiered medicine, our system, if it were judged from the vantage point of gradually producing equality of outcomes, would rightly be deemed a failure. This does not mean, however, that the original purpose of making adequate care available to the least privileged members of our society is invalid; equality is not necessary for that.

Even in procedural terms, equal treatment in the health system has a very restricted scope at least when it comes to waiting times (the topic of choice in the Chaoulli case). Very few major health institutions, if any, operate a central management of waiting lists as is well described in the paper by T. Sullivan *et al.* as well as Wright in this volume; mostly lists are specific to given physicians, especially surgeons, within a given institutions and, *a fortiori*, specific to different institutions. As a result, patients with identical conditions are now treated very differently in terms of ease of access according to where they live, which doctor they have and where they are hospitalized; are those differences like so many different 'tiers' in the system? The Quebec minister of health mooted the idea of publicizing waiting times across institutions for specific procedures so that patients in waiting could shop around for speedier access. This has not been independently assessed but everything suggests a very tepid response. In effect, 'jumping the queue' through private insurance would not be very different from the presently condoned practice of getting speedier attention by changing physician or changing hospital, a response that the ministerial initiative wanted to encourage in Quebec and seems to work in other provinces (see the Sullivan and Wright papers in this book).

Health services are expected to treat each and every individual in a 'personalized' way, in light of that person's individual needs. Needs, here, cannot be divorced from the person; they are not only strictly medical needs and they do not correspond to what is required by the 'average patient.' What makes a service acceptable to a given patient differs from what makes it acceptable to another. Quality of service needs to address the gap between expectations and execution; it needs to be sensitive to individual preferences, habits and cultures. That is why we have and cherish institutions that cater to different linguistic, dietary and cultural communities; some will say that lack of uniformity does not imply a departure from equality. So what is the common denominator? Money costs? But in acute care no two patients even with the same condition will generate rigorously the same costs; indeed the differences can be large. Health services are not a type of 'prêt a porter.'

There is a lack of candour in attempts to pretend that a uniform approach is taken in all cases and that differential access based on ability and willingness to pay never occurs. Even within the public sector, patients whose costs are defrayed by Workers' Compensation programs (that pay not only for treatments but replace lost wages) are often given speedier access to certain procedures. There are also some services that are not 'covered' such as in vitro fertilization, that are never provided except against private payment. But there are also complementary items for which a charge is made: this is a potentially very important domain. Since this practice is not officially condoned, it is not reported and therefore impossible to document statistically. T. Sullivan refers to the private provision of intravenous cancer agents provided privately but not considered insured services. Indeed, the more one looks for it, the more one hears about examples: differentially 'better' lenses inserted at the moment of cataract surgery, non ionizing contrast media, some expensive drug therapies, some orthopedic prostheses, some implantable devices... in these (and other) cases some patients willing and able to pay can opt for the up-grade. This is done discreetly; when discussed (in private) it is officially frowned upon but it goes on nevertheless at least in some institutions. Beyond all that, a 'grey market' exists for access to some surgeries (orthopedic procedures, hernia repair, plastic surgery, obesity surgery) and a great range of diagnostic procedures.

There is a logic that is inexorably at work here. There is increasing pressure for 'evidence-based' care: new procedures, equipment and drugs are more and more subjected to the test of evaluative studies. For instance mechanical hearts were assessed and found cost effective in certain cases after their experimental installation for evaluative purposes, which was itself funded privately. Their public funding though probable is still awaited (as it is for the drug Herceptin). The use of evaluative methodologies to set thresholds for public coverage does not mean that such procedures or equipment could not be used outside of the approved indications: what if a non qualifying patient was willing to pay for one? Such issues are left unexamined and are outside the pall of polite debate at the present time. For how long, given the pressure on public finances and the growing scope of evaluative studies? Now, only new additions to the existing body of procedures are being subjected to such a test; however, many long standing procedures are being performed with no assurance about their effectiveness 'because we haven't got anything else.' Is it conceivable that one day the only 'insured services' are those that have been verifiably found effective? That would open up a huge field for private discretionary financing through supplementary private insurance.

Provincial governments should recognize that within publicly funded health services and institutions several services or service complements already are being paid for privately. In this regard, governments seem to be paying lip service to the twisted logic of comprehensiveness, to which I shall return later.[8] Better information about all this and a process to allow for a second opinion when a patient is denied access to public funding because of medical indications could only improve the process and make it more transparent. All this is bound to increase given the ever increasing pressure of innovations, the ensuing practice of rigorous evaluation: this may in time lead to a core of demonstrably effective procedures, equipment and drugs for which equal access and public funding is imperative. Around this core will emerge a growing aura of services, drugs and procedures that are 'nice to have' but not demonstrably indispensable or cost effective but that many people might want to pay for and that they cannot be justifiably be denied from having.

So after Chaoulli, there is room for private insurance and this should go much further than paying for speedier treatment. I am not clear whether existing health insurance policies allow such complementary services or supplies and up-grades to be covered. Nevertheless, if their existence was more openly recognized several consequences might follow: the problem of public funding would be recast with an additional degree of freedom. The concept of evidence-based medicine would take center stage rather than being confined to the margin of policy making as it is now and even the issue of queue jumping would be seen in a different context.

The point of the above is that the fight against 'two-tier health care,' while a very popular political slogan, is an oversimplification. There are good reasons why the observed differences persist; they are the natural consequences of the exercise of freedoms that people value more than equality: freedom to choose one's doctor, one's hospital, to legitimately use one's financial resources. Attempts to impose equality would considerably restrict or even eliminate such freedoms. There is certainly consensus in according everyone equality with regard to being treated with respect but beyond that equality would be an ambiguous improvement if it only resulted in having every patient, for example, waiting exactly the same time. Better efficiency in this regard is more important than more equality.[9]

III – Promises, Promises! Can They All be Honoured?

The often reiterated 'principles' of the Canadian health care system promise everything (comprehensiveness) to all (universality). This is assumed to be possible within the reasonable limits placed upon public expenditure by an already high level of taxation. The strains are visible and growing even after several years of more or less steady economic growth. The mid-term future provides no encouragement: expensive innovations in drugs and equipment, the diminishing ratio of working age to retirement age people having an impact mostly on revenues and secondarily on expenditures, a rising level of expectations with regard to service quality, everything points to the increased difficulty of keeping promises made in the more forgiving past. Some take a national accounting view of health care financing; according to this mode of thinking, private financing of health services provides no respite because public and private finances come from the same pool of national income. Like most accounting identities, this one is true by definition and therefore not of much use. What people spend as a consequence of a personal decision is not seen in the same light as a compulsory contribution and, more significantly, does not have the same impact on the economy.

So, is there no alternative to private financing of health services for the growing gap between public commitments and public means? It would be simplistic to make that assertion especially as some policy makers following Chaoulli are bound to strongly re-assert their commitment to public health care and to single tier medicine. What in practice, after the buzz of the press conference, could they possibly do to make good on their pledge?

They could commit to increase public spending. There is almost no operational problem that cannot be resolved when the top authority focuses both its attention and considerable resources to its solution. In Quebec, over the past two years, substantial, measurable progress has been made in reducing waiting times for many time-sensitive procedures (cataract surgery, heart surgery, cancer therapy…). While these successes are undeniable the approach taken raises some important questions: what will happen when the minister's attention is drawn in some other direction? Were the very important and targeted injections of funds and the accompanying shift of activity from teaching to community hospitals a temporary episode designed to catch up with bulging waiting lists that will end once a satisfactory situation has been established, for it later to recur after the special measures are withdrawn? Was this all a shift of activity and resources that solved a few highly visible problems at the cost of starving other needs? Finally, have these extra resources been paid for the system to do what it should have done all along within existing resources? Those are questions for which the answers are not known.

An affirmative answer to the initial question, namely, can increased public spending do the job, may therefore only lead to a very cautious yes. Confidence could be greatly increased by simultaneously addressing the fundamental dysfunctional characteristics of the system that the bureaucratic mania imbedded in government policies has produced (as argued above). Why cannot our public hospitals function as well for patients as private clinics? This is due to many things that can only be changed with great difficulty: medieval notions governing the relationship between physicians and the institutions they work in ('in' not 'for') whereby effective management of clinics and operating theatres is an oxymoron. Rigid union-negotiated labour contracts make the operation of public clinics in the evening (a patient friendly practice) impossibly expensive for the institution and not that rewarding for employees. Changing that and much else besides presupposes an unimaginable degree of social strife that makes by comparison the setting up of a private facility very attractive.

To reassure defenders of public health services and at the same time avoid throwing the baby out with the bath water, it is at the same time essential to take a realistic look at the possible financial contribution to health services to be expected from the private sector. A lot of it is uninsurable: public health is uninsurable; disability requiring long term care is for all practical purposes largely uninsurable. Among all levels of acute care, much of tertiary and quaternary care would probably be excluded by insurers themselves from private coverage in the name of cost containment as well as any coverage for those in the lowest quintile of the income distribution.[10] This still leaves a large potential for private insurance but it clearly is not a panacea. Finally, many of those who could afford the coverage offered would decline to do so and continue to rely on the public system.

My point is simple: there is room for both public finance and private finance in supporting health services. This is hardly new as the two have coexisted all along. However, after Chaoulli, there is a need to rethink their respective roles. Private financing through insurance can move from the margin to a more central position. The task of governments is to give a clear signal as to the new role of private financing (as well as service delivery) in health care that will maximize the benefits to Canadians by using the respective strengths of the two players, so to speak. This is what it might look like:

In fields of activities where public financing must remain the only game in town, there is enough to do, if it is to be done right, to absorb more than all the financial resources that could be freed up through a larger role for private financing in other areas. Public health, services for disability-inducing physical and mental illnesses as well as heavy chronic conditions and tertiary care services represent a growing burden where substantial progress is desirable. Even with some resources shifted over to these responsibilities from other fields, governments would need to simultaneously in terms of service delivery, move away from the command and control approach and foster private provision in a competitive environment with public institutions. Not only could this improve performance and help reduce expenditure increases but it would compel governments to clarify their objectives in terms of expected results and standards of delivery, sometime seldom done in the too widely held belief that public institutions automatically do the best thing without specific prompting. With regard to tertiary care, a greater focus on an evidence-based approach as a tool to define public insurance coverage would explicitly open a field for private insurance of nice to have up-grades. Conversely, in all these fields, drugs (and home care for that matter) should be included in public coverage, whether for institutionalized patients or not. Drugs are an essential ingredient of almost any therapy and their stand alone coverage (where it exists) is an anomaly.

With regard to secondary acute care services, given the Chaoulli decision, provincial governments should be inspired by the Chinese proverb 'welcome what you cannot avoid.' This welcome is justified for the following two reasons: first, provincial governments need private insurers to take as much room as they can to free up public financial resources needed in the other domains left to their responsibility as described above.

Second, provincial governments can make use of the competition from private providers to reverse the trend to bureaucratization and a monopolistic management style that refuses to link financing rules and performance. To achieve this result much more is needed than a passive acceptance of the creation of private providers in secondary care. While a full discussion of the required steps would largely lie outside the scope of this paper, relevant headings can be briefly mentioned:

1. Abandonment of budgetary allowances in favour of payments for episodes of treatment by public hospitals;
2 Spelling out clear and stringent quality of care standards and a neutral enforcement mechanisms on both private and public hospitals;

3. 'Making room': in the training of health care professionals for the expansion in demand for services that could result from private financing of some services so that this has a minimal impact on the health-specific inflation rate;
4. Devising a distinction within the public sector between the *service purchase* function and the *service delivery* function so that that both private insurers and public purchasers can indifferently obtain services from either public or private institutions.

When governments took over the financing of hospitals they confronted organizations they could relate to: many hospitals are larger than the typical government department. The process of inducting hospitals into a public administration type of regime, the command and control model, the rigid hierarchies, the unionization, all of that came naturally to governments.

Not so with primary care that is largely community based and non-institutionalized: a privately operated cottage industry. The inclusion of primary medical care within Medicare proceeded on the premise of continuing private delivery. There were clearly no alternative at the time but, in that context, this inclusion may have been a mistake. The average cost of primary health services by itself would not represent for the average family a very significant burden; a special program of financial help for the lowest quintile of households would be manageable: such a regime might have prevented the emergence of a problem which constitutes the second most frequently heard grievance against the Canadian health system: the seemingly growing difficulty of finding a family physician. What public financing of primary care achieved, in that regard, was to remove any monetary incentive for primary care providers to show flexibility in service delivery modes, to adapt to consumer preferences (as a condition for their own success and even survival) and to perform efficiently large volumes of procedures. There is little discussion in Canada about problems of access to dentists, pharmacists, and psychologists in private practice; there is no ground to suppose that privately provided primary medical care would be much different. Not only have primary care providers lost the direct incentive for meeting patients' expectations, but governments' later attempts at devising and implementing alternative delivery modes that required those providers' cooperation very often met with a cold shouldered reception or those initiatives were held to ransom.

While the Chaoulli case does not directly impact this issue, the need to take a broad view of where and why the publicly financed system of health care has demonstrated lack of effectiveness requires a redefinition of the boundaries between private and public spheres of responsibility. Most reports of studies of that system deal at length with primary care and the need to improve its performance. The implications should be clear: the present approach is not working. De-insuring primary care while (after careful consideration) channeling public funds (to guarantee financial accessibility to those for whom even the modest premiums would exceed their means), exclusively to an alternative model of primary care management and perhaps requiring private insurers to similarly confine their coverage to the same channel, might prove to be the necessary road to a reform of primary care that may otherwise never come.

Conclusions

I have tried to show that ideological premises dictate most of the discussions about the Canadian health care system. They are found in the arguments presented by provincial attorneys general in the Chaoulli case and are likely to loom large in provincial health ministers' reaction to the Supreme Court judgment. The survival of socialist conceptions down to the 21st century is difficult to account for in a society that otherwise fervently espouses individualistic values, the use of incentives and the emergence of profit in the pursuit of consumer satisfaction and the role of private initiative to promote innovation that together combine in the so-called capitalist system. The infatuation with socialist models of organization fifty or forty years ago among intellectuals and some politicians is not so surprising but the persistence of these ideas in that one sector deserves attention.

What continues to support socialist modes of thinking in health care is closely related to the role that sector of activity has come to assume in this country: the Canadian health care system is what for many people defines Canada. It is what defines Canada mostly vis-à-vis the United States, the country in regard to which this most needs to be done in clear, unmistakable form. Nationalism is a potent force whose effects we, like every one else, are much more astute to detect in others than in ourselves. Publicly financed health services can prosper, and indeed perform better, without the inhibiting institutional and ideological paraphernalia with which it is burdened; but without that it might not be as much the identity fetish of today. Canadian nationalists in pursuing their political ends are holding the Canadian health care system hostage. How much longer?

Notes

1 *Johns Rawls, A Theory of Justice*, rev. ed. (Oxford: Oxford University Press, 1999) 24.
2 I.M.D. Little, *The Critique of Welfare Economics*, 2nd ed. (Oxford: Oxford University Press, 1957).
3 Rawls.*supra* note 1 at 24.
4 The noted historian François Furet has brilliantly analyzed the Western democracies' infatuation with the socialist model of organization and in particular the command and control system of economic management in *Le passé d'une illusion, essai sur le communism au XXème siècle* (Paris: Editions Robert Laffond, 1995). Also available in English translation.
5 L.R.Q., ch. S-4.2
6 Monique Jerome-Forget and Claude E. Forget *Who is the master? A Blueprint for Canadian Health care Reform* (Montreal: IRPP, 1998).
7 Canada, Standing Senate Committee on Social Affairs, Science and Technology, 'The Health of Canadians – final report on the state of the health care system in Canada' vol. 6, (October 2002). Chapter 2 discusses at length alternative financing methods for hospitals and recommends 'service-based' funding.
8 The burden rests with provincial governments alone as they have always had the ultimate responsibility for defining what services they pay for. With block funding the Federal government has abandoned any pretence of influencing those decisions as was well demonstrated by the recent abandonment of suggestions to restore conditional programs (Kirby had recommended no less that 17 earmarked funds!).
9 It lies well beyond the scope of this paper to attempt to develop a theory of justice in the provision of health services. The masterful contributions of the past century to social ethics suggest that equality must be subordinated to other objectives in a full fledged ethical theory of justice. See John Rawls, *A theory of Justice* rev. ed., (Oxford: Oxford University Press,1999) and Robert Nozick, *Anarchy, State and Utopia* (New York: Basic Books, 1974).
10 A more complete analysis of the distinctions between, and the characteris-

tics of, various categories of health services as well as the implications of this for public vs. private finance and service delivery can be found in Claude Forget, 'Comprehensiveness in Public Health Care: an impediment to effective restructuring' 11 (3) Policy Matters (Montreal: IRPP, October 2002).

Politics and Paradoxes: *Chaoulli* and the Alberta Reaction

TIMOTHY CAULFIELD AND NOLA M. RIES

Introduction

It would be an understatement to say that the *Chaoulli* decision created a political stir across Canada. For many, including various national and provincial politicians, the case was viewed as a disastrous blow to the integrity of Canada's public health care system. In the face of such a potentially explosive decision, many provincial leaders strove to put a positive 'public health care' spin on the decision, suggesting that the case was a wake up call to provincial governments to do their best to provide adequate support to the public system. Likewise, the federal government implemented a damage control strategy that, in the end, amounted to little more than non-specific claims about how steps have already been taken to improve the waiting list issue.[1] For many in the academic community, the case generated shock and grave disappointment. One commentator lamented that the case could emerge as the 'Two-tier Magna Carta.'[2] It has been noted that the majority ruling of the Supreme Court of Canada casually dismissed available evidence regarding the implications of a private tier and mishandled the comparative analysis of other countries' health care systems.[3]

One province, however, met the *Chaoulli* decision with open arms.[4] Indeed, for Premier Ralph Klein and the Alberta Government, the Supreme Court decision could not have come at a better time. Amid plans to introduce a variety of controversial health care reform strategies that mix public and private options, the so-called 'Third Way,'[5] the *Chaoulli* decision provided the Alberta Government with powerful judicial affirmation.

In this chapter, we explore the Alberta reaction to the *Chaoulli* ruling.

In our view, Alberta is the jurisdiction most likely to use the decision as a catalyst for health care reform that embraces a larger role for private financing and insurance. Like Québec, Alberta's existing health insurance scheme bans private insurance,[6] so *Chaoulli* has clear legal ramifications for Alberta's legislative framework. However, one of the ironies of the situation is that Alberta is in an enviable financial position with resources to invest in public health care if it so chooses. However, it clearly suits the Klein government's ideological agenda to argue the public health care system is broken and the *Chaoulli* decision compels change.

The Alberta Reaction

Somewhat surprisingly, there are very few official statements from the Alberta government about the *Chaoulli* decision. However, the brief press release issued from the Premier's office the day of the ruling leaves little doubt that Premier Klein and the government view the ruling as a ringing endorsement of their suggested reform strategies. The press release, in its entirety, states:

> The Supreme Court of Canada has ruled that Canadians have the right to timely access to health services. This includes ruling that prohibiting patients from using private financing and private insurance where wait times are excessive, violates the Charter of Rights. The Alberta government is very pleased with this decision. Premier Klein fully supports any change that will allow Canadians more choice in getting timely access to the health care services they want.[7]

However, Premier Klein's July 30 editorial, published jointly in the Edmonton Journal and Calgary Herald newspapers, is the most telling account of *Chaoulli*'s impact on Alberta's political leadership.[8] While not an official statement of the government's position, the editorial reveals both Klein's views and how the case is seen in the context of the Third Way reform proposals. Not surprisingly, Premier Klein declares the case to be a crucially important moment in the history of health care reform in Canada, suggesting that there 'can be little doubt that the Supreme Court of Canada decision has forever changed our health-care landscape.'[9] On a personal level, Premier Klein clearly sees the case as a kind of declaration of victory in his long battle with public health care proponents over the evidence concerning the impact of privatization. He noted as follows:

> In rendering their judgment, the Supreme Court also took special care to demolish the myths that the defenders of the status quo have been telling Canadians for years. The people resistant to change in Canada's health-care system have maintained for years that an increase in the choice Canadians have in getting their health care would destroy our current health- care system. ... In other words, the hollow rhetoric and pointless scare-mongering is over. ... Case closed.[10]

Premier Klein then continues on to suggest that Albertans need a health care system with more 'choice' – the term 'choice' being the Klein government's long-standing euphemism for private options:

> Choice can be found in a supplementary insurance plan to privately fund non-emergency medical services, with the exception of mental health and clinical psychology. In simple terms, it means that if you are in pain or suffering and cannot wait in line, you should be able to buy the health care you need. The Supreme Court of Canada has ruled that governments cannot deny you this right.[11]

Premier Klein's almost gleeful acceptance of the Supreme Court ruling contrasts sharply with political statements that emerged from other provincial jurisdictions.[12] Elsewhere in Canada, the focus seemed to be on minimizing the impact of the case and crafting news strategies to insulate the health care system from a shift toward more privatization. For example, the Manitoba Minister of Health, Tim Sale, was quoted as stating that '[w]e may need to change how we protect medicare but there was determination from the two [Provincial Health Ministers] that I spoke with, and I've certainly heard the same from Saskatchewan, we want to defend a universal health care system.'[13] Prime Minister Paul Martin did his best to play down the decision and vowed 'we are not going to have a two-tier health-care system in Canada'[14] Federal Health Minister Ujjal Dosanjh used the case as justification to 'strengthen the public health care system so there is no need for a private system.'[15] And Québec Premier Jean Charest declared that his government is 'going to do what we have to do to preserve the health-care system in which we believe.'[16]

The 'Alberta Paradox'

From a political perspective, the Alberta Government's reaction to the *Chaoulli* decision is hardly surprising. As noted, the government, if not the majority of Alberta citizens, has long supported, explicitly and implicitly, the use of private market strategies as a means of addressing health care reform – such as the push to use for-profit health facilities within the publicly funded system.[17] Nevertheless, there are a number of reasons why the Alberta position is both ironic and inconsistent.

First, the Alberta Government has a history of being suspicious of 'judicial activism' (this distrust was most recently apparent during the gay-marriage debates) and Klein has often expressed frustration with the 'maddening trend toward judge-made law.'[18] Based on his past criticism of meddlesome judges, one would expect Klein to side with the dissent in *Chaoulli*, where Binnie, LeBel and Fish emphasized that '[t]he resolution of such a complex fact-laden policy debate does not fit easily within the institutional competence or procedures of courts of law.'[19]

However, with *Chaoulli*, the Alberta government finds itself in the inconsistent position of embracing that exact kind of judicial interference it has, in the past, decried. The *Chaoulli* ruling significantly erodes the Québec government's ability to make health care policy and represents a potential major expansion the scope of section 7 of the *Charter*, which arguably opens the door to more so-called judicial activism.[20] In fact, Klein even goes further than the Supreme Court justices, asserting that citizens 'have a constitutional right to be, and stay, healthy.'[21] Klein's vocal acceptance of both the conclusion in and reasoning behind the *Chaoulli* ruling seems, to say the least, ironic given his government's threats to use the notwithstanding clause in reaction to other Supreme Court rulings.[22] Can Klein have it both ways?

This ironic acceptance of the ruling is made all the more stark when one considers the Alberta government's tepid response to the Romanow Commission on the Future of Health Care in Canada. Klein dismissed the Romanow Report as 'a non-starter,'[23] maintained that many of its recommendations call for unconstitutional federal interference with provincial authority, and refused to participate in the Health Council of Canada.[24] As compared to the Supreme Court ruling in *Chaoulli*, the Commission report offered a far more comprehensive analysis of the issues associated with private health care and waiting lists.[25] The Commission largely rejected the use of a second tier as a means of addressing waiting lists:

[T]hose who argue that the public system is no longer able to manage the situation fail to take into account the progress that is being made in some jurisdictions. In addition, private facilities may improve waiting times for the select few who can afford to jump the queue, but may actually make the situation worse for other patients because much-needed resources are diverted from the public health care system to private facilities.[26]

The second reason Alberta's reaction can be considered ironic relates to the quality of the Alberta health care system. Though it is true that there are problems with all health care systems, Alberta is often touted as having the best health care in Canada. The Capital Health Authority, the region that includes Edmonton, has, on several occasions, been rated as the top in the country.[27] In addition, there is evidence that, in general, Albertans are satisfied with the existing system. A recent survey found that '[e]ighty nine percent of Albertans were very or somewhat satisfied' with the health care services they received in 2004 (up from 87% in 2003) and 74% were very satisfied or somewhat satisfied with the overall system.[28] The same survey found that most Albertans (61%) thought it was easy or very easy to access services. Only 3% stated that they were unable to get the services that needed. In addition, for those who used hospital services, almost all were very or somewhat satisfied with the access to emergency care (69%), outpatient care (77%), and inpatient services (75%).[29] Likewise, polls consistently show that Albertans want the government to invest in health care.[30] So, the Alberta government is in the odd situation of adopting the most aggressive reform strategies in the province that, to some degree, needs them the least (and, as discussed below, this may have implications for how *Chaoulli* would apply in Alberta).

Third, of any Canadian province, Alberta likely has the most resources available to address the waiting list issues within the public system. Due to the ongoing availability of oil revenue, the Alberta government often has a surplus and is now debt free. The provincial surplus is currently calculated at $2.8 billion, which the government has said it will invest in 'priority areas,'[31] but health care is not identified as one of them.[32] Alberta's rosy fiscal situation has been the source of ongoing tension with the federal government.[33]

In addition to its financial wealth, Alberta is also home to one of Canada's most comprehensive waiting list initiatives. The Western Canada Waiting List Project, based at the University of Calgary, has done considerable research on the complex nature and dynamics of waiting lists.[34] This and other Alberta initiatives have suggested that the first step in addressing wait lists is to deal with the management and monitoring of wait lists.[35] In addition, Alberta is also one of the few provinces that has a relatively complete waitlist registry that allows the public to access information about waiting times associated with specific procedures and individual practitioners.[36] One health care ethics commentator has described this registry as a 'good example of the sort of detailed reporting that should be available in all jurisdictions, and for all procedures ... .'[37]

Applying *Chaoulli* in the Alberta Context

The critical question for all jurisdictions across Canada is just how significant the *Chaoulli* impact will be. As Professor Peter Russell explains in pages 5–18 of this volume, the actual legal scope of the decision can be interpreted quite narrowly. Importantly, Deschamps points out that '[t]he appellants do not contend that they have a constitutional right to private insurance'[38] and McLachlin and Major comment that '[t]he appellants do not seek an order that the government spend more money on health care, nor do they seek an order that waiting times for treatment under the public system be reduced.'[39] So, in Professor Russell's view, '[w]hether Quebec allows the decision to stand, and whether other provinces that have prohibitions against private insurance follow Quebec will be decided by politicians ... .'

Although the legal applicability of *Chaoulli* outside Québec is debatable (since there is not a majority ruling that a legislative prohibition against private insurance violates the Canadian *Charter*), Premier Klein clearly seeks to 'embrace the change' and promises the 'Alberta Government is moving swiftly to remove those barriers to accessing health care, not just because it is a legal requirement, but because it is a moral responsibility.'[40]

Alberta is one of several provinces with health insurance legislation that imposes prohibitions against private insurance similar to Québec (along with British Columbia and Prince Edward Island).[41] The Alberta *Health Care Insurance Act*[42] prohibits private contracts of insurance for services covered under the public system.[43] Physicians may opt out of the public plan,[44] but they are not eligible for payment from the government.[45] Given this likeness to the impugned provisions in Québec, the

Alberta health insurance regime is subject to the same arguments that convinced the majority of the Supreme Court that the prohibition unjustifiably infringes on rights to life and personal security.

Yet, the mere existence of a legislative prohibition against private health insurance is not sufficient to trigger the application of fundamental constitutional rights (or quasi-constitutional rights, as in the case of the Québec *Charter of Human Rights and Freedoms*). The legislative prohibition must be combined with ill-managed wait lists and improperly-resourced public health care systems that increase risk of mortality and serious morbidity. The *Chaoulli* decision is premised on the perception that '*most* Quebeckers have no choice but to accept delays in the medical system and their adverse physical and psychological consequences.'[46] The McLachlin and Major decision clearly states that a ban on private health insurance 'might be constitutional in circumstances where health care services are reasonable as to both quality and timeliness.'[47]

If residents in other Canadian provinces, such as Alberta, generally have timely access to health care of reasonable quality, then the case cannot be made under s. 7 of the *Charter* for opening up the system to a second tier of private insurance. As noted earlier, polls indicate that the majority of Albertans are satisfied with their ability to access needed health care services through the public system. At present, we are unaware of evidence to suggest that most Albertans face delays that cause physical and mental hardships serious enough to trigger the application of s. 7 of the *Charter*.

Even according to the Fraser Institute, a proponent of market-driven health care reform, Alberta ranked only behind Manitoba and Ontario in having the third shortest wait between referral from a general practitioner and treatment (averaged across 12 specialties), with an average of 17.8 weeks, a reduction from the previous report.[48]

But what of the patients in Alberta – statistically, likely a very small number – who do face lengthy waits that seriously affect their quality of life and prognosis? Those patients could attempt to challenge the legislative prohibition on private insurance (if it remains in effect) and the *Chaoulli* ruling would clearly provide a strong precedent in their favour. Another option for such patients is to obtain needed care outside the province and seek reimbursement from Alberta Health, an option available under the Alberta Health Care Insurance Regulation.[49] The dissenting judges in *Chaoulli* specifically refer to this type of mechanism as a 'safety valve' for patients who face delays in accessing care:

The safety valve (however imperfectly administered) of allowing Québec residents to obtain essential health care outside the province when they are unable to receive the care in question at home a timely way is of importance. If, as the appellants claim, this safety valve is opened too sparingly, the courts are available to supervise enforcement of the rights of those patients who are directly affected by the decision on a case-by-case basis. Judicial intervention at this level on a case-by-case basis is preferable to acceptance of the appellants' global challenge to the entire single-tier health plan.[50] .

Evidence indicates that patients in Alberta do access this mechanism, but with varying degrees of success. In 2004–05, the Alberta Department of Health received 100 requests for reimbursement of out-of-country health care, but only approved 34.[51] In 2003–04, 95 claims were submitted and the Department reimbursed 44. Although out-of-country treatment may be reimbursed for medically necessary services that are unavailable in Alberta, the government reportedly indicated it 'has agreed to send Albertans to other countries for procedures that are available locally, such as hip replacements, if a patient's health is deemed at risk because of long waiting times.'[52]

If the public health care system generally meets the needs of patients, and if patients can seek coverage for out-of-country care in pressing circumstances, there is little, if any, basis to support fundamental changes to the existing system, and even less basis to argue the divided ruling in *Chaoulli* compels such change. Regrettably, however, the McLachlin and Major decision may create a perverse incentive for an ideologically driven government to under-resource the public system to bolster its argument that the system is failing and requires (privatized) reform.[53] It is not clear whether this is a strategy Klein will adopt.

However, post-*Chaoulli*, the Alberta government has already acted to implement legislative and policy changes in the health care arena. Approximately one month after the *Chaoulli* ruling, the government revealed amended regulations under the *Health Care Protection Act* that will remove restrictions on procedures private clinics can perform and the fees they can charge.[54] Several weeks later, the government updated its Third Way health reform strategy to include a consideration of 'how private, supplementary health insurance might play a role in funding accessible, high quality health care in Alberta.'[55] There can be little doubt that the *Chaoulli* ruling facilitated these moves.

The *Chaoulli* ruling and the Klein reaction has certainly perked up insurance company ears, which already sell policies to Albertans to purchase services in other jurisdictions, typically the United States.[56] A vice-president of the Canadian Life and Health Insurance Association told a Calgary newspaper that 'We're all watching this very carefully of course. It's certainly important and it has implications for the industry.'[57] A small number of private health insurance companies and health brokerage companies that arrange for out-of-country care have started to spring up in Alberta,[58] and more may follow.

Conclusion

At this early stage, it is difficult to predict how far the Alberta government may go in expanding private health care. However, Premier Klein's enthusiastic response to the *Chaoulli* ruling suggests he will swing that crack in the door as far open as is politically palatable. Yet, the Alberta government has a reputation for more talk than action in some of its previous controversial health reform suggestions. In 2002, the government-commissioned Mazankowski report[59] recommended numerous changes to Alberta's health care system, including delisting services and expanding private sector financing and delivery. The government soon endorsed all the report's recommendations and struck a committee to recommend services that should be de-insured. In an anti-climactic result, the Alberta Health Minister eventually admitted the committee could not reach agreement about what services should be excluded from public insurance, noting that '[w]hether something is beneficial or not to an individual is sometimes difficult to quantify. Answers don't come in black-and-white packages. They normally come in shades of grey.'[60]

At the end of the day, Klein's enthusiastic response to the *Chaoulli* ruling may be much hype and Alberta's proposed Third Way initiatives may lead to less than dramatic reform. In the words of a recent Calgary newspaper editorial, 'always the sizzle, never the steak.'[61]

However, the *Chaoulli* ruling clearly changes the legal landscape, despite its ostensible application only in Québec. Premier Klein readily interprets it as establishing a mandate for change in Alberta and the publicity the case generated may shift the attitudes of some Canadians to support greater choice in purchasing care privately.[62]

While other provinces scramble to protect public health care and reinforce efforts to reduce waiting times to '*Chaoulli*-proof' their systems, Alberta may well take another path. How paradoxical that the premier who scorns judicial activism may use a Supreme Court decision to justify a privatization agenda and how paradoxical that a province that rolls in wealth may refuse to sustain a public health care system where access is based on need, not ability to pay.

Acknowledgements

The authors thank Laura Inglis, Vincent Kurata, Megan Koper and David Busch for their quick and helpful research assistance.

Notes

1 See, for example, CBC News, 'Ottawa urged to meet with provinces over health-care decision' (9 June 2005) http://www.cbc.ca/story/canada/national/2005/06/10/healthcare050610.html, where it is noted that the federal government often refers to the $41 billion it has recently invested in health care.

2 Gregory Marchildon, 'The Chaoulli Case: Two-Tier Magna Carta?' (2005) (www.longwoods.com/product.php?productid=17190&page=1) (Aug 22, 2005).

3 See Colleen Flood and Terrence Sullivan, 'Supreme Disagreement: The Highest Court Affirms an Empty Right' (2005) 173 Canadian Medical Association Journal 142.

4 The contrast between the Alberta response and other jurisdictions was noted in an Edmonton Journal story that appeared the day after the decision was released. 'While other provincial governments reacted with anger, frustration or confusion Thursday to the Supreme Court of Canada's rebuke of the nation's medicare system, Alberta's expressed delight.' Jason Markusoff, 'Alberta Government very pleased with this decisions' *Edmonton Journal* (10 June 2005) A3 at A3.

5 News Release, Alberta Government, 'World-wide health system innovators to speak Third Way discussion' (www.gov.ab.ca/can/200504/178052F4D8C35-AFC8–4FBD-9) (Aug 22, 2005). The Third Way is comprised of twelve action areas. See online: Alberta Government *www.health.gov.ab.ca./about/reform/getting.htm* (last accessed Sept. 7th 2005).

6 See *Alberta Health Care Insurance Act*, R.S.A. 2000, c. A-20.

7 Alberta Government, News Release, 'Premier's Statement, Supreme Court Chaoulli decision' (9 June 2005).

8 Ralph Klein, 'Time to embrace change in health care: Albertans have a right to more choices in obtaining the health care they need' *Edmonton*

Journal (30 July 2005) A17, Ralph Klein, 'Opening access to health care choices is a moral duty, says Klein' *Calgary Herald* (30 July 2005) A15. This editorial was subsequently printed in the Toronto Star: Ralph Klein, 'Alberta moving ahead on private health care; Supreme Court ruling shows that province has a moral responsibility to act, says Ralph Klein' *Toronto Star* (9 August 2005) A13.

9   *Ibid.*

10   *Ibid.*

11   *Ibid.* Klein suggests that this is not 'queue jumping': 'Not jump the line, but move out of the line. Move out of the publicly-funded health-care system and into an expanded parallel system that has more capacity to end your pain and suffering, but to do so at your own cost.' Failing to see that private options are another way of injecting funds into health care (this is one reason the US spends more on health care than any country in the world), he states: 'The answer is not more money. The answer is more choice.' *Ibid.* But, as noted by Steven Lewis, 'Neither premiums, nor co-payments, nor surtaxes based on use, nor offloading programs will fix health care. They will merely increase citizens' and businesses' costs and erode equity.' Steven Lewis, 'Single payer, universal health insurance: still sound after all these years' (2004) 171 Canadian Medical Association Journal 600.

12   The positive, pro-private care, spin on the *Chaoulli* decision was found in many other Alberta news publications. See, for example, Kathleen Harris and Bill Kaufmann, 'Court Gives Two-Tier Health Big Booster Shot' (10 June 2005) *Edmonton Sun* 2 at 2: 'Yesterday's Supreme Court judgment says the government's 'monopolistic' grip over the system, as patients suffer and die on long waiting lists, is unconstitutional.'

13   Dennis Bueckert, Canadian Press 'Provinces to discuss how to respond after high court health care ruling' (10 June 2005) C-Health News (http://chealth.canoe.ca/health_news_details.asp?news_id=14804&news_channel_id=0. (Aug 24, 2005).

14   Kirk Makin, Jeff Sallot, Rheal Sequin, 'The New Face of Medicare' (10 June 2005) *Globe and Mail* A1 at A1.

15   CBC News (www.cbc.ca/news/background/healthcare/ruling_reaction.html) (Aug 29, 2005).

16   *Ibid.* at Al.

17   Timothy Caulfield, Colleen Flood and Barbara von Tigerstrom, 'Comment: *Bill 11, Health Care Protection Act*' (2000) 9 Health Law Review 22.

18   John Geddes, 'Bashing the Judges: Critics are Taking Aim at Judicial Activism' (8 March 1999) *Macleans* at 23.

19   Para. 164.

20 For example, the dissenting judges are very critical of the majority's expanded notion of what constitutes an arbitrary law and argue that '[i]f a court were to declare unconstitutional every law impacting 'security of the person' that the court considers unnecessary, there would be much greater scope for intervention under s. 7 than has previously been considered by this Court to be acceptable.' See para. 234.

21 Editorial, *supra* note 8. McLachlin C.J. and Major J. explicitly noted that '[t]he *Charter* does not confer a freestanding constitutional right to health care.' Para. 104.

22 See, for example, CBC News, 'Alberta May Invoke Notwithstanding Clause over Same-Sex Marriage' (27 July 2005) (www.cbc.ca/story/canada/national/2005/07/27/Alberta-same-sex). It is interesting to note that, not surprisingly, the Quebec Government suggested it was considering use of the notwithstanding clause in the context of the *Chaoulli* decision. See Markusoff, *supra* note 4 at A3.

23 As quoted in Vanessa Lu, 'Romanow strikes back at his critics' *Toronto Star* (4 December 2002).

24 Tom Olson, 'Angry Klein vows to keep Alberta out of new Health Council' *Edmonton Journal* (30 May 2003) A1.

25 Commission on the Future of Health Care in Canada, *Building on Values: The Future of Health Care in Canada* (Ottawa, 2002) at 139 [the Romanow Report]. Binnie and LeBel JJ. criticized the majority for selecting 'bits of evidence' from health care reports such as interim reports from the Kirby Senate Inquiry (see para. 229) and notes that 'the Court is sufficiently burdened with conflicting evidence about our own health system without attempting a detailed investigation of the merits of trade-offs made in other countries....' (para. 226).

26 *Ibid.*

27 See Robert Marshall, 'The Best Health Care' *Maclean's* (5 June 2000) http://www.macleans.ca/topstories/article.jsp?content=35423 (August 25, 2005). It was also ranked #1 out of 57 regions across the country, in 2003 (see http://www.edmonton.com/statistics/page.asp?page=90)) While the Maclean's survey is hardly a scientific study, it is a rough indication of how the quality of care is perceived.

28 Herbert Northcott and Jennifer Northcott, *The 2004 Public Survey About Health and the Health System in Alberta* (Population Research Laboratory, University of Alberta) (http://www.health.gov.ab.ca/resources/publications/pdf/Survey2004.pdf) at vi. Despite the Supreme Court's strong proclamation that 'delays in the public system are widespread and have serious, sometimes grave, consequences' (*Chaoulli*, at para. 112), there is

only anecdotal evidence that this is the case. As noted by Kao-Ping Chua: 'The lack of quality data on waiting lists from the Canadian government … makes it very difficult to conclude with any certainty the size of the true waiting list problem.' Kao-Ping Chua, 'Waiting Lists in Canada: Reality of Hype?' (www.amsa.org/studytours/WaitingTimes_primer.pdf) (August 22, 2005). See also, Claudia Sanmartin, Samuel Shortt, Morris Barer, Sam Sheps, Steven Lewis and Paul McDonald, 'Waiting for Medical Services in Canada: Lots of Heat, But Little Light' (2000) 162 Canadian Medical Association Journal: 'The Canadian debate about access to care, and waiting lists in particular, is characterized by disturbing chasms between widely held views and research evidence. This disjunction appears to be the product of a number of factors, including lack of standard approaches to measurement and reporting of waiting lists lengths and waiting times and a general ignorance (or disregard) of the effects of competing approaches to managing waiting lists in Canada and abroad.' In addition, the evidence about the risks associated with being on a waiting risk is complex and less than clear. See, for example, Jean-Francois Legare, Alex MacLean, Karen Buth and John Sullivan, 'Assessing the risk of waiting for coronary artery bypass graft surgery among patients with stenosis of the left main coronary artery' (2005) 173 Canadian Medical Association Journal 371 at abstract: 'For selected patients with stenosis of the left main coronary artery, waiting for CABG did not appear to be associated with increased mortality or morbidity.'

29 *Ibid.* at vi. However, a recent poll reveals that many respondents are supportive of the Alberta government's health reform proposals. An August 2005 Ipsos-Reid poll of 800 Albertans found 44% in favour of all 12 initiatives in Klein's Third Way plan, while only 24% are opposed and 30% need more information before deciding. 51% of Calgarians support the reform plan, while only 39% of Edmontonians do. The plan has greater support among respondents with higher education and income. See Ipsos News Centre, 'Albertans Offer Tentative Support To Klein's Health Care Reforms' (2 August 2005) online: http://www.ipsos-na.com/news/pressrelease.cfm?id=2745.

30 See, for example, Tammy Horne and Susan Abells , *Public Remedies, Not Private Payments:*

Quality Health Care in Alberta (University of Alberta: Parkland Institute, November 2004) (http://www.ualberta.ca/~parkland/research/studies/execsum/EShealth.pdf) at 2: 'Reputable public opinion surveys show that roughly twice as many Albertans want the government to prioritize health care and other social program investments than want tax cuts.'

31 Province of Alberta, News Release, 'Higher revenue allows for increased investments in priority areas' (29 August 2005), online: http://www.gov.ab .ca/acn/200508/18654C97741D0–9FD6–4070–927DAFBE805D645B.html.

32 Priority areas that are specifically mentioned include infrastructure projects and capital investments (e.g. for provincial highways), disaster and emergency assistance (e.g. associated with floods, forest fires and 'mad cow' disease), environmental issues (e.g. drinking water), and affordable housing.

33 Jason Markusoff, "Leave Us Alone' Klein Warns: Premier Fires Back as Feds, Ontario Reportedly Eye Alberta's Energy Riches' *Edmonton Journal* (26 August 2005) A1.

34 Tom Noseworthy, From Chaos to Order: Making Sense of Waiting Lists in Canada (Western Waiting List Project, March 2001) online: http:// www.wcwl.org/. See also, *Romanow Report, supra* note 25 at 143: '[T]he WCWLP has made important progress not just in understanding the reality of wait lists in western Canada, but also in developing tolls for physicians to rank urgency and to ensure that wait lists are managed in a comprehensive, objective and transparent manner.'

35 See, for example, The Provincial Hip and Knee Replacement Project (www. Health.gov.ab.ca/resources/TechBriefHipKnee.pdf). (Aug 20, 2005).

36 Alberta Waitlist Registry (*http://www.health.gov.ab.ca/waitlist/ WaitListPublicHome.jsp*).

37 Peter A. Singer, 'How Long Must We Wait?' *National Post* (25 August 2005) A18. Dr. Singer is director of the University of Toronto Joint Centre for Bioethics. While the Alberta site may be slow in updating its information, it remains ahead of the other provinces including Québec, which has yet to post any wait times, and Ontario which has yet to post any times for 2005. See *http://canadaonline.about.com/od/healthcarewaittimes/index_r.htm*.

38 Para. 14.

39 Para. 102.

40 Editorial, *supra* note 8.

41 As noted in the *Chaoulli* decision: para. 72.

42 R.S.A. 2000, c. A-20.

43 *Ibid.*, s. 26.

44 *Ibid.*, 8.

45 *Ibid.*, s. 6.

46 Para. 111. Emphasis added.

47 Para. 158. However, their decision is unclear as to why they used the conditional 'might.' It seems difficult to imagine why a system that pro-

vides reasonably timely and quality care would not pass constitutional
muster.

48 The Fraser Institute, *Waiting Your Turn: Hospital Waiting Lists in Canada*,
14th Edition, by Nadeem Esmail and Michael Walker (October 2004) at 3.

49 Section 26.1(1) of the Regulation provides: '… a resident may apply in
writing to OOCHSC [Out of Country Health Services Committee] for
approval of the payment of expenses to be incurred, or that have been
incurred, with respect to insured services or insured hospital services
received outside of Canada, where the resident or his dependant has
endeavoured to receive the services in Canada and they are not available
in Canada.' The Committee consists of four physicians appointed by the
Government and the person who is the Out-of-Province Claims Team
Leader in the provincial Health Department.

50 Para. 264.

51 Michelle Lang, 'Calgarians push for costs on cross-border surgery' *Calgary
Herald* (1 August 2005) A1.

52 *Ibid.*, referring to a comment by Howard May, spokesperson for Alberta
Health.

53 Previous Supreme Court rulings have been known to create unintended
results. Joel Bakan cites examples of *Tetrault-Gadoury v. Canada (Employment and Immigration)*, [1991] 2 S.C.R. 22 and *Schacter v. Canada*, [1992] 2
S.C.R. 679. These cases required the federal government to extend unemployment insurance benefits to certain groups who had previously been
ineligible. However, Bakan notes that, to comply with the Court's ruling,
the federal government 'raised revenue for these extensions by increasing
the number of weeks that a person must work before being eligible for UI
benefits, reducing the number of weeks a person can receive benefits, and
stiffen[ed] penalties for workers who quit without just cause or refused to
take suitable jobs or are fired for misconduct.' See Joel Bakan, *Just Words:
Constitutional Rights and Social Wrongs* (Toronto: University of Toronto
Press, 1997) at 59.

54 *Health Care Protection Regulation Amendment*, Alta. Reg. 140/2005 (not yet
in force).

55 Alberta Government, Health and Wellness, *Getting on with Better Health
Care* (www.health.gov.ab.ca/about/reform/getting.html) at 13/14 (August
24, 2005).

56 Michelle Lang, 'Private health policies already on sale: Albertans offered
range of coverage' *Calgary Herald* (30 July 2005) A1.

57 *Ibid.*, quoting Wendy Hope.

58 Two companies, Acure Health and PPI Financial Group, sell private

insurance and a Calgary-based brokerage company called Health Treks recently opened. *Supra* note 56 and Michelle Lang, 'Calgarians turn to health brokers to cut the pain of surgery wait lists' *Calgary Herald* (25 July 2005) A1.

59 Alberta, *Mazankowski report - A framework for reform : report of the Premier's Advisory Council on Health,* vol. 1,2 (Edmonton: Queen's Printer, 2001). Online: Alberta Government *http://www.gov.ab.ca/home/health_first/documents/PACH_report.pdf* Appendixes at: *http://www.gov.ab.ca/home/health_first/documents/PACH_appendices_final.pdf*

60 Darcy Henton 'Alberta plan to delist medical services has hit snag: health minister' *Canadian Press* (8 January 2003), quoting former Health Minister, Gary Mar.

61 Editorial, 'Cautious to a fault: Third Way health reforms have little sizzle, and less steak' *Calgary Herald* (14 July 2005) A20.

62 For example, a June 2005 Pollara survey of 1,263 Canadians found that 55% 'agree with the Supreme Court decision that they should have the right to buy private health insurance if the public system cannot provide medical services in a timely fashion.' 63% indicated a willingness to pay privately to obtain faster access to care. See Jane Taber, 'Majority would pay for faster health care, poll finds' *Globe and Mail* (8 July 2005) A14.

Private Insurance for Medicare: Policy History and Trajectory in the Four Western Provinces

GREGORY P. MARCHILDON*

I. Medicare: Policy History and Future Trajectories

Canadian Medicare is characterized by: 1) narrow but deep coverage for medically necessary/required services; 2) provincial/territorial (P/T) administration of single-payer insurance within broad, national principles; and 3) P/T legal and administrative regimes that prohibit or discourage private insurance of Medicare services.[1] It is the third feature in particular that makes the Canadian model of Medicare unique among OECD countries.[2] Historically, this meant that public Medicare insurance administered by governmental authorities eventually trumped alternative, public-private model of health insurance subsidization.[3] In today's context, this means that Canada stands alone among OECD countries in not permitting – or encouraging through subsidy – parallel private insurance for hospital and physician services.[4]

Medicare is often perceived as the product of two discrete public policy decisions in the postwar era; P/T introduction of single-payer hospital insurance between 1947 and 1961, followed by P/T introduction of single-payer medical care insurance between 1962 and 1972, decisions that were highly influenced by federal cost-sharing and standard-setting through intergovernmental negotiation and national legislation. But the policy history of Medicare is more accurately seen as an unfolding process in which the sustaining elements that make up the overall policy have been continually refashioned over time. For example, premiums were once an important part of Medicare in most jurisdictions, and user fees were an accepted part of Medicare in at least some provinces, whereas today premiums are restricted to a minority of jurisdictions and user fees are extremely rare. The same applies to the prohibition on private insurance. While six provinces currently prohibit private Medicare insurance, few provinces explicitly prohibited private hospital insurance in the 1940s and 1950s. While such prohibitions became more common with the introduction of public medical care insurance in the 1960s, there were important exceptions, including Saskatchewan, the originator of single-payer medical care insurance, and British Columbia, a province that initially made private medical care insurance carriers part of its public scheme.

Finally, viewing the policy of Medicare as a unfolding work in progress emphasizes the fact that the policy sustainability of the single-payer Medicare model, even after its adoption by all jurisdictions, continued (and continues) to be challenged. The reasons offered against it today – and the interests that would profit from an alternative policy – are strikingly similar to those posited a half century ago. But it would be a mistake to view the *Chaoulli* decision as simply the most recent in a long list of challenges to single-payer Medicare. Coming as it does from the Supreme Court of Canada, and based as it is on fundamental human rights, *Chaoulli* may end up having a more lasting impact on Medicare than the past policy choices made by provincial governments to protect the single-payer model as suggested by Andrew Petter [This Volume]. Whether or not *Chaoulli* has a permanent policy impact, the decision certainly provides considerable political ammunition to those individuals and governments currently advocating greater choice through private funding and delivery.[5]

Based upon the contrasting policy histories in the four western provinces, some predictions are made concerning the future of provincial prohibitions on private Medicare insurance. The western provinces were major protagonists in initiating publicly insurance for hospital and physician services in Canada. In the late 1940s and early 1950s, British Columbia, Alberta, and Saskatchewan pioneered forms of hospitalization well before the federal government introduced cost-sharing through the *Hospital and Diagnostic Services Act* in 1957. Although Manitoba waited for an agreement with the federal government on cost-sharing before stepping out with its own plan, it was the only western province to include a prohibition on private hospital insurance in its enabling legislation.

During the great debate over public insurance for physician services in the 1960s, British Columbia, Alberta, Saskatchewan, and Manitoba were again in the forefront, having implemented their own public programs in anticipation of the federal start date of July 1968. At the same time, these provinces were deeply divided, both among themselves and internally, concerning the desirability of government-administered single-payer medical care insurance. Today, the governments of the western provinces again disagree about the merits of single-payer Medicare.

In what follows, emphasis is placed on the ideological and political stance of individual western premiers towards Medicare, particularly those that dominated the political landscape of their respective provinces during the formative decades of Medicare. In the Westminster system of cabinet government, considerable power is concentrated in the office of first ministers. In the cases where first ministers remain in office for an extended period of time, they are capable not only of establishing an administrative style for future governments but also a leadership model that is emulated by ideologically-compatible successors.[6] Enjoying extraordinarily long tenure as premiers during the formative years of Medicare, E.C. Manning of Alberta (1943–68), W.A.C. Bennett of British Columbia (1952–72), and T.C. Douglas of Saskatchewan (1944–61) left an indelible legacy on the governments of like-minded premiers which followed in their wake.[7]

Alberta

Virtually alone among the premiers, Ralph Klein has openly welcomed the *Chaoulli* decision as an opportunity to introduce choice into the 'monopoly' of the current single-payer system. Stating that the Supreme Court decision 'has forever changed our health-care landscape,' Klein promises a policy response to the decision shortly in the form of parallel private insurance for elective (non-emergency) services within the Medicare basket.[8] If Alberta follows through, Klein and his government will naturally assume the leadership of the interests and governments in Canada opposed to the single-payer model, in the same way that an earlier predecessor led the anti-Medicare forces from the late 1940s until the late 1960s.

In his support of the private sector and his opposition to single-payer Medicare, Klein is an ideological throwback to his predecessor, Ernest Manning. In 1950, Manning went out of his way to create a decentralized and multi-payer hospital insurance system that would provide a clear alternative to the more centralized, single-payer hospital insurance systems established in Saskatchewan and British Columbia.[9] Based on subsidized private insurance for low income earners, voluntary provincial grants to municipalities, and user fees, Manning's hospital-ization plan was held out by Medicare opponents as a viable alternative to the single-payer plans in Saskatchewan and British Columbia.[10]

Ernest Manning's ideological perspective on Medicare comes very close to fitting the polarized form of libertarian ideology described by Alan Maynard [This Volume]. For Manning, individual freedom of choice was a goal in itself. Moreover, he believed that individuals rather than governments are in the best position to judge their own welfare. For this reason, he insisted on the 'voluntary' rather than 'compulsory' health insurance and was opposed to universality, believing that indi-viduals should decide whether or not they required health insurance without the interference of the state. Finally, he argued that achieve-ment would be properly rewarded under a private enterprise system, and that access to health care should be part of that reward system.

Manning also believed that the federal government should not meddle in areas of provincial jurisdiction including health care. But on this point, he was more pragmatic. Manning also wanted to receive shared-cost funding from Ottawa; he justified his position on the basis that Albertans would be required to contribute their taxes to support a national program even if Alberta refused to participate.[11] As a conse-quence, his government attempted to negotiate an arrangement that would preserve the operating principles of his hospitalization scheme and operating principles. Manning government's bargaining position eventually took the form of a law, the *Hospitalization Benefits Act* of 1957, the terms of which proved unacceptable to Ottawa given the require-ments of public administration and universality under the *Hospital Insurance and Diagnostic Services Act* of 1957.[12] However, by June 1958, Alberta finalized an agreement with the federal government that would allow it to receive shared cost dollars on a revised hospitalization plan. *The Hospitalization Benefits Act, 1959*, created a single-payer hospital insurance plan.[13] At the same time, however, Alberta retained its user fees (ranging from $1 to $2 per hospital day) despite the fact that Ottawa refused to cost-share the portion of Alberta's expenditures funded by such fees. Finally, there was no prohibition on the purchase or sale of private hospital insurance in the new law, presumably not a deal-breaker from the view of the federal negotiators at the time given the absence of similar prohibitions in many other provinces' hospital-ization legislation.

For Alberta, history would repeat itself during the medical care in-surance battle during the 1960s. In response to growing popular support of universal, single-payer medical care insurance despite the rancorous implementation of the system in Saskatchewan, Manning again felt the need to establish a subsidy model that incorporated his ideological principles. In 1963, the country was still awaiting the report of the Royal Commission on Health Services. Manning was not sure what the Commission and its chair – Supreme Court Justice Emmett Hall – would ultimately recommend but he felt that the working version of his plan would nudge the Hall Commission away from Saskatchewan's single-payer model to his multi-payer model. What Manning did not realize was that Hall's experience with organized medicine during the hearings had already pushed him towards the Saskatchewan model. Hall confided to his staff that he was furious with 'those damn doctors. They think they know everything; all I hear is propaganda and not a shred of evidence to support their opposition to a government-sponsored plan.'[14]

Unfortunately for Manning, the Alberta submission to the Hall Commission followed the same pattern as those presented by organized medicine. Similar to the physicians, it made the general philosophical argument that a 'socialized health and medical services' plan was 'incompatible with the rights and responsibilities inherent in a free and democratic society' because a single-payer system would remove 'all direct responsibility' from the individual for purchasing physician services.[15] While providing subsidies for very low income earners to purchase private medical care insurance, everyone else would continue to decide whether or not to have health insurance. Predictably, the Alberta approach – dubbed 'Manningcare' by the media – was held up by the Canadian Medical Association and the Canadian Health Insurers Association as a superior alternative to the universal, single-payer system in Saskatchewan.[16]

In a 1963 speech to the Saskatchewan College of Physicians and Surgeons – an organization that remained defiant despite the implementation of single-payer medical care insurance by the provincial government the year before – the Alberta Health Minister referred to the 'long and tiring hours spent' by both the insurance industry, including over 40 private health insurance companies operating in the province, and the province's physicians to 'develop the prototype that we all hope might be a model for other parts of our Canada.'[17] Subscription in the Alberta medical care plan was voluntary. This combined with the fact that government subsidies were limited meant a low overall subscription rate. But universality was not the goal of the new Alberta plan, and the health minister argued 'that unless people are prepared to assume a reasonable degree of personal responsibility for their various private needs, of which medical care is but a minor one, cost wise, then government should not improperly use the public treasury to purchase their favor.'[18]

Within a year of the Alberta plan's implementation, however, the Hall Commission rejected the Manningcare model in favour of the single-payer model. The Hall report, and what Manning perceived as the federal government's preference for a single-payer design, goaded the Alberta premier into taking the offensive. In a national television broadcast paid for by anti-Medicare business groups, Manning argued that single-payer, by replacing 'all existing medical insurance programs and companies' with a government 'monopoly,' would eliminate competition and consumer choice. He also claimed that the federal government had been convinced of the single-payer approach by a cabal of 'socialistic advisers,' a reference to Prime Minister's policy advisor Tom Kent as well as the former Saskatchewan bureaucrats who had moved into senior posts in Ottawa following the defeat of the provincial CCF government in 1964.[19] Ostensibly, Manning was being assisted in his crusade against socialized medicine by Ontario and British Columbia which had also adopted subsidy-based medical care plans. However, both of those governments were more willing to compromise on principle in order to obtain federal cost-sharing, and Alberta's efforts to produce a common provincial front based upon a private insurance model ultimately failed. Manning felt let down – even abandoned – by his 'fair weather' provincial allies.[20]

Alone among premiers, Manning could not prevent what he perceived as the federal imposition of the principles of public administration and universality through the passage into law of the *Medical Care Act* of 1966. However, he still expected that the divisions within the federal cabinet would delay implementation. But when the Pearson government stuck to its deadline of July 1, 1968, Manning reluctantly established a government-administered single-payer system of medical care insurance to obtain his province's share of medical care transfers.[21] That same year, Manning retired, and left it to his Social Credit successor, Harry Strom, to implement the legislation. The *Alberta Health Care Insurance Act* of 1969 created the Alberta Health Insurance Commission as the sole medical care insurer in the province. In explicit language, the new law made it an offence for any other insurer to sell medical care insurance.[22] While federal cash may have finally enticed the government of Alberta into the single-payer fold, this did not mean that the Social Credit government or its Progressive Conservative successors would ever fully accept the logic of single-payer administration or the goal of universality.

British Columbia

Premier Gordon Campbell's immediate response to *Chaoulli* was to suggest that it posed an immediate challenge to the federal government and the *Canada Health Act*.[23] In doing so, Campbell appeared to be giving vague support to Premier Klein's argument that the *Chaoulli* decision would force a reconsideration of what was, and was not, included in the Medicare basket of insured services. However, reflecting the pragmatic position taken by his predecessors in the 1950s and 1960s, and the exigencies imposed by a highly polarized electorate, Campbell played his Medicare cards very close to his chest.

British Columbia was the first jurisdiction to consider establishing publicly-administered health insurance. In 1932, the British Columbia Royal Commission on State Health Insurance recommended a social insurance plan in which all low and middle income wage earners, along with their employers, would be required to contribute to a central fund, while higher income earners could, if they chose, voluntarily opt-in.[24] Despite the positive reaction to the Commission's recommendation, the Conservative government of the day rejected the recommendations for ideological and fiscal reasons. Although the Conservatives were soon defeated by the Liberals, they too avoided implementing public health insurance.[25]

In the prosperity that followed the war, the pressure for government provision of health insurance mounted. In part to check its Co-operative Commonwealth Federation (CCF) opposition, a Liberal-Conservative coalition government implemented a comprehensive hospital insurance plan modeled, in part, on the Saskatchewan plan. When introduced in 1949, about 15 per cent of the provincial population had private hospital insurance and this insurance was neither terminated nor prohibited in the enabling legislation – the *Hospital Insurance Act*, R.S.B.C. 1948, c. 151. Moreover, unlike the Saskatchewan plan, subscription to the public plan was voluntary. However, given their inability to compete with the lower premiums and better benefits in the public plan, most private insurance companies, including the largest, Blue Cross, voluntarily exited from the business in order to focus on supplementary hospital insurance as well as medical care insurance. Two commercial companies hung on by providing niche insurance to cover payment of premiums but they also exited after premiums were abolished in 1954.[26]

While inadequate planning, ineffective administration, escalating premiums and user fees led to the defeat of the coalition government in 1952, W.A.C. Bennett's new Social Credit government decided to repair, rather than simply abandon, hospitalization. Bennett immediately lowered patient co-payments to $1 per hospital day. Two years later, he eliminated premiums so that only residency in the province determined eligibility for hospital insurance.[27] Joining Saskatchewan's Premier Tommy Douglas, Bennett strongly supported federal cost-sharing for hospital insurance in order to provide an extra source of revenue to fund the program. Given the universality of the province's program as well as the exit of private insurers, Bennett was not then concerned about the federal government's insistence on universality and the single-payer principle.[28] On July 1, 1958, when the federal *Hospital Insurance and Diagnostic Services Act* was implemented, British Columbia (along with Alberta, Saskatchewan, Manitoba and Newfoundland) was eligible immediately for cost-sharing.[29]

While Bennett viewed the question of private carriers as irrelevant in the case of public hospital insurance in the 1950s, he saw it as central in the case of public medical care insurance in the 1960s. By World War II, physicians in British Columbia were already responding to what they perceived as the threat of government-administered, single-payer medical care insurance by initiating their own not-for-profit (NFP) plan – the Medical Service Association (MSA). Although domestic administrative difficulties, federal gradualism and fiscal concerns on the part of all governments delayed for years the introduction of public medical care insurance, the Saskatchewan government's introduction of single-payer medical care insurance scheme in 1962 sent shock waves through the local medical community and the Bennett government. Supporting the Manning government's position in Alberta, Bennett's government made it clear from the beginning that, contrary to Saskatchewan, it would work in concert with physicians to develop a mutually satisfactory plan – one in which private insurers, including of course the physician-sponsored MSA, would play an important role.[30]

During the course of a series of dinner meetings between Bennett and the president of the British Columbia Medical Association (BCMA), a new medical care plan was hatched. While fundamentally diverging from the Saskatchewan model, it also differed in one important respect from Manningcare.[31] Instead of subsidizing the purchase of private insurance by residents, a crown corporation known as the British Columbia Medical Plan (BCMP) was established to provide discounted medical care insurance for low income earners and for those unable to obtain private insurance for reasons of age or health. The BCMP paid 50 per cent of the basic premium for subscribers with a taxable income of $1,000 or less, and 90 per cent without taxable income. By 1967, 20 per cent of the provincial population belonged to the BCMP.[32]

In effect, through the BCMP, the government was underwriting higher risk patients through a targeted public plan thereby leaving private insurers with lower risk patients and higher profits. Not surprisingly, the Bennett government's approach was supported by physicians, private insurers, and the business community at large. At the same time, however, Bennett was also eager to obtain federal cost-sharing pursuant to the federal *Medical Care Act* so he opened negotiations with Ottawa with a view of preserving as much of his scheme as possible. In this, Bennett would prove more skillful than Manning.

On the domestic front, Bennett's government drafted a bill that kept all options open to the government. While the bill gave the government blanket powers to license private carriers as well as renew, suspend and cancel the right of insurers to sell medical care insurance, it provided no details on program design. The government promised to spell out these design features in the regulations under the *Medical Services Act* – which passed into law in March 1967 – but only after the federal government accepted a more flexible definition of 'public administration.'[33] In fact, according to Malcolm Taylor, the federal government had already defined 'public administration' more broadly in the federal *Medical Care Act* of 1966 than it had in the *Hospital Insurance and Diagnostics Services Act* in part to placate British Columbia, Alberta, and Ontario. The new definition permitted private insurance companies to act as agents in a provincial scheme as long as they were non-profit, their books were subject to public audit, and 'their administration was responsible to the provincial government.'[34]

In late June 1968, on the very eve of implementation, Bennett finally announced that his 'voluntary' approach to medical care insurance had been accepted by the federal government. Six NFP private insurers, designated as approved carriers by the government, were permitted to sell medical care insurance under the supervision of the government-appointed Medical Services Commission, including the physician-owned

MSA. In addition, the government's own BCMP continued to pick up the poor risks.[35] Under the regulations of the *Medical Services Act* approved by cabinet on May 21, 1968, all non-licensed carriers – including all the for-profit insurance carriers – were prohibited from selling medical care insurance as of July 1, 1968, the implementation date for the federal *Medical Care Act*.[36]

Bennett's apparent success in creating a private-sector and multi-payer alternative to single-payer Medicare, however, would not last. Partly as a result of the tight regulation of premiums and benefits to meet the federal condition of universality, most of the private companies soon vacated medical care insurance to focus on the supplementary health insurance business. By 1972, there were only two NFP private companies still operating as licensed carriers under the Medical Services Plan of British Columbia, an evolution that paralleled developments in Saskatchewan.[37]

Eventually, all private insurance would be legally prohibited. In 1991, the British Columbia Royal Commission on Health Care and Costs – the Seaton Commission – came down firmly in favour of protecting the principles of Medicare and against private funding. Although no prohibition on private insurance was specifically recommended by the Seaton Commission, the new NDP government introduced a blanket prohibition (section 39) on private insurance in the *Medical and Health Care Services* of 1992, and repeated in the successor *Medicare Protection Act* of 1996.[38]

Saskatchewan

Immediately following the Supreme Court's decision in *Chaoulli*, the most vocal and negative reaction among the provincial premiers came from Saskatchewan's Lorne Calvert. Stating that he was very 'disturbed' about the possibility of the *Chaoulli* decision 'opening the door to an Americanized health-care system in Canada,' Calvert speculated on the 'legislative tools' that might be available at both levels of government to 'strengthen' the universal, single-payer system.[39]

That Calvert would be the most vocal defender of the single-payer system among the premiers was hardly surprising given the legacy of his province and his party. The Saskatchewan CCF government spurred Medicare nationally by pioneering single-payer hospital insurance in the 1940s as well as single-payer medical care insurance in the early 1960s. Tommy Douglas, the premier of the province for almost two decades and the province's health minister in its first term of government, was the single individual most responsible for these achievements. Employing Maynard's [This Volume] polarized forms of ideologies, Douglas's egalitarianism was at the opposite pole from Ernest Manning's libertarianism. Without doubt, Douglas placed equality of opportunity above individual freedom and was dogged in his belief that all members of society have equal rights to basic goods such as health care. Moreover, the community rather than the individual should decide what goods and services should be distributed on the basis of need rather than purchasing power. Believing that government was simply the community writ large, he also believed that collective mechanisms were essential to ensure equitable treatment as well as real equality of opportunity.

Douglas faced relatively few political obstacles when his government implemented single-payer hospital insurance in 1947. More so in Saskatchewan than any other province, the Great Depression devastated the incomes of patients and doctors.[40] As a consequence, most physicians welcomed single-payer hospital insurance even if they remained uneasy about aspects of government administration of the system. Almost non-existent in Saskatchewan, private hospital insurance was not prohibited in the *Saskatchewan Hospitalization Act, 1946*, or the detailed regulations under the law.[41] Even the not-for-profit (NFP) 'voluntary insurance movement' spearheaded by organized medicine in the early postwar years had limited traction in rural Saskatchewan and Alberta relative to Ontario, British Columbia and Manitoba.[42]

By the early 1960s, a sea change had taken place, with private medical care insurance covering over 30 per cent of the provincial population. In particular, the two physician-run plans – Medical Services Incorporated (MSI) and Group Medical Services (GMS) had penetrated deeply into the province's two major cities and were attempting to provide insurance on a municipal basis beyond the cities.[43] This was no accident. In the years following the introduction hospitalization, organized medicine had become radically opposed to the single-payer principle. The College of Physicians and Surgeons of Saskatchewan – an organization that combined the functions of self-regulation and advocacy – felt it was in a race against time to have the 'voluntary' insurance principle entrenched before the government was ready to implement a 'compulsory' single-payer scheme.[44]

The College could only look on with dismay when shared-cost financing for hospitalization was introduced in 1958. With new money flowing into the province from Ottawa, the Saskatchewan government finally had the fiscal elbow room to introduce public medical care insurance, living up to an electoral promise that dated back to 1944.[45] When Douglas first announced his government's intention in a by-election in April, 1959, the College demanded input into designing the new plan.[46] In a provincial radio broadcast, Douglas he also set out five non-negotiable principles: 1) compulsory prepayment through taxes and premiums; 2) universality of coverage; 3) maintenance of high quality of service; 4) public administration; and 5) a plan acceptable 'both to those providing the service and those receiving it.' The fifth principle was Douglas's attempt to tell physicians that his government would make the administrative features of program as palatable as possible within the framework of the first four non-negotiable principles.[47] While he did not identify single-payer as one of his non-negotiable principles, Douglas emphasized to his listeners that the administrative costs of the province's single-payer hospital plan – about 4 per cent – were a fraction of the administrative costs associated with private insurance.[48] However, as Robert Evans point out [This Volume], what a governments and taxpayers see as administrative waste, the insurance industry and its employees see as profit, salaries, and wages.

In the same radio broadcast, Douglas appealed to the College to nominate three representatives for the Advisory Planning Committee on Medical Care (soon to be known as the Thompson Committee after the chair W.P. Thompson) to help work out the details of the plan.[49] Immediately following Douglas's broadcast, the College prepared a standard form letter for all of its MSI and GMS subscribers describing how a 'compulsory government-operated medical scheme' would destroy the plans. The College also refused Douglas's offer to participate in the Thompson Committee unless the terms of reference were changed to allow for a voluntary, multi-payer medical care plan.[50]

For months, the College sparred with the government over the terms of reference for the Thompson Committee. By April, the government agreed to add a number of tasks to the Committee's mandate as the price of College representation. While Douglas's principles remained intact, the College would use the larger mandate to delay the work of the committee well beyond its original one-year deadline. The question of single-payer medical care insurance then became the major public issue during the provincial election in June 1960. The divide between the College and the government became a chasm as physicians openly campaigned against Douglas and the CCF. Labeling the idea of single-payer 'communist' and 'totalitarian,' the College called in outside help to fight against Medicare. The government was re-elected despite the College's scare tactics. A month following the election, Douglas shared his assessment with a friend in Oxford:

> The most interesting feature of the campaign was that for the first time in my experience the medical profession openly entered the campaign; brought in public relations experts from outside; printed literature and acted like a full-fledged political party. Unfortunately for them, their public relations experts had received most of their training in the United States under Dr. Fischbein, President of the American Medical Association. Consequently, they underestimated the intelligence of the Saskatchewan electorate. The cries of 'red medicine,' 'political medicine' and 'state control' which proved so effective in nullifying President Truman's health insurance proposals in 1950 only succeeded in causing amusement and latterly, growing resentment among a great many people in Saskatchewan.[51]

After the election, relations among the members of the Thompson Committee became even more polarized and poisonous. Frustrated, the chair offered his resignation to the government, citing the College's strategy of using the Committee to identify and price 'all conceivable gaps, defects, and deficiencies' in the single-payer hospitalization program in order to support its case that the government should not introduce medical care insurance until the government had fixed the existing system.[52] Douglas convinced Thompson to stay, hoping that the Committee would eventually reach a compromise solution.[53]

Thompson and his committee met constantly in the months following the election but no compromise could be reached. Finally, the government demanded that the Committee produce an interim report addressing at least the medical care insurance part of the mandate by September 1961. The result was a deeply divided report, with eight majority members recommending a universal, single-payer program and four minority members recommending a government-subsidized, multi-payer program operated by the private for-profit and NFP insurance companies.[54] The uncompromising position of the College combined with Douglas's desire to see the medical care bill in the house before taking on the national leadership of the New Democratic Party (NDP) moved the dispute into high gear. A special fall session was called and the *Saskatchewan Medical Care Insurance Act, 1961* was put before the House. Douglas argued that the private insurance-subsidy approach supported by the College would prevent universal coverage and allow sizeable public expenditures to escape democratic account-ability. During second reading of the Bill, Douglas described his hopes for the bill in a manner that could only have increased the College's anxiety level:

> I believe ... that if this medical care insurance program is successful, and I think it will be, it will prove to be the forerunner of a national medical care insurance plan. It will become the nucleus around which Canada will ultimately build a comprehensive health insurance program which will cover all health services – not just hospital and medical care – but eventu-ally dental care, optometric care, drugs and all the other health services which people require. I believe that such a plan operated by the federal and provincial governments jointly will ultimately come in Canada. But I don't think it will come unless we lead the way.[55]

Although the Liberal opposition decried the fiscal costs of the pro-gram and demanded a public referendum on the medical care plan, it nonetheless felt obliged to vote in favour of the bill given public senti-ment and the official position of the federal Liberal government. The provincial Liberals, however, encouraged the College of Physicians and Surgeons to block implementation by refusing to nominate members to the Medicare Care Insurance Commission, the body established to ad-minister the plan. When the doctors threatened to go on strike, Woodrow Lloyd, having just come to the Premier's Office, extended the April 1 deadline for implementation to July 1, 1962. Rather than produce a compromise as Lloyd had hoped, however, the delay emboldened the College which then prepared its membership for a province-wide strike. Lasting 23 days, the doctors' strike split the province into two.[56]

The doctors' strike would finally end with a ceasefire mediated be-tween the government and the College. The terms of the ceasefire were captured in the Saskatoon Agreement which in turn became the basis of an amended medical care law.[57] The College's perspective on the im-portance of private insurance was placed directly in the Saskatoon Agreement:

> Over the years, doctors and many of the citizens of Saskatchewan have built up voluntary, non-profit health insurance agencies. These include Group Medical Services, the Saskatoon Mutual Medical and Hospital

Benefits Association and Medical Services Incorporated. It is the wish of the College that they should continue to play a part when the Medical Care Scheme comes into full operation. The College considers that they can help to protect doctors from the possible risks of having only a single source of income, and can develop additional fringe benefits under which a broader range of services can be made available to citizens on an insurance basis. Accordingly, provision has been made in the amending legislation for these agencies to participate in association with the medical care plan and for safeguarding the interests of all concerned.[58]

This may have seemed a victory for the College but, in reality, the role for approved private insurers was limited to that of a 'post office' for the repayment of bills. In response to a letter from a rural resident trying to understand the curious and cumbersome arrangement shortly after its introduction, Health Minster Allan Blakeney sent this reply:

It is true that the majority of the physicians are not accepting direct payment from the Medical Care Insurance Commission. Patients of these doctors must either join one of the approved health agencies (e.g. Medical Services Incorporated) or accept the bill directly from the doctor and obtain reimbursement from the Commission. If he joins the approved health agency, the doctor bills the agency, which forwards the bill to the Commission, with the payment returning via the same route. When he does so, he agrees to accept Commission payment in full. The patient who elects to accept the bill himself, forwards it to the Commission for reimbursement. The Commission pays the patient the same amount it would pay the doctor for the services provided. While all this is somewhat more complicated that one would like, I think it is working with reasonable satisfaction to both doctor and patient.[59]

The Saskatoon Agreement in general, and this compromise in particular, upset the more ardent supporters of universal, single-payer Medicare.[60] Some argued that the provision permitted the majority of doctors to practice outside the terms of *The Saskatchewan Medical Care Act*, a charge that Blakeney quickly rebutted:

Approved health agencies are provided for in the Act, and their activities are strictly regulated under it. The physician who accepts payment through an approved health agency is subscribing to nearly all of the same conditions as a physician who accepts payment directly from the Commission, including acceptance of the payment as payment in full ... Naturally, we hope that over a period of time the number of physicians choosing to accept payment directly from the Commission will increase.[61]

On these points, Blakeney was correct. For physicians, there were no legal or administrative advantages to be gained by working through the private insurance firms, while for patients, there were clear advantages to having doctors willing to accept payment directly from the Medical Care Insurance Commission. Finally, the main insurance companies of the day increasingly viewed the arrangement as an annoyance, and instead, gradually shifted their focus to supplementary health insurance. At the same time, however, the long-lasting effects of the bitter conflict practically ensured that future provincial administrations would not re-open old wounds by introducing an amendment prohibiting private insurance.

Manitoba

In his immediate response to *Chaoulli*, Manitoba NDP Premier Gary Doer stated that the Supreme Court's decision did not mark the beginning of the end of Canadian Medicare. Instead, he viewed it as an 'alarm bell' concerning the importance of reducing waiting lists, especially for elective procedures such as hip and knee replacements.[62] This position is identical to Charles J. Wright's conclusion [This Volume] that the current priority should be to fix the waiting list problem rather than the overcoming the legal challenges that may follow in the wake of *Chaoulli*. This pragmatic response, which attempts to step around the ideological and partisan political fault lines, is also very much within the tradition of how past Manitoba governments dealt with Medicare. At the same time, Premier Doer's party has always strongly supported the single-payer model. In addition, Manitoba has prohibited private Medicare insurance longer than any other western province, a history which goes back to the late 1950s.

In 1957, a Liberal-Progressive coalition government led by Premier Douglas Lloyd Campbell had to go to the polls within the year. Politically, Campbell's centrist position was being squeezed from the left by the CCF and from the right by the Progressive Conservatives under the leadership of Duff Roblin. In part due to the introduction of hospitalization schemes in Saskatchewan, Alberta, and British Columbia, public sentiment in favour of public hospital insurance was growing in

Manitoba. Knowing that a universal hospital insurance plan might save his government, Campbell speeded up work. Fiscally conservative, however, he was not prepared to proceed without federal money. Rather than looking west, therefore, Campbell looked east to Ontario where Leslie Frost's government was preparing to set up its own hospital insurance system if it received shared-cost funding from Ottawa.[63]

Frost's government had worked out an arrangement in which the government would provide hospital insurance directly but only after purchasing the facilities of the private insurers and transferring their employees to the Ontario Hospital Services Commission. Private insurers would thereafter be left to focus only on non-insured hospital services or medical care insurance. Time was also built into the implementation process to allow the private hospital contracts to expire. To follow Ontario, however, Manitoba would also have to delay the implementation of hospitalization to 1959, well after the provincial election. But to proceed earlier meant that the Campbell government would have to resort to terminating private hospital insurance contracts through legislation.[64]

Campbell chose to go early. In an effort to mitigate the political fallout, Campbell's Minister of Health met with the insurance industry to explain the government's proposed scheme of health insurance as well as its decision to terminate insurance contracts.[65] In April, the bill was debated and then passed in the Legislature, the government setting an implementation date of July 1, 1958. Section 36(2) of the *Hospital Services Insurance Plan* stated that every hospital insurance contract would simply 'cease to have any force or effect' and declared that any person selling hospital insurance was 'guilty of an offence and liable, on summary conviction, to a fine not exceeding two thousand dollars.'[66] Despite the prohibition, the only member of the house to vote against the law was John McDowell, an independent member who was against the 'socialistic bill' on principle. Even he, however, seemed to be more concerned about the fact that enrollment in plan would be 'compulsory' for all Manitoba residents rather than any prohibition of private hospital insurance.[67] With an eye to the coming election, Roblin had his party members vote in favour of the legislation as well as a separate bill winding up the hospital insurance business of Blue Cross.[68]

Just weeks before the implementation date, the Campbell government went to the polls only to be defeated.[69] This left it up to Duff Roblin's new government to implement a single-payer hospital plan his party had supported in the Legislature as the official opposition. A decade later, however, the Roblin government found itself much more reluctant when it implemented a single-payer medical care insurance plan.

Stating that he preferred a voluntary, multi-payer system, Roblin argued that the federal government was forcing his government into establishing a single-payer system because of the conditions required to obtain cost-sharing.[70] However, given the eligibility of the medical care plans in British Columbia and Saskatchewan, neither of which prohibited private insurers, it seems improbable that the federal government would have insisted that Manitoba insert an explicit prohibition on private insurance. In the end, the Roblin government simply copied the prohibition from its earlier hospitalization legislation into its new *Medical Services Insurance Act*.[71]

Conclusion

In the aftermath of the *Chaoulli* decision, the western provinces remain divided among themselves on the future of single-payer Medicare. The simplest explanation for this difference lies in the ideological differences of the current governing parties – the governments of Alberta and British Columbia lean right while the governments of Saskatchewan and Manitoba lean left. While this explanation has some explanatory power, it does not capture the nuances among the governments, as well as the premiers which lead these governments, and their likely response to *Chaoulli*.

Given the policy and leadership legacy they have inherited, the premiers of Alberta and Saskatchewan are likely to take the most ideological position in the debate to come. Even before *Chaoulli*, Ralph Klein's government was pushing the envelope in terms of introducing private elements into its public Medicare system.[72] After *Chaoulli*, the government of Alberta issued an amendment to its existing action plan on health care reform. Issued on August 10, 2005, this update states that the provincial Minister of Health and Wellness is examining 'how private, supplementary health insurance might play a role in funding accessible, high quality health care in Alberta.'[73] In his eagerness to take advantage of *Chaoulli*, Klein is resurrecting the government of Alberta's historic opposition to the universal, single-payer system.[74]

Klein's most obvious provincial adversary will be Lorne Calvert and his NDP government in Saskatchewan. As noted above, Calvert has already been the most unequivocal about defending single-payer Medicare, a position that is in keeping with Saskatchewan's history as the birthplace of single-payer Medicare. Paradoxically, Calvert has no prohibition on private insurance to protect. Saskatchewan remains the only western province in which the purchase or sale of private Medicare insurance has never been prohibited. Instead, successive provincial administrations have simply discouraged the rise of parallel private Medicare insurance by preventing cross-subsidization and extra billing.[75] Nonetheless, Calvert's government will almost surely defend the prohibition in other provinces as a legitimate means of protecting single-payer Medicare.

In contrast, the premiers of British Columbia and Manitoba are more likely to keep a low-key in the immediate post-*Chaoulli* scramble. Their position, based upon a long-term policy trajectory, is likely to be very pragmatic relative to Alberta and Saskatchewan. Both will want to avoid the ideological and partisan aspects of the debate for as long as they can. Given their respective histories, British Columbia is far less likely than Alberta to launch a privatization agenda based on *Chaoulli*, and Manitoba is far less likely than Saskatchewan to launch an aggressive defence of the single-payer system through new legislation or the courts. However, if the single-payer debate escalates, the current Manitoba government would have little option but to vigorously defend any legal challenge to its current prohibition on parallel private Medicare insurance as part of an overall strategy to support single-payer Medicare. Similarly, if forced to choose sides at a later stage in the debate, the current government in British Columbia will file in behind Alberta.

Of course, governments are not islands and premiers are not omnipotent. As noted in the preceding historical analysis, the provincial medical associations as well as the Canadian Medical Association (CMA), have played a major role in influencing Medicare policy in the provinces. In their analysis of the CMA's *Chaoulli* motion of last August, Trudo Lemmens and Tom Archibald [This Volume] argue that the CMA's support for private Medicare insurance (though qualified) may signal that the end of a long, and often grudging accommodation, with Medicare, and a return to its historic opposition. If this is the case, then the government of Alberta may have a powerful ally in its post-*Chaoulli* effort to transform single-payer Medicare into multi-payer 'Choicecare.' We must also recognize that provincial government operate in a profoundly different international environment than the one in which private insurers originally exited – voluntarily and involuntarily – from the hospital and medical care insurance business in the 1950s and 1960s. If the government of Quebec permits private insurance in response to *Chaoulli*, then under the terms of the North American Free Trade Agreement (NAFTA), U.S.-based (and Mexican-based) insurers will have access to the Quebec market on the same terms and conditions as domestic firms. Tracey Epps and David Schneiderman [This Volume] point out that of the 126 companies currently selling supplementary health insurance, 65 are American carriers. Once a provincial government opens its Medicare insurance market, NAFTA would make it almost impossible for any future government to reverse the policy.

Finally, irrespective of the ideological or policy position on private taken by a western provincial government, all four have played a leading role in the country in initiating major waiting list reforms including the Saskatchewan Surgical Care Network and the collaborative Western Canada Waiting List Project. Thus, even while the *Chaoulli* debate rages, and western premiers take diametrically opposed positions, their governments are nonetheless working – both alone and cooperatively – to address the very problem which, according to the Supreme Court, triggered *Chaoulli*.

Notes

* The author is indebted to Meghan Cross for her general research assistance as well as the specialized research expertise of Roberta Lexier, Scott MacNeill and Nicole O'Byrne.

1 Flood, Colleen, and Tom Archibald. 'The illegality of private health care in Canada' (2001), 164 C.M.A.J. 825. The term 'Medicare' is limited to medically necessary or medically required health services provided on a universal basis without user fees as defined under the *Canada Health Act* which originated as medically necessary hospital/diagnostic services and medically required physician services as provided under provincial and territorial single-payer insurance systems. By capitalizing 'Medicare,' this phrase can be distinguished from 'medicare,' a concept that, historically speaking, was limited to universal medical care insurance.

2 Hurley, Jeremy, et al. 'Parallel private health insurance in Australia: a cautionary tale and lessons for Canada' (2002), Centre for Economic Policy Research, Australian National University, discussion paper no. 448.

3 Given the presence of workers' compensation health benefits, automobile insurance health benefits and similar exceptions, and federal health

benefits and services for defined groups, P/T government Medicare insurance has never enjoyed a complete monopoly.

4 There are other release valves, including the right to purchase the services of any physician who has opted out of the Medicare system, and the ability to purchase treatment in other countries.

5 See Peter Russell [This Volume]

6 Savoie, Donald J. *Governing from the Centre: The Concentration of Power in Canadian Politics* (Toronto: University of Toronto Press, 1999). Bernier, Luc, Keith Brownsey and Michael Howlett, eds. *Executive Styles in Canada: Cabinet Structures and Leadership Practices in Canadian Government* (Toronto: University of Toronto Press, 2005). Blakeney, Allan and Sandford Borins. *Political Management in Canada* 2nd ed. (Toronto: University of Toronto Press, 1998).

7 Though premier of Manitoba for a far shorter period of time, it could be argued that Duff Roblin (1958–67) also left an indelible mark on future governments.

8 Alberta. Premier Ralph Klein. Public statement and release to media, August 4, 2005.

9 By 1954, hospitals in Alberta received only 38.6 per cent of their income from the provincial government: this compares to rates of 73 per cent in British Columbia and 85.7 per cent in Saskatchewan in the same year. Taylor, *Health Insurance*, 170.

10 The legislative authority for Alberta's first hospitalization plan was *The Hospitalization and Treatment Services Act*, c. 56, S.A. 1953. Naylor, C. David. *Private Practice, Public Payment: Canadian Medicine and the Politics of Health Insurance, 1911–1966*. Montreal and Kingston: McGill-Queen's University Press, 1986, 163; Taylor, Malcolm G. *Health Insurance and Canadian Public Policy: The Seven Decisions that Created the Canadian Health Insurance System*, 2nd ed. Montreal and Kingston: McGill-Queen's University Press, 1987, 169–70. Provincial Archives of Alberta (hereafter PAA), E.C. Manning Papers, 69.289, Box 1720, letter, Manning to Archie Gillis, April 4, 1953.

11 PAA, E.C. Manning Papers, 77.173, Box 692b, letter, Manning to Dr. L.E. Beauchamp, June 30, 1967.

12 S.A. 1957, c. 30.

13 S.A. 1957, c. 31.

14 Hall quoted in: Vaughn, Frederick. *Aggressive in Pursuit: The Life of Justice Emmett Hall*. (Toronto: University of Toronto Press, 2004), 126. Emmett Hall was appointed to the Supreme Court of Canada on November 23, 1962, in the midst of his work on the Royal Commission on Health Services.

15 Alberta Minister of Health, Dr. J. Donovan Ross, quoted in Taylor, *Health Insurance, supra* note 10 at 338.
16 Naylor *Private Practice: Public Payment*, 219; Taylor *Health Insurance, supra* note 10 at 339. Traynor, Cam. 'Manning against Medicare' (1995), 43 *Alberta History* 7.
17 PAA, E.C. Manning Papers, 77.173, Box 22, 239, text of speech, J. Donovan Ross, M.D., to the College of Physicians and Surgeons of Saskatchewan, Oct. 16, 1963, p. 4.
18 Ibid., p.8.
19 PAA, E.C. Manning Papers, E.C. Manning's text for broadcast: 'Let's look before we leap,' 77.173, Box 22, 2416.
20 PAA, E.C. Manning Papers, 77.173: 245b, letter, Manning to Carmen Naylor, Sept. 22, 1965; 691, letter, J. Donovan Ross to Matthew Diamond, Ontario Minister of Health, Dec. 5, 1966;
21 Taylor, *Health Insurance, supra* note 10 at 341.
22 Section 29(2) of the *Alberta Insurance Act*, R.S.A. 1969, c. 43, stated: 'Effective on the plan commencement date, an insurer shall not enter into, issue, maintain in force or renew a contract or initiate or renew a self-insurance plan under which any resident or group of residents are provided with any prepaid basic health services or indemnification for all or part of the cost of any basic health services.'
23 Cotter, John. 'Provinces Respond to Ruling,' Canadian Press, June 9, 2005.
24 British Columbia. *Royal Commission on State Health Insurance and Maternity Benefits: Final Report*. Victoria: C.F. Banfield, 1932.
25 Naylor. *Private Practice: Public Payment*, 75–85.
26 British Columbia Legislative Library government documents (hereafter BCLL). 'Reference Material on the British Columbia Hospital Insurance Service, Jan. 1, 1949 to Jan. 1, 1963,' B.C. Hospital Insurance Service.
27 Barman, Jean. *The West beyond the West: A History of British Columbia*. Toronto: University of Toronto Press, revised ed., 1996, 298. Taylor, *Health Insurance*, 167–69.
28 BCLL, 'Sessional Address by Hon. Eric Martin, British Columbia Minister of Health and Welfare,' Feb. 8, 1956. Taylor, *Hospital Insurance*, 126.
29 Taylor, *Hospital Insurance*, 233.
30 BCLL, 'Address of the Hon. Eric Martin, Minister of Health Services and Hospital Insurance,' Feb. 18, 1963.
31 Naylor, *Private Practice, Public Payment*, 149–50.
32 BCLL, Legislature speech by Hon. W.D. Black, Provincial Secretary and Minister of Health Services and Hospital Insurance, Feb. 10, 1967. *Victoria*

Daily Times, advertisement for the British Columbia Medical Plan, Sept. 23, 1967, 5. Barman, *The West beyond the West*, 298.

33 S.B.C. 1967, c. 24. 'Medicare Bill Due in House,' *Victoria Daily Times*, March 3, 1967, 17. Ian Street, 'On that Medicare Bill,' *The Province*, March 9, 1967. 'Medicare Scope Black's Secret,' *Vancouver Sun*, March 9, 1967.

34 Taylor, *Health Insurance*, 375.

35 Taylor, *Health Insurance*, 369. 'B.C. Ready for Medicare,' *Victoria Daily Times*, Jan. 16, 1968. 'Groups Hope to be Agents for B.C. under Medicare,' *Financial Post*, June 15, 1968. 'Bennett Medicare 'Savior' for All Other Provinces,' *Victoria Times*, June 29, 1968, 3.

36 *B.C. Gazette, Part II*, June 6, 1968, regulations under the *Medical Service Act*, order in council no. 1567, regulation 4.05, approved May 21, 1968.

37 BCLL, brochure entitled 'The Overall Medical Services Plan of British Columbia, Nov. 1972.

38 R.S.B.C. 1992, c. 76, section 39, and R.S.B.C. 1996, c. 286, section 45. British Columbia. *Closer to Home: The Report of the British Columbia Royal Commission on Health Care and Costs*. Vol. 2. Victoria, BC: Crown Publications, 1991. There is no record in *Hansard* of any debate concerning the prohibition.

39 Provinces respond to ruling, Canadian Press, June 9, 2005.

40 Marchildon, Gregory P. 'The Great Divide' in Marchildon, Gregory P., ed., *The Heavy Hand of History: Interpreting Saskatchewan's Past* (Regina: Canadian Plains Research Centre, 2005).

41 S.S. 1946, c. 82. Saskatchewan Archives Board, Regina (hereafter SAB), T.C. Douglas Papers, R33.5, 123c, Health Services Planning Commission, regulations under *The Saskatchewan Hospitalization Act, 1946*, Order in Council No. 1569, Sept. 24, 1946.

42 Naylor, *Private Practice: Public Payment*, 143–52.

43 SAB, T.C. Douglas Papers, R33.1, 575c, 'Summary of material on a medical care program for Saskatchewan, Feb. 1960, and 'Proposals for a Medical Care Program for Saskatchewan, a report to Cabinet by the Interdepartmental Committee to Study a Medical Care Program,' Nov. 20, 1959;. By the latter part of the 1950s, physician-operated Medical Services Incorporated (MSI) of Saskatchewan had over 200,000 paying customers and Group Medical Services (GMS) had over 60,000 clients while an insurance cooperative – the Saskatoon Mutual Medical and Hospital Benefit Association – had just under 5,000 members. There is no accurate information on commercial (for-profit) medical care insurance, but it constituted only about one-third of the amount paid out through Workers' Compensation Board health benefits.

44 Naylor, *Private Practice: Public Payment.*
45 SAB, T.C. Douglas Papers, R33.1: 557 (14–11), Letter, R.G. Ellis, State Hospital and Medical League, to F.D. Mott, Sept. 14, 1949; 562 (14–16), T.J. Bentley memo to T.C. Douglas, Nov. 6, 1951.
46 SAB, T.C. Douglas Papers, R33.1: 562 (14–16), letters between G.W. Peacock (Registrar, College of Physicians and Surgeons of Saskatchewan) and T.C. Douglas, April 28 and May 1, 1959.
47 SAB, T.C. Douglas Papers, R33.1, 575a, Script for radio broadcast 'Prepaid Medical Care' by T.C. Douglas, Dec. 16, 1959.
48 SAB, T.C. Douglas Papers, R33.1, 575a, Script for radio broadcast 'Prepaid Medical Care' by T.C. Douglas, Dec. 16, 1959.
49 W.P. Thompson's own views on the establishment and work on the committee are briefly summarized in Thompson, W.P. *Medical Care: Programs and Issues.* Toronto: Clarke Irwin, 1964. SAB, T.C. Douglas Papers, R33.1, 575a (14–28–2), Douglas to W.P. Thompson, Dec. 1, 1959.
50 SAB, letter prepared by College of Physicians and Surgeons (Saskatchewan), special committee on public relations, Dec. 22, 1959.
51 SAB, T.C. Douglas Papers, R33.1, 573a (14–28), letter, Douglas to James McConica, Oxford, UK, July 5, 1960.
52 SAB, T.C. Douglas Papers, R33.1, 576 (14–28–3), letter, W.P. Thompson to Douglas, Nov. 7, 1960.
53 SAB, T.C. Douglas Papers, R33.1, 576 (14–28–3), letter, Douglas to W.P. Thompson, Nov. 15, 1960. Johnson, A.W. Dream No Little Dreams: A Biography of the Douglas Government of Saskatchewan. Toronto: University of Toronto Press, 2004, 261.
54 Thompson, Medical Care, 66.
55 Saskatchewan. *Hansard.* Oct. 13, 1961, 19.
56 Much has been written about the events physician's strike but this account is summarized from various sources including: Badgley and Wolfe. Doctors' Strike: Medical Care and Conflict in Saskatchewan. Toronto: Macmillan of Canada, 1967; and Johnson. Dream No Little Dreams.
57 Naylor, *Private Practice, Public Payment*, 210.
58 SAB, A.E. Blakeney Papers, R12.2, Memorandum of Agreement: Government of the Province of Saskatchewan and the College of Physicians and Surgeons of Saskatchewan, July 23, 1962.
59 SAB, A.E. Blakeney Papers, R12.2, 20–5, letter, Blakeney to Herman Kemper, Jan. 3, 1963.
60 SAB, A.E. Blakeney Papers, R12.2, 20–5, Statement by the Congress of Canadian Women, June 1, 1963.

61 SAB, A.E. Blakeney Papers, R12.2, 20–5, letter, Blakeney to Albert Cox, October 15, 1962.
62 Provinces respond to ruling. Canadian Press, June 9, 2005.
63 Public Archives of Manitoba (herafter PAM), D.C. Campbell Papers, GR 43, G291, federal government relations files; letter, A.J. Swanson (Ontario Hospital Services Commission) to R.W. Bend (Manitoba Minister of Health), June 7, 1957; and letter, R.W. Bend to Paul Martin Sr., May 14, 1957.
64 PAM, D.C. Campbell Papers, GR 43, G291, 1957 health insurance file, 3 page undated provincial government memorandum [1957].
65 PAM, D.L. Campbell Papers, GR 43, G306, 1958 hospital insurance file, agenda for meeting between R.W. Bend and representatives of the insurance industry, Feb. 28, 1958.
66 *Hospital Services Plan*, S.M. 1958, c. 24, s. 36(6).
67 'Plan Socialistic, McDowell Says.' *Winnipeg Free Press*, April 4, 1958.
68 'Blue Cross Ordered to Return $1 Million.' *Winnipeg Tribune*, April 3, 1958.
69 Immediately following his defeat, Campbell attempted to form a coalition with the CCF – their combined seats would have placed the two parties in a majority – but the CCF refused the offer.
70 S.M. 1967, c. 36. This is the same prohibition in the current *Health Service Insurance Act*, C.C.S.M., c. H35. *Financial Post*, April 1, 1967, 16. Manitoba. Hansard, various debates in March and April 1967.
71 Manitoba. *Hansard*. March 16, 1967, 1715, statement by Health Minister C.H. Whitney.
72 See Sullivan, Greenberg, Sawka, and Hudson [This Volume] and Caulfield and Ries [This Volume].
73 Alberta. Alberta Health and Wellness, Action Plan 2005.
74 Gordon Campbell's reaction in 'Premiers respond to ruling.' Canadian Press, June 9, 2005.
75 Saskatchewan. Factum of the Attorney-General of Saskatchewan (*Chaoulli v. Quebec*), 7.

A Just Measure of Patience: Managing access to cancer services after *Chaoulli*

T. SULLIVAN, A. GREENBERG, C. SAWKA, AND A. HUDSON

Excessive Waits with Limited Public Coverage

In this chapter we examine the issue of waiting and coverage. We consider the options to reduce wait times based on our experience with cancer services in Ontario, we comment on the promise of private provision versus private insurance in improving access, and we conclude with some of the immediate considerations for cancer services in the light of *Chaoulli v. Quebec (Attorney General)*.[1]

The rationing of services is intrinsic to all health care systems. Some systems ration on the basis of ability to pay and some ration on the basis of need. How health care systems set these priorities for access is a reflection of the underlying values associated with citizenship, the social consensus on what services should be covered in a public scheme, and how health services should be paid for (tax financed, payroll financed, or privately financed). In Canada, with its history of federally mandated coverage for physician and hospitals services (and frankly little else of a national standard), we believe we ration publicly financed services on the basis of need.

Waiting lists, when appropriately managed, can be one sign of a fair and equitable system that responds on the basis of need. Appropriate management however presumes that waiting for some period does not actually cause harm to patients. The challenge comes when waiting creates risks to the patient in the form of conventional outcomes (i.e. death or progression of disease beyond a recoverable period), or quality of life outcomes (i.e. psychological distress or functional deterioration). The Supreme Court of Canada's judgment in *Chaoulli* concerned the latter; excessive waiting was deemed by the majority to be a breach of the Quebec *Charter of human rights and freedoms* protection of the right to life, and to personal security, inviolability and freedom.[2] In Canada, *Chaoulli* has gripped our attention.

In our view, the practical impact of the *Chaoulli* decision in Ontario has been two-fold. First, the judgement has successfully challenged the assumption that everyone has appropriate access to necessary hospital and medical services, as they require them. This is well expressed by three of the seven judges, McLachlin C.J. and Major and Bastarache JJ. with reference to the *Canadian Charter of Rights and Freedoms*[3]:

> However, because patients may be denied timely health care for a condition that is clinically significant to their current and future health, s. 7 protection of security of the person is engaged. *Access to a waiting list is not access to health care.* As we noted above, there is unchallenged evidence that in some serious cases, patients die as a result of waiting lists for public health care. Where lack of timely health care can result in death, s. 7 protection of life itself is engaged. The evidence here demonstrates that the prohibition on health insurance results in physical and psychological suffering that meets this threshold requirement of seriousness.[4]

The Supreme Court has suggested that the remedy for a potentially life threatening access problem is to allow the provision of private health insurance. In making this large leap of faith, an important public debate has been opened, which many of us had presumed settled, on whether private health insurance will provide a remedy to our access woes. This second consequence of opening up the question of market solutions to financing has raised the matter of what kind of social consensus we actually have in Canada regarding the provision of basic coverage for physician and hospital services. As Alan Maynard, Stefan Gress, and den Exter respectively point out in this volume, drawing from the EU experience, established market economies finance their health sectors either through publicly financed insurance or very tightly regulated, non-commercial social insurance arrangements. The failure of commercial insurance markets to deliver comprehensive health insurance is not only a tenet of all welfare economics, but also the history of health insurance in the civilized world.[5] As Bob Evans succinctly points out in this volume, the regularly reborn promise of 'real,' comprehensive private health insurance is the marketing of powdered unicorn horn.

In Canada, as in other OECD countries with comprehensive insurance, waiting times for priority conditions have been growing over the last several years.[6] Compared to countries such as the UK and New Zealand, where parallel private health care sectors have been encouraged, Canada's waiting times appear to be either similar in length or shorter.[7] The Supreme Court's decision in *Chaoulli* underscores a growing consensus that waiting times for many health care services in Canada are becoming too long, and that the seeming inertia surrounding the improved management of waiting lists must end. Indeed it is probably an understatement to say that this message has finally been heard by Canadian governments who have collectively pledged to reduce waiting times in the most recent First Ministers agreement of September 2004.

The *Chaoulli* decision did not pronounce on what might be reasonable or appropriate waits for the condition at hand. However, an upcoming Quebec Superior Court case, *Cilinger v. Centre hospitalier de Chicoutimi*[8] expected to be heard in 2008, will deal with these issues. The case is being brought on behalf of 10,000 Quebec breast cancer patients who were not seen for radiation treatment within eight weeks following surgery. The claim being made by the petitioner is that eight weeks is a 'reasonable' amount of time, and that 12 weeks is the maximum a breast cancer patient should wait without suffering a considerable increase in the risk of adverse outcomes. The Quebec Court of Appeal recently denied leave to join the Quebec government to this class action *Cilinger c. Québec (Procureur général).*[9]

The courts in the *Cilinger* case to date seem to be unwilling to demand that governments be held responsible to ensure the delivery of timely and effective cancer service, but the Supreme Court appears ready to open up the delivery system to private insurance. There are several arguments as to why accountability might be demanded on the part of hospitals but not the government. But allowing judicial action to bear on the hospital sector for wait time policies directly influenced by public funding arrangements on the face of it hardly seems completely fair. Those of us in the cancer community will watch carefully the evolution of this case. In the case of *Cilinger*, the contentious matter of what is a 'risky' waiting period for breast cancer has developed into an important debate on the evidence of risk of recurrence for patients who wait beyond 12 weeks for radtiotherapy after surgery.[10]

Cancer: the canary in the mine

As with all health services, the *Chaoulli* decision has the potential to affect how cancer services are organized and delivered in the future.

Moreover, the upcoming *Cilinger* decision is likely to influence the cancer service providers, but possibly not the government, to an even greater extent. However, these cases are not the first wake up call for provincial cancer systems. When it comes to waiting, cancer services, particularly radiation treatment, represent the canary in the mine for Canadian health care. Although there are public and professional concerns for wait times for a number of procedures, including hip and knee replacement and cataract surgery, cancer as a life threatening illness has demonstrated for the rest of the health system what happens when waiting times for treatment reach crisis levels.

In the late 1990s, waiting times for radiation treatment in Ontario became unmanageably long and called into question the very sustainability of the provincial cancer system. The delivery system had failed to respond to a sure and steadily growing demand for treatment driven by a 3% annual rise in incidence associated with aging and population growth, as well as the intensification of services. Between 1999 and 2000, recognizing this, the Ontario Ministry of Health and Long-term Care was compelled by clinical leaders who feared excessive waits were truly compromising survival to fund the re-referral of over 1500 breast and prostate cancer patients to the United States for radiation treatment.[11] As a solution, this was a costly one since the care in the US was significantly more expensive than providing the treatment in Ontario. Over and above the costs of treating these patients in Buffalo or Detroit, the government also covered their out-of-country travel and accommodation. Moreover, it almost certainly set the government back in terms of public confidence in the cancer system.

In the intervening years, a number of initiatives have been introduced in Ontario to overcome this crisis, which we discuss in detail below. Of these, a crucial one has been the improved measurement and reporting of cancer treatment waiting times. We know from this data that over the past few years, waiting times for cancer surgery have risen and more recently have been holding steady, waiting times for chemotherapy and hormone therapy are rising marginally, and waiting times for radiation treatment appear to be falling slightly.[12] On the face of it, the Ontario cancer system does not currently appear to be in crisis. However, it is important to note that what these data on waits do not show is whether or not the waits cancer patients experience are appropriate (e.g. a median wait of five weeks for both chemotherapy and radiation treatment in 2004). Moreover waiting times do not tell us much about the appropriate rates of treatment (i.e. to account for under- or over-treatment), nor the system's ability to meet the future demand for cancer treatment; it is estimated that about 25% of Ontario cancer patients who should be referred to radiation treatment are not currently receiving care for a range of reasons related to proximity to cancer services, the failure to refer, and possibly other reasons.[13] Furthermore, over the next ten years, the number of new cancer patients is expected to grow from approximately 55,000 per year to over 80,000 each year, almost wholly due to population growth and aging.[14]

It is certainly true as Charles Wright points out elsewhere in this collection, that cardiac care is one where some wait list triage is clearly required to prevent sudden death. The majority of cancers, perhaps slightly less dramatically than the minority of cardiac cases, must be treated in a timely fashion to avoid premature and in most cases certain death. This is unlike most other priority conditions for wait list reductions, such as osteoarthritis of the hip and knee and cataracts. In addition, the process of detecting and treating cancers sooner most often (but not always) confers some therapeutic and survival advantages. Indeed it is for these reasons that the majority of cancer patients now live beyond five years, and some entirely disease free beyond initial treatment.

Consider the trajectory of colorectal cancer, a largely preventable disease which is the largest killer among non-smokers in the population. This type of cancer often develops when benign polyps form on the lining of the colon. Due to genetic alterations, these polyps can grow abnormally (become adenomatous), but still be pre-cancerous. Eventually, some of these polyps will become cancerous. For average risk individuals, the pre-cancerous polyp can grow silently over 10 to 20 years. However, once malignant, the tumour must be treated to prevent proliferation through the lumen of the bowel and then metastasis (spreading to other parts of the body). Once the tumour metastasizes, it is difficult for patients to ensure full recovery even with advanced treatments currently in place. This trajectory between the onset of disease and adverse health outcomes sets cancer treatment waiting list reduction efforts apart from that for other diseases. This is in contrast to a number of fast growing tumours including those of the head and neck. Cancer patients are likely to experience significantly greater distress from waiting than are other patients, precisely because timely treatment really is vital to prevent death in most cases.

This clinical digression is intended to illustrate three unique realities for cancer. First, cancer is not one disease but in fact represents over 100 different diseases, each with a complicated treatment pathway in which patients must see multiple specialists often in different clinic settings, and therefore often experience many sequential waits for different services. This makes determining 'appropriate' waits for particular patients very difficult. Second, interventions to improve cancer service 'access' exist at multiple points in the soujourn of various cancers. This means access is not just definitive final treatment, but begins with prevention and screening, potential removal of polyps with endoscopy for early diagnosis, to treatment with evidence based surgical resection to effective radiotherapy, systemic and adjuvant therapy. Third and perhaps important for the *Chaouilli* decision, for cancer patients distress is driven by the real and imminent fear of death. With few exceptions however, we do not have clear cut points for the risk of passing the point of no return, or raising the risk of early recurrence in the course of waiting for treatment following initial surgery.[15] While the evidence basis is slim, consensus-based recommendations informed by current evidence and practice leaders for appropriate classification of waits for cancer patients will be forthcoming in Ontario by the end of 2005 for major cancer treatments.

While the focus may be on definitive treatments for those with advanced disease, there is no effective screening for colorectal cancer in Canada on a population basis, despite bullet proof international evidence for improved survival from screening.[16]

Options and Tools to Reduce Waiting Times for Cancer Service

What can be done about growing or excessive waiting times for cancer service? The *Chaoulli* decision has tended to constrain the terms of the debate to a choice between single payer versus a private insurance option. Canada has always had a multi-payer structure for services other than inpatient care and physician services. What *Chaoulli* has done is open up the debate about whether inpatient care should be open to a private insurance option, without actually suggesting how this should be done in any practical fashion. More importantly, the judgement does not even discuss a host of other options available to governments to reduce waiting times systematically and improve access to care as Colleen Flood and her colleagues note in their contribution in this volume.

Put simply, there are four principal means to reduce waiting times and improve access to cancer care. As a comprehensive proposal to reduce waiting times and increase access to care, these core strategies have been described in detail elsewhere.[17] Governments, health care managers and providers can:

1. Reduce the demand for services by investing in cancer prevention and early detection,
2. Target new investments in cancer services capacity to meet the growing demand (physical plant, human resources, and new agents and technologies),
3. Better coordinate access to cancer services, and
4. Make more efficient use of existing resources.

This section reviews a series of selected and promising approaches to reduce waiting times in the context of cancer care, and describes the specific tactics that have been implemented in Ontario's cancer system.

Investing in prevention and early detection

As a solution for reducing waiting times, investing in cancer prevention and early detection is easily overlooked. The benefits, including lower rates of and less advanced disease, are well known and substantiated,[18] but progress against the disease, like the incubation rate for many cancers, can take several years (and electoral cycles) to be realized.[19] Still, given that at least half of all cancers are preventable,[20] the overall future demand for services can be significantly reduced.

Investing in tobacco control, obesity prevention, and population-based organized cancer screening have all been shown to lower the burden of disease, which directly reduces the pressures on the healthcare delivery system. It is ironic that the Supreme Court struck down laws preventing tobacco advertising in *RJR-McDonald Inc. v. Canada (Attorney General)* concluding that there was a lack of sufficient evidence of a link between advertising and consumption,[21] as discussed by Sujit Choudhry in this volume. Long-term planning, including forecasting the coming demand for cancer services and devising ways to reduce it are more important than ever in light of the changing age structure of the population.

Public reporting

Internationally, the measurement and reporting of health performance information for quality improvement has become standard practice.[22] The public reporting of cancer treatment waiting times to stimulate reductions is equally widespread.[23] As with all performance reporting, there are three key objectives in publicly reporting cancer treatment waiting times: to indicate where there are problems, to monitor progress over time, and to demonstrate system accountability to the public.

To our knowledge, no studies to date have demonstrated the specific impact of publicly reporting treatment waiting times on subsequent performance,[24] however, a recent controlled experiment conducted in Wisconsin sheds light on the long-term effects of performance reporting more generally. The study, which included 115 hospitals in the state, showed significantly greater quality improvements among those hospitals whose performance data was released publicly compared with hospitals receiving either private reports or no reports at all.[25] Furthermore, the improvements analyzed were specific to the clinical areas covered in the performance reports.

In 2003, for the first time, Cancer Care Ontario began to post radiation therapy waiting times publicly on its web site.[26] The information is displayed by type of cancer and by cancer centre. Making comparative and timely waiting time information transparent to the public was intended to demonstrate and strengthen the accountability of the system. The public reports result in continued media attention[27] and create pressure on lower performing centres to act. In addition, public reporting has the benefit of driving 'purification through utilization' by creating an imperative for centres to provide the most accurate data as possible.

In 2005, public reporting of cancer performance information in Ontario was expanded in the form of the Cancer System Quality Index. The Index consists of the results of 25 quality indicators, with expanded reporting of waiting times including cancer assessment, surgery, chemotherapy and radiation treatment.[28] Cancer Care Ontario has mandated each of the regional cancer leaders to integrate the annual results of the Index into their planning and quality improvement cycles. The long-term impact of publicly reporting this performance information is currently being evaluated through a number of peer-reviewed grants.

Use of triage tools

To be efficient, a waiting list must reflect a prioritization of patients in the queue according to need. Patients needing a service or procedure sooner should be higher up on the list. To accurately assess the relative priority of different patients waiting for cancer services, standard and valid methods are needed to weigh symptoms, severity of disease and urgency.

The Western Canada Waiting List Project has developed waiting list management tools for five clinical areas: cataract surgery, children's mental health, general surgery, joint replacement and MRI scanning.[29] Although not specific to cancer, these tools have been validated and allow physicians to score different patients according to disease-specific criteria and are a useful model for managing waits for other conditions. These triage tools although viewed with growing regard by clinical leaders and managers in the health care sector nationally, were not mentioned in the *Chaoulli* decision.

Setting targets

Similar to triage tools, identifying an agreed upon 'appropriate' or 'reasonable' amount of time for a patient to wait for a particular treatment or service is critical for targeting reduction efforts and resources. Without the ability to run controlled experiments to determine precisely how long it is safe to wait, this is typically achieved through expert panel reviews and syntheses of the available evidence from observational studies. For example, in 2000 the UK established a two week waiting time rule for referrals to cancer specialists.[30] A recent systematic review in the UK was unable to determine the effectiveness of this policy on cancer patient waits[31]. A more recent discussion with the leader of the cancer program in the UK suggest progress toward the two week rule is in fact progressing well, driven in part by the huge influx of new capacity and resources for cancer in the UK.[32] In Canada, the Saskatchewan Surgical Care Network has set a waiting time target of three weeks for all cancer surgeries.[33]

In Ontario, consensus-based urgency classifications and target maximum waiting times have been developed and will be forthcoming for cancer surgery by the end of the year. Currently the Canadian Association of Radiation Oncologists suggest four weeks as a maximum time from referral to treatment with a radiation oncologist. It is important to note that none of these waiting targets (for the multitude of cancer diseases) has a strong base of evidence on which to base the time frames.

Central management of waiting lists

In most jurisdictions in Canada, individual physicians maintain their own, usually paper-based, waiting lists. This makes it almost impossible to organize care so that patients waiting unreasonably long times are identified and given the opportunity to be referred to another physician.

Saskatchewan was the first province in Canada to implement a province-wide registry to manage surgical care in order to remedy this problem.[34] The centralized registry enables consistent measurement of waiting times, the monitoring of capacity across the province, and the use of standard tools to prioritize patients in the queue.

In Ontario, the current government has a platform to reduce waiting times for five priority procedures: cancer, cardiac, cataract, and joint replacement surgeries, and for MRI and CT scans. To achieve this goal, the government launched the Ontario Wait Times Strategy in the fall of 2004. With a deadline of December 2006, the strategy has two main components: investment in additional surgical volumes and the development of an electronic province-wide surgical registry.

Building on the Saskatchewan Surgical Care Network's surgical registry model, the Ontario Wait Time Strategy team is in the process of developing a provincial surgical registry and a provincial diagnostic imaging registry. As a result, Ontario will soon have standard metrics for measuring waiting times across the five priority procedures. Further, each registry will include information on which provider a patient is waiting for, the urgency of his or her condition, how long he or she has been in the queue, and how many patients in total are waiting. In short, the registry will provide important information for providers and hospitals to manage and report waiting times. To support waiting list management through the registry, urgency scales and benchmark waiting times have been developed by expert panels for each of the five procedures. This will be an important initiative not only for the patients who will benefit from it but also because it will stand as a tool for the effective management of waiting times, and a rebuttal to accusations of management inaction in the face of long waits in a post-*Chaoulli* Ontario.

Process innovations and system redesign

Excessive waiting times are often a symptom of bottlenecks in the care process. For example, patients waiting for cancer surgery commonly experience delays in obtaining biopsies and other diagnostic tests and pathology results.[35] Finding new ways of organizing care through streamlined diagnostic assessment units,[36] or expanding the scope of practice of nurses to bolster screening programs[37] are common approaches to remove these types of access bottlenecks.

System redesign initiatives, in which entire care processes within and between clinics are analysed and reconfigured, are larger scale efforts to remove a series of bottlenecks.[38] This strategy is particularly important in cancer in which the patient journey crosses multiple providers, treatments and care settings and can result in multiple sequential waits. This approach has been used extensively in the UK's Cancer Services Collaborative.[39]

In 2004, Cancer Care Ontario received provincial funds to allocate to promising innovations in cancer care designed to reduce waiting times and improve patient access. The resulting program, the Access to Cancer Services Innovation Fund, awarded money to 22 promising innovations across the province following a proposal call and review.

The projects range from streamlined breast cancer diagnostic assessment units, to expanding the scope of practice of nurses to increase cancer screening rates, to a centralized waiting list tracking system. Each project is currently evaluating its success against agreed upon measures including waiting times and utilization rates.

New funding models and metrics

To reduce waiting times, governments may need to purchase more of a particular procedure. Since funding in the context of hospital global budgets is based largely on historical spending and is not tied to patient needs, there may be little incentive for providers to increase current volumes. Funding formulas that reflect needed increases in the rates for particular treatments or procedures, and account for differences in complexity are an important mechanism for improving access and reducing waiting times.

During the *Chaoulli* decision the idea of 'wait time guarantees' was advanced, originating from the Senate hearings led by Senator Kirby.[40] They have also been explored in the UK, where the guarantees have no direct patient remedy, other than reputational risk for the institution and possible employment for the chief executives. In addition, setting maximum acceptable wait times for many types of cancer and cancer treatments is a challenging task which might be better met with the classes of wait time targets used in Saskatchewan (broad windows of time for classes of treatment). Finally, while the fiscal imperatives associated with wait time guarantees have made the concept a difficult one for provincial governments struggling to manage their health envelopes, the concept still merits exploration with the public.

Tying accountability and funding to performance: new investments

As their health performance measurement systems evolve, many jurisdictions are beginning to link financial incentives to quality improvement, often referred to as 'Paying for performance.'[41] This includes payments to particular physicians or to hospitals, and typically involves bonuses for high performance or improvements against a series of explicit measures.

As a core measure of quality in the Canadian context, improved waiting times are one of several indicators that can be tied to funding. However, as noted in the previous section, assessment of waiting times must be done in the context of improving access to all patients in need of a particular service.

For Ontario's Wait Times Strategy, Cancer Care Ontario was responsible for designing the investment solution for additional cancer surgeries. The approach was explicitly intended to tie funding to performance. That is, in addition to adding almost 3000 more cancer surgeries this year than last, the 37 participating hospitals are required to have a multi-disciplinary practice setting, a commitment to developing tumour boards and surgical rounds, and a commitment to quality assurance and improvement, including a checklist approach to pathology reporting, and better capture and reporting of data on stage of cancer. Additionally, the extra funding requires participating hospitals to submit data to Cancer Care Ontario. To prepare for the downstream effects of increased access to cancer surgery, additional volumes are also being planned and purchased for chemotherapy and radiation treatment, and eight regional cancer centres are currently being expanded or newly constructed in Ontario.[42] This will help to prevent the re-referral of cancer patients to other parts of the province or out-of-province to receive needed treatment. Specifically, it will allow for the treatment of over 1500 new patients for chemotherapy and an equivalent number of new patients for radiation treatment by 2008.[43]

In summary, following a crisis in the late 1990s, Ontario's cancer system has been undergoing a comprehensive campaign to reduce waiting times and improve access to cancer services. This has included greater transparency in the reporting of waiting time information, building a significant amount of new treatment capacity in the province, purchasing additional volumes of treatment tied explicitly to performance, fostering innovations in service delivery to increase both productivity and quality, and development of a provincial wait times registry with urgency ratings to adjudicate and manage lengthy waits. It will take time for the effects of some of these initiatives to be apparent, however, as the data on waiting times for major cancer treatments in the province show, waiting times for most treatment modalities have generally been holding steady in the last few years, despite significant population growth. The most recent new investments in additional surgical procedures should reduce surgical waits, but may put new pressures on systemic therapy waits, a reality that has been anticipated in the current funding model.

Increasing Private Sector Involvement: delivery vs. insurance models

The *Chaoulli* decision brings the question of the effect of a parallel private sector on waiting times in the Canadian health system to the forefront. The assumptions underlying the call for parallel private financing are that it would help to reduce pressures on the public system and reduce waiting times. However, the available evidence shows that depending on the type of private sector involvement (e.g. increasing private insurance vs. private delivery), and its relationship to the existing public system, the effects will vary.[44] In our view, given the available evidence, the *Chaoulli* solution of increased options for private insurance would prove neither optimal nor effective, since the failure of private insurance markets are what brought about public health insurance in Canada to begin with. To borrow from Bob Evans, no powdered unicorn horn is likely to be found by sifting through the *Chaouilli* judgement.

In Australia, a 30% private health insurance rebate was introduced in 1999 to encourage the use of the private sector in order to reduce waiting pressures in the public system. A recent study, assessing the impact of the increased private activity on waiting times for elective procedures, found that the higher the proportion of public patients, the lower the public sector waiting times and vice versa.[45]

In contrast, the UK introduced an approach to increased private sector supply that should theoretically prevent the negative impact on the public sector seen in Australia. To increase capacity and reduce waiting times, the National Health Service (NHS) requested bids from the 'independent' sector to set up private diagnostic and treatment units. To avoid draining scarce human resources in the existing public system, the NHS set out to contract with internationally established providers who were external to the public providers in the NHS. These providers can contract with the NHS to perform an agreed upon number of procedures, based on a set price for each procedure, equal to public sector pricing.[46] Unlike in Australia, the private sector involvement being encouraged in the UK is for the *delivery* of care as opposed to its *insurance*. From the Canadian perspective, this kind of approach would allow the retention of the single payer model, including standard prices for specialized procedures would can be made more competitive with greater market segmentation. Moreover, by recruiting new professionals from outside the existing system, capacity is added while preserving the integrity of the public delivery system.

To date, there are no definitive studies on the effectiveness of the UK's private sector delivery model. However, a recent examination of the effects of private sector involvement in the health systems of five OECD countries suggested that depending on how it is structured, the expansion of private financing is more likely to weaken public coverage.[47] This is perhaps not surprising given the political consensus behind risk pooling for public coverage. As high-income contributors exit, the public commitment weakens.

Private delivery in Ontario: the CROS experiment

Seeking to increase the provincial supply of radiation treatment services during Ontario's crisis of the late 1990s, Cancer Care Ontario initiated an open bid process resulting in a contract with a private company, Canadian Radiation Oncology Service (CROS). Under the terms of the contract, CROS was required to treat 1000 patients per year without displacing staff in other clinics, in exchange for a flat fee equivalent to what the public insurance system would pay, plus a performance bonus.

The CROS approach consisted of renting existing space and using public equipment at the Toronto Sunnybrook Regional Cancer Centre during evenings and weekends – times when it would otherwise be idle.

The results of the CROS experiment included redesigning the care process, scheduling, and provided a savings over sending patients to the U.S. Essentially, however, CROS added capacity to the public delivery system, which up until recently had not been adding capacity rapidly enough to keep up with the growth of incident cancers. The CROS contract was not renewed the following year when similar incentives were provided to the public system and additional human resource capacity came on-stream. Critics of the experiment have argued that the CROS case mix was less challenging than in other clinics, and that displacement of staff in other clinics did occur.

While the Ontario cancer system has had limited experience with parallel private sector insurance or private delivery for public services, as the next section shows the *Chaoulli* decision and the advent of a new private chemotherapy infusion clinic are obliging Ontario to consider new options for some chemotherapy patients.

Access to Cancer services post-*Chaoulli:* Wait Time Appeal and Changing IV Drug Coverage?

The Justices of the Supreme Court that formed the majority in the *Chaoulli* decision did not address the question of how long a wait is too long for medically necessary services, although we will wait for any response to this question in the *Cilinger* case. From the perspective of risk to the patient in terms of his or her prognosis, this is a difficult question to answer. In the case of cancer, an unsafe delay in treatment can depend on the type, stage, pathology or genetic expression of the patient's disease, among other factors. Should the *Chaoulli* decision result in two-tier system across Canada where patients are permitted to purchase private access (either through insurance or out of pocket) for medically beneficial services, it is possible that the evidence-based approach to treatment of patients characteristic of cancer services may no longer endure. The ability to pay for medically necessary services through private insurance could supersede rationing on the basis of need. That is, any wait at all may be too long for patients with the means to seek private care. The risk for cancer patients is that private providers may offer services, which are neither based on evidence nor cost effective. The *Chaoulli* decision has shifted the national debate away from one about unreasonably long waiting times to one about access to care as noted earlier.

Perhaps the most constructive action arising from the *Chaouilli* judgement has been a burning imperative by governments already committed to drive down wait times at least within five priority areas including cancer services. A number of important initiatives are underway in Ontario to reduce waiting times within the public system, including targeted investments in imaging, increasing the volume of surgical procedures, central electronic registration and regional management and reporting of waiting lists. In our view, these investments will have a downward effect on waiting times for cancer services. All of this adds up to the likelihood that most falling wait times are *not* likely to be appealing as a judicial target. To the extent that governments and hospitals gird themselves with systematic methods to collect comparable data and reduce waiting times, they will be less vulnerable to challenges. The recourse to private insurance, as argued elsewhere is really an empty right with little consequence for the improvement of care other than the loud message to governments to get on with reducing wait times.[48]

The push for better access to care (not access to waiting) arising from the *Chaouilli* judgement in our view is and will continue to be a central public and a continued legal concern.

The emergence of the *Chaouilli* judgement alongside a national call for better and more timely provincial payment for blockbuster cancer drugs (like Herceptin) has the attention of cancer systems across the country. In oncology we are facing a variety of very good new cancer drugs that are both efficacious and cost effective. We also face a range of very expensive intravenous cancer drugs that have only modest medical benefits. Agents with modest survival or quality of life benefits which are not cost-effective are unlikely to make their way onto public formularies, but patients will want these agents even if the average cost of a life year gained exceeds $100,000. Both classes of drug are being licensed for sale in Canada and are being requested by patients and their families.

A slim majority of *oral* prescription drugs in Ontario are paid for through private insurance or out-of-pocket, however *intravenous* agents which require careful monitoring and infusion preparation have traditionally been delivered in the outpatient hospital setting and therefore within the public system, under the sweep of the *Canada Health Act*.[49] In a post-*Chaoulli* health care environment, what is the remedy for patients demanding services or drugs with modest benefits that the government does not make available in the public system? Is their recourse to cross the border for a higher priced remedy in the US, or should they have recourse to expensive life extending IV remedies at home? All formularies assess cost effectiveness and it seems a principled approach to scheduling drugs in a world of rapidly growing drugs costs. However, it probably is not a reasonable proposition to effectively prohibit access to agents which have benefit and for which oncologists will write prescriptions simply because the public payer has decided against adding these agents to a formulary.

Consider the recent opening of Provis Infusion Clinic, Inc. in Toronto. The clinic offers patients access to intravenous cancer agents that have some medical benefit, and have been approved for sale by Health Canada, but are not covered under the province's drug formulary because of either cost-effectiveness considerations or evidence considerations. Patients who have been referred to Provis by a medical oncologist and with the ability to pay, either out-of-pocket or through private insurance, can get access to infusion of drugs such as Velcade for multiple myeloma patients with advanced disease or Alimta for patients with mesothelioma. In short, the class of drugs offered to patients in this private clinic setting are those which are not paid for either because the assessment of evidence does not suggest they should or because such agents offer modest benefits without evidence of sufficient cost-effectiveness for the province to extend payment for all affected patients. In addition, the Provis delivery model requires patients to arrive at the clinic ready to be infused, having had the preparation work of installing chemotherapy lines performed within, and paid for by, the public system.

The increasing patient demand for expensive, cost-ineffective cancer drugs and the advent of Provis to satisfy this demand could have significant impacts on the public provision of intravenous drugs. One unintended adverse consequence of an enlarged access for cost ineffective drugs may be a reduced public pressure for cost-effective drugs to be covered by the public payer on a universal basis.

Moreover there is the real possibility of further proliferation of private infusion clinics across the province. Up until now, most Ontario cancer patients travelled to Buffalo to receive these types of expensive chemotherapy agents not covered in the public system. With the advent of a local clinic, the costs to each patient have been significantly reduced. While the particular impacts of Provis Infusion Clinic, Inc. on the public system may be relatively minor, the possibility of a growing market of such clinics could create significant impacts on the existing delivery system. These include a drain on human resources from the public system and a push to relax the focus on evidence and a growing marketing pressure for ineffective or unproven remedies. With very expensive and biologically targeted agents it is very important to know which patient populations will benefit and which will not, rather than simply selling agents to everyone without regard to the evidence of benefit. It is not inconceivable that private cancer clinics could be opened, providing a range of procedures for which there is no evidence of benefit to patients, effectively holding out false hope for money.

Unlike public hospitals, private clinics – like private insurers – have the ability to 'cream' cancer patients, providing services to the easiest cases and to offer care only at the final point of delivery (i.e. after chemotherapy preparation). Finally, should adverse reactions occur due to the infusion of chemotherapy agents at the private clinic, patients will need to be referred back to the public system for care.

Since only a minority of cancer patients will have the means to purchase unfunded intravenous chemotherapy agents, the advent of private infusion clinics represents an important new development in the Canadian health care system following the Supreme Court's decision on *Chaouilli*. The national standard for all intravenous drugs was public coverage and universal accessibility guided the approach. How we handle a growing group of expensive and modestly beneficial intravenous agents may signal an important departure in Canadian intravenous drug policy. In the absence of a national standard, a patchwork of solutions is being adopted in different provinces to respond to a growing consumer demand for these intravenous agents which do not satisfy cost-effectiveness criteria. The evolution of a national catastrophic drug scheme might at least make the decision rules consistent for all Canadians as distinct to making decisions thirteen times in Canada, but such an option is not apparent on the agenda of an apparently perplexed federal government.

Unlike Ontario, the Alberta health system offers private paying patients the ability to receive intravenous cancer drugs not covered by the provincial drug benefit program within public institutions. As discussed by Tim Caulfield and Nola Reis in this volume, this is in line with a range of initiatives underway in Alberta to combine public and private health care, and to promote a two-tiered system almost without regard for cost shifting from private to public or large cross subsidies between public and private care. As another example, breast cancer patients in Saskatchewan were able to pay for Herceptin within public hospitals prior to its being listed in the provincial drug formulary.

The range of expensive cancer agents that do not satisfy cost-effectiveness criteria is only likely to grow. The *Chaoulli* decision, the advent of the Provis clinic, and a lack of any effective national standard for prescription drugs are driving Ontario and other provinces to find a viable ongoing solution to this new access challenge for cancer services. Options range from allowing a parallel private delivery and privately financed system to grow for intravenous chemotherapy, to expanding the public system by permitting public hospitals to provide privately-financed drugs on a full cost recovery basis. Either solution will eventually require some regulatory framework to ensure quality and access within a principled framework. Finding the solution that is most likely to preserve the integrity and quality of the public system must take into account the plethora of cross-subsidy issues noted above; paying for the drugs privately covers only a portion of the cost of the service, and the remainder is picked up by the public system.

The *Chaoulli* judgement opens up a much broader set of access to care issues that have little to do with how long is too long for patients to wait for health care services. In particular, by advancing private insurance as a remedy for unreasonable waits, the decision has propelled a public debate on private financing and delivery of unfunded intravenous cancer agents for the minority of Canadian patients with the ability to pay for expensive intravenous drugs not covered by provincial formularies.

Notes

1 2005 SCC 35 [*Chaoulli*].
2 R.S.Q. c. C-12, s. 1.
3 Part I of the *Constitution Act, 1982*, being Schedule B to the *Canada Act 1982* (U.K.), 1982, c. 11.
4 *Supra* note 1 at para. 123.
5 D. Drache & T. Sullivan, eds., *Health Reform: Public Success, Private Failure* (London: Routledge, 1999).
6 Jeremy Hurst & Luigi Siciliani, *Tackling excessive waiting times for elective surgery: a comparison of policies twelve OECD countries* (Paris: Organisation for Economic Co-operation and Development, 2003), online: Organisation for Economic Co-operation and Development <http://www.oecd.org/dataoecd/24/32/5162353.pdf>.
7 *Ibid.* and Carolyn Hughes Tuohy, Colleen M. Flood & Mark Stabile, 'How

Does Private Finance Affect Public Health Care Systems? Marshalling the Evidence from OECD Nations' (2004) 29 J. Health Pol. 359 [Tuohy].

8 [2004] R.J.Q. 3083 (C.S.)[*Cilinger*].

9 [2004] R.J.Q. 2943.

10 V. Benk *et al.*, 'Impact of Radiation Wait Times on Risk of Local Recurrence of Breast Cancer: Early Stage Cancer with no Chemotherapy' (2004) 46 Technology Report, online: Canadian Coordinating Office for Health Technology Assessment <http://www.ccohta.ca/publications/pdf/155_breastcancerwl_tr_e.pdf >.

11 Ontario, Ministry of Health and Long-Term Care, *Report of the Cancer Services Implementation Committee* (Toronto: Cancer Services Implementation Committee, 2001), online: Ontario Ministry of Health <http://www.health.gov.on.ca/english/public/pub/ministry_reports/hudson/hudson.html>.

12 Cancer Care Ontario, 'Cancer System Quality Index' (2005), online: Cancer Care Ontario <http://www.cancercare.on.ca/qualityindex/>.

13 L. Barbera *et al.*, 'Defining the need for Raiotherapy for Lung Cancer in the General Population: A Criterion-based benchmarking approach' (2003) 41 Medical Care 1074.

14 Cancer Care Ontario, *Ontario Cancer Plan* (Toronto: Cancer Care Ontario, 2004), online: Cancer Care Ontario <http://cancercare.on.ca/index_ontarioCancerplan.htm>.

15 D. Hodgson *et al.*, 'Cancer Surgery' in J.V. Tu *et al.*, eds., *Access to Health Services in Ontario: ICES Atlas* (Toronto: Institute for Clinical Evaluative Sciences, 2005), online: Institute for Clinical Evaluative Sciences <http://www.ices.on.ca/webpage.cfm?site_id=1&org_id=67&morg_id=0&gsec_id=0&item_id=2862&type=atlas>.

16 'Colorectal cancer screening: recommendation statement from the Canadian Task Force on Preventive Health Care' (2001) 165 CMAJ 206.

17 Cancer Quality Council of Ontario, *Gaining access to appropriate cancer services: a four-point strategy to reduce waiting times in Ontario* (Toronto: Cancer Quality Council of Ontario, 2004), online: Cancer Care Ontario <http://www.cancercare.on.ca/documentsCQCOFourPointStrategy.pdf>.

18 See *e.g.* Dileep G. Bal *et al.*, 'California as a model' (2001) 15 J. Clin. Oncol. 69S, C. Summerbell *et al.*, 'Interventions for preventing obesity in children' (2005) 20 Cochrane Database Syst. Rev. CD001871, and Lazlo Tabar *et al.*, 'Beyond randomized controlled trials: organized mammographic screening substantially reduces breast carcinoma mortality' (2004) 11 J. Med. Screen 126.

19 Cancer Care Ontario, *Targeting Cancer: an action plan for cancer prevention and detection* (Toronto, Cancer Care Ontario, 2003), online: Cancer Care Ontario <http://www.cancercare.on.ca/OntarioCancerNewsArchives/200305/index_0305story2.html>.

20 Harvard Center for Cancer Prevention, *Harvard Report on Cancer Prevention*, vol. 2 (Boston: Harvard Center for Cancer Prevention, 1997), online: Harvard School of Public Health <http://www.hsph.harvard.edu/cancer/publications/reports.html>.

21 [1995] 3 S.C.R. 199.

22 Martin N. Marshall, Patrick S. Romano & Huw T.O. Davies, 'How do we maximize the impact of the public reporting of quality of care?' (2004) 16 Int. J. Qual. Health Care i57, Martin N. Marshall *et al.*, 'Public reporting on quality in the United States and the United Kingdom' (2003) 22 Health Aff. 134, Jerod M. Loeb, 'The current state of performance measurement in health care' (2004) 16 Int. J. Qual. Health Care i5 and Robert Gibberd *et al.*, 'Using indicators to quantify the potential to improve the quality of health care' (2004) 15 Int. J. Qual. Health Care i37.

23 See *e.g.* 'Cancer Waiting Time Statistics,' online: Department of Health <http://www.performance.doh.gov.uk/cancerwaits/>, 'Cancer Control in New Zealand,' online: Ministry of Health <http://www.moh.govt.nz/cancerwaitingtimes>, 'Waiting times against the 2005 target,' online: Scottish Executive <http://www.scotland.gov.uk/Topics/Health/health/cancer/cancerwaits>, 'Alberta Waitlist Registry: Cancer Services,' online: Alberta Health and Wellness <http://www.health.gov.ab.ca/waitlist/CancerServices.jsp?rhaID=All &loctnType=All&doSearch=Nl> and *supra* note 12.

24 Kathleen Morris & Jennifer Zelmer, Public Reporting of Performance Measures in Health Care (Ottawa: Canadian Policy Research Network, 2005), online: Canadian Policy Research Network <http://www.cprn.com/en/doc.cfm?doc=1176>.

25 Judith H. Hibbard, Jean Stockard & Martin Tusler. 'Hospital performance reports: impact on quality, market share, and reputation' (2005) 24 Health Aff. 1150.

26 Cancer Care Ontario, *Radiation Wait Times*, online: Cancer Care Ontario <http://www.cancercare.on.ca/index_waittimesRadiation.asp>.

27 See *e.g.* Peter Van Harten 'Radiation treatment wait times worsening' *The Hamilton Spectator* (13 January 2005) A1.

28 *Supra* note 12.

29 Tom W. Noseworthy *et al.*, 'Waiting for scheduled services in Canada:

development of priority-setting scoring systems' (2003) 9 J. Eval. Clin. Pract. 23.

30 W. Dodds *et al.*, 'Implementing the 2-week wait rule for cancer referral in the UK: general practitioner's views and practices' (2004) 13 Eur. J. Cancer Care (Engl) 82.

31 Centre for Reviews and Dissemination., *Two-week wait for cancer referrals* (York: University of York, 2005), online: Centre for Reviews and Dissemination <http://www.york.ac.uk/inst/crd/pdf/report27summ.pdf>.

32 Conversation between Dr. Mike Richards and Terrence Sullivan (10 September 2005)[unpublished].

33 Saskatchewan Surgical Care Network, 'Target Time Frames for Surgery,' online: Saskatchewan Surgical Care Network <http://www.sasksurgery.ca/target_timeframes.htm>.

34 P.A. Glynn *et al.*, 'The Saskatchewan Surgical Care Network – toward timely and appropriate access' (2003) 7 Hosp Q. 44.

35 Cancer Care Ontario, *Cancer surgery wait times measurement in the Greater Toronto Area: a pilot study conducted by the Surgical Oncology Program* (Toronto: Cancer Care Ontario, 2004), online: Cancer Care Ontario <http://www.cancercare.on.ca/pdf/SurgeryWaitTimesGTAPilot.pdf>.

36 Anna Gagliardi, William K. Evans & Eva Grunfeld. 'Evaluation of diagnostic assessment units in oncology: a systematic review' (2004) 22 J. Clin. Oncol. 1126.

37 G.S. Duthie *et al.*, 'A UK training program for nurse practitioner flexible sigmoidoscopy and a prospective evaluation of the practice of the first UK trained nurse flexible sigmoidoscopist' (1998) 43 Gut. 711 and .M. Palitz *et al.*, 'The colon cancer prevention program (CoCAP): rationale, implementation, and preliminary results' (1997), 11 HMO Pract. 5.

38 Baker, Ross & Farrah Schwartz. 'Innovation and access to cancer care services in Ontario' (2005) 3 Longwoods Review, online: Longwoods Publishing <http://www.longwoods.com product.php?productid=17194&cat=362&page=1>.

39 *Ibid.*

40 Canada, The Standing Senate Committee on Social Affairs, Science and Technology, *The Health of Canadians: The Federal Role*, vol. 6, online: Parliament of Canada <http://www.parl.gc.ca/37/2/parlbus/commbus/senate/com-e/soci-e/rep-e/repoct02v016highlights-e.htm>.

41 Cheryl L. Damberg *et al.*, 'Paying for performance: implementing a statewide project in California' (2005) 14 Qual. Manage. Health Care 79, Martin Roland, 'Linking physicians' pay to the quality of care - a major experi-

ment in the United Kingdom' (2004) 351 N. Engl. J. Med. 1448 and Meredith B. Rosenthal *et al.*, 'Paying For Quality: Providers' Incentives For Quality Improvement' (2004) 23 Health Aff. 127.

42 *Supra* note 14.
43 *Supra* note 14.
44 Tuohy, *supra* note 7.
45 Stephen J. Duckett, 'Private care and public waiting' (2005) 20 Aust. Health Rev. 87.
46 U.K., Department of Health, *Growing capacity: independent sector diagnosis and treatment centres* (London: Department of Health Publications, 2005), online: Department of Health <http://www.dh.gov.uk/assetRoot/04/02/05/27/04020527.pdf>.
47 Tuohy, *supra* note 7.
48 C.M. Flood & T. Sullivan, 'Supreme disagreement: the highest court affirms an empty right' (2005) 173 CMAJ 142.
49 R.S.C. 1985, c. C-6.

Section 7 'Safety Valves': Appealing Wait Times Within A One-Tier System

CAROLINE PITFIELD AND COLLEEN M. FLOOD

Introduction

In *Chaoulli*,[1] a majority of the Supreme Court struck down provisions in Quebec's health and hospital insurance legislation prohibiting private insurance for otherwise publicly funded health care services. Seven rather than the usual nine judges sat on this case, and by a majority of 4:3 concluded that the Quebec insurance provisions unjustifiably violated rights to life and security of the person protected by the Quebec Charter. On the critical issue of the application of the Canadian Charter, however, the Court was split 3:3 with Justice Deschamps choosing not to rule on this issue. Chief Justice McLachlin and Justice Major (writing on behalf of themselves and Justice Bastarache) found that the relevant provisions were in breach of section 7. Justices Binnie and Lebel (writing on behalf of themselves and Justice Fish), in a blistering dissent, found that the provisions did not breach either the Quebec or Canadian Charters.

In the context of a notably contentious decision, it is not surprising to find disagreement on the question of whether Quebec has an adequate 'safety valve' in its publicly funded health care system to allow individuals to access health care elsewhere in the event of serious delays.[2] What is significant, however, is that despite their different assessments of the evidence, the Court seemed to agree on the constitutional importance of this so-called 'safety valve.' All of these judges directly or indirectly suggested that the existence of an adequate appeal mechanism in Quebec's publicly funded health care system was an important determinant of whether or not the relevant Quebec laws prohibiting private health insurance were constitutional.[3]

The significance attributed to 'safety valves' suggests an important policy consideration for provinces responding to the *Chaoulli* decision – that is, that these mechanisms may be used to protect publicly funded health care systems from future section 7 challenges. This is not a new idea. The Senate Committee, lead by Senator Kirby, suggested that there should be a 'Health Care Guarantee' – a process through which individuals are able to access health care in another jurisdiction, including another country, in the face of undue delays.[4] Recently, Canada's medical establishment also began championing the use of such mechanisms to address wait times problems.[5] As provinces prepare to respond to the Court's decision, it is an option that should be considered in more detail.

The purpose of this paper is to explore whether the 'safety valve' in Ontario's public health care plan ('OHIP') renders the Province's prohibition against private health insurance more likely to withstand constitutional scrutiny. (Considerations are also applicable to other measures provinces used to protect the integrity of the publicly funded system, such as prohibitions preventing physicians from charging more in the private sector than the public sector tariff and/or from working in both the public and private sectors). OHIP has one of the most robust reimbursement and appeal processes in the country. Insured persons can apply to the General Manager of the plan for public payment of certain health care services performed out-of-country if equivalent services are unavailable in the Province, or unavailable without significant delay. In the event that this application is refused, they have a further right of appeal to the Ontario Health Services Appeal and Review Board – a quasi-judicial appeal board that allows claimants to make their case in person before independent decision-makers.

Because significant insight on the strengths and weakness of this 'safety valve' can be gleaned from the decisions of the Board, the focus of this paper will be on this stage of the process. Many of the conclusions drawn, however, have application to the process as a whole.

The Chaoulli Decision

On the preliminary question of whether section 7 of the *Charter* applied in the context of the case, six of the seven judges on the *Chaoulli* bench agreed that in certain circumstances, and in the face of undue delays in the publicly funded health care system, these rights could be engaged. What differed between these judges was their willingness to find that rights were actually violated in this case. Key in this regard, was their interpretation of whether the public monopoly over health insurance means that no alternative sources of health care are available to Quebeckers. The majority found that individuals were effectively trapped by the state in a closed and ineffective health system – to the point where their rights were breached by virtue of delays in accessing health care. They failed to identify any 'safety valve' or acceptable, alternative source of health care.

Justice Deschamps' opinion most explicitly acknowledged the potential significance of an effective safety valve. In considering whether delays, caused by waiting times constituted a breach of the right to 'inviolability' under the Quebec Charter, she dismissed the dissenting judges' suggestion that there was 'an internal mechanism' to safeguard the public health system. She wrote:

> According to them, Quebeckers may go outside the province for treatment where services are not available in Quebec. This possibility is clearly not a solution for the system's deficiencies. The evidence did not bring to light any administrative mechanism that would permit Quebeckers suffering as a result of waiting times to obtain care outside the province. The possibility of obtaining care outside Quebec is case-specific and is limited to crisis situations.[6]

Chief Justice McLachlin and Justice Major did not mention safety valves *per se*, but did explicitly find that the system was effectively closed and thus violated rights to security of the person. In so doing, they cited various passages from *Morgentaler* and concluded the following:

> In this appeal, delays in treatment giving rise to psychological and physical suffering engage the s. 7 protection of security of the person just as they did in *Morgentaler*. In *Morgentaler*, as in this case, the problem arises from a legislative scheme that offers health services. In *Morgentaler*, as in this case, the legislative scheme denies people the right to access alternative health care. (That the sanction in *Morgentaler* was criminal prosecution while the sanction here is administrative prohibition and penalties is irrelevant. The important point is that in both cases, care outside the legislatively provided system is effectively prohibited.) In *Morgentaler* the result of the monopolistic scheme was delay in treatment with attendant physical risk and psychological suffering. In *Morgentaler*, as here, people

in urgent need of care face the same prospect: unless they fall within the wealthy few who can pay for private care, typically outside of the country, they have no choice but to accept the delays imposed by the legislative scheme and the adverse physical and psychological consequences this entails. As in *Morgentaler*, the result is interference with security of the persons under section 7 of the *Charter*. [7]

Finally, the minority appeared to share the majority's understanding of how section 7 *might* apply in the circumstances – but disagreed with their factual characterization of the system and, in particular, the analogy with *Morgentaler.* Justices Binnie and LeBel, writing for themselves and Justice Fish, differentiated the facts of *Morgentaler* – which involved a right of access to medical treatment for a condition representing a danger to life or health without fear of criminal sanction – from those in *Chaoulli*.

The minority also referred to the 'importance' of 'allowing Quebec residents to obtain (publicly funded) essential health care outside of the province when unable to receive the case in question at home in a timely manner.'[8] They attributed access to out-of-province care, in combination with the prohibitions, with the responsibility of furthering the state's interest in distributing health care according to need and not ability to pay. Their judgment characterized Quebec's reimbursement scheme for out-of-province services as a form of 'safety valve' and noted that, through judicial review, courts were able to supervise the enforcement of the rights of patients directly affected by related administrative decisions on a case-by-case basis (i.e. when the 'safety valve was opened too sparingly'[9]). This kind of judicial intervention, they concluded, was preferable to the appellants' global challenge to the entire single-tier health plan.

The conclusions reached by the various judges in *Chaoulli* as to whether Quebec has a robust and effective appeal mechanism in its publicly funded health care system have implications for other provinces considering to what extent their own legislative provisions protecting one-tier medicine can withstand constitutional scrutiny. That said, as the disparity between the factual findings of these judges suggest, it is not just *any* appeal mechanism that can provide protection from such claims. Judging by the comments of the majority, an appeal mechanism operating in publicly funded health care systems would have to be able to address issues with respect to both the quality and the timeliness of access to health care services, as well as physical and psychological harm. We also speculate that this mechanism would have to be accessible to those facing potential harm and capable of expediting treatment for those in need when necessary. It would, therefore, have to employ an equitable, yet also quick and effective, process. The following section of this paper will evaluate the Ontario Health Services Appeal and Review Board in light of these requirements.

The Ontario Health Services Appeal and Review Board

A. The Mandate of the Ontario Health Services Appeal and Review Board

The Ontario Health Services Appeal and Review Board ('the Board') provides residents of Ontario with a limited, statutory right of appeal with respect to the availability and accessibility of insured health care services.

While the General Manager makes initial decisions about payment for out-of-country services on the basis of a paper application, on appeal before the Board, parties are provided with the opportunity to participate in an adjudicative hearing – to make argument (orally, by phone or in writing), provide new evidence and respond to opposing arguments from OHIP.[10] In essence, the Board operates like an informal court. Board Members are not 'expert' in the sense of clinical expertise; only three of them can be 'legally qualified medical practitioners,' none can be Crown employees and most are, in fact, lawyers by training.[11] They are intended to be like judges – 'independent' decision-makers appointed for fixed (three-year, renewable) terms. Decisions are made solely on the basis of evidence presented before them.

The Board's mandate with respect to payment claims for health care services is set out in Ontario's *Health Insurance Act*. Section 20(1) of the Act provides rights of appeal before the Board for 'insured persons' who have made payment claims for insured services that were refused by the General Manager. Rights of appeal also extend to those who have applied to the General Manager for OHIP coverage and been refused, and physicians and practitioners affected by certain directions. [12] Although the core part of the Board's work consists of appeals brought by individuals under this provision, it is a busy board and, as of 1998, hears appeals under thirteen other health-related statutes, including the *Long-Term Care Act* and the *Health Protection and Promotion Act*.

Entitlements to 'insured services,' for the purpose of the *Health Insurance Act*, are set out in Regulation 552.[13] 'Insured services' include insured physician services – which are services rendered by a physician in Ontario, if referred to in the schedule of benefits (essentially, a list of fees paid to physicians for providing certain services) – insured hospital services, insured dental-surgical services and various extended health care services, as further prescribed in the regulations. [14] This Regulation also provides a list of services that are specifically excluded from OHIP coverage[15] (such as treatment generally accepted within Ontario as experimental) and defines payment criteria for out-of-country services in certain circumstances.[16]

Amongst the entitlements provided in Regulation 552, the most relevant – in light of *Chaoulli* – is the 'safety valve' provision in section 28.4. Under this section, insured persons in the Province may obtain payment or repayment for services sought out of country, in hospitals or health facilities, under the following circumstances:

(2) Services that are part of a treatment and that are rendered outside Canada at a hospital or health facility are prescribed as insured services if,
  a) the treatment is generally accepted in Ontario as appropriate for a person in the same medical circumstances as the insured person;
  b) and either,
    i) that kind of treatment is not performed in Ontario by an identical or equivalent procedure; or
    ii) that kind of treatment is performed in Ontario but it is necessary that the insured person travel out of Canada *to avoid a delay that would result in death or medically significant irreversible tissue damage* [emphasis added]

Individuals who wish to seek treatment outside of OHIP under this provision must first apply to the General Manager for pre-approval in accordance with section 28.4(5). This section provides, in essence, that those seeking out-of-country services must have a 'physician who practices medicine in Ontario' submit an application to the General Manager containing written confirmation that, in his or her opinion, the conditions set out in section 28.4(2) are satisfied. The rationale for this is that OHIP is in a better position than the individual – or, individual physicians – to know what treatment is available in the Province and how accessible it is. Once the General Manager has reviewed the application, he will communicate his decision, with reasons, to the applicant by letter. The applicant, in turn, has 15 days to write a responding letter, informing both OHIP and the Board, of his or her intention to appeal a negative decision. For those granted pre-approval at this stage, the application process stops here; they can access treatment out-of-country and OHIP will cover the hospital bill as if the treatment had been provided at home.[17]

B. *Other Appeal Mechanisms in Provincial Health Care Systems*

The Board compares favorably to other administrative appeal mechanisms in other provinces. It is, for instance, one of the most independent boards in the country, with other boards often being comprised of or including governmental agents, and it offers appellants some of the most robust procedural protections. Comparatively, all decisions about public payment for out-of-country services in British Columbia involve the participation of a departmental representative. In that province, initial applications are made to the Medical Services Plan ('MSP') for administrative review; those applications that are refused by the MSP may be further assessed by a Review Panel, appointed on the request of the applicant and consisting of one representative from each of the Ministry, the provincial medical association and the general public.

Up until recently, Alberta's out-of-country services application process likewise lacked independence, according to the Provincial ombudsman. 'There was no formalized appeal mechanism and several investigations determined the initial decision-maker was subsequently reviewing his or her own decision on "appeal."' [18] Inadequate reasons for denial were also, apparently, supplied. Alberta now has a more independent appeal mechanism to challenge decisions made by the 'Out-of-Country Health Services Committee' comprised of six members appointed by the Minister: four physicians, an ethicist and a member of the public. However, the Panel apparently remains an informal mechanism, processing relatively few appeals a year, all in written form.

The Board also has a more specialized, more tailored mandate than other provincial appeal mechanisms. Quebec's 'Tribunal administratif du Québec' ('TAQ'), for instance, hears a very broad range of claims, of which health care claims with respect to out-of-country services represent a mere fraction.[19] It has jurisdiction to hear appeals with respect to administrative decisions made by virtually all government decision-makers in the province, including ministers, commissions, boards, municipalities and health institutions.[20] Claims with respect to health services arise as a result of applications for reimbursement under section 10 of Quebec's *Health Insurance Act* and ss. 23.1 and 23.2 of related regulations that have been declined by the Régie de l'assurance maladie de Quebec (the 'Régie'). [21]

A key complaint about Quebec's appeal process is the general, administrative nature of remedies provided. The regulations under which reimbursement is provided are quite vague – leaving vast discretion to the Régie with respect to applications – and corresponding decisions by the Board tend to be quite deferential. For this reason, as the minority judges in *Chaoulli* admit, the safety valve provided by TAQ may sometimes be opened 'too sparingly'[22] and, in some cases, unlawfully, as illustrated in a case called *Stein v. Tribunal administratif du Quebec*.[23] In this case, the Quebec Superior Court overturned a decision of the TAQ to deny a man reimbursement for the costs of health services received in the United States to treat metastasized colon cancer. It did so on the grounds that it was irrational, unreasonable and contrary to the purpose of provincial health insurance legislation to make Mr. Stein wait so long for surgery in the first place. It was patently unreasonable for the tribunal to not recognize that fact in upholding the decisions of both the Régie and TAQ.

Does The Board Provide An Adequate Safety Valve?

A. Substantive Dimension

The mandate of the Board appears to provide insured persons with some opportunity to appeal unreasonable wait times. However, like many administrative decision-makers, the Board is bound by a specific policy direction and does not have broad discretion to 'do justice' between the parties. Our review of Board decisions suggests that many appellants base their arguments before the Board on very personal understandings of medical necessity, often based on non-medical factors, such as psychological distress, compassion and financial or geographic efficiency. This is particularly the case when delays are at issue. But the Board has little ability to transcend the limits imposed by the Act and its Regulations in order to do justice and to provide parties with fair outcomes in the wider context of their personal circumstances.

As it is consistently required to remind appellants, it must simply apply the Act and its Regulations.[24] It has no explicit discretion to grant flexible, tailored remedies to suit the issues before it. It cannot order payment for non-insured services, grant partial reimbursement or take compassionate or efficiency (either financial or geographic) arguments into account. It does not have a policy-making function (except, perhaps, as an overseer of the General Manager's informal decision-making policies[25]) and has recently lost its jurisdiction to consider the constitutional validity of an Act or regulation. [26] It has also declined jurisdiction under the Canada Health Act[27] and will not consider private law issues, such as tort (negligence) or contract. [28] The most the Board can do is exercise a small margin of discretion in applying certain provision to the facts of the claim.

The result of this limited remedial power is that the Board is often unable to provide appellants with the redress that they are seeking. The success rate before the Board is relatively low. Out of a sample of approximately 121 appeals heard in 2002, only 10 were successful. [29] In the absence of information on the success rate of applications to the General Manager, it is difficult to gauge exactly what this statistic means. It is likely, at least in part, a reflection of excessively high appellant expectations, but it may also represent instances in which the 'safety valve' was opened too sparingly.

The following sections will critically examine Board decisions on section 28.4 with a view to determining how often the latter is the case – and, accordingly, whether the Board acts as an adequate section 7 'safety valve' for insured persons in Ontario.

Challenging the Range of Services Covered

Section 28.4(2) provides for repayment of out-of-country services when such services are recognized as appropriate for a person in the same circumstances as the insured but not performed in Ontario. The Board's decisions on this provision tend to focus on the first part of the general provision – section 28.4(2)(a) – which provides that the treatment sought must be 'generally accepted as appropriate for a person in the same medical circumstances as the insured person.'[30] Presumably this is because the second part of the test – determining whether or not the service is performed – is far easier to apply. Section 28.4(2)(a) is also relevant to the second branch, discussed below.

Initially, the reference to the 'insured person' in section 28.4(2)(a) appears to allow determinations in keeping with the appellant's own sense of medical necessity. Certainly appellants read it this way and tend to present evidence with respect to their own perceived need, and their own circumstances and context. What the provision actually requires, however, is consideration of what the profession accepts as appropriate for a person in the same *medical* circumstances as the appellant, but not necessarily the appellant himself. Although this may not be evident in this phrase alone, the administrative conditions provided in section 28.4(5) make it clear that Ontario physicians are the arbiters of generally acceptability (or, medical necessity) in this instance.

This test is often the source of appellant dissatisfaction with Board decisions. In addition to frustration because the Board cannot consider personal views on issues of medical necessity, appellants must contend with the reality that those responsible for the general quality of care provided in the health care system – that is, Ontario physicians and government bureaucrats – are also, effectively, responsible for determining circumstances in which care is available outside of that system. In most cases, this simply means that the services available to insured persons are limited to those considered appropriate – medically necessary – by Ontario physicians. In some instances, however, these judgments appear to include non-medical – sometimes inappropriate or even, seemingly, discriminatory – considerations.

For example, in one case, an appellant, who was a Jehovah's Witness, was denied approval for a certain prostate cancer treatment in the United States.[31] The evidence showed that this treatment was only offered to patients in Ontario (i.e. accepted as appropriate/non-experimental) after unsuccessful surgery and radiation treatment. Because the appellant was not willing to have surgery because of his religious beliefs, physicians would not provide him with access to the treatment. The rationale for denying treatment in this case was that it was not medically appropriate, but the decisive factor was the appellant's religious beliefs. Discrimination on the basis of age is likewise sometimes suggested in Board decisions. [32] While age may be a legitimate reason for depriving a patient of access to treatment, it can also be an easy way to cut costs or an excuse to avoid treating difficult patients. Age discrimination in medical judgments is particularly hard to identify, given the willingness of society to turn a blind eye to this kind of rationing (on the grounds that it is justifiable) and the ease with which it can be hidden under the 'linguistic guise of medical 'indications'.'[33] Medical judgment can also disguise discriminatory attitudes about certain medical conditions, like AIDS or mental illness.

This approach also means that moral issues are sometimes subsumed in 'medical circumstances.' This concern was illustrated in a recent decision of the Board that denied the appellant repayment for the costs of a living donor renal transplant performed in the United States because of ethical concerns about the connection between the (wealthy) appellant and his donor (his housekeeper).[34]

Discrimination aside – practically speaking, it is very difficult to ascertain what the profession 'generally accepts as appropriate' for someone in the same medical circumstances as the insured, particularly by resorting to the testimony of one or two physicians. The Board apparently has two ways of dealing with the problem. The first is to rely more heavily on the evidence presented by OHIP, because this is assumed to represent a composite of opinions from across the province. The second is to consider whether the treatment at issue is actually provided or performed in the province. [35] The problem with this approach is that it requires the Board to look at evidence that is supposed to be in support of section 28.4(2)(b)(i), – i.e. whether the 'treatment is not performed' in Ontario, a question that must be answered in the negative in order for an appellant to succeed. Thus, an appellant who provides good evidence in support of section 28.4(2)(b)(i)– i.e. that no one will perform the service – might actually find that this evidence is used to reject his or her claim on the basis of section 28.4(2)(a) – i.e. that it is not generally considered appropriate.[36]

All things considered, the mere existence of right of appeal with respect to the range of services that are publicly insured (as opposed to the timeliness of those services) is probably more than sufficient for the majority in *Chaoulli*. It should be recalled that the majority were very clear that the appellants were not asking for public funding for any new services or treatments. The Court's recent decision in *Auton*[37] also reflects a conservative view of claims for additions to the range of services that are publicly funded. Services that are not so included are free to be bought and sold in private markets and people may purchase private insurance coverage if it is available and they qualify. There is, as such, no 'public monopoly' hampering free choice (or as free as one's means will allow) and it is thus not evident that the Court's findings in Chaoulli would apply with respect to these services.

Nevertheless, in our view, a fairer appeal mechanism would allow appellants to challenge the standard of care in the system by reference to what is considered to be the standard of care in similarly situated jurisdictions, and would provide the Board with *explicit* discretion to override physician opinion in instances where such opinion appears to disclose discrimination or other illegitimate considerations. This would mean that the right of appeal in section 28.4(2)(b)(i) could be used to actually challenge the status quo and to sometimes question the quality of service provided by OHIP, which in turn might help ensure the perceived legitimacy of the system.

Challenging Long Wait Times

Section 28.4(2)(b)(ii) provides re-payment for treatment generally performed in Ontario, under circumstances in which it is 'necessary that the insured person travel out of Canada to avoid a delay that would result in death or medically significant irreversible tissue damage' – in essence, the kind of 'safety valve' sought by the judges on the *Chaoulli* bench, but limited to the physical dimension of harm.

While clearly preferable to the vague out-of-country service provisions in other provinces, section 28.4(2)(b)(ii) shares some of the same shortcomings as the first ---- including the need to determine whether the treatment at issue is considered appropriate for someone in the same medical circumstances as the insured person. Like section 28.4(2)(b)(i), it is also limited to instances in which purportedly objective, medical determinations about the necessity of out-of-country treatment can be made. Moreover, in order to secure repayment, appellants must show evidence from an Ontario physician demonstrating that delay in obtaining health care services *would* – and not *could* – result in death or medically significant irreversible tissue damage. Psychological harm is not considered relevant. At the same time, this section is prone to subjectivity in that those applying it sometimes exercise discretion in their evaluation of evidence and weigh it in light of their own appreciation of the significance of the delay. Given that the Board lacks any expert ability to measure such wait times, this approach is not surprising.

The requirements of section 28.4(2)(b)(ii) are such that the Board is most likely to reject a claim when the physical effect of delay is difficult to anticipate – i.e. when 'objective' determinations on the basis of the evidence are hard to come to and potential harms are unfathomable to the Board – regardless of other considerations. Thus, in one case, an appellant was refused re-payment for an MRI sought in the United States because of delay in receiving treatment here. She had been diagnosed with a serious brain tumour and told that delay in receiving treatment would not kill her, but that it was unknown whether it would cause tissue damage. Her appeal was declined because, on a retrospective review of the evidence, it was concluded that 'on a balance of probabilities' she would not have suffered medically significant irreversible tissue damage.[38] It appeared irrelevant to the Board that, at the time, physicians simply could not tell her what the exact effects of delay would be and that this fact itself was likely to cause serious anxiety.

As with the first provision, out-of-country service in the event of delay is also only available if Ontario physicians think it is appropriate. Thus, the Board's 2003 Annual Report refers to a case in which a woman, with a significant history for breast cancer, discovered a lump in her breast and was told to 'wait and see' by her physicians. Not satisfied with waiting for the lump to grow or change, she sought treatment in the United States. The Board dismissed her claim and found, on the basis of the evidence, that the 'wait and see' approach was considered appropriate.[39]

In our view, such a narrow characterization of the kind of harm resulting from delays that is worthy of redress does not amount to a sufficiently robust 'safety-valve' from a constitutional perspective.

One possible alternative approach, advocated by Monahan and Hartt (and by Stanley Hartt alone in this volume) and subsequently by the Senate Committee chaired by Senator Kirby,[40] is the establishment of a wait times guarantee. By adopting this approach, some of the problems currently associated with section 28.4.2(b)(ii) would be mitigated. In particular, Board members would no longer be required to determine, themselves, on the basis of medical evidence provided whether individuals had suffered too long or not; instead they would be guided by a list. The wait times set could be on the basis of the best medical evidence and could also allow for the fact that undue psychological suffering can occur as a result of having to wait too long for some procedures. From the Board's perspective, this would mitigate the issue of subjective decision-making that seems to be reflected in current decisions. What a wait list approach would not do is provide relief on an individualized basis – particularly in the event of psychological harm. It would be a one size fits all approach.

This last concern might be addressed by providing the Board with some explicit ability to exercise discretion in those instances where serious, psychological harm is at issue as a result of delay caused by the state – i.e. when a *Charter* right might otherwise be engaged. Significant consideration would have to be given to the appropriate parameters for the exercise of this discretion. Even so, determining those instances in which it should be exercised would presumably be difficult for the

Board to identify. (The Supreme Court of Canada itself shied away from addressing the question of actual, individual harm under section 7 in the *Chaoulli* decision – instead providing general definitions of an acceptable standard.[41]) Nevertheless, such a limited, exceptional remedy would ensure the Board's ability to fend off potential, subsequent section 7 challenges on these grounds without opening up the 'safety valve' too widely.

B. Procedural Fairness

In evaluating the ability of the Board to protect OHIP from section 7 challenges, its actual, practical accessibility is as important as its substantive ability to address relevant claims. Accordingly, the following section will discuss some of the barriers faced by appellants before the Board in terms of the Board's expertise, the complexity of its procedures, cost and delay.

1) Expertise and Interest Groups

Presently, Board Members are appointed and paid by the provincial Cabinet and can be re-appointed for as many terms as the Cabinet deems appropriate. Board Members tend to represent relatively elite professions – that is, they are lawyers, consultants and hospital executives. Most in fact are lawyers. Significantly, none of them represent patients, disease organizations, special interest groups or those who otherwise have a vested interest in making health care services available to those who most need them. The appointment process is completely closed and includes no public participation whatsoever.

   In terms of medical expertise, the *Health Insurance Act* provides that only three Board Members can be physicians and none can be Crown employees.[42] Technically, only a fraction of the Board's Members therefore represent parties otherwise already involved in making determinations about health care entitlements. The concern seems to have been that the Board not be co-opted by those who may have financial interests in expanding the range of services that attract public funding. The quid pro quo is a loss of clinical expertise. The Board cannot avail itself of this expertise through other means and must make decisions solely on the basis of the evidence provided by the parties before them. They are not authorized to use third party consultants or to otherwise supplement their understanding of the complex facts before them.

Determining the range of health services that should be funded is a complex process requiring a range of expertise. The reality is that all decisions to provide, or support the public provision, of any health care service involve a range of different considerations, including effectiveness, cost, and ethical or social concerns. Cost and effectiveness considerations are one component. Medical judgment is another. But more is required to build a satisfactory matrix of decision-making.

2) Complexity, Cost and Geographic Barriers

As more specialized alternatives to the legal system, administrative processes are supposed to offer 'speedy, informal and inexpensive dispute resolution backed by specialized expertise.'[43] In the case of applications to the General Manager – often made in the face of an imminent need – it is obviously important that this standard be met. For those who must bring a further right of appeal before the Board, the issues are slightly different. In some cases, the fact that more time has passed will make the urgency more acute; in others, treatment will already have been sought, at significant personal expense, so that it is repayment that individuals are after. Generally speaking, the most striking thing about issues of complexity, cost and delay before the Board is the disparity in these regards between the two parties.

Although the Board tells prospective appellants that they 'do not need a lawyer' to bring an appeal,[44] the reality is that given the complexity of the Board's procedures, many may need a lawyer to represent their claim (particularly if they are to succeed against OHIP, which is very familiar with the Board's processes and its mandate). In this regard it is relevant to note the amount of legal support Board Members themselves are provided with; despite the fact that over half of its Members are lawyers, the Board spent approximately $155,000, or almost a third of its overall budget, on legal training and legal counsel in the 2002–2003 fiscal year.[45]

Recognizing that its procedures are complex – and obviously aware of the fact that lawyers are no solution – the Board is attempting to address the fact that it may be daunting to some. In particular, in order to increase its accessibility, it has started to provide more information to prospective appellants, including the Rules of Practice and Procedures and pamphlets on the mandate and processes of the Board, in a low-cost and easy to obtain format though the establishment of a web-site.[46] It also has plans to revise the Rules in order to make them more accessible to unrepresented claimants.[47] While this is a step in the right direction, those looking to mount more sophisticated appeals still face many barriers.

Although there are plans to provide more sophisticated information in the future, through the publication of guidelines and practice directions[48], the best way to get such information for now is by consulting the Board's unreported decisions. Some of these are available on-line, but most are currently kept, in hard copy, at the Board's offices in Toronto. They are opened only during the day, Monday through Friday, making it difficult for appellants who live elsewhere in Ontario to look at them. Moreover, researching these decisions can be a very frustrating exercise. They are kept in binders and in alphabetical order. It is only recently that the Board has begun to file them in a relatively systematic fashion – that is, with files numbers, an index and some references to their subject matter. Still, not all decisions mentioned in the index are in the binders and not all decisions in the binder are represented in the index; there appear, for instance, to be far fewer procedural decisions and orders in the binder than are actually made by the Board. Finally, no decisions can be removed from the Board's office – which is understandable as they are otherwise unreported and unavailable elsewhere. For those wishing to continue researching at home, however, the Board's receptionist can copy decisions for 25 cents a page. [49]

In addition to the disparity of familiarity with the Board's procedures between appellants and OHIP, there are significant disparities between these parties when it comes to their ability to pay for the costs of an appeal and to also withstand the impact of those costs. Although obviously not as expensive as bringing an action before the general courts, costs are still significant, particularly if counsel is used and in light of the relatively modest rewards that claimants are seeking. Additional costs may be incurred in obtaining and presenting the necessary evidence and in traveling to, and staying in, Toronto, to attend at the Board's office, if necessary, to research past decisions and/or attend hearings. (In the latter case, physical costs may also be at issue.)

The Board cannot mitigate the costs that appellants incur in bringing an appeal, or the disparate impact that costs may have on the fairness of the appeal. All an appellant is likely to get after a successful appeal is payment or repayment for an insured service. The Board does not have the power to award financial damages, even when OHIP has misapplied the law or misinterpreted an application for pre-approval, acted negligently or otherwise caused an appellant to suffer real or financial harm by refusing to pay for an insured service. Its remedial powers are limited to ordering the General Manager to 'take such action as it considers the General Manager should take,' and there is no pre-judgment interest on such awards.[50] The only circumstances which may warrant a cost award, pursuant to the Board's own rules of Practice and Procedure, is when a party has acted unreasonably or in bad faith in the course of bringing or defending the action.[51] In practice, the Board is reluctant to exercise this power.[52]

3) Delay

Perhaps the most significant impediment for those with claims about access to health care services is timeliness – or delay.[53] Health care needs tend to be urgent, often too urgent to be dealt with through a court action, which can take years to work its way through the legal system, including the possibility of appeals.

Insofar as the General Manager and the Board process claims for medically required health care services, one might assume they prioritize timeliness. Clearly, in order to provide against a *Chaoulli*-style challenge in Ontario, the General Manager and the Board must ensure reasonable and timely access to alternative services when necessary. Timeliness has, however, only recently becomes an important goal for the Board, and even then only in certain aspects of its practice. Up until 1999–2000, it took the Board approximately a year to render its decisions and longer if any procedural issues were involved in the appeal. However, some effort was made to get rid of the backlog and reduce this lag time, so that the Board now provides written decisions within three months of the hearing.[54]

Despite significant efforts to render faster decisions, delays still exist in the Board's processes and as a result of its procedures – so that even if a decision is rendered within three months of a hearing, there may still be significant delays between the notice of appeal and the hearing itself. The Board's on-line information says that '[i]t takes about three months from the time you write the Board to request an appeal until the Board schedules your appeal hearing,' but it can take much longer for that hearing to actually occur, particularly if procedural matters arise in the interim.[55] In one case, a notice of appeal was filed in 2001 and still had not been heard two and a half years later.[56] In another, the appeal took four years to move through the Board's processes – including an appeal to the Divisional Court, which resulted in party and party costs for the appellant against OHIP[57] – only to end in an order for rehearing. Generally, the fact that twice as many appeals are not heard or are abandoned in a given year than are actually heard also suggests that there is significant delay in the processes leading up to a hearing.[58]

The Board is, apparently, very committed to the timeliness of its decision-making, despite an increasing number of appeals on increasingly complex issues, arising with respect to all fourteen statutes under which the Board has an appeal mandate. In order to maintain its ability to render timely decisions, for instance, it has proposed improvements to staff resources and decision-writing tools, and the implementation of fact sheets, guidelines and practice directions for the Board to use in making its decisions.[59] It also effectively requested an increase in Board membership from the Minister of Health in its last annual report.

In order to ensure the constitutionality of existing measures designed to prevent the flourishing of a two-tier system, the province must provide the resources for the Board to improve the timeliness of its decisions, including additional members. Other changes to consider include amending the *Health Insurance Act* to include a provision allowing the Board to impose costs on the government when it is responsible for creating delays in the appeal process and/or a provision specifically mandating expedited appeals, particularly when circumstances require them. Alberta, for instance, requires that a review happen within 30 days or less of being lodged[60] and that the Appeal Panel render its decision within five days[61]. Ontario might also consider reducing the Board's workload by establishing a second appeal mechanism to hear appeals brought under the other thirteen health statutes that provide for appeals to the Board.

Recommendations For Reform

The Ontario Board offers the potential to be a robust 'safety-valve' sufficient to stave off a constitutional challenge to laws designed to protect one-tier Medicare. However, reforms are required as presently, in the words of Justices Binnie and LeBel, appeals are allowed too sparingly.

Our first set of recommendations relate to the processes of decision-making. The Board's decisions should be available on-line. Resources need to be increased to allow the Board to hear and decide matters in an expeditious fashion. Hearings should occur within 30–60 days of an appeal being filed and decisions should be provided within five days. The Board should also have the ability to impose costs on the government when it is responsible for creating delays in the appeal process and to award, for example, pre-judgment interest. Consideration should also be given to including a wider range of expertise on the board that speaks to the multiple values that are at stake in determining how long is too long. The best medical evidence is certainly needed, but in and of itself is not sufficient. Considerations of cost-effectiveness and total governmental spending are also important and are presently bought to the table through the narrow windows of review provided for in the legislation. But other values are important too, particularly patient experience which can be bought to the decision-making table by appointment of patient representatives.

Our second set of recommendations relates to opening up the ability for a citizen to challenge a long wait time in Ontario. Some have argued for a wait list guarantee, and such a measure would certainly make adjudication on the part of the Board a more straightforward matter. As Stanley Hartt suggests in his contribution to this book, the test for the reasonableness of a delay could be based on the best insights and knowledge that medical science has at its disposal – in essence, something akin to the professional 'standard of care.' Resulting standards could be formally adopted at some stage of the process – by the government through regulation, by the General Manager through policies or guidelines – with the understanding that ignoring such standards for anything other than a bona fide medical reason would leave the plan explicitly vulnerable to section 7–type challenges.

But, in order to withstand a *Charter* challenge, Ontario's system of one-tier Medicare must allow the Board some discretion to respond to long wait times that cause psychological harms independent of adverse physical outcomes. A number of the Board's decisions bear witness to the psychological suffering endured by those who cannot meet the high standards of proof required by the existing legislation in order to be granted funding for treatment outside of Ontario. Absent a decision to restore the Board's constitutional jurisdiction, such decisions would be limited to the identification and redress of potential harms serious enough to give rise to a violation of rights to life, liberty or security of the person – but this would be enough to avert the harm and the subsequent, potential *Charter* challenge.

At core a health care system must balance individual rights and the communal good. This was not adequately addressed by the majority in *Chaoulli* but is strongly suggested as important in the minority judgment. The Board needs greater discretion in order to provide justice to individuals.[62] It must be available/accessible to address these claims in order to ensure that the valve works from a section 7 perspective, as reflected in the *Chaoulli* case. But at the same time, the public also has an interest in these cases and, accordingly, some limits on redress are constitutionally justifiable. In the end, what is important is not that the Board always provides access to alternative care in the face of concerns about wait times, but that it has the flexibility to do so when necessary.

Ultimately, improvements in the Board's operation and reinvigorating rights of appeal is important not just from a constitutional perspective but in a political perspective. Winning the constitutional argument will not be enough to sustain one-tier medicare – the system has to be viewed as both fair and responsive on the part of the citizens who fund it and the patients who it serves. Borrowing LaForest J.'s observation in *Eldridge*, 'effective communication is quite obviously an integral part of the provision of health care delivery,' whether at the clinical level or in the context of the system as a whole.[63] Because the Board is simply 'compelled to apply the Act and its regulations,' patient appeals have too often, seemingly fallen on deaf ears.

Notes

* The views of Ms. Pitfield are her own and do not reflect those of her employee, the Federal Department of Justice, Canada.
1 Chaoulli v. Quebec (Attorney General), 2005 SCC 35 (hereafter, 'Chaoulli').
2 See discussion below.
3 Insured persons in Quebec can apply for reimbursement for out-of-country services under s. 10 of Quebec's *Health Insurance Act*, R.S.Q. c. A-29and s.s 23.1 and 23.2 of the Province's *Regulation respecting the application of the Health Insurance Act*, R.Q. c. A-29, r.1 [hereafter, *Regulation respecting the Act*]. *Chaoulli, supra* note 1 at para. 264.
4 See Part III, The Health Care Guarantee, in: The Standing Senate Committee on Social Affairs, Science and Technology, *The Health of Canadians – The Federal Role, Vol. 6: Recommendations for Reform*, Final Report, (Ottawa: Sentate Standing Committee on Social Affairs, Science and Technology, 2002) (Chair: The Honourable Michael J.L. Kirby), available at http://www.parl.gc.ca/37/2/parlbus/commbus/senate/com-e/soci-e/rep-e/repoct02vol6–e.htm;, and *Chaoulli, supra* note 1 (Senator Michael Kirby and others Intervener's factum, at 15, available online at: <http://www.law.utoronto.ca/healthlaw/docs/chaoulli/Factum_Senate.pdf>).

5 Ruth Collins-Nakai, 'We need a safety valve,' *National Post*, August 22, 2005 and Andre Picard, 'Top MDs back wait-time remedy,' *Globe and Mail*, August 11, 2005 (copies available with the author, no page numbers available as printed from the internet).

6 *Chaoulli, supra* note 1 at para. 44.

7 *Chaoulli, supra* note 1 at para. 119.

8 *Chaoulli, supra* note 1 at para. 264.

9 *Ibid.*

10 *Health Insurance Act*, R.S.O. 1990, c. H.6, s. 21(1) (hereafter, the '*Health Insurance Act*'). Also, see Health Services Appeal and Review Board 'Frequently Asked Questions,' online: <http://www.hsarb.on.ca>.

11 See Health Services Appeal and Review Board, 'Annual Report: Fiscal Period April 1, 2002 to March 31, 2003' at page 15, online: <http://www.hsarb.on.ca/english/reports/default.htm> [Annual Report: 2002–2003].

12 *Health Insurance Act, supra* note 10, s. 20.1. The Board itself was established under the *Ministry of Health Appeal and Review Boards Act*, S.O. 1998, c. 18. This Act amalgamated five tribunals – the Health Services Appeal Board, the Health Facilities Appeal Board, the Health Protections Board, the Nursing Homes Review Board, and the Laboratory Review Board – to form a single Health Services Appeal and Review Board.

13 R.O. 552, amended to 374/05 (hereafter, 'Regulation 552').

14 *Health Insurance Act, supra* note 10, s. 11.2.

15 Regulation 552, *supra* note 13, s. 24(1).

16 Regulation 552, *supra* note 13, ss. 28.1–28.6.

17 Theoretically, it is after such an application is declined that insured persons may bring an appeal before the Board; in some cases, however, the Board will hear claimants that have not met these administrative conditions. See HSARB, Brown (File # s. 5297), August 13, 1996.

18 Office of the Ombudsman, 'Administrative Fairness Guidelines,' available online at: http://www.ombudsman.ab.ca/guidelines.html.

19 The TAQ Annual Report ('Rapport Annuel 2001–2002'), which is available online: Tribunal administratif du Québec Homepage <http://www.taq.gouv.qc.ca/publications-formulaires/depliants.jsp>, provides that of the 2,486 appeals heard by the social affairs section in 2001–2002, only three involved health care or worker's compensation issues (at 33 of the report).

20 For further information on the TAQ, see online: Tribunal administratif du Québec Homepage at: <http://www.taq.gouv.qc.ca>.

21 *Regulation respecting the Act, supra* note 3, s. 23.1.

22 *Chaoulli, supra* note 1 at para. 264.

23 *[1999] R.J.Q. 2416 (S.C.) (hereafter, 'Stein').*

24 HSARB, Duke (File # s. 6048), May 19, 2000 at 2. See also HSARB, Hureau (File # s. 6816), March 22, 2001. There is also an Ontario Divisional Court decision affirming these limits: *Mawani Estate v. Ontario (Health Insurance Plan, General Manager)* (1993) 62 O.A.C. 289 (Gen. Div.), [1993] O.J. No. 879 (QL).

25 In *Segal v. Ontario (Health Insurance Plan)*, (1994), 77 O.A.C. 31 (Gen. Div.) for instance, the Ontario Court of Justice allowed an appeal from a Board decision on the ground that the Board had not properly considered whether the application of the General Manager's general policy on hospital services was reasonable in the circumstances.

26 Drawing on various Supreme Court of Canada decisions – including, in particular, *Cuddy Chicks Ltd. V. Ontario (Labour Relations Board)* [1991] 2 S.C.R. 5 – the Board concluded that it had constitutional jurisdiction in a 2001 decision, HSARB, L.H. (File # 6492), September 19, 2001. Shortly thereafter, however, the government amended the Board's enabling statute in order to explicitly remove the power to 'inquire or make decisions concerning the constitutional validity of an Act or regulations.' Accordingly, the Board is now limited to interpreting and applying provisions in 'light of the *Charter*.'

27 HSARB, Credicott (File # s. 5258), May 14, 1996. See also *Collett v. Ontario (AG)* [1995] O.J. No. 776 (QL).

28 HSARB, Brennan, (File # 6029) May 20, 1998.

29 This approximation is based on the number of appeals granted according to the Board's indexes of decisions. These indexes have their own short-comings, as further discussed below.

30 The Board is also, often, required to consider the experimental treatment exclusion in s. 24 of Regulation 552 at this stage. Pursuant to this provision, treatment for a medical condition that is generally accepted in Ontario as experimental is excluded from OHIP coverage, whether sought in or out-of-country.

31 HSARB, Consorti (File # s. 6072) July 20 and October 30, 1998.

32 See, for instance, HSARB, Bardos (File # S. 5495), November 18, 1997.

33 Marshall B. Kapp, 'De Facto Health-Care Rationing by Age: The Law Has No Remedy' (1998) 19:3 J. of L. Med. 323 at 326. See HSARB, Bartolotti (File # s. 5387), October 21, 1997.

34 HSARB, Menkes (File #: 01–HIA-0005), August 24, 2001 at 9 (hereafter, 'Menkes'). See also HSARB, Flora (File #: s. 6681) March 5 and 6, 2001. The appellant in this case sought re-payment for the cost of a live related liver transplantation procedure performed in England. The Board split in its

final decision; two Members found that the procedure was not accepted as medically appropriate, and one Member found that it was.

35 *Menkes, supra* note 32.

36 In some cases, this problem is further exacerbated by the fact that the Board interprets 'performed' subjectively, not objectively. Thus in HSARB, Anderson (File # unavailable), October 17, 1994, the Board found that 'performed' does not mean 'theoretical availability,' but rather depends on the circumstances of the case.

37 Auton (Guardian ad litem of) v. British Columbia (Attorney General), 2004 SCC 78 (hereafter, '*Auton*')

38 HSARB, Bezugly (File # s. 5160), September 18, 1995.

39 'G.F. v. OHIP.' See Annual Report: 2002–2003, *supra* note 11 at page 10.

40 The Kirby Report, *supra* note 4 at 118.

41 In this respect, the Chief Justice and Justice Major found that the denial of timely health care for a condition that is clinically significant to their current and future health and any attendant, serious physical and psychological suffering engaged section 7. Justices Binnie and Lebel defined the relevant level of psychological harm as follows: 'The interference with one's mental well-being must rise above the ordinary anxiety caused by the vicissitudes of life, but it need not be so grave as to lead to serious mental anguish or nervous breakdown,' (*Chaoulli*, supra note at paras. 123 and 204 respectively).

42 As of March 2002, active Members of the Board include one physician and one cardiologist, seven lawyers (including one human rights lawyer), a nurse, a management consultant, and one hospital administrators. One lawyer was on a leave of absence. See Annual Report: 2002–2003, *supra* note 11 at 15.

43 Judith McCormack, 'Nimble Justice: Revitalizing Administrative Tribunals in a Climate of Rapid Change' (1995) 59 Sask L. Rev. 385, online: QL (AMPA) at 5 of QL version.

44 'Frequently Asked Questions,' *supra* note 10.

45 Annual Report: 2002–2003, *supra* note 11 at 17.

46 'Frequently Asked Questions,' *supra* note 9.

47 Annual Report: 2002–2003, *supra* note 11 at 7.

48 Health Services Appeal and Review Board, 'Annual Report: 2000–2001' and 'Annual Report: 2001–2002 available online at: http://www.hsarb .on.ca/english/reports/default.htm (hereafter, 'Annual Report: 2000–2001' and 'Annual Report 2001–2002').

49 The Board's 2002 Annual Report also provides a few, cursory summaries of selected Board decisions. However, it is not clear why these decisions

have been selected – they do not tend to be remarkable – and what they
are supposed to convey about the Board's practices and procedures. As the
following summary suggests, they provide little information on how the
Board approaches its task, how it applies the relevant provisions and what
it requires from those who come before it: 'In this appeal the Appellant
asked OHIP to insure insertion of an artificial vision device that would
alleviate his blindness. The Appeal Board heard evidence about the nature
of the treatment being performed in Portugal and was satisfied that the
treatment is 'generally accepted within Ontario as experimental.' ('Annual
Report: 2001–2002,' *supra* note 48 at 13).

50 HSARB, Feldman (File # s. 6600), October 28, 2002 at 5.

51 Rule 19 of the Board's Rules of Practice and Procedure, available online at:
http://www.hsarb.on.ca/english/rules/default.htm.

52 Although the Board may have exercised its powers to award costs, we did
not come across a cost award in the decisions, and there are no references
to such award in the indexes to the decisions. In one case, the Divisional
Court awarded party and party costs to a Board appellant on the grounds
that both OHIP and the Board had made mistakes and thus unduly prolonged the case. See HSARB, Ulcar (File # 01–HIA-0035), June 6, 2002 at 9.

53 It is also sometimes the case that individuals are themselves responsible
for some delay, i.e. in applying for reimbursement. In this case, the 12–
month limitation on applications dor such reimbursement provided in
Ontario Regulation 22/02, am ro O. Reg. 46/04 is an issue, particularly in
the case of minors. In this regard, see David Baker and Faisal Bhabha's
discussion on recent limitations periods with respect to accounts for
reimbursement of OHIP services at page 26 of 'Universality and Medical
Necessity: Statutory and Charter Remedies to Individual Claims to
Ontario Health Insurance Funding' (2004) 13:1 *Health L. Rev.* 25.

54 'Annual Report: 2001–2002, *supra* note at 1.

55 'Frequently Asked Questions,' *supra* note 10.

56 HSARB, Charles (File # 01–HIA-0055, 01–HIA-0132 etc.), unreported order,
April 3, 2003. The notice of appeal in this case was filed on June 28, 2001.

57 [2002] O.J. No.766 (SCJ).

58 'Annual Report: 2001–2002, *supra* note 48 at 19.

59 *Ibid.* at 8.

60 Alta. Reg. 216/81, consolidated up to 95/2005, at s. 28.07(3) (hereafter,
'Alta. Reg').

61 *Ibid.* at s. 28.07 (5).

62 The literature on HMO appeal mechanisms repeatedly makes this point.
Eleanor Kinney, for instance, identifies a broad scope of discretion as a key

attribute of these mechanisms. She writes, 'While counterintuitive, deci-sion-makers need to have the latitude to provide satisfactory relief to a patient. For example, the hard and fast application of coverage policies and medical practice guidelines may lead to undesirable outcomes that generate disputes. Giving decision-makers the flexibility to make deci-sions to meet patient objectives....may resolve a dispute and result in higher quality care for the patient.' Eleanor Kinney, 'Procedural Protec-tions for Patients in Capitated Health Plans' (1996) 22:2& 3 *Am. J. of L & Med.* 301 at 327.
63 *Eldridge v. British Columbia (A.G.)* [1997] 3 S.C.R 624, [1999] S.C.J. No. 86 (QL) at para.69.

Chaoulli and the Future of Medicare

Arbitrariness, Randomness and the Principles of Fundamental Justice

STANLEY H. HARTT Q.C.

Introduction

The recent decision of the Supreme Court of Canada in the matter of *Jacques Chaoulli et al v. The Attorney General of Quebec et al*[1] has commentators all a-twitter. Political biases shine through their reactions as beacons illuminating their inarticulate major premises.

Many see the landmark judgment as a courageous and brilliant blow struck by the judiciary, using the Charter as a sword, not a shield, for the right of human beings to insist that the State no longer be free to deprive them of life, or to cause them pain, suffering and deterioration of their health, by rationing scarce fiscal resources so that waiting times for medically necessary services are not delivered in a medically advisable time-frame.[2]

But many others choose to view it as either a disastrous interference with political decision-making or as the unraveling of the fundamental premise of our government-funded and delivered universal health care system, with predictions of dire social consequences, particularly for the poor and disenfranchised, resulting from the emergence of a dreaded 'two-tier' (or, if one is really hyperbolic about it, 'American-style') health care scheme.[3]

The truth is that the use of the Charter to fight the nefarious consequences of a much-beloved program is no more inappropriate than the almost two and one-half decade battle for equality rights. The mere fact that medicare has become associated with our very identity as Canadians does not justify the State arrogating to itself the monopoly provider role and then not providing timely care.

Canadians quite properly take comfort in the fact that the underlying principles of publicly funded health insurance are designed to ensure that none of us impoverish our families with the costs of a serious or prolonged or unexpected or final illness. But we have erected that laudable objective into a mantra that borders on the unreasonable, demanding that no one toy with the paradigm, even to improve it. Indeed, purporting to 'improve' medicare has joined the list of ideas that are greeted with droll derision, like 'trickle-down economics.'

Our precious medicare system has become a sort of opiate of the people. We want so much to believe the services will be there for us when we need them regardless of ability to pay that we fail to see around us the evidence that, in many unfortunate cases, beneficiaries suffer and die because wait times are too long.[4] Our beliefs intrude upon the evidence and obscure our vision. We don't want to see the hundreds and hundreds of cases where patients spend weeks on gurneys in hospital corridors because no beds are available, and harried resident physicians get to spend seconds with a needy person before being forced to race off to the next urgency. We permit our politicians to studiously under-fund, while pompously defending, the five principles of the Canada Health Act,[5] provided they repeat often and loudly enough that 'Canada will never have a two-tier health care system.'

And yet, when we examine what the Court decided, and what reasoning it adopted to reach that conclusion, the notion that the Court was treading as an unwelcome intruder on sanctified ground is unsustainable.

This paper begins with a review of the principal findings of the majority judgment and the logic and considerations that characterized their path to their decision. The dissenting minority's opinion is also examined, with particular critical emphasis on their finding that the impugned legislation should not be viewed as arbitrary. Finally, the notion of health care guarantees is explored and situated in the context of the majority's ruling.

The Majority's Reasons – Important Take-Aways

First, the Court did not limit itself to the circumstances of the Plaintiffs/ Appellants in this case. Dr. Jacques Chaoulli is a physician whose practice in Quebec showed him the fallacies of allowing funding decisions for medical services to be made by politicians and bureaucrats. He tried to create a mobile medical clinic that would revive the custom of doctors making house calls when patients could not conveniently visit hospitals, medical offices or CLSC's. He attempted to operate within the public system and outside it, but met in each and every instance the oppressive power of the State as it vigorously protected the one-size-fits-all model of Canadian health care delivery. As elsewhere, Quebec's governmental leaders seemed determined to 'defend' the medical care system by rendering it inhospitable to private initiatives.

Chaouilli's conclusion was that when he, as a patient, came to need medical services, he too would meet the insouciant rebuffs of the system and experience the feeling of helplessness, which his patients often suffered. His action for a declaratory judgment was not hypothetical, he argued, merely because he was relatively young and not sick at any time material to the case, or its long and slow progress through the judicial system, because it was a certainty that he would age and eventually require medical care and he had a very real interest in ensuring that such care was delivered in a timely manner.

He was young enough to insure himself now, so that, when the eventuality of serious illness occurred, he would not find himself, like the other Plaintiff, George Zeliotis, in agony but unable to get care anywhere but from the ponderous State system as Zeliotis did when he desperately needed hip replacements.

Zeliotis spent years in agony waiting for the new hips he badly required. He was in tears from the pain every morning before his feet hit the floor as he got out of bed. He was unable to work as a result of this and other, unrelated, health problems. He received his first hip replacement in 1994, about a year after his first appointment with the treating physician. The second took much longer. He was summoned to the hospital several times for his operation, once even prepped for surgery, and then each time sent home because other procedures had pre-empted the operating facilities. He was told this was because his hip replacement was deemed 'elective.' Zeliotis, of course, might be excused if he saw the 'elective' nature of his treatment as being purely in the eyes of the beholder!

Still, it would have been easy for the Supreme Court to do what Madame Justice Piché had done in her Quebec Superior Court decision. She essentially ducked the issue by following the legal reasoning of the Plaintiffs to the point where her pen was all but poised to render a favourable judgment, only to shrink at the last moment from the enormity of what she was about to do. Rather than signing a potential death warrant for the medicare system as Canadians know and cherish it, or at least pronouncing a dire diagnosis concerning its constitutionality, she fell back on notions of fundamental justice, of the greatest good for the greatest number and the alleged damage a system of parallel private insurance would cause to the existing structure. So did the three Justices of the Quebec Court of Appeal and the dissenting justices at the Supreme Court, all of whom concluded that the State should have the latitude to make financially motivated life and death decisions affecting individuals insured by provincial plans.

The Honourable Justices comprising the majority in the Supreme Court of Canada looked at and listened to all manner of information and evidence that went beyond the individual situations of Dr. Chaoulli and Mr. Zeliotis. The majority considered statistical information about waiting times in Canada and the practical impact of parallel public and private health care and insurance systems in a wide variety of countries. It drew a constitutional bright line in the sand, to guide legislators and the executive branches of governments toward a reasonable and non-anecdotal test of what obligations the Charter imposed on governments as monopoly provider of medical services (even if this role was assumed for good and sound public policy objectives).

Some of the questions asked from the bench clearly signaled that the Justices understood that judges too will one day be patients and that they saw no more reason than anyone else why their quest to prolong the length and improve the quality of their lives should be sacrificed to the single-payer ideology. For example, at page 87, line 6 ff of the transcript of the hearing, Justice Bastarache asked

'...si ma vie est menacée et que vous m'empêchez d'acheter des services privés, votre restriction sur mes droits n'est pas justifiée.....'

and, beginning at page 104, line 23, Justice Major asked

'...how do you respond to the patient who says, I need medical treatment and I can't get it, I can afford to buy it, the Government has promised me reasonable care within a reasonable time, they're not delivering, it's an offence if I go and see a doctor privately, it seems to me that those are essential issues that are more than policy.'

The refuge of an argument based on the principles of fundamental justice can not (including as it is expressed in the published reasoning of the minority) overcome the glaring point that absolutely nothing can be more contrary to those principles than the purely arbitrary and random manner in which actual patients are selected to be the ones whose care is delayed beyond reasonable and medically advisable waiting times. These decisions are made without any rational planning or case management but result from a variety of factors including which doctor has access to which hospital facilities, which locality is overburdened and which has spare capacity and other purely serendipitous circumstances over which the patient has no control or recourse.

Nothing about Mr. Zeliotis, his life, his age, or his medical profile justified his being the individual who, by rotten luck, was 'picked' by the system for so much pain, while others received the promised care and treatment in more satisfactory time frames. It is true that the judgment in the Superior Court pointed out that Zeliotis contributed to some of the delay by seeking a second opinion and pondering whether the intervention proposed by his doctors was the best way to proceed, but none of the decisions turned on that, quite normal, response from the patient. This is where the anecdotal and the juridical ought to merge – precisely because Zeliotis was an innocent victim of the system's inherent failings, failure to treat him as others had been treated should be seen as a severe breach of the principles of fundamental justice.

Second, McLachlin C.J. and Major J. (writing on behalf of themselves and Justice Bastarache) determined the Catch-22 of a monopoly medical care provider, namely that it did not provide timely access to care, was an untenable interference by the State with a citizen's rights to life and security of the person guaranteed by s. 7 of the Charter. They concurred with Justice Deschamps' reasoning that this was also an unjustified breach of the rights of life, personal security, inviolability and freedom, guaranteed by the Quebec Charter. However legitimate the goal of preserving the integrity, financial and structural, of the public health care and insurance plans, this objective must be weighed against the individual patient's right to fight for his or her life. In circumstances where Respondents could not justify the prohibition against purchasing private insurance, patients cannot be treated as conscripts, selected arbitrarily and randomly to die or suffer for the greater interest of the State.

It would be an error to make too much of the elegant choice by the majority to structure the judgment the way they did. No comfort for the biases of those who would preserve the status quo can be found in either judgment of McLachlin C.J. and Major J. on s. 7 of the Charter, or in the judgment of Justice Deschamps who rested her decision solely on the basis of the provisions of the Quebec Charter. Judges are political animals insofar as they understand what will produce push-back from politicians and the public, particularly in a case where they went as far away from deference to the legislative branch as they could possible go.

Quebec's Parti Québecois Opposition predictably began howling about the need for the Charest Government to invoke the notwithstanding provisions of section 33 of the Charter as soon as the province's politicians awakened from the slumber which had characterized their extraordinary inattention to this case even after it was argued. Imagine how much louder and effective those cries would have been if the basis of the decision had been other than one made in Quebec? In fairness to Madame Justice Deschamps, once she had decided that the Quebec Charter was enough to strike down the offending provisions of Quebec law, she did not need to wrestle with some of the more esoteric points of difference arising from a comparison of the wording of the relevant Quebec Charter provisions with those of section 7 of the Canadian Charter. Some have attempted to make elegant distinctions between the two,[6] but in a case of this nature, these amount to grasping at straws and, it is submitted, do not represent a strong argument that the reasoning in *Chaoulli* would not apply in another province.

Having Madame Justice Deschamps write the tie-breaking decision falls into the same camp as allowing the twelve month stay requested by Quebec subsequent to the publication of the judgment, in that it was based largely on the political environment and the need to make the landmark decision appear less intrusive. A stay was not requested by any of the Attorneys-General at the hearing before the Supreme Court of Canada, but rather by the ten members of the Senate of Canada who intervened. It was opposed by the Appellants and fully argued before the Court without a murmur from the A.G. Quebec. Since the judgment does not require Quebec to actually do anything, it is hard to see what the stay can accomplish. Moreover, if the majority believed what they said in their reasons for judgment, the stay will mean more people will suffer and die during the twelve-month period without any palpable effect on the medical care system in that province.[7]

It also needs to be said that the fact that the majority restricted itself to striking down two provisions of Quebec legislation that prohibited private medical insurance and did not deal with the laws of any other province does not mean that the principles enunciated by the Court are based on some peculiarity of Quebec law or practice and that the rest of medicare's defenders can breathe easily. It is simply a matter of granting to the Appellants what the Appellants sought, and not overstepping the original claim in a manner that would surely have been *ultra petita*.

In any event, it may well be moot whether the majority's reasoning is equally applicable in other provinces, because it is highly unlikely that the issue of timely availability of medical services will come before the courts again. Given the finding of the majority that people are dying on waiting lists, it would be politically impossible for any government to ask the courts to give it the right to continue this state of affairs. The only possible argument for an elected Attorney General to make in the future would be that wait times have been fixed and are no longer a problem, or that people are not in fact suffering and/or dying in the province.

The essence of the judgment in *Chaoulli* was that the Appellants were not required to satisfy the burden of establishing causality between the monopoly State system and the suffering and dying, or that removal of the restriction on private insurance would enhance their particular access. The Court was simply allowing them and others the opportunity to try to obtain timely care when the State couldn't provide it.

Third, the majority found, in essence, that none of the sky-is-falling scenarios concerning the consequences that might be in store for the public plan, advanced in hyperbolic earnestness by the Respondents, justifies the haphazard selection of particular individuals to contribute their bodies for suffering. The social policy dogma that the very existence of the public plan, or at least its quality, would be irreparably damaged if parallel health care services were to be allowed or encouraged, was found by the majority to be insupportable in the face of domestic and international evidence.

Canadian provinces are forced by budgetary constraints to restrict the supply of medical services by limiting admissions to medical schools, by capping the fees billed by physicians, by inducing early retirement for doctors and nurses, by refusing to adopt a rational plan to evaluate the credentials of qualified practitioners from other countries, among many other ways. The argument that private insurance would siphon resources away from the public system, leaving inferior service for those unable to pay for private insurance or private care, is only tenable if there is a fixed supply of medical services, which is patently false except in the short run.[8]

The cost of training a family physician or a specialist, and the time it takes, would presumably be the same whether the additional capacity was required to staff a private system or to supplement the public system's resources so that care can be delivered in a timely manner. The Court has found the status quo constitutionally untenable, so the additional resources will be required in any event.

The point is that arguments for or against single-payer health care systems (and, for that matter, for or against the *Chaoulli* judgment) seem to proceed more from an ideological than from a juridical starting point. The majority found that there was no reason grounded in fact to fear that the existence of a private regime alongside a public one would threaten, weaken or destroy the public system. They reached this conclusion by looking at evidence of the outcomes in the large number of countries that do operate parallel health care systems and found no basis for the qualms about deterioration of the standards of the publicly funded system advanced by the Respondents. This evidence, which was the foundation of the majority's view that the restrictions on private insurance in Quebec were arbitrary, was submitted to the Court by the ten members of the Senate of Canada who intervened in the proceedings, an intervention, incidentally, that was strenuously opposed by the federal Attorney General.

These are enormously important aspects of the Court's ruling.

Before *Chaoulli*, the well-intentioned State could attempt to keep the total cost of delivering medical services to Canadians low by virtue of the insurance principle (the larger the insured group, the lower the cost of insuring each member of the group, the universal group being, by definition, the largest). Budgets could be cut, then partially restored with great flourish (as in the recent Health Accord with the provinces, which held out the prospect of an additional $41 billion over ten years), but the decision was always political, based on what could be done given the competing claims on government revenues and the need for politicians to keep many other constituencies and lobbies happy.

After *Chaoulli*, governments are subject to what is known in Quebec law as an 'obligation of result.' Waiting times for medically necessary services (whether diagnosis or treatment) can not surpass the maximum time periods deemed, as to each condition, disease or symptom respectively, medically advisable by professional medical opinion generally, as the same may evolve from time to time. There is no ability to pay test, no deference to the right of the State to determine the allocation of its limited financial resources, no standard of the greatest good for the greatest number. Social policy engineering has given way, as it should have, to individual rights. If the State chooses to be the exclusive provider of medically necessary health care services, (and no one disputes that the State has the right, but not the obligation, to organize the health care system in this manner), then, if it fails to deliver timely access, it cannot prevent citizens from obtaining access from other sources.

Is Arbitrariness In The Law Or In The Outcomes?

The dissenting minority in the Supreme Court chose not to see the prohibition of private insurance imposed by the Quebec legislative scheme as arbitrary. They accepted the jurisprudentially-inherited test for arbitrariness, namely that, 'A law is arbitrary where 'it bears no relation to, or is inconsistent with, the objective that lies behind it" But Justices Binnie, LeBel and Fish concluded that, 'the prohibition against private health insurance is a rational consequence of Quebec's commitment to the goals and objectives of the *Canada Health Act.*'

Perhaps the problem is that, while no one disputes that Quebec's legislation was designed in a rational way and intended to provide equal access for all regardless of ability to pay, and that the legislator had no intention whatsoever of creating two tiers of patients, the lucky and the unlucky, the passage of time and the escalation of costs of equipment, fixed assets and personnel has resulted in particular individuals failing to receive the outputs promised by the laudable policy goals enshrined in Quebec's plan.

So the question arises – is the test of arbitrariness and the relationship of any law to, or its inconsistency with, its underlying objective to be measured only at the time and in the circumstances of its enactment? If not, can the law be constitutional when initially adopted and become unconstitutional when its operation produces effects and consequences unrelated to and inconsistent with the original intentions of the legislature?

The concept of a legislative scheme being constitutional in some circumstances, or in the first instance, but becoming unconstitutional as events materialize, is not unknown to the courts. For example, *Ford v Quebec (Attorney General)*[9] concerned a challenge to the prohibition of the use of English on commercial signs contained in Quebec's Charter of the French Language. The Court acknowledged, in an *obiter dictum,* that, because the survival of French was under external threat from a myriad of English-language influences, ranging from popular culture to state-of-the-art textbooks and professional and technical protocols, it would not be unconstitutional to require that French be predominant (as long as the use of English was not prohibited entirely) on public commercial signs in Quebec.

In *Quebec (Attorney General) v. Entreprises W.F.H. Ltée*,[10] the argument has been made that since the *Ford* ruling much time has elapsed and the French language is no longer threatened in Quebec. While this cases was unsuccessful at the Quebec Court of Appeal (because French was found to be sufficiently at risk in Quebec to justify the continuation of such a restriction - an application for leave to appeal to the Supreme Court of Canada was dismissed on 12 December 2002), the point was made that some laws may be constitutional at one point in time and not later, under different circumstances.

The minority believes firmly that the issues in *Chaoulli* are political, social policy issues. With the greatest of respect, when the State's inability to match its performance to its oratory actually kills people and produces physical suffering (as the majority found)[11] we have left the domain of social policy and entered the realm of constitutional law.

The minority, in order to demonstrate how non-judicial the issues raised in *Chaoulli* are (in their eyes), asks questions about the standards to be set for timely care and who is to set them:

> What is treatment 'within a reasonable time'? What are the benchmarks? How short a waiting list is short enough? How many MRIs does the Constitution require?

What would make Quebec's law arbitrary in the minds of the minority? Does the law need to single out persons named Chaoulli or Zeliotis, or persons identified by some other random characteristic, to be unconstitutional in the view of the minority? Or does the legislation lose the protection of its original rationality and relationship to the objectives and intent of its framers when, as a result of rising costs, the State no longer fulfills its goals and individuals pay the price in death and suffering?

The minority provides no answer to those individuals who, much as they may agree with the objectives of Quebec's health care legislation, believe they have a justiciable right to object when the parsimony of the State, and its impotence in trying to live up to its overblown and high-minded pontificating, result in people suffering, deteriorating and dying because of the unavailability of meaningful (*i.e.* timely) access to health care. So, how much health care is enough? Enough to ensure that the presumed beneficiaries of the plan suffer and die from their ill-

nesses and not from the unavailability of access to the services purportedly provided by the system. How many MRIs does the Constitution
require? Enough to ensure that the diagnostic information MRIs were
invented and built to provide is available to each patient's physician
while there is still time to do something about it. Otherwise, the objectives of the legislation are frustrated, and amount to nothing more than
speechmaking, and the State loses its right to preserve the monopoly
status of its public plan for failure to fund it to a minimal constitutional
standard.

The Health Care Guarantee

Ten Senators, members of the Standing Senate Committee on Social
Affairs, Science and Technology, chaired by Senator Michael Kirby,
sought and obtained intervener status in the *Chaoulli* case. In their
landmark report entitled *The Health of Canadians – The Federal Role*, the
Committee developed and explained a concept they called the Health
Care Guarantee.[12] The Guarantee, summarized in the most simple terms,
calls upon governments to match their promises to reality, and to make
the principle of accessibility in the Canada Health Act a fact by ensuring
that access is timely.

If governments wish to retain the monopoly provider role they have
carved out for themselves, for all the good social policy reasons the
Supreme Court minority recount, they cannot have it both ways. Each
individual must have an explicit promise from his or her provincial
plan that medically necessary health services will be delivered in a
medically timely manner.

The test of what is medically timely (and therefore 'reasonable')
would be based on the best insights and knowledge that medical science has at its disposal at any given time. It would not be up to the
Courts to come up with such outer limits for diagnosis or treatment, but
to the medical professions themselves. Even if there is a potential range
of responses that competent professionals would offer in a given situation, identifying the consensus standard of practice is not a new concept
in law. It arises regularly in professional negligence and malpractice
cases.

Based on the advice of the medical professions, the formal standards
would be formally set by the administrators of provincial health care
plans (exactly where the minority thinks they should be), with the
caveat that abusing patients to the advantage of the fisc by ignoring the

best available medical advice and stretching waiting times would have the potential consequence of more litigation to enforce the section 7 Charter rights of the patients affected.

Once the standards were set, governments would have to put their money where their mouths are, as the colloquial saying goes. In planning the treatment options for various patients in facilities within the province, authorities would have to bear the Guarantee in mind. If they could not schedule a place and time for care delivery within the vicinity of the patient's residence, they would have to begin planning for alternatives elsewhere within the province, or, if they really dropped the ball due to some confluence of circumstances, outside the province or even outside the country.

The hoped-for result would be the opposite of the most-feared consequence – budget-busting trips to far-off lands for what might have been available at home in a few more months. Like the self-assessment method of income tax collection, or the bargaining technique known as Final Offer Selection, the prospect of losing big would motivate the decision-makers not to go there in the first place. Care would in fact be made available to the patient who would otherwise be forced to travel. Remember, neither the patient nor the patient's family particularly want to go abroad at a time of great stress caused by the vicissitudes of serious illness. Nor does the government want to incur the financial penalty implicit in overlooking a potential Zeliotis, and so would behave rationally and pre-empt the big, unaffordable expense of avoidable medical travel by better case and treatment planning.

As the minority points out, the option of seeking treatment abroad is not one that does not exist at present. On the contrary, most, if not all, provinces have a provision that permits this in urgent cases. Unfortunately, the administration of this alternative has been stingy and cruel to put the best possible face on it, and, as a number of reported cases have demonstrated, patients are often forced to seek out and pay for such treatment abroad at their own expense and then claim reimbursement of the cost through the Courts.[13] Talk about two-tier medical care! A poor person would be obliged to suffer and die trying to overcome the bureaucracy which, motivated by financial caution alone, uses every ruse to deny patients access to this aspect of their provincial plans, including declaring a sought-after treatment 'experimental' merely because it was unavailable in the penny-pinching province in question (Quebec) and inviting the patient, instead, to resign himself to his fate and accept the inevitability of death (the 'Stein' case).[14]

The minority writes that the right place for the Courts to intervene is in cases of this nature, to right the wrongs occasioned by the finances-over-health-care bureaucrats. With respect, poor patients need the baseball bat of *Chaoulli* and the safety net of the Health Care Guarantee to avoid having to go through this Kafkaesque nightmare. Any judge who is aware of the law's delays will know that the Courts are precisely the wrong place to force civil servants to be reasonable where the plaintiff is a cancer or heart patient whose lifespan would not last beyond the initial interlocutory motions and discovery.

The beauty of the Health Care Guarantee is that it provides a self-regulating remedy to the constitutional dilemma of timely care and section 7. It could be enshrined as a principle by adding to the Canada Health Act language to require that accessibility (already guaranteed) must be timely in the medical sense. If all patients who benefited from the Guarantee were in fact receiving their diagnosis and treatment within the time parameters established from time to time using the best medical advice possible, they would, by definition, be receiving timely care and reasonable access in the constitutional sense. This measure would not avoid all future litigation over medical care, but it would establish a bright line where clear standards benefited everyone, rich and poor alike.

The only problem is that we might not be able to afford the Guarantee. The revenues and borrowing capacity of Canada, its Provinces and Territories, might not be sufficient to fund medical and hospital services to the level required. In that case, far from deferring to political decision-making mechanisms as to 'how much health care is enough,' Canadians should demand that their politicians stand down, blushing as they go, from the undeliverable promises they have been making to us for a generation.

The Health Care Guarantee is agnostic as to whether it is delivered by a public system, a private system or mixed or parallel systems. It stipulates only that, if the consensus of informed medical opinion is that chemotherapy should, for example, begin no more than X weeks after surgery for certain forms of breast cancer, the patient will not have to wait all or most of that time for her first appointment with the oncologist who will administer or supervise the treatment, with an additional wait tacked on before she can actually get to the front of the queue for the treatment itself. If that can be accomplished within a well funded, properly administered, single payer, state-monopoly system, fine. But if it cannot, all the hand wringing in the world cannot get our current system onside with the minimum constitutional requirements or square the Canada Health Act with section 7 of the Charter, and we should join the other OECD countries with public systems, which allow private options.[15]

As if to demonstrate that the theory of establishing a consensus on medically acceptable wait times can be translated into practice, the Globe and Mail reported on April 4, 2005 that Canada's doctors, acting through an organization known as the Wait Time Alliance of Canada, had issued the first in a series of standards for a variety of medical conditions: routine hip and knee replacements should be done within nine months (three months for consultation and a further six months for surgery); routine cataract surgery, four months; radiation therapy for cancer patients, 10 working days; non-urgent heart by-pass surgery, under six months; CT scans, MRIs and nuclear medicine diagnostic imaging, within seven days.[16]

The concept of reasonable wait times does not mean that the patient or patient's family who are nervous about gaining access to the system can demand immediate, next day access. There may be room for fine-tuning the times set out in the doctors' list. There certainly is a need to hear from the medical professions about other illnesses, diseases, conditions and afflictions so as to round out the list. Governments need to accept the burden of delivering meaningful (and, therefore, by definition, timely) care to the people they represent instead of grandstanding as the defenders of an ideal which exists only in the minds of the gullible.

Conclusion

Canada's health care system is, of course, not a disaster zone. Every day major and minor miracles are performed by skilled, hard-working and dedicated providers. Even as we, as a society, grind down their earning power, these well-trained and highly motivated professionals provide a wonderful product. But the legal issue is whether, at the margins, those individuals who the system fails (and there are large numbers of those), who wait for treatment in anxiety and fear and who, sometimes (and 'sometimes' is too often) deteriorate when they could have been cured, suffer when their pain could have been alleviated or die when they might have lived, have a constitutional right to complain. The Supreme Court of Canada has answered 'yes' and instead of grousing about it, Canada should get on with fixing its system.

The bankruptcy of political sloganeering was particularly illuminated immediately after the release of the judgment in *Chaoulli* (which neither the federal nor Quebec governments expected or prepared for and which journalists refused to treat as a serious possibility until after it had happened). At that time, the Prime Minister declared that Canada would never have a two-tier health care system, and then proceeded to press the House of Commons and the Senate to pass Bill C-48, the supplementary budget bill in which, to save its sorry political skin for a few weeks, the government promised to blow a precious $4.5 billion on other causes dictated to them by the New Democratic Party (NDP). The NDP claims parentage of the Canadian experiment of one-tier, one payer, publicly delivered and financed medical services and should have been demanding that C-48 be withdrawn and that every available cent be diverted to establishing and honouring a constitutionally self-fulfilling, Canada Health Act-preserving, Health Care Guarantee, but they did not. That is why life and death decisions about the timeliness of care delivery to plan beneficiaries in need should not and cannot be a political matter.

Ironically, it is only a matter of time before all of the political parties embrace the Health Care Guarantee. After *Chaoulli,* a constitutional challenge is available to those who don't receive timely care. The Guarantee is a way to deliver what Court has said that the public system must provide – access to the public system within a medically reasonable time frame. The decision about what kind of system, public, private or mixed, we will use to provide plan beneficiaries with the care they need is still up to Canadians, but governments need to look honestly at the resources available to them, and the competing claims on those resources, and come up with a realistic plan about what is in fact achievable. Wishing *Chaoulli* away won't work.

Notes

1 Chaoulli v. Quebec (Attorney General), 2005 SCC 35 [Chaoulli].
2 Kennedy, Mark. 'The Supreme Court decision that will change Canada.' *The Ottawa Citizen* 10 Jun 2005: A1; *Canadian Medical Association.* Medical News Today. 'Historic Supreme Court Decision: Access Delayed, Is Access Denied.' 12 Jun 2005<http://www.medicalnewstoday.com/medicalnews .php?newsid; Simpson, Jim. 'Supreme Court of Canada rules Quebec government health monopoly v fundamental rights.' *Ontario Medical*

Association <http://www.oma.org/Health/medicare/05quebec.asp; *British Columbia Medical Association.* 'Chaoulli Decision Acknowledges that Timely Access to Medical Care Must be a Priority.' 9 Jun 2005.<http://www.bcma.org/public/news_publications/releases2005/C haoulli

3 *Canadian Labour Congress.* 'Executive Council Statement on the Supreme Court of Canada Decision Re: Private Health Insurance.' 13 Jun 2005. *Canadian Union of Public Employees.* 'Chaoulli Supreme Court decision: Tell Ujjal Dosanjh to take action against private clinics.' 8 Jul 2005<http://www.cupe.ca/www/8/Chaoulli_health_care; *Canadian Health Coalition.* 'Reaction to the Chaoulli Decision.' 9 Jun 2005<http://www.medicare.ca; Chiarelli, Nina. 'Supreme Court ruling creates confusion; Future of medicare in doubt after decision on private insurance.' *The Saint John Telegraph Journal.* 10 Jun 2005:A1/A12; *The Council of Canadians.* 'What the Supreme Court Really Said.' 14 Jun 2005<http://www.canadians.org/news_updates .htm?COC.

4 Chaoulli *supra* note 1 at paras 112 ff, para 123

5 R.S.C. 1985, c. C-6

6 See the article by J.F. Gaudreault-Desbiens and C.M. Panaccio on the Quebec Charter in this volume.

7 See the article by Kent Roach in this volume.

8 See the article by Colleen M. Flood, Mark Stabile and Sasha Kontic in this volume.

9 1988 2 S.C.R. 790

10 2000 R.J.Q. 1222

11 *Chaoulli supra* note 1 at para 123. '…there is unchallenged evidence that in some serious cases, patients die as a result of waiting lists for public health care'

12 Standing Senate Committee on Social Affairs, Science and Technology, The Honourable Michael J.L. Kirby, Chair, The Honourable Marjory LeBreton, Deputy Chair. 'The Health of Canadians – The Federal Role,' Volume Six: Recommendations for Reform, page 109 ff.

13 See the article by Caroline Pitfield and Colleen Flood on Ontario's Health Services Appeal and Review Board in this volume.

14 Stein v. Tribunal administratif du Québec 1999 R.J.Q. 2416

15 See the article by André den Exter on the private insurance scheme in the Netherlands in this volume

16 Picard, André. 'MDs publish list of acceptable wait times.' *The Globe and Mail.* 4 Apr 2005: A8

In Search of a Mandate?

HONOURABLE ROY J. ROMANOW P.C., O.C., Q.C.

Introduction

In my view, there is no better window to the future of our nation, than the manner in which we collectively deal with Medicare. How we handle the issues arising from the recurrent debates on the provision of health care provides us with a glimpse of our future together — or not! Is the federation about to become an association? Will a particular ideology prevail, despite the preponderance of evidence that its tenets are contrary to Canadians' core values? Will this decision end the great social experiment known around the world as Canada? Are we seeing a disruption of our special balance between individual and community, and a movement against nation and toward enterprise? Whatever may be the eventual answers to these questions, we are at yet another serious crossroads in both health care and its contribution to nation building, Canadian identity, and, not least, health outcomes.

As we know, this book focuses on the legal debate concerning the role of private health care insurance in Canada, particularly in light of the Supreme Court of Canada's majority decision of June 9, 2005, in Chaoulli v. Quebec (Attorney General).[1]

Now I must admit that based on the evidence I have examined, as well as my understanding of the fundamental principles of health policy, and my involvement in the implementation of the *Canadian Charter of Rights and Freedoms*,[2] this decision came as a surprise to me. That four of the seven Supreme Court justices sitting on the case would rule in favour of Dr. Chaoulli, a physician looking to practice privately, and Zeliotis, a patient who had to wait for a hip operation, and essentially tell the Quebec government that its ban on private health insurance was in violation of Quebec's *Charter of human rights and freedoms*[3] and by clear implication the *Canadian Charter* as well, was in the words of one health policy expert, 'astonishing.'[4] The Court basically said that the prohibition of private health insurance enacted by a democratically elected provincial government was bad public policy – indeed, they described it as 'arbitrary.' Despite this, according to a June 2005 Statistics Canada report, over 80% of Canadians, including Quebeckers, are satisfied with the quality of health care they receive.[5]

This decision also touches upon a longstanding and related issue with respect to Canadian politics. Quebec has consistently held the position that the delivery of health care is an area of exclusive provincial jurisdiction. This view holds that provinces may deliver health care in any fashion they deem desirable. I do not subscribe to this view myself because I believe there is a constitutional and national role for the federal government to ensure that all Canadians in all regions have citizenship rights to equal access to Medicare services. But this decision—perhaps needlessly—has fuelled further the debate about which level of government is responsible for what policies and programs in Canada.

The Supreme Court's decision witnessed the Court move from deciding questions of constitutional law to matters of major public policy. Why? Were a few members of the Supreme Court in search of a mandate to venture into the world of politics? Seems so, and they did it in such a thunderous way! This remarkable level of activism on the part of the Court troubles even many of those who are sympathetic to the end result.[6]

That said, as we take a closer look at the issues arising from this somewhat startling decision, I want to suggest a touch of caution. It is my view that we need to distinguish between what the various justices have actually written and the intended or unintended permission that some proponents of private health care — high on ideology and low on evidence — have gleaned, even exploited, from this case.

The Expansion of Section 7 of the Canadian Charter of Rights and Freedoms?

Section 7 of the *Canadian Charter* is well known, but at the outset of this chapter it is perhaps worthwhile to restate what it says. Section 7 states: 'Everyone has the right to life, liberty and security of person and the right to not be deprived thereof except in accordance with the principles of fundamental justice.' Originally, the constitutional and political negotiators involved in the debate over the *Canadian Charter* and its entrenchment raised concerns over the meaning of this section and, in particular, the words 'in accordance with the principles of fundamental justice' as revealed by section 7. To Mr. Justice Barry Strayer, representing the federal government as counsel at the time, these words would '...cover the same thing as what is called procedural due process ... it ... does not cover the concept of what is called substantive due *process*, which would impose substantive requirements as to the policy of the law in question.'[7] Even for those who maintained their apprehensions about an entrenched *Canadian Charter,* this interpretation found favour. It reflected the consensus of the constitutional negotiators. I know because I had the extraordinary experience of serving as co-chair with Jean Chretien over an extended period of time during which politicians, academics, and legal experts debated the policy, the details, implications, and proposed compromises to be recommended to the First Ministers. One compromise was section 1, which mandated the courts to carefully balance their views with those of the elected lawmakers. It is a constitutional reminder for the courts that they need to establish such an appropriate balance between the interests of the individual and society when deciding cases of this nature.

The *Canadian Charter,* when finally accepted by all governments except Quebec, was understood to be a constitutional vehicle that would protect our most vulnerable communities, as Medicare does for those who cannot pay individually for their health care needs. Thus, as originally intended, and as court cases previous to *Chaoulli* have confirmed, 'section 7 did not protect against *economic deprivations or guarantee benefits* that might enhance life, liberty or security of person.'[8]

In fact, prior to the Supreme Court's decision on *Chaoulli* and even the gradual expansion of the applicability of section 7, the principles of fundamental justice were understood to reflect commitments to due process, sanctity of life, and domestic and international human rights guarantees.[9]

In the Quebec Court of Appeal's majority decision on *Chaoulli,* Delisile J.A. stated that, 'access to medicare was a fundamental right under section 7 and it was clear that the provision of health care did not extend to a right to purchase private health insurance since it was an economic claim not fundamental to human life.'[10]

Despite this, all seven justices sitting on the *Chaoulli* Court found that long waiting times in the public sector may, at least in some circumstances, engage section 7. But, Justices Binnie, LeBel, and Fish, in their dissenting opinion, were not persuaded that even when waiting engaged section 7 that the principles of fundamental justice were breached. They wrote: 'The courts can use s. 7 of the *Canadian Charter* to pre-empt the ongoing public debate only if the current health plan violates an *established 'principle of fundamental justice.'* That is not the case here.'[11]

The net legal effect of the *Chaoulli* decision is that in grappling with Medicare, the Court has ventured beyond constitutional and legal principles and into complex social policy, an area that has traditionally been in the domain of elected lawmakers. Will this outcome be a major turning point in the approach of the Court with respect to future cases on Medicare and other public policies that are of a social nature?

The whole of the history of section 7 jurisprudence has been marked by high sensitivity to the potentially expansive content of 'security of the person' and 'principles of fundamental justice.' The constrained context in which the Court has heretofore allowed these terms to be pleaded has served to preserve a healthy separation of legislative and judicial powers.

But not here! Here, there is a loose connection between any health care condition and the idea of a constitutionally protected 'security of the person.'

Here, justice is calculated by personal preference while broader social need is ignored.

Here, the imperative of markets and consumerism defines 'justice,' not the logic of responding equitably to human need and suffering.

Section 7, I can tell you with complete assurance, was not designed to expel broad social need from the forums of good government!

The implications of this decision could signal further attempts to seek major reversals to other public policies and programs. Will this lead to further attacks on the fundamental values of Canadians, which favour redistribution and social justice? As Professor John Whyte has written, 'the program of state distribution has been followed by an explanatory philosophy which has explicitly explored this political behaviour in terms of the idea of justice...it is now commonplace to think of the state's imposition of burdens and benefits as either promoting social justice or on the contrary, being fundamentally unjust.'[12] Not both.

Where's the Evidence?

There is another perplexing dimension to this decision. The majority found Quebec laws banning private health insurance to be arbitrary and they did so based on the evidence they had before them. But the evidence they heard was not from the millions of Canadians who receive great health care from public Medicare and who, notwithstanding their concerns about its future, continue to support it. Rather the evidence they reviewed came from others; for example, the Canadian Medical Association and individual physicians unhappy with the constraints of public Medicare. Granting intervener status to Senators, armed more with opinion than evidence, was odd in this regard. In the majority opinion, McLachlin C.J. and Major J., write, 'the evidence that the existence of the health care system would be jeopardized by human reactions to the emergence of a private system carries little weight.'[13] However, we are entitled to ask on what specific evidence is this statement made. Were unsubstantiated opinions offered by some interveners taken as fact?

Let us consider a few of the major studies that have chronicled the health care system in the United States; a system which, according to 2003 data compiled by the OECD, spends 15% of its GDP on health care. In Canada, by contrast, this figure amounts to 9.9%,[14] despite the fact that our vast geography and uneven demographics do us few favours in terms of economies of scale.

In a study on medical bankruptcies in the United States, which accounts for half of all bankruptcies in that country, Himmelstein *et al.* report that in 2001, between 1.9 and 2.2 million Americans filed for bankruptcy because of medical causes.[15] Moreover, another study reveals that in 1999, the cost of paper work for healthcare in the United States amounted to US$1059 per capita per year, while in Canada, the figure was US$307 per capita per year.[16] These differences demonstrate the inefficiencies associated with private for-profit delivery and, more precisely, how it would impact on, in the words of some of the justices, 'human reactions.' Why? Simply put, single-payer systems offering universal coverage obviate the need of thousands of hours being spent designing employee health benefit plans, selecting which HMO or provider to contract with and for what basket of services, variable deductibles, eligibility of family members for benefits, the costs of signing people on- and off - benefit plans based on their employment, and on and on. And that is before we get to the unique challenges of insuring those who frequently change employer, or who go from job to job, or who are simply too ill to work.

Additionally, if private insurance is much better in producing health outcomes and more cost efficient then why would the Japanese automaker Toyota build a new plant in Canada instead of the United States?

Well, according to Princeton economist Paul Krugman, writing in the New York Times, one of Canada's major selling points 'is its national health insurance system, which saves auto manufacturers large sums in benefit payments compared with their costs in the US.'[17]

The implied conclusion that timely access to health care services will be improved with the establishment of a parallel private scheme flies in the face of all of the evidence with which I grappled for 18 months as Royal Commissioner. The evidence that I speak of was gathered from numerous independent studies on this particular topic and others by some of the world's foremost experts. In addition, the evidence was gathered in roundtable deliberations of experts in London (UK), Paris, and Washington, D.C; meetings with OECD representatives in Ottawa in 2001; through actual site visits to hospitals and clinics both here in Canada and abroad in countries such as France and Sweden; and most importantly, from listening to thousands of Canadians about their concerns, solutions and values.

This gathering of evidence also closely examined those schemes that sought to graft the private onto the public. Today, this is described as the so-called 'Third-Way,' neither public nor private, but a mixture of both. It has arisen because we are told that no one wants the American model. However, the proposed 'Third Way' model has been tried and found wanting

Don't simply take my word for it. Commenting on this particular type of health system, Ted Marmor explains that:

> ...the experience of private supplementary insurance in Europe is that parallel financing persistently raises questions of fairness. They are a never ending source of complaint as illustrated by the controversies over pay beds in British NHS hospitals, private insurance coverage of co-payments in France, and the exiting from the public insurance 'pool' of those in Germany's top 10 percent of income earners.[18]

Still, proponents of private delivery advocate more of it, citing European — often non-existent hybrid — examples. Is this valid?

According to the OECD, in 2000 the average cost for health expenditures paid by the public sector was approximately 80%.[19] The comparison with other industrialized countries indicates that Canada is hardly the exception with respect to the public share of total health expenditures. In fact, Sweden, Germany, France, and the United Kingdom, all have larger public health care sectors than Canada.[20]

Canada devotes around 10% of its GDP to health care.[21] In this we are very close to several European countries: Germany and Switzerland consume over 11% of GDP and Norway and France around 10.5%.[22] But, the United States is at 15% of GDP and some reports have it reaching 19% of GDP by 2014.[23] So, where are the cost efficiencies? Where is the greater 'fairness' the Court is purportedly seeking?

The evidence that mixing and matching private and public with respect to the payment and delivery of health care services leads to the conclusion that, based on economics, health outcomes, and fundamental values, this type of system is very unlikely to succeed. As Marmor, who has studied these models, cautions: 'evaluating Canada's ban involves matters of judgement about what is fair and less costly, not what is simply possible to do.'[24]

The key point is this: if the ultimate objective is to inject substantial change in Medicare, then there needs to be evidence to justify these changes. The mantra of 'more choice' is insufficient. We know that Mr. Zeliotis' one-year wait for hip surgery was unreasonable in the eyes of the Supreme Court, yet the Court did not say what a reasonable wait time is. And, it did not say what a reasonable wait time should be in other individual cases for this procedure? What is more, it was loudly silent on the wait times associated with the thousands of other medical procedures and treatments that exist today.

Most important, whenever private pay is layered upon a public system, there has been a drift of human resources to the private side, providing timely care for the few, and making it worse for the many.

Accordingly, one may ask, does the Supreme Court of Canada now replace the professional health care providers in making these complicated determinations?

Where are we Headed?

To paraphrase noted British political scientist, Richard Rose, the best answers come from the questions we ask. Although this book has been framed in terms of considering the legal debate over access to justice and care, to me, the *Chaoulli* decision encompasses much broader issues. What is the political impact of this decision? How does it conform to public values? What is the effect on national unity? Will Canada be strengthened by the decision in the future?

Only three short years ago, when I delivered my health care report, it was made clear that 'Canadians embrace medicare as a public good, a national symbol and a defining aspect of their citizenship' and as such, there was little appetite for the inclusion of a parallel private system.[25] This sentiment, in fact, was not expressed simply by vested interests, but through an open and democratic process, which received input by Canadians from all walks of life. This indeed has to mean something. And as I have noted, these core Canadian sentiments were bolstered by evidence.

Predominantly, the *Chaoulli* decision suggests that the measure of a good health care system is centred on the amount of time that someone is on a waiting list. While this is important, I believe a values-based health care system encompasses much broader criteria.

Take, for example, the characteristics of a good and fair health care system as laid out by the World Health Organization (WHO). The WHO suggests that health consists of: (a) overall health—meaning the population is relatively healthy; (b) fair distribution of good health—meaning citizens have access to services regardless of where they happen to reside; (c) high degree of responsiveness—in terms of responding to people's expectations; and (d) a fair distribution of health care financing — meaning that people are not excluded from receiving adequate service because they are unable to pay for it.[26]

The wait list issue must be seen and dealt with in the context of overall reforms and health outcomes.

In sum, the Court's decision should be a clarion call to all — practitioners, policy experts, legal experts, and especially the public and the politicians they elect — to get on with badly needed reforms to Medicare before those clamouring for its destruction gather more momentum.

Whether you agree or disagree with my comments, I hope one idea forms the basis of common purpose today: health care is not an economic or legal construct, but rather, a political construct informed by fundamental values. And it is this view that has given Medicare its legitimacy. 'We all know,' as Greg Marchildon writes, 'that the demand for health care services is potentially limitless. After a protracted debate, we long ago decided, that at least for medicare services, rationing should be based upon urgency of need rather than ability to pay.'[27] The outcome of that debate signified that Medicare is, in fact, a public good and not an economic commodity.

We must return to evidence-based arguments and most important of all, demonstrate respect for the values of Canadians. We must strike the proper balance between the community and the individual.

Hopefully the Court will recalibrate in this direction and recognize that this decision was an aberration, not a move towards a broader mandate.

Martin Luther King Jr. once said: 'Of all the forms of inequality, injustice in health care is the most shocking and inhumane.' I believe that Canadians overwhelmingly share this sentiment. As a result, the rumours regarding the death of Medicare are greatly exaggerated. I believe Canada will find the courage to reform and sustain its most cherished social program.

Notes

1 2005 SCC 35 [*Chaoulli*].
2 Part I of the *Constitution Act, 1982,* being Schedule B to the *Canada Act 1982* (U.K.), 1982, c. 11 [*Canadian Charter*].
3 R.S.Q. c. C-12.
4 Steven Lewis 'Medicare's Fate: Are we Fiddlers or Firefighters?' *Winnipeg Free Press* (12 June 2005), online: Winnipeg Free Press <http://www.winnipegfreepress.com/westview/story/2847826p-3297880c.html>.
5 'Health Care' *CBC News Online* (10 June 2005), online: CBC News <http://www.cbc.ca/news/background/healthcare>.
6 See *e.g.* Norman Spector 'Blame the Boomers for the Supreme's Diagnosis' *The Globe and Mail* (12 June 2005) A13 and David Frum 'Bad Decision, Good Result' *National Post* (14 June 2005) A15.
7 J.D. Whyte, 'Fundamental Justice: The Scope and Application of Section 7 of the Charter' in P. Macklem *et al.*, eds., *Canadian Constitutional Law*, vol. 2 (Toronto: Emond Montgomery Publications Limited, 1994) at 517 [empha – sis added].
8 Martha Jackman, 'Section 7 of the Charter and Health-Care Spending' in Gregory P. Marchildon, Tom McIntosh & Pierre-Gerlier Forest, eds., *The Fiscal Sustainability of Health Care in Canada, Romanow Papers*, vol. 1 (Toronto: University of Toronto Press, 2004) at 115.
9 See *e.g. R. v. Parker* (2000), 49 O.R. (3d) 481 (C.A.) and *R. v. Morgantaler,* [1988] 1 S.C.R. 30.
10 *Chaoulli c. Québec (Procureure générale),* [2000] R.J.Q. 786, [2000] J.Q. no. 479 at para. 25 (C.S. civ.).
11 *Supra* note 1 [emphasis added].
12 *Supra* note 7 at 519.
13 *Supra* note 1 at para. 65.

14 'OECD Health Data 2005: How Does Canada Compare,' online: Organisation for Economic Co-operation and Development <http:// www.oecd.org/dataoecd/16/9/34969633.pdf>.

15 David Himmelstein *et al.*, 'MarketWatch: Illness and Injury as Contributors to Bankruptcy' (2005) 24:1 Health Aff. W5–63 at W5–63.

16 Steffie Woolhandler, Terry Campbell & David U. Himmelstein, 'Costs of Health Care Administration in
the United States and Canada,' (2003) 349:8 New Eng. J. Med. 768 at 772.

17 Paul Krugman 'Toyota, Moving Northward' *New York Times* (25 July 2005) A19.

18 Ted Marmor, 'An American in Canada—Making Sense of the Supreme Court Decision on Health Care' (2005) 6 Policy Options 63 at 64.

19 Canada, Commission of the Future of Health Care in Canada, Building on Values: The Future of Health Care in Canada, *Final Report* (Ottawa: National Library of Canada, 2002) at 27.

20 *Ibid.* at 26–27.

21 *Supra* note 14.

22 *Supra* note 14.

23 Julie Appleby 'Health Care Tab Ready to Explode: Costs could be 19% of economy by 2014' *USA Today* (24 February 2005) A1.

24 *Supra* note 18.

25 *Supra* note 19 at xviii.

26 World Health Organization, *The World Health Report 2000—Health Systems: Improving Performance* (Geneva: WHO, 2000) at 27–35.

27 Gregory P. Marchildon 'The Chaoulli case: Two-Tier Magna Carta?' *Law & Governance* (June 2005) 4, online: Longwoods Publishing < http:// www.longwoods.com/product.php?productid=17190&page=1>.

Appendix A

[The following is an edited and annotated English translation of the trial judge in *Chaoulli and Zeliotis v. Quebec*. The full judgment is reported at [2000] R.J.Q. 786, but this judgment has been edited to make it more accessible to audiences without legal training and to focus on the issues under s.7 of the Canadian Charter of Rights and Freedoms and s. 1 of the Quebec Charter of Rights and Freedoms. The editors acknowledge the assistance of the Canadian Medical Association and Borden, Ladner, Gervais LLP for providing access to a translated version of the trial judgment]

Trial Judgment of February 25, 2000

GINETTE PICHÉ J. PRESIDING

INTRODUCTION

'Those who forget history are doomed to repeat it.'

The present dispute concerning health and its current accessibility problems sometimes makes us forget the not too distant past, in which people who were sick did not obtain care because they simply did not have the means to do so. In a spirit of generosity and equality, Canadian society has decided that this shall no longer happen. At the present time, 'the public is expressing increasing concern about the short-term accessibility of health services.' This has prompted questions about the public system and the reasons why it might be desirable to have a parallel private health care system.

Should there be private sources of financing to make good the discrepancies between needs and the government's financial resources? These are political questions which the Court cannot answer. Nevertheless, they were present throughout the discussion in the proceeding before the Court.

The applicants submitted to the Court a motion for a declaratory judgment asking it to rule that ss. 15 of the Health Insurance Act ('HIA')and 11 of the Hospital Insurance Act ('HIA')are unconstitutional. Those provisions prohibit insured services being paid for by private insurance when they are furnished in Quebec. The provisions read as follows:

> Sec. 15. No person shall make or renew a contract of insurance or make a payment under a contract of insurance under which an insured service is furnished or under which all or part of the cost of such a service is paid to a resident of Quebec or to another person on his behalf.
> Sec. 11. (1) No one shall make or renew, or make a payment under a contract under which
> (a) a resident is to provided with or to be reimbursed for the cost of any hospital service that is one of the insured services;
> (b) payment is conditional upon the hospitalization of a resident; or
> (c) payment is dependent upon the length of time the resident is a patient in a facility maintained by an institution contemplated in section 2.

The applicants asked the Court to be allowed to obtain a private insurance policy to cover the costs inherent in private health services and hospital services when the latter are furnished by physicians not participating in the Quebec public health system.

The present dispute has obliged the Court to reflect on what is at stake behind the questions raised. Counsel for the coapplicant George Zéliotis in fact said 'I am arguing for the right of more affluent people to have access to parallel health services.' Why could they not purchase private insurance? Why prevent them? – and it may be added that even if such a proposal does not meet with the sympathy of some individuals, it deserves consideration ...

Were the applicants right to thus 'denounce' being unable to obtain private insurance? – and what about people who suffer lengthy delays before being operated on or, for example, receiving their chemotherapy treatments? Is all this not cruel? Will problems be solved by cutting away at the Canadian health system, the philosophy and principles of which, as we shall see, are altruistic and generous? Are the disputed provisions contrary to the principles of the Charter and would their disappearance lead in the more or less short term to the weakening and death of our present health system? ...

EVIDENCE

APPLICANTS' TESTIMONY

Account by George Zéliotis

It should be noted at the outset that it appeared from Mr. Zéliotis's testimony and the review of his medical file that Mr. Zéliotis did not really undergo all the problems and delays he alleged in his motion. Mr. Zéliotis is a man 67 years of age. The last few years of his life have not been easy. After working for Canadian Chemicals for 33 years he found himself unemployed, had to be treated for depression in March 1993, suffered a heart attack and had to be treated by the psychiatrist Dr. Vacaflor and by the cardiologists Dr. Schlezinger and Dr. Latter. In January 1994 the cardiologist Dr. Schlezinger recommended heart surgery. Mr. Zéliotis was operated on by Dr. Latter on March 24, 1994. Serious hip problems appeared in June 1994. He was seen by Dr. Yeardon. As it is this whole question which is the essence of Mr. Zéliotis's complaints, it is important to see exactly how he was treated by the health system.

(a) First hip operation
Mr. Zéliotis was examined by Dr. Yeardon on June 23, 1994. He was then referred by his family physician Dr. Giannakis to Dr. Fisher, an orthopedist, who saw him on January 10, 1995 On January 11 Dr. Fisher made his recommendations. Mr. Zéliotis himself hesitated: 'I wanted a second opinion.' On February 28, 1995 Dr. Fisher saw him and announced that he was not an ideal candidate for an operation. On March 27 Mr. Zéliotis went to the emergency department. On April 11, Dr. Fisher saw him again. On May 18, 1995 Mr. Zéliotis was operated on for an arthroplasty of the left hip.

(b) Mr. Zéliotis's other problems
Between July 1995 and December 1996 Mr. Zéliotis consulted a number

of people. In January 1996 he fell on his shoulder, in April he was operated on for a hernia, in February 1997 he met with Dr. Fisher, who decided that he should have an operation on his right hip. On September 4, 1997 an operation was finally performed on his other hip.

(c) Discussion
Mr. Zéliotis initiated a media campaign denouncing the delays in the health system. The truth is that, bearing in mind his personal medical obstacles, the fact that he was already suffering from depression, his indecision and his complaints which in many respects were unwarranted, it is hard to conclude that the delays that occurred resulted from lack of access to public health services, and in fact even the complaints made about the delays by Mr. Zéliotis may be questioned ...

It is possible to sympathize with Mr. Zéliotis, to understand the pain and anguish he felt, but one cannot conclude that the problems and delays he speaks of were solely caused by problems of access to Quebec health services. At the same time, the Court acknowledges that despite the fact that his medical file is not entirely conclusive he has an 'interest' in the broad sense in bringing the instant proceedings. So far as he was concerned, he had real problems getting an operation and this caused him suffering. He felt he would have had better access if there were a private system. We cannot say this is true, but it is his opinion and he is entitled to it.

Account of Dr. Jacques Chaoulli

(a) Who is the applicant and what did he say?
Dr. Chaoulli is 47 years old and obtained his doctorate in medicine in France. He is an immigrant and came to Quebec in 1977, first doing an M.Sc. in education at Laval University. He was denied the opportunity to do his internship in medicine in Quebec because of the quota. In early 1985, he was finally accepted at the Hôtel-Dieu in Québec and in 1986 obtained his licence to practise medicine in Quebec, after returning to France and practising there for eight months. When he came back to Quebec in 1986, he had as a completely new physician to practise for three years in a remote area from 1986 to 1989. He worked for two years at the Pontiac Hospital in Shawville. However, after two years he returned to Montréal. He explained his departure by saying that it was the director of professional services who released him after two years, telling him that he should not bill the RAMQ in an urban area for a year.

In June 1988 he went to the Montréal South Shore, working in emergency services for eight years. He obtained an emergency vehicle licence and created his own 'Médecins à domicile Rive-Sud' service in 1991. He had difficulty recruiting physicians and realized it was impossible for him to offer a twenty-four-hour service to the South Shore area. He related that the LCHC and the Longueuil police often called on his services.

Dr. Chaoulli wanted recognition for 'Médecins à domicile Rive-Sud.' He received some support but ran into a major problem: the refusal of the Régie régionale to recognize his services. In January 1995 he organized a public demonstration with fifty of his patients in Québec to explain to the Minister the importance of recognizing house calls with twenty-four-hour service. 'I was not doing this for the money,' he said, 'I was afraid I would no longer be able to provide this service.' The service made it possible to relieve the pressure on hospital emergency departments, he said. I was worried about the harmful consequences of the situation for my patients and my family,' he said ... 'I had,' he again said, 'a serious psychological trauma, not because of the financial aspect but because of the fact that the public could not have services at home. I felt a profound loss of esteem. I found it unfair that I could not give the public essential services.' It was in these circumstances that he took the decision by himself to initiate a hunger strike and claim, first, recognition of this activity, and secondly, a moratorium on the penalties. 'The hunger strike reflected my profound despair,' he said. 'It was a serious psychological trauma for me.' When he said these words, Dr. Chaoulli had tears in his eyes. He even said that the presence of his wife and daughter, who was five years old at the time, could no longer compensate for the problems he was having. 'I decided I would no longer live in a society where the government was so inhumane.' The hunger strike, he said, 'was one reason I did not commit suicide. I knew that my life was threatened, that human lives would be threatened because of the inaction and refusal of the government.'

In his opinion, not recognizing a house call service is criminal: human lives could be lost. At the end of the second week of his hunger strike he had himself taken to the Hôtel-Dieu in Québec to be rehydrated. He refused all food. He was sent to a psychiatrist, Dr. Anne Potvin, who found that he was rational. In the third week of the strike he went back to Parliament Hill to continue his strike. A verbal proposal was made to settle the financial penalty he had incurred in return for an end to his hunger strike. He refused: 'The proposal made was unacceptable.' At the end of the third week, passers-by asked him to halt his strike. He finally agreed and decided to get out of the public system and try to set up a private service hoping that private insurance would get involved 'I wanted to provide medicine for everyone, I thought the government would agree.'

On October 9, 1996 his status as a non-participant began. He decided to go to France and met there with a representative of the SAMU. I wanted to see the latest developments in prehospital services in France.' When he got back to Quebec, he advertised his services as a non-participating physician. He tried to make himself available 24 hours a day and operate an ambulance vehicle with rooflights and a siren. He had to have a licence. The Régie Régionale refused to give him the licence. He made house calls, and found that it was mostly wealthy people who called him. [TRANSLATION] 'That is not what I was looking for,' he said.

He subsequently contacted Hon. Dingwall, to whom he proposed a private non-profit hospital. 'I even suggested donating my already equipped emergency vehicle,' he said. On August 15, he received a reply from Hon. Allan Rock, who told him that his proposal was contrary to Canadian values. Canadians did not want a two-tier system. On August 8, he made a request to the Régie Régionale to be allowed to set up a private opted-out hospital. On March 19, 1998 he was again met with a refusal. The Régie did not recommend Dr. Chaoulli's proposal.

Since January 1997, he said,'I have significantly reduced my home medical practice. After Christmas 1997 I slowed down, I did not feel comfortable, either in the public or the private sector.' For fifteen months he withdrew and reduced his practice. 'I devoted my efforts to analysing the situation in Canada, the U.S. and Japan so I could be more useful to people.' He became a participant once more in July 1998 ...

He now says he feels great concern if he or his family were to fall ill. Dr. Chaoulli would like to obtain private insurance that could give him access to medical services and says he feels profound anguish that he cannot obtain private insurance. As a citizen he wishes to be allowed to pay a nonparticipating physician, if he so desires, for medically necessary service in a private non-convention hospital. He wishes to be allowed to obtain private insurance for access to pre-hospital emergency service, including airborne medical assistance (a helicopter) if necessary, from a private insurance source. 'In the event that I fall seriously ill,' he concluded, 'I want to be able to use my personal wealth to save my life rather than spend it on my funeral.' That is the gist of the testimony heard.

Discussion

... At the outset Dr. Chaoulli had to complete his initial contract in a remote region. He did not do this: he returned to Montréal and, contrary to what he was entitled to do, began practising on the South Shore. He then insisted on practising medicine as he wanted to do, disregarding what was decided by the Régie Régionale. Dr. Chaoulli also never testified that he received inadequate care or that the system did not respond to his personal health needs. He is still subject to significant penalties with the Régie de l'assurance-maladie of Quebec. He was released, returned to the public system, was still not satisfied. All of this leads the Court to raise questions about Dr. Chaoulli's real motives in this dispute. One cannot help being struck by the contradictions in the testimony and having the impression that Dr. Chaoulli embarked on a crusade which is now more than he can handle.

TESTIMONY OF SPECIALIST PHYSICIANS

(1) The applicants called five specialist physicians: Dr. Éric Lenczner, orthopedic surgeon in Montréal, Dr. Côme Fortin, ophthalmologist in Granby, Dr. Daniel Doyle, a surgeon and cardiologist in Québec, Dr. Abdenour Nabid, an oncologist in the Centre communautaire de l'Estrie and Dr. Michael Churchill-Smith, an internist in Montréal. All these physicians testified about the problems they had, about excessively long waiting lists, operation delays, the efforts they made every day to try and solve problems, to try and find solutions for the lack of system, organization and, shall we say, vision in the present day Quebec Régime de santé.

Dr. Lenczner spoke of 'huge problems in terms of access' for orthopedic surgeons which, even if they are not 'fatal,' are very incapacitating for those who can no longer walk, work and enjoy a normal life. Dr. Lenczner does not have enough time for operating at the hospital where he practises. He could operate on more patients if he was given more surgery time.

Dr. Fortin, an ophthalmologist, spoke of people who have cataracts, for example, who can no longer see properly and whose wait for surgery is greatly affecting their quality of life. Because of the nature of the disease, he said, waiting may even result in loss of vision. He had one day a week for operating himself, but this was not true of all his colleagues. He admitted that certain patients, doctors' children, and so on, were sometimes favoured. Nowadays, 'people have expectations, they want to be independent, they no longer want to wait,' he said.

Dr. Doyle is a thoracic and cardio-vascular surgeon and has been president of the cardio-vascular and thoracic surgeons of Quebec for five years. He now operates at the Hôpital Laval in Québec. He worked at the Hôpital Notre-Dame for ten years, now the CHUM, and is currently in Québec as he can have the desired operating time. He spoke of the priorities now existing for patients. Dr. Doyle explained that in 1992 there were two thousand patients on the waiting lists but the situation has improved considerably, as the government increased facilities in fall 1997. He spoke of surgeons trained in Quebec who had left for Ontario or the U.S., and the aggressive recruiting that takes place. 'Here we quickly become exhausted.' He said that Quebec patients are all very easygoing. They do not complain of having to wait, people accept it, they tell themselves that they have no choice. Dr. Doyle said that waiting should not exist in cardiology, that it is often a question of life or death, as cardiac illness is unpredictable. There is also a lack of nurses, erratic decisions which are made and so on. Despite the funds that private foundations are prepared to give, he cannot go ahead with certain projects because the government is not ready to invest for start-up and follow-up costs. 'There are a lot of political factors, we are five years behind Ontarians,' he said. 'Practising becomes demotivating.' At the same time, Dr. Doyle admitted that waiting exists everywhere. The population is growing older, it is now necessary to operate on people 85 years old. Dr. Doyle was not at all certain that the solution lay with private insurance. He related how, for example, insurance companies monitor patients who have operations with particular surgeons in the U.S., and so on.

Dr. Nabid was somewhat more pessimistic. He is a specialist in radio-oncology and has been president of the Quebec radiooncology specialists for four years. He said there is a lack of planning. Waiting lists have existed for several years. As we know, the population is growing older. There is a lack of technicians, a lot of pressure, a lack of equipment and of updating of equipment. 'Something is not working in the system when we have to send patients to Plattsburgh.' He said one has to 'put oneself in the patients' place, when they have been devastated by news of cancer.' For cancer patients, no delay is acceptable. 'We are dealing with human beings.' Like Dr. Doyle, he said that Quebecers are extremely likeable and easygoing people. Nevertheless, there should not be delays, he said.

Finally, Dr. Churchill-Smith testified. He is an internist, teaches at McGill and worked for ten years in the emergency department as a physician and department head at the Montréal General Hospital. Dr. Churchill-Smith has visited emergency departments in several countries, including France, where the approach is completely different from our own. There they have mobile emergency units which go to the patient. Currently, he said the government is studying various scenarios to find a solution. Money could be obtained from foundations to purchase helicopters, for example, if the operating costs could be guaranteed by the government.

DISCUSSION

The Court concludes from this testimony, first, that the physicians who testified were sincere and honest, wished to change things and unfortunately were powerless in view of the excessively long waiting lists. The Court accepts that waiting lists are too long and that even if the question is not always one of life or death all individuals are entitled to receive the care they need as promptly as possible. Yes, Quebeckers are patient and easygoing, but this does not mean that the health system should not be improved and transformed. Dr. Nabid even spoke of his profession as a sacred trust.

Further, the Court notes that despite the fact that some of these specialists indicated a desire to be free to obtain private insurance, no one completely and squarely supported the applicants' proposals, explaining that it was neither clear nor obvious a reworking of the system with a parallel private system would solve all the existing problems of delays and access. On the contrary, the specialists heard remained very cautious about a question which is complex and difficult.

OTHER TESTIMONY

(1) Barry Stein, Dr. André Roy

Among all the other witnesses heard there was the moving testimony of Barry Stein, a lawyer suffering from cancer whose sad story has been in the headlines. Mr. Stein related the events that occurred after his illness was diagnosed. He said he went to the CHUM, the Hôpital St-Luc, and recounted that his surgery was postponed three times. Mr. Stein said he went to the hospital to be operated on and was told that the operation would not take place that day. Finally, he decided to go and have an operation in New York. He contacted the Régie de l'assurance-maladie, which refused to pay for his surgery and hospitalization in New York. He went to court and obtained a judgment in his favour, ordering the RAMQ to pay his costs. ...

Dr. Roy gave the Court a different story from that provided by Mr. Stein. According to him, Mr. Stein's surgery only had to be postponed once and he could have been operated on the following week. Dr. Roy testified with aplomb and sincerity, giving various explanations about what happened to Mr. Stein, his patient, at St-Luc. What should we think of this? The Court remains uncertain as to what actually happened in this case. At the very least, the story is not conclusive ...

(3) Claude Castonguay

At the request of the applicants Clause Castonguay, Quebec Minister of Health in 1970, the 'father of health insurance in Quebec' and chair of the Castonguay Commission of Inquiry on Health and Social Welfare, testified. He testified with aplomb and restraint. Mr. Castonguay first noted that the purpose of the health insurance legislation adopted on November 1, 1970 was to give all individuals equal access to health care regardless of their income. He still supports that objective.

Mr. Castonguay explained that, however, in 1970 Quebec was in a period of prosperity and it was thought that this would continue. Quebec's debt was small, income from taxation was good. The aim of health insurance was to provide equal access to care for everyone. Nowadays, he explained, the situation has changed, public finances have deteriorated and the population has grown older. Despite this, the fundamental purpose of the plan should not change, Mr. Castonguay insisted. Instead, new solutions should be found for the health system. Mr. Castonguay said that he had never advocated what Dr. Chaoulli was advocating. In his opinion, the Quebec health system should remain public and accessible to the entire Quebec population. To do this there would have to be a new partnership with physicians, better organization of medical clinics and new investment in the health sector. According to Mr. Castonguay, a lot could be done to improve the present situation without adopting the solution advocated by the applicants Mr. Castonguay referred to the 1999 World Health Report which the Court feels may appropriately be considered here.

(4) WHO World Health Report 1999
The report by the World Health Organization is titled 'Making a Difference' and examines the situation in the world at the present time. This report results from the meeting of world Health Ministers and other leaders in Geneva in May 1999 for the last meeting of the World Health Assembly before the year 2000. Let us look at the statements by Dr. Brundtland, director general of the WHO:

> ... Our values cannot support market-oriented approaches that ration health services to those with the ability to pay. Not only do market-oriented approaches lead to intolerable inequity with respect to a fundamental human right, but growing bodies of theory and evidence indicate markets in health to be inefficient as well.
>
> . . . . .
>
> With the exception of only the United States, the high income market-oriented democracies mandate universal coverage. Their health outcomes are very high. They have contained expenditures to a much smaller fraction of GDP than has the USA (7–10% versus 14%). In the one country where it was studied – Canada – introduction of national health insurance had resulted in increased wages, reduced unemployment and improved health outcomes. Therein lies a lesson. ..

EXPERT WITNESSES: THEIR OPINIONS AND VIEWPOINTS

The Court should first say that it felt privileged to have heard such remarkable men. They all contributed greatly to the Court's analysis. It should be recalled, and we tend to forget this, that in Canada before the introduction of health insurance the situation was not a rosy one. There are those who will say that it is no better now, but this assertion can be seen to be clearly false when we really look back.

Fernand Turcotte is a physician and professor in the Faculty of Medicine at Laval University, holding degrees from the University of Montréal and Harvard, a specialist certified by the Royal College of Physicians and Surgeons of Canada, specializing in community medicine, and an Associate Member of the College. Dr. Turcotte is also the recipient of the De Fries medal, awarded for exceptional service to the public health of Canadians, in 1998. He is the author of a number of publications and research reports.

Dr. Fernand Turcotte first noted that health services and their provision have long been part of the field of social security. In fact, he said: ...

> In the early 1920s, it was recognized that illness had become the primary
> cause of the impoverishment of Canadians by the unemployment nearly
> always resulting from serious illness and by the using up of the family
> resources unavoidably resulting from the payment for care.

Nowadays, Dr. Turcotte said, 'people are no longer impoverished
because they have to go to hospital.' In the mid-1960s, this was not the
case. A person who was ill and was admitted to a private room might
after 30 days find himself or herself in a public room in unsatisfactory
conditions because he or she could no longer pay for the room. A
woman who had to go to hospital to give birth could be faced with a bill
for $5,000. Accordingly, costs had to be paid until Saskatchewan, Alberta
and British Columbia decided to adopt a hospital insurance system.
Subsequently, in Quebec, people also wanted to have their own system
and decided that they could afford one. It was necessary to acquire
universal insurance, transferable from one province to another ...

In Canada, the choice has been made to protect society against the
catastrophe caused by illness by making insurance available to everyone, subsidizing those who could not pay for it and making participation compulsory for everyone. This strategic choice frees insurance
from the obligation to constantly adjust the prices of its services to its
claim experience. The compulsory participation of all guarantees that
the effect of bad actuarial risks will be minimized in the larger number
of good risks which it is possible to assemble in a society. It also permits
a saving to be made on all the costs inherent in advertising and con-
tinual recruiting of participants. This in part explains the tremendous
administrative effectiveness of our health care system, the cost of managing which is nearly four times less than in the U.S.

In his report Dr. Turcotte noted that the Royal Commission on Health
Services, presided over by Emmet Hall J., was organized in 1960 to
determine whether the country's health services could respond to individual needs once financial accessibility to medical care was guaranteed and to identify what needed to be added in order to make them
able to cope, if problems were anticipated. In 1964, the Hall Commission concluded that Canada could offer all its citizens protection against
catastrophe resulting from illness without affecting existing health services. It recommended using types of insurance designed in the manner

of a social security program rather than a system of protection against disaster as provided in commercial insurance ...

Howard Bergman is a physician and a director of the geriatrics department at the Montréal General Jewish Hospital. At McGill University he is director of the geriatrics division and associate professor in the department of medicine and family medicine. He is a fellow of the American Geriatric Society and an associate professor of the University of Montréal, in the health administration department. He has prepared and participated in many publications and conferences ...

At the present time, Dr. Bergman said, overall expenditure control has become a subject of great concern. Canada is not the only country where this is happening. Thus, for example, in the U.S. the major concern is still overall expenditure, even though over 50% is private. At the same time, 'when a public system like our own is placed alongside the system of the former communist bloc, the comparison is ridiculous.' He noted that: 'Currently the Quebec health care system is one of the systems in which the private share is the largest. Over 30% of expenditure is private in Quebec, a proportion which has become one of the highest in the OECD. For the essential portion of medically necessary services, the Quebec health care system relies on a single payer and single management in which private participants are involved. Access is not based on the ability to pay.' Dr. Bergman voiced his concern at the erosion of the role of the government as single payer. Opening financing up to private sources would lead to a multi-speed system depending on the type of insurance each person could afford

... Dr. Bergman said that 'handicapped' persons might be excluded, as in Switzerland where, for example, mutual insurance companies have withdrawn from the poorest cantons. In cases where there are two systems, the public one becomes a 'safety net' where private hospitals transfer the worst economic risks. In Manitoba, it has been shown that health care providers who serve both private and public clientele give priority to the former, thereby lengthening the waiting period of patients in the public sector ... Once again, the U.S. may serve to illustrate the extreme situations that can occur. Hospitals there have two waiting rooms, the first serving private patients who 'go through' at once, the second being reserved for 'Medicaid' patients, who are poor and have public coverage: these patients are served 'otherwise' and act as a reservoir when the first waiting room empties, so as to absorb overhead.

Dr. Bergman related that already certain insurance companies are installing their offices on the second floor, with no elevator, to avoid having elderly or ill persons going to their offices to make insurance claims. On the second floor, it is thus possible to avoid applications by people who are short of breath or suffering from orthopedic problems. The insured must be young and in good health. What will happen to people who have AIDS or are suffering from heart ailments? The private system will make a hip replacement, but it is the public system which will cope if there are complications, Dr. Bergman said ...

Charles J. Wright is a physician specialized in surgery. He is a director of the Centre for Clinical Epidemiology, Evaluation at the Vancouver Hospital, Health Sciences Centre Faculty Member at the University of British Columbia and of the British Columbia Office of Health Technology. He was professor of surgery at the University of Saskatchewan and Head of the General Surgery at the Saskatchewan University and Hospital. He has given a large number of presentations at local, national and international meetings on Canadian health management ...

Dr. Wright said that our health care system is one of the most effective in the world in terms of 'ratio of productivity to administrative costs.' The Court feels that it must look here at what Dr. Wright said about the introduction of a private system alongside the public system. Once again the experience is contrary to the blandishments of those wishing to permit physician access to an alternative private system. The 'cream skimming' that goes on in the United States proprietary hospitals and in the health care insurance industry in the USA is well recognized. Certain occupations are blacklisted, and high-risk patients often refused coverage completely. In the hybrid system these costs would of course be borne by the public sector. In Britain, where there is no legal impediment to access to public or private systems, the private hospitals are definitely not the preferred place of treatment for complex or risky surgery or serious illness. They rarely have students or residents, nor do they have a full range of complex supporting services. In another analysis it was noted that for-profit hospitals do not provide care anymore efficiently or with greater public benefit than do nonprofit institutions, but they definitely distort service delivery patterns. They siphon off high revenue patients and vigorously try to avoid providing care to patient populations who are a financial risk ... .

Dr. Wright said:

... the existence of a dual system permits some insurance companies, business investors,and health care providers to reap more profit on the basis of the lower acuity level of the services that they provide. This shifts the overall load on the public system to the more complex high acuity end of the health care spectrum with consequent increased rather than decreased demand in the public system for certain services.

In concluding his report, Dr. Wright explained that:

> The principal argument for permitting a second tier private alternative system, namely that this would cause better overall access to care and relieve pressure on the public system, is not supported by any data. The information and studies compiled here suggest the opposite, namely that the major effect of allowing a private alternative would be to shift energy and resources from the public system into the private system, causing deterioration of public system access. This would only be to the advantage of those who could afford to pay or to purchase additional private health care insurance.

According to Dr. Wright, as a society we are capable of introducing the reforms now needed without rejecting the important principles of universal access that underlie our health care system ...

Theodore M. Marmor is professor of Public Policy and Management, School of Management, Yale University Professor of Political Science, Department of Political Science and Institution for Social and Policy Studies, Yale University, Ph.D. from Harvard university, in Politics and History, Graduate Research Fellow from Oxford. He is the author of books and edited volumes on health care reforms and has been an expert witness in numerous hearings in the United States and Canada and overseas. ...

Prof. Marmor was asked the following question: 'What would be the likely effects of permitting a parallel, private, regulated health insurance system to develop in Canada, one which would be permitted to pay for core services, now covered under the Canada Health Act, and accompanying provincial legislation?' He answered as follows, at p. 3 of his report:

> I do not believe it plausible that a private, parallel system of health insurance could be instituted in Canada without a number of undesirable side effects. By undesirable side effects I mean decreased support for Medicare from crucial groups of Canadian citizens, increased cost pressures on both systems, and increased administrative costs that regulating private insurance requires ... The case for changing the present Canadian

prohibition against parallel private health insurance for core medical services rests upon an appealing, but unrealistic theory. It is the view that parallel insurance can be introduced and operated so that no one in Canada would be worse off. On the analogy of 'gains from trade,' the assumption is that Canadians willing to pay for private coverage can exit the public system, free up space in waiting lists thereby ... The implicit assumptions behind this latter optimistic claim are that regulation can prevent the private system from growing too rapidly and that, given such constraints, a [sic] exit of anyone from the public insurance waiting lists must improve the chances to get care for Canadians left on those lists. This 'win-win' theory has a surface plausibility and, in some special contexts, might suggest a reasonable course of action. However, a closer examination reveals its theoretical and empirical flaws

Prof. Marmor added:

Doubts about the plaintiffs' assumptions are not only based on theoretical concerns. There is also considerable empirical basis for such skepticism. My studies of health care and financing systems in the OECD countries provides [sic] real world demonstrations of the dynamics that might well occur in Canada if a parallel system of private insurance were permitted to develop. In France, for example, there is continuous dispute about the role of cost sharing by patients in restraining demand for services in a fair and effective way.

Prof. Marmor then addressed the argument of waiting lists. The argument is as follows, Prof. Marmor explained:

There are waiting lists in Canada. If some of those on waiting lists made private arrangements for care at their expense (but eased by insurance options), and there were no change in Medicare, everyone would be better off. Those who jumped queues would be better off, as would the health care professionals who provided their care and received income. But even those remaining on queues would benefit, since the queues would be shortened. And so, why not permit this change?

Prof. Marmor explained that it is completely mistaken to think that there would be no change in our health system if a parallel private system were allowed to develop. He explained his conclusions as follows:

... waiting lists would persist in the public sector, and perhaps lengthen, as the number of patients in that system declined, since fewer hospital beds and professional staff would be serving them. (If resources were not diverted from the public system, unit costs would rise as fewer patients were treated in the same facilities, and new resources would be needed to service the private sector, increasing total Canadian spending on medical care.) Furthermore, the argument takes for granted that privately funded services can be organized as 'free-standing units.' Otherwise, such privately funded services would be unfairly subsidized by past and present public investment in research, capital improvements, and the easy availability of well-equipped modern hospitals. Thus I believe that allowing private insurance to be available as an alternative to Medicare would have profound negative impacts on the public system rather than none as is assumed. It would not increase availability of services in the public sector or reduce waiting lists. Instead, it would divert resources from the publicly financed program to be available to private activities and it would increase total Canadian expenditures on health. It also would give those able to secure private coverage an advantage over others.

Having a parallel private insurance system would produce substantial changes and damage the health system in Canada ...

The Australian experience, Prof. Marmor said,

... illustrates the difficulties with double coverage arrangements. The ban on age-rating (requiring a common premium) is an example of governmental unwillingness to bear the consequences of unregulated commercial insurance. The wealthy and older are those most able and inclined to exit a public system, but their expected use of a new privately insured system would produce prohibitively high premiums without regulation. With rate regulation, the government removes the core mechanism of private commercial insurance: namely risk rating. Consequently, the young and the healthy who would be most drawn to inexpensive, private insurance stay away from Australia's community-rated arrangements. More generally, where willingness to exit depends on income and health status, unregulated, private insurance markets cannot offer an alternative to public pooling of risk that is or has been acceptable to most OECD industrial democracies.

. . . . .

In the Canadian case, exiters would still be paying for public health insurance and thus would have a financial stake in reducing its funding. It is also the case that those who exit would be more likely to be affluent. As such, they a) have political influence disproportionate to their numbers; and b) currently finance a disproportionate share of Medicare, and would therefore have an especially strong interest in restraining its budget. From a social insurance standpoint, this degree of financial redistribution is fair, a mechanism for separating the provision of needed care from the financing of that care. But the expected impact of such a parallel system in Canada, given its current arrangements, would be an erosion of support, not its augmentation.

There will also be an increase in 'health costs.' Prof. Marmor said:

... what is proposed for Canada is not a cost-reducing innovation, but a cost-shifting program. And it is one that on the arguments proposed would almost certainly inflate overall Canadian health expenditures.

. . . . .

Finally, Canada now has what health economists metaphorically term 'single pipe' financing for basic medical care. The dominant view of health economists is that such funding with a global budget offers greater cost control ... .

Prof. Marmor concluded his report by saying:

Finally, the grounds used to bolster the arguments for parallel insurance are uniformly weak empirically ... Indeed, it is the stability of Canadian public health insurance, not its instability, that is the striking finding of comparative health policy research.

Finally, the applicant's expert Dr. J. Edwin Coffey testified. [He]is a graduate of McGill University in medicine specialized in obstetrics and gynecology. Fellow of the Royal College and of the American College of obstetricians and gynecologists. Established his practice in Montréal. Was Associate Professor in the Faculty of Medicine at McGill University. Interested in the political, economic and legislative affairs of the health care system since 1979 ... . Dr. Coffey submitted a voluminous report and testified at length. At p. 37 of his report he explained what he meant by the reform he was advocating:

... By structural reform, I mean a change in the method of financing and delivering health care and health insurance services, from an integrated system like the Quebec one ('système intégré') to a system based on contracting ('système du contrat') or to a system based on reimbursement ('système du remboursement') . . .

. . . . .

In Quebec efficiency will only be reached after the government decides to introduce a health care system based on contracting or reimbursement.

Dr. Coffey testified at length on the situation in the OECD countries (Organization for Economic Cooperation and Development). His conclusions compared the situation in Quebec and Canada with that of certain OECD countries. In his view:

The deteriorating health care and health insurance systems in Quebec and Canada are out of step with the health systems in other OECD countries. Quebec and Canada have failed to appreciate and apply many of the benefice [sic] public and private health system policies and reforms that the citizens of these OECD countries enjoy.
... In comparison to the health systems of all other OECD countries, and pointed out by the OECD reports, the unique and outstanding disadvantage that handicaps the health system in Quebec and Canada is the legislated prohibition of voluntary private health insurance and private hospital services that are medically necessary.

. . . . .

The ideologic and politically driven myths, that surround the Quebec and Canadian health systems, have overshadowed and presented [sic] evidence-based and practical reforms in the financing, insuring and delivery of medical and hospital services and have contributed to the dysfunctional state of our present health system ...

The Court notes that in his expert opinion and the conclusions at which he arrived, Dr. Coffey stood alone.

Before concluding, the Court should note that it felt it advisable to review here the gist of the testimony given by the experts heard. It quickly appeared to the Court that the issues were much broader than those discussed and it was the whole question of introducing a private health system parallel to the public system that was discussed by the applicants. In the circumstances, it became essential to look at both sides of the coin and see what the various experts heard in the course of the trial thought about it ...

[The trial judge then examined and dismissed the argument that the legislation prohibiting private insurance for services covered in the public system amounted to criminal law which can only be enacted by the Federal government and not the provinces.]

PARTIES' ARGUMENTS [under s.7 of the Charter]

The applicants argued that ss. 15 HIA and 11 HIA infringe the rights protected by s. 7 of the Charter and the rights mentioned in the Quebec Charter. Sec. 7. Everyone has the right to life, liberty and security of the person and the right not to be deprived thereof except in accordance with the principles of fundamental justice.

The applicants alleged that the public health system limits access to medically required care in terms of the available human, physical and financial resources. In their submission this fact, taken together with a prohibition from making use of a parallel private care system, infringes the right to life and security of the person.

They further argue that the right to liberty mentioned in s. 7 of the Charter extends to the individual's right to autonomy in the making of the personal decisions which he or she must make. In their submission, certain ancillary economic rights are capable of protection by s. 7 of the Charter. The applicants argued that the right to obtain private insurance or to pay for hospital services is an ancillary right relating directly to their right to obtain the health care which they need.

The Attorney General of Quebec, for her part, emphasized that anyone alleging an infringement of the Charter must present evidence of it on a balance of probabilities. It was argued that only an immediate or imminent risk to life, liberty or the security of the person is capable of infringing s. 7 and this was not established by the applicants to be the case. In the submission of the Attorney General of Canada, the infringement is entirely hypothetical and unsupported by the evidence.

The Attorney General of Quebec argued that in any case the 'rights' denied by ss. 15 HIA and 11 HIA are purely economic and cannot benefit from the protection of s. 7 of the Charter.

Finally, it was alleged that if there was an infringement of life, liberty or security in the case at bar, such infringement was consistent with the principles of fundamental justice, as the Court must exercise restraint toward governmental policy over health, weighing all the rights involved and the purposes sought by the disputed legislation.

DISCUSSION

As the Supreme Court has often said, analysis of the compatibility of legislation with the protection provided by s. 7 of the Charter must be undertaken in two stages. The first stage will thus consist here of determining whether the disputed provisions infringe the right to life, liberty or security of the person, while the second will involve determining whether such infringement is contrary to the rules of fundamental justice. If there is still an infringement, the latter must be analysed in terms of s. 1 of the Charter.

Purely economic rights and s. 7

The Court must point out that because of the range of meanings which may be given to the words used in s. 7, there has been no consensus as to the scope of this provision in the Supreme Court of Canada. Despite that, there is one rule that enjoys universal acceptance, namely that s. 7 was not designed to protect purely economic rights. The comments of McIntyre J. in Re Public Service Employee Relations Act [1987] 1 S.C.R. 313 at 405 are an illustration of this:

> For obvious reasons, the Charter does not give constitutional protection to all activities performed by individuals. There is, for instance, no Charter protection for the ownership of property, for general commercial activity, or for a host of other lawful activities.

McIntyre J. said that the Charter is concerned primarily with individual, political and democratic rights:

> The omission of similar provisions in the Charter, taken with the fact that the overwhelming preoccupation of the Charter is with individual, political and democratic rights with conspicuous inattention to economic and property rights, speaks strongly against any implication of a right to strike.

Two years later, in Irwin Toy Ltd. v. Quebec (A.G.) [1989] 1 S.C.R. 927 at

1003 a majority of the Supreme Court again ruled on the absence of any
protection for economic rights provided by s. 7:

> What is immediately striking about this section is the inclusion of 'secu-
> rity of the person' as opposed to 'property.' This stands in contrast to the
> classic liberal formulation, adopted, for example, in the Fifth and Four-
> teenth Amendments in the American Bill of Rights, which provide that no
> person shall be deprived 'of life, liberty or property, without due process
> of law.' The intentional exclusion of property from s. 7, and the substitu-
> tion therefor of 'security of the person' has, in our estimation, a dual effect.
> First, it leads to a general inference that economic rights are as generally
> encompassed by the term 'property' are not within the perimeters [sic] of
> the s. 7 guarantee. This is not to declare, however, that no right with an
> economic component can fall within 'security of the person.' Lower courts
> have found that the rubric of 'economic rights' embraces a broad spectrum
> of interests, ranging from such rights, included in various international
> covenants, as rights to social security, equal pay for equal work, adequate
> food, clothing and shelter, to traditional property – contract rights. To
> exclude all of the these at this early moment in the history of Charter
> interpretation seems to us to be precipitous.

It can be said that the Supreme Court, when it began interpreting the
Charter, did not wish to limit the guarantee in s. 7 in advance. At the
same time, it was clear that purely economic rights should in principle
not benefit from constitutional protection ...

In light of the preceding analysis, the Court feels that certain conclusions can be drawn regarding the guarantee contained in s. 7 of the
Charter. First, it is clear that the Charter is not designed to protect
purely economic rights. Second, it must be said that there is a body of
opinion on the Supreme Court that would extend the scope of s. 7 to
guarantee greater independence to individuals and, conversely, would
prevent undue interference by the state in people's personal choices.
The door is thus not closed to recognition of certain rights intimately
bound up with and inseparable from the right to life, liberty and security of the person. This will mean some measure of protection for rights
known as 'ancillary economic rights' ... .

The Court thus comes to the important question raised by the applicants: Can it then be concluded that the right to obtain private insurance
or the right to contract for hospital care, rights prohibited by ss. 15 HIA
and 11 HIA, are ancillary economic rights protected by s. 7 of the Charter?

The Court submits that such an interpretation is possible. The Court considers that the economic barriers set up by ss. 15 HIA and 11 HIA are closely linked to the opportunity to have access to health care. Without these rights, in view of the cost involved, access to private care is illusory. In this sense, these provisions are an obstacle to access to health services and are thus capable of infringing the life, liberty and security of the person. However, it should pointed out that s. 7 of the Charter does not protect a physician's right to practise his profession without constraint in the private sector.

Additionally, limitation of recourse to the private sector for care constitutes an infringement of the physical integrity of the person only in the event that the public system is not capable of effectively guaranteeing such access. If the public system makes the care in question available, there will not be any infringement of s. 7 of the Charter. The Court does not believe that a constitutional right exists to choose the source from which the medically required care will be obtained.

Sections 15 HIA and 11 HIA will thus not really infringe s. 7 if the public health system offers the same care and makes it accessible.

The Attorney General of Quebec clearly showed that ss. 15 HIA and 11 HIA constitute economic barriers only as regards care offered by the public system. In principle, these provisions do not deny access to care, they deny access to care from the private sector. The applicants, for their part, alleged that the public health system does not have unlimited resources and so there will be gaps and deficiencies in the availability of medically required care. In support of their arguments, they pointed to the waiting periods in emergency rooms and elsewhere. For these reasons, they submitted that obstacles to access to the private sector infringed their physical and psychological integrity ... .

Real or potential, and imminent, infringement

... In the Court's opinion, in view of the nature of the rights involved in s. 7, especially the rights to life and security of the person, this provision should be capable of offering preventive protection when an infringement is feared. The writers Brun and Tremblay have this to say on the point:

> The right to life, and to a certain extent the right to security, have no real meaning unless they are given a preventive aspect. This has been recognized by the Supreme Court, provided however that the infringement of

the right of a person alleging s. 7 has a degree of certainty that approaches probability ...

It can thus be concluded from the extracts reproduced above that the guarantee contained in s. 7 of the Charter will apply when a deprivation is actual or potential and is imminent. In the case at bar, the applicants' state of health is not under threat. They are not suffering from any illness for which they require medical care. However, they alleged the 'threat' of a deprivation in the event that their state of health requires care. Nevertheless, this is a threat which cannot really be described as actual, although it may be described as potential.

It is difficult to determine whether the threat is imminent simply because it is impossible to foresee the future state of health of an individual with certainty. In particular, it is impossible to predict in the majority of cases when an accident causing injury will occur. In view of this uncertainty we must conclude, as a person's state of health is unforeseeable, that there is an imminent threat of deprivation in the case at bar.

Conclusion [on Right to Life, Liberty and Security of the Person]

In light of the foregoing discussion, the Court comes to the following conclusions: (1) the Supreme Court has expressed the view that s. 7 of the Charter might embrace certain rights of an economic nature intimately bound up with the right to life, liberty and security of the person; (2) the right to obtain private insurance or the right to contract in the private sector to obtain health care, prohibited by ss. 15 HIA and 11 HIA, are capable of protection by s. 7 of the Charter when the care is not available through the public system; (3) the applicants can complain of a potential and imminent threat of deprivation.

The Court concludes that there is, first, an infringement of the applicants' rights to life, liberty and security of the person under s. 7. It remains to be seen whether such an infringement is in accordance with the rules of fundamental justice. As we have seen, the two parts of s. 7 are related and must be analysed together.

Principles of fundamental justice

To determine whether an infringement of the right to life, liberty or security of the person is contrary to the principles of fundamental justice reference must be made inter alia to the background of the legislation ...

In Cunningham v. Canada [1993] 2 S.C.R. 143 at 151, McLachlin J. said this on the point:

> Having concluded that the appellant has been deprived of a liberty interest protected by s. 7 of the Charter, we must determine whether this is contrary to the principles of fundamental justice under s. 7 of the Charter. In my view, while the amendment of the Parole Act to eliminate automatic release on mandatory supervision restricted the appellant's liberty interest, it did not violate the principles of fundamental justice. The principles of fundamental justice are concerned not only with the interest of the person who claims his liberty has been limited, but with the protection of society. Fundamental justice requires that a fair balance be struck between these interests, both substantively and procedurally ...

In undertaking an analysis of the principles of fundamental justice, therefore, the Court must consider the factors underlying the impugned legislation to see whether they are consistent with the values of the Charter. Further, it must take into account the balance which should exist between the protection of individual rights and the protection of society so as to determine whether the scope of the impugned legislation is overbroad and unreasonable.

The reasons for and principles underlying ss. 15 HIA and 11 HIA and their respective legislation have already been considered. The Health Insurance Act and the Hospital Insurance Act are legislation designed to create and maintain a public health system open to all residents of Quebec. They are legislation which seeks to encourage the overall health of all Quebecers without discrimination on the basis of their economic situation. In short, it is a measure by the government intended to promote the well-being of its population as a whole.

Clearly, ss. 15 HIA and 11 HIA raise economic barriers against access to private care. However, these are not really measures designed to limit access to care, but measures intended to prevent the creation of a parallel private care system. Underlying these provisions is the fear that the establishing of a private care system would have the effect of diverting a substantial portion of health resources at the expense of the public sector. The Quebec government adopted ss. 15 HIA and 11 HIA to guarantee that virtually all health resources existing in Quebec would be at the disposal of the Quebec population as a whole. That is clear.

The disputed provisions seek to guarantee access to health care which is equal and adequate for all Quebecers. The adoption of ss. 15 HIA and 11 HIA was prompted by considerations of equality and human dignity, and hence it is clear that there is no conflict with the general values expressed by the Canadian Charter or the Quebec Charter of Human Rights and Freedoms.

In closing, let us consider the question of the balance that should exist between individual rights and those of society. The Quebec public health system does not enjoy unlimited and inexhaustible resources; all the expert witnesses said so. The same might indeed be said for every health system existing in the world. In such circumstances, it is entirely justifiable for a government, having the best interests of its people at heart, to adopt a health policy solution which is designed to favour the largest possible number of people. The government limits the rights of a few to ensure that the rights of all citizens in the society will not be adversely affected.

The evidence showed that the right to have recourse to a parallel private health care system, advocated by the applicants, would have repercussions on the rights of the public as a whole. We cannot act like ostriches. The result of creating a parallel private health care system would be to threaten the integrity, sound operation and viability of the public system. Sections 15 HIA and 11 HIA prevent this from happening and guarantee the existence of a quality public health system in Quebec.

Further, the Court considers that ss. 15 HIA and 11 HIA do not have an overbroad application. The only way of ensuring that all health resources will benefit all Quebecers without discrimination is to prevent a parallel care system from being established. That is precisely what the disputed provisions in the case at bar do. ... In the Court's opinion the infringement of the right to life, liberty and security of the person in the case at bar is not 'unnecessarily broad, going beyond what is needed to accomplish the governmental objective.'

Consequently, the infringement of the right to life, liberty and security of the person in the case at bar is done in accordance with the principles of fundamental justice.

Section 1 of Charter

In view of the fact that there is no infringement of s. 7 or of the Quebec Charter, the Court considers that there is no need to analyse s. 1 of the

Charter. At the same time, the Court considers that an analysis under s. 1 would show that the impugned provisions in the case at bar are a reasonable limit in a free and democratic society.

[The Court then concluded that the impugned law did not violate the right against the imposition of cruel and unusual punishment under s.12 of the Charter or equality rights under s.15 of the Charter]

CONCLUSIONS

... the Court found that the Supreme Court has left the way open to extending the scope of s. 7 of the Charter so as to guarantee greater autonomy to individuals without excessive interference by the state. The Court also considers that if access to the health system is not possible, it is illusory to think that rights to life and security are respected. The Court feels that the economic barriers created by ss. 15 HIA and 11 HIA are related to the opportunity of access to health care.

In the case at bar, the applicants are not in a situation where their state of health requires care. At the same time, the Court considers that the right to health and even to some extent the right to security has no real meaning unless it is given a preventive scope. The 'threat' or deprivation must be real or imminent. Here it is imminent, but the infringement is done in accordance with the principles of fundamental justice and so cannot be regarded as conflicting with s. 7 of the Charter.

The disputed provisions were adopted on the basis of considerations of equality and human dignity and are not in conflict with the values embodied in the Charter or the Quebec Charter of Human Rights and Freedoms.

It is entirely understandable that a government with the best interests of the public at heart should adopt a solution that will benefit the largest number of individuals ...

Finally, there is no infringement of s. 15 of the Charter ... The impugned provisions serve to promote legitimate social interests. There is no inconsistency with the principles found in the Charter. The Court notes what the highest court in the land said in Edwards Books and Art Ltd [1986] 2 S.C.R. 713 at 779:

In interpreting and applying the Charter I believe that the courts must be cautious to ensure that it does not simply become an instrument of better situated individuals to roll back legislation which has as its object the improvement of the condition of less advantaged persons.

Before concluding, the Court should say that solutions to the problems in the health system are not to be found through legal channels. Thirty years have passed since health insurance was introduced. In La Presse of November 17, 1999, Claude Castonguay wrote 'a revision of the Quebec system is inevitable and we will have to change the way we do things.' At the start of this judgment, the Court noted that we should not forget past times in which persons with illness could not obtain health care because they lacked the means. 'Those who forget history are doomed to repeat it.'

The expert witnesses heard stated that the Canadian health care system is an altruistic and generous effort by society and its problems will not be solved by undermining its foundation. Does this also mean that there is no scope for reform?

The Court will say no more on this question, as it is a political question which the Court cannot answer, that being the function of legislature.

FOR THESE REASONS, THE COURT:

DISMISSES the motion;

WITH costs.

GINETTE PICHÉ J.S.C.

Appendix B

[The following is an edited translated version of the Quebec Court of Appeal's decision rejecting the appeal of Dr. Chaoulli and Mr. Zeliotis from the trial judgment as excerpted in Appendix A. The official and full version of this judgment is reported at [2002] R.J.Q. 1205. We have focused on the issue decided under s.7 of the Canadian Charter. We thank Charles Maxime Panaccio who did the translation and the University of Toronto Faculty of Law for financial assistance.]

Reasons of Delisle J. A.

Section 7 of the Canadian Charter

> Everyone has the right to life, liberty and security of the person and the right not to be deprived thereof except in accordance with the principles of fundamental justice.

[22] ... the analysis of section 7 of the Canadian Charter follows two steps. First, there must be an infringement of the right to life, liberty or security of a person and, second, the infringement must not be in accordance with the principles of fundamental justice.

[23] The first instance judge has followed this approach. First, she has concluded that there was an infringement of the rights guaranteed by section 7 of the Canadian Charter, and then she concluded that this infringement was in accordance with the principles of fundamental justice.

[24] Unlike the first instance judge, I am of the view that section 7 of the Canadian Charter does not apply, for three reasons.

[25] First, the right to enter into a contract which is forbidden by sections 11 HOIA and 15 HEIA is an *economic* right which is not *fundamental* to the life of the person. One must not invert the relevant principles and render fundamental an ancillary economic right to which, moreover, less well-off individuals would not have access. The relevant fundamental right is that of offering to all a public health protection regime, which the prohibitions provided for by the above-cited sections aim at safeguarding. It has not been demonstrated in the present case that the infringement to the economic right was of such a nature as to jeopardize this fundamental right.

[26] Indeed, in order to invoke a violation of section 7 of the Canadian Charter, it must be proved that there exists a real or potential and imminent infringement of the right guaranteed by that section.

[27] A real infringement has not been demonstrated here; the health of the appellant is not involved.

[28] He however wishes to protect his future rights in case he would be in need of health care.

[29] For an infringement to be imminent, it must present a certain degree of proximity and be predictable. It cannot be remote and uncertain.

[30] Finally, section 7 of the Canadian Charter cannot be used to judicially second-guess the appropriateness of a societal choice, as observed by Justice Lamer in *Reference Re. ss. 193 and 195.1 (1) c) Criminal Code Manitoba* [1990] 1 S.C.R. 1123, 1176:

> In the area of public policy what is at issue are political interests, pressures and values that no doubt are of social significance, but which are not 'essential elements of a system for the administration of justice,' and hence are not principles of fundamental justice within the meaning of s. 7. The courts must not, because of the nature of the institution, be involved the realm of pure public policy; that is the exclusive role of the properly elected representatives, the legislators. To expand the scope of s. 7 too widely would be to infringe upon that role.

[31] The second ground of appeal is rejected.

[The judge then upheld the trial judge's decision that the impugned legislation did not violate ss. 12 or 15]

Articles 1, 4, 5 and 6 of the Quebec Charter

1. Every human being has a right to life, and to personal security, inviolability and freedom. He also possesses juridical personality.

4. Every person has a right to the safeguard of his dignity, honour and reputation.

5. Every person has a right to respect for his private life.

7. Every person has a right to the peaceful enjoyment and free disposition of his property, except to the extent provided by law.

[49] The appellant raises, with respect to these articles, the same arguments than those raised with respect to the Canadian Charter.

[50] For the reasons already mentioned, sections 11 HOIA and 15 HEIA infringe none of those rights.

Section 1 of the Canadian Charter and Article 9.1 of the Quebec Charter

[51] Given the conclusion that there is no infringement to any of the rights invoked by the appellant, it is not necessary to analyse this ground of appeal.

Conclusion

[52] The appeal must be rejected, with costs ...

Reasons of Forget J.A.

[53] I am in agreement with the conclusion suggested by Justice Delisle and with the whole of his reasons, except as they concern section 7 of the Canadian Charter.

[54] I do not believe that the right invoked by the appellant can be described as a right of a purely economic nature. In fact, the appellant asks for a right of access to health services. He claims that the public health care system is not able to provide the care that the private sector could provide him. Without private insurance, he would thus not have access to quality health services.

[55] I am of the view that the economic question is incidental and that section 7 of the Canadian Charter can here be applied. On thus issue I share the conclusion of the first instance judge, who, following a long discussion, writes:

> The Court finds that the economic barriers established by sections 15 HEIA and 11 HOIA are intimately related to the possibility of access to health care. Without these rights, given the costs, access to private care is illusory. In that sense, these provisions are a barrier to access to health services and are thus susceptible to affect life, liberty and security of the person.

[56] The right to security aims at protecting every person's physical and psychological integrity.

[57] The appellant must show that the infringement is real or potential and imminent.

[58] I acknowledge, like Justice Delisle, that the infringement is not real since the health of the appellant is not in cause but, in my view, and with respect, it is certainly potential since most humans are one day or another confronted to health problems which require adequate care.

[59] Secondly, the infringement must be imminent. In this regard, Justice Delisle writes that it must have a certain degree of proximity and be predictable. I am generally in agreement with these characteristics, but I cannot convince myself to apply them strictly in relation to health care. To force a person to wait until he or she is gravely ill (or he of she be implicated in a grievous accident) before launching proceedings in order to obtain adequate health services would have the effect, in a majority of cases, to render the claim illusory, given the unpredictability of illness and of its evolution.

[60] As to the second stage of the analysis of section 7 of the Canadian Charter, I also share the view of the first instance judge, who has

concluded that the infringement did not go against the principles of fundamental justice.

[61] The analysis must establish a balance between the claimed individual rights and the rights of society. The first instance judge summarizes thus the State's desire to privilege access to health care for all citizens:

> Clearly, sections 15 HEIA and 11 HOIA create economic barriers against access to private care. However, they are not really measures aiming at limiting access to care, they are rather *measures aiming at avoiding the establishment of a parallel private health care system*. The ground of these provisions is the fear that the establishment of a private care system would have the effect of robbing a substantial part of health resources to the detriment of the public sector. *The Quebec government has adopted sections 15 HEIA and 11 HOIA in order to guarantee that the quasi-totality of health resources existing in Quebec be at the disposition of all the population of Quebec. This is clear.*

> The impugned provisions *aim at guaranteeing equal and adequate access to health services for all Quebeckers*. The adoption of sections 15 HEIA and 11 HOIA was motivated by considerations of equality and human dignity and, therefore, it is clear that there is no conflict with the general values found in the Canadian charter of the Quebec charter of rights and freedoms.

[62] The first instance judge has concluded that 'the right to access a parallel private health care system [...] would have repercussions on the rights of all the population.'

[63] The State has chosen to privilege collective interests; the infringement is thus in accordance with the principles of fundamental justice.

[64] Like Justice Delisle, I suggest that the appeal be rejected, with costs.

Reasons of Brossard J.A.

[65] I am in complete agreement with my colleague Justice Delisle's opinion, save for one reservation which is related to the reasons expressed by Justice Forget. I use the term 'reservation' rather than 'diver-

gence' because I do not believe that it is necessary, on the one hand, to qualify in a formal and definitive way the nature of the right conferred by sections 11 HOIA and 15 HEIA in order to solve the present case, whereas, on the other hand, I am not convinced that there exists a true divergence between the reasons expressed by my colleagues.

[66] Like Justice Delisle, I am of the view that the right to enter into a contract forbidden by sections 11 HOIA and 15 HEIA is an economic right which, in itself and in isolation from its possible consequences, is not fundamental to the life of the person. Hence, to the extent that, in the present case, it has not been demonstrated that the infringement to this right jeopardized the appellant's fundamental right to health and life, it does not seem necessary to me to dwell on it any longer.

[67] On a theoretical plane, on the other hand, I share Justice Forget's view. In other words, if we consider the possibility that, in other circumstances, it could be demonstrated that that there is a risk, be it only a potential one, for the health or life of one or many persons, resulting from the impossibility to obtain the required medical care within appropriate delays, as a consequence of the withdrawal of this person's right to get insurance which would enable him or her to have access to such care outside of the public regime, we should then conclude that this withdrawal constitutes an infringement of the fundamental right protected by article 7 of the Canadian Charter.

[68] Although I agree with Justice Forget on this aspect, I however abstain from expressing an opinion as to whether such an infringement would then be contrary to the principles of fundamental justice. Indeed, in light of the evidence, this seems neither necessary nor appropriate in the present case.

[69] Like my colleagues, I am of the view, in the present case, to reject the appeal, with costs, but without expressing a definitive opinion on what precedes.

Appendix C

[The following is an edited version of the Supreme Court's decision which reversed the decisions of the trial judge and the Court of Appeal found in appendices A and B by a 4: 3 decision. The judgment has been edited to make it more accessible to the lay reader. The full text of the judgment is reported as *Chaoulli v. Quebec (Attorney General)*, 2005 SCC 35 and is available at *http://www.lexum.umontreal.ca/csc-scc/en/index.html*. Note that the paragraph numbers in the original judgment have been retained although some have been edited out.

The majority of the Court is composed of the separate judgment of Justice Deschamps and those of Chief Justice McLachlin and Justice Major with the agreement of Justice Bastarache. The dissenting judgement is written by Justices Binnie and Le Bel with the agreement of Justice Fish.

Some words of explanation are required because the four judges that composed the majority only agreed that Quebec's prohibition on private medical insurance for services covered in the public system violated the Quebec Charter of Rights and Freedoms and not the Canadian Charter of Rights.

Justice Deschamps, unlike all the other judges who heard the case, decided only the issues arising under the Quebec Charter of Rights and not the Canadian Charter of Rights. She found that Quebec's laws violated the right to life, and to personal security, inviolability and freedom under s.1 of the Quebec Charter. This right does not, as under s.7 of the Charter, require that the rights be deprived in a manner that does not accord with the principles of fundamental justice. Justice Deschamps also found that the Quebec government had not justified the violation under s.9.1 of the Quebec Charter which provides that 'in exercising his fundamental rights and freedoms, a person shall maintain a proper regard for democratic values, public order and the general well-being of the citizens of Quebec.' This justification provision has been interpreted in a manner similar to section one of the Canadian Charter which provides that Charter rights are 'subject only to such reasonable limits prescribed by law as can be demonstrably justified in a free and democratic society.' Having decided the impugned law was invalid under the Quebec Charter, Justice Deschamps did not decide whether it also violated the Canadian Charter.

In contrast, Chief Justice McLachlin and Justice Major with the agreement of Justice Bastarache decided that the Quebec law violated not only the Quebec Charter but s.7 of the Canadian Charter and had not been justified under s.1 of the Canadian Charter. Justice Binnie and Le Bel with the agreement of Justice Fish decided that the Quebec law violated neither the Quebec or Canadian Charter.

The result is that three judges (Chief Justice McLachlin, Justices Major and Bastarache) on the Supreme Court concluded that a prohibition on private medical insurance for services covered in the public system was an unjustified violation of s.7 of the Canadian Charter and three judges (Justices Binnie, Le Bel and Fish) concluded that such a prohibition did not violate the Charter. The seventh judge, Justice Deschamps, has not decided the issue under the Canadian Charter. but has decided that it is unjustified violation of the Quebec Charter.

Two judges presently on the Court, Justices Abella and Charron, were not on the Court when the appeal was heard. In addition, Justice Major will retire in December, 2005. In many ways, this state of affairs leaves the questions under the Canadian Charter to be resolved by subsequent decisions of the courts]

1 **DESCHAMPS J.** – Quebeckers are prohibited from taking out insurance to obtain in the private sector services that are available under Quebec's public health care plan. Is this prohibition justified by the need to preserve the integrity of the plan?

2 As we enter the 21st century, health care is a constant concern. The public health care system, once a source of national pride, has become the subject of frequent and sometimes bitter criticism. This appeal does not question the appropriateness of the state making health care available to all Quebeckers. On the contrary, all the parties stated that they support this kind of role for the government. Only the state can make

available to all Quebeckers the social safety net consisting of universal and accessible health care. The demand for health care is constantly increasing, and one of the tools used by governments to control this increase has been the management of waiting lists. The choice of waiting lists as a management tool falls within the authority of the state and not of the courts. The appellants do not claim to have a solution that will eliminate waiting lists. Rather, they submit that the delays resulting from waiting lists violate their rights under the Charter of human rights and freedoms, R.S.Q., c. C-12 ('Quebec Charter'), and the Canadian Charter of Rights and Freedoms ('Canadian Charter').They contest the validity of the prohibition in Quebec, as provided for in s. 15 of the Health Insurance Act, R.S.Q., c. A-29 ('HEIA'), and s. 11 of the Hospital Insurance Act, .S.Q., c. A-28 ('HOIA'), on private insurance for health care services that are available in the public system. The appellants contend that the prohibition deprives them of access to health care services that do not come with the wait they face in the public system.

3   The two sections in issue read as follows:

   15.   No person shall make or renew a contract of insurance or make a payment under a contract of insurance under which an insured service is furnished or under which all or part of the cost of such a service is paid to a resident or a deemed resident of Québec or to another person on his behalf. ...

   11.   (1) No one shall make or renew, or make a payment under a contract under which

   (a) a resident is to be provided with or to be reimbursed for the cost of any hospital service that is one of the insured services;

   (b) payment is conditional upon the hospitalization of a resident; or

   (c) payment is dependent upon the length of time the resident is a patient in a facility maintained by an institution contemplated in section 2. ...

4   In essence, the question is whether Quebeckers who are prepared to spend money to get access to health care that is, in practice, not accessible in the public sector because of waiting lists may be validly pre-

vented from doing so by the state. For the reasons that follow, I find that the prohibition infringes the right to personal inviolability and that it is not justified by a proper regard for democratic values, public order and the general well-being of the citizens of Quebec.

5   The validity of the prohibition is contested by the appellants, George Zeliotis and Jacques Chaoulli. Over the years, Mr. Zeliotis has experienced a number of health problems and has used medical services that were available in the public system, including heart surgery and a number of operations on his hip. The difficulties he encountered prompted him to speak out against waiting times in the public health care system. Mr. Chaoulli is a physician who has tried unsuccessfully to have his home-delivered medical activities recognized and to obtain a licence to operate an independent private hospital ... .

13   Given that I have had the opportunity to read the reasons of Binnie and LeBel JJ., I think it would be appropriate to highlight the main points on which we agree and disagree before addressing the issues raised by the appellants.

14   As I mentioned at the beginning of my reasons, no one questions the need to preserve a sound public health care system. The central question raised by the appeal is whether the prohibition is justified by the need to preserve the integrity of the public system. In this regard, when my colleagues ask whether Quebec has the power under the Constitution to discourage the establishment of a parallel health care system, I can only agree with them that it does. But that is not the issue in the appeal. The appellants do not contend that they have a constitutional right to private insurance. Rather, they contend that the waiting times violate their rights to life and security. It is the measure chosen by the government that is in issue, not Quebeckers' need for a public health care system.

15   To put the problem in context, the legislative framework of the impugned provisions must first be explained. Considering the provisions in their legislative context will make it possible to address the division of powers argument. I will then explain why, in my opinion, the case must first be considered from the standpoint of the Quebec Charter. Next, I will examine the appeal from the standpoint of s. 1 of the Quebec Charter before considering whether the prohibition is justi-

fied under s. 9.1 of the Quebec Charter. Because I conclude that the Quebec Charter has been violated, it will not be necessary for me to consider the arguments based on the Canadian Charter.

Legislative Context

16   Although the federal government has express jurisdiction over certain matters relating to health, such as quarantine, and the establishment and maintenance of marine hospitals (s. 91(11) of the Constitution Act, 1867), it is in practice that it imposes its views on the provincial governments in the health care sphere by means of its spending power ... In order to receive federal funds, a provincial plan must conform to the principles set out in the Canada Health Act, R.S.C. 1985, c. C-6: it must be administered publicly, it must be comprehensive and universal, it must provide for portability from one province to another and it must be accessible to everyone. These broad principles have become the hallmarks of Canadian identity. Any measure that might be perceived as compromising them has a polarizing effect on public opinion. The debate about the effectiveness of public health care has become an emotional one. The Romanow Report stated that the Canada Health Act has achieved an iconic status that makes it untouchable by politicians (Building on Values: The Future of Health Care in Canada: Final Report (2002), at p. 60 (Romanow Report)). The tone adopted by my colleagues Binnie and LeBel JJ. is indicative of this type of emotional reaction. It leads them to characterize the debate as pitting rich against poor when the case is really about determining whether a specific measure is justified under either the Quebec Charter or the Canadian Charter. I believe that it is essential to take a step back and consider these various reactions objectively. The Canada Health Act does not prohibit private health care services, nor does it provide benchmarks for the length of waiting times that might be regarded as consistent with the principles it lays down, and in particular with the principle of real accessibility.

17   In reality, a large proportion of health care is delivered by the private sector. First, there are health care services in respect of which the private sector acts, in a sense, as a subcontractor and is paid by the state. There are also many services that are not delivered by the state, such as home care or care provided by professionals other than physicians. In 2001, private sector services not paid for by the state accounted for

nearly 30 percent of total health care spending (Canadian Institute for Health Information, Public and Private Shares of Total Health Expenditure, by Use of Funds, Canada, 2001). In the case of private sector services that are not covered by the public plan, Quebeckers may take out private insurance without the spectre of the two-tier system being evoked. The Canada Health Act is therefore only a general framework that leaves considerable latitude to the provinces. In analysing the justification for the prohibition, I will have occasion to briefly review some of the provisions of Canada's provincial plans. The range of measures shows that there are many ways to deal with the public sector/private sector dynamic without resorting to a ban ...

Priority Given to Arguments Based on the Quebec Charter

27   In the instant case, s. 7 of the Canadian Charter and s. 1 of the Quebec Charter have numerous points in common:

Canadian Charter
7.   Everyone has the right to life, liberty and security of the person and the right not to be deprived thereof except in accordance with the principles of fundamental justice.

Quebec Charter
1.   Every human being has a right to life, and to personal security, inviolability and freedom.

28   The similarities between these two provisions probably explain in part why the Superior Court and the Court of Appeal considered only the Canadian Charter in their decisions. With regard to certain aspects of the two charters, the law is the same. For example, the wording of the right to life and liberty is identical. It is thus appropriate to consider the two together. Distinctions must be made, however, and I believe that it is important to begin by considering the specific protection afforded by the Quebec Charter for the reason that it is not identical to the protection afforded by the Canadian Charter.

29   The most obvious distinction is the absence of any reference to the principles of fundamental justice in s. 1 of the Quebec Charter. The analysis dictated by s. 7 of the Canadian Charter is twofold. Under the approach that is generally taken, the claimant must prove, first, that a

deprivation of the right to life, liberty and security of the person has occurred and, second, that the deprivation is not in accordance with the principles of fundamental justice. If this is proved, the state must show under s. 1 of the Canadian Charter that the deprivation is justified in a free and democratic society.

30   According to established principles, the onus is on the claimant to prove a violation of constitutional rights ... Under s. 7 of the Canadian Charter, the claimant would thus have a dual burden. The effect of placing this burden of proof on the claimant is that it makes his or her task more onerous. There is no such dual burden of proof under the Quebec Charter because the principles of fundamental justice are not incorporated into s. 1 of the Quebec Charter. For this reason, the Quebec Charter has a scope that is potentially broader. This characteristic should not be disregarded.

31   Ruling on the points in issue by applying the Quebec Charter enhances an instrument that is specific to Quebec; this approach is also justified by the rules of Canadian constitutional law.

32   Before getting into the heart of the debate regarding s. 1 of the Quebec Charter, I must address three preliminary arguments raised by the respondent Attorney General of Quebec: (a) that the protection of the right to freedom and life is limited to situations involving the administration of justice, (b) that the right asserted is economic and is not a fundamental right, and (c) that the appellants do not have standing.

Preliminary Objections

Scope of Section 1 of the Quebec Charter

33   The trial judge adopted a liberal approach to applying the protection afforded by s. 7 of the Canadian Charter. She expressed the opinion that the protection is not limited to situations involving the administration of justice. This Court has not yet achieved a consensus regarding the scope of this protection ... In my opinion, the same question of law does not arise in the context of the Quebec Charter. The Quebec Charter has a very broad scope of application. It extends to relationships between individuals and relationships between individuals and the state.

Limiting the scope of s. 1 of the Quebec Charter to matters connected with the administration of justice is not justified in light of the general scope of this quasi-constitutional instrument.

Economic Right or Fundamental Right

34   Delisle J.A. accepted the argument of the Attorney General of Quebec and declined to apply s. 7 of the Canadian Charter on the basis that the right in issue, which in his opinion is an economic right, is not protected by the Charter. This appeal does not require the Court to establish a general rule including or excluding economic rights in or from the scope of s. 1 of the Quebec Charter. The Superior Court judge made the following observation in this regard :

> [TRANSLATION] ... 'the economic barriers ... are closely related to the possibility of gaining access to health care. Having regard to the costs involved, access to private care without the rights in question is illusory. Accordingly, those provisions are an impediment to access to health care services and therefore potentially infringe the right to life, liberty and security of the person.' [Emphasis deleted.]

Piché J.'s analysis is correct. Limits on access to health care can infringe the right to personal inviolability. The prohibition cannot be characterized as an infringement of an economic right.

Standing

35   Clearly, a challenge based on a charter, whether it be the Canadian Charter or the Quebec Charter, must have an actual basis in fact. However, the question is not whether the appellants are able to show that they are personally affected by an infringement. The issues in the instant case are of public interest and the test from Minister of Justice of Canada v. Borowski, [1981] 2 S.C.R. 575, applies. The issue must be serious, the claimants must be directly affected or have a genuine interest as citizens and there must be no other effective means available to them. These conditions have been met. The issue of the validity of the prohibition is serious. Chaoulli is a physician and Zeliotis is a patient who has suffered as a result of waiting lists. They have a genuine interest in the legal proceedings. Finally, there is no effective way to challenge the validity of the provisions other than by recourse to the courts ... .

Infringement of the Rights Protected by s. 1 of the Quebec Charter

37   The appellant Zeliotis argues that the prohibition infringes Quebeckers' right to life. Some patients die as a result of long waits for treatment in the public system when they could have gained prompt access to care in the private sector. Were it not for s. 11 HOIA and s. 15 HEIA, they could buy private insurance and receive care in the private sector.

38   The Superior Court judge stated 'that there [are] serious problems in certain sectors of the health care system' (at p. 823). The evidence supports that assertion. After meticulously analysing the evidence, she found that the right to life and liberty protected by s. 7 of the Canadian Charter had been infringed. As I mentioned above, the right to life and liberty protected by the Quebec Charter is the same as the right protected by the Canadian Charter ... .

39   Not only is it common knowledge that health care in Quebec is subject to waiting times, but a number of witnesses acknowledged that the demand for health care is potentially unlimited and that waiting lists are a more or less implicit form of rationing ... Waiting lists are therefore real and intentional. The witnesses also commented on the consequences of waiting times.

40   Dr. Daniel Doyle, a cardiovascular surgeon, testified that when a person is diagnosed with cardiovascular disease, he or she is 'always sitting on a bomb' and can die at any moment. In such cases, it is inevitable that some patients will die if they have to wait for an operation. Dr. Doyle testified that the risk of mortality rises by 0.45 percent per month. The right to life is therefore affected by the delays that are the necessary result of waiting lists ...

42   In the instant case, Dr. Eric Lenczner, an orthopaedic surgeon, testified that the usual waiting time of one year for patients who require orthopaedic surgery increases the risk that their injuries will become irreparable. Clearly, not everyone on a waiting list is in danger of dying before being treated. According to Dr. Edwin Coffey, people may face a wide variety of problems while waiting. For example, a person with chronic arthritis who is waiting for a hip replacement may experience considerable pain. Dr. Lenczner also stated that many patients on non-

urgent waiting lists for orthopaedic surgery are in pain and cannot walk
or enjoy any real quality of life.

43   Canadian jurisprudence shows support for interpreting the right to
security of the person generously in relation to delays. In R. v.
Morgentaler, [1988] 1 S.C.R. 30, at p. 59, Dickson C.J. found, based on
the consequences of delays, that the procedure then provided for in s.
251 of the Criminal Code, R.S.C. 1985, c. C-46, jeopardized the right to
security of the person. Beetz J., at p. 105, with Estey J. concurring, was of
the opinion that the delay created an additional risk to health and
constituted a violation of the right to security of the person. ..

44   In the opinion of my colleagues Binnie and LeBel JJ., there is an
internal mechanism that safeguards the public health system. According to them, Quebeckers may go outside the province for treatment
where services are not available in Quebec. This possibility is clearly
not a solution for the system's deficiencies. The evidence did not bring
to light any administrative mechanism that would permit Quebeckers
suffering as a result of waiting times to obtain care outside the province.
The possibility of obtaining care outside Quebec is case-specific and is
limited to crisis situations ... .

Justification for the Prohibition

46   Section 9.1 of the Quebec Charter sets out the standard for justification. It reads as follows:

> 9.1. In exercising his fundamental freedoms and rights, a person
>   shall maintain a proper regard for democratic values, public
>   order and the general well-being of the citizens of Québec.

In this respect, the scope of the freedoms and rights, and limits to
their exercise, may be fixed by law.

48   ... The analytical approach developed in R. v. Oakes, [1986] 1
S.C.R. 103, must be followed [under s.9.1 of the Quebec Charter]. This
approach is well known. First, the court must determine whether the
objective of the legislation is pressing and substantial. Next, it must
determine whether the means chosen to attain this legislative end are
reasonable and demonstrably justifiable in a free and democratic soci-

ety. For this second part of the analysis, three tests must be met: (1) the existence of a rational connection between the measure and the aim of the legislation; (2) minimal impairment of the protected right by the measure; and (3) proportionality between the effect of the measure and its objective ... It is the minimal impairment analysis that has proven to be the most delicate stage in the instant case. The other stages cannot, however, be bypassed.

Purpose of the Statute

49   The prohibitions are set out in the HOIA and the HEIA. The general objective of these statutes is to promote health care of the highest possible quality for all Quebeckers regardless of their ability to pay. Quality of care and equality of access are two inseparable objectives under the statutes ... .

55   Section 11 HOIA and s. 15 HEIA convey [the intention to limit private services].. clearly. They render any proposal to develop private professional services almost illusory. The prohibition on private insurance creates an obstacle that is practically insurmountable for people with average incomes. Only the very wealthy can reasonably afford to pay for entirely private services. Assuming that a permit were issued, the operation of an institution that is not under agreement is the exception in Quebec. In fact, the trial judge found that the effect of the prohibition was to 'significantly' limit the private provision of services that are already available under the public plan.. This observation relates to the effects of the prohibition. These effects must not be confused with the objective of the legislation. According to the Attorney General of Quebec, the purpose of the prohibition is to preserve the integrity of the public health care system. From this perspective, the objective appears at first glance to be pressing and substantial. Its pressing and substantial nature can be confirmed by considering the historical context ...

Proportionality

Rational Connection

57   The next question is whether the prohibition on private insurance has a rational connection with the objective of preserving the public

plan. Does this measure assist the state in implementing a public plan
that provides high-quality health care services that are accessible to all
residents of Quebec?

58   According to the trial judge, the effect of the measure adopted by
the state is to 'significantly' limit private health care. Although the
effect of a measure is not always indicative of a rational connection
between the measure and its objective, in the instant case the consequences show an undeniable connection between the objective and
the measure. The public plan is preserved because it has a quasi-
monopoly.

Minimal Impairment

60   The burden of proof does not rest on the appellants. Under s. 9.1 of
the Quebec Charter, the onus was on the Attorney General of Quebec to
prove that the prohibition is justified. He had to show that the measure
met the minimal impairment test. The trial judge did not consider the
evidence on the basis that there was a burden on the Attorney General
of Quebec.

61   To determine whether the Attorney General of Quebec has discharged this burden, I will begin by analysing the expert evidence
submitted to the Superior Court ...

The Experts Who Testified at Trial and Whose Evidence was Accepted by the Superior Court Judge

62   As can be seen from the evidence, the arguments made in support
of the position that the integrity of the public system could be jeopardized by abolishing the prohibition can be divided into two groups. The
first group of arguments relates to human reactions of the various
people affected by the public plan, while the second group relates to the
consequences for the plan itself.

63 Human reactions

1. Some witnesses asserted that the emergence of the private sector
    would lead to a reduction in popular support in the long term
    because the people who had private insurance would no longer

see any utility for the public plan. Dr. Howard Bergman cited an article in his expert report. Dr. Theodore Marmor supported this argument but conceded that he had no way to verify it.

2. Some witnesses were of the opinion that the quality of care in the public plan would decline because the most influential people would no longer have any incentive to bring pressure for improvements to the plan. Dr. Bergman cited a study by the World Bank in support of his expert report. Dr. Marmor relied on this argument but confirmed that there is no direct evidence to support this view.

3. There would be a reduction in human resources in the public plan because many physicians and other health care professionals would leave the plan out of a motive for profit: Dr. Charles D. Wright cited a study done in the United Kingdom, but admitted that he had read only a summary and not the study itself. Although Dr. Marmor supported the assertion, he testified that there is really no way to confirm it empirically. In his opinion, it is simply a matter of common sense.

4. An increase in the use of private health care would contribute to an increase in the supply of care for profit and lead to a decline in the professionalism and ethics of physicians working in hospitals. No study was cited in support of this opinion that seems to be based only on the witnesses' common sense.

64   It is apparent from this summary that for each threat mentioned, no study was produced or discussed in the Superior Court. While it is true that scientific or empirical evidence is not always necessary, witnesses in a case in which the arguments are supposedly based on logic or common sense should be able to cite specific facts in support of their conclusions. The human reactions described by the experts, many of whom came from outside Quebec, do not appear to me to be very convincing, particularly in the context of Quebec legislation. Participation in the public plan is mandatory and there is no risk that the Quebec public will abandon the public plan. The state's role is not being called into question. As well, the HEIA contains a clear provision authorizing the Minister of Health to ensure that the public plan is not jeopardized by having too many physicians opt for the private system (s. 30 HEIA).

The evidence that the existence of the health care system would be jeopadized by human reactions to the emergence of a private system carries little weight.

65 Impact on the public plan

1. There would be an increase in overall health expenditures: the alleged increase would come primarily from the additional expenditures incurred by individuals who decide to take out private insurance; the rest of the increase in costs would be attributable to the cost of management of the private system by the state.

2. Insurers would reject the most acute patients, leaving the most serious cases to be covered by the public plan.

3. In a private system, physicians would tend to lengthen waiting times in the public sector in order to direct patients to the private sector from which they would derive a profit.

66 Once again, I am of the opinion that the reaction some witnesses described is highly unlikely in the Quebec context. First, if the increase in overall costs is primarily attributable to the individual cost of insurance, it would be difficult for the state to prevent individuals who wished to pay such costs from choosing how to manage their own finances. Furthermore, because the public plan already handles all the serious cases, I do not see how the situation could be exacerbated if that plan were relieved of the clientele with less serious health problems. Finally, because of s. 1(e), non-participating physicians may not practise as participants; they will not therefore be faced with the conflict of interest described by certain witnesses. As for physicians who have withdrawn (s. 1(d) HEIA), the state controls their conditions of practice by way of the agreements (s. 1(f) HEIA) they are required to sign. Thus, the state can establish a framework of practice for physicians who offer private services ...

68 ... the judge's finding that the appellants had failed to show that the scope of the prohibition was excessive and that the principles of fundamental justice had not been violated was based solely on the 'fear' of an erosion of resources or a 'threat [to] the integrity' of the

system (at p. 827; emphasis deleted). But the appellants did not have the burden of disproving every fear or every threat. The onus was on the Attorney General of Quebec to justify the prohibition. Binnie and LeBel JJ. rely on a similar test in asserting that private health care would likely have an impact on the public plan. This standard does not meet the requirement of preponderance under s. 9.1 of the Quebec Charter. It can be seen from the evidence that the Attorney General of Quebec failed to discharge his burden of proving that a total prohibition on private insurance met the minimal impairment test.

69   There is other evidence in the record that might be of assistance in the justification analysis. In this regard, it is useful to observe the approaches of the other Canadian provinces because they also operate within the financial framework established by the Canada Health Act.

Overview of Other Provincial Plans

70   The approach to the role of the private sector taken by the other nine provinces of Canada is by no means uniform. In addition to Quebec, six other provinces have adopted measures to discourage people from turning to the private sector. The other three, in practice, give their residents free access to the private sector.

71   Ontario (Health Care Accessibility Act, R.S.O. 1990, c. H.3, s. 2), Nova Scotia (Health Services and Insurance Act, R.S.N.S. 1989, c. 197, s. 29(2)) and Manitoba (Health Services Insurance Act, R.S.M. 1987, c. H35, s. 95(1)) prohibit non-participating physicians from charging their patients more than what physicians receive from the public plan. In practice, there is no financial incentive to opt for the private sector. It is worth noting that Nova Scotia does not prohibit insurance contracts to cover health care obtained in the private sector. Ontario and Manitoba prohibit insurance contracts but refund amounts paid by patients to non-participating physicians.

72   Alberta (Alberta Health Care Insurance Act, R.S.A. 2000, c. A-20, s. 9(1)), British Columbia (Medicare Protection Act, R.S.B.C. 1996, c. 286, s. 18(2)) and Prince Edward Island (Health Services Payment Act, R.S.P.E.I. 1988, c. H-2, ss. 10, 10.1 and 14.1) have adopted a very different approach. In those provinces, non-participating physicians are free to set the amount of their fees, but the cost of the services is not refunded

and contracts for insurance to cover services offered by the public plan are prohibited. This is the same policy as has been adopted by Quebec.

73   Saskatchewan (Saskatchewan Medical Care Insurance Act, R.S.S. 1978, c. S-29, s. 18(1.1)), New Brunswick (Medical Services Payment Act, R.S.N.B. 1973, c. M-7, s. 2.01(a), and General Regulation – Medical Services Payment Act, N.B. Reg. 84-20, Sch. 2, para. n.1), and Newfoundland and Labrador (Medical Care Insurance Act, 1999, S.N.L. 1999, c. M-5.1, s. 10(5), and Medical Care Insurance Insured Services Regulations, C.N.L.R. 21/96, s. 3) are open to the private sector. New Brunswick allows physicians to set their own fees. In Saskatchewan, this right is limited to non-participating physicians. The cost is not refunded by the public plan, but patients may purchase insurance to cover those costs. Newfoundland and Labrador agrees to reimburse patients, up to the amount covered by the public plan, for fees paid to non-participating physicians. In Newfoundland and Labrador, patients may subscribe to private insurance to cover the difference.

74   Even if it were assumed that the prohibition on private insurance could contribute to preserving the integrity of the system, the variety of measures implemented by different provinces shows that prohibiting insurance contracts is by no means the only measure a state can adopt to protect the system's integrity. In fact, because there is no indication that the public plans of the three provinces that are open to the private sector suffer from deficiencies that are not present in the plans of the other provinces, it must be deduced that the effectiveness of the measure in protecting the integrity of the system has not been proved. The example illustrated by a number of other Canadian provinces casts doubt on the argument that the integrity of the public plan depends on the prohibition against private insurance. Obviously, since Quebec's public plan is in a quasi-monopoly position, its predominance is assured. Also, the regimes of the provinces where a private system is authorized demonstrate that public health services are not threatened by private insurance. It can therefore be concluded that the prohibition is not necessary to guarantee the integrity of the public plan ... .

Overview of Practices in Certain OECD Countries

77   Mr. Chaoulli, echoed by at least one of the witnesses (Dr. Coffey), argued that Canada is the only OECD country to prohibit insurance for

health care provided by non-participating physicians. This assertion must be clarified as it relates to Canada: it is true of only six provinces. It must also be qualified in the international context: while no such prohibition is found in any other OECD country, it should nonetheless be mentioned that measures to protect the public plan have been implemented in a number of countries, even some of the countries whose health care plans have been provided as models. There is no single model; the approach in Europe is no more uniform than in Canada.

78   In a number of European countries, there is no insurance paid for directly out of public funds. In Austria, services are funded through decentralized agencies that collect the necessary funds from salaries. People who want to obtain health care in the private sector in addition to the services covered by the mandatory social insurance are free to do so, but private insurance may cover no more than 80 percent of the cost billed by professionals practising in the public sector. The same type of plan exists in Germany and the Netherlands, but people who opt for private insurance are not required to pay for the public plan. Only nine percent of Germans opt for private insurance.

79   Australia's public system is funded in a manner similar to the Quebec system. However, Australia's system is different in that the private and public sectors coexist, and insurance covering private sector health care is not prohibited. The government attempts to balance access to the two sectors by allowing taxpayers to deduct 30 percent of the cost of private insurance. Insurance rates are regulated to prevent insurers from charging higher premiums for higher-risk individuals (C. H. Tuohy, C. M. Flood and M. Stabile, 'How Does Private Finance Affect Public Health Care Systems? Marshaling the Evidence from OECD Nations' (2004), 29 J. Health Pol. 359).

80   The United Kingdom does not restrict access to private insurance for health care. Nor does the United Kingdom limit a physician's ability to withdraw from the public plan. However, physicians working full-time in public hospitals are limited in the amounts that they may bill in the private sector to supplement income earned in the public sector (at p. 40). Only 11.5 percent of Britons had taken out private insurance in 1998 (Tuohy, Flood and Stabile, at p. 374),and only eight percent of hospital beds in the United Kingdom are private. New Zealand has a plan similar to that of the United Kingdom with the difference that

40 percent of New Zealanders have private insurance (Tuohy, Flood and Stabile, at p. 363).

81   Sweden does not prohibit private insurance, and the state does not refund the cost of health care paid for in the private sector. Private insurance accounts for only two percent of total health care expenditures and there are only nine private hospitals.

82   It can be seen from the systems in these various OECD countries that a number of governments have taken measures to protect their public plans from abuse. The measures vary from country to country depending on the nature of their specific systems. For example, in the United Kingdom, there are limits on the amounts physicians may earn in the private sector in addition to what they receive from the public plan. Australia has opted to regulate insurance premiums, but it is alone in this respect.

83   As can be seen from the evolution of public plans in the few OECD countries that have been examined in studies produced in the record, there are a wide range of measures that are less drastic, and also less intrusive in relation to the protected rights. The Quebec context is a singular one, not only because of the distinction between participating physicians, non-participating physicians and physicians who have withdrawn (s. 1 HEIA), but also because the Minister may require non-participating physicians to provide health services if he or she considers it likely that the services will not be provided under uniform conditions throughout Quebec or in a particular region (s. 30 HEIA). A measure as drastic as prohibiting private insurance contracts appears to be neither essential nor determinative.

84   It cannot therefore be concluded from the evidence relating to the Quebec plan or the plans of the other provinces of Canada, or from the evolution of the systems in place in various OECD countries, that the Attorney General of Quebec has discharged his burden of proof under s. 9.1 of the Quebec Charter. A number of measures are available to him to protect the integrity of Quebec's health care plan. The choice of prohibiting private insurance contracts is not justified by the evidence. However, is this a case in which the Court should show deference?

Level of Deference Required

87   It cannot be said that the government lacks the necessary resources to show that its legislative action is motivated by a reasonable objective connected with the problem it has undertaken to remedy. The courts are an appropriate forum for a serious and complete debate. As G. Davidov said in 'The Paradox of Judicial Deference' (2000–2001), 12 N.J.C.L. 133, at p. 143, '[c]ourts do not have to define goals, choose means or come up with ideas. They do not have to create social policies; they just have to understand what the other branches have created. No special expertise is required for such an understanding.' In fact, if a court is satisfied that all the evidence has been presented, there is nothing that would justify it in refusing to perform its role on the ground that it should merely defer to the government's position. When the courts are given the tools they need to make a decision, they should not hesitate to assume their responsibilities. Deference cannot lead the judicial branch to abdicate its role in favour of the legislative branch or the executive branch.

88   The question submitted by the appellants has a factual content that was analysed by the trial judge. One part of her findings must be adapted to the context of s. 9.1 of the Quebec Charter. The other findings remain unchanged. The questions of law are not complex.

89   The courts have a duty to rise above political debate. They leave it to the legislatures to develop social policy. But when such social policies infringe rights that are protected by the charters, the courts cannot shy away from considering them. The judicial branch plays a role that is not played by the legislative branch. Professor Roach described the complementary role of the courts vis-à-vis the legislature as follows (K. Roach, 'Dialogic Judicial Review and its Critics' (2004), 23 Sup. Ct. L. R. (2d) 49, at pp. 69–71):

> [Some] unique attributes of courts include their commitment to allowing structured and guaranteed participation from aggrieved parties; their independence from the executive, and their commitment to giving reasons for their decisions. In addition, courts have a special commitment to make sense of legal texts that were democratically enacted as foundational documents.

... The pleader in court has a guaranteed right of participation and a right to a reasoned decision that addresses the arguments made in court, as well as the relevant text of the democratically enacted law. ...

Judges can add value to societal debates about justice by listening to claims of injustice and by promoting values and perspectives that may not otherwise be taken seriously in the legislative process.

90   From this perspective, it is through the combined action of legislatures and courts that democratic objectives can be achieved. In their analysis of the Quebec secession reference, Choudhry and Howse describe this division of constitutional responsibilities accurately (S. Choudhry and R. Howse, 'Constitutional Theory and The Quebec Secession Reference' (2000), 13 Can. J. L. & Jur. 143, at pp. 160-61):

[I]nterpretive responsibility for particular constitutional norms is both shared and divided. It is shared to the extent that courts are responsible for articulating constitutional norms in their conceptually abstract form. But interpretive responsibility is divided because beyond the limits of doctrine, constitutional interpretation is left to the political organs. The image which emerges is one of 'judicial and legislative cooperation in the molding of concrete standards through which elusive and complex constitutional norms ... come to be applied.' ...

95   In short, a court must show deference where the evidence establishes that the government has assigned proper weight to each of the competing interests. Certain factors favour greater deference, such as the prospective nature of the decision, the impact on public finances, the multiplicity of competing interests, the difficulty of presenting scientific evidence and the limited time available to the state. This list is certainly not exhaustive. It serves primarily to highlight the facts that it is up to the government to choose the measure, that the decision is often complex and difficult, and that the government must have the necessary time and resources to respond. However, as McLachlin J. (as she then was) said in RJR-MacDonald Inc. v. Canada (Attorney General), [1995] 3 S.C.R. 199, at para. 136, '... care must be taken not to extend the notion of deference too far.'

96   The instant case is a good example of a case in which the courts

have all the necessary tools to evaluate the government's measure. Ample evidence was presented. The government had plenty of time to act ... . Governments have promised on numerous occasions to find a solution to the problem of waiting lists. Given the tendency to focus the debate on a sociopolitical philosophy, it seems that governments have lost sight of the urgency of taking concrete action. The courts are therefore the last line of defence for citizens.

97   For many years, the government has failed to act; the situation continues to deteriorate. This is not a case in which missing scientific data would allow for a more informed decision to be made. The principle of prudence that is so popular in matters relating to the environment and to medical research cannot be transposed to this case. Under the Quebec plan, the government can control its human resources in various ways, whether by using the time of professionals who have already reached the maximum for payment by the state, by applying the provision that authorizes it to compel even non-participating physicians to provide services (s. 30 HEIA) or by implementing less restrictive measures, like those adopted in the four Canadian provinces that do not prohibit private insurance or in the other OECD countries. While the government has the power to decide what measures to adopt, it cannot choose to do nothing in the face of the violation of Quebeckers' right to security. The government has not given reasons for its failure to act. Inertia cannot be used as an argument to justify deference.

98   In the instant case, the effectiveness of the prohibition has by no means been established. The government has not proved, by the evidence in the record, that the measure minimally impairs the protected rights. Moreover, the evidence shows that a wide variety of measures are available to governments, as can be seen from the plans of other provinces and other countries.

Proportionality

99   Having found that s. 15 HEIA and s. 11 HOIA do not meet the minimal impairment test, I do not need to consider proportionality. If the prohibition is not minimally impairing, it obviously cannot be regarded as a measure that sufficiently addresses the effect of the measure on the protected rights.

Conclusion

100   The relief sought by the appellants does not necessarily provide a complete response to the complex problem of waiting lists. However, it was not up to the appellants to find a way to remedy a problem that has persisted for a number of years and for which the solution must come from the state itself. Their only burden was to prove that their right to life and to personal inviolability had been infringed. They have succeeded in proving this. The Attorney General of Quebec, on the other hand, has not proved that the impugned measure, the prohibition on private insurance, was justified under s. 9.1 of the Quebec Charter. Given that this finding is sufficient to dispose of the appeal, it is not necessary to answer the other constitutional questions.

The reasons of McLachlin C.J. and Major and Bastarache JJ. were delivered by

102   **THE CHIEF JUSTICE AND MAJOR J.** – We concur in the conclusion of our colleague Deschamps J. that the prohibition against contracting for private health insurance violates s. 1 of the Quebec Charter of Human Rights and Freedoms, and is not justifiable under s. 9.1. On the argument that the anti-insurance provision also violates s. 7 of the Canadian Charter of Rights and Freedoms ('Charter'), we conclude that the provision impermissibly limits the right to life, liberty and security of the person protected by s. 7 of the Charter and has not been shown to be justified as a reasonable limit under s. 1 of the Charter.

103   The appellants do not seek an order that the government spend more money on health care, nor do they seek an order that waiting times for treatment under the public health care scheme be reduced. They only seek a ruling that because delays in the public system place their health and security at risk, they should be allowed to take out insurance to permit them to access private services.

104   The Charter does not confer a freestanding constitutional right to health care. However, where the government puts in place a scheme to provide health care, that scheme must comply with the Charter. We are of the view that the prohibition on medical insurance in s. 15 of the Health Insurance Act, and s. 11 of the Hospital Insurance Act, violates s. 7 of the Charter because it impinges on the right to life, liberty and

security of the person in an arbitrary fashion that fails to conform to the principles of fundamental justice.

105   The primary objective of the Canada Health Act, R.S.C. 1985, c. C-6, is 'to protect, promote and restore the physical and mental well-being of residents of Canada and to facilitate reasonable access to health services without financial or other barriers' (s. 3). By imposing exclusivity and then failing to provide public health care of a reasonable standard within a reasonable time, the government creates circumstances that trigger the application of s. 7 of the Charter.

106   The Canada Health Act, the Health Insurance Act, and the Hospital Insurance Act do not expressly prohibit private health services. However, they limit access to private health services by removing the ability to contract for private health care insurance to cover the same services covered by public insurance. The result is a virtual monopoly for the public health scheme. The state has effectively limited access to private health care except for the very rich, who can afford private care without need of insurance. This virtual monopoly, on the evidence, results in delays in treatment that adversely affect the citizen's security of the person. Where a law adversely affects life, liberty or security of the person, it must conform to the principles of fundamental justice. This law, in our view, fails to do so.

107   While the decision about the type of health care system Quebec should adopt falls to the Legislature of that province, the resulting legislation, like all laws, is subject to constitutional limits, including those imposed by s. 7 of the Charter. The fact that the matter is complex, contentious or laden with social values does not mean that the courts can abdicate the responsibility vested in them by our Constitution to review legislation for Charter compliance when citizens challenge it. ..

108   The government defends the prohibition on medical insurance on the ground that the existing system is the only approach to adequate universal health care for all Canadians. The question in this case, however, is not whether single-tier health care is preferable to two-tier health care. Even if one accepts the government's goal, the legal question raised by the appellants must be addressed: is it a violation of s. 7 of the Charter to prohibit private insurance for health care, when the result is to subject Canadians to long delays with

resultant risk of physical and psychological harm? The mere fact that this question may have policy ramifications does not permit us to avoid answering it.

Section 7 of the Charter

109   Section 7 of the Charter guarantees that 'everyone has the right to life, liberty and security of the person and the right not to be deprived thereof except in accordance with the principles of fundamental justice.' The disposition of this appeal therefore requires us to consider (1) whether the impugned provisions deprive individuals of their life, liberty or security of the person; and (2) if so, whether this deprivation is in accordance with the principles of fundamental justice ...

Deprivation of Life, Liberty or Security of the Person

110   The issue at this stage is whether the prohibition on insurance for private medical care deprives individuals of their life, liberty or security of the person protected by s. 7 of the Charter.

111   The appellants have established that many Quebec residents face delays in treatment that adversely affect their security of the person and that they would not sustain but for the prohibition on medical insurance. It is common ground that the effect of the prohibition on insurance is to allow only the very rich, who do not need insurance, to secure private health care in order to avoid the delays in the public system. Given the ban on insurance, most Quebeckers have no choice but to accept delays in the medical system and their adverse physical and psychological consequences.

112   Delays in the public system are widespread and have serious, sometimes grave, consequences. There was no dispute that there is a waiting list for cardiovascular surgery for life-threatening problems. Dr. Daniel Doyle, a cardiovascular surgeon who teaches and practises in Quebec City, testified that a person with coronary disease is 'sitting on a bomb' and can die at any moment. He confirmed, without challenge, that patients die while on waiting lists: Inevitably, where patients have life-threatening conditions, some will die because of undue delay in awaiting surgery ...

114 Dr. Eric Lenczner, an orthopaedic surgeon, testified that the one-year delay commonly incurred by patients requiring ligament reconstruction surgery increases the risk that their injuries will become irreparable (A.R., vol. 2, at p. 334). Dr. Lenczner also testified that 95 per cent of patients in Canada wait well over a year, and many two years, for knee replacements. While a knee replacement may seem trivial compared to the risk of death for wait-listed coronary surgery patients, which increases by 0.5 per cent per month, the harm suffered by patients awaiting replacement knees and hips is significant. Even though death may not be an issue for them, these patients 'are in pain,' 'would not go a day without discomfort' and are 'limited in their ability to get around,' some being confined to wheelchairs or house bound.

115 Both the individual members of the Standing Senate Committee on Social Affairs, Science and Technology who intervened in this appeal and the Canadian Medical Association cited a Statistics Canada study demonstrating that over one in five Canadians who needed health care for themselves or a family member in 2001 encountered some form of difficulty, from getting an appointment to experiencing lengthy waiting times ... Thirty-seven per cent of those patients reported pain ... .

118 The jurisprudence of this Court holds that delays in obtaining medical treatment which affect patients physically and psychologically trigger the protection of s. 7 of the Charter. In R. v. Morgentaler, [1988] 1 S.C.R. 30, Dickson C.J. concluded that the delay in obtaining therapeutic abortions, which increased the risk of complications and mortality due to mandatory procedures imposed by the state, was sufficient to trigger the physical aspect of the woman's right to security of the person. He found that the psychological impact on women awaiting abortions constituted an infringement of security of the person. Beetz J. agreed with Dickson C.J. that '[t]he delays mean therefore that the state has intervened in such a manner as to create an additional risk to health, and consequently this intervention constitutes a violation of the woman's security of the person.'

119 In this appeal, delays in treatment giving rise to psychological and physical suffering engage the s. 7 protection of security of the person just as they did in Morgentaler. In Morgentaler, as in this case,

the problem arises from a legislative scheme that offers health services. In Morgentaler, as in this case, the legislative scheme denies people the right to access alternative health care. (That the sanction in Morgentaler was criminal prosecution while the sanction here is administrative prohibition and penalties is irrelevant. The important point is that in both cases, care outside the legislatively provided system is effectively prohibited.) In Morgentaler the result of the monopolistic scheme was delay in treatment with attendant physical risk and psychological suffering. In Morgentaler, as here, people in urgent need of care face the same prospect: unless they fall within the wealthy few who can pay for private care, typically outside the country, they have no choice but to accept the delays imposed by the legislative scheme and the adverse physical and psychological consequences this entails. As in Morgentaler, the result is interference with security of the person under s. 7 of the Charter ... .

121 ... In Morgentaler, as here, the system left the individual facing a lack of critical care with no choice but to travel outside the country to obtain the required medical care at her own expense ... .

123   Not every difficulty rises to the level of adverse impact on security of the person under s. 7. The impact, whether psychological or physical, must be serious. However, because patients may be denied timely health care for a condition that is clinically significant to their current and future health, s. 7 protection of security of the person is engaged. Access to a waiting list is not access to health care. As we noted above, there is unchallenged evidence that in some serious cases, patients die as a result of waiting lists for public health care. Where lack of timely health care can result in death, s. 7 protection of life itself is engaged. The evidence here demonstrates that the prohibition on health insurance results in physical and psychological suffering that meets this threshold requirement of seriousness.

124   We conclude, based on the evidence, that prohibiting health insurance that would permit ordinary Canadians to access health care, in circumstances where the government is failing to deliver health care in a reasonable manner, thereby increasing the risk of complications and death, interferes with life and security of the person as protected by s. 7 of the Charter. ..

Deprivation in Accordance with the Principles of Fundamental Justice

126 Having concluded that the ban on private medical insurance constitutes a deprivation of life and security of the person, we now consider whether that deprivation is in accordance with the principles of fundamental justice. Our colleagues Binnie and LeBel JJ. argue that the record here provides no ground for finding that the deprivation violates the principles of fundamental justice. With respect, we cannot agree. ..

128 The principle of fundamental justice implicated in this case is that laws that affect the life, liberty or security of the person shall not be arbitrary. We are of the opinion that the evidence before the trial judge supports a finding that the impugned provisions are arbitrary and that the deprivation of life and security of the person that flows from them cannot therefore be said to accord with the principles of fundamental justice ... .

130 A law is arbitrary where 'it bears no relation to, or is inconsistent with, the objective that lies behind [it].' To determine whether this is the case, it is necessary to consider the state interest and societal concerns that the provision is meant to reflect...

Whether the Prohibition on Private Medical Insurance is Arbitrary

135 The government argues that the interference with security of the person caused by denying people the right to purchase private health insurance is necessary to providing effective health care under the public health system. It argues that if people can purchase private health insurance, they will seek treatment from private doctors and hospitals, which are not banned under the Act. According to the government's argument, this will divert resources from the public health system into private health facilities, ultimately reducing the quality of public care.

136 In support of this contention, the government called experts in health administration and policy. Their conclusions were based on the 'common sense' proposition that the improvement of health services

depends on exclusivity. They did not profess expertise in waiting times for treatment. Nor did they present economic studies or rely on the experience of other countries. They simply assumed, as a matter of apparent logic, that insurance would make private health services more accessible and that this in turn would undermine the quality of services provided by the public health care system.

137 The appellants, relying on other health experts, disagreed and offered their own conflicting 'common sense' argument for the proposition that prohibiting private health insurance is neither necessary nor related to maintaining high quality in the public health care system. Quality public care, they argue, depends not on a monopoly, but on money and management. They testified that permitting people to buy private insurance would make alternative medical care more accessible and reduce the burden on the public system. The result, they assert, would be better care for all. The appellants reinforce this argument by pointing out that disallowing private insurance precludes the vast majority of Canadians (middle-income and low-income earners) from accessing additional care, while permitting it for the wealthy who can afford to travel abroad or pay for private care in Canada.

138   To this point, we are confronted with competing but unproven 'common sense' arguments, amounting to little more than assertions of belief. We are in the realm of theory. But as discussed above, a theoretically defensible limitation may be arbitrary if in fact the limit lacks a connection to the goal.

139   This brings us to the evidence called by the appellants at trial on the experience of other developed countries with public health care systems which permit access to private health care. The experience of these countries suggests that there is no real connection in fact between prohibition of health insurance and the goal of a quality public health system.

140   The evidence adduced at trial establishes that many western democracies that do not impose a monopoly on the delivery of health care have successfully delivered to their citizens medical services that are superior to and more affordable than the services that are presently available in Canada. This demonstrates that a monopoly is not necessary or even related to the provision of quality public health care.

141   In its report The Health of Canadians – The Federal Role, the Standing Senate Committee on Social Affairs, Science and Technology discussed in detail the situations in several countries, including Sweden, Germany and the United Kingdom. The following discussion of the health care systems in these three countries is drawn directly from the findings in volume 3 of the report The Health of Canadians – The Federal Role, vol. 3, Health Care Systems in Other Countries, Interim report (2002) ('Kirby Report').

142   In Sweden, as in Canada, access to public health care is universal. The public health care system is financed predominantly by the public sector through a combination of general taxation and social insurance (i.e., employer/employee contributions) and employs a user fee mechanism. Unlike in Canada, private health care insurance that covers the same benefits as public insurance is 'legal' in Sweden. However, only a small minority of the population purchase private insurance. The result is a system of public health care coverage that provides quality care on a broader basis than in Canada and encompasses physicians, hospital services, drugs and dental care. In Sweden, the availability of private health care insurance appears not to have harmed the public health care system.

143   In Germany, public health care insurance is administered by 453 Sickness Funds – private non-profit organizations structured on a regional task or occupational basis. Sickness Fund membership is compulsory for employees with gross incomes lower than approximately $63,000 Canadian, and voluntary for those with gross incomes above that level. Although all Sickness Funds are regulated at the federal level through what is known as the 'Social Code Book,' they are essentially run by representatives of employees and employers. As in Sweden, public health care coverage is broader in Germany than in Canada, including physician services, hospitals, prescription drugs, diagnostic services, dental care, rehabilitative care, medical devices, psychotherapists, nursing care at home, medical services by non-physicians (physiotherapists, speech therapists, occupational therapists, etc.) and income support during sick leave.

144   In Germany, as in Sweden, private health insurance is available to individuals at a certain income level who may voluntarily opt out of the Sickness Funds. Private coverage is currently offered by 52 private

insurance companies that are obliged to offer an insurance policy with the same benefits as the Sickness Funds at a premium that is no higher than the average maximum contribution to the Sickness Funds. Private health care coverage is also available to self-employed people who are excluded from the Sickness Funds and public servants who are de facto excluded from participating in Sickness Funds as their health care bills are reimbursed at the rate of 50 per cent by the federal government. Private insurance covers the remainder.

145   Despite the availability of alternatives, 88 per cent of the German population are covered by the public Sickness Funds: this includes 14 per cent to whom private insurance is available. Of the remaining 12 per cent, only 9 per cent are covered by private insurance and less than 1 per cent have no health insurance at all. The remaining 2 per cent are covered by government insurance for military and other personnel.

146   The United Kingdom offers a comprehensive public health care system – the National Health Service (NHS) – while also allowing for private insurance. Unlike Canada, the United Kingdom allows people to purchase private health care insurance that covers the same benefits as the NHS if these services are supplied by providers working outside of the NHS. Despite the existence of private insurance, only 11.5 per cent of the population have purchased it. Again, it appears that the public system has not suffered as a result of the existence of private alternatives.

147   After reviewing a number of public health care systems, the Standing Senate Committee on Social Affairs, Science and Technology concluded in the Kirby Report that far from undermining public health care, private contributions and insurance improve the breadth and quality of health care for all citizens, and it ultimately concluded, at p. 66:

> The evidence suggests that a contribution of direct payments by patients, allowing private insurance to cover some services, even in publicly funded hospitals, and an expanded role for the private sector in the delivery of health services are the factors which have enabled countries to achieve broader coverage of health services for all their citizens. Some countries like Australia and Singapore openly encourage private sector participation as a means to ensure affordable and sustainable health services.

148   Nor does it appear that private participation leads to the eventual demise of public health care. It is compelling to note that not one of the countries referred to relies exclusively on either private insurance or the public system to provide health care coverage to its citizens. Even in the United States, where the private sector is a dominant participant in the field of health care insurance, public funding accounts for 45% of total health care spending.

149   In summary, the evidence on the experience of other western democracies refutes the government's theoretical contention that a pro-hibition on private insurance is linked to maintaining quality public health care.

150   Binnie and LeBel JJ. suggest that the experience of other countries is of little assistance. With respect, we cannot agree. This evidence was properly placed before the trial judge and, unless discredited, stands as the best guide with respect to the question of whether a ban on private insurance is necessary and relevant to the goal of providing quality public health care. The task of the courts, on s. 7 issues as on others, is to evaluate the issue in the light, not just of common sense or theory, but of the evidence ... .

151   Binnie and LeBel JJ. also suggest that the government's continued commitment to a monopoly on the provision of health insurance cannot be arbitrary because it is rooted in reliance on 'a series of authoritative reports [that analysed] health care in this country and in other coun-tries' (para. 258); they are referring here to the reports of Commissioner Romanow (Building on Values: The Future of Health Care in Canada: Final Report (2002)), and Senator Kirby. We observe in passing that the import of these reports, which differ in many of their conclusions, is a matter of some debate, as attested by our earlier reference to the Kirby Report. But the conclusions of other bodies on other material cannot be determinative of this litigation. They cannot relieve the courts of their obligation to review government action for consistency with the Char-ter on the evidence before them.

152   When we look to the evidence rather than to assumptions, the connection between prohibiting private insurance and maintaining qual-ity public health care vanishes. The evidence before us establishes that

where the public system fails to deliver adequate care, the denial of private insurance subjects people to long waiting lists and negatively affects their health and security of the person. The government contends that this is necessary in order to preserve the public health system. The evidence, however, belies that contention.

153   We conclude that on the evidence adduced in this case, the appellants have established that in the face of delays in treatment that cause psychological and physical suffering, the prohibition on private insurance jeopardizes the right to life, liberty and security of the person of Canadians in an arbitrary manner, and is therefore not in accordance with the principles of fundamental justice.

Section 1 of the Charter

154   Having concluded that the prohibition on private health insurance constitutes a breach of s. 7, we must now consider whether that breach can be justified under s. 1 of the Charter as a reasonable limit demonstrably justified in a free and democratic society. The evidence called in this case falls short of demonstrating such justification.

155   The government undeniably has an interest in protecting the public health regime. However, given the absence of evidence that the prohibition on the purchase and sale of private health insurance protects the health care system, the rational connection between the prohibition and the objective is not made out. Indeed, we question whether an arbitrary provision, which by reason of its arbitrariness cannot further its stated objective, will ever meet the rational connection test under R. v. Oakes, [1986] 1 S.C.R. 103.

156   In addition, the resulting denial of access to timely and effective medical care to those who need it is not proportionate to the beneficial effects of the prohibition on private insurance to the health system as a whole. On the evidence here and for the reasons discussed above, the prohibition goes further than necessary to protect the public system: it is not minimally impairing.

157   Finally, the benefits of the prohibition do not outweigh the deleterious effects. Prohibiting citizens from obtaining private health care insurance may, as discussed, leave people no choice but to accept exces-

sive delays in the public health system. The physical and psychological suffering and risk of death that may result outweigh whatever benefit (and none has been demonstrated to us here) there may be to the system as a whole.

158   In sum, the prohibition on obtaining private health insurance, while it might be constitutional in circumstances where health care services are reasonable as to both quality and timeliness, is not constitutional where the public system fails to deliver reasonable services. Life, liberty and security of the person must prevail ... if the government chooses to act, it must do so properly.

159   We agree with Deschamps J.'s conclusion that the prohibition against contracting for private health insurance violates s. 1 of the Quebec Charter of Human Rights and Freedoms and is not justifiable under s. 9.1. We also conclude that this prohibition violates s. 7 of the Canadian Charter of Rights and Freedoms and cannot be saved under s. 1.

The reasons of Binnie, LeBel and Fish JJ. were delivered by

BINNIE AND LEBEL JJ. (DISSENTING) –

Introduction

161   The question in this appeal is whether the province of Quebec not only has the constitutional authority to establish a comprehensive single-tier health plan, but to discourage a second (private) tier health sector by prohibiting the purchase and sale of private health insurance. The appellants argue that timely access to needed medical service is not being provided in the publicly funded system and that the province cannot therefore deny to those Quebeckers (who can qualify) the right to purchase private insurance to pay for medical services whenever and wherever such services can be obtained for a fee, i.e. in the private sector. This issue has been the subject of protracted debate across Canada through several provincial and federal elections. We are unable to agree with our four colleagues who would allow the appeal that such a debate can or should be resolved as a matter of law by judges. We find that, on the legal issues raised, the appeal should be dismissed.

162   Our colleagues the Chief Justice and Major J. state at para. 105:

> By imposing exclusivity and then failing to provide public health care of a reasonable standard within a reasonable time, the government creates circumstances that trigger the application of s. 7 of the Charter.

163   The Court recently held in Auton (Guardian ad litem of) v. British Columbia (Attorney General), [2004] 3 S.C.R. 657 that the government was not required to fund the treatment of autistic children. It did not on that occasion address in constitutional terms the scope and nature of 'reasonable' health services. Courts will now have to make that determination. What, then, are constitutionally required 'reasonable health services'? What is treatment 'within a reasonable time'? What are the benchmarks? How short a waiting list is short enough? How many MRIs does the Constitution require? The majority does not tell us. The majority lays down no manageable constitutional standard. The public cannot know, nor can judges or governments know, how much health care is 'reasonable' enough to satisfy s. 7 of the Canadian Charter of Rights and Freedoms ('Canadian Charter') and s. 1 of the Charter of Human Rights and Freedoms, R.S.Q. c. C-12 ('Quebec Charter'). It is to be hoped that we will know it when we see it.

164   The policy of the Canada Health Act, R.S.C. 1985, c. C-6, and its provincial counterparts is to provide health care based on need rather than on wealth or status. The evidence certainly established that the public health care system put in place to implement this policy has serious and persistent problems. This does not mean that the courts are well placed to perform the required surgery. The resolution of such a complex fact-laden policy debate does not fit easily within the institutional competence or procedures of courts of law. The courts can use s. 7 of the Canadian Charter to pre-empt the ongoing public debate only if the current health plan violates an established 'principle of fundamental justice.' Our colleagues McLachlin C.J. and Major J. argue that Quebec's enforcement of a single-tier health plan meets this legal test because it is 'arbitrary.' In our view, with respect, the prohibition against private health insurance is a rational consequence of Quebec's commitment to the goals and objectives of the Canada Health Act.

165   Our colleague Deschamps J. states at para. 4:

In essence, the question is whether Quebeckers who are prepared to spend money to get access to health care that is, in practice, not accessible in the public sector because of waiting lists may be validly prevented from doing so by the state. [Emphasis added.]

This is so, but of course it must be recognized that the liberty and security of Quebeckers who do not have the money to afford private health insurance, or who cannot qualify for it, or who are not employed by establishments that provide it, are not put at risk by the absence of 'upper tier' health care. It is Quebeckers who have the money to afford private medical insurance and can qualify for it who will be the beneficiaries of the appellants' constitutional challenge.

166   The Quebec government views the prohibition against private insurance as essential to preventing the current single-tier health system from disintegrating into a de facto two-tier system. The trial judge found, and the evidence demonstrated, that there is good reason for this fear. The trial judge concluded that a private health sector fuelled by private insurance would frustrate achievement of the objectives of the Canada Health Act. She thus found no legal basis to intervene, and declined to do so. This raises the issue of who it is that should resolve these important and contentious issues. Commissioner Roy Romanow makes the following observation in his Report:

Some have described it as a perversion of Canadian values that they cannot use their money to purchase faster treatment from a private provider for their loved ones. I believe it is a far greater perversion of Canadian values to accept a system where money, rather than need, determines who gets access to care.

(Building on Values: The Future of Health Care in Canada: Final Report (2002), at p. xx ('Romanow Report'))

Whether or not one endorses this assessment, his premise is that the debate is about social values. It is not about constitutional law. We agree. ...

175   The argument for a 'two-tier system' is that it will enable 'ordinary' Canadians to access private health care. Indeed, this is the view

taken by our colleagues the Chief Justice and Major J. who quote the appellants' argument that 'disallowing private insurance precludes the vast majority of Canadians (middle-income and low- income earners) from accessing' private health care (para. 137). This way of putting the argument suggests that the Court has a mandate to save middle-income and low-income Quebeckers from themselves, because both the Romanow Report and the Kirby Report found that the vast majority of 'ordinary' Canadians want a publicly financed single-tier (more or less) health plan to which access is governed by need rather than wealth and where the availability of coverage is not contingent on personal insurability. Our colleagues rely in part on the experience in the United States (para. 148) and the fact that public funding in that country accounts for only 45 per cent of total health care spending. But if we look at the practical reality of the U.S. system, the fact is that 15.6 per cent of the American population (i.e. about 45 million people) had no health insurance coverage at all in 2003, including about 8.4 million children. As to making health care available to medium and low-income families, the effect of 'two-tier' health coverage in the U.S. is much worse for minority groups than for the majority. Hispanics had an uninsured rate of 32.7 per cent, and African Americans had an uninsured rate of 19.4 per cent. For 45 million Americans, as for those 'ordinary' Quebeckers who cannot afford private medical insurance or cannot obtain it because they are deemed to be 'bad risks,' it is a matter of public health care or no care at all.

176   It would be open to Quebec to adopt a U.S.-style health care system. No one suggests that there is anything in our Constitution to prevent it. But to do so would be contrary to the policy of the Quebec National Assembly, and its policy in that respect is shared by the other provinces and the federal Parliament. As stated, Quebec further takes the view that significant growth in the private health care system (which the appellants advocate) would inevitably damage the public system. Our colleagues the Chief Justice and Major J. disagree with this assessment, but governments are entitled to act on a reasonable apprehension of risk of such damage. ... While the existence of waiting times is undoubted, and their management a matter of serious public concern, the proposed constitutional right to a two-tier health system for those who can afford private medical insurance would precipitate a seismic shift in health policy for Quebec. We do not believe that such a seismic shift is compelled by either the Quebec Charter or the Canadian Charter. ...

The Canadian Charter of Rights and Freedoms

[The Right to Life, Liberty and Security of the Person under s.7 of the Charter]

191   Like our colleagues McLachlin C.J. and Major J., we accept the trial judge's conclusion that in some circumstances some Quebeckers may have their life or 'security of the person' put at risk by the prohibition against private health insurance. ...

201   We do not agree with the appellants, however, that the Quebec Health Plan puts the 'liberty' of Quebeckers at risk. The argument that 'liberty' includes freedom of contract (in this case to contract for private medical insurance) is novel in Canada, where economic rights are not included in the Charter and discredited in the United States. In that country, the liberty of individuals (mainly employers) to contract out of social and economic programs was endorsed by the Supreme Court in the early decades of the 20th century on the theory that laws that prohibited employers from entering into oppressive contracts with employees violated their 'liberty' of contract; see, e.g., Lochner v. New York, 198 U.S. 45 (1905), at p. 62:

> ... a prohibition to enter into any contract of labor in a bakery for more than a certain number of hours a week, is, in our judgment, so wholly beside the matter of a proper, reasonable and fair provision, as to run counter to that liberty of person and of free contract provided for in the Federal Constitution.

Of this line of cases, which was not brought to an end until West Coast Hotel Co. v. Parrish, 300 U.S. 379 (1937), Professor L. H. Tribe has written that the Supreme Court of the United States:

> ... relied on the Fourteenth Amendment's Due Process Clause to strike down economic legislation that the Court saw as improperly infringing on contractual liberty, but in which the Court was widely (even if not always correctly) perceived to be substituting its own judgment, in the absence of any actual constitutional mandate, for that of the legislature.

(American Constitutional Law (3rd ed. 2000), vol. 1, at p. 1318)

202   Nor do we accept that s. 7 of the Canadian Charter guarantees Dr. Chaoulli the 'liberty' to deliver health care in a private context. The trial judge correctly concluded that 's. 7 of the Canadian Charter does not protect a physician's right to practise his or her profession without restrictions in the private sector. That is a purely economic right' (p. 823). The fact that state action constrains an individual's freedom by eliminating career choices that would otherwise be available does not in itself attract the protection of the liberty interest under s. 7. The liberty interest does not, for example, include the right to transact business whenever one wishes ... : We would therefore reject Dr. Chaoulli's claim on behalf of care providers that their liberty interest under either the Canadian Charter or the Quebec Charter has been infringed by Quebec's single-tier public health system ... .

207   As stated, the principal legal hurdle to the appellants' Charter challenge is not the preliminary step of identifying a s. 7 interest potentially affected in the case of some Quebeckers in some circumstances. The hurdle lies in their failure to find a fundamental principle of justice that is violated by the Quebec health plan so as to justify the Court in striking down the prohibition against private insurance for what the government has identified as 'insured services.'

Principles of Fundamental Justice [under Section 7 of the Canadian Charter]

209   ... the formal requirements for a principle of fundamental justice are threefold. First, it must be a legal principle. Second, the reasonable person must regard it as vital to our societal notion of justice, which implies a significant societal consensus. Third, it must be capable of being identified with precision and applied in a manner that yields predictable results. These requirements present insurmountable hurdles to the appellants. The aim of 'health care to a reasonable standard within reasonable time' is not a legal principle. There is no 'societal consensus' about what it means or how to achieve it. It cannot be 'identified with precision.' As the testimony in this case showed, a level of care that is considered perfectly reasonable by some doctors is denounced by others. Finally, we think it will be very difficult for those designing and implementing a health plan to predict when its provisions cross the line from what is 'reasonable' into the forbidden territory of what is 'unreasonable,' and how the one is to be distinguished from the other ... .

210   Much of the argument pursued by the Chief Justice and Major J., as well as by Deschamps J. in her reasons relating to the Quebec Charter, revolves around the vexing issue of waiting lists, which have notoriously fuelled major public debates and controversies. ...

221   Waiting times are not only found in public systems. They are found in all health care systems, be they single-tier private, single-tier public, or the various forms of two-tier public/private. Waiting times in Canada are not exceptional. The consequence of a quasi- unlimited demand for health care coupled with limited resources, be they public or private, is to ration services ...

222   The expert witnesses at trial agreed that waiting lists are inevitable ... The only alternative is to have a substantially overbuilt health care system with idle capacity. This is not a financially feasible option, in the public or private sector.

Who Should Be Allowed to Jump the Queue?

223   In a public system founded on the values of equity, solidarity and collective responsibility, rationing occurs on the basis of clinical need rather than wealth and social status ... In general, the evidence suggests that patients who need immediate medical care receive it. There are of course exceptions, and these exceptions are properly the focus of controversy, but in our view they can and should be addressed on a case-by-case basis.

Availability of Public Funding for Out-of-Province Medical Care

224   Section 10 of the Health Insurance Act provides that in certain circumstances Quebeckers will be reimbursed for the cost of 'insured services' rendered outside Quebec but in Canada (Regulation respecting the application of the Health Insurance Act, R.R.Q. 1981, s. 23.1), or outside Canada altogether (s. 23.2). There is no doubt that the power of reimbursement is exercised sparingly, and on occasion unlawfully; see for example Stein v. Tribunal administratif du Québec, [1999] R.J.Q. 2416 (S.C.). One of the difficulties in assessing the effectiveness of this individual remedy is that neither Dr. Chaoulli nor Mr. Zeliotis is before the Court with an actual medical problem. (The trial judge, as stated, dismissed Mr. Zeliotis' personal health complaints as unsubstantiated.) The reimbursement scheme for out-of-province services exists as a form

of safety valve for situations in which Quebec facilities are unable to respond. As Stein shows, there are lapses of judgment, as there will be in the administration of any government plan. The existence of the individual remedy, however, introduces an important element of flexibility, if administered properly ... .

264   The safety valve (however imperfectly administered) of allowing Quebec residents to obtain essential health care outside the province when they are unable to receive the care in question at home in a timely way is of importance. If, as the appellants claim, this safety valve is opened too sparingly, the courts are available to supervise enforcement of the rights of those patients who are directly affected by the decision on a case-by-case basis. Judicial intervention at this level on a case-by-case basis is preferable to acceptance of the appellants' global challenge to the entire single- tier health plan. It is important to emphasize that rejection of the appellants' global challenge to Quebec's health plan would not foreclose individual patients from seeking individual relief tailored to their individual circumstances.

The Evidence Relied on by the Chief Justice and Major J. Did Not Satisfy the Trial Judge and Is Not, in Our View, Persuasive

225   The Chief Justice and Major J. cite Dr. Lenczner as an authority at para. 114 but the trial judge pointed out that Dr. Lenczner had not been qualified as an expert witness and counsel for Mr. Zeliotis agreed. Dr. Lenczner's comments were largely anecdotal and of little general application. He described a patient who was a golfer, and thus lost his access to his golf membership for that season. He also stated that a tear can increase over time and get to the point of being irreparable, but no studies or general evidence was adduced to show the incidence of such cases in Quebec. Our colleagues comment at para. 112 that 'a person with coronary disease is 'sitting on a bomb' and can die at any moment.' This is true, of course. He or she can die at home, or in an ambulance on the way to a hospital. Again, our colleagues write, 'patients die while on waiting lists' (para. 112). This, too, is true. But our colleagues are not advocating an overbuilt system with enough idle capacity to eliminate waiting lists, and such generalized comments provided no guidance for what in practical terms would constitute an appropriate level of resources to meet their suggested standard of 'public health care of a reasonable standard within reasonable time' (para. 105).

226   We have similar concerns about the use made by the appellants of various reports in connection with other OECD countries. These 'country' reports were included in an Interim Kirby Report but not in its final version. The Final Kirby Report's recommendation was to stick with a single-tier system. We think the Court is sufficiently burdened with conflicting evidence about our own health system without attempting a detailed investigation of the merits of trade-offs made in other countries, for their own purposes. A glance at the evidence shows why.

227   Our colleagues the Chief Justice and Major J. state, at para. 142, that in Sweden only a very small minority of the population actually utilize private insurance. Yet, the Interim Kirby Report goes on to take note of more recent trends:

> The growing rate of the number of insured, or people on private health care insurance, is some 80% or something like that now. It is growing very fast due to the normal waiting lists and the problems within the system today. ...

229   We are not to be taken as disputing the undoubted fact that there are serious problems with the single-tier health plan in Canada. Our point is simply that bits of evidence must be put in context. With respect, it is particularly dangerous to venture selectively into aspects of foreign health care systems with which we, as Canadians, have little familiarity. At the very least such information should be filtered and analysed at trial through an expert witness.

230   ... We thus conclude that our colleagues' extracts of some of the tour d'horizon data published in the Interim Kirby Report do not displace the conclusion of the trial judge, let alone the conclusion of the Kirby Report itself. Apart from everything else, it leaves out of consideration the commitment in principle in this country to health care based on need, not wealth or status, as set out in the Canada Health Act ... .

Arbitrariness

233   We agree with our colleagues the Chief Justice and Major J. that a law is arbitrary if 'it bears no relation to, or is inconsistent with, the objective that lies behind [the legislation]' (para. 130). We do not agree with the Chief Justice and Major J. that the prohibition against private

health insurance 'bears no relation to, or is inconsistent with' the preservation of access to a health system based on need rather than wealth in accordance with the Canada Health Act. We also do not agree with our colleagues' expansion of the Morgentaler principle to invalidate a prohibition simply because a court believes it to be 'unnecessary' for the government's purpose. There must be more than that to sustain a valid objection ...

235   Rejecting the findings in the courts below based on their own reading of the evidence, our colleagues the Chief Justice and Major J. state (at para. 128):

> We are of the opinion that the evidence before the trial judge supports a finding that the impugned provisions are arbitrary and that the deprivation of life and security of the person that flows from them cannot therefore be said to accord with the principles of fundamental justice.

We note that our colleagues refer to the evidence before the trial judge rather than the view taken of that evidence by the trial judge. The trial judge reached a contrary conclusion on the facts, and deference is due to her view of that evidence ...

243   The appellants' argument in favour of a parallel private regime is one of a 'win/win' prediction; i.e. that waiting times in the public regime will be reduced if those who can afford private insurance leave the public waiting lists in order to receive private health care. However, the Kirby Report states flatly that 'allowing a private parallel system will ... make the public waiting lines worse' (vol. 4, at p. 42 (emphasis added)). This conclusion is supported by the Romanow Report (p. 139: '[P]rivate facilities may improve waiting times for the select few ... but ... worse[n them for the many]') ...

245   The Australian experience, as reported by Dr. Wright, is that at present delays in the Australian public system are caused largely by surgeons' reluctance to work in public hospitals and by their encouragement of patients to use the private system on a preferential basis ...

246   The same is true for the United Kingdom, which has a two-tier health system where physicians who want to practise privately are required to practise a minimum number of hours in the public system.

There, an Audit Commission of the National Health Service reported that surgeons do on average a third to half again as many operations for private fees as they do in the public system, and that they spend less time than they are contracted for working in the public system in order to conduct private practice ...

247   Both the Romanow Report and the Kirby Report examine the current shortage of health care professionals in Canada ... an in rural parts of Canada in particular ... Dr. Wright testified that the experience in all jurisdictions with two-tier health care systems (e.g., the United Kingdom, Australia, New Zealand and Israel) demonstrates a diversion of energy and commitment by physicians and surgeons from the public system to the more lucrative private option ...

249   The evidence suggests that parallel private insurers prefer to siphon off high income patients while shying away from patient populations that constitute a higher financial risk, a phenomenon known as 'cream skimming' ... The public system would therefore carry a disproportionate burden of patients who are considered 'bad risks' by the private market by reason of age, socio-economic conditions, or geographic location ... .

252   The expert witnesses at trial (other than the appellants' witness Dr. Coffey) and the Romanow Report and the Kirby Report all agree that the most cost-effective method of providing health care is through public single-tier financing. Dr. Wright testified at trial that the 'public administration criterion [of the Canada Health Act] renders the Canadian health care system one of the most efficient in terms of the ratio of productivity to administrative costs in the world' ...

255   With respect to the impact on the financial resources of the public system, the experts testified that the introduction of a parallel private health regime would likely increase the overall cost of health care to Canadians ...

Conclusion on 'Arbitrariness'

256   For all these reasons, we agree with the conclusion of the trial judge and the Quebec Court of Appeal that in light of the legislative objectives of the Canada Health Act it is not 'arbitrary' for Quebec to

discourage the growth of private sector health care. Prohibition of private health insurance is directly related to Quebec's interest in promoting a need-based system and in ensuring its viability and efficiency. Prohibition of private insurance is not 'inconsistent' with the state interest; still less is it 'unrelated' to it.

257 In short, it cannot be said that the prohibition against private health insurance 'bears no relation to, or is inconsistent with' preservation of a health system predominantly based on need rather than wealth or status ...

258 As to our colleagues' dismissal of the factual basis for Quebec's legislative choice, the public has invested very large sums of money in a series of authoritative reports to analyse health care in this country and in other countries. The reports uniformly recommend the retention of single-tier medicine. People are free to challenge (as do the appellants) the government's reliance on those reports but such reliance cannot be dismissed as 'arbitrary.' People are also free to dispute Quebec's strategy, but in our view it cannot be said that a single-tier health system, and the prohibition on private health insurance designed to protect it, is a legislative choice that has been adopted 'arbitrarily' by the Quebec National Assembly as that term has been understood to date in the Canadian Charter jurisprudence.

The Morgentaler Case Is Not Applicable

259 Our colleagues the Chief Justice and Major J. rely substantially on comments made by Beetz J. (concurred in by Estey J.) in Morgentaler when he invoked a principle of 'manifest unfairness.' Nowhere in his analysis pertaining to the principles of fundamental justice did Beetz J. use the words 'arbitrary' or 'arbitrariness.' Moreover the context for his remarks was the prospect of a criminal prosecution of a pregnant woman. Section 251(2) of the Criminal Code stated that a pregnant woman who used 'any means or permit[ed] any means to be used' for the purpose of procuring her own miscarriage was guilty of an indictable offence punishable with imprisonment for two years. Parliament provided a defence if the continued pregnancy would or would be likely to, in the opinion of a therapeutic abortion committee, 'endanger her life or health' (s. 251(4)(c)). The Court struck down the criminal prohibition because the prohibition was designed to operate only with the statutory de-

fence, and the Court found that in practice these committees operated unevenly and that the statutory scheme 'contain[ed] so many potential barriers to its own operation that the defence it create[ed would] in many circumstances be practically unavailable to women who would prima facie qualify ...' (at pp. 72–73, per Dickson C.J.). For Beetz J., too, a key issue was that a significant proportion of Canada's population is not served by hospitals in which therapeutic abortions could lawfully be performed (pp. 94–95) ... .

Conclusion Under Section 7 of the Canadian Charter

265   For the foregoing reasons, even accepting (as we do) the trial judge's conclusion that the claimants have established a deprivation of the life and security of some Quebec residents occasioned in some circumstances by waiting list delays, the deprivation would not violate any legal principle of fundamental justice within the meaning of s. 7 of the Canadian Charter.

The Appellants' Challenge Under The Quebec Charter

271   Section 1 of the Quebec Charter, in essence, covers about the same ground as s. 7 of the Canadian Charter, but it does not mention the principles of fundamental justice.

272   Under s. 1 of the Quebec Charter, as at the first stage of a s. 7 analysis, the claimant bears the burden of establishing, on a balance of probabilities, that the impugned law infringes his or her protected rights and interests. If such a claim is made out, the focus of the analysis may shift to s. 9.1 of the Quebec Charter in order to determine whether the claimed exercise of the right is made with due regard for 'democratic values, public order and the general well-being of the citizens of Québec.'

273   In our view, on the evidence, the exercise by the appellants of their claimed Quebec Charter rights to defeat the prohibition against private insurance would not have 'proper regard for democratic values' or 'public order,' as the future of a publicly supported and financed single-tier health plan should be in the hands of elected representatives. Nor would it have proper regard for the 'general well-being of the citizens of Québec,' who are the designated benefi-

ciaries of the health plan, and in particular for the well-being of the less advantaged Quebeckers.

274   Those who seek private health insurance are those who can afford it and can qualify for it. They will be the more advantaged members of society. They are differentiated from the general population, not by their health problems, which are found in every group in society, but by their income status. We share the view of Dickson C.J. that the Charter should not become an instrument to be used by the wealthy to 'roll back' the benefits of a legislative scheme that helps the poorer members of society ... The concern, of course, is that once the health needs of the wealthier members of society are looked after in the 'upper tier,' they will have less incentive to continue to pressure the government for improvements to the public system as a whole ... .

276   This is not a case, in our view, where the onus of proof determines the outcome. The evidence amply supports the validity of the prohibition of private insurance under the Quebec Charter. The objectives are compelling. A rational connection is demonstrated. The decision boils down to an application of the minimal impairment test. In respect of questions of social and economic policy, this test leaves a substantial margin of appreciation to the Quebec legislature. Designing, financing and operating the public health system of a modern democratic society like Quebec remains a challenging task. It calls for difficult choices. In the end, we find that the choice made a generation ago by the National Assembly of Quebec remains within the range of options that are justifiable under s. 9.1. Shifting the design of the health system to the courts is not a wise choice.

277   In this respect, we should bear in mind that the legislative provisions challenged under s. 1 concern all citizens of Quebec. They address concerns shared by all and rights belonging to everyone. The legislative solution affects not only individuals but also the society to which all those individuals belong. It is a problem for which the legislature attempted to find a solution that would be acceptable to everyone in the spirit of the preamble of the Quebec Charter:

WHEREAS every human being possesses intrinsic rights and freedoms designed to ensure his protection and development;

Whereas all human beings are equal in worth and dignity, and are entitled to equal protection of the law;

Whereas respect for the dignity of the human being and recognition of his rights and freedoms constitute the foundation of justice and peace;

Whereas the rights and freedoms of the human person are inseparable from the rights and freedoms of others and from the common well-being;

278   The evidence reviewed above establishes that the impugned provisions were part of a system which is mindful and protective of the interests of all, not only of some.

279   We would dismiss the appeal.

[Subsequent to the release of this decision on June 9, 2005, the Attorney General of Quebec requested a re-hearing and a suspension of the judgment for 18 months. Many of the parties and intervenors made supplementary submissions on this request. On August 4, 2005, the seven judges who sat on the case issued the following ruling: 'The motion for a partial rehearing is granted. The Court's judgment is stayed for a period of 12 months from the date such judgment was issued, namely June 9, 2005.']